Microsoft Exchange 2000: Programming Collaborative Web Applications

ISBN 0-13-061827-6

PRENTICE HALL PTR MICROSOFT® TECHNOLOGIES SERIES

NETWORKING

- An Administrator's Guide to Windows 2000 TCP/IP Networks
  Wilson
- IP Solutions for Windows 2000
  Ammann
- Microsoft Technology: Networking, Concepts, Tools
  Woodard, Gattuccio, Brain
- NT Network Programming Toolkit
  Murphy
- Building COM Applications with Internet Explorer
  Loveman
- Understanding DCOM
  Rubin, Brain
- Web Database Development for Windows Platforms
  Gutierrez

PROGRAMMING

- Windows 2000 Kernel Debugging
  McDowell
- Windows Script Host
  Aitken
- The Windows 2000 Device Driver Book, Second Edition
  Baker, Lozano
- Win32 System Services: The Heart of Windows 98 and Windows 2000, Third Edition
  Brain, Reeves
- Programming the WIN32 API and UNIX System Services
  Merusi
- Windows CE 3.0: Application Programming
  Grattan, Brain
- The Visual Basic Style Guide
  Patrick
- Windows Shell Programming
  Seely
- Windows Installer Complete
  Easter
- Windows 2000 Web Applications Developer's Guide
  Yager
- Developing Windows Solutions with Office 2000 Components and VBA
  Aitken
- Multithreaded Programming with Win32
  Pham, Garg
- Developing Professional Applications for Windows 98 and NT Using MFC, Third Edition
  Brain, Lovette
- Introduction to Windows 98 Programming
  Murray, Pappas
- The COM and COM+ Programming Primer
  Gordon
- Understanding and Programming COM+: A Practical Guide to Windows 2000 DNA
  Oberg
- Distributed COM Application Development Using Visual C++ 6.0
  Maloney
- The Essence of COM, Third Edition
  Platt
- COM-CORBA Interoperability
  Geraghty, Joyce, Moriarty, Noone
- MFC Programming in C++ with the Standard Template Libraries
  Murray, Pappas
- Introduction to MFC Programming with Visual C++
  Jones
- Visual C++ Templates
  Murray, Pappas
- Visual Basic Object and Component Handbook
  Vogel
- Visual Basic 6: Error Coding and Layering
  Gill
- ADO Programming in Visual Basic 6
  Holzner
- Visual Basic 6: Design, Specification, and Objects
  Hollis
- ASP/MTS/ADSI Web Security
  Harrison

BACKOFFICE

- Microsoft Exchange 2000: Programming Collaborative Web Applications
  Ammann
- Microsoft SQL Server 2000 Optimization Guide
  Fields
- BizTalk: Implementing Business-To-Business E-Commerce
  Kobielus
- Designing Enterprise Solutions with Microsoft Technologies
  Kemp, Kemp, Goncalves
- Microsoft Site Server 3.0 Commerce Edition
  Libertone, Scoppa
- Building Microsoft SQL Server 7 Web Sites
  Byrne
- Optimizing SQL Server 7
  Schneider, Goncalves

ADMINISTRATION

- Tuning and Sizing Windows 2000 for Maximum Performance
  Aubley
- Windows 2000 Cluster Server Guidebook
  Libertone
- Windows 2000 Hardware and Disk Management
  Simmons
- Windows 2000 Server: Management and Control, Third Edition
  Spencer, Goncalves
- Creating Active Directory Infrastructures
  Simmons
- Windows 2000 Registry
  Sanna
- Configuring Windows 2000 Server
  Simmons
- Supporting Windows NT and 2000 Workstation and Server
  Mohr
- Zero Administration Kit for Windows
  McInerney
- Windows NT 4.0 Server Security Guide
  Goncalves
- Windows NT Security
  McInerney

CERTIFICATION

- Core MCSE: Windows 2000 Edition
  Dell
- Core MCSE: Designing a Windows 2000 Directory Services Infrastructure
  Simmons
- MCSE: Implementing and Supporting Windows 98
  Dell
- Core MCSE
  Dell
- Core MCSE: Networking Essentials
  Keogh
- MCSE: Administering Microsoft SQL Server 7
  Byrne
- MCSE: Implementing and Supporting Microsoft Exchange Server 5.5
  Goncalves
- MCSE: Internetworking with Microsoft TCP/IP
  Ryvkin, Houde, Hoffman
- MCSE: Implementing and Supporting Microsoft Proxy Server 2.0
  Ryvkin, Hoffman
- MCSE: Implementing and Supporting Microsoft SNA Server 4.0
  Mariscal
- MCSE: Implementing and Supporting Microsoft Internet Information Server 4
  Dell
- MCSE: Implementing and Supporting Web Sites Using Microsoft Site Server 3
  Goncalves
- MCSE: Microsoft System Management Server 2
  Jewett
- MCSE: Implementing and Supporting Internet Explorer 5
  Dell
- Core MCSD: Designing and Implementing Desktop Applications with Microsoft Visual Basic 6
  Holzner
- MCSD: Planning and Implementing SQL Server 7
  Vacca
- MCSD: Designing and Implementing Web Sites with Microsoft FrontPage 98
  Karlins

PRENTICE HALL PTR MICROSOFT® TECHNOLOGIES SERIES

Microsoft Exchange 2000: Programming Collaborative Web Applications

Paul T. Ammann

PH PTR

Prentice Hall PTR, Upper Saddle River, NJ 07458
www.phptr.com

Library of Congress Cataloging-in-Publication Data

Ammann, Paul T.
　　Microsoft Exchange 2000: programming collaborative Web applications /
Paul T. Ammann.
　　　　p. cm. – (Prentice Hall PTR Microsoft technologies series)
　　　ISBN 0-13-061827-6
　　　　1. Internet programming 2. Web sites–Design.
　　3. Microsoft Exchange server. I. Title. II. Series.
　　QA76.625.A456 2001
　　005.7'13769–dc21　　　　　　　　　　　　　　　　　　　2001031506

Editorial/Production Supervision: *Jan H. Schwartz*
Acquisitions Editor: *Jill Harry*
Marketing Manager: *Dan DePasquale*
Manufacturing Manager: *Alexis R. Heydt*
Manufacturing Buyer: *Maura Zaldivar*
Cover Design Direction: *Jerry Votta*
Cover Design: *Anthony Gemmellaro*
Interior Series Design: *Gail Cocker-Bogusz*
Interior Series Design: *Meg VanArsdale*
Editorial Assistant: *Justin Somma*
Composition: *Eileen Clark with Maureen Brigham*

```
PH     © 2002 by Prentice Hall PTR
PTR    Prentice-Hall, Inc.
       Upper Saddle River, NJ 07458
```

Prentice Hall books are widely used by corporations and government agencies for training, marketing, and resale.

The publisher offers discounts on this book when ordered in bulk quantities. For more information, contact Corporate Sales Department, phone: 800-382-3419; fax: 201-236-7141; email: corpsales@prenhall.com or write Corporate Sales Department, Prentice Hall PTR, One Lake Street, Upper Saddle River, NJ 07458.

All product names mentioned herein are the trademarks or registered trademarks of their respective companies, organizations, or owners.

All rights reserved. No part of this book may be reproduced, in any form or by any means, without permission in writing from the publisher.

Printed in the United States of America

10 9 8 7 6 5 4 3 2 1

ISBN 0-13-061827-6

Pearson Education LTD.
Pearson Education Australia PTY, Limited
Pearson Education Singapore, Pte. Ltd.
Pearson Education North Asia Ltd.
Pearson Education Canada, Ltd.
Pearson Educación de Mexico, S.A. de C.V.
Pearson Education – Japan
Pearson Education Malaysia, Pte. Ltd.
Pearson Education, Upper Saddle River, New Jersey

Dedication

This book is dedicated to my wife, Eve, for her love, support, and patience while I worked on this book.

CONTENTS

Preface xxv

ONE Introduction to the Web Storage System 1

Accessing Items Using URLs 1
Knowledge Management 2
Web Storage System Schema 2
Web Storage System Forms 3
Collaboration Data Objects 3
Web Storage System Events 4
WorkFlow Support 5
Web Application Development 5
Exchange 2000 Server Web Storage System 6

Web Storage System Access APIs and Protocols 6

OLE DB and ADO Access 7
HTTP/WebDAV Access 9
File System Access 10
MAPI Access 11
Additional Web Storage System Access Protocols 11

Web Storage System Item Properties 12

Namespaces and Property Names 12
Namespace URLs and URNs 13
Default Web Storage System Namespaces 13
Custom Properties 15
  Namespace Guidelines 15
  Custom Properties and MAPI 16
Property Names and the Exchange OLE DB Provider 16
Property Names and HTTP/WebDAV 17
Property Names and XML 18
Property Data Types 19
The Item Default Stream Property 21
Automatic Property Promotion from the Stream 22

▼ TWO Web Storage System Schema and Search Engine 25

Web Storage System Schema 25

Content Classes 25
    Content Class Inheritance 27
Schema Definition Items 29
    Content Class Definitions 29
    Property Definitions 30
Schema Scope 31
Folder Expected Content Class 32
Application and Schema Folders 33

Web Storage System Search 34

The SELECT Statement 35
The SELECT * Statement 36
Search Scope 36
Property and Full-Text Indexing 38
    Property Indexing 38
    Full-Text Indexing 38
    Customizing Full-Text Indexing 39

Web Storage System Search Folders 40

Search Folder Properties 41
Search Folder Items 41
HTTP/WebDAV Search Folder Creation Protocol Command 42
    Example Search Folder HTTP Request and Response 43

▼ THREE Web Storage System Security 45

Item Access Rights 46

Folder Item Access Rights 46
Nonfolder Item Access Rights 47
Standard Access Rights 48

Web Storage System XML Security Descriptor Format 48

Security Identifiers in XML 49
XML Security Descriptor XML Elements 50
Discretionary Access Control Lists XML Elements 51
System Audit Control Lists XML Elements 53
Example Descriptor in XML 55

Accessing Item Descriptors 56
New Item Descriptor Inheritance 57
Exchange 5.5 Access Rights and the Web Storage System 57

▼ FOUR Web Storage System Forms and Events 81

An Introduction to Web Storage System Forms 81

Web Storage System Form Registration 81

Web Storage System Forms Registry 82
Schema Collection Ref 83
Form Definition Properties 84
Form Registration Examples 86
  HTTP/WebDAV Example 86
  Testapp Example 87
Order of Precedence 88
Default Form Registration 88

Reusing Elements of Outlook Web Access 89

Working with Default Views 89
Controlling the Navigation Bar 90
URL Parameters 90

An Introduction to Web Storage System Events 91

Web Storage System Event Terms 92

Events Overview 92

Exchange Calls Event Methods 93
Multiple Events 94
Multiple Sinks 95
OLE DB and ADO 96

Events and Event Sink Interfaces 96

  System Events 97
Synchronous Events 97
Synchronous Event Details 97
Asynchronous Events (Notifications) 100
  Asynchronous Event Details 100
System Events 100
Additional Event Sink Interfaces 101
Support Interfaces 102

Event Registration 103
    The Event Registration Item 103
    Registration Steps 104
    Recursive Events 104
        Registering for MDB-Wide Events 104
    Event Notification Priority 105
    The RegEvent Script 106
        Remarks 108
    Event Registration Guidelines 108
    Event Registration Security 108
    Event Registration Modification 109
Event Reliability 109
Working in an Event Sink 110
    Loop Recursion 110
    Information Passed to an Event Method 110
    Contextual Information in an Event Registration 110
    Security in an Event Sink 111
        COM+ Applications 111
The Script Host Sink 112
Event Naming 112
Sink Monitoring 113
    Event Logs 113
    Performance Monitor Counters 114

▼ FIVE Collaboration Data Objects 115
CDO Components 116
CDOEX Server 116
CDOW 118
CDOEXM 118
CDO and ADO 119
Differences between CDO and ADO 120
    Synchronized Streams and Properties 120
    Binding to Items in the Web Storage System 121
    Updating Items in the Web Storage System 122

CDO and ADSI 122
The IDataSource Interface 123
Data Sources and Binding 123
The Configuration Object 124

▼ SIX Messaging 125

Internet Standard Message Formats 126
The RFC 822 Message Format 126
The UUENCODE Attachment Format 127
The MIME Message Format 127
- MIME Message Body Parts 128
- Content Body Parts 129
- Multipart Body Parts 130
- MIME Hierarchies of Body Parts 131
- Messaging and the Exchange Web Storage System 132

Messaging Content Classes 132
Automatic Message Property Promotion 133
The Exchange Mail Submission URI 135
Messaging with CDO for Exchange 2000 Server 136
CDO Messaging COM Interfaces 136
CDO Messaging COM Classes 137
CDO BodyPart Object Hierarchies 137
- Example 1: Alternative Representations of a Message 138
- Example 2: Alternative with Attachments 138
- Example 3: Alternative with MHTML Formatting 140

CDO BodyPart Fields and Streams 140
- BodyPart Content Streams 141
- BodyPart Streams 142

CDO Message Fields and Streams 143
- Message Fields 144
- Message Streams 144
- Message Stream and Property Synchronization 146

CDO Messaging Configuration 146
   Configuration Fields 147
CDO Messaging and ADO 149
   When to Use CDO or ADO for Messaging 150

▼ SEVEN Calendaring and Contacts 151

Calendars in Exchange 2000 Server 152
Calendars on the Internet 152
The Calendar Object Model 154
Time Zones 155
Specifying the Time Zone 156
Making Time Zones Work with Outlook 157
Using Recurring Appointments with Time Zones 158
Time Zone to CdoTimeZoneId Map 158
Contacts 161
Working with the CDO Person Object 161

▼ EIGHT Workflow 163

Workflow Overview 163
Using Built-In Workflow Functionality 165
   Modeling Business Processes 166
   Developing Typical Workflow Applications 167
Creating Workflow Event Sinks and Tools 168
   Developing Advanced Workflow Applications 168
   Application Architecture 173
   Workflow Components 174
      Workflow Engine 175
      Workflow Event Sink 176
   Workflow Variations 178
      Web-Based and Email Workflow Compared 178
      Default and Ad Hoc Process Definitions 180

Workflow Process Definition 182
   Defining the ActionTable 182
   Setting Security and Audit Properties 186

Workflow Security Modes 186
   Privilege Checking 188
   Restricted Mode 188
   Privileged Mode 189

Managing Workflow Deployment 189
   Adding the Workflow System Account 189
   Registering a Workflow Event Sink 190
   Privileged Workflow Authors 192

Testing and Debugging Workflow Applications 193
   Using an Audit Trail 193
   Using Script Debugger 193

▼ NINE Server and Recipient Management 195

Overview 196
   Typical Uses 196

DLLs and Installation 196

Web Storage System Configuration 197

Rules about Folder Trees and MDBs 198

Folder Tree Replication 199

Active Directory and CDOEXM 200

Building Active Directory Paths 200

Retrieving Folder Tree URLs 202

Web-Based Management 204

Exchange Management Security 205

Managing the Exchange Server 205

Setting Up a Store 206

Managing Mail Recipients 208

Recipient Management Interfaces 208

Using the Interfaces in Context 209

Recipients, Folders, and Groups 211
Accessing Mailboxes and Folders 211
Email Addresses Stored as Active Directory Paths 212
Error Checking with CDOEXM Objects 213

▼ TEN Constructing Web Storage System URLs 215

Constructing OLE DB URLs 215
The File: URL Scheme 216
The HTTP: URL Scheme 218
Constructing Web Storage System HTTP URLs 220
Using Relative URLs 221
Getting the Host Domain Name 224
Getting Well-Known Mailbox Folder URLs 229

▼ ELEVEN Working with Folders and Items 233

Creating Folders 233
Creating Items 236
Getting Existing Items 241
Accessing Item Streams 244
Copying Items 249
Deleting Items 251
Deleting Items Using a Recordset 252
Moving Items 255
Working with Item Properties 256
    Printing Item Property Names, Types, and Values 256
    Working with Multivalued Properties 259
    Setting and Retrieving Custom Properties 263
Getting a List of Folders 266
Using Transactions 268

▼ TWELVE Using the HTTP/WebDAV Protocol 277

Creating Items (HTTP/WebDAV) 277
Creating Folders (HTTP/WebDAV) 279
Getting an Item's Stream (HTTP/WebDAV) 280
Deleting Items (HTTP/WebDAV) 281
Copying Items (HTTP/WebDAV) 282
Moving Items (HTTP/WebDAV) 282
Getting Item Property Values (HTTP/WebDAV) 283
Constructing XML with XMLDOM 285
Modifying Item Property Values (HTTP/WebDAV) 286
Searching Folders (HTTP/WebDAV) 288
Specifying Row Ranges in a Search 290
Rendering Search Results with XSL 290
Creating Search Folders 293

▼ THIRTEEN Search Tasks 297

Simple Query 298
Schema Scope 299
Specifying a Deep Traversal 301
Word and Character Matching 302
Specifying a Date Range 305
Getting Item Counts with GROUP BY 307
Enumerating Search Results 309

▼ FOURTEEN Using Schema 311

Creating Property Definitions 312
Creating Content Class Definitions 316
Specifying Expected Content Classes for Folders 318

Configuring a Folder's Schema Scope 319
    Setting the Schema Collection Reference for a Folder 320
    Setting the Base Schema Path for a Schema Folder 323
Testing Your Schema 327
Displaying Icons Based on Item Content Class 329
Using Folder Content Class 330

▼ FIFTEEN Security Tasks 331

Getting an Item's XML Security Descriptor 331
Creating Web Storage System Descriptors in XML 334
    Creating an ACE in XML 334
    Modifying an Item's DACL 335
Updating an Item's Security Descriptor 337

▼ SIXTEEN Using Web Storage System Forms 339

Registering a Web Storage System Form 339
Form Definition Properties 339
    Syntax 340
    Registering a Web Storage System Form Using PROPPATCH 341
    Using ADO to Set the SCR and Default Document Properties 342
    Binding Messages to Custom Forms 344
Reusing Outlook Web Access Components in a Web Page 346
    Loading an Outlook Web Access View in an IFrame 346
    Loading an Outlook Web Access View in a Frame 347

▼ SEVENTEEN Using Store Events 349

Implementing Synchronous Event Sinks 350
    Implementing an OnSyncSave Event Sink 350
    Implementing an OnSyncDelete Event Sink 352
Implementing Asynchronous Event Sinks 354
    Implementing an OnSave Event Sink 354
    Implementing an OnDelete Event Sink 356

Contents   **xix**

Implementing System Event Sinks 358
    Implementing an OnMdbStartup Event Sink 358
    Implementing an OnMdbShutdown Event Sink 359
    Implementing an OnTimer Event Sink 359

Managing Event Registrations 360
    Adding an Event Registration for a Folder 360
    Removing an Event Registration for a Folder 363
    Enumerating Event Registrations for a Folder 364

Managing Event Registrations with RegEvent.vbs 367
    Registering for an Asynchronous Event 367
    Registering for an OnSyncSave Event 367
    Registering for a System Event 368
    Registering for an OnTimer Event 368
    Deleting Event Registrations 369
    Enumerating Event Registrations 369

▼ **EIGHTEEN** Messaging 371

Creating a Message 371

Configuring the Message Object 372
    Setting Language and Time-Zone Information 373
    Setting the Send and Post Methods 373
    Sending or Posting Using the Network 375
    Sending or Posting Using the Pickup Directory 376
    Sending or Posting Using Exchange 377
    Configuring Network Authentication Information 379
    Setting Network Proxy Information 380
    Using Default Configuration Settings 381

Addressing the Message 381

Setting Subject and TextBody Fields 384

Setting Message Header Fields 387

Adding Attachments 389

Manually Adding Attachments 391

Creating MIME-Formatted Messages 394

Adding BodyPart Objects to the MIME Hierarchy 395
Setting Header Fields on Body Parts 399
Creating MHTML-Formatted Messages 400
Specifying the Header Fields Character Set 403

Sending and Posting Messages 405
Sending Using Exchange 406
Posting Using Exchange 409
Replying to Messages 411
Forwarding Messages 413
Extracting Embedded Messages 415
Embedding a Message 416
Loading Messages from within ADO Stream Objects 418
Saving Messages into ADO Stream Objects 420
Listing Inbox Contents Using ADO 422

▼ NINETEEN Calendaring and Contacts 425

Creating Appointments and Meeting Requests 425
Adding an Appointment to the Calendar 425
Sending a Meeting Request 427
   Addressing a Calendar Message 430
   Checking Free/Busy Status 431
   Publishing an Appointment 434
Creating Recurring Appointments and Meetings 436
   Specifying Exceptions to Recurring Appointments and Meetings 441
   Using Calendar Folder Query 443
Adding Attachments to Appointments and Meetings 445

Processing a Calendar Message 446
Responding to a Meeting Request 449
Processing Meeting Responses 452
Processing Meeting Cancellations 453
Processing Recurring Meeting Exceptions 455

Updating Appointments and Meetings 456
Getting Appointments and Meetings from Folders in Exchange 457

Sending Meeting Updates 459
Canceling Appointments and Meetings 462
   Canceling an Appointment 462
   Canceling a Meeting 463
   Canceling Recurring Appointments and Meetings 464
   Declining a Previously Accepted Meeting 467

Inviting Additional Attendees 468
Inviting Attendees to a Meeting in the Calendar Folder 469
Forwarding a Meeting Request 470

Configuring the Appointment Object 471

Using Contacts 472

Creating Contacts 472
Creating a Contact in the Web Storage System 472
Creating a Contact in Active Directory 473

Searching for Contacts 474

Getting a Contact's VCard Stream 475

▼ TWENTY   Managing Workflow 477

Using the WorkflowSession Object 477
Managing Run-Time Errors 478

Caching Custom Properties 478
Accessing Active Directory Properties 480
Using WorkflowSession Item Security 481
   ItemAuthors 481
   ItemReaders 482
Using Audit Trail 484
Deleting Workflow Items 484
Working with ReceivedMessage 484
Accessing and Modifying a ProcessInstance 487

Advanced Developer Tasks 488
Creating Action Table Columns 488
Adding Action Table Rows 490
Specifying the Common Script File 490
Creating the ProcessDefinition 491
Registering a Workflow Event Sink in a Folder 492

TWENTY ONE Server and Recipient Management 497

Server Management Tasks 497
- Enumerating Storage Groups and Stores 497
- Retrieving Folder Tree URLs 499
- Creating a Folder Tree 502
- Deleting a Folder Tree 503
- Creating a Storage Group 505
- Deleting a Storage Group 506
- Creating a Public Store 508
- Deleting a Public Store 511
- Creating a Mailbox Store 513
- Deleting a Mailbox Store 515
- Checking for CDOEXM Errors 517

Recipient Management Tasks 518
- Creating a Mail-Enabled Recipient 519
- Creating a Mailbox-Enabled Recipient 520
- Creating a Recipient Using ADSI 523
- Disabling a Mail Recipient 525
- Creating a Contact 526
- Moving a Mailbox 530
- Deleting a Mailbox 533
- Setting Mailbox Storage Limits 534
- Controlling Mailbox Cleanup 535
- Enumerating Recipients 536
- Enumerating Groups 538
- Enumerating Contacts 539
- Setting Proxy Addresses 540
- Building a Restricted Address List 541
- Enabling a Folder for Mail 542

APPENDIX MIME, SMTP, and RFCs 545

MIME Encapsulation of Aggregate HTML Documents (MHTML) 545
- Key Concepts of MHTML 546
- CDO Support for MHTML 547

MIME Extensions to Internet Mail 547

MIME Capabilities 548
Sample MIME Message 548
MIME Headers 550
- *Content-Type 551*
- *Content-Type: Application 551*
- *Content-Type: Audio 552*
- *Content-Type: Image 552*
- *Content-Type: Message 552*
- *Content-Type: Multipart 553*
- *Content-Type: Text 556*
- *Content-Type: Video 557*
- *Content-Transfer-Encoding 557*
- *Content-Transfer-Encoding: 7Bit 558*
- *Content-Transfer-Encoding: 8Bit 558*
- *Content-Transfer-Encoding: Base64 558*
- *Content-Transfer-Encoding: Binary 558*
- *Content-Transfer-Encoding: Quoted-Printable 558*
- *Content-Transfer-Encoding: X-Token 559*
- *Content-Disposition 559*
- *Content-Disposition: Attachment 559*
- *Content-Disposition: Inline 559*

Internet Mail RFCs 559

Internet Messages and SMTP 560

About Simple Internet (RFC 822) Messages 560
Simple Internet Mail Message: An Example 561
About SMTP 562
Summary of RFC 822 562
- *RFC 822: Introduction 562*
- *RFC 822: Notational Conventions 563*
- *RFC 822: Lexical Analysis of Messages 564*
- *RFC 822: Message Specification 565*
- *RFC 822: Date and Time Specification 566*
- *RFC 822: Address Specification 566*
- *RFC 822: Appendixes 567*

SMTP/NNTP Transport Event Sinks with CDO 567

▼ INDEX 569

PREFACE

Accelerate your development productivity with the expert insights and instructive code samples in this hands-on guide. This book delivers the detailed information you need to use the leading edge Web Storage System technology in Microsoft Exchange 2000 Server to build powerful applications for calendaring, contact management, workflow, and more. You'll dig deep into the architecture and schema of the Web Storage System to see how it provides easy access to email, documents, and Web pages, and you'll explore the systems support for XML and other Internet standards. This highly technical expert guide will help you

- *Understand Exchange 2000 Server development.* Develop quickly with the Exchange 2000 Server and Web Storage System platform, master tools for building Web Storage System applications, organize data within the store, and get to that data from most clients without using any code.
- *Learn how to access data.* Define and access custom content classes and properties, use OLE DB and the Microsoft ActiveX Data Objects (ADO) 2.5 Object Model to access the Web Storage System, use Collaboration Data Objects (CDO) for Exchange to develop messaging and calendaring applications, and interact with Microsoft Active Directory services.
- *Extend your application.* Go beyond the core features of Exchange 2000 Server to use Web Storage System events, design workflow applications, and develop for Microsoft Outlook 2000.
- *Build for the Web.* Explore applications and tools for the Web, build Web Storage System forms that replace the standard Microsoft Outlook Web access forms, and create Web pages that use XML and XSL for added flexibility in your Web applications. Prepare for the enterprise: Build secure applications with the Windows 2000 security model, set up your own test environment, secure your middle-tier components by using the COM+ role-based security model, and understand key issues to watch out for when deploying a custom enterprise application.

Developers learn how to build innovative messaging, collaboration, and knowledge management solutions with this expert guide to Microsoft Exchange 2000 Server. The first product to feature Microsoft's new Web Store technology, Exchange 2000 provides a rich, state-of-the-art environment for creating Web-enabled business and workflow applications. In the first part of the book, developers dig into Web Store architecture and schema and explore the technology's leading edge support for XML and other Internet standards.

Subsequent chapters provide skillful guidance and practical examples to help programmers get to work, teaching them how to apply their existing expertise with Office 2000 and Visual Studio 6 to this new platform, and extending their knowledge with timely insights on Windows 2000. Topics include using OLE DB and the ActiveX Data Objects (ADO) 2.5 Object Model to access the Web store, working with Collaboration Data Objects (CDO) 3.0, extending applications with Web Store events, building security into applications with the Windows 2000 security model, building Exchange-based Web forms, using XML, and developing for Outlook 2000.

The developer's guide to building powerful server-side applications with Exchange 2000 and Web Store. The developer's guide to building powerful server-side applications with Exchange 2000 and Web Store

Rich in hands-on guidance and instructive code samples, this book delivers expert, just-in-time information for using Microsoft's new Web Store technology.

Key book benefits are as follows:

- Delivers practical insights, instruction, and code samples to accelerate developer productivity with the new Web Store technology in Exchange 2000.
- Takes developers inside Web store architecture demonstrating how it provides easy access to email, documents, Web pages, and other business information from a variety of client software and familiar development tools.
- Provides how-to information for building applications for instant messaging, real-time collaboration, calendaring, contact management, workflow, and other business applications using minimal code.

Microsoft Exchange 2000 Server enables a wide range of collaborative activities, including group scheduling, team customer and task lists, document routing, and discussion groups that are designed to help knowledge workers become more productive. Exchange 2000 significantly expands the Exchange infrastructure for collaboration and business applications through its use of the new Web Store.

The Web Store provides a single point of management and collaboration for knowledge stored and shared through email, documents, and applications. It integrates Web content such as Web pages, rich storage for documents, extensive messaging and collaboration services, and complete application hosting and workflow services.

The Exchange platform has an increasingly strong story for developers in the enterprise. A few companies, such as ECMS and MicroEye, are making progress toward building large-scale collaboration applications on Exchange, and their visible success has served to validate the potential of the platform.

O N E

Introduction to the Web Storage System

The Microsoft Web Storage System is a database technology that you can use to store, share, and manage many types of data. For example, you can store email messages, Web content, multimedia files, and Microsoft Office documents together in the Web Storage System.

The Web Storage System is organized much like a traditional file system—a hierarchy of folders. Each folder can contain any number of items, including other folders. You can access items in the Web Storage System using many protocols and Application Programming Interfaces (APIs), including

- HTTP and WebDAV (HTTP/WebDAV)
- Microsoft ActiveX Data Objects (ADO) 2.5
- OLE DB 2.5
- Collaboration Data Objects for Microsoft Exchange 2000 Server (CDOEX)
- Messaging Application Programming Interface (MAPI)
- Through the file system and by using several other industry-standard wire protocols

Accessing Items Using URLs

All items in the Web Storage System are identified using URLs when using the following protocols and components:

- *HTTP/WebDAV.* When accessing an item using the HTTP/WebDAV protocol, the items constructed use the standard HTTP URL scheme—for example,

    http://server.microsoft.com/public/reports/report1.doc

- *Exchange OLE DB provider.* When using the Exchange OLE DB provider (ExOLEDB), the URL for the item is constructed using a URL based on either the HTTP or file URL scheme—for example,

  http://server.domain.tld/public/folder1/item2.doc

  file://./backofficestorage/domain.microsoft.com/public folders /reports/report1.doc
- *File system.* You can use standard file URLs to identify items in the Web Storage System. These URLs are constructed the same way as a standard file URL pointing to any file on the file system—for example,

  file:///M:\backofficestorage\somewhere.microsoft.com\MBX\user1 \inbox\report.eml

Knowledge Management

Critical to any collaborative application's success is its ability to enable users to easily organize, find, search, secure, and access information. When using the Web Storage System, you have a repository that makes this easy to do. For example,

- You can intuitively organize content in hierarchies of folders. You can store information about the content for fast and efficient indexing. Changing the folder hierarchies and items within these folders is easy.
- You can control access to items using Extensible Markup Language (XML)-formatted security descriptors.
- You can search entire folder hierarchies using a simple and straightforward Structured Query Language (SQL) syntax, which is the same syntax used by Microsoft Indexing Service.
- You can access content using a wide variety of protocols and APIs, including HTTP/WebDAV, ADO, OLE DB, the file system, and MAPI.
- You can provide discoverable schema information about the content within your application's folders, including the content's intended purpose or function and the set of properties relevant to the content.

Web Storage System Schema

The Web Storage System gives you the ability to define schemas for your applications. Web Storage System schemas center around the content class, a name identifying the intent or purpose of an item along with a set of properties that items of this content class normally will have had defined for them. When creating schema definitions for your applications, you define your content classes and associated properties. The Web Storage System comes with a large number of predefined content classes and properties that you can either use or extend when building your own applications.

The schema information that pertains to a particular application is controlled through a folder's schema scope. A folder's schema scope is a set of folders, traversed in a particular order, that contain schema definition items. You can extend the schema on a folder-by-folder basis by defining the list of folders in the Web Storage System in which you are storing your schema information. You can always extend the base schema provided by the Web Storage System to tailor your application items with a rich set of extended classes and properties.

One benefit of Web Storage System schemas is that they provide a way for schema-aware applications and tools to discover the names of content classes and properties that apply to a particular application. One example of a schema-aware application built in to the Web Storage System is the Search Query processor. By defining your own schemas, you can extend the list of properties returned when users execute a SELECT * statement or an HTTP/WebDAV PROPFIND command in your application folder.

Web Storage System Forms

The Web Storage System can automatically render item data in HTML display format when requested over the network, using the HTTP/WebDAV protocol. You define the format for this display information using an HTML Web Storage System Form. Creating and registering form templates is easy and straightforward.

You need not be concerned in your application with identifying the capabilities of the user's browser software; the Web Storage System form-rendering engine handles this for you. The Web Storage System form-rendering engine is geared toward generating rich HTML content for Microsoft Internet Explorer 5.0 or later, but it will also automatically detect less powerful browser software and generate content in HTML 3.2.

Collaboration Data Objects

Collaboration Data Objects (CDO) is a powerful set of Component Object Models (COM) that you can use to manage folders, messages, Exchange mailboxes, public stores and public folder trees, appointments, contacts, and all other items in the Web Storage System. The CDO components support Internet standards and protocols for messaging, contact management, and appointment/calendar exchange. In addition to providing intuitive and straightforward object models, CDO components provide direct access to OLE DB interfaces when required for optimum performance. Additionally, application developers interested in maintaining compatibility with MAPI clients such as Microsoft Outlook are encouraged to use CDO.

CDOEX is made up of the following components:

- *CDOEX Server.* This component provides you with core collaboration functionality such as raw folder and item access, messaging, calendaring, and contact management.
- *CDO Workflow for Exchange 2000 Server.* This component provides you with workflow management tools.
- *CDO Management Objects for Exchange 2000 Server.* This component provides management functionality for the Web Storage System and Exchange 2000.

All CDO components integrate seamlessly with the ADO 2.5 component to provide you with a consistent data-access interface to the Web Storage System and Microsoft Windows 2000 Active Directory. As you set values to CDO properties or access Web Storage System properties, CDO saves data to the correct locations for you, whether in the Web Storage System or Active Directory.

CDO interface properties provide the essential functionality for creating collaborative applications using the Web Storage System. There are situations, however, in which using ADO or OLE DB might be easier or more appropriate.

Web Storage System Events

The Web Storage System provides a powerful set of store and system events. An event is the occurrence of some activity or action within a folder, a store, or the system. You can write applications called event sinks that receive these notifications either synchronously or asynchronously and take some application-appropriate action, such as sending a message or aborting the operation that is triggering the event. Event sinks are COM objects that provide an implementation of a Web Storage System-defined set of COM interfaces. All Web Storage System event sinks run out of process with respect to the event source, thereby protecting the server process from exceptions and faults generated by the sink. The event source is the process or thread that invokes the event method on a sink when an event occurs for which that sink is registered.

Synchronous events are used to intercept a particular operation before it is actually committed to the store. The event is called synchronous because sinks run at the time the operation is being performed. For example, when a user requests to save an item to the store, the OnSyncSave event occurs. Event sinks registered for notification of this event are run as part of the actual save operation, and each sink can possibly abort the operation before its completion.

Asynchronous events run at some point after a particular operation has completed. These sinks cannot abort the operation as it occurs; instead, they are simply notified after the event has occurred.

Event sinks interact with data in the Web Storage System using the ExOLEDB provider and ADO. Additionally, CDO integrates with the ExOLEDB/ADO data access layer to provide a seamless and consistent way to manipulate this data.

WorkFlow Support

Web Storage System events can drive a workflow tracking process such as workflow objects implemented by CDO for Exchange. The CDO workflow engine provides a systematic process to control state transitions for documents in the Web Storage System. The engine relies on a user-defined table of actions—called the action table—to evaluate and execute transitions for documents saved in the application folder. You can think of the action table as a state-machine graph of document state transitions.

The workflow engine runs in response to certain system and Web Storage System events. It encapsulates the logic for advancing the state of your workflow documents. This enables you to control the status of documents that you are tracking or guiding. You define a workflow process and set it up to be executed based on events occurring in your application folder or in the system. These events, for which you register your application, cause the workflow event sink to run. They include the OnSyncSave and OnSyncDelete Web Storage System events and the OnTimer system event. These events invoke the workflow engine if you have registered the workflow event sink on your workflow application folder.

Web Application Development

The Web Storage System is a great environment for running a Web site that uses ASP and HTML files. Your ASP pages do not have to be in the Web Storage System, but with ASP pages in the Web Storage System you can manage in the same way that you manage other items.

The Web Storage System provides access to content through the HTTP/WebDAV protocol. The native format for property requests in WebDAV is XML. You can take advantage of the XML-related tools provided with Windows 2000 and Internet Explorer 5.0 or later to build client-side front ends for Web Storage System applications. Among the XML tools is the MSXML DOM parser and the XMLHTTPRequest COM object. You can use the XMLHTTPRequest object to send and receive XML-formatted HTTP requests for properties and item searches and then render the data in the browser by using the Extensible Style Language (XSL) templates, behaviors, and ActiveX controls. In this manner, you can separate data from display on the client, and you can handle data transactions between the client and the Web Storage System without round tripping to the server for new display information such as you would with an ASP page.

Exchange 2000 Server Web Storage System

Microsoft Exchange 2000 Server is the first to use Web Storage System technology and serves as the basis for both public and private stores.

An Exchange 2000 private store is the default storage location for a user's mailbox, containing private messages, appointments, contacts, and other Outlook folders and items. You can store private mailboxes in multiple private stores. This feature is transparent to end users as well as developers because each mailbox is accessed under a single virtual root—under MBX when using the ExOLEDB provider or under Exchange when using the HTTP/WebDAV protocol. MAPI clients can also access mailboxes transparently in any private store.

Exchange 2000 supports hosting public folder trees in multiple public stores. One public store is accessible to MAPI clients, and all others can be accessed by using the new protocols and APIs, for example, through the server-side ExOLEDB provider, through the HTTP/WebDAV protocol, or through the file system.

Web Storage System Access APIs and Protocols

Earlier versions of Microsoft Exchange Server provided access to items in stores by using MAPI. With the Web Storage System, several new APIs and protocols are available for accessing items and item properties.

The ExOLEDB provider is available on the server, enabling you to use ADO 2.5 and CDO for Exchange in your server-side applications. Such applications include ASP pages, COM+ components, and Web Storage System event sinks.

The Web Storage System also provides access using the HTTP protocol. This industry-standard protocol has been enhanced through the WebDAV specification to support an additional set of protocol commands, such as MOVE, COPY, DELETE, and MKCOL. More importantly, you can request or set properties for items using the PROPFIND, PROPPATCH, and SEARCH commands. The format for transferring property data is XML.

For many applications, access to an item's content—but not its properties—is all that is required. You can access item streams using the Microsoft Win32 file APIs. All public and private stores are available through the native operating system's file system. You cannot access an item's properties through the file system. To access these, you must use the ExOLEDB provider, the HTTP/WebDAV protocol, or MAPI.

The following topics introduce you to the APIs and protocols provided by the Web Storage System:

- OLE DB and ADO access
- HTTP/WebDAV access
- File System access
- MAPI access

OLE DB and ADO Access

Exchange 2000 provides a new, high-performance OLE DB provider that you can use on the local server to access Web Storage System items using OLE DB, ADO 2.5, and CDO.

Because the ExOLEDB provider is a server-side component, it can be used only to access public and mailbox stores that reside locally on the server. The ExOLEDB provider is ideal for use in COM+ components, ASP, and Web Storage System Event sinks that run on the server. To access remote public and mailbox stores, use the HTTP/WebDAV protocol, a shared file system, or MAPI and derived components, such as CDO 1.2.1.

Exchange registers this provider for the file URL namespace with the OLE DB 2.5 root binder on the local server. The root binder eliminates the requirement that you explicitly specify an ADO Connection object when accessing items through OLE DB, which means that you can bind an ADO Record object directly to an item only by using a file-type URL. To bind to items by using the HTTP URL scheme through the ExOLEDB provider, you must specify the ExOLEDB provider binder with an ADO Connection object (Connection.Provider = "ExOLEDB.DataSource"). In most cases, it is best that you specify this provider explicitly to avoid needing to figure out whether an ADO Connection object is required to bind an item using ExOLEDB.

Table 1–1 summarizes how specific ADO 2.5 objects can be used effectively in Web Storage System applications.

TABLE 1-1 *How specific ADO 2.5 objects can be used effectively in Web Storage System applications*

ADO 2.5 object	Usage

Record	Use the Record object to access any item in the Web Storage System. You have full access to the item's set of properties and its associated stream. For example:
	`Dim Rec As New ADODB.Record`
	`Dim Conn as New ADODB.Connection`
	`Dim Stm as ADODB.Stream`
	`Conn.Provider = "ExOLEDB.DataSource"`
	`Conn.Open "http://server/folder"`
	`Rec.Open "http://server/folder/item.txt", Conn`
	`Set Stm = Rec.Fields(adDefaultStream).Value`

8 Chapter 1 ● **Introduction to the Web Storage System**

TABLE 1-1 *How specific ADO 2.5 objects can be used effectively in Web Storage System applications (continued)*

ADO 2.5 object	Usage

Recordset	Use the Recordset object to issue SQL SELECT commands in folders. Consider these examples:
	`Dim Conn as New ADODB.Connection`
	`Conn.Provider = "ExOLEDB.DataSource"`
	`Conn.Open RootFolderURL`
	`Dim Rs as New ADODB.Recordset`
	`Set Rs.ActiveConnection = Conn`
	`"select ""DAV:displayname"" " _`
	`& "from scope('shallow traversal of ""URL""')" _`
	`& "Where ""DAV:ishidden"" = False"`

Stream	Use the ADO Stream object to access an item's stream. For example:
	`Dim Stm As ADODB.Stream`
	`Dim Rec as New ADODB.Record`
	`Dim Conn as New ADODB.Connection`
	`Conn.Provider = "ExOLEDB.DataSource"`
	`Conn.Open Url`
	`Rec.Open Url, Conn`
	`Set Stm = Rec.Fields(adDefaultStream).Value`
	`' Or, alternately`
	`Dim Stm2 as New ADODB.Stream`
	`Stm2.Open Rec, adModeRead, adOpenStreamFromRecord`

Connection	Use the ADO Connection object to bind to a particular public or private store, handle transactions, and share across Record and Recordset objects to avoid continually rebinding to stores. Consider the following:
	`Dim Conn as New ADODB.Connection`
	`Conn.Provider = "ExOLEDB.DataSource"`
	`Conn.Open RootFolderURL`
	`Conn.BeginTrans`
	`   Rec.Open ItemURL, Conn, adModeReadWrite`
	`..' ..`
	`Conn.CommitTrans`
	Placing Connection object references in ASP Session or Application objects and reusing this connection from one ASP page to another is ideal for optimal server-side performance.

TABLE 1-1 *How specific ADO 2.5 objects can be used effectively in Web Storage System applications (continued)*

ADO 2.5 object	Usage

Fields
Field
	Use the ADO Fields collection and the ADO Field object to access an item's properties. For example:
	`Dim Rec as New ADODB.Record`
	`Dim Conn as New ADODB.Connection`
	`Conn.Provider = "ExOLEDB.DataSource"`
	`Conn.Open Url`
	`Dim Flds as ADODB.Fields`
	`Dim Fld as ADODB.Field`
	`Rec.Open Url, Conn, adModeReadWrite`
	`Set Flds = Rec.Fields`
	`For Each Fld in Flds`
	`    '...`
	`Next Fld`
	`...`

Each of the following CDO objects provides an ADO Fields collection on its default interface, allowing you to access Web Storage System item properties directly, as if the object was an ADO Record or Recordset object:

- Addressee
- Appointment
- BodyPart
- Configuration
- Exception
- Folder
- Item
- Message
- Person

HTTP/WebDAV Access

Items in the Web Storage System can be accessed remotely by using the HTTP/WebDAV protocol, defined in RFC 2518. This protocol extends the HTTP/1.1 protocol, defined by RFC 2616, to provide additional methods and capabilities. For example, it provides a means to access not only an item's contents but also an extensible set of associated properties. The protocol also defines methods used to move, copy, delete, and make collections of items. XML, defined in the World Wide Web Consortium Recommendation REC-xml-19980210, is the encoding format used to transfer item properties across the network.

Microsoft Internet Explorer 5.0 provides the Microsoft XML (MSXML) COM component, a powerful XML parser and set of related tools. The

XMLHTTPRequest COM class integrates with MSXML COM objects to simplify the management of client-side HTTP protocol requests and responses that contain XML bodies. Response XML data can easily be cast into HTML-formatted data by using the XSL transformation capabilities of the MSXML component.

File System Access

You can access the Web Storage System using Microsoft Windows Explorer and Microsoft Win32 file-system APIs through the Exchange Installable File System (ExIFS). Each store (there can be many on a single host) exists as a file system folder mounted under drive M on the host server. If drive M is already in use, the next available letter in the alphabet is used. Figure 1–1 shows the Windows Explorer view of a typical server. Note the Web Storage System folders under drive M.

You can share drive M as you would any other drive. End users can use Windows Explorer or Microsoft MS-DOS commands at a command prompt to update items used by Web Storage System applications. You can also restrict users without permissions from editing documents and jeopardizing data integrity.

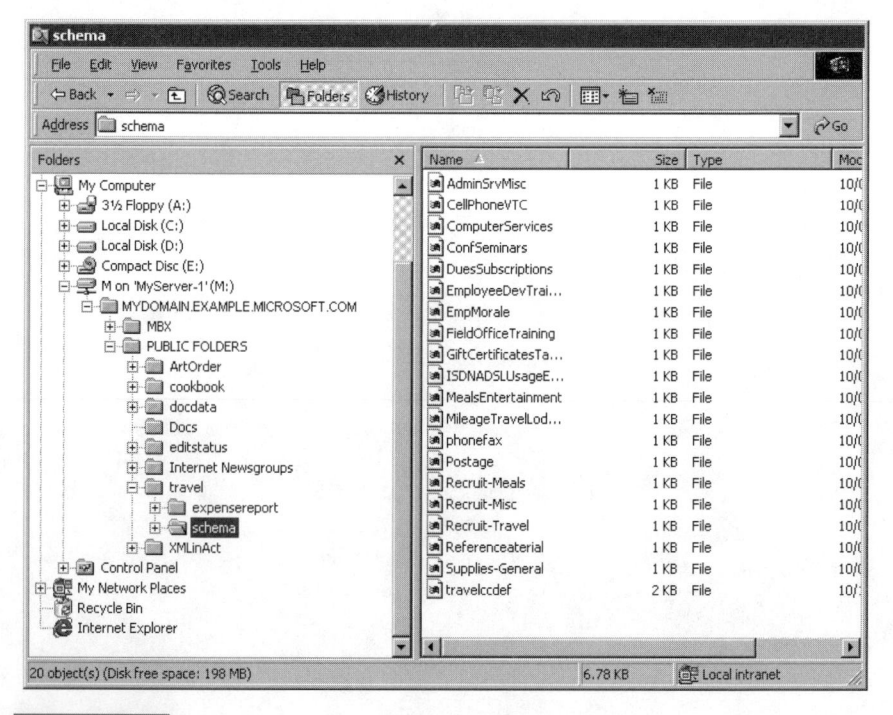

FIGURE 1–1 *An example of the Windows Explorer view of a typical server*

The default names for the first public and private stores are Public Folders and MBX, respectively.

When using Win32 file-system APIs, no mechanism is present to access properties for an item; you can access only each item's stream. To access item properties, you need to use an alternate mechanism, such as the WebDAV protocol, the ExOLEDB provider, or MAPI.

MAPI Access

MAPI can be used not only to access the items and folders within a public and private store, but also to access the rich set of properties stored along with each item. MAPI is used by various industry-standard email clients, such as the Microsoft Exchange client, all versions of Microsoft Outlook, and Microsoft Outlook Express, and many versions of proprietary clients, including those sold by QUALCOMM Incorporated (Eudora) and Netscape Communications Corporation. Previous versions of Exchange Server provided stores that were accessed primarily by using MAPI providers.

Exchange 2000 Server continues to provide access to MAPI clients, such as Microsoft Outlook, through the Web Storage System MAPI message-store provider. MAPI clients can access mailboxes in any private store on the server transparently. MAPI clients can access only *one* public folder tree per server. This public folder tree is designated as the MAPI public folder tree and is normally specified as the "/public" virtual root through HTTP and the "Public Folders" top-level folder through the ExOLEDB provider. To access data within other public folder trees and associated public stores, you must use the new APIs and protocols, such as the HTTP/WebDAV protocol, the ExOLEDB provider, or the file system.

Additional Web Storage System Access Protocols

The following protocols are supported, primarily for accessing private Web Storage System mailboxes:

- *Post Office Protocol version 3.0 (POP3).* Used to access private Inbox folders. Resources in a private store are available through this reliable, yet simple wire protocol. This protocol is ubiquitous in modern email–client applications, such as Outlook Express.
- *Internet Message Access Protocol version 4 (IMAP4).* Used for rich access to private-folder hierarchies, including the Inbox folder. Resources in a private store and within various public stores are available through this industry-standard wire protocol. Users need only an IMAP4-supporting application to access resources through the protocol.

Web Storage System Item Properties

Using the Web Storage System, you can easily store any number of properties (also called fields) along with each item. You can access the value of each property, and you can search and group items having properties that match certain conditions.

Any number of properties can be stored with each item, and the set of properties for each item can be different. Unlike with a relational database, you do not need to add a column to a table to set an item property.

Web Storage System item properties have names made up of a namespace and a local name. The namespace is a unique string that acts as a scope for the name. Using a namespace guarantees that each property with a shared local name is unique within the store. Namespaces are defined using the Uniform Resource Identifier (URI) syntax. Examples of URI values used are urn:schemas:httpmail: and *http://schemas.microsoft.com/exchange/*.

Namespaces and Property Names

By convention, property names for Web Storage System items are composed of a URI and a local name. The URI portion of the property name ensures that it is globally unique and unambiguous. Two properties with the same local name can therefore be differentiated using namespaces.

For example, one application might use a property called state. In one case, "state" may refer to a country, and in another case it may refer to a state of some document in a process. Both properties are made unambiguous for an item by adding a URI prefix to the property names, as in the following example:

```
urn:schemas-domain1-tld:state
urn:schemas-domain2-tld:state
```

The two names are broken down into the parts shown in Tables 1–2 and 1–3.

TABLE 1-2 *urn:schemas-domain1-tld:state*

URI component	Value
Namespace URI	urn:schemas-domain1-tld:
Property name (local part)	state
Full name	urn:schemas-domain1-tld:state

Table 1-3 *urn:schemas-domain2-tld:state*

URI component	Value
Namespace URI	urn:schemas-domain2-tld::
Property name (local part)	state
Full name	urn:schemas-domain2-tld:state

Namespace URLs and URNs

A namespace is a URI, in the form of a character string, which is used to identify a resource on the Internet. The two most common URI schemes currently being used are the URL and the Uniform Resource Name (URN):

- *URL.* An address for a resource on the Internet. Web browsers use URLs to locate Internet resources. A URL defines the protocol used to access the resource (such as http://), the host on which the resource is available, and path information required to access the resource on the host. For example, *www.microsoft.com/default.asp* is a URL.
- *URN.* A name for a resource on the Internet. URNs uniquely identify (name) Internet resources, without regard to where they are located. As such, URNs are intended only to generate unique names and do not normally imply protocols, hosts, or path information.

Both URLs and URNs are forms of URIs.

With the Web Storage System, URLs are used both as URIs in item property names and to identify particular items. URNs are used only with property names. For example, an item's URL could be *file:///./backofficestorage/ domain.tld/public folders/folder1/*. That item will also have properties named *http://schemas.microsoft.com/exchange/security/descriptor* and DAV:contentclass. The first property name is composed of the namespace URI *http:// schemas.microsoft.com/exchange/security/* and the local name *descriptor*. The second property name is composed of the namespace URI "DAV:" and the local name "contentclass."

Namespace URIs are commonly expressed using the URL scheme. However, the URL is used only to scope the local part of the property name and does not imply that a resource or item exists at this URL or that it can be downloaded.

Default Web Storage System Namespaces

The Web Storage System defines and reserves the namespaces listed in Table 1-4. These namespaces can be used in property names.

Chapter 1 • Introduction to the Web Storage System

TABLE 1-4 *Web Storage System Namespaces*

Namespace	Description
DAV:	Properties defined for the Web-based Distributed Authoring and Versioning (WebDAV) protocol, including properties for general data access (such as DAV:href) and for determining hierarchical information (such as DAV:isfolder).
http://schemas.microsoft.com/exchange/	Properties specific to Microsoft Exchange 2000 Server and Web Storage System.
http://schemas.microsoft.com/exchange/events/	Properties used to create event-sink binding items.
urn:schemas-microsoft-com:office:forms	Properties used to register HTML forms in the Web Storage System.
http://schemas.microsoft.com/exchange/security/	Properties specific to security features for items in the Web Storage System.
urn:schemas:microsoft-com:datatypes:	Definitions for data types used when creating schema items.
urn:schemas:microsoft-com:exch-data:	Definitions for Exchange-specific data types used for Web Storage System properties.
urn:schemas:microsoft-com:xml-data:	Definitions for XML namespaces that incorporate dynamic data typing and binding.
urn:schemas:microsoft-com:office:office	Properties specific to Microsoft Office files.
urn:schemas:calendar:	Properties used for calendaring. The following properties are also available for CDO calendar objects: Appointment, CalendarMessage, CalendarPart, Exception, RecurrencePattern, and Addressee.
urn:schemas:contacts:	Properties for managing contacts. Several properties are also available for the CDO Person object.
urn:schemas:httpmail:	Fields used to create and process the body of a message. For fields in the header of a message, use the mail header namespace.
urn:schemas:mailheader:	Standard mail header properties for messages. Several properties are also available for the CDO Message object.

When adding your own properties to items, you use your own namespace URI in the property name to make each one unique.

Custom Properties

Although the Web Storage System provides a large number of predefined properties used for standard applications, you can store any number of additional properties along with each item; these are called custom properties. Each item can have a completely different set of custom properties that you define.

A custom property is persisted with its associated item and can be requested by name when examining the item. When you bind directly to items using the ExOLEDB provider or ADO or when you issue a PROPFIND command with a depth of 0 through the HTTP/WebDAV protocol, the Web Storage System returns all custom properties for the item. Custom properties are not visible to an SQL 'SELECT *' statement or a PROPFIND command for all item properties with a depth of 1, unless they are defined as part of the item's content class. Therefore, to make your properties discoverable to schema-aware applications such as the Web Storage System query processor, you must add property and content class definitions to the application folder's schema scope.

When searching for custom properties using an SQL statement, you should use the CAST element for all properties that are not of the string type. Custom properties should be cast in both the SELECT list and the WHERE clause portions of the SQL statement.

NAMESPACE GUIDELINES

When creating a name for a custom property, you should use a namespace URI to provide scope and uniqueness for the name. The following guidelines are recommended:

- If your company or organization has registered a domain name with InterNIC, use this name when constructing a namespace for your custom properties.
- Make sure to use a valid URI scheme for your namespaces. This guarantees that no problems are encountered when transmitting these custom properties through the HTTP/WebDAV protocol.
- Avoid using a namespace scheme that denotes standard properties, such as urn:content-classes:, urn:schemas:, and so on. Make sure you incorporate your domain name in the namespace. For example, use

  ```
  urn:schemas-domain-tld:
  http://schemas.domain.tld/myschema/
  ```

  where tld denotes the top-level domain.

- Define custom properties as part of an application schema. This provides a mechanism for discoverability as well as the ability to return custom properties when a SELECT * statement is executed on a folder

containing resources that use custom properties. For more information, see "Web Storage System Schema" in Microsoft's *Software Development Kit* (SDK).
- If your company or organization does not have a registered domain name, try to generate a namespace that will render your property names as unique as possible. One way to guarantee it is to use a globally unique identifier (GUID) you generate on one of your computers in the namespace, as in the following:

```
urn:uuid:c2f41010-65b3-11d1-a29f-00aa00c14882/
```

This mechanism, although guaranteed to render the namespace unique, is not simple to read, and it may be difficult to present to users in Microsoft Outlook or Web forms.
- Make sure you understand how fully qualified names are constructed when setting custom properties using the WebDAV protocol. For example, when constructing the XML code to set custom properties, omitting either the colon (:) or the forward slash (/) at the end of the XML namespace reference causes the number sign (#) to be used as a separator. If you later request the property by concatenating the property to the namespace with the appropriate separator character, the ExOLEDB provider returns an error, indicating that the property is not defined. Note that you can always verify the name of a property by requesting all properties through a WebDAV PROPFIND command or by binding the associated item directly by using ADO or OLE DB.

CUSTOM PROPERTIES AND MAPI

Custom properties that you set by using either the HTTP/WebDAV protocol or the ExOLEDB provider are available for use by MAPI clients, including MAPI Outlook forms. All custom properties are accessible on items as named properties within the PS_PUBLIC_STRINGS MAPI namespace.

Property Names and the Exchange OLE DB Provider

When you access item properties using the server-side ExOLEDB provider, you construct the property names by combining the namespace URI and the local name, as shown in Table 1-5.

When combining the namespace URI and the local name to form the full name, the following rules are used to determine the separation character:

1. If the namespace ends with the character '/', ':', or '?', the two parts of the name are simply joined; for example, "DAV:" + "contentclass" gives "DAV:contentclass".
2. Otherwise, the "#" character is appended to the namespace URI and is used to separate the namespace URI from local name. For example,

"urn:schemas-microsoft-com:office:office" + "Author" gives "urn:schemas-microsoft-com:office:office#Author". Adding "urn:schemas-domain-tld#" + "casenumber" yields "urn:schemas-domain-tld##casenumber".

TABLE 1-5 Construct the property names by combining the namespace URI and the local name

Namespace URI	Local name	Full name
DAV:	contentclass	DAV:contentclass
urn:schemas:mailheader:	to	urn:schemas:mailheader:to
http://schemas.microsoft.com/exchange/security/	descriptor	http://schemas.microsoft.com/exchange/security/descriptor
urn:schemas-microsoft-com:office:office	Author	urn:schemas-microsoft-com:office:office#Author

The reverse of these rules is used to separate a namespace from a local name when transmitting properties using the HTTP/WebDAV protocol.

Full names are used regardless of whether you are requesting access to the property through an SQL statement, an ADO Fields collection, or an OLE DB IRow or IRowset interface.

Property Names and HTTP/WebDAV

When you access item properties using the HTTP/WebDAV protocol, the property names are represented as namespace-scoped XML elements complying with the Namespaces in XML Recommendation. For example, a property accessible through the ExOLEDB provider with the name "DAV:contentclass" is represented through HTTP/WebDAV as

```
<a:contentclass xmlns:a="DAV:">[value]</a:contentclass>
```

The prefix "a" in this example acts only as a placeholder for the URI "DAV:" and is not part of the property name.

A typical response to the PROPFIND HTTP/WebDAV command:

```
PROPFIND /path/resource.eml HTTP/1.1
Content-Type: text/xml
Content-Length: XXX

<?xml version="1.0" encoding="UTF-8"?>
<d:propfind xmlns:d="DAV:">
 <d:prop><d:displayname/></d:prop>
 <d:prop><d:getcontentlength/></d:prop>
 <d:prop><d:resourcetype/></d:prop>
 <d:prop><d:iscollection/></d:prop>
</d:propfind>
```

might look like this:

```
<?xml version='1.0'?>
<a:multistatus
  xmlns:a="DAV:"
  xmlns:b="urn:uuid:c2f41010-65b3-11d1-a29f-00aa00c14882/">
<a:response>
<a:href>http://microsoft.com/path/resource.eml</a:href>
<a:propstat>
  <a:status>HTTP/1.1 OK</a:status>
  <a:prop>
    <a:displayname>resource.eml</a:displayname>
    <a:getcontentlength>367</a:getcontentlength>
    <a:resourcetype><a:collection/></a:resourcetype>
    <a:iscollection b:dt="boolean">0</a:iscollection>
  </a:prop>
</a:propstat>
```

In this example, the properties "DAV:displayname", "DAV:getcontentlength", "DAV:resourcetype", and "DAV:iscollection" were requested for the item at the URL *http://microsoft.com/path/resource.eml*. Note that the prefixes ("a" and "d") used as placeholders for the "DAV:" URI are different in the two XML strings. Table 1–6 shows full names and example-scoped XML elements side by side.

Note The prefix used as a placeholder for the namespace URI is random and always refers to a namespace URI.

TABLE 1–6 *Full names and example-scoped XML elements side by side*

Full name	Example-scoped XML element
DAV:resourcetype	<a:resourcetype xmlns:a="DAV:"/>
DAV:iscollection	<b:iscollection xmlns:b="DAV:"/>
DAV:getcontentlength	<c:getcontentlength xmlns:c="DAV:"/>
DAV:iscollection	<d:iscollection xmlns:d="DAV:"/>

Property Names and XML

When an application accesses a Web Storage System property by using HTTP/WebDAV protocol, the property name, when placed in an XML stream, is disassembled into its namespace and name parts. When the property name is taken out of the XML stream, it is reassembled and then saved to the item in the Web Storage System. This happens transparently within the WebDAV service itself. The following rules are used to identify the namespace and the name portions of a fully qualified property name when disassembling it for transport using HTTP:

- Valid URL and URN schema-separator characters, which delimit namespace names from property names, are:

  forward slash (/)

  colon (:)

  semicolon (;)

  number sign (#)

  question mark (?)

  When disassembling a property name into a namespace URI and a local name, the string is scanned from right to left until one of the characters listed in the preceding paragraph is found.

- If the separator character is the number sign (#), the namespace is the entire string to the left of the character. The property name is the string to the right of it.
- If the separator is not the number sign, the namespace name is the entire string to the left of the property name. The property name is the string to the right of the separator character.

Table 1-7 shows how a fully qualified property name is disassembled into its parts.

TABLE 1-7 *How a fully qualified property name is disassembled into its parts name*

Namespace	Name	Full name
urn:schemas-microsoft-com:	prop1	urn:schemas-microsoft-com:prop1
http://microsoft.com/schema	prop2	http://microsoft.com/schema#prop2
http://exchange.microsoft.com/schema/	prop3	http://exchange.microsoft.com/schema/prop3
urn:property#	prop4	urn:property##prop4
urn:property?	prop5	urn:property?prop5

Property Data Types

A rich set of single- and multivalue data types is provided for item properties in the Web Storage System. Table 1–8 lists these types, using the XML-data representation for each one. Table 1–9 lists the mappings between the data types and the types presented using OLE DB and MAPI.

Table 1–9 lists the mappings between types in OLE DB (ExOLEDB provider), MAPI, and XML (HTTP/WebDAV).

Table 1-8 Item properties in the Web Storage System using the XML-data representation

Type (XML)	Description
Boolean	A Boolean value, either True or False. In an XML string, this value is either "1" for True or "0" for False.
i2 mv.i2	2-byte integer.
int mv.int	4-byte integer.
i8 mv.i8	8-byte integer.
dateTime.tz mv.dateTime.tz	Date and time.
r4 mv.r4	4-byte floating-point number.
fixed.14.4 mv.fixed.14.4	Fixed floating-point number.
float mv.float	Floating-point number.
uuid mv.uuid	GUID in string format.
string mv.string	2-byte character string (Unicode).
bin.base64 mv.bin.base64	Binary data (base 64-encoded).

Table 1-9 Data Type Mappings

XML-data type	OLE DB type	MAPI type
boolean	DBTYPE_BOOL	PT_BOOLEAN
i2 mv.i2	DBTYPE_I2 DBTYPE_ARRAY | DBTYPE_I2	PT_I2 PT_MV_I2
int mv.int	DBTYPE_I4 DBTYPE_ARRAY | DBTYPE_I4	PT_LONG PT_MV_LONG
i8 mv.i8	DBTYPE_I8 DBTYPE_ARRAY | DBTYPE_I8	PT_I8 PT_MV_I8
dateTime.tz mv.dateTime.tz	DBTYPE_FILETIME DBTYPE_ARRAY | DBTYPE_FILETIME	PT_SYSTIME PT_MV_SYSTIME
dateTime.tz mv.dateTime.tz	DBTYPE_FILETIME DBTYPE_ARRAY | DBTYPE_FILETIME	PT_APPTIME PT_MV_APPTIME

TABLE 1-9 *Data Type Mappings (continued)*

XML-data type	OLE DB type	MAPI type
r4	DBTYPE_R4	PT_R4
mv.r4	DBTYPE_ARRAY | DBTYPE_R4	PT_MV_R4
fixed.14.4	DBTYPE_CY	PT_CURRENCY
mv.fixed.14.4	DBTYPE_ARRAY | DBTYPE_CY	PT_MV_CURRENCY
float	DBTYPE_DOUBLE	PT_DOUBLE
mv.float	DBTYPE_ARRAY | DBTYPE_DOUBLE	PT_MV_DOUBLE
uuid	DBTYPE_GUID	PT_CLSID
mv.uuid	DBTYPE_ARRAY | DBTYPE_GUID	PT_MV_CLSID
string	DBTYPE_WSTR	PT_UNICODE
mv.string	DBTYPE_ARRAY | DBTYPE_WSTR	PT_MV_UNICODE
string	DBTYPE_STR	PT_STRING8
mv.string	DBTYPE_ARRAY | DBTYPE_STR	PT_MV_STRING8
bin.base64	DBTYPE_BYTES	PT_BINARY
mv.bin.base64	DBTYPE_ARRAY | DBTYPE_BYTES	PT_MV_BINARY
Not supported	DBTYPE_ERROR	PT_ERROR
Not supported	DBTYPE_NULL	PT_NULL
Not supported	DBTYPE_IUNKNOWN	PT_OBJECT
Not supported	Not supported	PT_UNSPECIFIED

The Item Default Stream Property

Each item in the Web Storage System that is not a collection has a special property called the default stream. This property contains any sequence of characters or bytes of any length, just like a file on the file system. At first glance, the stream for an item might appear to be equivalent to another property whose type is text or binary. The primary differences are as follows:

- The default stream for an item is always available using the same name or index, regardless of the item.
- The stream can contain a sequence of characters or bytes of any length. Regular text or binary properties have limited size. Text properties can be up to 50 KB.
- Only the item's stream is available through the Microsoft Win32 file system APIs. In this way, item default streams are the same as the contents of a file on the file system.

When using ADO or CDO, you access the item's stream by requesting the property with the value adDefaultStream in the Fields collection. The returned Field object contains a reference to an ADO Stream object (_Stream interface). With OLE DB, the property is requested using the DBGUID_DEFAULTSTREAM flag. The stream is accessed using the returned IStream interface reference. The ADO Stream object differentiates between binary and text streams. No differentiation exists when using the raw IStream interface.

No inherent relationship exists between an item's properties and its stream, with a few notable exceptions: Items that are messages and Office documents, both of which are handled in a special way.

Automatic Property Promotion from the Stream

The Web Storage System provides special handling called property promotion for messages and office documents when their content streams are saved. Typically, when you create an item in the Web Storage System, no inherent relationship exists between the item's properties and its stream. With messages and Microsoft Office documents, however, the item stream is automatically examined as it is being saved to the store, and property values are extracted from this stream and set for the item. Note, however, that this is a one-way action; if properties are subsequently set on the item, the stream is not automatically updated.

Property promotion is triggered in one of two ways: through file extensions or through content type when using the HTTP/WebDAV protocol. A Web Storage System item saved with the one of the file name extensions listed and described in Table 1–10 has its stream content automatically examined for properties that are then promoted as fields for the item.

For example, if you copy a message in a file called *item.eml* to the Web Storage System using the file system, the Web Storage System assumes that the file contains a message. It parses the message content stream and sets the various messaging-related fields for the item, such as urn:schemas:httpmail:subject. Similarly, if you copy a Microsoft Word file to the Web Storage System using the file system, the Web Storage System examines the file's structured storage for standard Office properties, extracts the values, and automatically sets them for the item. For example, the Author document property value is used to set the urn:schemas-microsoft-com:office:office#Author property for the item.

When you put items in the Web Storage System using the HTTP/WebDAV protocol, Office and message and application content types also trigger property promotion. For example, if you issue a PUT command and the content type of the body of the HTTP request is "message/rfc822", the Web Storage System assumes that the inbound stream is an RFC 822 (and possibly MIME)-formatted stream, parses the stream, and promotes the various messaging-related headers to properties for the item. Similarly, the content type "application/msword" triggers the promotion of the document's structured storage properties to item properties.

TABLE 1-10 *File name extensions used in the Web Storage System*

File name extension	Description
.eml	Denotes an RFC 822-formatted message. Typically, messages are further formatted using the Multipurpose Internet Mail Extensions (MIME). The message stream is parsed, and the value of various mail header fields such as To: and From: are added ("promoted") to the item as properties. The DAV:contentclass for the item is also set appropriately (e.g., urn:content-classes:message, and urn:content-classes:calendarmessage).
.doc, .xls, .ppt and other Office extensions	Results in the item being created with DAV:contentclass set to urn:content-classes:document. For Office documents that have standard extensions such as .doc, .xls, or .ppt, document properties available within the file's standard structured storage are added as item properties.

T W O

Web Storage System Schema and Search Engine

Web Storage System Schema

The Web Storage System provides a means to define schema information for items. By using the schema capabilities of the Web Storage System, you can make schema information about your application discoverable to schema-aware applications such as the Web Storage System Structured Query Language (SQL) query processor. Schema information is not rigidly enforced in the Web Storage System as it would be in a relational database system such as Microsoft SQL Server. Instead, schema information in the Web Storage System is primarily used to provide a mechanism for schema-aware applications to discover the names of content classes and associated properties used for items in a particular application.

Content Classes

A Web Storage System content class defines the intent or purpose of an item along with the names of properties that are intended for items in this class.

A content class is different from a content type. A content type defines the type of data that is stored in an item's stream. For example, a common content type is "application/msword"; this content type value indicates that the item's stream contains a Microsoft Word document in binary form. However, it neither defines the intent or purpose of the Microsoft Word file to an application nor specifies what properties are stored with the item. For instance, one such file might be a Ph.D. thesis and another might be a resume.

A good example of a content class is an expense report. An expense report can be in the format of a Microsoft Excel worksheet, a Microsoft Word document, or an email message. However, regardless of the format, there may be a common set of properties stored with the expense report. For example, an expense-tracking application might store the date range in the report, the total dollar amount in the report, and the approval state of the report. Each item stored by the application can have these properties defined, irrespective of the item's content type (email message or Microsoft Office document).

A content class is used frequently by applications to do the following:

- Indicate what processing should occur for the specified item.
- Instantiate an object to render or manipulate the specified item.
- Enhance the user interface, such as by displaying an icon appropriate for the specified content class.
- Render items using forms that are based on the specified item's content class.

Figure 2–1 shows the relationship between property and content class definitions and how you can extend a content class, thereby refining and inheriting both its intent and its associated properties.

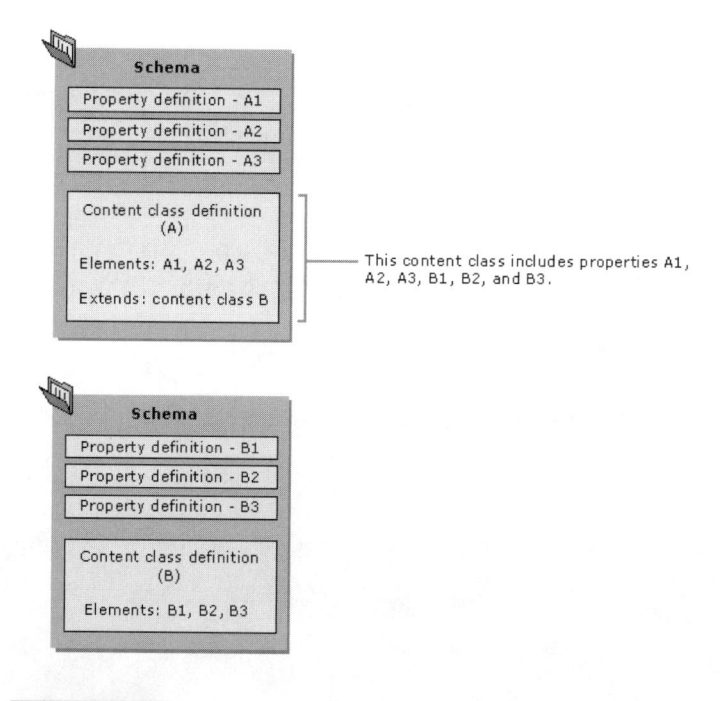

Figure 2–1 *The relationship between property and content class definitions and how you can extend a content class*

CONTENT CLASS INHERITANCE

When you create a content class definition, you can inherit properties and semantics defined by other content classes. To extend or refine a content class, you specify its name in the new class urn:schemas-microsoft-com:xml-data#extends property. An extended (or "derived") content class inherits both the intent of the base class and the properties of the extending content class. The concept of content class inheritance parallels that of class inheritance in programming languages such as C++.

SINGLE INHERITANCE • An example of single inheritance is extending the urn:content-classes:person content class for a contact-management application. Your new content class, urn:schemas-domain-tld:content-classes:salesperson, can define additional marketing properties for the contact. Rather than redefining all the properties used with the urn:content-classes:person class for the urn:schemas-domain-tld:content-classes:salesperson class, you instead inherit these properties through extension. Figure 2–2 depicts this inheritance.

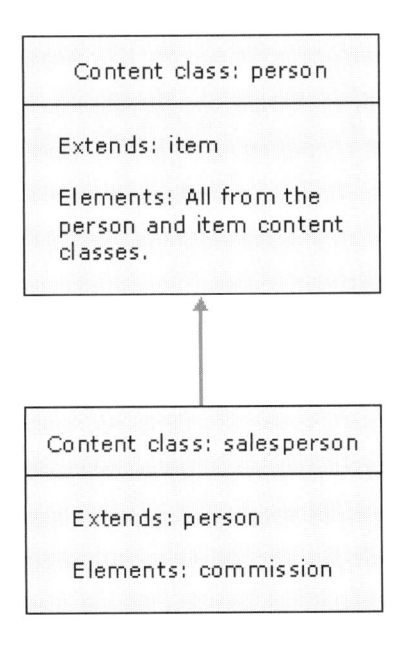

FIGURE 2–2 *An example of single inheritance is extending the urn:content-classes:person content class for a contact-management application*

MULTIPLE INHERITANCE • A scenario that demonstrates multiple inheritance and an effective use of content classes is an expense report tailored for delivery as either an email message or a document. To create an application for electronically mailing expense reports, you need access to expense report and message properties; for applications generating expense report documents, you need access to expense report and document properties.

In Figure 2–3, three content classes (top row) extend the Item content class: message, expensereport, and document. They also serve as base classes for other content classes. The illustration also shows two derived content classes (bottom row): expensemessage and expensedocument. These content classes need properties from their base classes, message and document, respectively. And both classes share a need for expense report properties from expensereport. They do not need to have any additional property definitions.

The email expense report application will use the expensemessage content class, and the document expense report application will use the expensedocument content class. Of course, you can define a content class that inherits from all the base classes; it depends entirely on the needs of the application.

The benefits of inheritance are not only for applications designed for a newer, derived content class, but also for any older applications that can now understand their properties in extended content classes.

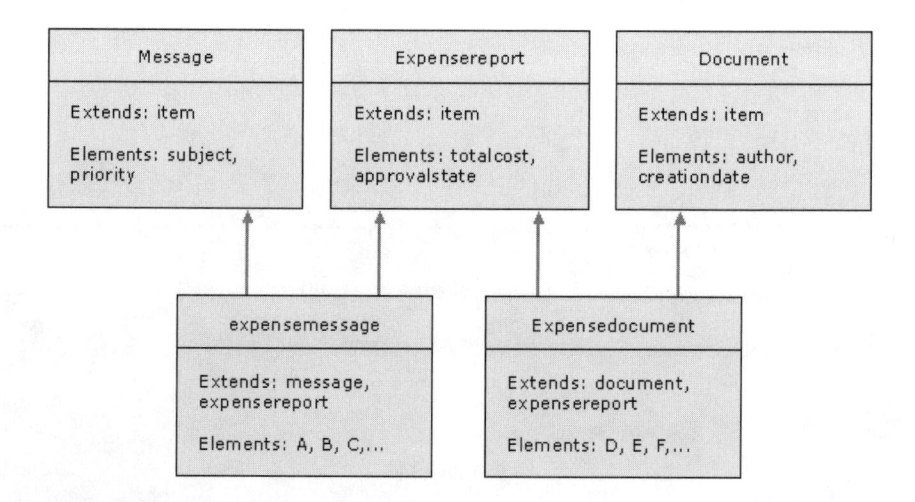

Message	Expensereport	Document
Extends: item	Extends: item	Extends: item
Elements: subject, priority	Elements: totalcost, approvalstate	Elements: author, creationdate

expensemessage	Expensedocument
Extends: message, expensereport	Extends: document, expensereport
Elements: A, B, C,...	Elements: D, E, F,...

FIGURE 2–3 *Three content classes extend the Item content class: message, expensereport, and document*

Schema Definition Items

In the Web Storage System, schema information is defined using two types of items:

- *Content class definition items.* These define the intent or purpose of an item, along with a set of property names that pertain to content of the item's class. Content class definitions also imply a set of semantic requirements for the item. For example, an item having content class urn:content-classes:mdn (Mail Delivery Notification, or MDN) is a message, and it has all the same properties defined as does the urn:content-classes:message content class. However, the semantics applied to the message are different in that the MDN class denotes a message that is a notification of delivery of some kind.
- *Property definition items.* These define information about a property, such as its name and type. To make a custom property visible to schema-aware applications, you create a definition for the property and then refer to it in a content class definition.

You are not required to create schema information for your application. You can simply add properties to an item if you want, and you do not have to define each property for the content class or property definition.

CONTENT CLASS DEFINITIONS

Content class definition items contain properties that define aspects of content stored in the Web Storage System. Table 2–1 lists and describes the properties used to define content classes.

TABLE 2–1 *Properties used to define content classes*

Property name	Value
urn:schemas-microsoft-com:xml-data#name	The name of the content class. By convention, content class names are constructed using the same mechanism as property names. For example: urn:schemas-domain-tld:content-classes:classA
DAV:contentclass	urn:content-classes:contentclassdef This designates the item as a content class definition item.
urn:schemas-microsoft-com:xml-data#element	A multivalue string containing the names of properties associated with the specified content class. Each referenced property must have a corresponding property definition item within scope.

TABLE 2–1 Properties used to define content classes (continued)

Property name	Value
urn:schemas-microsoft-com:xml-data#extends	A multivalue string containing the names of content classes that the specified class extends or inherits from. Each name must have a corresponding content class definition item within scope.
urn:schemas-microsoft-com:exch-data:expected-content-class	If defining a folder content class, this property is a multivalue string containing the names of content classes expected for items in a folder that belong to this class.

The urn:schemas-microsoft-com:exch-data: namespace contains several other properties that can be attributed to a content class for informational purposes.

PROPERTY DEFINITIONS

Property definitions are items, typically in a designated schema folder, which contain schema information about properties. To create a property definition, create an item and then specify its property values, as described in Table 2–2.

TABLE 2–2 Create a property definition by creating an item and then specify its property values

Fully qualified property name	Value
urn:schemas-microsoft-com:xml-data#name	The name of the property. For example: urn:schemas-domain-tld:propA
urn:schemas-microsoft-com:datatypes#type	The property's data type. See Data Types.
DAV:contentclass	urn:content-classes:propertydef
urn:schemas-microsoft-com:exch-data:isvisible	True or False. Used to indicate to schema-aware applications whether the property is visible to the client. Typically, you set this to False for properties that your application uses internally, but which you do not intend to be viewed by the application user.
urn:schemas-microsoft-com:exch-data:isindexed	True or False. Indicates whether the property is to be indexed.
urn:schemas-microsoft-com:exch-data:isrequired	True or False. Indicates to schema-aware applications whether the property is required for the specified items.
urn:schemas-microsoft-com:exch-data:ismultivalued	True or False. Indicates to schema-aware applications whether the property is a multivalue property.

Schema Scope

Each folder in the Web Storage System has a schema scope. The schema scope is a set of folders, traversed in a particular order, which can contain schema definition items. Each folder can have a different schema scope. The scope can be simple, consisting of only the global schema folder, or complex, containing a large list of folder URLs.

The following two properties from the urn:schemas-microsoft-com:exch-data: namespace are examined on folder items to define a schema scope:

- schema-collection-ref

   This property is a URL for a folder in which to search for content class and property definitions. This is the first folder searched for schema definition items and is always the first folder in a folder's schema scope. If this property is not set, the default is that store's *non_ipm_subtree/Schema* folder, which contains the Web Storage System default schema definition items.

- baseschema

   This property is a multivalue string containing URLs for one or more other folders. You extend the schema scope for a folder by identifying other folders that contain schema definition items.

Applying these two properties to folders, you create a virtual tree of folders in a store that contains schema definition items, starting with the folder identified by schema-collection-ref. When a schema-aware application constructs the schema information for a particular folder, it traverses the entire scope, breadth first, collecting definition items as they are encountered. Figure 2–4 presents one possible schema scope for a folder.

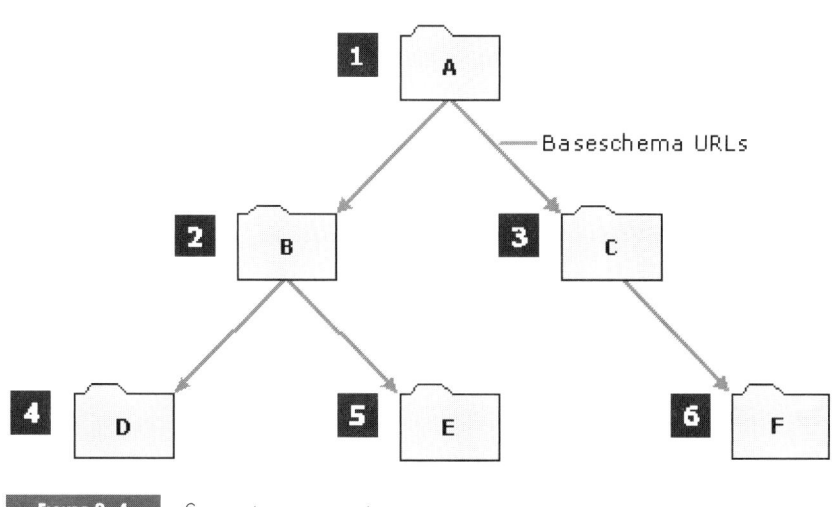

FIGURE 2–4 *Scope tree concept*

In Figure 2–4, we find the following:

- An application folder (not shown in the diagram) identifies folder *A* as its schema collection folder in its schema-collection-ref property.
- Folder *A* is the first folder searched for schema definition items.
- Folder *A* has baseschema URLs pointing to folders *B* and *C*, which are subsequently searched (in that order) for schema definition items.
- Folder *B* has baseschema URLs pointing to folders *D* and *E*, which are subsequently searched (in that order) for schema definition items.
- Folder *C* has a baseschema URL pointing to folder *F*, which is the last folder in the scope and the last one searched. Typically, this folder is set to the *non_ipm_subtree/Schema* folder for that store.

> **Note** The scope tree descends in breadth-first fashion. A breadth-first search works as follows: *A* is searched first, followed by *B* and *C*, and then *D*, *E*, and *F*. This algorithm is not of the recursive-descent type (i.e., *A*, *B*, *D*, *E*, *C*, *F*).

Also notice that the scope tree need not, and normally does not, correlate to the actual folder hierarchy in the Web Storage System. This scope tree is virtual in that sense.

In most cases, you should have one folder in your application folder's schema scope that has a baseschema property with one entry pointing to the *non_ipm_subtree/Schema* folder in that store. This folder contains the default global schema provided by the Web Storage System. If your scope does not contain the *non_ipm_subtree/Schema* folder, the global schema definition items are not included in your application folder's schema definition.

Folder Expected Content Class

The urn:schemas-microsoft-com:exch-data:expected-content-class property enables you to define the names of expected content classes for items in a particular folder. The list of expected content classes for a folder is information that applications typically use when creating aggregate views of properties for items in that folder. For example, when you issue an HTTP/WebDAV PROPFIND command for all properties in a folder (Depth = 1), or you issue a SELECT * statement, the list of properties returned is calculated using the definitions of the folder's expected content classes.

There are two ways to set expected content classes:

- *For a specified folder*
    Update the urn:schemas-microsoft-com:exch-data:expected-content-class property for the folder item.

- *As part of a content class definition*
  This technique is suitable for defining a folder content class, such as with urn:content-classes:contactfolder, which usually contains items having a content class of urn:content-classes:person.

Application and Schema Folders

Schema definition items can be placed in any folder in a particular store and then used to define schemas for your application. By appropriately setting the schema-collection-ref and baseschema properties for various folders, you can bring these definitions into scope.

To avoid complexity when designing and managing your application's schema, plan and organize your schema information. For example, create folders under your top application folder that are designated as schema folders. Figure 2-5 shows a single schema folder under the application folder.

FIGURE 2–5 *A single schema folder under the application folder*

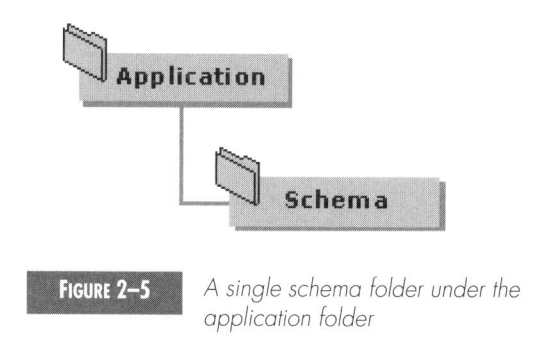

Table 2–3 lists possible URLs to the folders in the preceding illustration.

TABLE 2–3 *Possible URLs to the folders in Figure 2–5*

Folder display name	Example URL
application	*file://./backofficestorage/domain.microsoft.com/public folders/application/*
schema	*file://./backofficestorage/domain.microsoft.com/public folders/application/schema/*

By placing all schema definition items in designated folders, you decrease the complexity of managing and debugging your application's schema. This is shown in Figure 2–6.

Chapter 2 ● **Web Storage System Schema and Search Engine**

FIGURE 2–6 *Decrease the complexity of managing and debugging your application's schema*

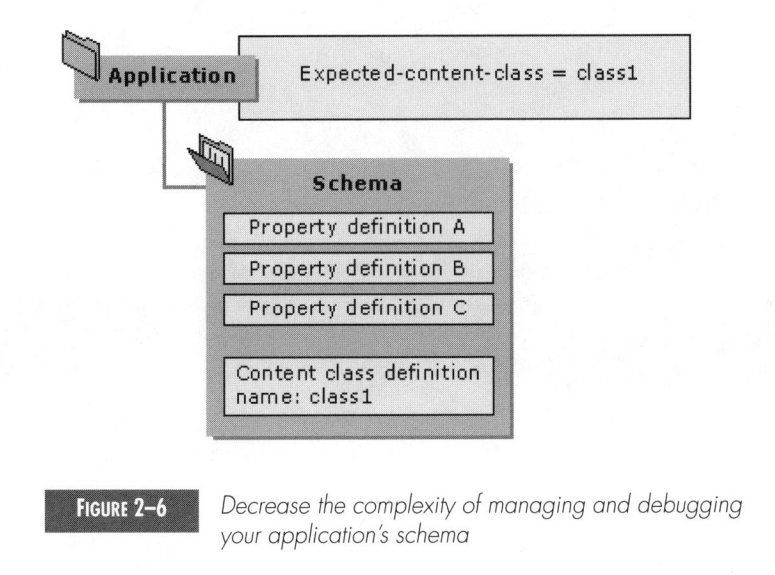

Arrange the hierarchy of application and schema folders any way you want. As you refine your application, organization is easier with additional schema subfolders.

Web Storage System Search

The Web Storage System is a vast store of resources in a single infrastructure, and search capabilities are provided to locate specific items or create views of resource data. You can search for items in the Web Storage System using a familiar SQL syntax, which is based on the syntax defined by the Microsoft Indexing Service Query Processor.

When searching the Web Storage System using Microsoft ActiveX Data Objects (ADO) or OLE DB, search results are returned in Recordset or Rowset objects. When searching using Web Distributed Authoring and Versioning (WebDAV), results are returned as Extensible Markup Language (XML) elements in the body of an HTTP response.

Indexing properties and implementing full-text indexing improves search performance. For more information about these capabilities, see "Property and Full-Text Indexing" in the SDK.

If you are using WebDAV, you can create Search Folders to persist search results in a folder addressable by URLs and also searchable by other queries.

The Microsoft Indexing Service search engine operates by using a system account, enabling it to read all stores, including private mailboxes. To maintain security, Rowsets objects returned from an SQL query are evaluated against the access control lists (ACL) of the item or folder searched and the security identifier of the user. Any row in which grant access is restricted is removed before the search result is returned.

The SELECT Statement

You can use a SELECT statement to return the values of properties for items in a particular folder or folders within a store. The SELECT statement has the following syntax:

```
SELECT select-list | *
FROM SCOPE(resource-list)
[WHERE search-condition]
[order-by-clause]
```

To request specific properties, you enclose each property name in quotation marks and separate each property name with a comma. For example:

```
SELECT "DAV:href", "DAV:displayname" ...
```

The search scope to execute is the combination of a folder URL and a traversal depth. This is shown in the following example:

```
'shallow traversal of "/folder1/"'
'deep traversal of "/folder1/folder2/"'
```

A full URL can be used as well, as in the following example:

```
'shallow traversal of "http://server/vroot/folder1"'
'shallow traversal of
"file://./backofficestorage/domain.tld/pub2/f1"'
```

A FROM clause does not require an explicit SCOPE element, in which case a shallow traversal is assumed. For example:

```
FROM "http://server/vroot/folder1"
```

If a SCOPE element is specified in the SQL query statement, but a depth is not, the Web Storage System query processor assumes a *deep* traversal, as in the following example:

```
FROM SCOPE("http://server/vroot/folder1") (deep traversal here)
```

The Web Storage System does not support deep traversals in the public store designated for MAPI clients, such as Microsoft Outlook. If either an explicit or implicit deep traversal is requested, the Web Storage System query processor returns an error.

Tokens, which are properties in a select list or values in a WHERE clause, must be delimited by single quotations marks. A token can contain only alphabetic characters, unless it is also enclosed in double quotation marks. In the following SQL WHERE clause, a full-text search is requested, and "this" and "that" are tokens:

```
WHERE CONTAINS (' "this" AND "that" ')
```

This clause does not work:

```
WHERE CONTAINS ('10 dollars')
```

To fix the clause, surround the token with double quotation marks within the single quotation marks:

```
WHERE CONTAINS ('"10 dollars"')
```

Use of the CONTAINS clause is restricted to properties that are marked for full-text indexing, and only if full-text searching has been enabled for that particular store.

The SELECT * Statement

A SELECT * statement returns all the properties defined by the content classes identified in the expected content class list for the specified folder. When constructing this list of properties to return, the schema scope for the folder is used. If any required schema definition items are not present within this schema scope, only the default properties for items are returned.

Similarly, sending a PROPFIND command using the HTTP/WebDAV protocol with a depth of 1 to find all item properties returns only the properties defined by the expected content classes of the folder.

Using SELECT * can be an unnecessarily broad use of an SQL query. In most instances, queries with specified property names and other search criteria allow for a much more optimized result. When using SELECT * there are server processing tasks that will be performed due to the unnecessarily broad request, which in most situations is not needed for retrieving a subset of data.

Search Scope

Instead of querying a table as you would a database, you issue a query on a folder scope. A scope is defined as a folder specified by a URL and a depth. You can specify a deep traversal to search a folder and all of its subfolders, or a shallow traversal to search only in the specified folder.

You cannot perform a deep traversal in the MAPI client public store installed by Microsoft Exchange 2000 Server, but you can perform deep traversals of private stores and in any other public folder trees.

You define a search scope using the SCOPE SQL element. Within the SCOPE element, you define the depths and URLs for the folders to be searched. For shallow searches, you specify "shallow traversal of"; for deep searches, you specify "deep traversal of". After specifying the depth, you specify the URL for each folder. The syntax for this statement is as follows:

```
SCOPE('shallow traversal of "URL1"' , ['shallow traversal of "URL2"'])
SCOPE('deep traversal of "URL1"', ['deep traversal of "URL2"'])
```

For example, to find all child folders contained within a particular folder, you execute the following SQL statement:

```
SELECT "DAV:href", "DAV:displayname"
FROM SCOPE('shallow traversal of "URL"')
WHERE "DAV:isfolder" = True and "DAV:ishidden" = False
```

This query returns all visible folders in the folder specified by a URL string variable. The traversal is shallow, so subfolders are not searched.

When you execute SQL SELECT commands using the ExOLEDB provider, you can use URLs relative to the top-level public folder. Each SELECT command is executed within the context of an OLE DB session (ADO connection) that implicitly defines the store being searched.

Use of the SCOPE element is optional. If the element is not used, the search depth defaults to shallow. If you specify a SCOPE element but do not specify a depth for a folder, the search defaults to deep traversal. For example, the following statement defaults to a shallow traversal:

```
SELECT "DAV:href" FROM "URL"
```

This statement defaults to a deep traversal:

```
SELECT "DAV:href" FROM SCOPE('"URL"')
```

When specifying multiple folders in your SCOPE element, you must use the same depth for each folder. You cannot mix deep and shallow searches within the same SQL command.

Only shallow traversal of a single folder is supported in the public folder tree designated for MAPI clients. If you specify deep traversal or multiple folders, an error is returned.

Each SELECT command is executed within the context of an OLE DB session (ADO connection) that implicitly defines the store (public or mailbox) and the folder tree being searched. When you execute SQL SELECT commands using the ExOLEDB provider, you can use URLs relative to the OLE DB session scope.

Property and Full-Text Indexing

You can improve search performance by implementing full-text indexing and by creating indexes for properties you define in the Web Storage System.

PROPERTY INDEXING

You can create indexes on custom properties using schema.

To create an index on a custom property,

1. Set the property definition urn:schemas-microsoft-com:exch-data:isindexed to TRUE. (This setting alone does not create the index.)
2. Define a content class that includes the custom property.
3. Include that content class in a folder's expected content class. This folder is typically the application folder containing the items that hold your data.
4. Use CREATE INDEX to create indexes on all properties that are defined in the folder's expected content class. (This function indexes all items in a folder, rather than individually.)

The indexed property is now quickly accessible by SQL queries.

Note Indexes cannot be created in the installable file system M: drive. Indexes cannot be created on properties of the existing default Web Storage System namespaces, such as the DAV: namespace.

FULL-TEXT INDEXING

By implementing full-text indexing, you can do fast full-text searches by using the CONTAINS and FREETEXT predicates in an SQL query. The full-text indexing process indexes words in message and document bodies and additionally indexes words within message properties of the urn:schemas:mailheader: namespace. Full-Text indexing also enables Microsoft Outlook users to search for documents as well as messages. Nonbinary attachments are also indexed.

To implement full-text indexing, use the Microsoft Exchange System manager to navigate to the store to be indexed. Right-click on the store and click **Create Full-Text Index**. After you create the index, you can specify options on the **Full-Text Indexing** tab of the store's **Properties** to set the update interval, type of population, and other settings.

Full-text indexing creates indexes on words in the bodies of the following document types: .doc, .xls, .ppt, .html, .htm, .asp, .txt, and .eml.

Full-text indexing creates search catalogs for use by the search engine; however, there is no programmatic way to manipulate search catalogs in the Web Storage System.

The properties that participate in full-text indexing are listed in Table 2–4. The first parameter of the CONTAINS and FREETEXT predicates allow you to include searching the content in one or all of these properties in addition to searching the message or document body.

TABLE 2-4 *Properties that participate in full-text indexing*

MAPI Properties	urn:schema:httpmail properties
PR_SUBJECT, PR_SUBJECT_W	urn:schemas:httpmail:subject
PR_BODY, PR_BODY_W	urn:schemas:httpmail:textdescription
PR_SENDER_NAME, PR_SENDER_NAME_W	urn:schemas:httpmail:sendername
PR_SENT_REPRESENTING_NAME, PR_SENT_REPRESENTING_NAME_W	urn:schemas:httpmail:fromname
PR_DISPLAY_TO, PR_DISPLAY_TO_W	urn:schemas:httpmail:displayto
PR_DISPLAY_CC, PR_DISPLAY_CC_W	urn:schemas:httpmail:displaycc
PR_DISPLAY_BCC, PR_DISPLAY_BCC_W	urn:schemas:httpmail:displaybcc
PR_SENDER_EMAIL_ADDRESS, PR_SENDER_EMAIL_ADDRESS_W	urn:schemas:httpmail:senderemail

CUSTOMIZING FULL-TEXT INDEXING

You can add properties to participate in full-text indexing and add or remove noise words that are excluded in a search.

ADDING PROPERTIES • If you are familiar with adding keys to the Microsoft Windows registry, you can set up other properties to be full-text indexed in addition to the httpmail namespace properties listed in Full-Text Indexing. You create a text file of properties that are referred to in the registry by the following key:

> HKEY_LOCAL_MACHINE\Software\Microsoft\Search\1.0\ExchangeParameters\SchemaTextFilePathName

To add properties for full-text indexing,

1. Create a text file of a list of properties you want to be full-text indexed. The full name for each property must be on a separate line.

Note The DAV:href and DAV:displayname properties cannot be full-text indexed.

2. Start the Registry Editor by entering regedt32 at a command prompt.
3. Activate the HKEY_LOCAL_MACHINE window.
4. Navigate to the key Software\Microsoft\Search\1.0.

5. If it does not already exist, add a key under 1.0 with the name ExchangeParameters.
6. If it does not already exist, add a key under ExchangeParameters with name SchemaTextFilePathName.
7. Add a value to the SchemaTextFilePathName key, with the name SchemaTextFilePathName, a data type of REG_SZ, and a string value of the path to the text file of properties, such as "E:\Exchsrvr\fulltextprops.txt."
8. Close the registry editor.
9. The properties will be full-text indexed the next time full-text indexing is run as configured in the Microsoft Exchange System Manager.

EDITING NOISE WORDS • Noise words are words that the MsSearch engine excludes from a full-text search, such as "but" and "or." Noise word files are in the *\Program Files\Common Files\System\MSSearch\Data\Config* folder on the Exchange 2000 server. There are noise words for different languages, and the English noise word is noise.eng.

You can add or remove noise words in these files. The changes won't take effect until the next time full-text indexing is run.

Web Storage System Search Folders

You can create collections of items that are the results of an SQL search directly in the Web Storage System within a search folder when using the HTTP/WebDAV protocol. Like other folders in the Web Storage System, persisted search folders are addressable using a URL and can be accessed and queried in the same manner as other folders.

Using search folders in the Web Storage System frees you from having to write your own code to save SQL search results for subsequent use by your clients. You can create search folders in private stores and public folders, except for the public folder tree designated for MAPI clients. Search folders can be created only using the HTTP/WebDAV protocol.

The items stored in a search folder are those items that exist within the folder scope and match the conditions you specify with an SQL SELECT statement when you create the search folder. That is, the folder does not contain *copies* of the items, but rather links to the items themselves. This is made possible through the Web Storage System's single-instancing technology.

Although search folders are based on an SQL SELECT statement, they provide a mechanism far more powerful than simply storing the results returned by a standard SQL SELECT command. Using persisted search folders, you can arbitrarily group items within a particular folder scope that match the criteria you specify and then place them in another folder for subsequent searching or monitoring by your application.

For example, one part of your application may need to routinely return various property values for all items belonging to the hypothetical content class urn:schemas-myorganization-tld:statusreport that exist within your application's folder hierarchy, which could be many levels deep. Rather than continuously executing a deep-traversal search for the property values on items belonging to this content class, you could instead create a search folder for the application's folder hierarchy with the condition that each matched item in the folder belongs to the specified content class urn:schemas-myorganization-tld:statusreport. After the search folder is constructed, you could then routinely query it to retrieve property values for these items only. Because the Web Storage System SQL engine need not retraverse the entire folder scope and refilter these items, search performance is greatly improved.

The Web Storage System constructs search folders asynchronously with respect to client requests. That is, when a successful creation request is made and the client receives this response from the service, not all items that match the SQL request have yet been linked to the search folder.

Search Folder Properties

Search folders are like normal folders: Once created, they contain standard properties defined for folders, and they can be searched for items and then deleted when no longer needed. However, the Web Storage System sets special properties on persisted search folders. Table 2–5 lists these properties and their descriptions.

TABLE 2–5   *The Web Storage System sets special properties on persisted search folders*

Property	Description
DAV:searchtype	The Web Storage System sets this property to "dynamic."
DAV:searchrequest (Read-Only)	The Web Storage System places the SQL query statement used to populate the search folder in this property.
DAV:resourcetype	The Web Storage System sets this property to the value "DAV:collection/ DAV:searchresults/" for search folders.

Search Folder Items

When you create a search folder, you specify an SQL command that the Web Storage System uses to populate the folder with items. After the folder has been populated, links to all items that match your request are placed in the folder. Additionally, each item's complete set of properties is also available. Because of this, the list of properties you specify when creating the search folder does not limit which properties you can access or search for within the search folder itself. You can issue PROPGET and SEARCH commands for items in the folder in the normal way. The most important aspect of the SQL command used to construct the folder is the WHERE clause condition.

If you issue a SELECT * search command or an HTTP/WebDAV PROPFIND command (depth 1) with a scope that contains the search folder, you receive the properties defined by the original containing folder's schema. That is, the list of properties returned by the SELECT * command for a search folder is not controlled by the search folder's schema, but rather by the item's containing folder itself. This also holds true when you issue a PROPGET command. In summary, the normal schema rules for items in a folder still apply as if the items were being accessed in their actual containing folder.

You cannot add new items to a search folder manually. If you issue a PUT, POST, or normal MKCOL command for an item in the search folder, the Web Storage System returns an error. You can, however, nest-search folders.

HTTP/WebDAV Search Folder Creation Protocol Command

You create a search folder just as you would create a standard folder using the HTTP/WebDAV MKCOL command. However, along with the MKCOL request, you specify an XML request body containing a value for the folder's DAV:searchrequest property. The value of this property is set to an SQL query used to construct the contents of the persisted search folder. Note that when setting a value for the DAV:searchrequest property, you specify the SQL statement within a DAV:sql subelement, as in the following example:

```
<a:searchrequest xmlns:a="DAV:">
  <a:sql>select * from scope(...)</a:sql>
</a:searchrequest>
```

The following is an example of a persisted search folder HTTP/WebDAV request (the XML portion has been formatted with extra spaces to aid readability and need not be formatted this way in your applications):

```
MKCOL /folderpath/search_folder/ HTTP/1.1
Host: somedomain.microsoft.com
Content-Length: XXX
Content-type: text/xml

<?xml version="1.0"?>
<a:propertyupdate xmlns:a="DAV:" >
    <a:set>
        <a:prop>
            <a:searchrequest>
                <a:sql>
                    Select "DAV:displayname"
                    FROM Scope('shallow traversal of
                         "/exchange/user1/inbox"')
                </a:sql>
```

Web Storage System Search Folders

```
      </a:searchrequest>
    </a:prop>
  </a:set>
</a:propertyupdate>
```

EXAMPLE SEARCH FOLDER HTTP REQUEST AND RESPONSE

In the following sample client/server dialog, the client requests the creation of a search folder at the URL *http://somedomain.microsoft.com/public2/ps1/* that contains the items that satisfy the following SQL search command:

```
SELECT *
FROM scope('shallow traversal of
   "http:// somedomain.microsoft.com/public2/templates/"')
WHERE "DAV:ishidden"     = False
AND   "DAV:contentclass" = "urn:schemas-mydomain-tld:reporttemplate"
```

CLIENT REQUEST • The client connects to port 80 (HTTP) on the host with Domain Name Service (DNS) name somedomain.microsoft.com and sends the command in the following example to the server. (Note that, for purposes of brevity and clarity, some standard headers that are usually sent with these requests [such as Accept-Language:] have been omitted from this example:

```
MKCOL /pub2/templates/search_folder/ HTTP/1.1
Host: somedomain.microsoft.com
Content-Length: XXX
Content-type: text/xml

<?xml version="1.0"?>
<a:propertyupdate xmlns:a="DAV:">
  <a:set>
    <a:prop>
      <a:searchrequest>
        <a:sql>
        SELECT *
        FROM scope('shallow traversal of
           "http://somedomain.microsoft.com/pub2/templates"')
        WHERE "DAV:ishidden" = False
        AND "DAV:contentclass" = "urn:schemas-mydomain-tld:reporttemplate"
        </a:sql>
      </a:searchrequest>
    </a:prop>
  </a:set>
</a:propertyupdate>
```

Chapter 2 • Web Storage System Schema and Search Engine

SERVER RESPONSE • The server then sends the following response to the client:

```
HTTP/1.1 207 Multi-Status
Server: Microsoft-IIS/5.0
Date: Tue, 22 Feb 1999 12:54:46 GMT
WWW-Authenticate: Negotiate AADAB...
MS-Exchange-Permanent-URL:
     http://hostname/pub2/-FlatUrlSpace-/ab7e2af09631
b745981c6d39445456f2-17/
Location: http://hostname/pub2/templates/search_folder/
Timeout: Infinity
Repl-UID:
<rid:ab7e2af09631b745981c6d39445456f2000000001371>
Content-Type: text/xml
Content-Length: XXX
ResourceTag: <rt:ab7e2af09631b745981c6d39445456f200000000
1371ab7e2af09631b745981
c6d39445456f2000000001573>

<?xml version="1.0"?>
<a:multistatus xmlns:a="DAV:">
  <a:response>
    <a:href>
     http://hostname/pub2/templates/search_folder
    </a:href>
    <a:status>HTTP/1.1 201 Created</a:status>
    <a:propstat>
       <a:status>HTTP/1.1 200 OK</a:status>
       <a:prop><a:searchrequest/></a:prop>
    </a:propstat>
  </a:response>
</a:multistatus>
```

After this successful response has been sent, the Web Storage System begins populating the search folder with the items that satisfy the SQL request. Be aware that not all items that match the criteria appear in the search folder until the Web Storage System completes the construction of the folder.

Note Note that the server has sent a different Timeout value for the search. The Location header returned can be different from the value sent by the client when the MKCOL request was made.

THREE

Web Storage System Security

You can control access to an item and its properties using a security descriptor. Using Web Storage System security descriptors, you can

- Both grant and deny a trustee access rights to an item and its properties.
- Identify trustees using a Microsoft Windows security identifier (SID).
- Set, retrieve, and modify the descriptor in Extensible Markup Language (XML) format.
- Access the descriptor using both the Microsoft Exchange OLE DB (ExOLEDB) provider and the HTTP/WebDAV protocol in XML format.

Each item's security descriptor is accessed through the item's *http://schemas.microsoft.com/exchange/security/descriptor* property. This property is the item's descriptor in XML format. The descriptor is physically stored and replicated in a Microsoft Exchange 2000 Server-specific binary format, which is internally based on the standard Microsoft Windows 2000 descriptor format. The XML representation of the descriptor is not stored directly for the item. When you request this property for an item, the XML string is generated and then returned. When you set this property for an item, the XML string is parsed and the binary descriptor for the item is updated.

The following topics introduce you to the features of Web Storage System security:

- Item Access Rights
- Web Storage System XML Security Descriptor Format

Item Access Rights

A Microsoft Windows security descriptor defines access rights to a securable object through definition of the object's owner and through a set of access control entries (ACE) in the descriptor's discretionary access control list (DACL). Each ACE in the DACL either grants or denies a trustee a certain set of access rights to the securable object. The set of rights granted or denied by a particular ACE is contained in its access mask. The access mask is a 32-bit number in which the upper 16 bits define standard and generic access rights and the lower 16 bits define access rights that are object specific.

The following topics list the access rights available for items in the Web Storage System:

- Folder Item Access Rights
- Nonfolder Item Access Rights
- Standard Access Rights

Folder Item Access Rights

Table 3–1 lists the access rights for items that are folders in the Web Storage System.

TABLE 3–1 Access rights for items that are folders in the Web Storage System

Access right	Mask (Hex)	Description
fsdrightListContents	0x00000001	Same as FILE_LIST_DIRECTORY. Trustee can list file contents.
fsdrightCreateItem	0x00000002	Same as FILE_ADD_FILE. Trustee can add a file to a folder.
fsdrightCreateContainer	0x00000004	Same as FILE_ADD_SUBDIRECTORY. Trustee can add a subfolder.
fsdrightReadProperty	0x00000008	Same as FILE_READ_EA.
fsdrightWriteProperty	0x00000010	Same as FILE_WRITE_EA.
fsdrightReadAttributes	0x00000080	Same as FILE_READ_ATTRIBUTES. Reserved for future use.
fsdrightWriteAttributes	0x00000100	Same as FILE_WRITE_ATTRIBUTES. Reserved for future use.
fsdrightWriteOwnProperty*	0x00000200	The trustee can modify his or her own items.
fsdrightDeleteOwnItem	0x00000400	The trustee can delete his or her own items.
fsdrightViewItem*	0x00000800	The trustee can view items.

Item Access Rights

TABLE 3–1 *Access rights for items that are folders in the Web Storage System (continued)*

Access right	Mask (Hex)	Description
fsdrightOwner*	0x00004000	The trustee is the owner of the folder. This right corresponds to the frightsOwner right in previous versions of Exchange and is provided for backward compatibility.
fsdrightContact*	0x00008000	Not used for security. Identifies the user as the contact for the folder. This right corresponds to the frightsContact right in previous versions of Exchange and is provided for backward compatibility.

* Denotes an Exchange-specific right.

Note For a folder item, the mask containing all the rights in this table is 0xcfff. This does not include the standard access rights that reside above the 16th bit in the mask. (See Standard Access Rights.) An example of a mask with all folder item rights and all standard access rights is 0x1fcfff.

Nonfolder Item Access Rights

Table 3–2 lists the access rights for items that are not folders. Many of these access rights are equivalent to their counterparts in Windows 2000 NTFS file system security.

TABLE 3–2 *Access rights for items that are not folders*

Access right	Mask (Hex)	Description
FsdrightReadBody	0x00000001	Same as FILE_READ_DATA.
FsdrightWriteBody	0x00000002	Same as FILE_WRITE_DATA.
FsdrightAppendMsg	0x00000004	Same as FILE_WRITE_DATA. Ignored.
FsdrightReadProperty	0x00000008	Same as FILE_READ_EA.
FsdrightWriteProperty	0x00000010	Same as FILE_WRITE_EA.
FsdrightExecute	0x00000020	Same as FILE_EXECUTE. Ignored.
FsdrightReadAttributes	0x00000080	Same as FILE_READ_ATTRIBUTES.
FsdrightWriteAttributes	0x00000100	Same as FILE_WRITE_ATTRIBUTES.
FsdrightWriteOwnProperty*	0x00000200	Trustee can modify his or her own items.
FsdrightDeleteOwnItem*	0x00000400	Trustee can delete his or her own items.
FsdrightViewItem*	0x00000800	Trustee can view items.

* Denotes an Exchange-specific right.

Note For a nonfolder item, the mask containing all the above rights is 0x0fbf. This does not include the standard access rights that reside above the 16th bit in the mask. (See Standard Access Rights.) An example of a mask with all nonfolder item rights and all standard access rights is 0x1f0fbf.

Standard Access Rights

The standard access rights listed in Table 3–3 are defined by the Windows security system and are presented here for completeness. These access rights pertain to the security descriptor. Note that trustees can access or modify portions of the descriptor.

TABLE 3–3 *Standard access rights*

Access right	Mask (Hex)	Description
FsdrightDelete	0x00010000	DELETE (standard right)
FsdrightReadControl	0x00020000	READ_CONTROL (standard right)
FsdrightWriteSD	0x00040000	WRITE_DAC (standard right)
FsdrightWriteOwner	0x00080000	WRITE_OWNER (standard right)
FsdrightSynchronize	0x00100000	SYNCHRONIZE (standard right)

An example of an access mask with all standard access rights is 0x1f0000.

Web Storage System XML Security Descriptor Format

Each item in the Web Storage System has an associated security descriptor that you can access in XML format using the ExOLEDB provider or the HTTP/WebDAV protocol. Any client that can parse and assemble well-formed XML strings that follow the security grammar discussed in this and the following topics can examine and modify the item's descriptor, privileges permitting. For example, all clients that have Microsoft Internet Explorer 5.0 have access to the MSXML COM component that contains a DOM parser, the XMLHTTP COM class, and various other XML-related tools.

The following example provides an outline of the security descriptor grammar in XML (all elements and attributes reside in the *http://schemas.microsoft.com/security/* namespace):

```
<security_descriptor
xmlns="http://schemas.microsoft.com/security/">
 <revision>...</revision>
```

```
<owner>...</owner>
<group>...</group>
<dacl>...</dacl>
<sacl>...<sacl>
</security_descriptor>
```

The structure of the descriptor closely follows the standard structure for Windows 2000 security descriptors.

Security Identifiers in XML

Security identifiers are used in security descriptors to identify trustees. In Web Storage System XML format, security identifiers are represented with the XML elements listed in Table 3–4. All elements and attributes reside in the *http://schemas.microsoft.com/security/namespace*.

TABLE 3–4 *Security identifiers are represented with the XML elements*

Element name	Possible child elements or contents
sid	string_sid? nt4_compatible_sid? type? ad_object_guid? display_name?
string_sid	Windows security identifier in string format; for example, "S-1-1-0".
nt4_compatible_sid	Microsoft Windows NT Security Accounts Manager (SAM)-compatible name, for example, "Domain\User".
type	One of the following strings: user group domain alias well_known_group deleted_account invalid unknown computer
ad_object_guid	A globally unique identifier (GUID) in standard string format. This GUID corresponds to the objectGUID attribute for the Microsoft Active Directory object identified by this SID.
display_name	A display name for the specified trustee; for example, Administrator. This display name is derived from the Microsoft Windows 2000 Active Directory object for this trustee.

The following is an example of a SID in XML format:

```
<sid>
  <string_sid>S-1-1-0</string_sid>
  <nt4_compatible_name>\Everyone</nt4_compatible_name>
  <type>well_known_group</type>
  <ad_object_guid>{GUID}</ad_object_guid>
  <display_name>Everyone</display_name>
</sid>
```

SIDs in this format appear in the descriptor's DACL and system audit control list and are used to define the item's owner and primary group.

When a security descriptor is retrieved for an item, all available elements contained in a SID element are present. However, when you set a security descriptor, you should specify only one of the elements in the SID structure. The most efficient element to use when identifying a trustee is the <string_sid> element. If you don't know the trustee's SID before you update the descriptor, you can specify (in order of decreasing lookup efficiency) the <nt4_compatible_name> element, the <ad_object_guid> element, or the <display_name> element. From one of these three elements, the Web Storage System determines the trustee's SID by searching Active Directory or a local SAM account database. Using the <display_name> element can cause ambiguity when searching for the user object and should be avoided whenever possible. If multiple entries are present in the SID element, the most efficient element (as previously mentioned) is used.

XML Security Descriptor XML Elements

As seen in Table 3–5, each item's security descriptor is represented in XML with the elements and attributes listed in the tables in this and the following topics. Each security identifier is expressed by using the XML syntax described in the topic Security Identifiers in XML. Note that all items and attributes reside in the *http://schemas.microsoft.com/security/* namespace.

TABLE 3–5 *Security Descriptor is Represented in XML with the Elements and Attributes*

Element name	Child elements or contents
Security_descriptor	Revision?
	Owner?
	Group?
	DACL?
	A system access-control list (SACL)?

TABLE 3-5 *Security Descriptor is Represented in XML with the Elements and Attributes (continued)*

Element name	Child elements or contents
Revision	Decimal number (32 bits)
Owner Attributes: Defaulted=boolean	SID (See "Security Identifiers in XML" earlier in this chapter.)
Primary_group Attributes: Defaulted=boolean	SID (See "Security Identifiers in XML" earlier in this chapter.)
DACL Attributes: Defaulted=boolean protected=boolean autoinherited=boolean	revision? effective_aces? subcontainer_inheritable_aces? subitem_inheritable_aces? (See "Discretionary Access Control Lists XML Elements" in the SDK.)
SACL Attributes: Defaulted=boolean protected=boolean autoinherited=boolean	revision? audit_always? audit_on_failure? audit_on_success?
audit_always	(See "System Audit Control Lists XML Elements" in the SDK.)
audit_on_failure	(See "System Audit Control Lists XML Elements" in the SDK.)
audit_on_success	(See "System Audit Control Lists XML Elements" in the SDK.)

Discretionary Access Control Lists XML Elements

In DACLs, the dacl XML element can contain the elements revision, effective_aces, subitem_inheritable_aces, and subcontainer_inheritable_aces. Table 3-6 lists the content models for these elements.

TABLE 3-6 *Discretionary Access Control Lists XML Elements*

Element name	Child elements or contents
DACL Attributes defaulted=boolean protected=boolean autoinherited=boolean	revision? effective_aces? subitem_inheritable_aces? subcontainer_inheritable_aces?
revision	String; revision for the DACL; for example, 2.

Chapter 3 • Web Storage System Security

TABLE 3–6 *Discretionary Access Control Lists XML Elements (continued)*

Element name	Child elements or contents
effective_aces	access_allowed_ace* access_denied_ace* access_allowed_object_ace* access_denied_object_ace*
subcontainer_inheritable_aces	access_allowed_ace* access_denied_ace* access_allowed_object_ace* access_denied_object_ace*
subitem_inheritable_aces	access_allowed_ace* access_denied_ace* access_allowed_object_ace* access_denied_object_ace*
access_allowed_ace Attributes: inherited =boolean (no_propagate_inherit=boolean)[1]	access_mask SID
access_denied_ace Attributes: inherited =boolean (no_propagate_inherit=boolean)[1]	access_mask SID
access_allowed_object_ace Attributes: inherited =boolean (no_propagate_inherit=boolean)[1] (inherited_object_type=GUID)[1]	access_mask SID object_type?
access_denied_object_ace Attributes: inherited =boolean (no_propagate_inherit=boolean)[1] (inherited_object_type=GUID)[1]	access_mask SID (object_type | property_name)?
access_mask	A hexadecimal number in string format; for example, "1fc9ff". This number is the 32-bit access mask for the ACE. This mask identifies the access rights that the ACE grants or denies a trustee.
SID	See Security Identifiers in XML.
object_type	A GUID in standard string format. The GUID identifies the property to which this ACE applies.
property_name	The name of the property—for example, urn:schemas:mailheader:from.

[1] Denotes attributes present in inheritable ACEs. These entries are present in the subcontainer_inheritable_aces and subitem_inheritable_aces elements of the dacl element.

Web Storage System XML Security Descriptor Format

The following example presents an ACL within a descriptor's DACL, in XML format:

```
<S:dacl S:defaulted="0" S:protected="0" S:autoinherited="1">
  <S:revision>2</S:revision>
  <S:effective_aces>
   <S:access_allowed_ace S:inherited="1">
     <S:access_mask>1f0fbf</S:access_mask>
     <S:sid>
      <S:string_sid>S-1-5-21-507921405-507921405-507921405-500</S:string_sid>
      <S:type>user</S:type>
      <S:nt4_compatible_name>DOMAIN\Administrator</S:nt4_compatible_name>
      <S:ad_object_guid>{446ca8b5-58b5-48b5-88b5-ae41ef9038b5}</S:ad_object_guid>
      <S:display_name>Administrator</S:display_name>
     </S:sid>
   </S:access_allowed_ace>
   <S:access_denied_ace S:inherited="1">
     <S:access_mask>1f0fbf</S:access_mask>
     <S:sid>
      <S:string_sid>S-1-5-7</S:string_sid>
      <S:type>well_known_group</S:type>
      <S:nt4_compatible_name>NT AUTHORITY\ANONYMOUS LOGON</S:nt4_compatible_name>
     </S:sid>
   </S:access_denied_ace>
   <S:access_allowed_ace S:inherited="1">
     <S:access_mask>120ea9</S:access_mask>
     <S:sid>
      <S:string_sid>S-1-1-0</S:string_sid>
      <S:type>well_known_group</S:type>
      <S:nt4_compatible_name>\Everyone</S:nt4_compatible_name>
     </S:sid>
   </S:access_allowed_ace>
  </S:effective_aces>
</S:dacl>
```

System Audit Control Lists XML Elements

In system ACLs, the sacl XML element can contain the elements revision, audit_always, audit_on_success, and audit_on_failure. Table 3–7 lists the content models for these elements.

TABLE 3–7 *System Audit Control Lists XML Elements*

Element name	Child elements or contents
SACL Attributes: defaulted ="boolean" protected ="boolean" autointerhited="boolean"	revision? audit_always? audit_on_failure? audit_on_success?
revision	String. A revision for the SACL; for example, "2".
audit_always	revision? effective_aces? subitem_inheritable_aces? subcontainer_inheritable_aces?
audit_on_failure	revision? effective_aces? subitem_inheritable_aces? subcontainer_inheritable_aces?
audit_on_success	revision? effective_aces? subitem_inheritable_aces? subcontainer_inheritable_aces?
system_audit_ace Attributes: inherited =boolean (no_propagate_inherit=boolean)[1]	access_mask SID
system_audit_object_ace Attributes: inherited =boolean (no_propagate_inherit=boolean)[1] (inherited_object_type=GUID)[1]	access_mask SID (object_type | property_name)?
access_mask	A hexadecimal number in string format; for example, "1fc9ff". This number is the 32-bit access mask for the ACE.
SID	See Security Identifiers in XML.
object_type	A GUID in standard string format. The GUID or the name identifies the property to which this ACE applies.
property_name	The name of the property—for example, urn:schemas:mailheader:from.

[1] Denotes attributes present in inheritable ACEs. These entries are present in the subcontainer_inheritable_aces and subitem_inheritable_aces elements.

Example Descriptor in XML

The following example represents a security descriptor in XML format:

```xml
<S:security_descriptor xmlns:S="http://
schemas.microsoft.com/security/"
      xmlns:D="urn:uuid:c2f41010-65b3-11d1-a29f-
00aa00c14882/"
      D:dt="microsoft.security_descriptor">
 <S:revision>1</S:revision>
 <S:owner S:defaulted="0">
  <S:sid>
   <S:string_sid>S-1-5-44-444</S:string_sid>
   <S:type>alias</S:type>
<S:nt4_compatible_name>BUILTIN\Administrators</
S:nt4_compatible_name>
  </S:sid>
 </S:owner>
 <S:primary_group S:defaulted="0">
  <S:sid>
   <S:string_sid>S-1-5-21-555555555-555555555-55555555555-
555</S:string_sid>
   <S:type>group</S:type>
   <S:nt4_compatible_name>DOMAIN\Domain Users</
S:nt4_compatible_name>
   <S:ad_object_guid>{2bdc2b0c-a8e1-a8e1-a8e1-
1a12ec24a8e1}</S:ad_object_guid>
  </S:sid>
 </S:primary_group>
<S:dacl S:defaulted="0" S:protected="0"
S:autoinherited="1">
  <S:revision>2</S:revision>
  <S:effective_aces>
   <S:access_allowed_ace S:inherited="1">
    <S:access_mask>1f0fbf</S:access_mask>
    <S:sid>
     <S:string_sid>S-1-5-21-5555555555-5555555555-
555555555-599</S:string_sid>
     <S:type>user</S:type>
<S:nt4_compatible_name>DOMAIN\Administrator</
S:nt4_compatible_name>
     <S:ad_object_guid>{48b548b5-48b5-48b5-48b5-
48b548b548b5}</S:ad_object_guid>
     <S:display_name>Administrator</S:display_name>
    </S:sid>
   </S:access_allowed_ace>
   <S:access_denied_ace S:inherited="1">
    <S:access_mask>1f0fbf</S:access_mask>
    <S:sid>
```

```
    <S:string_sid>S-1-5-7</S:string_sid>
    <S:type>well_known_group</S:type>
    <S:nt4_compatible_name>NT AUTHORITY\ANONYMOUS LOGON</
S:nt4_compatible_name>
   </S:sid>
  </S:access_denied_ace>
  <S:access_allowed_ace S:inherited="1">
   <S:access_mask>120ea9</S:access_mask>
   <S:sid>
    <S:string_sid>S-1-1-0</S:string_sid>
    <S:type>well_known_group</S:type>
<S:nt4_compatible_name>\Everyone</S:nt4_compatible_name>
   </S:sid>
  </S:access_allowed_ace>
 </S:effective_aces>
 </S:dacl>
</S:security_descriptor>
```

Accessing Item Descriptors

When generating the XML version of any given descriptor, the item's security properties are not returned automatically. To view or modify an item's descriptor in XML format, you must bind to the item and request the property directly, as in the following example:

```
Dim Rec as New ADODB.Record
Dim Conn as New ADODB.Connection
Dim Flds as ADODB.Fields
Dim strXMLDesc as String
Dim strXMLAdminDesc as String

Conn.Provider = "ExOLEDB.DataSource"
Conn.Open strItemURL
Rec.Open strItemURL, Conn
Set Flds = Rec.Fields
strXMLDesc=Flds("http://schemas.microsoft.com/exchange/
    security/descriptor")
```

Note that access to the item's security descriptor itself is specified using the following standard access rights:

- READ_CONTROL Only trustees (users and groups) granted the standard READ_CONTROL access right can examine the security descriptor.
- WRITE_DAC Only trustees granted the WRITE_DAC access right can modify the discretionary ACL.
- WRITE_OWNER Only trustees granted the WRITE_OWNER access right can change the item's owner.

New Item Descriptor Inheritance

When new items are created in folders, they are secured using the ACEs present in the subitem_inheritable_aces section of the parent folder's discretionary ACL. In a sense, the item inherits a "virtual" descriptor from its parent folder. If the parent folder's descriptor changes, the item automatically inherits the changes.

When you set the descriptor for an item, the "virtual" inheritance is no longer used, and the item's descriptor is used to control access. Therefore, if you make changes to the parent folder's descriptor, items that have had their descriptors set directly do not inherit these changes.

The default behavior described in the preceding paragraphs emulates the folder-based access control system used in earlier versions of Microsoft Exchange. The drawback to using parent-folder inheritance for items is that the access rights granted or denied to trustees apply uniformly to all items within a given folder that have not had their associated descriptors explicitly set.

Exchange 5.5 Access Rights and the Web Storage System

Previous versions of Microsoft Exchange 2000 Server supported a custom access control system using the PR_ACL_TABLE table for folders in the store. This ACL granted users access rights for each such folder and the items within it. With the Web Storage System, all mailbox stores and one public store are accessible using MAPI and backward compatibility with this access control system. You can use MAPI or COM components (such as the ACL.DLL component) to grant users the access rights listed in Table 3–8.

TABLE 3–8 *Use MAPI or COM components to grant users the access rights*

Access right	Enables you to	Mask (Hex)
frightsReadAny	Read any items.	0x001
frightsCreate	Create items.	0x002
frightsEditOwned	Edit any items owned by the user.	0x008
frightsDeleteOwned	Delete any items owned by the user.	0x010
frightsEditAny	Edit any item.	0x020
frightsDeleteAny	Delete any item.	0x040
frightsCreateSubfolder	Create subfolders for the specified folder.	0x080
frightsOwner	Set permissions on the specified folder.	0x100
frightsContact	Appear as the contact on the specified folder. Not part of rightsAll.	0x200
frightsFolderVisible	Make the specified folder visible to the trustee.	0x400

Note Unlike in previous versions of Microsoft Exchange, in which ACLs were used only at the folder level to grant a user a particular access right, all Web Storage System items (folders and nonfolders) can have these rights appear in ACEs that either grant or deny that access right to a trustee.

In the PR_ACL_TABLE property, you identify trustees by using a long-term entry identifier for the user or group in Active Directory. When the PR_ACL_TABLE table for a folder is updated, the Web Storage System makes adjustments to the item's actual security descriptor.

Access rights for nonfolder items and properties cannot be represented using the PR_ACL_TABLE property for a folder. However, property tags for the XML security descriptor are provided in the *EDKMDB.h* header file in the MSDN Library, Platform SDK section.

THE EXCHANGE CANONICAL ACL FORMAT • MAPI clients such as Microsoft Outlook 2000 display security settings for a folder using information found in the folder's PR_ACL_TABLE property. To give MAPI clients the ability to properly view these settings for folders in the Web Storage System, you need to structure the ACL using the Exchange Canonical ACL format. When you use this format, the PR_ACL_TABLE property is correctly populated with access rights that map to the earlier Exchange security model.

In this format, there are two logical sections in the DACL for a folder:

1. ACEs that apply to the folder itself constitute one section.
2. ACEs that apply only to items (messages) in the folder make up the other section. These ACEs are found only in the subitem_inheritable_aces section of the DACL.

Within each of these subsections, the ACEs must be in a particular order, as in the following example:

```
REPEAT <n>
   GRANT ACCESS RIGHT FOR USER A
   DENY ACCESS RIGHT FOR USER A
REPEAT <m>
   GRANT ACCESS RIGHT FOR DL B
   GRANT ACCESS RIGHT FOR DL C
REPEAT <m>
   GRANT ACCESS DENY FOR DL B
   GRANT ACCESS DENY FOR DL C
REPEAT <0 or 1>
   GRANT ACCESS RIGHT FOR EVERYONE
```

Both *n* and *m* can be *0* (zero).

For example, the descriptor that follows Table 3–9 is in Exchange Canonical ACL format. It defines the security settings presented in that table when viewed in Outlook 2000. The settings are based on the permission roles presented on the Security property page for the folder item.

TABLE 3-9 *Exchange Canonical ACL format*

Trustee	Outlook permissions role
Default	Author
user8, test (DOMAIN\testuser8)	None
user7, test (DOMAIN\testuser7)	Contributor
user6, test (DOMAIN\testuser6)	Reviewer
user5, test (DOMAIN\testuser5)	Nonediting author
user4, test (DOMAIN\testuser4)	Author
user3, test (DOMAIN\testuser3)	Publishing author
user2, test (DOMAIN\testuser2)	Editor
user1, test (DOMAIN\testuser1)	Publishing editor
user0, test (DOMAIN\testuser0)	Owner
Anonymous	Contributor
testgroup1 (DOMAIN\testgroup1)	Reviewer
testgroup2 (DOMAIN\testgroup2)	Publishing author

```
<S:security_descriptor xmlns:S="http://
schemas.microsoft.com/security/"
   xmlns:D="urn:uuid:c2f41010-65b3-11d1-a29f-00aa00c14882/"
   D:dt="microsoft.security_descriptor">
 <S:revision>1</S:revision>
 <S:owner S:defaulted="0">
  <S:sid>
   <S:string_sid>S-1-5-32-544</S:string_sid>
   <S:type>alias</S:type>

<S:nt4_compatible_name>BUILTIN\Administrators</
S:nt4_compatible_name>
  </S:sid>
 </S:owner>
 <S:primary_group S:defaulted="0">
  <S:sid>
   <S:string_sid>S-1-5-21-527237240-507921405-1708537768-
513</S:string_sid>
   <S:type>group</S:type>
   <S:nt4_compatible_name>DOMAIN\Domain Users</
S:nt4_compatible_name>
   <S:ad_object_guid>{2bdc2b0c-a8e1-4fd3-8135-
1a12ec24d256}</S:ad_object_guid>
  </S:sid>
```

```xml
    </S:primary_group>
    <S:dacl S:defaulted="0" S:protected="0"
S:autoinherited="1">
      <S:revision>2</S:revision>
      <S:effective_aces>
        <S:access_allowed_ace S:inherited="0">
         <S:access_mask>1208a9</S:access_mask>
         <S:sid>
          <S:string_sid>S-1-5-21-527237240-507921405-1708537768-
1117</S:string_sid>
          <S:type>user</S:type>

<S:nt4_compatible_name>DOMAIN\testuser8</
S:nt4_compatible_name>
          <S:ad_object_guid>{74116535-9aad-4995-957e-
99e6640fb69b}</S:ad_object_guid>
          <S:display_name>user8, test</S:display_name>
         </S:sid>
        </S:access_allowed_ace>
        <S:access_denied_ace S:inherited="0">
         <S:access_mask>dc916</S:access_mask>
         <S:sid>
          <S:string_sid>S-1-5-21-527237240-507921405-1708537768-
1117</S:string_sid>
          <S:type>user</S:type>

<S:nt4_compatible_name>DOMAIN\testuser8</
S:nt4_compatible_name>
          <S:ad_object_guid>{74116535-9aad-4995-957e-
99e6640fb69b}</S:ad_object_guid>
          <S:display_name>user8, test</S:display_name>
         </S:sid>
        </S:access_denied_ace>
        <S:access_allowed_ace S:inherited="0">
         <S:access_mask>1208ab</S:access_mask>
         <S:sid>
          <S:string_sid>S-1-5-21-527237240-507921405-1708537768-
1116</S:string_sid>
          <S:type>user</S:type>

<S:nt4_compatible_name>DOMAIN\testuser7</
S:nt4_compatible_name>
          <S:ad_object_guid>{a145c819-2769-4ed7-b8c5-
01ac0829d004}</S:ad_object_guid>
          <S:display_name>user7, test</S:display_name>
         </S:sid>
        </S:access_allowed_ace>
        <S:access_denied_ace S:inherited="0">
         <S:access_mask>dc914</S:access_mask>
         <S:sid>
```

Web Storage System XML Security Descriptor Format   61

```xml
      <S:string_sid>S-1-5-21-527237240-507921405-1708537768-
1116</S:string_sid>
      <S:type>user</S:type>
<S:nt4_compatible_name>DOMAIN\testuser7</
S:nt4_compatible_name>
      <S:ad_object_guid>{a145c819-2769-4ed7-b8c5-
01ac0829d004}</S:ad_object_guid>
      <S:display_name>user7, test</S:display_name>
     </S:sid>
    </S:access_denied_ace>
    <S:access_allowed_ace S:inherited="0">
     <S:access_mask>1208a9</S:access_mask>
     <S:sid>
      <S:string_sid>S-1-5-21-527237240-507921405-1708537768-
1115</S:string_sid>
      <S:type>user</S:type>
<S:nt4_compatible_name>DOMAIN\testuser6</
S:nt4_compatible_name>
      <S:ad_object_guid>{f70d1982-9804-4a7e-8eff-
553d193a2756}</S:ad_object_guid>
      <S:display_name>user6, test</S:display_name>
     </S:sid>
    </S:access_allowed_ace>
    <S:access_denied_ace S:inherited="0">
     <S:access_mask>dc916</S:access_mask>
     <S:sid>
      <S:string_sid>S-1-5-21-527237240-507921405-1708537768-
1115</S:string_sid>
      <S:type>user</S:type>
<S:nt4_compatible_name>DOMAIN\testuser6</
S:nt4_compatible_name>
      <S:ad_object_guid>{f70d1982-9804-4a7e-8eff-
553d193a2756}</S:ad_object_guid>
      <S:display_name>user6, test</S:display_name>
     </S:sid>
    </S:access_denied_ace>
    <S:access_allowed_ace S:inherited="0">
     <S:access_mask>1208ab</S:access_mask>
     <S:sid>
      <S:string_sid>S-1-5-21-527237240-507921405-1708537768-
1114</S:string_sid>
      <S:type>user</S:type>
<S:nt4_compatible_name>DOMAIN\testuser5</
S:nt4_compatible_name>
      <S:ad_object_guid>{fb3f5f39-11b1-4071-8956-
e1452831ff57}</S:ad_object_guid>
```

Chapter 3 • Web Storage System Security

```xml
    <S:display_name>user5, test</S:display_name>
   </S:sid>
  </S:access_allowed_ace>
  <S:access_denied_ace S:inherited="0">
   <S:access_mask>dc914</S:access_mask>
   <S:sid>
    <S:string_sid>S-1-5-21-527237240-507921405-1708537768-1114</S:string_sid>
    <S:type>user</S:type>

<S:nt4_compatible_name>DOMAIN\testuser5</S:nt4_compatible_name>
    <S:ad_object_guid>{fb3f5f39-11b1-4071-8956-e1452831ff57}</S:ad_object_guid>
    <S:display_name>user5, test</S:display_name>
   </S:sid>
  </S:access_denied_ace>
  <S:access_allowed_ace S:inherited="0">
   <S:access_mask>1208ab</S:access_mask>
   <S:sid>
    <S:string_sid>S-1-5-21-527237240-507921405-1708537768-1113</S:string_sid>
    <S:type>user</S:type>

<S:nt4_compatible_name>DOMAIN\testuser4</S:nt4_compatible_name>
    <S:ad_object_guid>{ec73ab98-1b80-42a6-9887-545400d08c9b}</S:ad_object_guid>
    <S:display_name>user4, test</S:display_name>
   </S:sid>
  </S:access_allowed_ace>
  <S:access_denied_ace S:inherited="0">
   <S:access_mask>dc914</S:access_mask>
   <S:sid>
    <S:string_sid>S-1-5-21-527237240-507921405-1708537768-1113</S:string_sid>
    <S:type>user</S:type>

<S:nt4_compatible_name>DOMAIN\testuser4</S:nt4_compatible_name>
    <S:ad_object_guid>{ec73ab98-1b80-42a6-9887-545400d08c9b}</S:ad_object_guid>
    <S:display_name>user4, test</S:display_name>
   </S:sid>
  </S:access_denied_ace>
  <S:access_allowed_ace S:inherited="0">
   <S:access_mask>1208af</S:access_mask>
   <S:sid>
    <S:string_sid>S-1-5-21-527237240-507921405-1708537768-1141</S:string_sid>
    <S:type>user</S:type>
```

```xml
<S:nt4_compatible_name>DOMAIN\testuser3</S:nt4_compatible_name>
    <S:ad_object_guid>{67f9fe57-b2be-4ea5-bf43-bd3888390aaf}</S:ad_object_guid>
    <S:display_name>test user3</S:display_name>
   </S:sid>
  </S:access_allowed_ace>
  <S:access_denied_ace S:inherited="0">
   <S:access_mask>dc910</S:access_mask>
   <S:sid>
    <S:string_sid>S-1-5-21-527237240-507921405-1708537768-1141</S:string_sid>
    <S:type>user</S:type>

<S:nt4_compatible_name>DOMAIN\testuser3</S:nt4_compatible_name>
    <S:ad_object_guid>{67f9fe57-b2be-4ea5-bf43-bd3888390aaf}</S:ad_object_guid>
    <S:display_name>test user3</S:display_name>
   </S:sid>
  </S:access_denied_ace>
  <S:access_allowed_ace S:inherited="0">
   <S:access_mask>1208ab</S:access_mask>
   <S:sid>
    <S:string_sid>S-1-5-21-527237240-507921405-1708537768-1112</S:string_sid>
    <S:type>user</S:type>

<S:nt4_compatible_name>DOMAIN\testuser2</S:nt4_compatible_name>
    <S:ad_object_guid>{2ab61a07-e6c0-4c1b-a7fe-ff841ffb240e}</S:ad_object_guid>
    <S:display_name>user2, test</S:display_name>
   </S:sid>
  </S:access_allowed_ace>
  <S:access_denied_ace S:inherited="0">
   <S:access_mask>dc914</S:access_mask>
   <S:sid>
    <S:string_sid>S-1-5-21-527237240-507921405-1708537768-1112</S:string_sid>
    <S:type>user</S:type>

<S:nt4_compatible_name>DOMAIN\testuser2</S:nt4_compatible_name>
    <S:ad_object_guid>{2ab61a07-e6c0-4c1b-a7fe-ff841ffb240e}</S:ad_object_guid>
    <S:display_name>user2, test</S:display_name>
   </S:sid>
  </S:access_denied_ace>
```

```xml
     <S:access_allowed_ace S:inherited="0">
      <S:access_mask>1208af</S:access_mask>
      <S:sid>
       <S:string_sid>S-1-5-21-527237240-507921405-1708537768-1140</S:string_sid>
       <S:type>user</S:type>
<S:nt4_compatible_name>DOMAIN\testuser1</S:nt4_compatible_name>
       <S:ad_object_guid>{0724e453-7b94-4161-b224-3f5f45497203}</S:ad_object_guid>
       <S:display_name>test user1</S:display_name>
      </S:sid>
     </S:access_allowed_ace>
     <S:access_denied_ace S:inherited="0">
      <S:access_mask>dc910</S:access_mask>
      <S:sid>
       <S:string_sid>S-1-5-21-527237240-507921405-1708537768-1140</S:string_sid>
       <S:type>user</S:type>
<S:nt4_compatible_name>DOMAIN\testuser1</S:nt4_compatible_name>
       <S:ad_object_guid>{0724e453-7b94-4161-b224-3f5f45497203}</S:ad_object_guid>
       <S:display_name>test user1</S:display_name>
      </S:sid>
     </S:access_denied_ace>
     <S:access_allowed_ace S:inherited="0">
      <S:access_mask>1fc9ff</S:access_mask>
      <S:sid>
       <S:string_sid>S-1-5-21-527237240-507921405-1708537768-500</S:string_sid>
       <S:type>user</S:type>
<S:nt4_compatible_name>DOMAIN\testuser0</S:nt4_compatible_name>
       <S:ad_object_guid>{386ca8b5-5a21-4cf7-8d0a-ae41ef903ae6}</S:ad_object_guid>
       <S:display_name>user, test0</S:display_name>
      </S:sid>
     </S:access_allowed_ace>
     <S:access_allowed_ace S:inherited="1">
      <S:access_mask>2</S:access_mask>
      <S:sid>
       <S:string_sid>S-1-5-7</S:string_sid>
       <S:type>well_known_group</S:type>
       <S:nt4_compatible_name>NT AUTHORITY\ANONYMOUS LOGON</S:nt4_compatible_name>
      </S:sid>
```

Web Storage System XML Security Descriptor Format

```xml
    </S:access_allowed_ace>
    <S:access_denied_ace S:inherited="1">
     <S:access_mask>1fc9bd</S:access_mask>
     <S:sid>
      <S:string_sid>S-1-5-7</S:string_sid>
      <S:type>well_known_group</S:type>
      <S:nt4_compatible_name>NT AUTHORITY\ANONYMOUS LOGON</S:nt4_compatible_name>
     </S:sid>
    </S:access_denied_ace>
    <S:access_allowed_ace S:inherited="0">
     <S:access_mask>1208a9</S:access_mask>
     <S:sid>
      <S:string_sid>S-1-5-21-527237240-507921405-1708537768-1142</S:string_sid>
      <S:type>group</S:type>
      <S:nt4_compatible_name>DOMAIN\testgroup1</S:nt4_compatible_name>
      <S:ad_object_guid>{57395759-90f4-4a78-9590-709b86613d06}</S:ad_object_guid>
      <S:display_name>testgroup1</S:display_name>
     </S:sid>
    </S:access_allowed_ace>
    <S:access_allowed_ace S:inherited="0">
     <S:access_mask>1208af</S:access_mask>
     <S:sid>
      <S:string_sid>S-1-5-21-527237240-507921405-1708537768-1143</S:string_sid>
      <S:type>group</S:type>
      <S:nt4_compatible_name>DOMAIN\testgroup2</S:nt4_compatible_name>
      <S:ad_object_guid>{feb5d452-9f83-4765-8e71-1045f01a2e1d}</S:ad_object_guid>
      <S:display_name>testgroup2</S:display_name>
     </S:sid>
    </S:access_allowed_ace>
    <S:access_denied_ace S:inherited="0">
     <S:access_mask>dc916</S:access_mask>
     <S:sid>
      <S:string_sid>S-1-5-21-527237240-507921405-1708537768-1142</S:string_sid>
      <S:type>group</S:type>
      <S:nt4_compatible_name>DOMAIN\testgroup1</S:nt4_compatible_name>
      <S:ad_object_guid>{57395759-90f4-4a78-9590-709b86613d06}</S:ad_object_guid>
      <S:display_name>testgroup1</S:display_name>
```

Chapter 3 • Web Storage System Security

```xml
       </S:sid>
      </S:access_denied_ace>
      <S:access_denied_ace S:inherited="0">
       <S:access_mask>dc910</S:access_mask>
       <S:sid>
        <S:string_sid>S-1-5-21-527237240-507921405-1708537768-1143</S:string_sid>
        <S:type>group</S:type>

<S:nt4_compatible_name>DOMAIN\testgroup2</S:nt4_compatible_name>
        <S:ad_object_guid>{feb5d452-9f83-4765-8e71-1045f01a2e1d}</S:ad_object_guid>
        <S:display_name>testgroup2</S:display_name>
       </S:sid>
      </S:access_denied_ace>
      <S:access_allowed_ace S:inherited="1">
       <S:access_mask>1208ab</S:access_mask>
       <S:sid>
        <S:string_sid>S-1-1-0</S:string_sid>
        <S:type>well_known_group</S:type>

<S:nt4_compatible_name>\Everyone</S:nt4_compatible_name>
       </S:sid>
      </S:access_allowed_ace>
     </S:effective_aces>
     <S:subcontainer_inheritable_aces>
      <S:access_allowed_ace S:inherited="0" S:no_propagate_inherit="0">
       <S:access_mask>1208a9</S:access_mask>
       <S:sid>
        <S:string_sid>S-1-5-21-527237240-507921405-1708537768-1117</S:string_sid>
        <S:type>user</S:type>

<S:nt4_compatible_name>DOMAIN\testuser8</S:nt4_compatible_name>
        <S:ad_object_guid>{74116535-9aad-4995-957e-99e6640fb69b}</S:ad_object_guid>
        <S:display_name>user8, test</S:display_name>
       </S:sid>
      </S:access_allowed_ace>
      <S:access_denied_ace S:inherited="0" S:no_propagate_inherit="0">
       <S:access_mask>dc916</S:access_mask>
       <S:sid>
        <S:string_sid>S-1-5-21-527237240-507921405-1708537768-1117</S:string_sid>
        <S:type>user</S:type>
```

```xml
<S:nt4_compatible_name>DOMAIN\testuser8</S:nt4_compatible_name>
    <S:ad_object_guid>{74116535-9aad-4995-957e-99e6640fb69b}</S:ad_object_guid>
    <S:display_name>user8, test</S:display_name>
   </S:sid>
  </S:access_denied_ace>
  <S:access_allowed_ace S:inherited="0" S:no_propagate_inherit="0">
    <S:access_mask>1208ab</S:access_mask>
    <S:sid>
    <S:string_sid>S-1-5-21-527237240-507921405-1708537768-1116</S:string_sid>
    <S:type>user</S:type>

<S:nt4_compatible_name>DOMAIN\testuser7</S:nt4_compatible_name>
    <S:ad_object_guid>{a145c819-2769-4ed7-b8c5-01ac0829d004}</S:ad_object_guid>
    <S:display_name>user7, test</S:display_name>
   </S:sid>
  </S:access_allowed_ace>
  <S:access_denied_ace S:inherited="0" S:no_propagate_inherit="0">
    <S:access_mask>dc914</S:access_mask>
    <S:sid>
    <S:string_sid>S-1-5-21-527237240-507921405-1708537768-1116</S:string_sid>
    <S:type>user</S:type>

<S:nt4_compatible_name>DOMAIN\testuser7</S:nt4_compatible_name>
    <S:ad_object_guid>{a145c819-2769-4ed7-b8c5-01ac0829d004}</S:ad_object_guid>
    <S:display_name>user7, test</S:display_name>
   </S:sid>
  </S:access_denied_ace>
  <S:access_allowed_ace S:inherited="0" S:no_propagate_inherit="0">
    <S:access_mask>1208a9</S:access_mask>
    <S:sid>
    <S:string_sid>S-1-5-21-527237240-507921405-1708537768-1115</S:string_sid>
    <S:type>user</S:type>

<S:nt4_compatible_name>DOMAIN\testuser6</S:nt4_compatible_name>
    <S:ad_object_guid>{f70d1982-9804-4a7e-8eff-553d193a2756}</S:ad_object_guid>
```

```xml
      <S:display_name>user6, test</S:display_name>
    </S:sid>
  </S:access_allowed_ace>
  <S:access_denied_ace S:inherited="0"
S:no_propagate_inherit="0">
    <S:access_mask>dc916</S:access_mask>
    <S:sid>
      <S:string_sid>S-1-5-21-527237240-507921405-1708537768-1115</S:string_sid>
      <S:type>user</S:type>

<S:nt4_compatible_name>DOMAIN\testuser6</S:nt4_compatible_name>
      <S:ad_object_guid>{f70d1982-9804-4a7e-8eff-553d193a2756}</S:ad_object_guid>
      <S:display_name>user6, test</S:display_name>
    </S:sid>
  </S:access_denied_ace>
  <S:access_allowed_ace S:inherited="0"
S:no_propagate_inherit="0">
    <S:access_mask>1208ab</S:access_mask>
    <S:sid>
      <S:string_sid>S-1-5-21-527237240-507921405-1708537768-1114</S:string_sid>
      <S:type>user</S:type>

<S:nt4_compatible_name>DOMAIN\testuser5</S:nt4_compatible_name>
      <S:ad_object_guid>{fb3f5f39-11b1-4071-8956-e1452831ff57}</S:ad_object_guid>
      <S:display_name>user5, test</S:display_name>
    </S:sid>
  </S:access_allowed_ace>
  <S:access_denied_ace S:inherited="0"
S:no_propagate_inherit="0">
    <S:access_mask>dc914</S:access_mask>
    <S:sid>
      <S:string_sid>S-1-5-21-527237240-507921405-1708537768-1114</S:string_sid>
      <S:type>user</S:type>

<S:nt4_compatible_name>DOMAIN\testuser5</S:nt4_compatible_name>
      <S:ad_object_guid>{fb3f5f39-11b1-4071-8956-e1452831ff57}</S:ad_object_guid>
      <S:display_name>user5, test</S:display_name>
    </S:sid>
  </S:access_denied_ace>
  <S:access_allowed_ace S:inherited="0"
S:no_propagate_inherit="0">
```

```xml
    <S:access_mask>1208ab</S:access_mask>
    <S:sid>
     <S:string_sid>S-1-5-21-527237240-507921405-1708537768-1113</S:string_sid>
     <S:type>user</S:type>

<S:nt4_compatible_name>DOMAIN\testuser4</S:nt4_compatible_name>
     <S:ad_object_guid>{ec73ab98-1b80-42a6-9887-545400d08c9b}</S:ad_object_guid>
     <S:display_name>user4, test</S:display_name>
    </S:sid>
   </S:access_allowed_ace>
   <S:access_denied_ace S:inherited="0" S:no_propagate_inherit="0">
    <S:access_mask>dc914</S:access_mask>
    <S:sid>
     <S:string_sid>S-1-5-21-527237240-507921405-1708537768-1113</S:string_sid>
     <S:type>user</S:type>

<S:nt4_compatible_name>DOMAIN\testuser4</S:nt4_compatible_name>
     <S:ad_object_guid>{ec73ab98-1b80-42a6-9887-545400d08c9b}</S:ad_object_guid>
     <S:display_name>user4, test</S:display_name>
    </S:sid>
   </S:access_denied_ace>
   <S:access_allowed_ace S:inherited="0" S:no_propagate_inherit="0">
    <S:access_mask>1208af</S:access_mask>
    <S:sid>
     <S:string_sid>S-1-5-21-527237240-507921405-1708537768-1141</S:string_sid>
     <S:type>user</S:type>

<S:nt4_compatible_name>DOMAIN\testuser3</S:nt4_compatible_name>
     <S:ad_object_guid>{67f9fe57-b2be-4ea5-bf43-bd3888390aaf}</S:ad_object_guid>
     <S:display_name>test user3</S:display_name>
    </S:sid>
   </S:access_allowed_ace>
   <S:access_denied_ace S:inherited="0" S:no_propagate_inherit="0">
    <S:access_mask>dc910</S:access_mask>
    <S:sid>
     <S:string_sid>S-1-5-21-527237240-507921405-1708537768-1141</S:string_sid>
     <S:type>user</S:type>
```

```xml
<S:nt4_compatible_name>DOMAIN\testuser3</
S:nt4_compatible_name>
    <S:ad_object_guid>{67f9fe57-b2be-4ea5-bf43-
bd3888390aaf}</S:ad_object_guid>
    <S:display_name>test user3</S:display_name>
  </S:sid>
 </S:access_denied_ace>
 <S:access_allowed_ace S:inherited="0"
S:no_propagate_inherit="0">
    <S:access_mask>1208ab</S:access_mask>
    <S:sid>
    <S:string_sid>S-1-5-21-527237240-507921405-1708537768-
1112</S:string_sid>
    <S:type>user</S:type>

<S:nt4_compatible_name>DOMAIN\testuser2</
S:nt4_compatible_name>
    <S:ad_object_guid>{2ab61a07-e6c0-4c1b-a7fe-
ff841ffb240e}</S:ad_object_guid>
    <S:display_name>user2, test</S:display_name>
  </S:sid>
 </S:access_allowed_ace>
 <S:access_denied_ace S:inherited="0"
S:no_propagate_inherit="0">
    <S:access_mask>dc914</S:access_mask>
    <S:sid>
    <S:string_sid>S-1-5-21-527237240-507921405-1708537768-
1112</S:string_sid>
    <S:type>user</S:type>

<S:nt4_compatible_name>DOMAIN\testuser2</
S:nt4_compatible_name>
    <S:ad_object_guid>{2ab61a07-e6c0-4c1b-a7fe-
ff841ffb240e}</S:ad_object_guid>
    <S:display_name>user2, test</S:display_name>
  </S:sid>
 </S:access_denied_ace>
 <S:access_allowed_ace S:inherited="0"
S:no_propagate_inherit="0">
    <S:access_mask>1208af</S:access_mask>
    <S:sid>
    <S:string_sid>S-1-5-21-527237240-507921405-1708537768-
1140</S:string_sid>
    <S:type>user</S:type>

<S:nt4_compatible_name>DOMAIN\testuser1</
S:nt4_compatible_name>
    <S:ad_object_guid>{0724e453-7b94-4161-b224-
3f5f45497203}</S:ad_object_guid>
```

```xml
      <S:display_name>test user1</S:display_name>
     </S:sid>
   </S:access_allowed_ace>
   <S:access_denied_ace S:inherited="0"
S:no_propagate_inherit="0">
     <S:access_mask>dc910</S:access_mask>
     <S:sid>
      <S:string_sid>S-1-5-21-527237240-507921405-1708537768-1140</S:string_sid>
      <S:type>user</S:type>
<S:nt4_compatible_name>DOMAIN\testuser1</S:nt4_compatible_name>
      <S:ad_object_guid>{0724e453-7b94-4161-b224-3f5f45497203}</S:ad_object_guid>
      <S:display_name>test user1</S:display_name>
     </S:sid>
   </S:access_denied_ace>
   <S:access_allowed_ace S:inherited="0"
S:no_propagate_inherit="0">
     <S:access_mask>1fc9ff</S:access_mask>
     <S:sid>
      <S:string_sid>S-1-5-21-527237240-507921405-1708537768-500</S:string_sid>
      <S:type>user</S:type>
<S:nt4_compatible_name>DOMAIN\testuser0</S:nt4_compatible_name>
      <S:ad_object_guid>{386ca8b5-5a21-4cf7-8d0a-ae41ef903ae6}</S:ad_object_guid>
      <S:display_name>user0, test</S:display_name>
     </S:sid>
   </S:access_allowed_ace>
   <S:access_allowed_ace S:inherited="1"
S:no_propagate_inherit="0">
     <S:access_mask>2</S:access_mask>
     <S:sid>
      <S:string_sid>S-1-5-7</S:string_sid>
      <S:type>well_known_group</S:type>
      <S:nt4_compatible_name>NT AUTHORITY\ANONYMOUS LOGON</S:nt4_compatible_name>
     </S:sid>
   </S:access_allowed_ace>
   <S:access_denied_ace S:inherited="1"
S:no_propagate_inherit="0">
     <S:access_mask>1fc9bd</S:access_mask>
     <S:sid>
      <S:string_sid>S-1-5-7</S:string_sid>
      <S:type>well_known_group</S:type>
      <S:nt4_compatible_name>NT AUTHORITY\ANONYMOUS LOGON</
```

```xml
S:nt4_compatible_name>
    </S:sid>
  </S:access_denied_ace>
  <S:access_allowed_ace S:inherited="0"
S:no_propagate_inherit="0">
    <S:access_mask>1208a9</S:access_mask>
    <S:sid>
      <S:string_sid>S-1-5-21-527237240-507921405-1708537768-1142</S:string_sid>
      <S:type>group</S:type>

<S:nt4_compatible_name>DOMAIN\testgroup1</S:nt4_compatible_name>
    <S:ad_object_guid>{57395759-90f4-4a78-9590-709b86613d06}</S:ad_object_guid>
    <S:display_name>testgroup1</S:display_name>
    </S:sid>
  </S:access_allowed_ace>
  <S:access_allowed_ace S:inherited="0"
S:no_propagate_inherit="0">
    <S:access_mask>1208af</S:access_mask>
    <S:sid>
      <S:string_sid>S-1-5-21-527237240-507921405-1708537768-1143</S:string_sid>
      <S:type>group</S:type>

<S:nt4_compatible_name>DOMAIN\testgroup2</S:nt4_compatible_name>
    <S:ad_object_guid>{feb5d452-9f83-4765-8e71-1045f01a2e1d}</S:ad_object_guid>
    <S:display_name>testgroup2</S:display_name>
    </S:sid>
  </S:access_allowed_ace>
  <S:access_denied_ace S:inherited="0"
S:no_propagate_inherit="0">
    <S:access_mask>dc916</S:access_mask>
    <S:sid>
      <S:string_sid>S-1-5-21-527237240-507921405-1708537768-1142</S:string_sid>
      <S:type>group</S:type>

<S:nt4_compatible_name>DOMAIN\testgroup1</S:nt4_compatible_name>
    <S:ad_object_guid>{57395759-90f4-4a78-9590-709b86613d06}</S:ad_object_guid>
    <S:display_name>testgroup1</S:display_name>
    </S:sid>
  </S:access_denied_ace>
  <S:access_denied_ace S:inherited="0"
S:no_propagate_inherit="0">
```

Web Storage System XML Security Descriptor Format 73

```xml
      <S:access_mask>dc910</S:access_mask>
      <S:sid>
       <S:string_sid>S-1-5-21-527237240-507921405-1708537768-1143</S:string_sid>
       <S:type>group</S:type>

<S:nt4_compatible_name>DOMAIN\testgroup2</S:nt4_compatible_name>
       <S:ad_object_guid>{feb5d452-9f83-4765-8e71-1045f01a2e1d}</S:ad_object_guid>
       <S:display_name>testgroup2</S:display_name>
      </S:sid>
    </S:access_denied_ace>
    <S:access_allowed_ace S:inherited="1" S:no_propagate_inherit="0">
      <S:access_mask>1208ab</S:access_mask>
      <S:sid>
       <S:string_sid>S-1-1-0</S:string_sid>
       <S:type>well_known_group</S:type>

<S:nt4_compatible_name>\Everyone</S:nt4_compatible_name>
      </S:sid>
    </S:access_allowed_ace>
   </S:subcontainer_inheritable_aces>
   <S:subitem_inheritable_aces>
    <S:access_denied_ace S:inherited="0" S:no_propagate_inherit="0">
      <S:access_mask>1f0fbf</S:access_mask>
      <S:sid>
       <S:string_sid>S-1-5-21-527237240-507921405-1708537768-1117</S:string_sid>
       <S:type>user</S:type>

<S:nt4_compatible_name>DOMAIN\testuser8</S:nt4_compatible_name>
       <S:ad_object_guid>{74116535-9aad-4995-957e-99e6640fb69b}</S:ad_object_guid>
       <S:display_name>user8, test</S:display_name>
      </S:sid>
    </S:access_denied_ace>
    <S:access_denied_ace S:inherited="0" S:no_propagate_inherit="0">
      <S:access_mask>1f0fbf</S:access_mask>
      <S:sid>
       <S:string_sid>S-1-5-21-527237240-507921405-1708537768-1116</S:string_sid>
       <S:type>user</S:type>
```

```xml
    <S:nt4_compatible_name>DOMAIN\testuser7</S:nt4_compatible_name>
      <S:ad_object_guid>{a145c819-2769-4ed7-b8c5-01ac0829d004}</S:ad_object_guid>
      <S:display_name>user7, test</S:display_name>
    </S:sid>
   </S:access_denied_ace>
   <S:access_allowed_ace S:inherited="0" S:no_propagate_inherit="0">
    <S:access_mask>1208a9</S:access_mask>
    <S:sid>
     <S:string_sid>S-1-5-21-527237240-507921405-1708537768-1115</S:string_sid>
     <S:type>user</S:type>

    <S:nt4_compatible_name>DOMAIN\testuser6</S:nt4_compatible_name>
      <S:ad_object_guid>{f70d1982-9804-4a7e-8eff-553d193a2756}</S:ad_object_guid>
      <S:display_name>user6, test</S:display_name>
    </S:sid>
   </S:access_allowed_ace>
   <S:access_denied_ace S:inherited="0" S:no_propagate_inherit="0">
    <S:access_mask>1f0716</S:access_mask>
    <S:sid>
     <S:string_sid>S-1-5-21-527237240-507921405-1708537768-1115</S:string_sid>
     <S:type>user</S:type>

    <S:nt4_compatible_name>DOMAIN\testuser6</S:nt4_compatible_name>
      <S:ad_object_guid>{f70d1982-9804-4a7e-8eff-553d193a2756}</S:ad_object_guid>
      <S:display_name>user6, test</S:display_name>
    </S:sid>
   </S:access_denied_ace>
   <S:access_allowed_ace S:inherited="0" S:no_propagate_inherit="0">
    <S:access_mask>120ca9</S:access_mask>
    <S:sid>
     <S:string_sid>S-1-5-21-527237240-507921405-1708537768-1114</S:string_sid>
     <S:type>user</S:type>

    <S:nt4_compatible_name>DOMAIN\testuser5</S:nt4_compatible_name>
      <S:ad_object_guid>{fb3f5f39-11b1-4071-8956-e1452831ff57}</S:ad_object_guid>
      <S:display_name>user5, test</S:display_name>
```

Web Storage System XML Security Descriptor Format 75

```xml
      </S:sid>
    </S:access_allowed_ace>
    <S:access_denied_ace S:inherited="0"
S:no_propagate_inherit="0">
      <S:access_mask>1f0716</S:access_mask>
      <S:sid>
        <S:string_sid>S-1-5-21-527237240-507921405-1708537768-
1114</S:string_sid>
        <S:type>user</S:type>

<S:nt4_compatible_name>DOMAIN\testuser5</
S:nt4_compatible_name>
        <S:ad_object_guid>{fb3f5f39-11b1-4071-8956-
e1452831ff57}</S:ad_object_guid>
        <S:display_name>user5, test</S:display_name>
      </S:sid>
    </S:access_denied_ace>
    <S:access_allowed_ace S:inherited="0"
S:no_propagate_inherit="0">
      <S:access_mask>120ea9</S:access_mask>
      <S:sid>
        <S:string_sid>S-1-5-21-527237240-507921405-1708537768-
1113</S:string_sid>
        <S:type>user</S:type>

<S:nt4_compatible_name>DOMAIN\testuser4</
S:nt4_compatible_name>
        <S:ad_object_guid>{ec73ab98-1b80-42a6-9887-
545400d08c9b}</S:ad_object_guid>
        <S:display_name>user4, test</S:display_name>
      </S:sid>
    </S:access_allowed_ace>
    <S:access_denied_ace S:inherited="0"
S:no_propagate_inherit="0">
      <S:access_mask>1f0716</S:access_mask>
      <S:sid>
        <S:string_sid>S-1-5-21-527237240-507921405-1708537768-
1113</S:string_sid>
        <S:type>user</S:type>

<S:nt4_compatible_name>DOMAIN\testuser4</
S:nt4_compatible_name>
        <S:ad_object_guid>{ec73ab98-1b80-42a6-9887-
545400d08c9b}</S:ad_object_guid>
        <S:display_name>user4, test</S:display_name>
      </S:sid>
    </S:access_denied_ace>
    <S:access_allowed_ace S:inherited="0"
S:no_propagate_inherit="0">
      <S:access_mask>120ea9</S:access_mask>
```

```
      <S:sid>
        <S:string_sid>S-1-5-21-527237240-507921405-1708537768-
1141</S:string_sid>
        <S:type>user</S:type>

<S:nt4_compatible_name>DOMAIN\testuser3</
S:nt4_compatible_name>
        <S:ad_object_guid>{67f9fe57-b2be-4ea5-bf43-
bd3888390aaf}</S:ad_object_guid>
        <S:display_name>test user3</S:display_name>
      </S:sid>
    </S:access_allowed_ace>
    <S:access_denied_ace S:inherited="0"
S:no_propagate_inherit="0">
      <S:access_mask>1f0716</S:access_mask>
      <S:sid>
        <S:string_sid>S-1-5-21-527237240-507921405-1708537768-
1141</S:string_sid>
        <S:type>user</S:type>

<S:nt4_compatible_name>DOMAIN\testuser3</
S:nt4_compatible_name>
        <S:ad_object_guid>{67f9fe57-b2be-4ea5-bf43-
bd3888390aaf}</S:ad_object_guid>
        <S:display_name>test user3</S:display_name>
      </S:sid>
    </S:access_denied_ace>
    <S:access_allowed_ace S:inherited="0"
S:no_propagate_inherit="0">
      <S:access_mask>1f0fbf</S:access_mask>
      <S:sid>
        <S:string_sid>S-1-5-21-527237240-507921405-1708537768-
1112</S:string_sid>
        <S:type>user</S:type>

<S:nt4_compatible_name>DOMAIN\testuser2</
S:nt4_compatible_name>
        <S:ad_object_guid>{2ab61a07-e6c0-4c1b-a7fe-
ff841ffb240e}</S:ad_object_guid>
        <S:display_name>user2, test</S:display_name>
      </S:sid>
    </S:access_allowed_ace>
    <S:access_allowed_ace S:inherited="0"
S:no_propagate_inherit="0">
      <S:access_mask>1f0fbf</S:access_mask>
      <S:sid>
        <S:string_sid>S-1-5-21-527237240-507921405-1708537768-
1140</S:string_sid>
        <S:type>user</S:type>
```

Web Storage System XML Security Descriptor Format

```xml
<S:nt4_compatible_name>DOMAIN\testuser1</S:nt4_compatible_name>
    <S:ad_object_guid>{0724e453-7b94-4161-b224-3f5f45497203}</S:ad_object_guid>
    <S:display_name>test user1</S:display_name>
    </S:sid>
  </S:access_allowed_ace>
  <S:access_allowed_ace S:inherited="0" S:no_propagate_inherit="0">
    <S:access_mask>1f0fbf</S:access_mask>
    <S:sid>
     <S:string_sid>S-1-5-21-527237240-507921405-1708537768-500</S:string_sid>
     <S:type>user</S:type>

<S:nt4_compatible_name>DOMAIN\testuser0</S:nt4_compatible_name>
    <S:ad_object_guid>{386ca8b5-5a21-4cf7-8d0a-ae41ef903ae6}</S:ad_object_guid>
    <S:display_name>user0, test</S:display_name>
    </S:sid>
  </S:access_allowed_ace>
  <S:access_denied_ace S:inherited="1" S:no_propagate_inherit="0">
    <S:access_mask>1f0fbf</S:access_mask>
    <S:sid>
     <S:string_sid>S-1-5-7</S:string_sid>
     <S:type>well_known_group</S:type>

<S:nt4_compatible_name>NT AUTHORITY\ANONYMOUS LOGON</S:nt4_compatible_name>
     </S:sid>
  </S:access_denied_ace>
  <S:access_allowed_ace S:inherited="0" S:no_propagate_inherit="0">
    <S:access_mask>1208a9</S:access_mask>
    <S:sid>
     <S:string_sid>S-1-5-21-527237240-507921405-1708537768-1142</S:string_sid>
     <S:type>group</S:type>

<S:nt4_compatible_name>DOMAIN\testgroup1</S:nt4_compatible_name>
    <S:ad_object_guid>{57395759-90f4-4a78-9590-709b86613d06}</S:ad_object_guid>
    <S:display_name>testgroup1</S:display_name>
    </S:sid>
  </S:access_allowed_ace>
  <S:access_allowed_ace S:inherited="0" S:no_propagate_inherit="0">
```

```xml
      <S:access_mask>120ea9</S:access_mask>
      <S:sid>
       <S:string_sid>S-1-5-21-527237240-507921405-1708537768-
1143</S:string_sid>
       <S:type>group</S:type>

<S:nt4_compatible_name>DOMAIN\testgroup2</
S:nt4_compatible_name>
       <S:ad_object_guid>{feb5d452-9f83-4765-8e71-
1045f01a2e1d}</S:ad_object_guid>
       <S:display_name>testgroup2</S:display_name>
      </S:sid>
     </S:access_allowed_ace>
     <S:access_denied_ace S:inherited="0"
S:no_propagate_inherit="0">
      <S:access_mask>1f0716</S:access_mask>
      <S:sid>
       <S:string_sid>S-1-5-21-527237240-507921405-1708537768-
1142</S:string_sid>
       <S:type>group</S:type>

<S:nt4_compatible_name>DOMAIN\testgroup1</
S:nt4_compatible_name>
       <S:ad_object_guid>{57395759-90f4-4a78-9590-
709b86613d06}</S:ad_object_guid>
       <S:display_name>testgroup1</S:display_name>
      </S:sid>
     </S:access_denied_ace>
     <S:access_denied_ace S:inherited="0"
S:no_propagate_inherit="0">
      <S:access_mask>1f0716</S:access_mask>
      <S:sid>
       <S:string_sid>S-1-5-21-527237240-507921405-1708537768-
1143</S:string_sid>
       <S:type>group</S:type>

<S:nt4_compatible_name>DOMAIN\testgroup2</
S:nt4_compatible_name>
       <S:ad_object_guid>{feb5d452-9f83-4765-8e71-
1045f01a2e1d}</S:ad_object_guid>
       <S:display_name>testgroup2</S:display_name>
      </S:sid>
     </S:access_denied_ace>
     <S:access_allowed_ace S:inherited="1"
S:no_propagate_inherit="0">
      <S:access_mask>120ea9</S:access_mask>
      <S:sid>
       <S:string_sid>S-1-1-0</S:string_sid>
       <S:type>well_known_group</S:type>
```

```
        <S:nt4_compatible_name>\Everyone</S:nt4_compatible_name>
       </S:sid>
      </S:access_allowed_ace>
     </S:subitem_inheritable_aces>
    </S:dacl>
</S:security_descriptor>
```

FOUR

Web Storage System Forms and Events

An Introduction to Web Storage System Forms

The Microsoft Web Storage System form is a Web-based forms technology that is built on Internet standards. A Web Storage System form is a Web page that is registered in the Web Storage System. The registration itself is a single record in the Web Storage System store.

This topic covers the following information:

- Web Storage System Form Registration
- Reusing Elements of Outlook Web Access

Web Storage System Form Registration

Web Storage System form registration controls when Microsoft Exchange 2000 Server displays a custom form. For example, the form can be

- Displayed as the default view for a folder.
- Displayed in response to a command such as Open or Edit.
- Displayed when the user opens an item of a particular content class.

HOW WEB STORAGE SYSTEM FORMS WORK • Web Storage System forms are designed to work with browsers that comply with the HTML 3.2 standard. Web Storage System Forms require HTML 3.2 features. Browsers that support those features include Microsoft Internet Explorer 3 or later and Netscape Navigator 3 or later.

Web Storage System Forms support any browser specified in the Microsoft Internet Information Services (IIS) *Browsecap.ini* configuration file.

Everything in the Web Storage System is URL addressable. When accessed on the Web, Microsoft Outlook Web Access provides a default rendering for all items in the Web Storage System. The forms registry allows developers to override the default rendering in Outlook Web Access.

When Exchange receives an HTTP request from the user's browser, the request is transferred to Microsoft Internet Information Services (IIS). IIS which invokes an ISAPI DLL. This is the same DLL that the Web Storage System uses to process all HTTP/DAV requests. The ISAPI DLL checks the form registry for a form registration. The form registration provides a set of form-specific attributes such as content class, user action, language, browser type, and item state.

Information read from the HTTP request header is processed and compared against browser information stored in *Browsecap.ini* to derive browser capabilities.

The ISAPI DLL uses a best-fit comparison with the forms registry information to determine which form to display.

The registry passes these two parameters to the renderer:

- DataURL (URL to item being requested)
- FormURL (value in formurl parameter)

In the form registration, developers can specify one of the following in the executeURL field:

- A custom ASP script
- A custom ISAPI filter

Each of these is mutually exclusive. In addition, if an .asp file is listed, it generates the entire response.

Note For the ASP script or the ISAPI filter to be executed, the execute permissions must be turned on in Exchange System Manager.

To adjust Execute Permissions,

1. Open the Exchange System Manager.
2. Select the Exchange Virtual Server.
3. Select the virtual server (often Public).
4. Right click the server icon.
5. Select Access.
6. Turn on script for ASP and script and executables for the ISAPI filter.

Web Storage System Forms Registry

The Web Storage System forms registry provides a method of storing form registrations. The registration can specify customized forms and actions based on a set of properties. This provides a simple means to register and query forms associated with an item of a particular content class. Form registrations are stored in the Web Storage System in the same way as schema or event registrations.

Registrations can be performed on a per-folder basis. For example, in a tracking application, you could create a schema subfolder and store the registration and schema information for your application in that schema folder.

Registration on a per-folder basis simplifies the administration of an application because everything (forms and form definitions) is stored in the same location.

Note The Web Storage System Forms Registry is a new technology. It is not the Microsoft Windows registry or the COM registry.

ABSOLUTE OR RELATIVE REGISTRATION • Forms can be registered with an absolute or relative reference to the registration item. The Form URL can now take one of the following formats :

- /forms/form.htm (A relative URL, relative to the form registration.)
- /public/webapps/app/forms/form.htm (This is relative to the virtual server from the HTTP request.)
- <http://server/public/webapps/app/forms/form.htm> (No processing happens in the rendering engine, and the form is passed to the executeUrl method unchanged.)

Note Although absolute registration is supported, it is not recommended. Use relative registration whenever possible.

RECOMMENDED SERVER AND PUBLIC FOLDER CONFIGURATION • Data and forms must be stored on a single server. If the data is on one server, but the form is on another server, the forms renderer is unable to access what it needs.

To have a distributed setup, full public folder replication must be activated for the Web application.

Users should only access the Web application on a server where it physically resides. The forms renderer should not be accessed directly.

Schema Collection Ref

Objects in Web Storage System define the location of their schema through the schema collection ref (SCR). The SCR is the URL of the starting location start searching for schema information.

If the SCR is not set, the default starting location is the schema folder. The URL can point to the current folder or to another folder that is known to contain schema information.

The form definition sets the SCR property to a URL that indicates a folder in the store—for example, *http://servername.microsoft.com/public/myschema*.

The baseschema property is a multivalued string that defines the URLs to search for schema information. This is different from the Schema Collection Ref because the baseschema property contains all the locations that will be searched. The Schema Collection Ref simply specifies where to start.

> **Note** Because there is no HTTP proxy between backend Exchange servers, the SCR must point to a folder in the store where the object exists.

In searching for schemas, Exchange uses the following look-up order:

- The SCR on the item's parent folder. (Most folders have a defined SCR.)
- The multivalued base schema property of an item's parent folder.

> **Note**
> 1. If the item is itself a folder, its SCR is used. If the item does not have an SCR, its parent folder is not used.
> 2. Forms look-up follows the same lookup path as the Exchange schema.

Form Definition Properties

Form definitions have the properties shown in Table 4–1.

TABLE 4–1 *Form definitions*

Property name	Description
urn:schemas-microsoft-com:office:forms#browser	Case insensitive; indicates the type of browser. An asterisk (*) indicates a wildcard. Example: Microsoft Internet Explorer.
urn:schemas-microsoft-com:office:forms#cmd	Case-insensitive string denoting the action or behavior being performed on an object. This is the first parameter after the command (?Cmd= of the URL returned from IIS roughly corresponding to the ISAPI QUERY_STRING.) The QUERY_STRING is delimited by ampersands (&) that represent modifiers of the action. Example: NewArt.

TABLE 4-1 *Form definitions (continued)*

Property name	Description
urn:schemas-microsoft-com:office:forms#contentclass	The content class for which the form is registered. Case insensitive; associated with a set of schemas and a set of forms. Example: urn:content-classes:message.
urn:schemas:microsoft-com:office:forms#contentstate	This property is used to match forms against the *http://schemas.microsoft.com/exchange/contentstate* that can be set on any item. Case insensitive. Example: mySample.
urn:schemas-microsoft-com:office:forms#executeparameters	Parameters to pass to the form-rendering engine specified by the executeurl property. This property must be URL escaped. An ampersand (&) is used to separate multiple values. Examples: param1=mySample& m2=url%20escaped.
urn:schemas-microsoft-com:office:forms#executeurl	The URL to execute to render a form. An ISAPI filter or ASP page. Example: process.asp
urn:schemas-microsoft-com:office:forms#formurl	The URL of the form or template being handled and rendered; the item that is denoted by the current URL. Example: ExpenseForm.htm.
urn:schemas-microsoft-com:office:forms#language	Automatically provided as part of the HTTP request headers, this is the language of the form. This attribute corresponds to a case-insensitive ISO language-country value in the Accept-Language HTTP header. Example: en
urn:schemas-microsoft-com:office:forms#majorver	The major version of the browser.
urn:schemas-microsoft-com:office:forms#messagestate	State of the item. Case-insensitive; values include normal, submitted, read, unread, and importance.
urn:schemas-microsoft-com:office:forms#minorver	The minor version of the browser.
urn:schemas-microsoft-com:office:forms#platform	The platform of the browser to be matched against for forms registrations. Case insensitive. Same format as in *browscap.ini*. Example: WINNT.
urn:schemas-microsoft-com:office:forms#request	Property used to specify whether the form uses GET or POST requests. Case insensitive. There are two possible values: GET and POST. GET queries for information, POST writes information. Examples: GET, POST.

Form Registration Examples

A form registration is a set of form-specific properties. The forms registry uses the form registration to choose which form to display. The form definition is a single record in an application schema folder in the Web Storage System store.

The form registration records the form definition properties.

The content class of items displayed by this form is required; all other form registration properties are optional.

The most basic form registration would consist of:

- The DAV content class of the form registration
- The form's content class
- The form's URL (not necessary in some scenarios)
- The executeURL field

REGISTRATION SECURITY • To register a form in a folder, you must have permissions to modify items in that folder.

Security is based on the Windows 2000 and Microsoft Windows NT security model and on the security identifiers (SIDs) of real network users. Discretionary access control lists (DACLs) can be set on any item in the Web Storage System.

NAMESPACES • An Extensible Markup Language (XML) namespace is a label that accompanies a set of elements or attributes. The namespace uniquely identifies these elements or attributes by limiting the scope:

```
Example of Dav Namespace URI
xmlns:d="DAV:"
xmlns:f="urn:schemas-microsoft-com:office:forms"
```

For the server and client examples that follow, the following XML namespaces have been declared:

```
xmlns:d="DAV:"
xmlns:b="urn:schemas:mailheader:"
xmlns:f="urn:schemas-microsoft-com:office:forms"
xmlns:sales="sales:"
xmlns:s="urn:schemas-microsoft-com:exch-data:"
xmlns:c="urn:schemas:calendar:">
```

HTTP/WEBDAV EXAMPLE

This example creates a form registration for messages. The form that will be displayed is Form1.htm:

```
<?xml version="1.0"?>
<g:propertyupdate xmlns:g="DAV:"  xmlns:form="urn:schemas-microsoft-com:office:forms">
```

```
    <g:set>
       <g:prop>
     <g:contentclass>urn:schemas-microsoft-
com:office:forms#registration</g:contentclass>
       </g:prop>
       <g:prop><form:browser>*</form:browser></g:prop>
       <g:prop><form:cmd>*</form:cmd></g:prop>
       <g:prop><form:contentclass>urn:content-
classes:message</form:contentclass></g:prop>

<g:prop><form:contentstate>*</form:contentstate></g:prop>

<g:prop><form:executeurl>process.asp</
form:executeurl></g:prop>

<g:prop><form:formurl>/myforms/form1.htm</form:formurl>
</g:prop>
       <g:prop><form:language>en</form:language></g:prop>
       <g:prop><form:majorver>*</form:majorver></g:prop>

<g:prop><form:messagestate>*</form:messagestate></g:prop>
       <g:prop><form:minorver>*</form:minorver></g:prop>
       <g:prop><form:platform>WinNT</form:platform></g:prop>
       <g:prop><form:request>GET</form:request></g:prop>
    </g:set>
</g:propertyupdate>
```

TESTAPP EXAMPLE

Testapp is a folder inside the public folder. The major version is "=5," which represents Microsoft Internet Explorer 5 or later.

Note   If the major version is less than five, it is listed as &lt5. The < is required; <5 is not interpreted correctly.

```
<resource>
<href>testapp/editsales.html</href>
<contenttype>text/html</contenttype>
<prop>
<b:contentclass>urn:schemas-microsoft-
com:office:forms#registration</b:contentclass>
<f:formurl>/testapp/editsalesman.html</f:formurl>
<f:cmd></f:cmd>
<f:contentclass>urn:content-classes:salesman</
f:contentclass>
<f:executeurl>/exchweb/bin/process.asp</f:executeurl>
<f:browser>*</f:browser>
<f:contentstate>*</f:contentstate>
```

```
<f:language>*</f:language>
<f:majorver>=5</f:majorver>
<f:minorver>*</f:minorver>
<f:messagestate>*</f:messagestate>
<f:platform>*</f:platform>
<f:request>GET</f:request>
</prop>
</resource>
```

Order of Precedence

Form definition properties are used to determine which version of a form to use. The registry uses the following order of precedence:

1. HTTP request
2. URL action (Cmd)
3. Message-State
4. Content-State
5. Browser capability (browser type and version)
6. Version
7. Platform
8. MajorVer
9. MinorVer
10. Language

For the first seven of these, a nonwildcard value has highest precedence, a wildcard value has middle precedence, and a null value has lowest precedence.

For the version properties, the precedence order (highest to lowest) is =, <=, >=, <, >, *, and then null.

> **Note** Except for the browser capability, attributes must match exactly. Browser capability comparisons are as follows:
>
> = equals
> <= less than or equal to
> >= greater than or equal to
> < less than
> > greater than

Default Form Registration

Opening a public folder in Outlook Web Access reveals a list of the contents of that folder, which is displayed by default. However, a Web Storage System form can be registered as the default form. If a Web Storage System form is registered as the default form, you will see it instead of the usual list of items.

To register a default form,

1. Create the form.
2. Set the SchemaCollectionRef.
3. Create a form registration for the content class of urn:content-classes:folder. Set CMD=* and Request=* or GET.

Note Registering a form overrides the setting in the DAV:defaultdocument property.

Reusing Elements of Outlook Web Access

Developers can create customized Web pages simply by reusing pieces of Outlook Web Access. These pieces can be embedded in a Web page. Tables, frames, and iframes can be used to arrange the Outlook Web Access pieces.

For example, a Web page could contain the user's inbox and the group calendar. It could have a brand or company identifier in one corner and current news and links to internal tools in another corner.

Working with Default Views

Outlook Web Access provides default views for everyday tasks—for example, viewing an inbox or outbox. Default views can be manipulated by specifying additional parameters.

The syntax of a default view is

http://"ServerName"/"exchange"/"UserName"/parameter

For example, if you want to see the deleted items for a user named "User1" on a server named Finance, you type the following URL:

http:// "Finance"/"exchange"/"User1"/deleted%20items

Parameter names include Inbox, Outbox, Calendar, Contacts, Deleted Items, Drafts, and Sent Items.

Note Spaces in names are represented with the characters %20.

Controlling the Navigation Bar

The Outlook bar normally appears in a frame on the left side of the browser window. The Outlook bar allows the user to navigate between different views, such as Inbox and Outbox.

However, you may want to display the Outlook Web Access contents in the browser window without the Outlook bar. You can do this by adding ?Cmd=contents to the URL.

You can display just the navigation bar by adding ?Cmd=navbar to the URL.

The code in the following example shows the contents of the inbox without the navigation bar:

http://servername/exchange/user1/inbox/?Cmd=contents

URL Parameters

URL parameters can be used to show calendar views, view open messages, and perform other tasks in the browser window. The parameters can be broken into two categories: commands and options. (See Tables 4–2 and 4–3, respectively.) Commands handle information; options control how the information is viewed.

TABLE 4–2 *Commands—New, Get, Post, Reply, Forward, Save, and Send*

Parameter name	Description
Post	Defines how data is submitted to the server.
Get	Defines how data is requested from the server.
New	Creates a new item.
Reply	Replies to a message.
Forward	Forwards a message.
Save	Saves a message.
Send	Sends a message.

TABLE 4–3 *Options—Date, Page, Sort, and View*

Parameter name	Description
Page=x	Displays page x.
View=x	Displays Outlook view named x.
Sort=x	Sorts by column x.
Date=x	Displays date in calendar.

CMD EXAMPLES • The syntax for the cmd parameter is *http://server_name/ Exchange_v-root/folder/item_name ?Cmd=action[&modifier [&modifier]]*.

TABLE 4-4 *Syntax for the Cmd parameter*

To do this	Use this syntax (examples)
View an Existing Object	*http://server_name/v-root/folder/item_name?Cmd=action*
Create a New Message	*http:// server_name/v-root /user_name/Drafts/?Cmd=new*
View or Change Options	*http://ServerName/exchange/UserName/?Cmd=options*
Open a Message in the User's Inbox	*http://server_name/exchange_v-root/folder/inbox/ messagename.EML?Cmd=open* Messagename is the subject that the sender types. It is also the file name in the folder.
View a Calendar by Month or by Week	*http:// server_name /v-root /user_name/calendar/ ?View=Monthly* *http:// server_name / v-root /user_name/calendar/ ?View=Weekly & Date = 11/09/1999*

An Introduction to Web Storage System Events

The following topic covers how you can programmatically respond to events that occur in the Microsoft Web Storage System. With events, you can write your own custom logic that executes on the server in response to changes in the data in the Web Storage System.

This topic explains how to register, modify, and monitor events; how to write event sink COM classes; and how to respond to event notifications when the event sink class receives them. The topic covers the following information:

- Web Storage System Event Terms
- Events Overview
- Events and Event Sink Interfaces
- Event Registration
- Working in an Event Sink
- The Script Host Sink
- Sink Monitoring

Web Storage System Event Terms

Event, Store Event
> A change in the store for which you can receive programmatic notification by means of an event sink.

Event Sink
> A custom COM class or script that is called to process an event that occurs in the store, according to the properties specified in an event registration.

Event Methods
> Methods in the event sink that Microsoft Exchange calls to notify you that an event occurred.

Event Registration
> A logical connection between an event and an event sink that is created by a special type of store item. The connection is such that when an event occurs that meets the event registration criteria, the appropriate event method is called in the event sink.

Event Notification
> The process whereby Exchange detects an event occurrence that matches an event registration's criteria, creates an instance of the event sink specified in the event registration, and calls the appropriate event method.

Top-Level Folders
> Folders in Messaging Databases (MDBs) that have no parent folders (root folders).

Events Overview

Events occur when Web Storage System items are saved, deleted, moved, copied, or modified; when a MDB is started or stopped; or when a specific time interval has elapsed. You can write event sinks (COM objects or scripts) that can receive notification of these events. Typical applications that use event sinks include the following:

Timers
> You can register to receive notifications at specified times. A timer can be used to synchronize information external to the store, periodically clean up the store, remind people of pending tasks, or trigger batch processing.

Notifications
> You can register to receive an event, and then in the event sink, you can notify other parties that the event has occurred.

Automatic Categorization
> An item being saved to the store could be analyzed and categorized so that data is properly stored and information about the data is kept up to date.

Workflow Applications
> You can register to receive event notifications when workflow items are moved in the Web Storage System. The event sink can programmatically handle the workflow item as it moves along on its workflow path.

Item Validation
> Event sinks can validate or check items when they are saved to the store. The event sink might process a delete notification by checking a custom criterion to see if the person deleting the item has the rights to do so. When a save event occurs, you might check the formatting of the item being saved.

Store Maintenance
> Whenever an item is deleted from a particular location in the store, other items that are outside the Web Storage System may need to be modified or deleted. The event sink could automatically handle this task.

Exchange Calls Event Methods

The event sink can be a COM class with interfaces and event methods defined by Exchange. To notify the event sink, Exchange creates an instance of the event sink COM class, obtains the appropriate interface, and invokes the appropriate event method.

Figure 4–1 shows how Exchange calls the event sink.

FIGURE 4-1 How Exchange calls the event sink

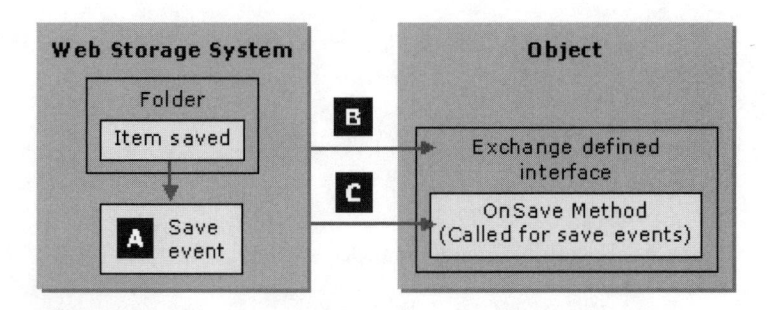

A
    An item is saved to the store, causing a store event.

B
    Exchange obtains the required interface in the event sink.

C
    Exchange calls the event method for the given event notification.

Note   This same process takes place if the event sink is a script, except that a special COM object (the Script Host) is called, which then runs the appropriate event method in the script.

Multiple Events

Figure 4-2 shows that events can occur anywhere in the Web Storage System and that the same event sink class can be called for numerous Web Storage System events.

You register with the server to receive event notifications by saving a registration item to the store. Where you save the item defines the scope (location and range) of where event notification will fire. Event scope is covered in the "Recursive Events" section of "Event Registration."

Note   Exchange runs each event sink notification on a unique out-of-process thread on the local machine.

Events Overview

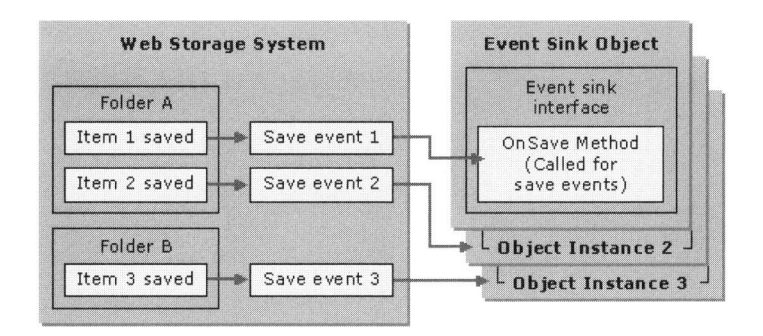

FIGURE 4–2 *Events can occur anywhere in the Web Storage System*

Multiple Sinks

You can have multiple event sinks for the same event. Figure 4–3 shows multiple events responding to a single event.

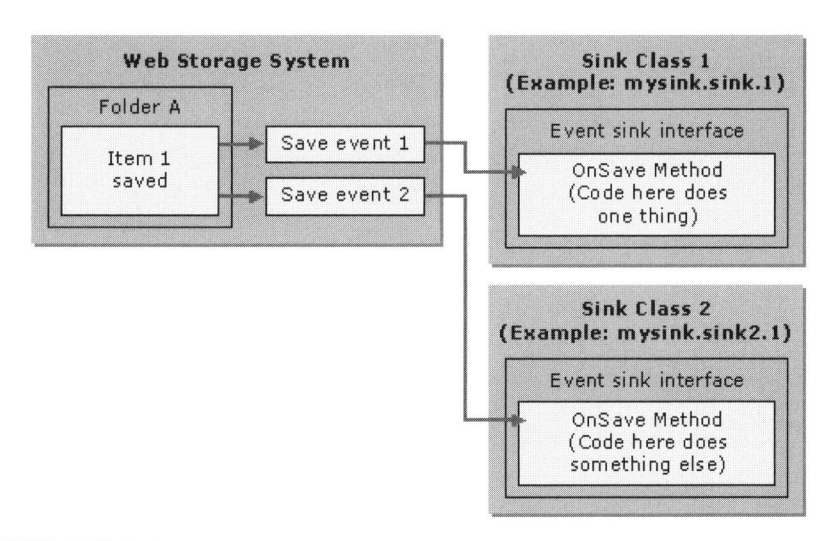

FIGURE 4–3 *Multiple events responding to a single event*

OLE DB and ADO

You can use OLE DB and Microsoft ActiveX Data Objects (ADO) to access data from within the event sinks. ExOLEDB is the Microsoft Exchange 2000 Server OLE DB implementation for Exchange 2000 Server. ExOLEDB is a core component of Exchange and is registered automatically when Exchange 2000 Server is installed.

Events and Event Sink Interfaces

Exchange has defined interfaces that you can implement to handle synchronous, asynchronous, and system events. The following tables list the interfaces and their event methods. The subtopics in this section explain the concepts behind each interface and method.

SYNCHRONOUS EVENTS • Synchronous events occur before the item is committed to the store. The IExStoreSyncEvents has two methods, as shown in Table 4–5.

TABLE 4–5 *Methods of IExStoreSyncEvents*

Name	When the event is called (by Exchange)
OnSyncSave	When an item is saved to the store, before the changes are committed.
OnSyncDelete	When an item is deleted from the store, before the delete is committed.

ASYNCHRONOUS EVENTS • Asynchronous events occur *after* the item is committed to the store. The IExStoreAsyncEvents has two methods, as shown in Table 4–6.

TABLE 4–6 *Methods of IExStoreAsyncEvents*

Name	When the event is called (by the event sink source)
OnSave	When an item is saved to the store, after the changes are committed.
OnDelete	When an item is deleted from the store, after the delete is committed.

Note Other events, such as moving or copying an item, are handled by the save and delete events. When an item is copied in the store, it generates a save event. A move causes both the save and delete events.

SYSTEM EVENTS

The IExStoreSystemEvents has three methods, as shown in Table 4–7.

TABLE 4–7 *Methods of IExStoreSystemEvents*

Name	When the event is called (by the event sink source)
OnTimer	After a certain period of time.
OnMDBStartUp	When an MDB is started.
OnMDBShutdown	When an MDB is shut down.

Synchronous Events

Synchronous events are processed in the context of an OLE DB transaction and occur before the item has been committed. Each synchronous event is called twice, once for the begin phase and once for the commit or abort phase. The begin phase is called first, in prioritized order, for all qualifying sinks, then the commit or abort phase is called for the same sinks. Exchange waits for each synchronous event sink notification to finish before calling the next.

Exchange provides synchronous event notifications by calling the IExStoreSyncEvents interface methods shown in Table 4–8.

TABLE 4–8 *Interface methods of IExStoreSyncEvents*

Name	Description
OnSyncSave	Called before an item is saved to the Web Storage System.
OnSyncDelete	Called before an item is deleted from the Web Storage System.

While it runs, the synchronous event sink has exclusive control over the store item that triggered the event. No other process or request can access the item until all event sinks have finished running.

Synchronous Event Details

The following information is important to know when you develop synchronous event methods:

- Moving a folder does not cause events to occur on any items in the folder.
- Copying a folder causes events to occur on all items in the folder.
- Deleting a folder does not cause events to occur on items (messages and documents) in the folder. However, it causes events to occur on the subfolders.

- Synchronous events are processed in a specific order.
- The item causing the event is passed into the sink in the context of an OLE DB local transaction.
- An item passed to a synchronous event sink transaction does not exist in the Web Storage System until the transaction has been committed.
- When the event sink is processing a synchronous event, it can abort the OLE DB local transaction. If the transaction is aborted, no further synchronous event notifications occur for this event. Also, the synchronous events in this transaction that have already been notified (processed) are again notified that the transaction was aborted (the abort phase). This notification allows you to clean up data or undo activities if the event is aborted. For example, the method that handles the synchronous OnSyncSave event may create an associated file outside the Web Storage System. Upon notification of failure, your method could delete that external file.
- Aborting the transaction associated with a delete event prevents the item from being deleted. If you abort an event that is the result of a move, both the save and delete steps of the move are aborted. This means that the original item is not deleted and the new item is not saved.

Figure 4-4 illustrates how event sinks affect a Web Storage System item.

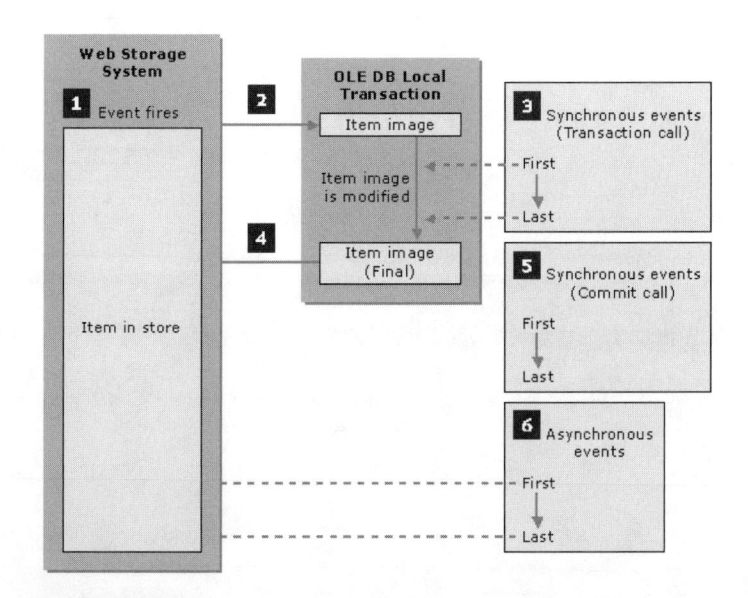

Figure 4-4 How event sinks affect a Web Storage System item

EVENT SINK SEQUENCE FOR A WEB STORAGE SYSTEM ITEM

1. The event occurs in the store.
2. A "transaction" image of the item is created.
3. Synchronous event methods receive event notification of the begin phase, in which they modify the image.
4. The image is committed to the store as the item (from the OLE DB transaction).
5. Synchronous event methods receive event notification of the commit phase.
6. Asynchronous interface methods in sink classes receive notifications. The store item is directly modified.

Note Asynchronous events are processed in no specified or guaranteed order. The event source does not wait for asynchronous events to finish.

As the previous illustration shows, synchronous events are always called twice—once for the begin phase and once for the commit or abort phase. It is important to add code in your methods for handling synchronous events to determine which type of call is being made. The filter in an IExStoreSyncEvents::OnSyncSave method could look like the following example:

```
[C++]
if( lFlags & EVT_SYNC_BEGIN ) {
    Log(pLog,"-----------EVT_SYNC_BEGIN-----------\r\n");
    //Handle the sink here.
}
else if( lFlags & EVT_SYNC_COMMITTED ) {
    Log(pLog,"---------EVT_SYNC_COMMITTED---------\r\n");
    //Handle the commit here.
}
else if( lFlags & EVT_SYNC_ABORTED ) {
    Log(pLog,"----------EVT_SYNC_ABORTED----------\r\n");
    //Handle the abort here.
}
```

Asynchronous Events (Notifications)

An asynchronous event is essentially a notification that an event occurred.

Exchange provides asynchronous event notifications by calling the IExStoreAsyncEvents interface methods shown in Table 4–9.

TABLE 4-9 *Interface methods of IExStoreAsyncEvents*

Name	Description
OnSave	Called when an item is saved to the Web Storage System.
OnDelete	Called when an item is deleted from the Web Storage System.

When you process an asynchronous event, Exchange processes the return value. Returning S_OK indicates that the event notification was handled successfully. Returning S_PENDING indicates that you are handling the event notification in a separate process. When you return S_PENDING, you must notify Exchange (from the separate process) after you have finished handling the event by calling IAsyncNotify Completed.

ASYNCHRONOUS EVENT DETAILS

The following list presents conceptual details about asynchronous events:

- Asynchronous events do not have any firing priority.
- Moving a folder does not cause events to fire on any items in the folder.
- Copying a folder causes events fire events on all items in the folder.
- Deleting a folder does not cause events to fire on items (messages and documents) in the folder. However, it causes events to fire on the subfolders.
- When the OnDelete event is called, the item has already been deleted.
- There is no guarantee as to how soon asynchronous event notifications are called after the event occurs.
- Asynchronous events are not processed if a synchronous event aborts the event.

System Events

System events give timed notifications or notify the event sink that databases have started up or shut down.

Exchange provides system event notifications by calling the IExStoreSystemEvents interface methods shown in Table 4–10.

TABLE 4–10 Interface methods of IExStoreSystemEvents

Name	Description
OnTimer	Called after a certain period of time.
OnMDBStartUp	Called when a MDB is started.
OnMDBShutDown	Called when a MDB is shut down.

Exchange runs each system event notification in a separate process. Exchange does not wait for the notification process to finish. System events do not lock items in the store.

You can use timer events for repeated calls, such as scheduling routine tasks. They can also be used for a one-time event.

System events are not tied to a particular item or location in the store (scope). However, where you save the OnTimer event registration can provide a context in the event notification. For example, you may want to perform periodic checking on items in a specific folder. You place the OnTimer event registration in that folder so that when the event method is called, you know where to perform the checking tasks.

Additional Event Sink Interfaces

You can implement additional interfaces in the event sink to have further control over the registration for events in your sink. You do not register for the event system to call these methods. If the interface methods are implemented in your sink, they are automatically called at the appropriate times.

ICREATEREGISTRATION • The optional ICreateRegistration interface method shown in Table 4–11 is called by the event sink source.

TABLE 4–11 Interface method of ICreateRegistration

Name	Description
Register	Called by Exchange when an event registration item is saved, copied, moved, or replicated. Use this method to reject event registration requests or to respond to registration items that have been modified, moved, copied, or replicated.

Whenever an event registration item that specifies the event sink is saved, copied, moved, or replicated, Exchange automatically queries the event sink for this interface. This gives you an opportunity to perform your own custom checks for event registration and handle event registrations when they are changed, copied, moved or replicated.

Support Interfaces

Some support interfaces exist for you to work with event sinks. Some interfaces are for use within an event, and others are for use when registering events.

Some interfaces are for use in an event sink. They allow you to access sink-related store information and perform tasks in the store. Some of these interfaces are passed as arguments in the event method calls. In all cases, the interfaces can be obtained from Exchange objects. You do not need to implement them.

Table 4–12 describes available support interfaces.

TABLE 4–12 *Available support interfaces*

Name	Description
IAsyncNotify	Allows an asynchronous event handler to notify Exchange that it has finished processing an event.
IexoledbUrlMapper	Methods for converting paths to different types.
IexStoreEventInfo	Used to retrieve event information and control the event transaction (passed to every method that the store calls for event sink notification).
IexStoreDispEventInfo	OLE Automation-compatible version of the IExStoreEventInfo.
IexStoreEventLogonInfo	Used to provide information about the user who caused the event and the store in which the event occurred.
IexStoreEventRegistrationURL	Returns the URL of the event registration item.
IgetSourceURL	Used for getting the URL of the source row.
IstoreGUIDFromURL	Gets the MDB globally unique identifier (GUID) from the given URL (cocreatable).
IuserData	Used as a temporary place to persist data for the duration of the synchronous event (from the begin phase to the commit or abort phase).

Event Registration

You must register with Exchange to receive event notifications by creating and saving Event Registration Items. This section addresses the concepts behind Event Registration.

- The Event Registration Item
- Registration Steps

The Event Registration Item

An item becomes an event registration item when you set the content-class to urn:content-class:storeeventreg.

The following defines the event properties for an Event Registration item:

http://schemas.microsoft.com/exchange/events/ namespace.

TABLE 4–13 *Exchange OLE DB provider logs events*

Property	Required	Use
Criteria	No	An SQL Where clause that specifies the conditions that will cause the event to fire.
Enabled	No	Boolean to enable the event to be fired.
EventMethod	Yes	Defines which event or events cause notification.
MatchScope	No	Defines where the event will fire relative to where it is saved.
Priority	No	The priority of the event.
ScriptUrl[1]	Yes	The name of the script if the event is a script being run by the Script Host Sink.
Sinkclass	Yes	The Class ID (CLSID) or Program ID (progID) of the object containing the event sink.
TimerExpiryTime[2]	No	Time to end an OnTimer event.
TimerInterval[2]	Yes	Interval, in minutes, for an OnTimer event.
TimerStartTime[2]	Yes	Start time for an OnTimer event.

1. Required only if using a script to handle the event.
2. Used only for OnTimer events.

Registration Steps

To register to receive notification of specific events,

1. If the event sink is a COM class (not a script), you must register it in the Microsoft Windows operating system.
2. Create a store item with a content class of urn:content-class:storeeventreg. (It is now an event registration item.)
3. Set properties on the item.
4. Save the item to the store location where you want to keep the event notifications. (The registration is now complete.)

Recursive Events

You save the event registration item to where you want to store event notifications. For synchronous and asynchronous events, you further specify what items the event covers (items, folders, children). When an event sink is registered for a folder and its subfolders, it is called a recursive event.

RECURSIVE EVENT SCOPE • You can register for recursive events only in Top-Level Folders. (Top-Level Folders have no parent in the MDB.)

Permissions for the event sink to handle recursive events are determined only for the folder in which the event is registered. This means that if you have rights to register and receive notifications for events in the parent folder, you can receive notification in all child folders. Manage the folder hierarchy so that child folders are created only in parent folders with trustworthy recursive events. You can perform additional checks during event registration and by checking the context of the event notification when handling the event.

To register for a recursive event scope, the application must save the event registration item to the root folder from which the sink is to recur. The application must also set the item property, *http://schemas.microsoft.com/exchange/events/MatchScope*, to "DEEP."

> **Note** If you register for a recursive event scope, use criteria to specify whether you want the event to fire on folders, items, or both.

REGISTERING FOR MDB-WIDE EVENTS

Global events can only be registered in the following folders:
   For private mailbox stores, use

```
File://./backofficestorage/ADMIN/%
userdnsdomain%/MBX/SystemMailbox
{GUID}/Storeevents/GlobalEvents
```

For public folders, use

```
File://./backofficestorage/ADMIN/%
userdnsdomain%/Public Folders/Non_ipm_subtree/StoreEvents
{GUID}/GlobalEvents
```

Global events can be registered only by an administrator, a member of the domain administrators group, or users in the exchange administrators role. It is not enough to be a member of the administrators group or the exchange server group. Use the Exchange Administration Delegation Wizard in the Exchange Management console to make a user an Exchange Administrator.

The following code registers for a private MDB-wide event:

```
dim igetSG
dim regURL
dim WshShell
dim Return

set igetSG=CreateObject("Exoledb.StoreGuidFromUrl.1")
'Get the guid for the registration process
guid = igetSG.StoreGuidFromUrl("file://./backofficestorage/
    " + Anystoreitem)
'Anystoreitem is just that—any store item in the store will
get you the 'store url. It might be something like:
'    "theserver.microsoft.com/MBX/user1/inbox"

'Build the registration URL (using
   "theserver.microsoft.com")
   regURL = "file://./backofficestorage/ADMIN/
   theserver.microsoft.com/MBX/SystemMailbox" & guid & "/
   StoreEvents/GlobalEvents/my_event"

set WshShell=WScript.CreateObject("WScript.Shell")
Return = WshShell.Run ("cscript c:\regevent.vbs add
onsyncsave mysink.sink " & regURL & " -m ANY", 4 , TRUE)

WScript.Echo Return
```

Note Serverwide events are not supported.

Event Notification Priority

When registering for synchronous event notifications, you set a priority that dictates when the notification will occur relative to the other event registrations waiting on the same event. The registration priority can have any value in the ranges shown in Table 4–14.

TABLE 4-14 *Event notification priority*

Priority	Integer value	Hex value
Highest (first to be notified)	0	0
Default	65535	0x0000ffff
Lowest (last to be notified)	2147483647	0x7fffffff

Event Registrations with the same priority can fire in any order. Figure 4–5 depicts synchronous sink execution by priority.

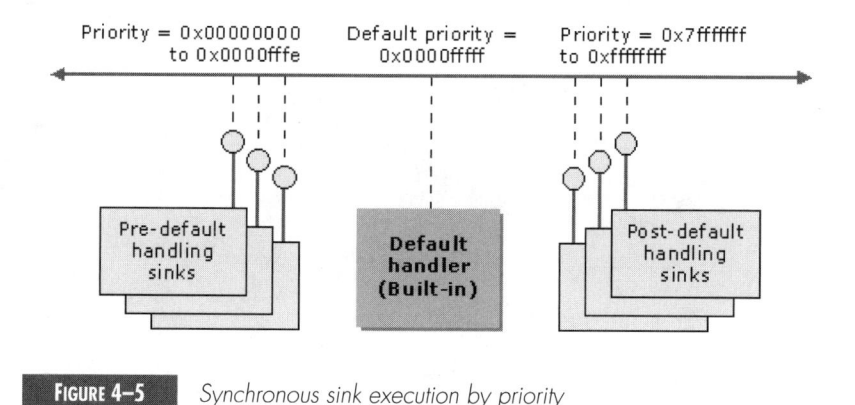

FIGURE 4-5 *Synchronous sink execution by priority*

Register the priority using the decimal value.

Priorities do not apply to asynchronous event registrations.

RECURSIVE SINK FIRING ORDER • Recursive event notifications occur before event notifications in the subfolders.

The RegEvent Script

The Exchange 2000 Server documentation provides a useful script that you can use to register, enumerate, and delete event registrations. The Microsoft Visual Basic Scripting (VBScript) edition code may also prove useful for you in developing your own registration scripts.

Running the RegEvent.vbs with no arguments returns the parameters as well as examples of use. The following defines the parameters for the RegEvent.vbs script:

```
cscript RegEvent.vbs Add|Delete|Enum
                     EventMethod
                     SinkClass
                     Registration Item Name(Scope)
                     StartTime
                     Interval
                     [-p Priority]
                     [-m MatchScope]
                     [-f CriteriaFilter]
                     [-file ScriptFilePath]
                     [-url ScriptUrl]
                     [-e ExpiryTime]
```

EventMethod (Add)

The name of the store or system event should be one or more of the following:

OnSave, OnDelete, OnSyncSave, OnSyncDelete, OnMdbStartup, OnMdbShutDown, or OnTimer.

Case is ignored. Multiple events can be specified in the same registration by placing semicolons (;) between the names of each event, for example, "OnSave;OnDelete".

SinkClass (Add)

The class identifier (in registry format) or programmatic identifier (progID) of your event sink—for example, "MySinks.SaveSink.1".

Registration Item Name (Add | Delete | Enum)

The name of the event registration item. The event scope is defined by where you save it—for example,

file://./backofficestorage/domain/public%20folders/myfolder/EventRegItem1

registers for events in "myfolder".

StartTime (OnTimer)

When to start the OnTimer event—for example, "8/4/98 01:50:00 AM".

Interval (OnTimer)

The time, in minutes, between each OnTimer event notification.

Priority (Add for OnSyncSave and OnSyncDelete)

[optional] The registration's priority. See Event Notification.

MatchScope (add for synchronous and asynchronous notifications)

[optional] The scope for the Event Registration. Can be one of the following: DEEP | SHALLOW | EXACT | ANY. Defaults to EXACT.

CriteriaFilter (Add)
[optional] An SQL WHERE clause of conditions for notification—for example, WHERE "DAV:ishidden" = FALSE. See "Remarks," later in this topic.

ScriptFilePath (Add)
[optional] The full file path to the event sink script file. If a script host is specified (by the sinkclass progid or clsid), then ScriptFilePath points to a script file in the file system.

ScriptUrl (Add)
[optional] The full HTTP URL to the event sink script file. If a script host is specified (by the sinkclass progid or clsid), ScriptURL points to a script in the Web Storage System.

ExpiryTime (OnTimer)
[optional] When to stop the OnTimer event—for example, "8/4/99 01:50:00 AM".

REMARKS

Exchange must be running for you to create event registrations.

You cannot register for the OnTimer event with any other events.

You cannot register for system events and synchronous or asynchronous events in the same command. (For example, "Regevent Add OnSave;OnMDB-Startup" is not allowed.)

Event Registration Guidelines

The scope of a sink is restricted to a single MDB.

Event registration items are automatically hidden when saved.

Event sinks in a DLL need to have a surrogate host defined for when they are instantiated by Exchange. Wrapping the DLL in a COM+ application assigns the surrogate host automatically.

Event Registration Security

To register for an event, the user saving the event registration item must be a member of the Folder Owner role for the folder in which the event registration is saved.

You can also implement the ICreateRegistration::Register method in the event sink. This method gives you a programmatic means to evaluate and abort event registration requests.

Event Registration Modification

You change event registrations by modifying and saving the original event registration item.

Enumerating Event Registrations
Event registrations can be enumerated programmatically or by using the regevent.vbs script.

Deleting an Event Registration
An event registration is removed by deleting the event registration item. Deleting a folder removes all event registrations in the folder and the folder's subfolders.

Moving or Copying an Event Registration
If you move or copy an event registration, it will automatically register in the new location.

Stopping or Starting an Event Registration
To stop an event registration from providing notification without deleting the registration, set the event registration item's enabled property to false.
Setting the enabled property to true will start the event registration again.
For related information, see "The Event Registration Item."

Event Reliability

Both synchronous and asynchronous event notifications are reliable under normal conditions. That is, no notification is skipped on an event. However, if there is a failure in the store, Exchange might call your event method multiple times. For example, Exchange might shut down after three of five event notifications have been invoked. When Exchange restarts, the three previous event notifications might or might not be invoked a second time. An event method that fails after being notified will not be notified again for that specific event.

Working in an Event Sink

Developing code in an event sink depends on several key concepts. The following topics cover those concepts:
- Loop Recursion
- Information Passed to an Event Method
- Contextual Information in an Event Registration

Loop Recursion

An asynchronous event method can modify the item that caused the event notification. This, in turn, can fire an event for the same item, thereby causing a recursive event loop. The event sink must ensure that looping does not occur.

Information Passed to an Event Method

Exchange passes information to the event methods through the event notification. Interfaces are passed into the event sinks, and other interfaces can be obtained from within the event sink.

The event methods that handle synchronous events receive the IExStoreEventInfo Interface and an image of the item that caused the event to fire.

The event methods that handle asynchronous events receive the IExStoreEventInfo Interface and the URL of the item that caused the event to fire.

The OnTimer event method receives the URL for the event registration item.

The MDBStartUp and MDBShutDown methods receive the MDB GUID and MDB name.

It is possible to pass custom information from the event registration item to the event sink.

Contextual Information in an Event Registration

This topic assumes an understanding of Event Registration.

You can store contextual information in custom properties on the Event Registration Item. Information properties can include event location, users the event is for, a search query needed to notify users of an event, and so on.

Event methods can retrieve these properties by accessing the event registration item through the IExStoreEventInfo.EventBinding property or the IExStoreDispEventInfo.EventRecord property. Both of these properties point to the registration item.

To pass custom data from the event registration item to the event sink,

1. Add custom properties at registration to the event registration. Use Fields.Append to do this.
2. Retrieve the custom properties from the event item in the event sink. Use the Fields("<property name>") method to retrieve the property values.

Note — You can change the properties in the event registration item from within the event sink.

Security in an Event Sink

Synchronous events can obtain an OLE DB session object from the IExStoreEventInfo interface that is passed to the method handling the event in the sink. This provides a session logged on as the user who caused the event to occur. Therefore, the event sink has access to the event item, the mailbox, or the public folder in which the event occurred, and any items in the MDB in which the event occurred that the logon has access to.

Note — Logons are scoped within sessions and therefore cannot access more than one store. Hence, a synchronous sink handling an item in a public folder does not have access to the mailbox of the user who caused the event.

The OnTimer event has neither context nor scope.

COM+ APPLICATIONS

You can wrap the event sink (a COM class) in a COM+ application (previously called an MTS package). A COM+ application can provide a user context for the event to run in. This is advantageous because the event may now access the store with the privileges of the package's security context without having to log on.

Note — COM+ application wrappers can have only one security context per registered sink class. In cases where the same sink class requires different security contexts, you can wrap the sink class multiple times and register each wrapped class as different sink class.

One COM object that typically must be wrapped by a COM+ application package is the Script Host Sink.

It is also possible to create COM+ applications that run at startup. In some cases, this can be useful for initialization purposes.

ADDITIONAL SECURITY RESTRICTIONS • Individual event sinks can enforce additional security restrictions by employing role-based security at the component, interface, or method level.

The Script Host Sink

The Script Host Sink is provided and registered with Exchange 2000 Server for running all event methods in scripts. The Script Host Sink runs the scripts in process. To run a script, you specify the Script Host Sink as the event sink class and then specify the script in the event registration item's ScriptUrl property.

The Script Host resides in *exodbesh.dll*. It is registered with the installation of Exchange as ExOleDB.ScriptEventSink.1.

Event Naming

In COM class event sinks, you name event methods by prefixing the event name with the interface name. Use the following event method names:

```
IExStoreSyncEvents_OnSyncSave
IExStoreSyncEvents_OnSyncDelete
IExStoreAsyncEvents_OnSave
IExStoreAsyncEvents_OnDelete
IExStoreSystemEvents_OnMDBStartUp
IExStoreSystemEvents_OnMDBShutDown
IExStoreSystemEvents_OnTimer
```

For example, the OnSave event method is declared as follows:

```
Private Sub IExStoreAsyncEvents_OnSave
(pEventInfo,URLItem,Flags)
   'sink code
End Sub
```

When implementing event methods as scripts, you prefix all event methods with "ExStoreEvents_." For example, the OnSyncSave event in a script would be ExStoreEvents_OnSyncSave.

In Visual Basic, you can use the Implements declaration to specify that you are going to implement methods in a Visual Basic class. The following code declares the interfaces:

```
Implements IExStoreAsyncEvents
Implements IExStoreSyncEvents
Implements IExStoreStoreEvents
```

Sink Monitoring

Event sinks can be monitored. The following topics cover sink monitoring:

- Event Logs
- Performance Monitor Counters

Event Logs

The Exchange OLE DB provider logs events in the Windows 2000 Application event log. Those events are shown in Table 4–15.

TABLE 4–15   *ExOLEDB events*

Severity	Symbol	Description
Error	EVENTS_BINDING_DISABLED	Exchange OLE DB has disabled the event registration due to the problems in the event sink.
Error	EVENTS_INVALID_BINDING	Exchange OLE DB was unable register the event.
Error	EVENTS_INVALID_CRITERIA_FILTER	Exchange OLE DB was unable to process the specified event criteria filter.
Error	EVENTS_INVALID_PROPERTY_VALUE	Exchange OLE DB was unable to initialize the event registration.
Error	EVENTS_INVALID_SINK_CLASS	Exchange OLE DB was unable either to create an event sink object or get the necessary interface or interfaces from the sink class.
Error	EVENTS_MISSING_PROPERTY	Exchange OLE DB was unable to initialize event registration due to a missing property value.
Error	EVENTS_UNABLE_TO_INITIALIZE_SOURCE	Exchange OLE DB was unable to initialize event registration for the store.
Error	EVENTS_UNABLE_TO_REGISTER_BINDING	Microsoft Exchange OLE DB was unable to initialize an event registration.
Error	EXOLEDB_FAILED_TO_REGISTER_OBJECTS	Exchange OLE DB was unable to successfully register event sink COM objects.

Performance Monitor Counters

System Monitor counters are fully supported for each event. For the core OLE DB functions, these counters are the same as the store counters. For Exchange-specific implementations, such as the various event interfaces, the OLE DB layer in the store supports counters for discovering how an out-of-process sink affects the performance of the overall system. In addition, the OLE DB provider creates counters for each virtual server instance. This is similar to what is done by other Internet Information Services, such as Simple Mail Transport Protocol (SMTP), Network News Transfer Protocol (NNTP), and HTTP services.

Each event (for example, ONSYNCSAVE) appears as an instance of the following counters (all rate counters are per second):

- Submitted Rate
- Submitted Total
- Completed Rate
- Completed Total

FIVE

Collaboration Data Objects

CDOEX Server is a server-side collaborative component that is used in conjunction with Microsoft ADO 2.5 and Microsoft Active Directory Services Interfaces (ADSI). You use CDO to create Web collaboration solutions based on the Microsoft Web Storage System and Active Directory service in Microsoft Windows 2000. Whereas OLE DB, ADO, and ADSI provide the fundamental data access mechanisms to the Web Storage System and Active Directory, CDO provides extended collaborative functionality that includes the creation and management of the following:

- Folders and nonfolder items
- Messages
- Appointments
- Meeting request messages and the associated correlation of individual responses (accept, accept tentative, decline) to the request
- Contacts
- Mailboxes, recipients and the Microsoft Web Storage System folder hierarchies and settings
- Store event-driven workflows that manage process-driven applications

In Microsoft Exchange 2000, most components of CDOEX are available only on the same computer (or cluster) as Exchange 2000 itself. In addition, CDOEX can access data only in the local Exchange 2000 public and mailbox stores. It cannot directly access data residing in different Exchange 2000 stores.

Note   The CDO for Exchange Management (CDOEXM) component of CDO for Exchange can be used from remote servers. You can install CDOEXM along with the Exchange 2000 Administration tools.

CDO Components

CDO is a set of components with which you can build rich collaborative applications on the Web Storage System platform. Table 5–1 lists the COM components that are provided with CDO, along with a brief description of each.

TABLE 5–1 *CDO components*

Component	Description
CDOEX	Provides fundamental collaboration tools for managing messages, appointments, calendar messages, and contacts.
CDO Workflow Objects for Exchange (CDOWF)	Provides tools for writing and managing workflows by using the Web Storage System.
CDOEXM	Provides tools for managing the Exchange 2000 Server and public and private stores.

CDOEX and CDOWF are installed on the same computer as Exchange 2000. These components cannot be installed remotely or used directly through distributed COM (DCOM). You can use these components in ASP, COM+ server-side components, Web Storage System event sinks, advanced workflow applications, and Microsoft Windows services that run on the Exchange 2000 server.

You can install the CDOEX component on separate computers and use it to manage your Exchange 2000 servers remotely. For example, you can use CDOEXM in Microsoft Management Console snap-ins and extensions; you can also create scripts by using the Windows Scripting Host and run them on remote machines. However, you can also use the CDOEX component on the server running Exchange 2000.

CDOEX Server

CDOEX Server provides the fundamental tools you need for building collaboration applications that use the Web Storage System and Active Directory. CDOEX provides the fundamental interfaces and COM classes that are used to manage most types of items in the Web Storage System. The CDOWF and the CDOEX COM components extend this core component to provide additional functionality.

By using CDOEX Server, you can do the following:

- Manage items in the Web Storage System (both folders and nonfolder items).
- Create, modify, delete, send, and post messages in Internet formats.
- Manage all aspects of calendar and appointment interchange and related messages, including the messages that contain meeting requests and that respond to meeting requests.
- Manage appointments in a user's calendar folder or in public folders.
- Manage contact information in a user's contacts folder, in public folders, and in Active Directory.

Table 5–2 lists the CDOEX COM classes and interfaces along with a brief description of each.

TABLE 5–2 *CDO for Exchange 2000 Server*

CDO COM class	CDO interface	Description
Configuration	IConfiguration	Used to configure CDO objects.
Item	IItem IDataSource	Used to manage items in the Web Storage System.
Folder	IFolder IDataSource	Used to manage folder items in the Web Storage System.
Appointment	IAppointment IBodyPart IDataSource	Used to create and manage appointment items in the Web Storage System.
Person	IPerson IDataSource IMailbox IMailRecipient* IMailboxStore*	Used to create and manage user and contact information in the Web Storage System and Active Directory.
Message	IMessage IBodyPart IDataSource	Used to create, send, respond to, and manage message items in the Web Storage System.
CalendarMessage	ICalendarMessage IMessage IBodyPart IDataSource	Used to create, send, reply to, and manage messages in the Web Storage System that contain calendar-related information.
Addressee	IAddressee IDataSource	Used to resolve addresses in Active Directory and retrieve a user's free or busy status.
Attendee	IAttendee	Used to add attendees to appointments.

* Denotes an interface that is available only if the CDOEX Objects Library is installed.

You can use the CDOEX component as a foundation upon which to build your application's COM/COM+ components. You can aggregate the CDO Item and Folder COM objects in your COM objects at run time, and thereby expose consistent, CDO-based implementations of the CDO IItem and IFolder interfaces to clients.

CDOEX Server supports various Internet Standard formats for messages, calendar information exchange, and contact information exchange, including RFC 822, MIME, iCalendar, and VCard formats.

CDOW

CDOW provides the tools you need to add workflow to your Web Storage System applications. Driven by the Web Storage System event architecture, CDOW provides a built-in workflow engine along with custom COM components that you can use to create process definitions and action tables that model your application's workflow processes.

CDOEXM

CDOEXM is a collection of COM objects and interfaces aggregated into CDO and ADSI objects. With CDOEXM you can programmatically manage Exchange 2000 Server, items in the stores, and store recipients (users). You can create, move, copy, reconfigure, monitor, or delete these items.

CDOEXM is useful for system administrators who need to do such things as archive stores every week, monitor the stores, or manage the server remotely. You can also use CDOEXM for server applications typically used in Internet applications, such as automatic registration of users and email management. CDOEXM encapsulates and simplifies many programmatic tasks that are specific to managing Exchange 2000 Server.

This section describes the objects and interfaces in CDOEXM. It also covers CDOEXM security issues, scripting, remote management, and lists requiring DLLs.

For a complete description of CDOEXM, see "Server and Recipient Management," in the SDK.

In this section, you will find the following topics, which cover overview information about managing the store:

- Active Directory and CDOEXM
- DLLs and Installation
- Exchange Management Security
- Web-based Management

In addition, you will find the following topics, which cover the CDOEXM objects and aggregated interfaces:
- Managing the Exchange Server
- Managing Mail Recipients

CDO and ADO

CDO and ADO are designed to work in conjunction with one another. Applications use ADO to navigate, search, and modify the properties of items in the Web Storage System; they use CDO to create and manage specific types of items, such as messages, contacts, appointments, messages containing meeting requests, and folders. Whereas ADO provides raw data access, CDO provides added functionality, which

- Handles the creation and management of various Internet standard stream formats for items such as messages, appointments, and contacts. These formats include the RFC 822 message format, the MIME format, the iCalendar format (for appointment exchange), and the vCard contact format. Unlike ADO objects, CDO objects automatically keep the item's stream in synchrony with the item's properties.
- Provides business logic that makes it easier to work with the raw data in many objects in the Web Storage System and Active Directory. For example, the CDO Person object alleviates the need to remember all of the various attribute names of User objects in Active Directory when performing the most routine tasks due to schema differences.
- Encodes and decodes data into Internet standard transfer formats, such as base64 and quoted-printable.
- Correlates meeting request responses into a master appointment in a user's calendar folder or a public folder.

Both CDO and ADO rely directly on the ExOLEDB Provider to access data residing in the Web Storage System.

Note You can use the Microsoft OLE DB Provider for Internet Publishing (MSDAIPP) with ADO to remotely access information in the Web Storage System. Using CDOEX or CDOWF with the MSDAIPP provider is not supported.

In addition, the MSDAIPP provider relies on the WinInet API to manage HTTP connections. The WinInet API is not supported in middle-tier or server-side applications. Therefore, you should not use MSDAIPP in middle-tier or server-side applications.

CDO objects can also be bound to ADO objects directly; this increases performance by not requiring separate bindings to the item in a particular store. When bound, changes made with a CDO object can be saved back to the ADO object, therefore, you need only one session when you process items by using both CDO and ADO.

Differences between CDO and ADO

Although both ADO and CDO rely on the ExOLEDB provider for access to items in Exchange 2000 stores, the semantic behaviors of each are different in many respects. The following sections outline these differences:

- Synchronized Streams and Properties
- Binding to Items in the Web Storage System
- Updating Items in the Web Storage System

Synchronized Streams and Properties

Many items in the Web Storage System contain an associated stream of data that represents the item in serialized format. The properties for the item, therefore, are represented in the stream by using a related Internet standard format. For example, a message item normally contains properties that identify to whom the message is addressed, who the message is from, and a subject. The values of these properties reside in two places: as properties for the item and in the message stream, formatted according to RFC 822 and RFC 1522 (MIME). Table 5–3 represents such an item.

TABLE 5–3 *Synchronized Streams and Properties*

Property	Value
urn:schemas:mailheader:to	"User 1" <user1@microsoft.com>
urn:schemas:mailheader:from	"User 2" <user2@microsoft.com>
urn:schemas:mailheader:subject	You're late for the meeting!
urn:schemas:mailheader:textdescription	We're in room 3607. Come by if you can!
adDefaultStream (-1)	To: "User 1" <user1@microsoft.com> From: "User 2" <user2@microsoft.com> Subject: You're late for the meeting! We're in room 3607. Come by if you can!

When the item is accessed using an ADO Record object, all of the data, including the stream, is presented in a fields collection. The stream, which has a special semantic definition within the ADO 2.5 specification, is accessed using the ADO Stream object from within the Fields collection. However, ADO assumes no correlation between the properties for the item and the default stream. That is, if you were to change the urn:schemas:mailheader:to property to `"User 3" <user3@microsoft.com>`, only the property would change, and the stream would not be updated to reflect the new value. You would have to update the message stream manually.

CDO, on the other hand, keeps the list of properties and the associated stream synchronized for items of certain content classes. If the item in the preceding table were accessed using the CDO Message object, the properties and stream would be coupled, and changes made to properties would be reflected in the stream, and vice versa.

Binding to Items in the Web Storage System

The ADO Record object uses only one method to bind items in a Web Storage System: the _Record.Open method. This method is used not only to bind to existing items, but also to create new ones. You control the behavior of the Open method, such as whether to create a new item or overwrite an existing item, by using various parameters of the method. For example, to open and bind an item for both read and write access, you specify the adModeReadWrite flag in the third parameter. To force the creation of a new item, you specify the adCreateCollection or adCreateNonCollection option in the fourth parameter; adCreateCollection creates a folder item (a collection of other items) and adCreateNonCollection creates a file (noncollection).

CDO objects bind directly to items in the Web Storage System by using the IDataSource Open, SaveTo, and SaveToContainer methods. Both the Open and SaveTo methods are similar to the ADO Open method except that with CDO objects, the initial direction of data flow is defined as part of the method—Open first copies data from the item into the object, and SaveTo saves the data in the object to the item. In both cases, when the operation completes, the CDO object is bound to the item in the store. The SaveToContainer method is just a variation on the SaveTo method that frees the caller from having to invent a unique name for the item in the folder.

When using ADO, you get an item's associated stream by requesting the adDefaultStream (-1) property from the object's fields collection. When using CDO, the method is different: the CDO IItem and IMessage interfaces define the GetStream method that returns the item's stream directly.

Updating Items in the Web Storage System

There are operational differences between CDO and ADO when you update items in the Web Storage System. First, we examine the procedures used to update items when using ADO, and then examine the procedure used with CDO. Finally, the differences are highlighted.

When you access an item in the Web Storage System by using an ADO Record or Recordset object, a copy of the requested properties is copied into the ADO object. If you decide to make changes to the item's properties, you first alter, append, or delete the values by using the associated fields collection, and then save these changes back to the store by using the Fields.Update method. To recopy the values stored in the store back to the ADO object, you use the Fields.Resync method. If the item has an associated stream, you make changes to it by first retrieving it from the fields collection by using the special ADO index value of -1. The value of this field is a reference to an ADO Stream object. After modifying the content within the Stream object, you call _Stream.Flush to commit the changes to the store. The important thing to remember is that there is no inherent correlation between the stream and the properties; both are treated as separate data values for the item.

CDO objects that modify items with streams, on the other hand, do maintain a correlation between the stream and the item's properties. Because of this correlation, modifications to the CDO object's fields collection are not committed directly to the store when the Fields.Update method is called. Instead, you must invoke the IDataSource.Save method to commit the changes. When the Save call is executed, the item's stream is recreated and saved to the store along with the property values.

CDO and ADSI

CDO and ADSI objects are also designed to work together. You can use CDO and ADSI objects together to:

- Create new users and their associated Exchange 2000 Server mailboxes.
- Manage user and contact information in Active Directory by using the same objects and logic.
- Easily identify the URLs for a particular user's mailbox folders, such as the Inbox, Calendar, Drafts, and Contacts folders.
- Manage Public Folder tree information and related information in Active Directory, when you use the CDOEX component.

The IDataSource Interface

The CDO object model defines the core IDataSource interface for accessing data in other ADO, CDO, and ADSI objects, or as saved data in the Web Storage System and Active Directory. All top-level CDO objects expose an implementation of this interface.

CDO objects are bound to items in the Web Storage System by using the IDataSource.Open, IDataSource.SaveTo, and IDataSource.SaveToContainer methods. The Open method first binds the specified store item, which is identified by a URL, and then copies the data to the object. The SaveTo method first binds the item and then saves the current data stored in the CDO object to the store item. The SaveToContainer method is similar to SaveTo, except that you need only specify the folder (container) in which to save the item; the actual name for the item is a GUID that is generated internally.

All CDO objects provide the ability to bind other CDO, ADO, and ADSI objects. What types of objects a certain CDO can bind to is not part of the core IDataSource interface definition, but is left to the particular implementation. Object binding follows a similar pattern to Web Storage System item binding. The OpenObject method first binds the target object and then copies the data in the target object to the opening CDO object. Similarly, the SaveToObject first binds the object and then saves the data in the binding CDO object to the target object:

```
CDO Object    <----- OpenObject ------- Target
CDO Object    -------SaveToObject ----> Target
```

After a CDO object has been bound to a Web Storage System item or another object, changes made within the CDO object can be saved into the bound data source.

Data Sources and Binding

The term *data source* is intended to be generic, meaning any object or store that can act as a repository of data. Examples of data sources include CDO objects, ADO objects, Web Storage System items, and Active Directory objects. The term *binding* refers to the state of two objects being associated—or linked—at runtime. When you use an OLE DB provider to create or modify an item in the Web Storage System, you first bind the object in the store, and then make changes to its properties or streams. After the data source is bound, the data in the data source can be modified, deleted, created, and so on.

After a binding has occurred, there are two copies of data present: the data in the Binding object (the binder) and the data source. For example, when you use an ADO Record object to bind to an existing item in the Web Storage System, the data in the Record object is a copy of the data in the store. Similarly, when you use a CDO Message object to bind to an ADO Record object, the data in the Record object is copied to the Message object. When you make changes to the data in the Binding object, these changes are not saved back to the data source automatically; you must commit the changes by using an appropriate method call.

Both ADO and CDO objects can bind to items in the Web Storage System by using an appropriate OLE DB provider. Thus, both ADO and CDO objects can have Web Storage System items as data sources. CDO objects, on the other hand, can have other objects as data sources. For example, a CDO Message object can bind to an ADO Record object, an ADO Stream object, a CDO BodyPart object, or any object exposing an implementation of the IStream interface.

The Configuration Object

The CDO object model is designed to support a single CDO Configuration object that is shared across a wide array of objects. Each top-level CDO object stores a reference to this central Configuration object through a Configuration property on an associated interface. Table 5–4 lists these top-level COM classes and the interface through which the Configuration reference is set.

TABLE 5–4   *Top-level COM classes*

Class	Configuration interface property
Item	IItem.Configuration
Folder	IFolder.Configuration
Message	IMessage.Configuration
CalendarMessage	ICalendarMessage.Configuration
Appointment	IAppointment.Configuration
Person	IPerson.Configuration
Addressee	IAddressee.Configuration

SIX

Messaging

Messaging is a platform for users and processes to send and receive electronic messages. In any collaboration application, users and processes need to communicate and coordinate their efforts. Microsoft Exchange 2000 Server provides a powerful platform for users to send messages by using a variety of tools with Exchange 2000, including HTTP/WebDAV, the Microsoft Web Storage System OLE DB provider, Simple Mail Transport Protocol (SMTP), Network News Transfer Protocol (NNTP), Internet Message Access Protocol (IMAP) protocols, and through MAPI. Users receive messages in their private mailbox folders in the Web Storage System, which can be accessed using HTTP/WebDAV, POP3, IMAP, and MAPI. These messages are natively stored in the RFC 822 and MIME formats.

The CDO for Exchange 2000 COM component provides a set of COM classes you can use in your application to create, access, modify, and send messages in Internet standard formats. CDO messaging objects can directly bind to messages in the Web Storage System by using the Web Storage System OLE DB Provider, and can send messages using a variety of tools, including SMTP, NNTP, and directly by using the Web Storage System OLE DB Provider.

The following sections introduce the concepts and technologies you can use to enhance your collaborative applications with messaging functionality by using Microsoft Exchange 2000 Server.

This topic covers the following information:
- Internet Standard Message Formats
- Messaging and the Exchange Web Storage System
- Messaging with CDOEX 2000 Server

Internet Standard Message Formats

The Microsoft Web Storage System, Microsoft Exchange 2000 Server, and the CDOEX 2000 Server COM components are designed to support Internet standard message formats that specify how electronic messages should be formatted when transferred over a network. Messages are stored in Internet standard formats in the Web Storage System and transferred in these formats across the network using the SMTP. When using the CDO for Exchange 2000 COM component, you can create applications that automatically construct, send, receive, and interpret messages in these Internet standard formats.

The following Internet standard message format specifications are described in this section:

- The RFC 822 Message Format
- The UNIX-to-UNIX encode (UUENCODE) Attachment Format
- The MIME Message Format

The RFC 822 Message Format

The RFC 822 specification defines an electronic message format consisting of header fields and an optional message body. The header fields contain information about the message, such as the sender, the recipient, and the subject. If a message body is included, it is separated from the header fields by an empty line (\r\n).

The following example illustrates a message in the RFC 822 message format:

```
From: someone@microsoft.com
To: someone_else@microsoft.com
Subject: An RFC 822 formatted message

This is the plain text body of the message. Note the blank
line between the header information and the body of the
message.
```

The RFC 822 message format is the basis for other message formats. The following example illustrates the Usenet article/message format specified by RFC 850:

```
From: someone@<yourcompany>.com
Subject: A basic RFC 850 formatted message
Newsgroups: comp.<yourcompany>.test

The body of this message is plain text. Note the blank line
between the header information and the body of the message.
```

The UUENCODE Attachment Format

The UUENCODE format provided one of the earliest ways to add attachments to messages. In the UUENCODE format, attachments are appended to the message body after being encoded using the UUENCODE algorithm. Each attachment is prefixed with the file name and the encoding end string. Multiple attachments are individually appended in sequence and separated by a blank line. In the UUENCODE attachment format, the message body consists of only two basic parts—the message text and the message attachments.

The following example shows a message body formatted using the UUENCODE attachment format that contains the message text and an attached Microsoft Word file:

```
To: "User 1" <user1@microsoft.com>
From: "User 2" <user2@microsoft.com>
Subject: My latest draft.

I've attached my latest draft.
Regards,
User 2

begin 644 mydraft.doc
AAAAAAAAAFDFAAAAFAFAF....
```

Although the UUENCODE format provides a way to add attachments to messages, it does not define ways to:

- Indicate the type of the attachment, except through the file's extension.
- Specify alternate character encoding for the message text to support international languages.
- Relate groups of attachments.
- Indicate that the message text is a form of rich text, such as HTML or Rich Text Format (RTF) formatted text.
- Provide future enhancements to a structure of complex message bodies. The UUENCODE attachment format is neither flexible nor descriptive.

The next section, The MIME Message Format, describes a message format that enables each of these enhancements.

The MIME Message Format

The MIME specification enables the exchange of messages with more complex content than RFC 822.

The body of a MIME-formatted message is subdivided into body parts. Body parts contain parts of a message—for example an image, spreadsheet, text formatted using HTML, an alternate representation of the message text, a sound file, or an executable program. The MIME specification also defines additional mail header fields to describe aspects of each message body part. The MIME header fields enable you to do the following:

- Specify the type of content within the body part, such as an image, an application file, an executable program, and so on.
- Specify the class of content within the body part. For example, a Microsoft Word document attachment would be of the type application/msword, but its purpose or class could be an expense report or specification. Distinct from the type of content, the class defines the intent or purpose of the content.
- Specify the encoding for each content part when encoding is necessary—for example, in a binary file.
- Specify a character encoding other than U.S. ASCII for each separate text body part.
- Specify the intended disposition of a body part, for example, inline or attachment.
- Specify a base URI for resources referenced in HTML content.

Body parts can be organized into groups formed in a hierarchy. With this hierarchy, you can relate multiple body parts in the body of a message. For example, you can indicate that a body part consists of the following:

- Multiple representations of the same message, such as plain text, HTML, and audio
- Multiple parts with related resources that are to be assembled when displayed to the reader—for example an HTML page that consists of HTML, images, style sheets, frames, JavaScript files, and so on
- Multiple parts that vary in purpose, some being alternate representations, some attachments, and some groups of related resources

MIME Message Body Parts

A message body formatted according to the MIME specification is subdivided into parts that are organized as a hierarchy. As with any hierarchy, some parts contain other parts called descendants, and all parts have ancestors except for the top part, called the root. Each part or subdivision of the body is defined as a body part. Body parts that do not contain other body parts are defined as content body parts, and body parts that do contain other body parts are defined as multipart body parts. The following example shows a hierarchy of parts, at the top of which is the root body part, labeled R, which has direct descendants, labeled A1 and A2:

```
R
  A1
    A1.1
    A1.2
  A2
    A2.1
    A2.2
```

The body parts R, A1, and A2 are multipart body parts because they contain descendants; A1.1, A1.2, A2.1, and A2.2 are content body parts because they do not contain descendants. These body parts contain the actual content of the message, such as the plain-text version of the message, an attachment, an HTML page, and so on.

In the MIME formatting scheme, multipart body parts contain only other body parts and do not directly contain the content of the message. Their purpose is to define the relationship of their descendants.

The MIME specification defines the header Content-Type to indicate the type of body part. For example, the body part type indicates what kind of data the body part contains. Values for the Content-Type header contain a primary- and secondary-type indicator separated by a forward slash (/)—for example, image/gif and multipart/related. Multipart body parts always have a primary type of multipart. All nonmultipart body parts have some other type of multipart—for example, an image, an application, a text, and so on. For additional information, see "MIME Extensions to Internet Mail" in the Appendix, "MIME, SMTP, and RFCs."

Content Body Parts

A content body part contains content and header fields, which provide information about the content. The content is any array of bytes, from a binary file to HTML-formatted text. When necessary, the content is encoded so that the entire body of the message complies with the RFC 822 specification. The MIME specification defines the Content-Transfer-Encoding header to specify how the body was encoded if encoding was required. Additional information about the body part can be specified using header fields. The Content-Disposition header field is used to indicate whether the content is intended as a message attachment or to be displayed inline with content from other body parts in the message body. The Content-Type header field indicates what type of content is contained in the body part. When the content is text, the header normally indicates the character encoding used in the message.

If you send a message that includes an image called *picture.gif*, and the image is an attachment, your email program must encode the image binary data into U.S. ASCII characters so that the message can be transmitted over the network using the SMTP protocol. To correctly decode and display the image, the recipient must know the Content-Type, how it was encoded, and how it should be handled. The headers must convey that

- The type of content in the body part is an image in GIF format (image/gif).
- The binary data in the body part was encoded using the base64-encoding algorithm.
- The body part is intended as an attachment to the message.
- The suggested file name is *picture.gif*.

The following example shows the headers that convey this information to the recipient's email program:

```
Content-Type: image/gif;
   name="picture.gif"
Content-Transfer-Encoding: base64
Content-Disposition: attachment;
   filename="picture.gif"

[encoded content here]
```

Multipart Body Parts

The MIME specification defines several multipart content types that are used to describe the relationship of descendant body parts. For example, when a message contains both a U.S. ASCII text message and an image attachment, the body is subdivided into three parts: the root body part, the body part containing the U.S. ASCII message text, and the body part containing the image attachment. The root body part has a Content-Type of multipart and mixed and contains the other two body parts. Therefore, the text and the attachment are descendants of the root body part. These descendant body parts have Content-Type text/plain and Content-Type image/XXX, respectively.

Another example is when alternate representations of a message are present in a message. Each representation is stored in a body part that is a descendant of a body part with Content-Type set to multipart/alternative. This Content-Type value indicates to recipients that the body part contains alternative representations of a single message—for example, in U.S. ASCII text, HTML marked-up text, and audio.

For more information on body parts, content types, and the MIME specification, see "MIME Extensions to Internet Mail" in Appendix A.

MIME Hierarchies of Body Parts

A MIME-formatted message is divided into a hierarchy of body parts. Multipart body parts define the relationships between descendant body parts, and content body parts contain the actual content of the message. The illustration that follows (Figure 6–1) represents a typical MIME hierarchy for a message that contains the following content:

- Alternative versions of the message, in U.S. ASCII plain text and HTML
- A related image used to render the HTML content
- A Word attachment

Content body parts are displayed in a shaded box labeled *Content*. Multipart body parts act as structural nodes in the hierarchy and define the relationships among the descendant content body parts.

The format of a MIME header is specified by RFC 2045. For a complete description of the MIME message format, see RFC 2045, RFC 2046, RFC 2047, RFC 2048, and RFC 2049.

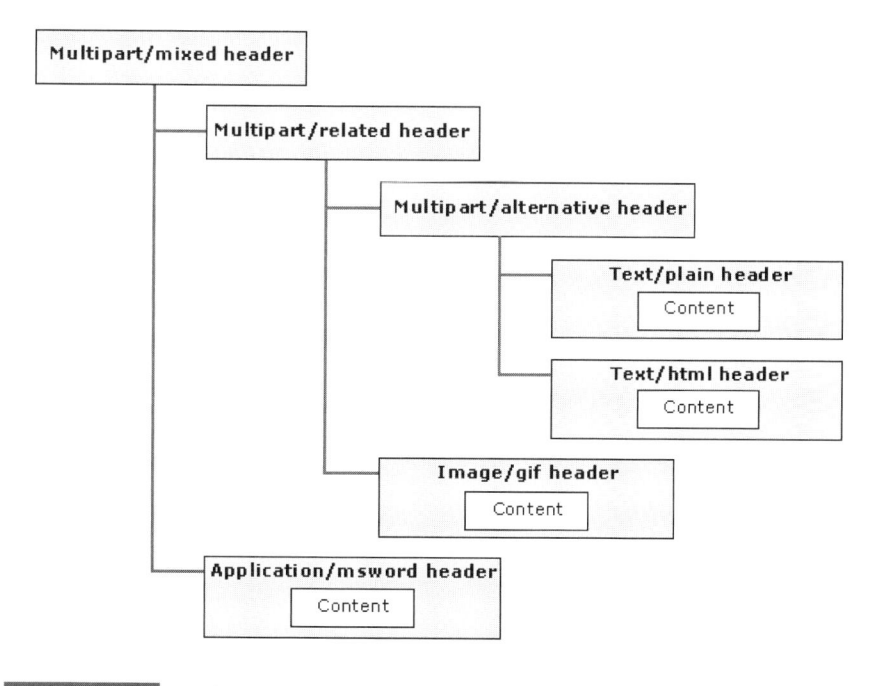

FIGURE 6–1 *Multipart/mixed structure*

Messaging and the Exchange Web Storage System

The following section introduces the new messaging technology and the related content classes provided by the Web Storage System and Microsoft Exchange 2000 Server:

- *Messaging Content Classes.* The Web Storage System and messaging applications use content classes to define the intent or purpose of an item. A rich set of content classes used with messaging applications is provided, and your applications can extend these classes to define in finer detail the purpose of messaging items present in the Web Storage System.
- *Automatic Message Property Promotion.* The Web Storage System automatically sets properties for messaging items from values contained in the saved message stream.
- *The Exchange Mail Submission URI.* Each Exchange private information store provides a special URI for each mailbox that you can use to send messages. Similar to the SMTP, you can send messages using this URI with the ExOLEDB provider and with the HTTP/WebDAV protocol.

Messaging Content Classes

The Web Storage System provides a set of content classes to identify items that are messages. Table 6–1 lists the content classes along with a brief description of each.

TABLE 6–1 *Messaging Content Classes*

Content class	Description
urn:content-classes:message	The base content class for all messages. This content class defines an item that is a message and a set of properties that describes the item.
urn:content-classes:calendarmessage	Extends the urn:content-classes:message content class and identifies a message that contains meeting requests, appointments, and so on.
urn:content-classes:reportmessage	Extends the urn:content-classes:message content class and identifies a message that is a report. Such messages include Delivery Status Notifications (DSNs) and Mail Disposition Notifications (MDNs).

Table 6-1 *Messaging Content Classes (continued)*

Content class	Description
urn:content-classes:dsn	Extends the urn:content-classes:reportmessage content class and identifies a message that is a DSN.
urn:content-classes:mdn	Extends the urn:content-classes:reportmessage content class and identifies a message that is an MDN.
urn:content-classes:recallmessage	Extends the urn:content-classes:message and identifies a message that is used to recall a previously sent message.
urn:content-classes:recallreport	Extends the urn:content-classes:recallmessage content class and identifies a message that contains a report about a recalled message.

The following illustration shows the hierarchy of these classes:

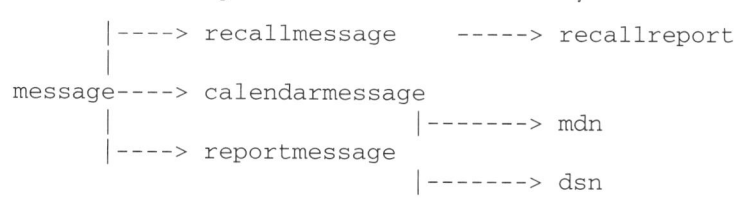

```
              |----> recallmessage      -----> recallreport
              |
message----> calendarmessage
              |                         |-------> mdn
              |----> reportmessage
                                        |-------> dsn
```

Note   The *recallmessage, recallreport, reportmessage*, MDN, and DSN content classes identify a refined intent or purpose for items beyond simply being a message; no additional properties are defined for these classes. These content classes are good examples of the practice of using content class to refine the intended purpose of an item in the Web Storage System. Content class definitions do not need to specify additional properties if those defined by the base class are sufficient. In your applications, you can use similarly defined hierarchies of content classes for the same purpose, such as making the intent or purpose of various items more specific. The *calendarmessage* content class, on the other hand, defines the additional urn:schemas:calendar:method property, which is specific to these types of message items.

Automatic Message Property Promotion

The Web Storage System automatically sets properties for messaging items when the associated stream is saved. You control this behavior through the file name extension of the item. When you create an item with an .eml extension, and write the item's stream, the Web Storage System assumes that the stream is formatted according to the RFC 822 and MIME standards. It examines the inbound stream for various messaging-related values, such as mail header fields and message text, and automatically sets these properties for the item. This is referred to as property promotion; the promotion is from data within the stream to properties for the item. The Web Storage System checks the stream for all properties defined by the urn:content-classes:message content class for promotion.

In the following example, you create an item in your inbox with the name *mymessage.eml* and you also save and commit the following stream to the item in the Web Storage System:

```
To: "User 1" <user1@microsoft.com>
From: "User 2" <user2@microsoft.com>
Subject: My latest draft.
```

This is the text portion of the message.

Table 6–2 lists the properties for the items after saving the stream.

Table 6–2 *Automatic Message Properties*

Property	Value
urn:schemas:mailheader:to	"User 1" <user1@microsoft.com>
urn:schemas:httpmail:to	"User 1" <user1@microsoft.com>
urn:schemas:httpmail:displayto	User 1
urn:schemas:mailheader:from	"User 2" <user2@microsoft.com>
urn:schemas:httpmail:from	"User 2" <user2@microsoft.com>
urn:schemas:httpmail:frome-mail	user2@microsoft.com
urn:schemas:httpmail:fromname	User 2
urn:schemas:mailheader:subject	My latest draft.
urn:schemas:httpmail:subject	My latest draft.
urn:schemas:httpmail:textdescription	This is the text of the message.
urn:schemas:httpmail:date	10/5/98 11:49 AM
urn:schemas:httpmail:datereceived	10/5/98 11:52 AM
DAV:contentclass	urn:content-classes:message
urn:schemas:httpmail:hasattachments	False

Note The Web Storage System does not automatically update the stream for the message when the properties are changed using OLE DB or Microsoft ADO. You must update the stream separately. To avoid updating the stream separately, use the CDO Message object or the CalendarMessage object when you modify existing items in the Web Storage System. These objects automatically ensure that messaging properties and the item stream remain synchronized.

The Exchange Mail Submission URI

Exchange 2000 provides a new process for sending messages using the HTTP/WebDAV protocol and the ExOLEDB provider. You can send messages using a special URI called the Exchange mail submission URI. A user's mail submission URI is found by retrieving the value of the urn:schemas:httpmail:sendmsg property of the user's private mailbox folder. To send messages using the URI, the sending agent must have the user's credentials or Send On Behalf Of rights for that mailbox.

To send a message, you have the following two options:

- Write an RFC 821 stream to the item's stream. With HTTP, you do this with the PUT protocol command. With the Exchange OLE DB provider, you retrieve the item's default stream (adDefaultStream in ADO) and write the message stream to it. The portion of the stream containing the message must be in the format defined by RFC 822 and the MIME specification. The entire stream must contain the RFC 821 SMTP protocol commands listed at the beginning, as shown in the following example:

```
MAIL FROM:: "User 1" <user1@fake.microsoft.com>
RCPT TO: "User 2" <user2@fake.microsoft.com>
RCPT TO: "User 3" <user3@fake.microsoft.com>

(Message Stream)
```

- The SMTP DATA protocol command is not needed and is assumed after the first blank line designated by the first "\r\n\r\n" sequence in the stream.
- When sending a message over HTTP, the sender must be authenticated as either the owner of the mailbox or a user with Send On Behalf Of rights for this mailbox.
- Write the properties for the message defined for the urn:contentclasses:message content class. This is similar to sending messages using MAPI—the Web Storage System automatically generates the message stream for you when you commit the properties to the item. When sending a message using the ExOLEDB provider, the sender must be authenticated as either the owner of the mailbox or a user with Send On Behalf Of rights for this mailbox. When using this process, you cannot add attachments or send a complex MIME-formatted message.

Unlike the user's outbox folder, the mail submission URI is neither a folder nor an item in the user's mailbox. It is a virtual item used only to send messages by using the HTTP protocol or the ExOLEDB provider.

Messaging with CDO for Exchange 2000 Server

You can use the CDO for Microsoft Exchange 2000 Server COM component provided by Exchange 2000 Server to manage all aspects of message construction and manipulation. Like its predecessor, CDO for Microsoft Windows 2000, you can use CDO for Exchange 2000 Server to construct, process, and respond to messages formatted according to the Internet RFC 822 and MIME specifications. Such formats are the native storage format for messages in the Web Storage System.

Messages, like other nonfolder items in a Web Storage System repository, consist of a stream of data and a set of associated properties defined by the various messaging content classes. Working directly with the properties might satisfy the needs of your application. For example, working with the properties would suffice if you are working with simple messages that contain only U.S. ASCII text or HTML and have no attachments. You can use Microsoft ADO or OLE DB to create and transmit such messages, leaving the stream construction to Exchange.

In the case of existing messages in the Web Storage System, you can also rely solely on the message item's properties for your application. However, if you need to manipulate or send more complex messages, such as those with attachments or MIME-formatted bodies, you must be able to parse, interpret, or construct the message's associated MIME stream. ADO provides access to the item's properties and stream, but does not provide any facilities for the management of the item's stream. The CDO for Exchange 2000 messaging components provide this functionality.

CDO Messaging COM Interfaces

The CDO for Exchange COM component defines several COM interfaces that are used to construct and manage messages.

- IBodyPart Interface defines methods and properties that are used to manage a body part of a message.
- IBodyParts Interface defines a collection interface that is used to manage a collection of body parts.
- IMessage Interface defines methods and properties that is used to manage a message.

Each of these interfaces is dual. You can use these interfaces with programming languages such as Microsoft Visual C++, Microsoft Visual Basic, Microsoft VBScript, and Microsoft JScript.

The following interfaces are used when constructing SMTP or NNTP transport event sinks using CDO for Exchange:

- ISMTPOnArrival
- INNTPOnPostEarly
- INNTPOnPost
- INNTPOnPostFinal

For more information on transport event sinks and CDO, see "SMTP/NNTP Transport Event Sinks with CDO," on the SDK.

CDO Messaging COM Classes

The CDO for Exchange COM component provides the following implementations of the CDO COM interfaces discussed in the previous section:

- The BodyPart COM Class represents a message body part.
- The Message COM Class represents a message.
- The CalendarMessage COM Class represents a message containing calendar items.

The CalendarMessage COM class is discussed in detail in Chapter 7 of this documentation.

CDO BodyPart Object Hierarchies

Message bodies are organized in CDO as hierarchies of BodyPart objects. In MIME-formatted messages, each body part in the hierarchy is a BodyPart object. The root of the hierarchy is either a Message or CalendarMessage object. Figure 6–2 illustrates a possible hierarchy.

Navigation through the body-part hierarchy is facilitated through the IBodyPart.BodyParts collection and the IBodyPart.Parent property on each BodyPart object.

When you need to construct messages using only the UUENCODE format, you set the IMessage.MIMEFormatted property to False. In this case, the message text and each attachment to the message are contained in a BodyPart object.

Chapter 6 • Messaging

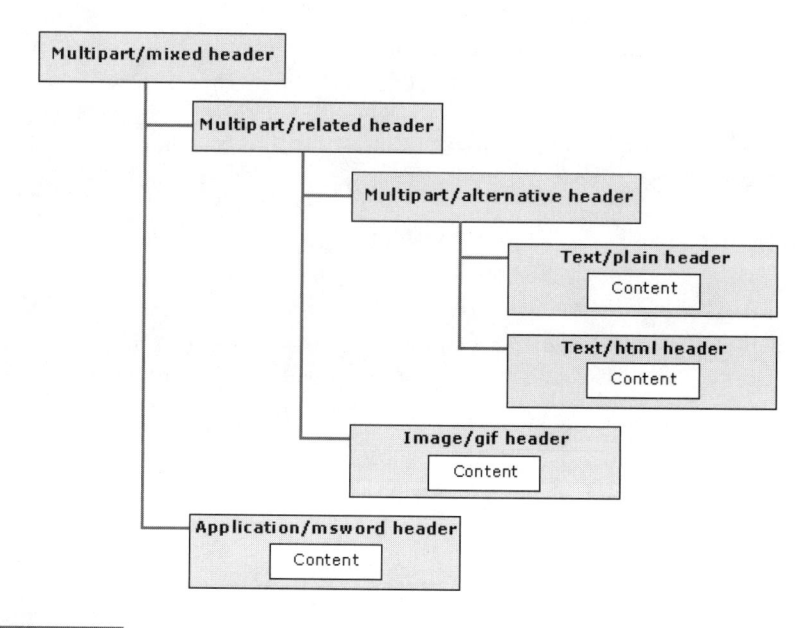

FIGURE 6-2 *Example BodyPart hierarchy*

Example 1: Alternative Representations of a Message

Many messages are commonly sent with alternative representations of the message text, for example in both HTML and plain text. With MIME, you can indicate to the recipient that the message contains these alternative representations of a message. Figure 6-3 shows what the hierarchy of CDO objects for such a message might look like.

The Message object is itself a body part with a Content Type equal to "multipart/alternative." Because of this, its content stream is empty. Its IBodyPart.BodyParts collection has two items, which are both BodyPart objects. Each descendant body part has a content stream with the particular alternative representation of the message.

Example 2: Alternative with Attachments

If the message in the previous example had attachments, such as an image and a Microsoft Word file, the hierarchy of objects might look like the representation in Figure 6-4.

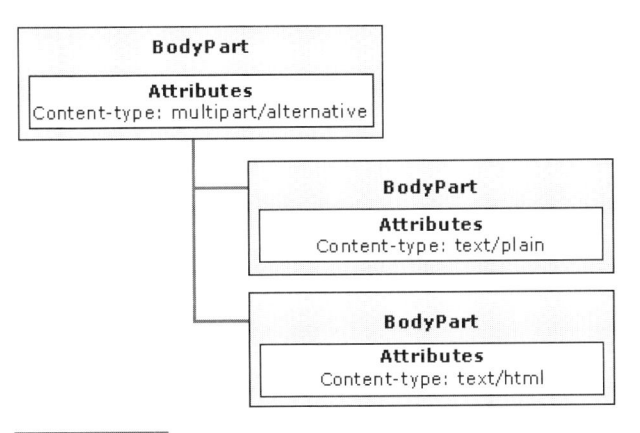

```
                    ┌──────────────────────────────────────┐
                    │             BodyPart                 │
                    │ ┌──────────────────────────────────┐ │
                    │ │          Attributes              │ │
                    │ │ Content-type: multipart/alternative│ │
                    │ └──────────────────────────────────┘ │
                    └──────────────────────────────────────┘
                              │
                              ├────┌──────────────────────────────┐
                              │    │          BodyPart            │
                              │    │ ┌──────────────────────────┐ │
                              │    │ │       Attributes         │ │
                              │    │ │ Content-type: text/plain │ │
                              │    │ └──────────────────────────┘ │
                              │    └──────────────────────────────┘
                              │
                              └────┌──────────────────────────────┐
                                   │          BodyPart            │
                                   │ ┌──────────────────────────┐ │
                                   │ │       Attributes         │ │
                                   │ │ Content-type: text/html  │ │
                                   │ └──────────────────────────┘ │
                                   └──────────────────────────────┘
```

FIGURE 6–3   *Alternative representation BodyPart hierarchy*

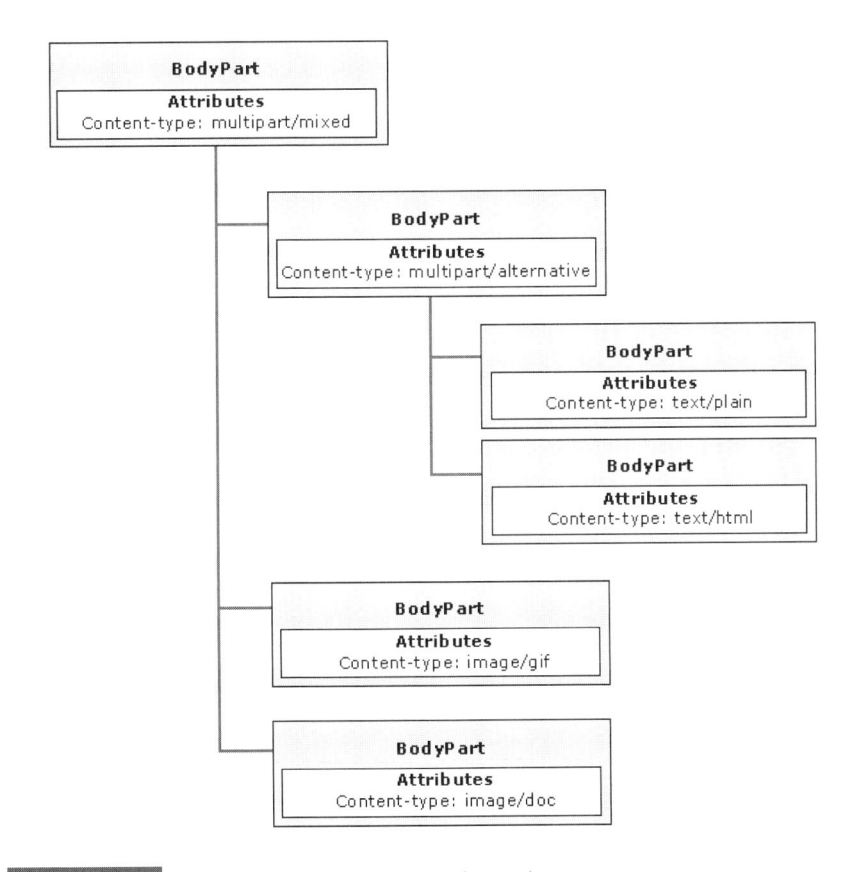

[Figure 6–4: BodyPart hierarchy with outer multipart/mixed containing a multipart/alternative BodyPart (with text/plain and text/html children) and two additional BodyPart attachments with content-types image/gif and image/doc.]

FIGURE 6–4   *Alternative representation with attachments*

Example 3: Alternative with MHTML Formatting

You can send images, style sheets, scripts, and other related materials along with the message to enable clients to properly render the HTML-formatted message. You can do this by using the MHTML MIME format. Figure 6–5 shows what the body part hierarchy might look like.

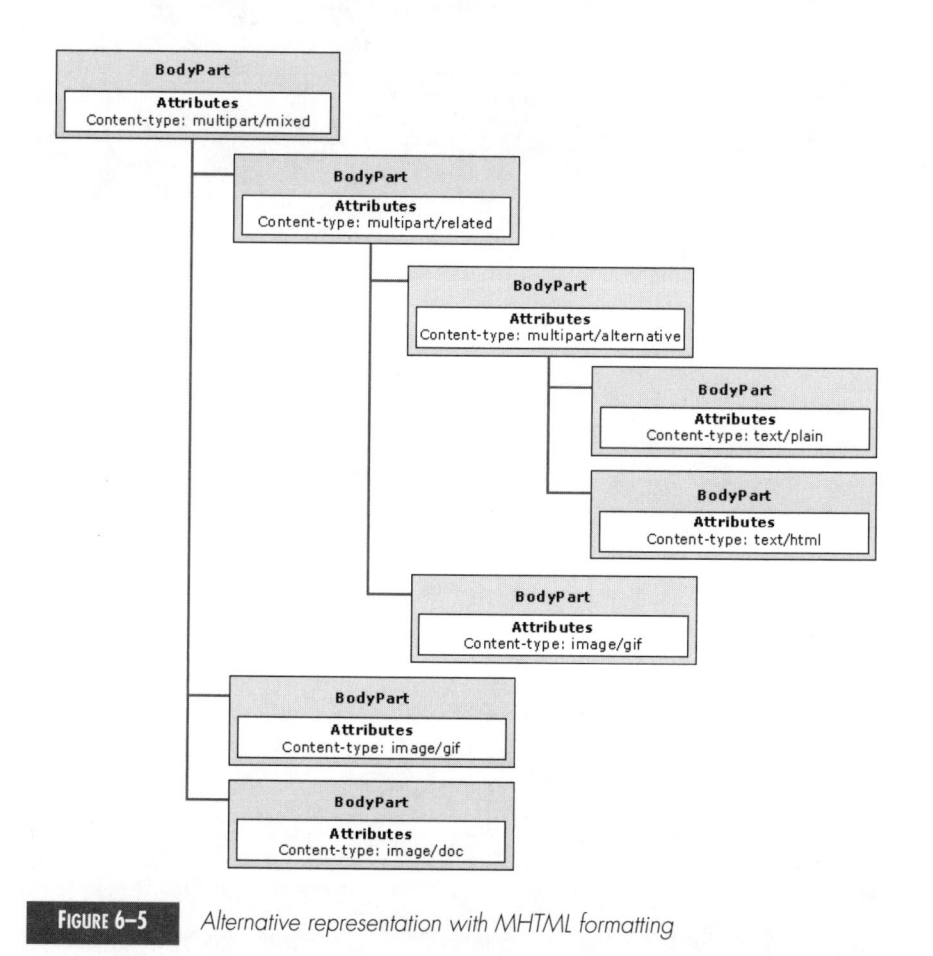

FIGURE 6–5 *Alternative representation with MHTML formatting*

CDO BodyPart Fields and Streams

Each body part has a set of fields and possibly some content. To access the fields for a body part, you use the IBodyPart.Fields collection. To access the content of the body part, you use the IBodyPart.GetEncodedContentStream and

IBodyPart.GetDecodedContentStream methods. Each method returns the content in either encoded or decoded format. To access the entire body part MIME-formatted stream, you use the IBodyPart.GetStream method. Each stream is returned in an ADO Stream object. Figure 6–6 shows the relationship of the fields collection and the various streams associated with a body part.

Body part fields are not stored directly as fields for the item in the Web Storage System; they are stored in the MIME-formatted message stream. To manipulate the fields for a body part, use a CDO Message object to open the item from the Web Storage System.

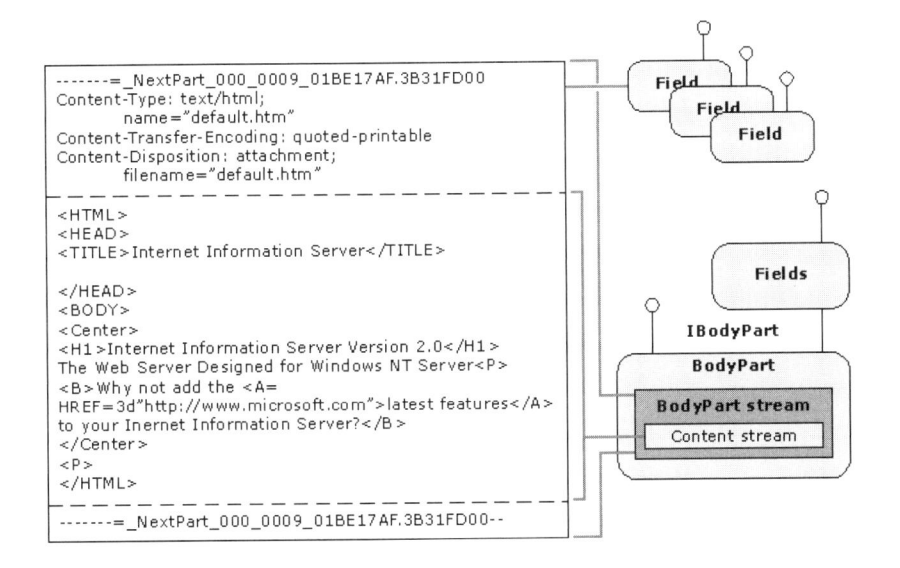

FIGURE 6–6 *The relationship of the fields collection and the various streams associated with a body part*

BodyPart Content Streams

Each content BodyPart object contains a content stream that can be requested using IBodyPart.GetDecodedContentStream and IBodyPart.GetEncodedContentStream. The encoding process is defined by the urn:schemas:mailheader:content-transfer-encoding property in the fields collection. This corresponds to the Content-Transfer-Encoding mail header field defined by the MIME specification.

For example, a body part containing the message in HTML format in a multipart/alternative hierarchy could have the following decoded content stream:

```
<html><p>Here is a simple <b>message</b>.
```

A body part containing a binary attachment or file, such as an image or Word document, would contain totally different streams for the encoded and decoded content. For the encoded content stream, the binary stream would be encoded using an algorithm such as base64 and returned as U.S. ASCII text. For the decoded stream, a raw binary stream is returned. In addition, the ADO Stream object has a _Stream.Type property that indicates whether the content is binary or text. For text streams, the character set is identified using the _Stream.Charset property. Changes made to the stream can be saved back to the body part using the _Stream.Flush method. In a sense, the Stream object is bound to the body part as if the BodyPart object were its storage location. To manipulate the content of a body part, always use the decoded content stream.

Body parts that have Content-Type set to multipart do not have an associated content stream in the CDO object model. These body parts exist solely to create the hierarchy and relationships between descendant body parts. Requesting their content streams raises an exception, but all BodyPart objects have a stream.

BodyPart Streams

All BodyPart objects can generate a stream that is the portion of the MIME-formatted message body starting with that BodyPart object in the hierarchy. This stream is different from a content stream, which contains only the raw content for the body part. The MIME stream is returned by the IBodyPart.GetStream method in an ADO Stream object. When constructed, the MIME stream for the BodyPart object and all descendants are included.

You can use this stream to copy body-part hierarchies between different messages. For example, you might build a complex MIME hierarchy and want to copy the entire hierarchy from one message to another. You can generate the stream for that portion of the first message and save it as the stream of a BodyPart object in another message. Once saved, the MIME-formatted data is parsed and the appropriate BodyPart hierarchy is constructed automatically.

To clarify the difference between a body part's content stream and stream, consider the following example, which illustrates a stream for a body part containing the HTML portion of a message:

```
Content-Type: text/html;
     charset="iso-8859-1"
Content-Transfer-Encoding: 7bit

<html><p>Here is a simple <b>message</b>
```

The *content stream* for the body part would be

```
<html><p>Here is a simple <b>message</b>.
```

Another example is a hypothetical multipart/alternative body part stream:

```
Content-Type: multipart/alternative;
        boundary="----=_NextPart_000_0000_01BED789.F54D7C60"
```

This is a multipart message in MIME format.

```
------=_NextPart_000_0000_01BED789.F54D7C60
Content-Type: text/plain;
        charset="iso-8859-1"
Content-Transfer-Encoding: 7bit

Here is a simple message.
------=_NextPart_000_0000_01BED789.F54D7C60
Content-Type: text/html;
        charset="iso-8859-1"
Content-Transfer-Encoding: 7bit

<html><p>Here is a simple <b>message</b>.
------=_NextPart_000_0000_01BED789.F54D7C60--
```

Note In this case, the BodyPart object used to generate this MIME stream does not contain content; it only defines the relationship of its descendant BodyPart objects. If you call the IBodyPart.GetDecodedContentStream or IBodyPart.GetEncodedContentStream for this BodyPart object, an exception is raised.

CDO Message Fields and Streams

Message objects, like BodyPart objects, have an associated Fields collection and a method used to generate the message object's stream. The Fields collection can be retrieved using either the IBodyPart or IMessage interfaces. The Field objects within each Fields collection are identical. The IMessage interface defines the GetStream method that you use to retrieve the content for an entire message.

The set of messaging fields for a message is defined by the urn:content-classes:message content class. When you set message properties using properties on the IMessage interface, many of these fields are generated automatically.

The format of the message stream is controlled using the IMessage.MIMEFormatted property. If IMessage.MIMEFormatted is set to False, only a plain text message is constructed, and all attachments are added using the UUENCODE format.

Message Fields

The set of fields stored with the message is defined by the urn:content-classes:message content class. Many fields defined for messaging content classes refer to the same underlying message data, but they return this data as different data types. For example, every message header field for a Message object can be accessed in the urn:schemas:mailheader: namespace, but all are returned as U.S. ASCII strings, with any non-U.S. ASCII characters encoded by the process defined in RFC 1522. Similarly named fields within the urn:schemas:httpmail: namespace return the same information, but in a different data format. In the urn:schemas:httpmail: namespace, field values are decoded and returned as unicode characters. Another example is the *http://schemas.microsoft.com/exchange/sensitivity* field that returns an enumerated value rather than a string identifying the sensitivity of the message.

When accessing fields in the urn:schemas:mailheader: namespace, the OLE DB type for the majority of fields is DBTYPE_STR. The ADO Field interface is dual and Automation compatible. Single-byte characters are returned as wide, two-byte (wchar_t) characters. However, encoded characters are not decoded before being returned.

Message Streams

When you request the message stream by using the IMessage.GetStream method, the CDO Message object internally constructs the stream. The object formats the stream using the process defined by RFC 822 and places the output into the ADO Stream object. If you have set the IMessage.MIMEFormatted property to False, the Message object uses the UUENCODE attachment format for the stream. Otherwise, the Message object generates the stream using the MIME format. By default, the IMessage.MIMEFormatted property is set to True. Setting this property to False limits the type of data you can send with your message. Use MIME formatting whenever possible.

The following example shows a typical MIME-formatted message generated by CDO for a message having HTML, plain text message, and an attached XSL style sheet:

```
Thread-Topic: This is a test
From: "User 1" <user1@microsoft.com>
To: "User 2" <user2@microsoft.com>
Subject: This is a test
MIME-Version: 1.0
Content-Type: multipart/mixed;
        boundary="----
=_NextPart_000_0000_01BED78B.61E13E10"
Thread-Index: Ab7Xxg4EDFQD/RrtQVCb0K8odOtcJA
Content-Class: urn:content-classes:message
X-MimeOLE: Produced By Microsoft MimeOLE V5.00.2918.2701
```

CDO Message Fields and Streams   145

```
This is a multi-part message in MIME format.

------=_NextPart_000_0000_01BED78B.61E13E10
Content-Type: multipart/alternative;
        boundary="----=_NextPart_001_0001_01BED78B.61E13E10"

------=_NextPart_001_0001_01BED78B.61E13E10
Content-Type: text/plain;
        charset="iso-8859-1"
Content-Transfer-Encoding: 7bit

Here is a simple message.

------=_NextPart_001_0001_01BED78B.61E13E10
Content-Type: text/html;
        charset="iso-8859-1"
Content-Transfer-Encoding: 7bit

<html><p>Here is a simple <b>message</b>.
------=_NextPart_001_0001_01BED78B.61E13E10--

------=_NextPart_000_0000_01BED78B.61E13E10
Content-Type: text/xml;
        name="test.xsl"
Content-Transfer-Encoding: quoted-printable
Content-Disposition: attachment;
        filename="test.xsl"

<xsl:stylesheet xmlns:xsl=3D"http://www.w3.org/TR/WD-xsl">
<xsl:template>
  <xsl:copy>
      <xsl:apply-templates select=3D"@*"/>
      <xsl:apply-templates select=3D"* | text()"/>
  </xsl:copy></xsl:template><xsl:template =
match=3D"@*"><xsl:copy><xsl:value-of/></xsl:copy></xsl:template>
</xsl:stylesheet>
------=_NextPart_000_0000_01BED78B.61E13E10--
```

This example was generated using CDO for Exchange, using the IMessage.GetStream method for a Message object and written to console using the _Stream.ReadText method of the resulting ADO Stream object.

Note   For a Message object, the IMessage.GetStream and the IBodyPart.GetStream methods return identical streams.

Message Stream and Property Synchronization

Unlike many items in the Web Storage System, there is an assumed relationship between a message item's fields and stream. For example, the urn:schemas:mailheader:to property for the message item is normally the same as the value of the To: header field in the RFC 822 message stream. When you save items that have an .eml extension, the Web Storage System parses the inbound item stream, extracts the values for the various messaging fields, and automatically sets these fields for you. The stream is therefore always synchronized with the messaging fields for the item.

However, if you open an existing message using an ADO Record object and change the item's messaging fields directly, the Web Storage System does not regenerate the message stream. In this case, you must update the message stream manually. If you do not update the stream manually, the item's messaging fields no longer reflect the data contained within the stream.

To avoid these difficulties, use the appropriate CDO messaging object to manipulate messages. The CDO Message and CalendarMessage objects automatically synchronize the message fields and the stream when changes are made to either object. Avoid using an ADO Record object to change the messaging fields of an existing message. If you do use a Record object to change an existing message, update its stream rather than its messaging fields. These fields are set automatically when the message stream is saved and parsed.

CDO Messaging Configuration

The configuration information for CDO top-level objects is stored in an instance of the Configuration COM class. A Configuration object contains information such as the method used to deliver messages, the paths to the pickup directories for SMTP and NNTP servers, a user's mailbox URI, and so forth. When you create a Configuration object, CDO fills in the default configuration information by collecting information from Microsoft IIS for Microsoft Windows 2000 and Microsoft Outlook Express, provided they are installed on the computer running CDO.

If you do not create a Configuration object, CDO creates one each time you send or post a message. When sending many messages, create a single Configuration object and use it with each Message object to maximize application performance. For example, you can store this object in an ASP Session or Application object, and retrieve it when you need to send a message.

Passwords specified in Outlook Express are not picked in the Configuration object's field collection. These passwords are specified in a dialog box when you select My Server Requires Authentication in Outlook Express. For outbound mail authentication, however, you can provide a write-only password using the sendpassword field on the Configuration object.

Configuration Fields

Configuration information is stored in an ADO Fields collection in the Configuration object. Most configuration fields reside in the *http://schemas.microsoft.com/cdo/configuration/* namespace. Table 6–3 provides a list of common configuration fields along with a brief description of each.

TABLE 6–3 *Common Configuration Fields*

Configuration property	Description
activeconnection	An ADO Connection object used to send messages by using the Exchange OLE DB provider. If this object is not specified, a new Connection object is created to send the message. This Connection object is used only when sending messages in Exchange. You control how messages are sent by setting the sendusing and postusing configuration fields.
mailboxurl	Used to specify the URI to a user's mailbox when sending messages using the Exchange OLE DB provider. If this property is not specified, the mailbox URI for the user specified in the sendusername or postusername is constructed using data retrieved from Active Directory.
sendusing	Used to specify whether to send the message using the local SMTP service drop directory, over the network using the SMTP protocol, or by using the Exchange mail submission URI.
Postusing	Used to specify whether to post the message using the local NNTP service drop directory, over the network using the NNTP protocol, or by using the Exchange mail submission URI.
sendusername postusername	Specifies the username to use for credentials when sending or posting messages over the network. Additionally, when sending or posting messages using Exchange, these values are used to look up the user's mailbox URI in Active Directory. You can bypass the lookup by setting the mailbox property in the configuration just discussed.
sendpassword postpassword	The passwords associated with sendusername/postusername for credentials when sending messages over the network.
smtpserver nntpserver	Used to indicate the DNS name of the SMTP or NNTP service host, if messages are sent using the SMTP/NNTP protocols.

TABLE 6–3 *Common Configuration Fields (continued)*

Configuration property	Description
smtpserverport nntpserverport	Used to indicate the transmission control protocol/Internet protocol (TCP/IP) port of the SMTP or NNTP service, if messages are sent using the SMTP/NNTP protocols. This field is always used in conjunction with smtpserver/nntpserver field.
smtpauthenticate nntpauthenticate	Used to identify the authentication process, if any, when sending or posting messages using the SMTP/NNTP protocols.
hardlinklist	Contains the URLs to public folders in which to post a message when using Exchange. This property is multivalued, but currently only one URL can be specified.
urlproxyserver	Indicates the proxy server and port used to access external network resources.
timezoneid	(urn:schemas:calendar: namespace) Defines the time zone used to format Date (DATE) values returned by the Message object. This property is set using the CdoTimeZoneId enumeration.
languagecode	Determines what locale identifier is used when localizing message response text. This text can automatically be included in the Message object generated by IMessage.Reply, IMessage.ReplyAll, IMessage.Forward, and IMessage.PostReply. This behavior is controlled using the usemessageresponsetext field in the Configuration object.
usemessageresponsetext	Used to control whether or not message response text is added automatically within messages created using the IMessage.Reply, IMessage.ReplyAll, IMessage.Forward, and IMessage.PostReply methods. The response text is localized using the locale identified by the languagecode configuration field.

The CDO component provides string constants (in this case, cdoSMTPServerPort) that you can use in your program to identify properties and avoid typographical errors. By using the constant instead of the actual string, you can also take advantage of the syntax auto-complete function that is included in Microsoft Visual Studio.

CDO Messaging and ADO

CDO for Exchange integrates with ADO 2.5 objects to provide a consistent interface for accessing item data in the Web Storage System. CDO objects are similar to ADO objects. Like ADO Record and Recordset objects, the Message, CalendarMessage, BodyPart, and CalendarPart objects expose a Fields collection and a way to access an item's stream. CDO objects facilitate binding to Web Storage System items through the CDO IDataSource interface Open, SaveTo, and SaveToContainer methods.

[C++, IDL] The CDO objects listed in the previous section also implement the OLE DB CoType TRow interfaces. You can use this set of interfaces on the CDO object as if it were an instance of an OLE DB Row object. For example, you may write a set of high-performance functions in C++ that operate using a passed IRow interface. If you have a CDO object such as a Message or BodyPart object, it is not necessary to create a separate OLE DB Row object to pass to the function. Instead, you can pass the IRow interface on to the CDO object. If necessary, the function can always determine whether the object is a CDO object by calling QueryInterface for some CDO-specific interface such as IDataSource or IMessage.

The CDO Message and CalendarMessage objects can bind directly to other objects by using the IDataSource.OpenObject and IDataSource.SaveToObject methods. The types of objects you should bind to include the following:

- ADO Record and Stream objects that are possibly bound to items in the Web Storage System that have a messaging content class. Use the CalendarMessage object to bind objects that have at least the content class urn:content-classes:calendarmessage, or some class derived from this class. Use the Message object to bind objects that have at least the content class urn:content-classes:message or some class derived from this class. You bind the CDO object to these ADO objects using either the _Record or Stream interface.
- OLE DB Row and Stream objects that are bound to items in the Web Storage System. You bind the CDO object to these OLE DB objects using either the IRow or IStream interface, respectively.
- CDO BodyPart and Item objects. You embed messages by saving them to a BodyPart object in another Message object's BodyPart hierarchy. You bind to these objects using either the IBodyPart or IItem interface, respectively.

An example of binding a CDO object to an ADO or OLE DB object is when you are writing a synchronous Web Storage System event sink. When an event occurs, the sink is passed a reference to an OLE DB/ADO object containing the triggering item. If the triggering item is a message, you can bind a CDO message object to the object to examine and manipulate it.

When to Use CDO or ADO for Messaging

You can use both CDO and ADO objects to send messages. Use the guidelines described here to decide when to use CDO or ADO objects in your messaging applications.

Use ADO objects to do the following:

- Identify items in the Web Storage System that are types of messages.
- Search folders and folder hierarchies for messages.
- Set custom properties for messages when the messaging properties are not to be altered.

Use CDO objects to do the following:

- Create any kind of new message items.
- Send messages in applications that run on the server.
- Modify an existing message item, including any associated messaging properties.
- Synchronize a messaging item's properties and stream if they are out of synchronization.

If you bind an item in the Web Storage System using an ADO object, and later you require use of a CDO Message or CalendarMessage object, bind the CDO object to the ADO object using the IDataSource.OpenObject or IDataSource.SaveToObject methods. You do not need to rebind the CDO object to the item in the Web Storage System to access and modify the item's contents.

In some cases, you must bind a CDO Message object to a Record object. For example, if you create a Web Storage System OnSyncSave event sink, the item causing the event to run is not committed to the Web Storage System when the sink executes. However, the sink passes a reference to an ADO Record object that represents the item in memory. If the item represents a message, create an instance of the Message COM class and bind it to the Record object using the IDataSource.OpenObject method. After you modify the content using the Message object, call IDataSource.Save to commit the changes back to the Record object.

[C++, IDL] If you write a Web Storage System event sink using C++, and you plan to use the OLE DB interfaces rather than the ADO interfaces, you can bind the item using the IDataSource.OpenObject method. Pass the IRow interface to the method to bind the CDO object to the OLE DB Row object housing the item data in memory.

SEVEN

Calendaring and Contacts

Calendaring is the process of creating and maintaining appointments and meetings. Appointments and meetings are stored in calendars, which are folders in the Web Storage System. An appointment represents an activity that takes place on a particular date and at a specific time. A meeting is an appointment that involves more than one individual.

You can use calendaring with Microsoft Exchange 2000 Server to:

- Create single or recurring appointments.
- Send requests to others to invite them to a meeting.
- Check when others are free or busy.
- Schedule the use of conference rooms and other resources.

Exchange 2000 Server provides a calendar for each mailbox. In addition, appointments and meetings can be placed in public folders for group calendars.

Appointments and meetings typically have a start time and an end time. Recurring appointments and meetings have multiple instances that follow a pattern. For example, you can schedule meetings that always occur at 10:00 A.M. on the first Monday of each month.

Meeting requests are sent out to invite attendees to participate in a meeting. The person sending the meeting request is called the organizer. Meeting requests are a special type of message. An attendee can respond to a meeting request by accepting, tentatively accepting, or declining. Meeting responses are also special types of messages. The organizer's copy of the meeting maintains a list of attendees and their responses.

If you send a meeting request, and later you want to make changes to the meeting, you can send an update to the attendees. As the meeting organizer, you can cancel the meeting and send a message to inform the attendees of the cancellation. Attendees cannot cancel a meeting; however, they can decline a meeting that they have already accepted.

Instead of inviting attendees to a meeting, you can publish an appointment. For example, you can send employees the list of company holidays. A published appointment has no attendees.

Finally, appointment and meeting requests can have attachments. When you send a meeting request, the attachment is sent as part of the message. An attachment can be almost anything, for example, a map showing a meeting location.

This topic covers the following information:

- Calendars in Exchange 2000 Server
- Calendars on the Internet
- The Calendar Object Model
- Time Zones

Calendars in Exchange 2000 Server

In Microsoft Exchange 2000 Server, each mailbox usually has an associated calendar folder. However, when you first create a mailbox, it does not have an associated calendar folder. The calendar folder is created in one of the following ways:

- Microsoft Outlook creates a calendar folder the first time it accesses a mailbox.
- Exchange 2000 Server creates a calendar folder the first time it delivers a message to a mailbox.

You can view your calendar by using Outlook, Outlook Web Access, applications that use CDO, or any combination of the three. Exchange 2000 Server can also store appointments in public folders; typically this is done for team or project schedules.

Calendars on the Internet

New Internet standards enable you to send meeting requests to users who have various calendaring systems. The iCalendar specification (RFC 2445) defines the format of calendar information sent between calendar user agents. Calendar user agents (CUAs) are client programs such as Microsoft Outlook. You can use CDO to send calendar information to any CUA that complies with the iCalendar specification.

CDO also creates a plain-text representation of calendar messages. When you send a meeting request or response to users who do not have an iCalendar-compliant email client, they see the plain-text version of the meeting, including the start and end times, location, subject, and meeting description.

Microsoft Exchange 2000 Server supports the iCalendar specification as an interchange format. Exchange 2000 automatically converts calendar information to the correct format for client programs, including CDO, Outlook, and Schedule+.

iCalendar information is transported across the Internet formatted as MIME. The MIME body part containing iCalendar information has a content type of text/calendar. The following example shows a typical iCalendar meeting request:

```
X-Receiver: someone@microsoft.com
X-Receiver: another@microsoft.com
X-Sender: user12@exchange.microsoft.com
thread-index: Ab76K9YbzaPyz4RUTJWwZL3wQ+HxyA==
Content-Class: urn:content-classes:calendarmessage
From: <user12@exchange.microsoft.com>
Sender: <user12@exchange.microsoft.com>
To: <someone@microsoft.com>
Cc: <another@microsoft.com>
Subject: Documentation Review Meeting
Date: Wed, 8 Sep 1999 11:56:19 -0700
Message-ID:
<000201befa2b$d62c2e70$79b41eac@exchange.microsoft.com>
MIME-Version: 1.0
Content-Type: multipart/alternative;
    boundary="----=_NextPart_000_0003_01BEF9F1.29D23870"
Content-Transfer-Encoding: 7bit
X-Mailer: Microsoft CDO for Exchange Server
X-MimeOLE: Produced By Microsoft MimeOLE V5.00.2919.5500

This is a multi-part message in MIME format.

------=_NextPart_000_0003_01BEF9F1.29D23870
Content-Type: text/plain;
    charset="us-ascii"
Content-Transfer-Encoding: 7bit

Type         : Single Meeting
Organizer    : MAILTO:user12@exchange.microsoft.com
Start Time   : 09/09/1999 10:00
End Time     : 09/09/1999 11:30
Time Zone    : Local time
Location     : Executive Conference Room

*~*~*~*~*~*~*~*~*~*

------=_NextPart_000_0003_01BEF9F1.29D23870
Content-Class: urn:content-classes:calendarmessage
```

```
Content-Type: text/calendar;
   method=REQUEST;
   charset="utf-8"
Content-Transfer-Encoding: 7bit

BEGIN:VCALENDAR
METHOD:REQUEST
PRODID:Microsoft CDO for Microsoft Exchange
VERSION:2.0
BEGIN:VEVENT
DTSTAMP:19990908T185620Z
DTSTART:19990909T100000
SUMMARY:Documentation Review Meeting
UID:{A6DEF157-DFCE-40F4-AC77-217563191E7B}
ATTENDEE;ROLE=REQ-PARTICIPANT;PARTSTAT=NEEDS-
ACTION;RSVP=TRUE:MAILTO:someone@microsoft.com
ATTENDEE;ROLE=OPT-PARTICIPANT;PARTSTAT=NEEDS-
ACTION;RSVP=TRUE:MAILTO:another@microsoft.com
ORGANIZER;ROLE=REQ-
PARTICIPANT;PARTSTAT=ACCEPTED;RSVP=TRUE:MAILTO:
user12@exchange.microsoft.com
LOCATION:Executive Conference Room
DTEND:19990909T113000
SEQUENCE:0
PRIORITY:5
CLASS:Personal
CREATED:19990908T185620Z
LAST-MODIFIED:19990908T185620Z
STATUS:CONFIRMED
TRANSP:OPAQUE
X-MICROSOFT-CDO-BUSYSTATUS:BUSY
X-MICROSOFT-CDO-INSTTYPE:0
END:VEVENT
END:VCALENDAR

------=_NextPart_000_0003_01BEF9F1.29D23870--
```

For more information on the iCalendar format, see RFC 2445 in the SDK.

The Calendar Object Model

CDO objects provide the necessary logic to work with appointments, meetings, messages, and other calendaring items. These objects make it easier for you to write calendaring applications. For an overview diagram, see "CDO for Exchange 2000 Server objects" in the SDK.

In CDO, the Appointment object represents appointments and meetings. Meetings have attendees, each represented by an Attendee object in the Attendees collection.

Recurring appointments and meetings are those that occur more than once and follow a pattern. A pattern is defined by using one or more RecurrencePattern objects in the Appointment object's RecurrencePatterns collection. The Exception objects in the Exceptions collection define modifications to the pattern.

You invite attendees to a meeting and attendees respond to the invitation by using messages represented by CalendarMessage objects. These messages are also used to update or cancel an existing appointment. The CalendarMessage object exposes the IMessage interface; therefore, a calendar message has all of the capabilities of any other CDO message.

The CalendarMessage object encapsulates information about one or more appointments in CalendarPart objects in the CalendarParts collection. When you process calendar messages, you extract the Appointment objects from the CalendarPart objects.

Appointment objects can have attachments. Each attachment is a BodyPart object in the appointment's Attachments collection.

Microsoft Exchange 2000 Server stores the free or busy status of each calendar user in a special public folder. You can use the Addressee object to verify user names in the directory and to get a user's free or busy status.

The Configuration object stores information, such as the location of the user's calendar folder and the identity of the user. In general, you need to associate a Configuration object with each Appointment and CalendarMessage object.

Time Zones

Appointments are stored in the Microsoft Web Storage System and are based on coordinated universal time (UTC). When you view an appointment, you need to convert the appointment to local time. Clients such as Microsoft Outlook automatically convert appointments to the local time of the client computer.

CDO automatically converts date and time values in the properties of CDO objects to local time. CDO does this based on the time-zone information in the corresponding CDO Configuration object. When you save an appointment or create a calendar message, CDO converts the local time specified in the StartTime and EndTime properties of the Appointment object to UTC, based on the time-zone information in the Configuration object. When CDO expands recurring appointments into individual instances, it uses the time-zone information from the Appointment object.

Date and time values in the Fields collection and in the stream of CDO objects are converted to local time. This is done by using the time-zone information from the Configuration object. By default, the CDO Appointment and Configuration objects use the system time-zone value from the computer that is running CDO.

For example, you are in Brussels (UTC + 1:00 hour) and you want to schedule a telephone conference with colleagues in Bangkok (UTC + 7:00 hours). You create a meeting for 9:00 a.m. local time and send a meeting request. The appointment is stored in Microsoft Exchange 2000 Server as 08:00:00 UTC. When your colleagues in Bangkok view the appointment, their calendar client programs convert UTC to local time and display the start time as 3:00 p.m.

You can also create floating appointments. Floating appointments are appointments that are not adjusted for time zones. For example, you may want to have an appointment on your calendar for lunch every day from 12:00 noon to 1:00 p.m., regardless of the time zone. You would not want lunch to convert from noon to 6:00 p.m. when you travel from Brussels to Bangkok.

Specifying the Time Zone

CDO offers two ways to specify the local time zone: the timezoneid field and the timezone field. The urn:schemas:calendar:timezoneid field uses the values from the CdoTimeZoneId enumeration. These values correspond to the Microsoft Win32 time-zone values that are used by the operating system. This field is easy to work with and should be sufficient for most applications.

The urn:schemas:calendar:timezone field provides greater flexibility, but is more complicated to use. You can use this field to specify a time zone that is not included in the CdoTimeZoneId enumeration.

The urn:schemas:calendar:timezone field is a string that contains a VTIMEZONE block, as defined by the iCalendar standard. If this field is specified, the urn:schemas:calendar:timezoneid field is ignored.

Both the Configuration object and the Appointment object have the urn:schemas:calendar:timezoneid and urn:schemas:calendar:timezone fields. CDO does not set the time zone of the Appointment object from the Configuration time zone.

The example that follows shows how to create a custom time zone by using the urn:schemas:calendar:timezone field. This example creates a time zone that is the same as the United States and Canada, Pacific Time:

[Visual Basic]

```
Dim Config As New CDO.Configuration
Dim timezone As String

timezone = timezone & "BEGIN:VTIMEZONE" & vbCrLf
timezone = timezone & "TZID:Same as Pacific" & vbCrLf
timezone = timezone & "BEGIN:STANDARD" & vbCrLf
timezone = timezone & "DTSTART:16010101T020000" & vbCrLf
timezone = timezone & "TZOFFSETFROM:-0700" & vbCrLf
timezone = timezone & "TZOFFSETTO:-0800" & vbCrLf
timezone = timezone &
"RRULE:FREQ=YEARLY;WKST=MO;INTERVAL=1;BYMONTH=10;BYDAY=-1SU" & vbCrLf
timezone = timezone & "END:STANDARD" & vbCrLf
timezone = timezone & "BEGIN:DAYLIGHT" & vbCrLf
timezone = timezone & "DTSTART:16010101T020000" & vbCrLf
timezone = timezone & "TZOFFSETFROM:-0800" & vbCrLf
timezone = timezone & "TZOFFSETTO:-0700" & vbCrLf
timezone = timezone &
"RRULE:FREQ=YEARLY;WKST=MO;INTERVAL=1;BYMONTH=4;BYDAY=1SU"
& vbCrLf
timezone = timezone & "END:DAYLIGHT" & vbCrLf
timezone = timezone & "END:VTIMEZONE" & vbCrLf

Config.Fields(cdoTimeZoneURN) = timezone
Config.Fields.Update
```

Making Time Zones Work with Outlook

Outlook converts appointments from UTC to the local time of the computer running Outlook when it displays them from the Web Storage System. Conversely, Outlook converts appointments from local time to UTC when it saves them in the Web Storage System. As long as appointments are saved with the correct local time zone, they are displayed correctly by Outlook.

Outlook does not support floating appointments. Outlook interprets floating appointments as UTC. For example, a floating appointment with a start time of 1:00 p.m. is displayed by Outlook as 6:00 a.m in Bangkok (UTC + 7:00 hours).

Using Recurring Appointments with Time Zones

When a recurring appointment spans standard time and daylight savings time, CDO automatically adjusts the individual appointment instances. For example, you have scheduled meetings to occur each Monday at 2:00 p.m. for an entire year. When you view any instance of the meeting during the year, the adjusted time is 2:00 p.m. The UTC value in the Web Storage System varies plus or minus the daylight savings offset, so that when the local time conversion is made, the resulting value is still 2:00 p.m.

CDO uses the time-zone information from the Appointment object when expanding recurring appointments. Start and end times are automatically adjusted for standard time and daylight savings time.

Time Zone to CdoTimeZoneId Map

Table 7–1 lists the mapping of time zones presented by the Microsoft Windows operating system and the corresponding CdoTimeZoneId enumerated values.

TABLE 7–1 *Time Zone to CdoTimeZoneId map*

Time zone	CdoTimeZoneId Enum	Value
(GMT) Casablanca, Monrovia	cdoMonrovia	31
(GMT) Greenwich Mean Time: Dublin, Edinburgh, Lisbon, London	cdoLisbon	2
(GMT+01:00) Amsterdam, Berlin, Bern, Rome, Stockholm, Vienna	cdoBerlin	4
(GMT+01:00) Belgrade, Bratislava, Budapest, Ljubljana, Prague	cdoPrague	6
(GMT+01:00) Brussels, Copenhagen, Madrid, Paris	cdoParis	3
(GMT+01:00) Sarajevo, Skopje, Sofija, Vilnius, Warsaw, Zagreb	(None)	(None)
(GMT+01:00) West Central Africa	(None)	(None)
(GMT+02:00) Athens, Istanbul, Minsk	cdoAthens	7
(GMT+02:00) Bucharest	cdoEasternEurope	5
(GMT+02:00) Cairo	cdoCairo	49
(GMT+02:00) Harare, Pretoria	cdoHarare	50
(GMT+02:00) Helsinki, Riga, Tallinn	(None)	(None)
(GMT+02:00) Jerusalem	cdoIsrael	27
(GMT+03:00) Baghdad	cdoBaghdad	26

TABLE 7-1 *Time Zone to CdoTimeZoneId map (continued)*

Time zone	CdoTimeZoneId Enum	Value
(GMT+03:00) Kuwait, Riyadh	(None)	(None)
(GMT+03:00) Moscow, St. Petersburg, Volgograd	cdoMoscow	51
(GMT+03:00) Nairobi	(None)	(None)
(GMT+03:30) Tehran	cdoTehran	25
(GMT+04:00) Abu Dhabi, Muscat	cdoAbuDhabi	24
(GMT+04:00) Baku, Tbilisi, Yerevan	(None)	(None)
(GMT+04:30) Kabul	cdoKabul	48
(GMT+05:00) Ekaterinburg	(None)	(None)
(GMT+05:00) Islamabad, Karachi, Tashkent	cdoIslamabad	47
(GMT+05:30) Calcutta, Chennai, Mumbai, New Delhi	cdoBombay	23
(GMT+05:45) Kathmandu	(None)	(None)
(GMT+06:00) Almaty, Novosibirsk	cdoAlmaty	46
(GMT+06:00) Astana, Dhaka	(None)	(None)
(GMT+06:00) Sri Jayawardenepura	(None)	(None)
(GMT+06:30) Rangoon	(None)	(None)
(GMT+07:00) Bangkok, Hanoi, Jakarta	cdoBangkok	22
(GMT+07:00) Krasnoyarsk	(None)	(None)
(GMT+08:00) Beijing, Chongqing, Hong Kong SAR, Urumqi	cdoBeijing	45
(GMT+08:00) Irkutsk, Ulaan Bataar	(None)	(None)
(GMT+08:00) Kuala Lumpur, Singapore	cdoHongKong	21
(GMT+08:00) Perth	(None)	(None)
(GMT+08:00) Taipei	(None)	(None)
(GMT+09:00) Osaka, Sapporo, Tokyo	cdoTokyo	20
(GMT+09:00) Seoul	(None)	(None)
(GMT+09:00) Yakutsk	(None)	(None)
(GMT+09:30) Adelaide	cdoAdelaide	19
(GMT+09:30) Darwin	cdoDarwin	44
(GMT+10:00) Brisbane	cdoBrisbane	18
(GMT+10:00) Canberra, Melbourne, Sydney	(None)	(None)
(GMT+10:00) Guam, Port Moresby	cdoGuam	43
(GMT+10:00) Hobart	cdoHobart	42
(GMT+10:00) Vladivostok	(None)	(None)

TABLE 7-1 *Time Zone to CdoTimeZoneId map (continued)*

Time zone	CdoTimeZoneId Enum	Value
(GMT+11:00) Magadan, Solomon Is., New Caledonia	cdoMagadan	41
(GMT+12:00) Auckland, Wellington	cdoWellington	17
(GMT+12:00) Fiji, Kamchatka, Marshall Is.	cdoFiji	40
(GMT+13:00) Nuku'alofa	(None)	(None)
(GMT-01:00) Azores	cdoAzores	29
(GMT-01:00) Cape Verde Is.	(None)	(None)
(GMT-02:00) Mid-Atlantic	cdoMidAtlantic	30
(GMT-03:00) Brasilia	cdoBrasilia	8
(GMT-03:00) Buenos Aires, Georgetown	cdoBuenosAires	32
(GMT-03:00) Greenland	(None)	(None)
(GMT-03:30) Newfoundland	cdoNewfoundland	28
(GMT-04:00) Atlantic Time (Canada)	cdoAtlanticCanada	9
(GMT-04:00) Caracas, La Paz	cdoCaracas	33
(GMT-04:00) Santiago	(None)	(None)
(GMT-05:00) Bogota, Lima, Quito	cdoBogota	35
(GMT-05:00) Eastern Time (US and Canada)	cdoEastern	10
(GMT-05:00) Indiana (East)	cdoIndiana	34
(GMT-06:00) Central America	cdoCentral	11
(GMT-06:00) Central Time (US and Canada)	(None)	(None)
(GMT-06:00) Mexico City	cdoMexicoCity	37
(GMT-06:00) Saskatchewan	cdoSaskatchewan	36
(GMT-07:00) Arizona	cdoArizona	38
(GMT-07:00) Mountain Time (US and Canada)	cdoMountain	12
(GMT-08:00) Pacific Time (US and Canada); Tijuana	cdoPacific	13
(GMT-09:00) Alaska	cdoAlaska	14
(GMT-10:00) Hawaii	cdoHawaii	15
(GMT-11:00) Midway Island, Samoa	cdoMidwayIsland	16
(GMT-12:00) Eniwetok, Kwajalein	cdoEniwetok	39

Contacts

Contacts are collections of information about a person or business, such as phone numbers, email addresses, and pager numbers. You can store contact information in the Microsoft Web Storage System, Microsoft Windows 2000 Active Directory, or both.

Some of the benefits of using contacts with Microsoft Exchange 2000 Server are as follows:

- The CDO Person object enables faster development by creating and managing contact information stored in the Web Storage System and Active Directory.
- The CDO Person object enables easy conversion of contact information into the Internet-industry VCARD format.
- The software offers predefined Web Storage System schema.
- Contact information may be manipulated through the CDO Person object and Microsoft Outlook.

Working with the CDO Person Object

The CDO Person object defines methods and properties for managing contact items in the Web Storage System or Active Directory. Contacts that exist in Active Directory can be saved to the Web Storage System and, conversely, from the Web Storage System to Active Directory. CDO handles the underlying information that maps between ADSI and a schema in the Web Storage System.

The CDO Person Object has the Person COM class that represents a single person who might have a mailbox in the Web Storage System. The IPerson interface contains a comprehensive set of personal and business information properties that can be set and retrieved programmatically.

The IPerson interface contains a Fields property that provides access to a Microsoft ADO Fields collection of contact-related schema fields. These fields provide additional settings, such as BusinessHomePage, that are not CDO properties.

For compatibility with other contact and personal information managers (PIM) programs, the IPerson interface contains the GetVCardStream method for saving contact information to a file in a VCARD-compliant MIME format.

The DataSource property provides access to the IDataSource interface on contact items for saving and opening contact items to and from the Web Storage System or Active Directory. Script users can use the GetInterface method to access the IDataSource interface.

EIGHT

Workflow

Workflow is an application that models a business process. CDO Workflow is built-in functionality provided with Microsoft Exchange 2000 Server. It enables you to design workflow applications without having to write the fundamental code that accesses, modifies, and controls data. CDO Workflow for Exchange 2000 Server includes a workflow engine, modeling tools, and an event sink.

This chapter discusses the following topics:

- Workflow Overview
- Using Built-in Workflow Functionality
- Creating Workflow Event Sinks and Tools
- Workflow Security Modes
- Managing Workflow Deployment
- Testing and Debugging Workflow Applications

Workflow Overview

The term workflow describes applications that are modeled on business processes, such as an expense report approval system. Typical workflow applications include the following:

- Forms routing and approval
- Document review and publishing
- Issue tracking

You could write these kinds of applications from scratch in almost any programming language, but you can simplify the task by using the built-in workflow engine and specialized workflow modeling tools provided with Exchange 2000 Server.

Modeling tools enable you to specify the overall design or flow of a business processing a simple, high-level representation called a process definition. In an expense report, for example, you could define a process in which reports totaling less than $50 are routed directly to your accounting department, whereas reports equal to or greater than $50 are routed to a manager for approval.

The modeling tools enable you to define the various states of the document—for example, submitted, needs approval, or approved. You define transitions between states by using actions in VBScript. You can easily modify or extend the process definition without rewriting all of the fundamental application code.

You use the tool to associate the process definition with a folder. When anything happens in the folder, the Workflow Event Sink calls the workflow engine, which runs your application. The workflow engine executes and manages individual instances of a process definition; these are also called process instances.

CDO Workflow objects for Microsoft Exchange provide a built-in workflow engine and an object model for programming that engine. You can create process definitions, which consist of a table of actions or rules that define the business process. Table 8–1 shows a single, simplified row from an action table.

Table 8–1 *Simplified Row from an Action Table*

Row ID	Caption	State	NewState	EventType	Condition	Action
"1"	"Create"	""	"Submitted"	"OnCreate"	"IsValidExpenseForm()"	"CheckDollarAmount"

The workflow engine evaluates the process definition to see which actions it needs to run. Next, it executes scripts or COM objects to perform application-specific business logic.

CDO Workflow Event Sink makes it easier for you to integrate workflow into existing applications. For example, you can register the event sink in a folder, where the event sink intercepts all changes made in that folder, and it automatically calls the workflow engine on the application's behalf. If you have existing applications in that folder, they continue to create, modify, or delete items. The event sink also connects to the system timer events to automate expiring items, overdue work, or other cleanup tasks. The event sink works well in scenarios in which users are creating or editing documents using off-the-shelf applications such as Microsoft Word or Microsoft Excel.

CDO Workflow applications build on the Microsoft Web Storage System architecture and they must run on a server running Exchange 2000 Server. You install workflow applications into either a public folder or a private Inbox folder. You register the Workflow Event Sink in folders that you own. Server administrators must determine the following for each server:

- Who is authorized to register workflows on that computer?
- Who might write unlimited workflow scripts as opposed to "sandboxed" workflow scripts?

Some earlier versions of Microsoft Exchange Server (5.5 with Service Pack 1 and later) included Routing Objects libraries, which are helper objects for building simple document routing applications. Whereas Routing Objects are in some ways similar to the new CDO Workflow objects, they were designed only for MAPI-based email routing applications and don't take advantage of the new Web Storage System features. Exchange 2000 Server is still compatible with existing MAPI applications, including Routing Objects. If you want to build a routing application that runs on both Exchange Server 5.5 and Exchange 2000 Server, you use MAPI and the Routing Objects libraries. If you want to write Web-based workflow applications or use new Web Storage System features, you should use Exchange 2000 Server and CDO Workflow objects.

Using Built-In Workflow Functionality

Workflow application developers should have a working knowledge of VBScript. They can use VBScript with the Exchange Workflow Designer and built-in CDO Workflow functionality to create workflow applications. The built-in functionality includes the workflow engine and workflow event sink. These are installed by default with Exchange 2000 Server.

Microsoft also provides a GUI application tool called Microsoft Workflow Designer for Exchange 2000 Server. This tool can be installed on the server or on a client computer. Use Exchange Workflow Designer to create workflow applications that take advantage of built-in workflow functionality. For detailed information on how to use Exchange Workflow Designer, see the "Exchange Workflow Designer Help," in the MS Exchange SDK.

Before using Exchange Workflow Designer, you need to do the following:

1. Get workflow registration privileges. You need to be a member of the Can register workflow role of the workflow event sink COM+ package.

2. Get workflow author privileges. You can have either a restricted or a privileged workflow author role. To have a restricted role, there's nothing you need to do. To have a privileged author role, you must be added to the COM+ role for the workflow event sink.

3. Create a new public folder. You need to be the folder owner to run Exchange Workflow Designer on the folder.

After you have installed Exchange Workflow Designer, established yourself as a workflow author and registrar and created a new folder for your workflow design, you can use VBScript to associate your business logic with events in your folder, such as creating an item, changing an item, or deleting an item.

The following topics provide an overview of Exchange Workflow Designer and of workflow objects:

- Modeling Business Processes
- Developing Typical Workflow Applications

Modeling Business Processes

Microsoft Workflow Designer for Exchange 2000 Server is a tool for constructing a diagram that is translated by the tool into an ActionTable. It provides workflow authors with a visual tool for creating their own ProcessDefinition logic. You can use Exchange Workflow Designer to do the following:

- Model the workflow logic.
- Add script actions and conditions to the logic.
- Save the ProcessDefinition in a workflow folder.

Figure 8–1 shows the default process when you start Exchange Workflow Designer.

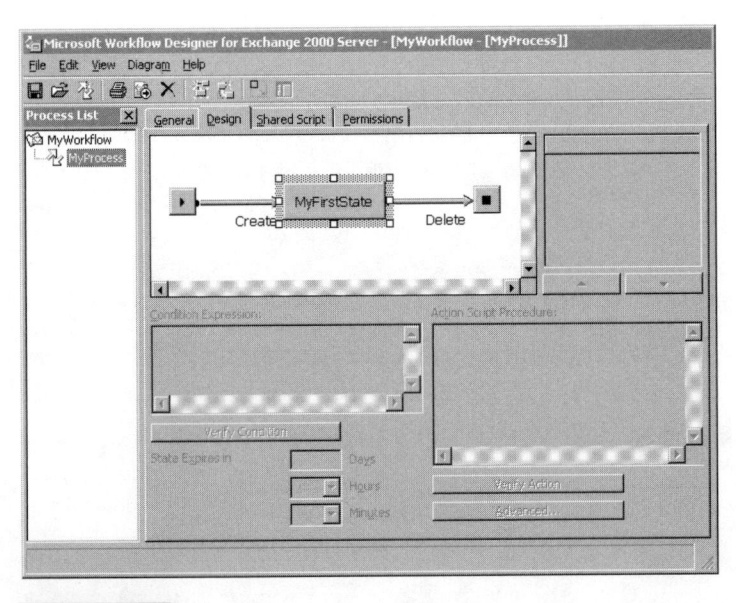

FIGURE 8–1 *Exchange Workflow Designer*

Developing Typical Workflow Applications

Exchange 2000 Server workflow components include the workflow engine and workflow event sink. The engine and event sink create the run-time objects that implement your design and provide your script with the correct data. You can use the WorkflowSession object in condition and action scripts that you add with Exchange Workflow Designer. The WorkflowSession object is the staple of the typical application developer. Its properties expose the functionality of the IAuditTrail, ISessionProps, IMembers, and IWorkflowMessage interfaces.

WorkflowSession Object

The workflow engine passes this intrinsic object to the script host environment. The WorkflowSession object provides the following functionality to your script:

- A Fields collection representing the ProcessInstance that is undergoing transition. Your scripts can modify this row to create desirable side effects for a state transition. For instance, new contact information gets saved in a folder, so your script adds sales region ID and regional manager ID fields to the row and inserts data into those fields.
- Write access to the AuditTrail. Your script can pass errors and other information back to the WorkflowSession object that is logged by your audit trail provider. An audit trail provider is any registered COM object that implements the IAuditTrail interface.
- A method for sending and tracking email notifications and responses associated with a specific ProcessInstance in its TrackingTable property. This property returns a recordset. Your script can use the recordset to tabulate responses or work with custom form data.
- The ability to control item-level security of the item undergoing transition. The WorkflowSession object exposes the ItemReaders and ItemAuthors collections. Your scripts can modify these collections to give readers and authors exclusive privileges to documents.
- Run-time environment information such as the names of the domain and server that Workflow is running on and the context of the user who triggered the workflow transition.

You can see a graphical representation of the WorkflowSession object model in CDO for Workflow Objects.

AuditTrailEventLog Object

You can access the audit trail using the IWorkflowSession object by calling AddAuditEntry. Microsoft provides the AuditTrailEventLog coclass with the workflow components. This is a sample provider that you can use to write to the application log in Event Viewer. Exchange Workflow Designer uses this provider by default. Advanced developers can develop providers by implementing the IAuditTrail interface.

WorkflowMessage Object

The WorkflowMessage object provides several useful email features for workflow applications. Using this object, you can:

- Send email in restricted mode, which prevents object instantiation.
- Track responses to workflow emails.
- Make workflow emails part of the workflow transaction so that a "send" is aborted if the transaction fails.

A WorkflowMessage object is not cocreatable; you access its functionality through the WorkflowSession object. The WorkflowSession object provides the GetNewWorkflowMessage method for sending email notifications. The IWorkflowMessage interface contains a subset of the IMessage interface and adds one unique method—SendWorkflowMessage.

Creating Workflow Event Sinks and Tools

Advanced developers may want to create their own event sink or designer tool. If you are an advanced developer, you can use the interfaces provided by the CDO Workflow objects to make direct calls to the workflow engine; you can also design workflow processes.

To use the engine with your event sink or designer tool, you should be familiar with how the workflow engine operates. The following topics describe how the workflow engine controls the current state of a document in a workflow:

- Developing Advanced Workflow Applications
- Application Architecture
- Workflow Components
- Workflow Variations
- Workflow Process Definition
- Workflow Security

Developing Advanced Workflow Applications

You can develop your own workflow applications by making direct calls to the ProcessDefinition object. You can use ADO, OLE DB, or WebDAV to create the necessary data bindings.

To develop a workflow application using any language that supports COM:

1. Define an action table.
2. Develop script functions or custom COM objects to represent your business logic.
3. Create a ProcessDefinition.
4. Register the workflow event sink in the workflow folder.

The first three steps constitute your workflow design. In the final step, you save your workflow design as an item in a public folder and create an association between the workflow event sink and synchronous Web Storage System events.

Defining an ActionTable

The ActionTable encapsulates the logic of your design. You define the ActionTable by laying out the rules for documents that are saved or posted in the specified folder. A rule tells the workflow engine, "If a document is in a given state and a given condition is true, then execute the given action." Each row in the table addresses a combination of state, condition, and action. The ActionTable schema includes 14 properties that are explained in IProcessDefinition Interface.

Developing Script Functions

ActionTable fields include Condition, Action, and CompensatingAction. You can include script functions within these fields of the ActionTable, and you can have a reference to a CommonScript function in any of these fields. You can declare the CommonScript as a separate item or include it as the default stream of the ProcessDefinition item.

If you are a privileged workflow author, you can use a COM object as a Condition, Action, or CompensatingAction, in which case the ActionTable contains the ProgID for your COM object in the respective field(s). The ActionTable requires you to set flags indicating whether conditions and actions contain COM objects or script.

Creating a ProcessDefinition

After you have created the two critical pieces of your workflow design—the ActionTable and the CommonScript—you can associate them with a ProcessDefinition object. You can then set other important properties of your design, such as:

- The security mode under which you want the process to execute (Mode).
- The logging tool you want to use for monitoring and debugging your design (AuditTrailProvider).

After you set the ProcessDefinition properties, you save it as an item in the workflow folder by using its DataSource property. You can also use the ADO Fields collection with the Web Storage System schema property names to set these values. If you have physical access to the server, you can use CDO Workflow interfaces to set these properties. For remote scenarios, you need to use ADO.

Registering the Workflow Event Sink

The workflow event sink handles OnSyncSave, OnSyncDelete, and OnTimer events in any Microsoft Web Storage System folder where it is registered. When a user saves or deletes an item in a folder, an event occurs. When the event occurs in a folder, the Web Storage System process looks for an event registration item in the folder. The registration item tells the Web Storage System which process handles the event. You need to tell the Web Storage System that you want the workflow event sink process to handle **OnSyncSave**, **OnSyncDelete**, and **OnTimer** events in your folder. This is called registering the workflow event sink in a folder.

The following rules govern the registration of an event sink:

- The event type must be one of the three supported types: OnSyncSave, OnSyncDelete, or OnTimer.
- The user who registers the workflow must be a member of the Can Register Workflow role. The "Deployment" topic in the MS Exchange explains how to do this.
- You cannot set the MatchScope Field of the registration to ANY.
- You cannot register the event sink for a synchronous event with DEEP **MatchScope Field** if it is already registered in a subfolder of the same folder.
- You cannot register the event sink in a folder where it is already registered by a DEEP **MatchScope Field** registration in a parent folder.
- When you set the **OnTimer** interval, it should not be smaller than necessary, because the **OnTimer** event occurs for every workflow folder on the server.
- **OnTimer** events can have DEEP **MatchScope Field** only on a public folder tree that you create. DEEP **MatchScope Field** for **OnTimer** events is not supported in the default public folder tree.

The following code registers your workflow application folder for the **OnTimer** system event, the **OnSyncSave** store event, and the **OnSyncDelete** store event. In this example, the **OnTimer** event causes the workflow event sink to run every 15 minutes.

[Visual Basic]

```
Dim EventRuleItem As String
Dim sEvtRegURL As String
Dim ProcessDefinitionURL As String
```

Creating Workflow Event Sinks and Tools   171

```
'''''''''''''''''''Register OnTimer Event

  EventRuleItem = "OnTimerRule"

  sEvtRegURL = sFolderURL & EventRuleItem

  'The event registration item (sEvtRegURL) must be saved
  'in the folder for which you want to register
  'the workflow sink.

  Dim Rec As ADODB.Record
  Set Rec = New ADODB.Record

  Rec.Open sEvtRegURL, , adModeReadWrite, _
           adCreateNonCollection Or adCreateOverwrite, _
           adDelayFetchFields
If Err.Number <> 0 Then
  Debug.Print "Failed to open event registration record." &
Err.Description
  End If

  Dim Flds As ADODB.Fields
  With Rec
    Set Flds = .Fields
    Flds("DAV:contentclass") = "urn:content-
class:storeeventreg"
    Flds("http://schemas.microsoft.com/exchange/events/
EventMethod") = "OnTimer"
    Flds("http://schemas.microsoft.com/exchange/events/
SinkClass") = "CdoWfEvt.EventSink.1"
    Flds("http://schemas.microsoft.com/exchange/events/
TimerStartTime") = #5/1/1999#
    Flds("http://schemas.microsoft.com/exchange/events/
TimerInterval") = 720
    Flds("http://schemas.microsoft.com/exchange/events/
TimerExpiryTime") = #8/4/2000#
    Flds.Update
    .Close
  End With

'''''''''''''''''''Register OnSyncSave and OnSyncDelete
Events

  EventRuleItem - "OnSyncSave_OnSyncDelete_Rule"

  sEvtRegURL = sFolderURL & EventRuleItem

  ProcessDefinitionURL = sProcDefURL
```

```
Rec.Open sEvtRegURL, , adModeReadWrite, _
          adCreateNonCollection Or adCreateOverwrite, _
          adDelayFetchFields
  If Err.Number <> 0 Then
    Debug.Print "Failed to open event registration
record." & Err.Description
  End If

With Rec
  Set Flds = .Fields
Flds("DAV:contentclass") = "urn:content-
class:storeeventreg"
    Flds("http://schemas.microsoft.com/exchange/events/
EventMethod") = "OnSyncSave;OnSyncDelete"
    Flds("http://schemas.microsoft.com/exchange/events/
SinkClass") = "CdoWfEvt.EventSink.1"
    Flds("http://schemas.microsoft.com/exchange/events/
Criteria") = "WHERE $DAV:ishidden$ AND $DAV:iscollection$ =
FALSE"
    Flds("http://schemas.microsoft.com/cdo/workflow/
defaultprocdefinition") = ProcessDefinitionURL
    Flds("http://schemas.microsoft.com/cdo/workflow/
adhocflows") = 0
    Flds("http://schemas.microsoft.com/cdo/workflow/
enabledebug") = True
    Flds("http://schemas.microsoft.com/cdo/workflow/
disablesuccessentries") = False
    Flds.Update
    .Close
  End With
```

Calling IProcessInstance Advance

You can also develop your own workflow event sink for calling the workflow engine (Advance) directly, by using the IProcessInstance object. Use ADO, OLE DB, or WebDAV to create the necessary bindings.

At a minimum, your event sink must:

- Bind to the Web Storage System item that initiated the event.
- Open a ProcessInstance object on the item.
- Call the IProcessInstance member method Advance.
- Save the ProcessInstance item.

Application Architecture

A workflow application consists of forms and documents that a user manipulates; it also consists of tools on the server that manage those documents according to a predetermined set of rules. The application architecture includes two layers, which are discussed in the following topics:

- Presentation Layer
- Business Logic Layer

Presentation Layer

A workflow application includes forms or documents with which the user interacts directly. This layer is called the presentation layer of the application. The presentation layer could be a Microsoft Word document, a Web form, a Microsoft Outlook form, or some other type of presentation layer that you design. All of these things work because workflows are triggered by any save or post in the workflow folder and because the Web Storage System provides heterogeneous document storage. What you use as your presentation layer is up to you; it has no relationship to the functionality of CDO Workflow objects. The presentation layer, illustrated in Figure 8–2, is independent of CDO Workflow objects; it usually runs on a client computer.

Business Logic Layer

You use CDO Workflow objects to design and run workflow applications. These applications contain the business rules that govern your document approval and routing processes. Whereas the presentation layer usually runs on a separate client computer, the business rules run on the same server as the Web Storage System, where the target documents are stored. Your business logic or workflow layer, as seen in Figure 8–3, operates in a process separate from the Web Storage System process.

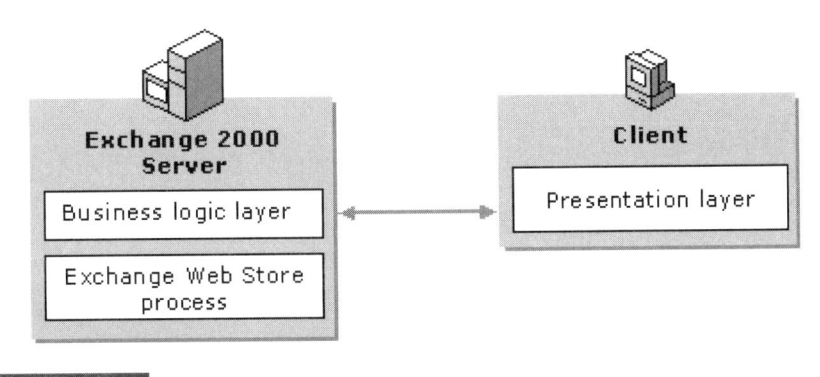

FIGURE 8–2   *The Presentation Layer*

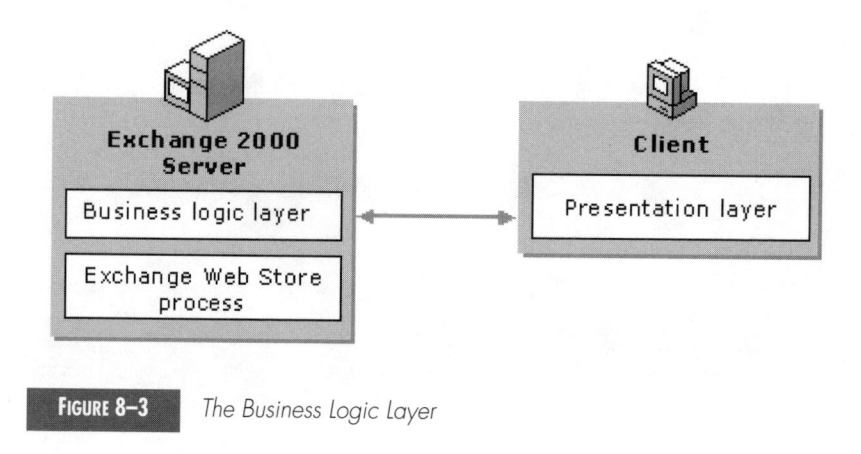

FIGURE 8–3 *The Business Logic Layer*

Workflow Components

Workflow components are installed automatically with Exchange 2000 Server. They include the workflow engine and the workflow event sink.

Workflow components (see Figure 8–4) run in the event sink host process. This process is separate from the Web Storage System process. The event sink host process includes the workflow event sink, the workflow engine, and the script host. The rest of this section focuses on the workflow engine and event sink, which make up the core functionality of a workflow application.

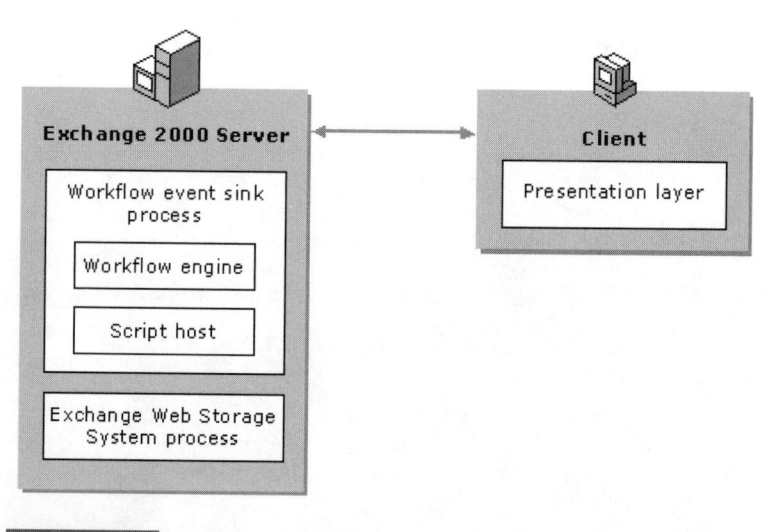

FIGURE 8–4 *Workflow component architecture*

WORKFLOW ENGINE

Exchange 2000 Server includes an in-process server (CDOWF.DLL) that implements the IProcessInstance Advance method, also known as the workflow engine. The workflow engine controls the state changes to documents in your workflow folder. The workflow event sink (CDOWFEVT.DLL) calls the engine when an event fires in your workflow folder.

The sequence diagram in Figure 8–5 shows the flow of information between the processes in the workflow run-time environment.

Application developers do not call the engine directly, unless they are writing their own event sink, advanced ASP application, or other middle-tier component. Event sinks, ASP applications, and middle-tier components can use the workflow engine by making direct calls to the IProcessInstance Advance method. The engine maintains document integrity based on the parameters that the event sink passes.

The engine checks your process design when it is notified of an event. You define a workflow process and set it up to be executed based on Web Storage System events or system events. The process design encapsulates the logic for advancing the state of your workflow documents. It includes script or COM actions and conditions. Figure 8–6 shows an application folder with a default ProcessDefinition and several ProcessInstances.

In Figure 8–6, the engine attempts to find a match between the event notification that it received and a rule in the process logic. When it finds a match, it executes the prescribed action. The engine and the script host run in the workflow event sink process and have access to the ProcessInstance and the user context. Figure 8–7 shows the workflow event sink process hosting the script host and the workflow engine.

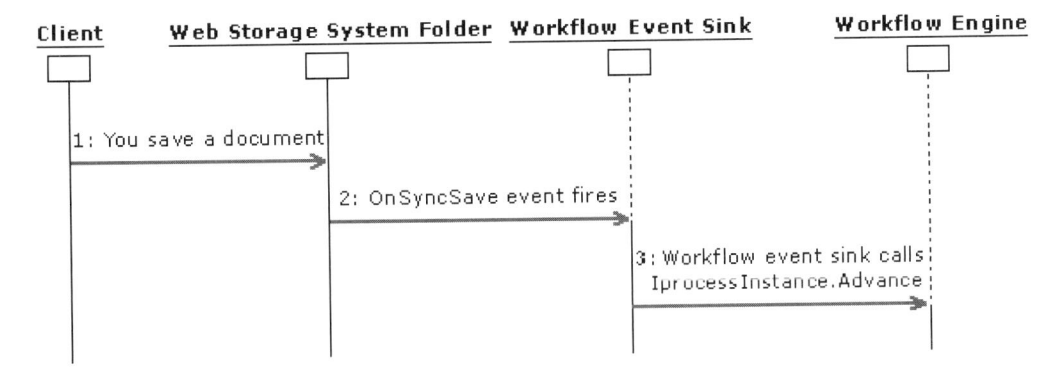

FIGURE 8–5 *The flow of information between the processes in the workflow run-time environment*

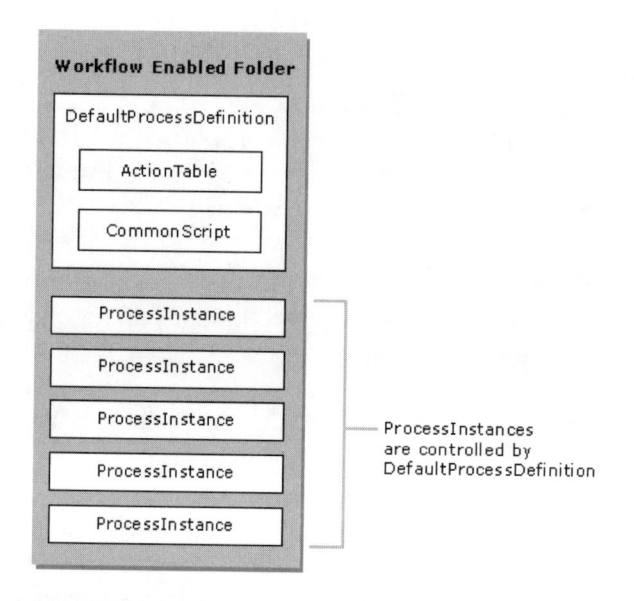

FIGURE 8–6 *An application folder with a default ProcessDefinition*

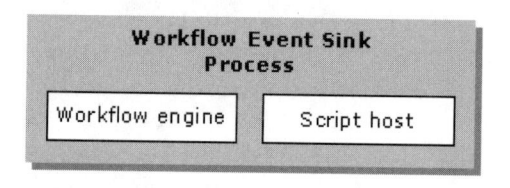

FIGURE 8–7 *Workflow event sink process*

When the workflow engine finds an action table match and executes the action script or COM object, it passes to the host environment a WorkflowSession object with a Fields collection representing the ProcessInstance undergoing transition. Only the workflow engine can change the status of a ProcessInstance directly. The workflow engine ignores any changes to the current state property made by the user or by a script. Figure 8–8 shows how workflow operates.

WORKFLOW EVENT SINK

The workflow event sink is the interface between the Web Storage System process and the workflow engine. The event sink is automatically registered

Creating Workflow Event Sinks and Tools 177

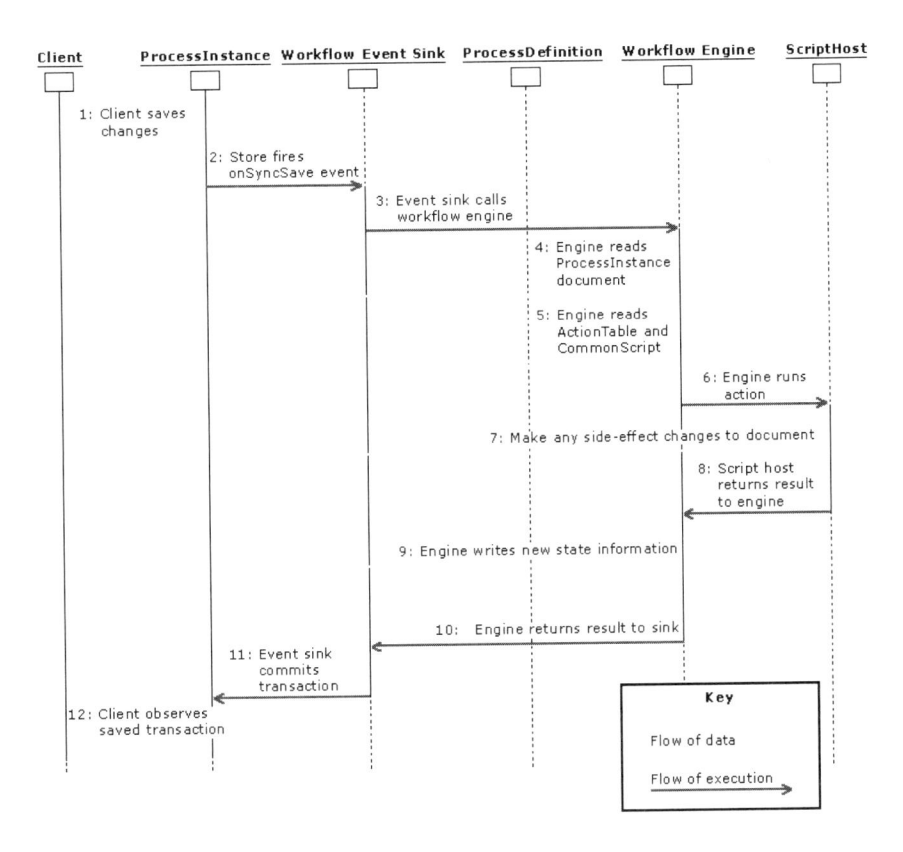

FIGURE 8-8 *Workflow sequence diagram*

as a COM+ application package when you install Exchange 2000 Server. You can view this package through the Component Services console, which is accessed on the Administrative Tools menu. Figure 8–9 shows the Component Services console in Microsoft Management Console (MMC) with the workflow event sink COM+ package installed.

The workflow event sink receives event notifications from the Web Storage System process and makes the appropriate call to the workflow engine. See "Workflow Engine" earlier in this chapter for an illustration of the calling sequence. Applications that wish to use the CDO Workflow event sink must create the appropriate Web Storage System Event Registration items in their folder. If you are using the Exchange Workflow Designer, it registers the event sink for you automatically.

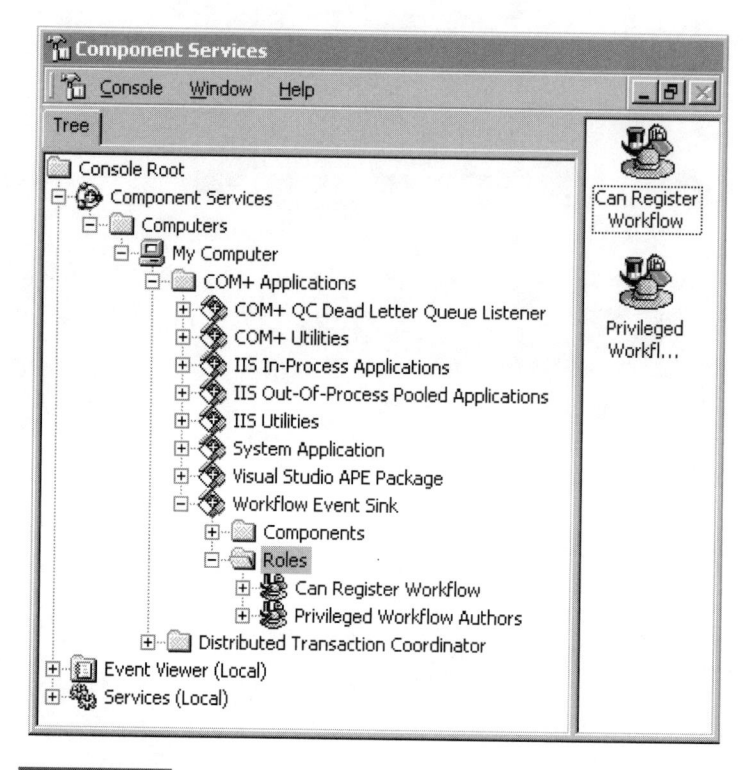

FIGURE 8-9 *Component Services console in MMC*

Workflow Variations

The following topics discuss how users access the workflow folder and how a workflow instance gets its process definition.

- Web-based and email Workflow Compared
- Default and Ad Hoc Process Definitions

WEB-BASED AND EMAIL WORKFLOW COMPARED

CDO Workflow objects support both Web-based workflows and email workflows. The following sections explain the two types of workflow.

Web-Based Workflow

In Web-based workflow, users can connect directly to the Web Storage System through the corporate network. Users can access and update Web Storage System items directly through their network credentials. If a client application updates a property on the work item, you update the workflow state depending on the value of this property. For example, a manager clicks an Approve box on a form (client) and saves it. Your workflow design moves the item from a 'needs approval' state to an 'approved' state.

You can use email in this type of application only to send notification messages to users. These notification messages contain a URL that links to the actual work item that needs to be updated.

Because the user who connects directly to the Web Storage System has been authenticated by Microsoft Windows 2000 security, you can control access to data based on the user's identity. The WorkflowSession, ItemReaders, and ItemAuthors collections provide easy mechanisms to control access to individual items as they move through the workflow process. Figure 8–10 shows the client computer directly connected to the Web Storage System server through the corporate network.

Email Workflow

In email workflow, users need not be directly connected to the corporate network. Offline users can participate in workflow through the Internet by transmitting data in email. In this case, CDO Workflow updates the workflow state upon receipt of a message that correlates to an existing workflow process instance. Direct authentication of such messages by Windows 2000 is not possible. Figure 8–11 shows a client participating in email workflow without network credentials.

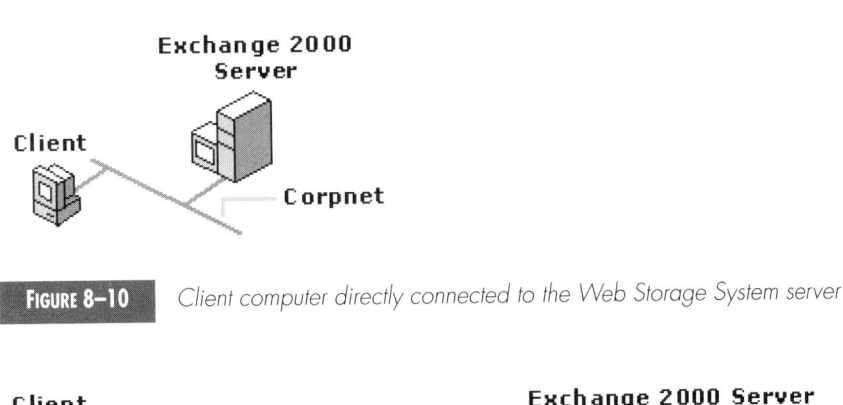

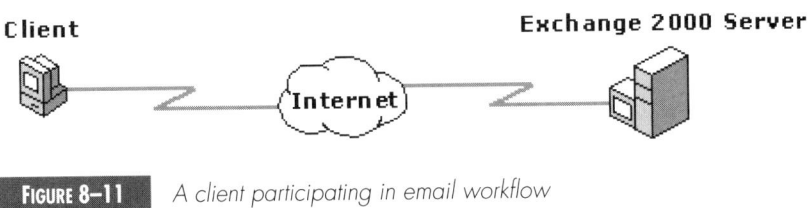

FIGURE 8–10   *Client computer directly connected to the Web Storage System server*

FIGURE 8–11   *A client participating in email workflow*

The system compares incoming messages to existing workflow process instances. If the system fails to correlate an incoming message, it considers that message a new process instance and starts a new workflow. Standard SMTP mail does not always contain sufficient information for correlation. For example, some mailers have a message ID and some do not; or a message header can get rewritten. CDO Workflow implements a reliable process to make sure that each outgoing and incoming workflow item or response has a unique correlation ID. The correlation ID feature requires Microsoft Outlook as the email client.

DEFAULT AND AD HOC PROCESS DEFINITIONS

You can specify that new workflow items use a default workflow process or an ad hoc workflow process. There are four ways to define processes:

- A client uses the default workflow process in a folder.
- A client picks from one of many processes installed in a folder. In this scenario, the process definition must be hidden to prevent unintended editing or viewing.
- A client picks a process definition from another folder. This requires that ad hoc workflow be enabled. Ad hoc workflows can run only in restricted mode. In this scenario, the process definition must be hidden to prevent unintended editing or viewing.
- A client submits an item with an embedded process definition. This requires that ad hoc workflow be enabled. Ad hoc workflows can run only in restricted mode.

Default Process Definition

In a default process workflow (see Figure 8–12), all documents in a workflow folder follow the same process definition. In this case, the process definition is stored at the folder level. Every new document created in that folder inherits a URL to the default process definition for that folder. You implement this type of process definition by setting the *http://schemas.microsoft.com/cdo/workflow/defaultprocdefinition* property on the OnSync-Save registration item in the workflow folder.

Client-Specified Process Definition

A client may specify one of many process definitions installed in a folder, depending on the class of document, or the client may specify a process from another folder. For example, you might have different classes of documents that have different approval behaviors. You use a relative URL to specify the process definition (e.g., MyProcessDesign1.wdm). To specify a process from another folder, you must set the CDO enumeration CdoWfAdhocFlows_Enum flag directly with the Web Storage System schema property. This is part of the event sink registration. Ad hoc workflows can run only in restricted mode.

[FIGURE 8-12 diagram: Workflow Enabled Folder containing DefaultProcessDefinition (with ActionTable and CommonScript) and multiple ProcessInstance items controlled by DefaultProcessDefinition]

FIGURE 8-12   *Workflow default process definition*

Ad Hoc Process Definitions

If your workflow process is truly ad hoc (see Figure 8-13), then upon saving the document the user decides how it should be routed for review. You implement this type of ActionTable by setting the *http://schemas.microsoft.com/cdo/workflow/adhocflows* property on the OnSyncSave registration item in the workflow folder. Ad hoc workflows can run only in restricted mode.

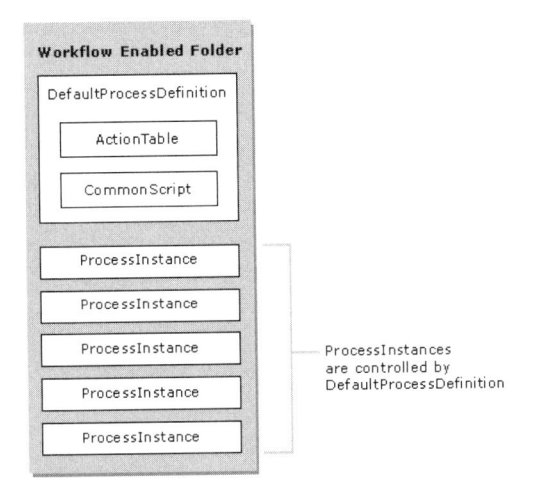

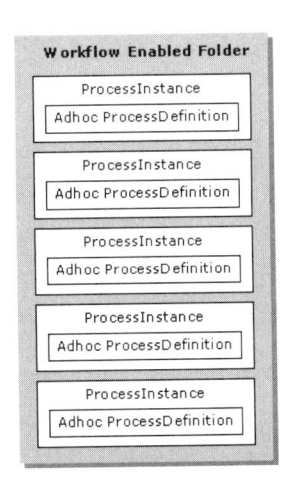

[FIGURE 8-13 diagram: Workflow Enabled Folder containing multiple ProcessInstance items, each with its own Adhoc ProcessDefinition]

FIGURE 8-13   *Workflow ad hoc process definitions*

Workflow Process Definition

The process definition is the design that you create to control the flow of documents in your workflow folder. If you are using the Exchange Workflow Designer, the process definition is generated automatically from the diagram and script code that you create. Advanced developers can use the Process-Definition object directly in ASP applications and middle-tier components. The ProcessDefinition object encapsulates the business logic in its Action-Table property and specifies which script file to use for conditions and actions that are executed at run time. In addition, you specify the security mode for your workflow and how you want to audit workflow processes.

This section includes the following topics:

- Defining the ActionTable
- Setting Security and Audit Properties

DEFINING THE ACTIONTABLE

The ActionTable is an ADO recordset stored as a property of the ProcessDefinition object. The action table distills your business rules into a list of possible state transitions. Exchange Web Storage System events drive a workflow tracking process with CDO Workflow objects. The workflow engine provides a systematic process to control state transitions for documents in the Web Storage System. The engine relies on a user-defined table of actions (called the ActionTable) to evaluate and execute transitions for documents saved in the application folder. Table 8–2 illustrates a simplified subset of a typical row in the action table. A complete row in the ActionTable includes fourteen fields.

TABLE 8–2 *A Simplified Subset of a Typical Row in the Action Table*

Row ID	Caption	State	NewState	EventType	Condition	Action
"1"	"Create"	""	"Submitted"	"OnCreate"	"IsValidExpenseForm()"	"CheckDollarAmount"

Table 8–3 illustrates a variety of actions that could be in an action table.

TABLE 8–3 *A Variety of Actions that Could Be in an Action Table*

State	NewState	EventType	Condition	Action	ExpiryInterval
""	"Initial"	"OnCreate"	"IsValid()"	"SendMail(Mgr)"	
"Initial"	"Assigned"	"OnChange"	"IsDelegated()"	"SendMail(Worker)"	
""	"Assigned"	"OnEnter"	"True"		"15"
"Assigned"	"Completed"	"OnChange"	"IsBalanced()"	"TimeStamp() SendMail(Mgr)"	
"Completed"	""	"OnDelete"	"HasTimeStamp()"	"Archive()"	
"Initial"	""	"OnExit"	"True"	"MarkInitialized()"	

The following sections describe how to use the action table:

- Row Evaluation Order
- Workflow Event Types
- Conditions and Actions

Row Evaluation Order

When the workflow engine finds more than one match for a single state transition, it evaluates action table rows in a clearly defined order. Table 8–4 shows two rows from a larger table; the workflow engine matches both rows 4 and 5 when a document is saved in the workflow folder for the first time.

TABLE 8–4   *Two Rows from a Larger Table*

ID	Event	CurrentState	NewState	Condition	Action	ExpiryInterval
4	OnCreate	""	Submitted	True	NotifyMgr()	
5	OnEnter	""	Submitted	True		15 minutes

In the example illustrated in the Table 8–4, the engine follows this order:

1. Matches the OnCreate row first and executes its action.
2. Matches the OnEnter event and executes its action.

The workflow engine obeys the following rules in all cases:

1. Looks for an OnChange row to match the current state and next state fields.
2. Finds an OnChange row match and looks for an OnExit row match.
3. Finds an OnExit row match and executes the OnExit action.
4. After executing the OnExit action, executes the OnChange action.
5. Looks for an OnEnter row to match. If it finds a matching OnEnter row, it executes its action script.

The two tables that follow illustrate the evaluation rules for all cases. Table 8–5 represents an action table with symbols for the different states, conditions, and actions. Table 8–6 shows the order in which the engine performs the actions.

TABLE 8–5   *An Action Table with Symbols for the Different States*

Event	State	Condition	Action	NewState
OnChange	A	X	I	B
OnExit	A	Y	II	
OnEnter		Z	III	B

From the information given in Table 8–5, the order shown in Table 8–6 applies.

TABLE 8–6 *The Order in Which the Engine Performs the Actions*

Order	Condition/Script
1st	Condition X returns true
2nd	Evaluate condition Y
3rd	Evaluate action II
4th	Evaluate action I
5th	Evaluate condition Z
6th	Evaluate action III

The ActionTable includes an EvaluationOrder column for making clear decisions about multiple matching rows during a single document transition. If this column is blank, no order is guaranteed when more than one row matches.

Event Types

There are two sets of event types in workflow:

- *The workflow event sink* uses the CdoWfEventType enumeration when it calls ProcessInstance Advance (workflow engine).
- *The ActionTable* uses event types to characterize document transitions.

Using CdoWfEventTypes in Calls to Advance

You use the following CdoWfEventTypes when you develop your own event sink to use the workflow engine:

- cdowfOnCreate
- cdowfOnChange
- cdowfOnDelete
- cdowfOnExpiry
- cdowfOnReceive

Using Event Types with an Action Table

Use event types when you design the ActionTable to define which events you want a rule to fire for. Your ActionTable can include states that have more than one path of entry or exit. You might take certain actions with a workflow item regardless of how it reached a given state. When you want an action to fire for a particular state, no matter how the ProcessInstance entered or exited that state, the ActionTable EventTypes include two types for you to use. OnEnter and OnExit allow you to specify an action for a given state whenever a ProcessInstance enters or leaves that state. Table 8–7 lists the values that you can use in the ActionTable EventType field.

Creating Workflow Event Sinks and Tools

TABLE 8–7 *Values that may be used in the ActionTable EventType Field*

Name	Value	Description
OnCreate	1	Document was created.
OnChange	2	Document was modified.
OnDelete	3	Document was deleted.
OnEnter	4	New state is entered. This is where Exchange Workflow Design usually sets the expiry interval.
OnExit	5	Old state is exited.
OnExpiry	6	Document has been in the current state too long.
OnReceive	7	Received an email response correlating to the document.

Conditions and Actions

Conditions and Actions are scripts or COM objects that implement your business logic. These scripts are contained in the following action table fields:

- Condition
- Action
- Compensating Action

The preceding fields can contain inline script, calls to script functions in a global script file, or the ProgIDs of custom (COM) objects. You tell the workflow engine what combination of scripts and objects are in an action table row by setting the flags in the last column of the action table row. The Flags field represents a binary OR'd value of CdoWfTransitionFlags constants. Table 8–8 shows the possible combinations.

TABLE 8–8 *Conditions and Actions*

Flag Value	Condition	Action	CompensatingAction
0x00	Script	Script	Script
0x01	Script	Object	Script
0x02	Object	Script	Script
0x03	Object	Object	Script
0x04	Script	Script	Object
0x05	Script	Object	Object
0x06	Object	Script	Object
0x07	Object	Object	Object

Note — In most cases the condition field should not be empty. If you leave the field empty, and you use the ProcessDefinition object to define your workflow, you get an error when the ProcessDefinition validates the ActionTable. Also, the engine must find at least one TRUE condition per state and EventType in your ActionTable, otherwise it returns the following failure code: CDOWF_NO_CONDS_MATCHED.

SETTING SECURITY AND AUDIT PROPERTIES

Setting Security

You use the ProcessDefinition object to set the security mode for the workflow. The IProcessDefinition interface has a mode property that tells the workflow engine the mode in which you want the workflow to execute. In restricted mode, you are not able to use COM objects in the ActionTable or to create objects in memory from script. In privileged mode, you can use COM objects in the ActionTable and cocreate almost any object in script. If you fail to set the mode property, it defaults to zero (0). Zero is neither restricted nor privileged; your application will not run with a zero value for the mode property. You must explicitly set the security mode. Security modes are covered in more detail in the next section.

Setting Audit Trail Provider

You also use the ProcessDefinition object to tell the workflow engine what tool to use for logging information, warnings, and error messages. These messages are useful for monitoring and debugging your workflow application. The default AuditTrail provider that comes with Exchange 2000 writes all auditing information to the Windows 2000 Server event log.

Workflow Security Modes

When your action table includes scripts and COM objects that run on your server, workflow security becomes a big issue. You can prevent workflow applications from disrupting your server by using workflow security modes. Use security modes to differentiate between trusted and nontrusted developers. Security modes provide users the most flexibility within appropriate limitations.

Table 8–9 summarizes the two modes of security that you can implement with CDO Workflow.

You use restricted mode for nontrusted workflows. Users should be free to set up one-off workflow designs to track documents, but you don't want them to be able to run any script or COM object.

The security mode is a property of the process definition, which you set at design time. You can set this property to either restricted or privileged mode. For your workflow to run in privileged mode, however, you must be a member of the PrivilegedWorkflowAuthors group, which is checked at run

Workflow Security Modes

TABLE 8–9 *Two Modes of Security that may be Implemented with CDO Workflow*

Factors to consider	Restricted mode	Privileged mode
Script access	Only the current Web Storage System item (ProcessInstance) is accessible.	Scripts and objects can access enterprise databases as security context allows.
Security context	EUSER_EXSTOREEVENT (guest privileges)	Workflow System Account defined by system administrator *and* ActiveConnection of user who triggered workflow event
Cocreatable COM objects	None	Unlimited registered components. Allows you to integrate with other systems such as SQL databases and other business applications that provide COM components.
Microsoft Active Directory access	Limited Active Directory lookups through the WorkflowSession GetUserProperty method.	Can use LDAP and Active Directory.

time. PrivilegedWorkflowAuthors is a built-in group to which a system administrator must add you. Figure 8–14 shows Component Services in MMC, where you can view the workflow event sink COM+ package with the Privileged-WorkflowAuthors role and its members.

The following section explains Privilege Checking in more detail.

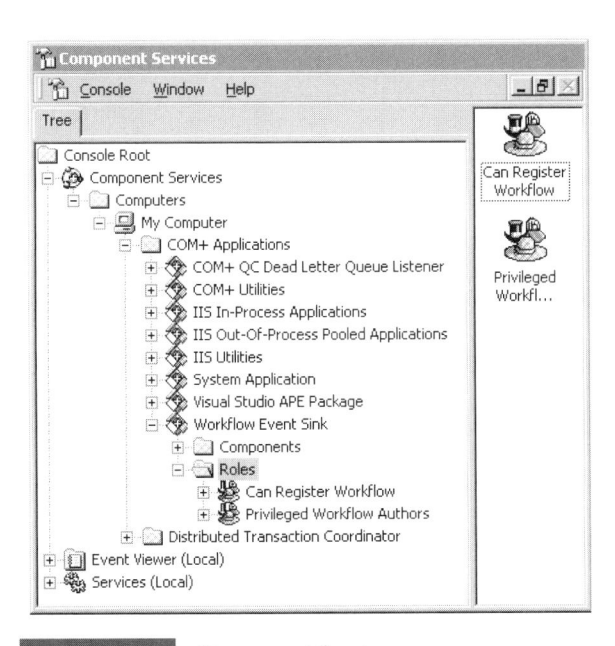

FIGURE 8–14 *Component Services*

PRIVILEGE CHECKING

The workflow event sink enforces security by checking privileges at run time. The event sink performs this check to prevent an unauthorized person from tampering with the scripts, workflow process design, or other application data. For privileged mode workflows, the event sink verifies that all of the following design-time pieces of a workflow were last modified by a member of the PrivilegedWorkflowAuthors role:

- ProcessDefinition
- CommonScript
- Event Sink Registration document

After checking privileges, the event sink calls Advance. The call to Advance fails if any of these were last modified by anyone other than a member of the PrivilegedWorkflowAuthors role.

Exchange 2000 Server Setup creates the COM+ application package for the workflow event sink and installs the PrivilegedWorkflowAuthors role.

This section includes the following subtopics:

- Restricted Mode
- Privileged Mode

RESTRICTED MODE

Restricted mode is for nontrusted developers. This mode has a limited set of permissions and allows access only to the intrinsic WorkflowSession object. Table 8–10 summarizes restricted mode characteristics.

TABLE 8–10 *Restricted Mode Characteristics*

Feature	Description
Script execution only	The workflow conditions and actions must be written in script. You cannot use COM objects in this mode.
Sandboxed script only	The workflow engine configures the script host to disallow the use of CreateObject. The script can modify the row undergoing the workflow using the IWorkflowSession interface.
Script runs as EUSER_EXSTOREEVENT (guest privileges by default)	Before running any condition or action scripts, the event sink logs on and impersonates the system's anonymous account. This prevents the script from doing anything outside the restricted scope. *Note*: You must configure the workflow event sink account to act as part of the operating system by using the Domain Controller Security Policy Management console.

PRIVILEGED MODE

You can configure the workflow application to run in privileged mode. When it runs in privileged mode, the workflow engine verifies that your design-time objects are authored by someone with proper privileges. Table 8–11 recapitulates the privileged mode characteristics.

TABLE 8–11 *Privileged Mode Characteristics*

Feature	Description
Script or COM actions	The workflow actions can be either script or calls to a registered COM object.
No script sandboxing	The workflow engine allows the use of CreateObject for any valid classID on the system, including the FileSystem object, all CDO, or ADO objects, etc.
Script runs as Workflow System Account	The script host executes the script under the same Windows 2000 security account as the caller. No impersonation occurs. In the default case for the CDO Workflow event sink, this means that the script will run in the Workflow System Account, which typically has full-administrative permissions to most Exchange 2000 Server resources.

Managing Workflow Deployment

You manage workflow deployment through Active Directory Users and Computers console and the Components Services console. The following sections describe the steps involved in workflow deployment:

- Adding the Workflow System Account
- Registering a Workflow
- Privileged Workflow Authors

Adding the Workflow System Account

You need to add a Workflow System Account as a member of Domain EXServers group for the workflow event sink to run with proper privileges. You use Active Directory Users and Computers and Component Services to do this. Exchange 2000 Server Setup installs Workflow components by default.

Perform the following steps to add the Workflow System Account:

- Pick an existing account from your Microsoft Windows 2000 domain or create a new account. These instructions assume that you have created an account named Workflow System Account. Set the account's password to never expire.

- Ensure that the Workflow System Account has an Exchange mailbox. If your application uses email-based workflow (IWorkflowMessage SendWorkflowMessage method), the Workflow System Account mailbox folder must be on the same physical server as the application folder where you are registering the workflows. This restriction does not apply to the IWorkflowMessage Send method, which uses SMTP.
- Make the Workflow System Account a member of the Windows 2000 group named Domain EXServers. This enables the CDO Workflow event sink to execute with proper privileges.
- In the console tree of Component Services, select your computer. Then select the COM+ application named **Workflow Event Sink**. In the **Action** menu, click **Properties**.
- Click the **Identity** tab. Click **This user**, and type the name and password for the Workflow System Account.
- Use the Domain Controller Security Policy management console to configure the Workflow Event Sink account to act as part of the operating system. If you are configuring a member server (rather than a domain controller), use the Local Security Policy management console.
- Add the Workflow System Account to the Privileged Workflow Authors role in the COM+ application package for the workflow event sink.

Registering a Workflow Event Sink

You control who can register the workflow event sink in a Web Storage System folder. Anyone can create a workflow design as long as the author is the folder owner and is authorized to register the CDO Workflow event sink. You can control who registers the event sink by populating the Can Register Workflow role of the Workflow Event Sink COM+ package. Figure 8–15 shows the Component Services dialog box where you populate this role.

Note — Before you add users to roles or modify Workflow Event Sink properties, you must shut down the COM+ application if it is running.

Workflow for Exchange 2000 Server supports three events: OnSyncSave, OnSyncDelete, and OnTimer. You enable the workflow folder by registering the event sink for these events in the folder where you want to enforce the workflow process.

Note — Please read this FAQ in the MS Exchange SDK about replicating workflow enabled folders to Exchange 5.5 servers.

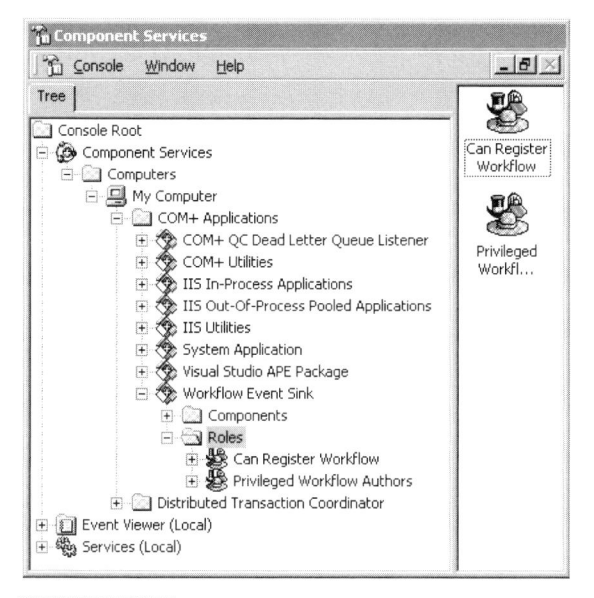

Managing Workflow Deployment

FIGURE 8-15 *Component Services dialog box where you populate the Workflow Event Sink role*

You can register the event sink with DEEP scope, which means that all subfolders inherit the same workflow process. Certain rules apply to registering the event sink with DEEP scope. The topic Registering Workflow Event Sink in a Folder covers these rules in detail.

You can use the event registration item to set the following four properties for the workflow application:

- *http://schemas.microsoft.com/cdo/workflow/defaultprocdefinition* identifies the default ProcessDefinition for the folder in which the event fires. You can use either an absolute or a relative URL for this property.
- *http://schemas.microsoft.com/cdo/workflow/adhocflows* determines whether ad hoc workflows are allowed in the folder where the event fires.
- *http://schemas.microsoft.com/cdo/workflow/enabledebug* determines whether the workflow engine enables JIT script debugging for the folder that the event fires in.
- *http://schemas.microsoft.com/cdo/workflow/disablesuccessentries* determines that the workflow engine does not log success entries to the audit trail.

You never use the OnTimer registration item to set these properties. You must set the defaultprocdefinition and adhocflows properties with the OnSyncSave registration item. The enabledebug and disablesuccessentries properties are optional, and you can set them on either the OnSyncSave or the OnSyncDelete registration items, or on both. Table 8–12 summarizes where to set these properties.

TABLE 8–12 *Properties for the Workflow Application*

Property	Set with OnSyncSave registration item?	Set with OnSyncDelete registration item?	Set with OnTimer registration item?
http://schemas.microsoft.com/cdo/workflow/defaultprocdefinition	Yes, mandatory, except for ad hoc workflow	No	No
http://schemas.microsoft.com/cdo/workflow/adhocflows	Yes, mandatory	No	No
http://schemas.microsoft.com/cdo/workflow/enabledebug	Yes, optional	Yes, optional	No
http://schemas.microsoft.com/cdo/workflow/disablesuccessentries	Yes, optional	Yes, optional	No

Privileged Workflow Authors

You enable privileged authors, as seen in Figure 8–16, to design powerful workflow applications by making them members of the PrivilegedWorkflowAuthors built-in role. You grant this permission per computer, so you must do this on every server on which you want people to have a privileged author role.

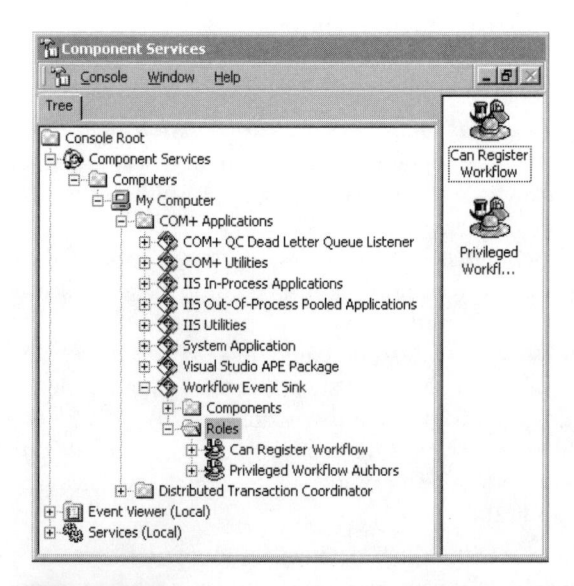

FIGURE 8–16 *Privileged Workflow Authors*

Testing and Debugging Workflow Applications

Built-in workflow functionality enables you to test and debug a process design. You can use the audit trail to follow the success or failure of state transitions during the testing phase. In addition, you can enable the workflow engine to start the Microsoft Script Debugger when you get a script run-time error. The following sections describe these features:

- Using an Audit Trail
- Using Script Debugger

Using an Audit Trail

The workflow components include a built-in audit trail provider. The AuditTrailEventLog provider writes messages to the application log in Event Viewer.

CDO Workflow defines an IAuditTrail interface that you can use to develop your own auditing tool. You can use any component that supports this interface as an audit trail logging tool. You specify the programmatic identifier (ProgID) of your component in the AuditTrailProvider property of the ProcessDefinition object when you design the workflow application.

You can use the audit trail to gather information about where your process succeeded or failed. For example, it tells you whether the source of the audit event was the event sink or the workflow engine. It also records the nature of the transition, so that you can tell where you are in the process.

Sometimes you get run-time errors for which the audit trail can't help you determine the cause. In those cases you might need to debug the script code. The following section describes how the script debugger works with workflow Using_Script_Debugger.

Using Script Debugger

Use script debugger when you get unexpected results from a save or delete operation on the client. This usually means that your script caused a run-time exception. If you are using Exchange Workflow Design, you use a checkbox to enable JIT script debugging. JIT starts script debugger when the error occurs. The debugger starts on the server, so you need to have access to the server. Developers creating their own tools can enable JIT using the Web Storage System schema property. To enable JIT script debugging, set enabledebug equal to true for the OnSyncSave and OnSyncDelete event registration items in the workflow folder. The workflow engine uses the value of this property with the EnableDebug() method of the IProcessInstance interface to configure the script host before running any script.

For JIT to work correctly, the server environment must be set up properly. The following three requirements must be met:

- The workflow event sink COM+ identity must be set to "interactive user" in component services.
- The registry key "HKCU/Software/Microsoft/Windows Script/Settings/JITDebug" must be set to REG_DWORD "1".
- If Microsoft Visual InterDev is installed on the server, JIT must be enabled in Tools|Options|Debugger|General.

Note You may have to create the registry key.

By default, a workflow script aborts after 15 minutes (900 seconds). You can configure the maximum time a script executes using the following registry key:

HKLM\SOFTWARE\Microsoft\Exchange\Workflow\Maximum execution time for scripts in seconds

Set it higher to give yourself more time to debug the script. Specify maximum time a script executes in seconds with a setting of type DWORD. You have to set this key on any machine that you want to configure the maximum time a script executes. (You may have to create the registry key.)

Note The minimum setting supported is 5 minutes (300 seconds).

NINE

Server and Recipient Management

CDOEXM is a collection of COM classes and interfaces aggregated into CDO and ADSI classes. You can use CDOEXM to programmatically manage the Microsoft Exchange 2000 Server, items in the Message Databases (MDBs), and the store recipients (users). You can create, move, copy, reconfigure, monitor, or delete these items. You can use CDOEXM objects on your server or remotely.

CDOEXM encapsulates and simplifies many programmatic tasks that are specific to managing the Exchange 2000 server. CDOEXM is useful for system administrators, who need to perform tasks such as periodically archiving their MDBs, monitoring performance, or managing the server remotely. You can also use CDOEXM to perform server-side Internet application tasks, such as automatically creating and registering users, managing data in public MDBs, and managing email.

The following topics cover overview information about server and recipient management:

- Overview
- DLLs and Installation
- Web Storage System Configuration
- Active Directory and CDOEXM
- Exchange Management Security
- Web-Based Management

The following topics cover the CDOEXM classes and aggregated interfaces:

- Managing the Exchange Server
- Managing Mail Recipients

Overview

You can use CDOEXM COM classes to manage the Exchange 2000 server and its databases. Interfaces aggregated into CDO and ADSI classes allow you to manage recipients and their mailboxes. CDOEXM can be used on the same computer as the Exchange 2000 server or can be used remotely.

TYPICAL USES

CDOEXM allows you to develop applications such as the following:

Business Critical Applications
Business applications can use the management tools to programmatically manage Web Storage System information and recipients according to business logic or business rules.

System Administration
System administrators can build custom programs to move items in an MDB, mount a public store, create and enable recipients, move recipients, change forwarding addresses, and so on. These programs can be built quickly by using the recipient management interfaces.

MMC Snap-ins
CDOEXM is intended for use in developing your own MMC snap-ins for Exchange.

Remote Management
CDOEXM can be used to develop server-side objects that can manage the Exchange 2000 Server. These management objects can be invoked remotely by using ASP pages.

Automated Services
Automatic services (or tools) can use CDOEXM. One such tool can service Web-based clients to allow them to register in a Microsoft Web Storage System as new users, grant them access to public stores, and give them mailboxes.

DLLs and Installation

Table 9–1 shows the DLL that contains the CDOEXM classes and aggregated interfaces.

TABLE 9–1 *The DLL that contains the CDOEXM Classes and Aggregated Interfaces*

DLL Name	Description
CDOEXM.DLL	CDOEXM

Installation of CDOEXM

When you install Exchange, CDOEXM is automatically installed when you install Exchange Management Components. Exchange Management Components is also installed as part of the Exchange Management User Interface installation.

You may want to develop or use the CDOEXM components on a computer that does not have Exchange installed. To do this, you can install the Exchange Management Components from the Exchange 2000 Server installation package.

Dependent DLLs

CDOEXM can use the following DLLs:

- ACTIVEDS.DLL
- ADVAPI32.DLL
- CLUSAPI.DLL
- COMCTL32.DLL
- EXCHMEM.DLL
- KERNEL32.DLL
- MSVCP50.DLL
- MSVCRT.DLL
- NETAPI32.DLL
- OLE32.DLL
- OLEAUT32.DLL
- RESUTILS.DLL
- RPCRT4.DLL
- SECURITY.DLL
- USER32.DLL
- VERSION.DLL

Web Storage System Configuration

The Web Storage System is made up of public stores and mailbox stores. The Exchange 2000 server keeps these stores in MDBs.

In Exchange, administrators use CDOEXM to manage storage groups, in which they create public and mailbox stores. Administrators access and use storage groups; storage groups do not provide any representation to users or applications that access the Web Storage System.

Users and applications see Web Storage System data as paths that can be accessed by using HTTP-DAV paths or *file:///./ paths*. Data in public stores is presented in the Web Storage System, in folder trees. To access data in the public stores, you use the paths of a folder tree. To access data in a mailbox store, you use paths to mailboxes and subfolders in the mailboxes.

For a more sequential look at configuring an Exchange store, see "Setting Up a Store" later in this chapter.

As you configure your public and mailbox stores, you can view your current Server configuration by using the Exchange System Manager MMC snap-in.

Folder Trees

Folder trees organize public folder data in hierarchical folders for access by Web Storage System applications, Microsoft Outlook, and custom applications using Exchange 2000 Server. Typically, a folder tree represents the data in a single MDB. In Exchange 2000 Server, however, it is possible to have a folder tree distributed across multiple MDBs.

Using folder trees, you can replicate stores on other servers. For more information about replication, see "Folder Tree Replication" later in this chapter.

MDBs

All store data is kept in MDBs, which in the Exchange 2000 Server are Jet databases. In many cases, each public or mailbox store has its own MDB on a single server. With Exchange 2000 Server, however, a store can have multiple MDBs. The MDBs can be placed on different servers to improve performance and simplify MDB maintenance.

Rules about Folder Trees and MDBs

Logical constraints to using folder trees include the following:

- Each MDB must have only one folder tree.
- An MDB cannot have the folder tree of another MDB on the same server.
- An MDB can have a folder tree of an MDB on another server. For more information, see "Folder Tree Replication."

Figure 9–1 shows how these rules are applied in an incomplete folder tree and server configuration.

Public Store B must have a folder tree, but it cannot be Folder Tree 1 (because Folder Tree 1 already belongs to a store on the server).

Folder Tree 2 cannot be assigned to Public Store A (because Public Store A already has a folder tree).

Public Store 2A can be assigned Folder Tree 1 (because it is on a remote server). Public Store 2A becomes a replica of Public Store A.

Folder Tree Replication

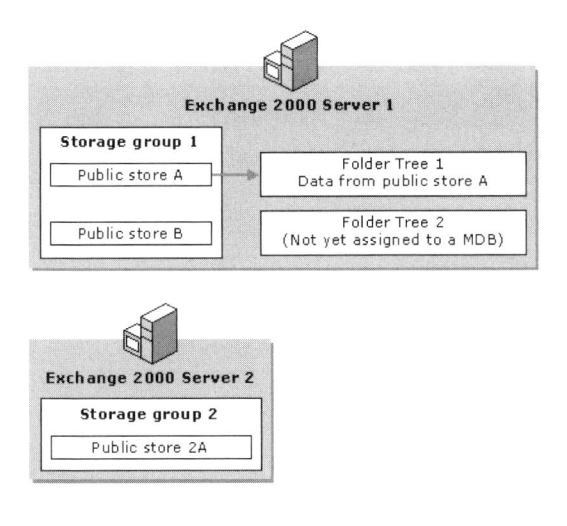

FIGURE 9-1 How rules are applied in an incomplete folder tree and server configuration

Folder Tree Replication

You can replicate folder trees on multiple servers (see Figure 9-2). Each folder tree will have its own MDB and the server will keep the information mirrored.

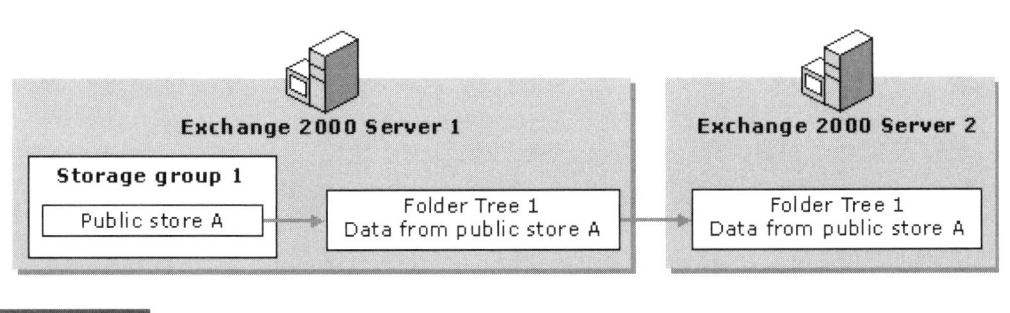

FIGURE 9-2 Folder tree replication

Note Replicating and configuring what is displayed in a folder tree is performed outside CDOEXM.

For related information, see "Setting Up a Store."

Active Directory and CDOEXM

Performing management with CDOEXM involves gathering and modifying information in the Exchange 2000 Server and Microsoft Active Directory directory service in Microsoft Windows 2000. Active Directory information is configured in namespaces by using the Lightweight Directory Access Protocol (LDAP). It is important to understand the role of Active Directory for Exchange 2000 Server.

In CDOEXM classes, the IDataSource2 interface is provided for opening, managing, and deleting Exchange-related Active Directory objects.

CDOEXM and ADSI

The Exchange 2000 Server data that resides in Active Directory can be accessed by using ADSI. ADSI is a generic API, however, that has no specific functions for managing the Exchange data in Active Directory. Also, ADSI cannot access data in Exchange 2000 Server.

CDOEXM encapsulates and simplifies Exchange management tasks so that data in both Active Directory and Exchange are managed as needed.

For information about a class for obtaining and building Active Directory paths, see the "IADS Pathname" section in the Platform SDK in the Microsoft MSDN Library.

Building Active Directory Paths

You can programmatically build Active Directory paths by using CDOEXM COM classes. The following example shows how you can use each CDOEXM object to enumerate storage groups, public and mailbox stores in the storage groups, and the folder trees in which the stores appear:

[Visual Basic]

```
Private Sub EnumerateStore()

  Dim iExs As New CDOEXM.ExchangeServer
  Dim isg As New CDOEXM.StorageGroup
  Dim ipsDB As New CDOEXM.PublicStoreDB
  Dim imbxDB As New CDOEXM.MailboxStoreDB
  Dim ift As New CDOEXM.FolderTree

  Dim ds2 As IDataSource2
  Set ds2 = iExs

  Debug.Print Chr(13) + Chr(13) + Chr(13) +
"================================="
```

```vb
  Dim server_nm As String
  server_nm = Environ("COMPUTERNAME") 'The computer name is
the servername.

  ds2.Open server_nm
  Debug.Print "ExchangeVersion = " + iExs.ExchangeVersion

  Debug.Print "DirectoryServer = " + iExs.DirectoryServer

  Dim storegroup As Variant
  Dim pubstore As Variant
  Dim mbx As Variant


  For Each storegroup In iExs.StorageGroups
    Debug.Print "StorageGroup    = " + storegroup + Chr(13)
    isg.DataSource.Open storegroup

    For Each pubstore In isg.PublicStoreDBs

      Debug.Print "Public Store   = " + pubstore
      ipsDB.DataSource.Open pubstore
      Debug.Print "         Name      = " + ipsDB.Name +
Chr(13)

      Debug.Print "FolderTree     = " + ipsDB.FolderTree
      ift.DataSource.Open ipsDB.FolderTree
      Debug.Print " RootFolderURL = " + ift.RootFolderURL
      Debug.Print "            Name = " + ift.Name + Chr(13)

    Next 'public store
    For Each mbx In isg.MailboxStoreDBs

      Debug.Print "Mailbox        = " + mbx
      imbxDB.DataSource.Open mbx
      Debug.Print "           Name = " + imbxDB.Name +
Chr(13)

    Next 'mailbox
  Next 'storage group


  Set iExs = Nothing
  Set isg = Nothing
  Set ipsDB = Nothing
  Set imbxDB = Nothing
  Set ift = Nothing

End Sub
```

Retrieving Folder Tree URLs

Folder tree URLs are required for various store management operations. The following code locates a folder tree by name on a given server and returns the full URL, which you can use when creating a public store:

[Visual Basic]

```
'//////////////////////////////////////////////////////////////////////////////
'// Function:   GetFolderTreeURL
'// Purpose:    To get the Folder Tree Hierarchies URL
'// Input:      strComputerName = contains the name of the Exchange 2000 Server
'//             strFHName = contains the name of the Folder Tree Hierarchy to be found
'// Output:     True = the Folder Tree Hierarchy was found
'//             False = there were errors and Folder Tree Hierarchy wasn't found
'//
'// Notes:      The function is useful for checking to see if this folder tree url
'//             is already in use.  Also it is useful when creating a new
'//             public or mailbox store (since they require a folder tree URL).
'//
'//////////////////////////////////////////////////////////////////////////////

Public Function GetFolderTreeURL(ByVal strComputerName As String, _
                                 ByRef strFHName As String) As Boolean
    On Error Resume Next
    Dim Result      As Boolean
    Dim RootDSE     As IADs
    Dim conf        As IADs

    Dim conn        As New ADODB.Connection
    Dim comm        As New ADODB.Command
    Dim rs          As ADODB.Recordset

    'Get the default IExchangeServer interface
    Dim iServer     As New CDOEXM.ExchangeServer

    Dim strPath         As String
    Dim strDSAdminName  As String
    Dim strDSAdminPass  As String
```

```
    Dim strDNFolder     As String

    Result = True

    strFHName = ""

    ' Bind to the Exchange Server
    iServer.DataSource.Open strComputerName
    Result = Result And CheckError("Open Server in function
GetFolderTreeURL")

    Set RootDSE = GetObject("LDAP://" +
iServer.DirectoryServer + "/RootDSE")
    strPath = "LDAP://" & iServer.DirectoryServer & "/" &
RootDSE.Get("configurationNamingContext")

    ' Set the Provider for the connection object
    conn.Provider = "ADsDSOObject"

    'You will need to provide login credentials if you are
not logged in
    'with an administrator security context.
'    conn.Properties("user id") = "Administrator"
'    conn.Properties("Password") = ""
'    conn.Properties("Bind Flags") = 1

    ' Open connection
    conn.Open
    Result = Result And CheckError("Open Connection in
function GetFolderTreeURL")


    ' Set command to connection object
    Set comm.ActiveConnection = conn
    Result = Result And CheckError("Set Active Connection
in function GetFolderTreeURL")


    comm.CommandText = "<" & strPath & ">" &
";(objectClass=msExchPFTree);ADsPath,distinguishedName,Name
;subtree"

    ' Execute command
    Set rs = comm.Execute
    Result = Result And CheckError("Execute Command in
function GetFolderTreeURL")

    ' Get the Default FolderTreeHierarcy
    Do While Not (rs.EOF)
```

```
            'You can print access folder tree information here
            'Debug.Print rs.Fields("ADsPath").Value
            'Debug.Print rs.Fields("distinguishedName")
            'Debug.Print rs.Fields("Name")
            strDNFolder = rs.Fields("distinguishedName")
            'cut the folder name to get the Folder Hierarchies
            strFHName = Mid(strDNFolder, InStr(2, strDNFolder,
    "CN="))
            If strFHName <> "" Then
                Exit Do
            Else
                rs.MoveNext
            End If
        Loop
        ' test if the URL to the FolderTreeHierarcy is empty
        If strFHName = "" Then
            Debug.Print "No Folder Hierarchy Name Found."
            Result = False
        End If

        'Cleanup
        Set RootDSE = Nothing
        Set conf = Nothing

        Set conn = Nothing
        Set comm = Nothing
        Set rs = Nothing
        Set iServer = Nothing

        GetFolderTreeURL = Result
    End Function
```

See "Checking for CDOEXM Errors," in the MS Exchange SDK to see the function CheckError().

Web-Based Management

Remote management over the Web can use server-side ASP pages to run scripts or create COM objects to perform Exchange management tasks.

Scripts have security restrictions when they are run out of the administrator's process (such as from a server-side ASP page). For running scripts out of process, take one of the following two actions to have administrator rights:

- Run the scripts within a Script Host that has administrator privileges.
- Use the script to create objects that obtain administrator privileges. Then, perform the management tasks from within the objects.

For obtaining administrative privileges outside of an administrator's process, see the next section "Exchange Management Security."

Exchange Management Security

CDOEXM objects must be run in a security context that is sufficient to perform management tasks. This is also true for the CDO and ADSI objects with aggregated CDOEXM recipient interfaces. CDOEXM uses the Windows 2000 security model for accessing Exchange 2000 Server. Authentication as a Windows 2000 user will give you the administrative rights associated with that user. The following items suggest ways to obtain administrative privileges for CDOEXM objects:

Log On as an Administrator
As an administrator, you can create objects to perform system management.

Wrap the COM classes using COM+
In many automated processes, you may want to allow users without administrative privileges to perform some specific Exchange management tasks—for example, allowing them to register at your Web site and gain access to public stores. You can set up a server-side ASP page that can run management objects within their own security contexts.

To give your management objects security contexts, you can wrap them in COM+ applications (formerly called an MTS package). COM+ applications allow you to specify the identity, and thus the security context, of that object as a user with administrative rights. For more information, see "Security in COM+" in the COM+ section of the Platform SDK in the Microsoft MSDN Library.

Managing the Exchange Server

CDOEXM provides five COM classes for managing Exchange 2000 Server and its MDBs. The CDOEXM object models are at CDO Exchange Management.

All CDOEXM interfaces are Automation compatible and thus can be used in Microsoft Visual Basic and scripting.

The classes and their uses are briefly described next.

The Server COM Class
The Server COM class is for managing the overall Exchange 2000 Server. The IExchangeServer interface on this class allows you to obtain information such as the name of the server, the type of the server, version of the server,

and the storage groups that are on the server. You can also set server characteristics such as enabling or disabling message tracking or setting the number of days before log files are removed.

The FolderTree COM Class

The FolderTree COM class is for managing folder trees as they relate to MDBs. The IFolderTree interface allows you to manage the folder tree and the tree replicas.

For more information, see "Web Storage System Configuration" earlier in this chapter.

The StorageGroup COM Class

The StorageGroup COM class allows you to manage groups of public and mailbox stores. When you create a store, you must place it in a storage group. The storage group management tasks include managing log files for the group and resetting the database for the stores. The IStorageGroup interface allows you to access your MDB's underlying Jet database configuration information.

For more information, see "Setting Up a Store" later in this chapter.

The PublicStoreDB COM Class

The PublicStoreDB COM class is for managing public stores in Exchange 2000 Server. The IPublicStoreDB interface allows you to create, modify, and delete public stores.

Users of the Web Storage System access public stores through folder trees.

The MailboxStoreDB COM Class

The MailboxStoreDB COM class is for managing the Exchange 2000 Server mailbox stores. Individual mailboxes are created in and managed from mailbox stores. The IMailboxStoreDB interface allows you to move, mount, or dismount a mailbox store or to access and set information pertaining to a mailbox store.

For related information, see "Setting Up a Store" in the "Server Management Tasks" section in the MS Exchange SDK.

Setting Up a Store

The following section discusses the sequence for creating public folders and mailboxes in Exchange 2000 Server with CDOEXM objects.

Create a Storage Group

A default storage group is created when Exchange 2000 Server is installed. When you create stores, you can use this default storage group or create a new storage group.

For a code sample of creating a storage group, see "Creating a Storage Group" in the "Server Management Tasks" section in the MS Exchange SDK.

Create a Folder Tree

You must create a folder tree before you create public or mailbox stores, because it is necessary to identify an existing folder tree when you create a store.

> **Note** You can also use the default folder tree that is created when Exchange 2000 Server is installed.

For a code sample of creating a Folder Tree, see "Creating a Folder Tree" in the MS Exchange SDK.

Create Public and Mailbox Stores

You can now create public and mailbox stores. When creating stores, you must specify both a storage group in which the store is to be managed and a folder tree in which the store's content is to appear.

For public and mailbox store code samples, see "Creating a Public Store and Creating a Mailbox Store."

Your store now looks like Figure 9–3.

Create Public Folders and Mailboxes

You can now create public folders and mailboxes. You can also give users permissions to create public folders and create their own mailboxes.

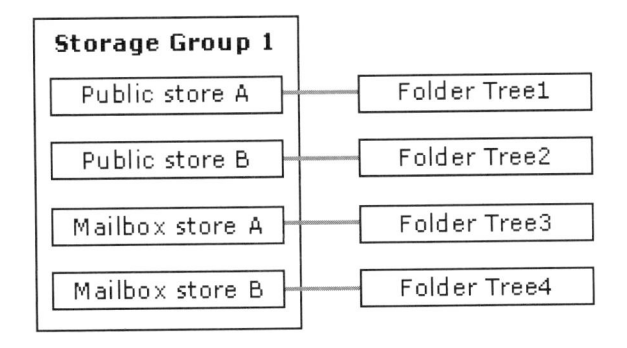

```
Storage Group 1
  Public store A   ── Folder Tree1
  Public store B   ── Folder Tree2
  Mailbox store A  ── Folder Tree3
  Mailbox store B  ── Folder Tree4
```

FIGURE 9–3   *Public and Mailbox Stores*

For an example of how to create a folder, see "Creating Folders" in the MS Exchange SDK.

For information and examples of creating and managing mailboxes, see "Managing Mail Recipients" later in this chapter.

Managing Mail Recipients

This topic covers how mail recipients can be programmatically managed in Exchange 2000 Server. The management is provided by CDOEXM interfaces that are aggregated into CDO and ADSI objects capable of acting as recipients.

The CDOEXM recipient interfaces are used in conjunction with information in CDO and ADSI objects for tasks such as creating, moving, and deleting recipients. These interfaces also provide the means for setting mailbox properties such as limits, forwarding properties, proxy addresses, and alias names.

See the following subtopics for more information:

- "Recipient Management Interfaces" discusses the interfaces and where they fit into the CDO and ADSI models.
- "Recipients, Folders, and Groups" discusses the store items that can be managed as recipients.

Recipient Management Interfaces

Table 9–2 lists the CDOEXM interfaces and the CDO and ADSI objects into which they are aggregated.

TABLE 9–2 *CDOEXM Interfaces and the CDO and ADSI Objects*

Aggregated CDOEXM interface	CDO and ADSI COM classes
ImailRecipient	CDO.Person
	CDO.Folder
	ADSI Contact (IADS)
	ADSI Group (IADSGroup)
	ADSI User (IADSUser)
ImailboxStore	CDO.Person
	ADSI User (IADSUser)
IdistributionList	ADSI Group (IADSGroup)

The CDOEXM IMailRecipient interface is used to specify storage policies for all mail recipients. After a recipient is in a mailbox store, the recipient can appear in an address book or other information servers designed to access Exchange 2000 Mailbox Stores.

The CDOEXM IMailboxStore interface is used to specify storage policies for mailbox-enabled recipients, such as how long to keep deleted messages.

For more information, see "Creating a Mail-Enabled Recipient" in the MS Exchange SDK.

Using the Interfaces in Context

The CDOEXM recipient interfaces (IMailRecipient and IMailboxStore) are aggregated into existing CDO and ADSI classes because they are used in relation to those classes. Recipient management is implemented by using properties on the object, in addition to properties and methods on the IMailRecipient interface. Although all pertinent properties are not always exposed on the IMailboxStore and IMailRecipient interfaces, they may be used within the IMailRecipient and IMailboxStore methods.

For important information about accessing recipient mailboxes and folders by using ADSI or ExOLEDB, see "Accessing Mailboxes and Folders" later in this chapter.

The following example demonstrates the coordinated use of the CDO.Person interface (and its underlying object) with the IMailBoxStore interface to create a mailbox-enabled recipient:

[Visual Basic]

```
Function CreateMailboxCDOPerson(strFirstName As String, _
                                strLastName As String, _
                                strHomeMDBUrl As String)
As Boolean
'strHomeMDBUrl should look like this
'strHomeMDBUrl = "CN=Mailbox Store (MYSTORE),CN=First
Storage Group,
'
CN=InformationStore,CN=MYSTORE,CN=Servers,
'             CN=First Administrative
Group,CN=Administrative Groups,
'             CN=IASI,CN=Microsoft
Exchange,CN=Services,CN=Configuration,
'
DC=mydomain,DC=extest,DC=microsoft,DC=com"

    Dim oPerson         As New CDO.Person
    Dim oMailbox        As CDOEXM.IMailboxStore
```

Chapter 9 • Server and Recipient Management

```
    Dim strUserName     As String
    Dim strURL          As String
    Dim strContainerName As String
    Dim Result          As Boolean

    Result = True

    strUserName = strFirstName & strLastName

    strContainerName = "Users"
    ' Create URL for the user
    Result = Result And CreateUserURL(strURL,
strContainerName, False, strUserName)

    oPerson.FirstName = strFirstName
    oPerson.LastName = strLastName

    oPerson.DataSource.SaveTo strURL
    Result = Result And CheckError("SaveTo " & strURL)

    Set oPerson = New CDO.Person
    ' Bind
    oPerson.DataSource.Open strURL
    Result = Result And CheckError("Bind to CDO User " &
strUserName)

    ' Create Mailbox
    Set oMailbox = oPerson
    oMailbox.CreateMailbox strHomeMDBUrl
    Result = Result And CheckError("Create Mailbox for CDO
User " & strUserName)

    ' Save
    oPerson.DataSource.Save
    Result = Result And CheckError("Save CDO User " &
strUserName)

    'CleanUp
    Set oPerson = Nothing
    Set oMailbox = Nothing

    CreateMailboxCDOPerson = Result
End Function
```

Recipients, Folders, and Groups

A recipient can be a person (user), a folder, or a group. The following list defines the types of recipients with respect to their objects and mailbox types:

- Mailbox-enabled recipients have both a mail address and an Exchange mailbox.
- Mail-enabled recipients have a mail address, but do not have an Exchange mailbox. Mail sent to this type of recipient is typically forwarded to another email location outside Exchange.
- Mail-enabled folders are folders in which items can be posted.
- Mail-enabled groups are distribution lists.

Table 9–3 defines the characteristics of these mail recipient types.

TABLE 9–3 *Characteristics of Mail Recipient Types*

Recipient type	Email address	Actual mailbox in store
Mailbox-enabled recipient	Address can be a store mailbox or be set to a forwarding address.	The mailbox is private for the recipient.
Mail-enabled recipient	Mail is forwarded to this address.	No mailbox.
Mail-enabled folder	An address to the folder.	The mailbox is a folder in which items are posted.
Mail-enabled group	A group address. (Mail is routed to those in the group.)	No mailbox. The group serves essentially as a distribution list.

When any of these recipient types is disabled, Exchange 2000 Server does not provide access to them by standard email protocols. From an email perspective, the server does not recognize the address unless it is enabled.

Accessing Mailboxes and Folders

When managing recipients, the CDOEXM recipient interfaces access and modify items in both Active Directory and Exchange 2000 Server.

For more information about the use of Active Directory in Exchange, see "Active Directory and CDOEXM" earlier in the chapter.

Person and User Objects Use LDAP

Recipients are defined in both Active Directory and Exchange 2000 Server. The principal location to bind to a recipient is in Active Directory. Thus, the CDOEXM interfaces in the Person and User objects bind to Active Directory by using an LDAP URL. The following example illustrates this:

```
Dim objPerson As New CDO.Person
objPerson.DataSource.Open
"LDAP://MYSERVER1/CN=jamessmith,CN=users,
DC=CompanyADomain,DC=Dev,DC=com"
```

The LDAP URL consists of the following parts:

```
"LDAP://servername/CN=RecipientName,CN=FolderAlias,
DC=DomainNamePart,DC=DomainNamePart2,DC=DomainNamePartn"
```

For related information, see "Building Active Directory Paths" earlier in the chapter.

Folder Objects Use ExOLEDB

Public folders can serve as mailboxes for recipients. To use CDOEXM interfaces in the Folder object, you connect directly to a store by using the ExOLEDB provider. Connect to the store by providing a "File://./" URL. An Open statement might look like the following:

```
Dim objFolder As New CDO.Folder
fullurl = "file://./backofficestorage/
MyDomain.wherever.com/Public Folders/Folder3"
objFolder.DataSource.Open fullurl, , adModeReadWrite,
adFailIfNotExists
```

The File URL parts are defined as follows:

```
fullurl = "file://./backofficestorage/DomainName/
FolderName"
```

For an example of working with a folder, see "Building a Restricted Address List" in the MS Exchange SDK.

Email Addresses Stored as Active Directory Paths

Email addresses are converted (stored) as Active Directory paths when specific CDOEXM interface properties are set. Some of these properties can receive recipients as email addresses (such as IMailboxStore, ForwardTo, or Delegates).

For example, setting IMailboxStore.ForwardTo to user1@somewhere.microsoft.com results in the ForwardTo value being set to the Active Directory path (for example, cn=Private MDB,cn=First Storage Group,...).

To complete an LDAP URL by using an Active Directory path, you typically must add "LDAP://*server/*" and "CN=*first tree item*."

For more information about the use of Active Directory in Exchange, see "Active Directory and CDOEXM."

Error Checking with CDOEXM Objects

CDOEXM objects support the Visual Basic ISupportErrorInfo that logs errors into the global VBA.ErrorObject.

For an error-checking code sample, see "Checking for CDOEXM Errors" in the MS Exchange SDK.

T E N

Constructing Web Storage System URLs

The following sections outline in detail how to construct URLs for items in the Web Storage System.

The method you use to construct URLs depends upon the URL scheme, for example, whether you use the file: or http: scheme. In addition, which URL you use to address an item depends on the access protocol or component you use to access it. For example, you can use both file: and http: URLs to identify items and folders when using the server-side Microsoft Exchange 2000 Server OLE DB Provider. You must use http: URLs when addressing items that use the HTTP/WebDAV protocol.

This topic consists of the following sections:

- Constructing Web Storage System OLE DB URL
- Constructing Web Storage System HTTP URLs
- Using Relative URLs
- Getting the Host Domain Name
- Getting Well-Known Mailbox Folder URLs

Constructing OLE DB URLs

When you use the server-side ExOLEDB Provider, you can use either the `file:` or the `http:` URL scheme to identify items in the Web Storage System. These URLs are applicable for use with any component that uses this provider to access items, including ADO version 2.5 and CDOEX.

The following sections discuss how to construct URLs by using these schemes:

- The File: URL Scheme
- The HTTP: URL Scheme

215

The File: URL Scheme

In constructing URLs using the `file:` scheme for use with the ExOLEDB Provider, each URL has the following two forms:

```
file://./backofficestorage/domain-name/MBX/user-alias/path
file://./backofficestorage/domain-name/public-folder-tree-
   name/path
```

`domain-name`

You use the first form to access a user's base mailbox folder. You use the second form to access items in public folder trees. This is fully qualified name of the domain in which the store resides, for example, "mydomain.microsoft.com." Note that this domain name does not include the name of the server itself.

`public-folder-tree-name`

For private mailboxes, this is always "MBX". For items stored in a public store, this is the name of the public folder tree in which the item resides. Note that it is not the name of the public store that houses the public folder tree.

Table 10–1 lists the default names provided by Exchange 2000 to access private mailboxes and the default public folder tree.

TABLE 10–1 *Default Folder Tree Names*

Default folder tree name	Description
MBX	Contains all private mailboxes.
Public Folders	Contains the default public store installed with Exchange 2000.

When you add new public stores and associated public folder trees, you use the name of that public folder tree in the URL. To access mailboxes in additional private stores, you always use "MBX".

`user-alias`

This is the user's Exchange mailbox alias, for example, User1.

`path`

This is the folder path to the item. This path consists of a series of folder names separated by "/" characters.

The ExOLEDB Provider registers the `file:` OLE DB URL namespace with the OLE DB root binder. Therefore, you need not specify this provider explicitly when you use OLE DB, ADO, or CDO objects to access items by using the `file:` URL scheme.

The URLs in the following examples use the `file:` scheme:

```
file://./backofficestorage/sample.microsoft.com/public
folders/reports/report1.doc
file://./backofficestorage/sample.microsoft.com/public
folders/reports/schema/

file://./backofficestorage/sample.microsoft.com/MBX/User1/
Inbox
file://./backofficestorage/sample.microsoft.com/MBX/User1/
Calendar
file://./backofficestorage/sample.microsoft.com/MBX/User1/
Drafts

file://./backofficestorage/sample.microsoft.com/
application1/app1/
file://./backofficestorage/sample.microsoft.com/
application1/app1/schema
```

The URLs presented in Table 10–2 point to a user's mailbox folders (English).

TABLE 10–2 URLs of a User's Mailbox Folder

Folder	URL
Calendar	`file://./backofficestorage/microsoft.com/MBX/UserAlias/Calendar`
Contacts	`file://./backofficestorage/microsoft.com/MBX/UserAlias/Contacts`
Drafts	`file://./backofficestorage/microsoft.com/MBX/UserAlias/Drafts`
Inbox	`file://./backofficestorage/microsoft.com/MBX/UserAlias/Inbox`
Journal	`file://./backofficestorage/microsoft.com/MBX/UserAlias/Journal`
Notes	`file://./backofficestorage/microsoft.com/MBX/UserAlias/Notes`
Outbox	`file://./backofficestorage/microsoft.com/MBX/UserAlias/Outbox`
Sent Items	`file://./backofficestorage/microsoft.com/MBX/UserAlias/Sent%20Items`
Tasks	`file://./backofficestorage/microsoft.com/MBX/USerAlias/Tasks`

Note The URLs in the preceding table are only examples; you should not construct them manually in your application. You can retrieve all the URLs in a user's localized mailbox folder by using the IMailbox interface on a CDO Person object or by retrieving properties on the base mailbox folder, such as urn:schemas:httpmail:inbox or urn:schemas:httpmail:calendar.

The HTTP: URL Scheme

When you construct URLs by using the `http:` scheme for use with the ExOLEDB Provider, you follow the same procedure as you would when accessing the item over the network using the HTTP protocol. The structure of the URL is as follows:

`http://servername/virtual-directory/virtual-path`

servername

   This is the local server name. You can use the local server's fully qualified domain name, but this is not required with the ExOLEDB Provider. The DNS is *not* used to resolve this name into an IP address, and the network is *not* used to access the item. The URL serves only to uniquely identify an item in the local computer's Web Storage System. Only URLs for items that reside in private or public stores on the same server can be used; you cannot access items in stores on remote servers by using the ExOLEDB Provider.

virtual-directory

   This is the Exchange HTTP Virtual Server virtual directory mapped to the public folder. Table 10-3 shows the default virtual directory names for all private stores and the default public folder "Public Folders."

TABLE 10-3 *Default Virtual Directory Names*

Virtual directory name	Description
Exchange	All private mailboxes in any private store are available through this virtual directory.
Public	This virtual directory is mapped to the top public folder in the default public folder tree. The default public folder name is "Public Folders".

   Each virtual path starts with an Exchange HTTP Virtual Server virtual directory name.

virtual-path

   This is the virtual path to the item. The path is *virtual* because multiple Exchange virtual directories can exist as a hierarchy below the first Exchange virtual directory. Each virtual subdirectory can map to a noncontiguous public folder housed in any public store. If the subfolder is not an Exchange virtual directory, the path is identical to the physical hierarchy below the public folder.

Note When you use http: URLs with the ExOLEDB Provider, you must explicitly specify the ExOLEDB Provider binder when binding the item. This provider has the programmatic identifier "ExOLEDB.DataSource". The OLE DB Provider for Internet Publishing (MSDAIPP) is registered as the *default* provider for the `http:` URL scheme. If you do not specify the ExOLEDB Provider, the MSDAIPP provider attempts to service the request. This provider is not supported for use with CDO for Exchange, nor should it be used in server applications that need to scale.

The URLs in the following examples use the `http:` scheme:

```
http://server.microsoft.com/public/reports/report1.doc
http://server.microsoft.com/public/reports/schema/

http://server.microsoft.com/exchange/User1/Inbox
http://server.microsoft.com/exchange/User1/Calendar
http://server.microsoft.com/exchange/User1/Drafts

http://server.microsoft.com/application1/app1/
http://server.microsoft.com/application1/app1/schema
```

The URLs in Table 10–4 are examples of common file: URLs for a user's mailbox folders (English).

TABLE 10–4 *URLs for a User's Mailbox Folders*

Folder	URL
Calendar	`http://server.microsoft.com/exchange/UserAlias/Calendar`
Contacts	`http://server.microsoft.com/exchange/UserAlias/Contacts`
Drafts	`http://server.microsoft.com/exchange/UserAlias/Drafts`
Inbox	`http://server.microsoft.com/exchange/UserAlias/Inbox`
Journal	`http://server.microsoft.com/exchange/UserAlias/Journal`
Notes	`http://server.microsoft.com/exchange/UserAlias/Notes`
Outbox	`http://server.microsoft.com/exchange/UserAlias/Outbox`
Sent Items	`http://server.microsoft.com/exchange/UserAlias/Sent%20Items`
Tasks	`http://server.microsoft.com/exchange/UserAlias/Tasks`

Note The URLs in the preceding table are only examples; you should not construct them manually in your application. You can retrieve all the URLs in a user's localized mailbox folder by using the IMailbox interface on a CDO Person object or by retrieving properties, such as urn:schemas:httpmail:inbox or urn:schemas:httpmail:calendar, on the base mailbox folder.

Constructing Web Storage System HTTP URLs

When you construct URLs by using the `http:` scheme, you follow the same procedure as when you identify a resource accessible through the HTTP protocol. The structure of the URL is:

`http://servername/virtual-directory/virtual-path`

servername

This is the Web server name. The server's name must resolve to the IP address of the host through the mechanism that is provided, for example DNS, Microsoft Windows Internet Naming Service (WINS), LMHOSTS file, etc.

virtual-directory

This is the Exchange HTTP Virtual Server virtual directory mapped to the public folder. Table 10–5 shows the default virtual directory names for all private stores and the default public folder "Public Folders."

TABLE 10–5   *Default Virtual Directory Names*

Virtual directory name	Description
Exchange	All private mailboxes in any private store are available through this virtual directory.
Public	This virtual directory is mapped to the top public folder in the default public folder tree. The default public folder name is "Public Folders."

Each virtual path starts with an Exchange Virtual Server virtual directory.

virtual-path

This is the virtual path to the item. The path is virtual because multiple Exchange virtual directories can exist as a hierarchy below the first Exchange virtual directory. Each virtual subdirectory can map to a noncontiguous public folder housed in any public store. If the subfolder is not an Exchange virtual directory, the path is identical to the physical hierarchy below the public folder.

The URLs in the following examples use the `http:` scheme:

```
http://server.microsoft.com/public/reports/report1.doc
http://server.microsoft.com/public/reports/schema/

http://server.microsoft.com/exchange/User1/Inbox
http://server.microsoft.com/exchange/User1/Calendar
http://server.microsoft.com/exchange/User1/Drafts
```

```
http://server.microsoft.com/application1/app1/
http://server.microsoft.com/application1/app1/schema
```

The URLs in Table 10–6 are examples of common http: URLs for a user's mailbox folders (English).

TABLE 10–6 *Examples of Common http: URLs for a User's Mailbox Folders*

Folder	URL
Calendar	`http://server.microsoft.com/exchange/UserAlias/Calendar`
Contacts	`http://server.microsoft.com/exchange/UserAlias/Contacts`
Drafts	`http://server.microsoft.com/exchange/UserAlias/Drafts`
Inbox	`http://server.microsoft.com/exchange/UserAlias/Inbox`
Journal	`http://server.microsoft.com/exchange/UserAlias/Journal`
Notes	`http://server.microsoft.com/exchange/UserAlias/Notes`
Outbox	`http://server.microsoft.com/exchange/UserAlias/Outbox`
Sent Items	`http://server.microsoft.com/exchange/UserAlias/Sent%20Items`
Tasks	`http://server.microsoft.com/exchange/UserAlias/Tasks`

Note The URLs in the previous table are only examples; you should not construct them manually in your application. You can retrieve all the URLs in a user's localized mailbox folder by using the IMailbox interface on a CDO Person object or by retrieving properties, such as urn:schemas:httpmail:inbox or urn:schemas:httpmail:calendar, on the base mailbox folder.

Using Relative URLs

When using the ExOLEDB provider, all operations on items in a particular public or mailbox store run in an OLE DB session. After this session has been established with a particular store, you can refer to items in that store by using relative URLs. These operations are called *scoped operations*, the scope being the folder tree residing in that particular store. With http: URLs, the relative URLs must include the entire path, starting from the root virtual directory. With file: URLs, the path starts with the first folder below the top-level folder. You can also use relative URLs when you construct SQL queries for folders in a store.

With ADO, the OLE DB session object that houses the current session information is wrapped using an instance of an ADO Connection object. After you have established the session (Connection) to a particular store, you can then dispense with generating the fully qualified URL for items in that store when you use ADO Record and Recordset objects.

For example, the following functions demonstrate this functionality in a public store:

- The getConnection function returns an ADO Connection object that is connected to a particular store. To create the Connection using the file: URL scheme, you need only specify the name of the top-level public folder within that store. The fully qualified domain name is retrieved using the ADSystemInfo object. This is all the information you need to connect to a public folder tree in a public store. However, for mailboxes, you also need the user's alias.
- The getRecord_ro function returns a read-only ADO Record object bound to the item specified using a relative URL in a particular store. The caller can pass either an open Connection object or the name of the top-level public folder. In the latter case, the function uses the getConnection function internally to retrieve a Connection to the store identified by the specified top-level public folder.
- The getRecord_rw function returns a read-write ADO Record object bound to the item specified using a relative URL. The caller can pass either an open Connection object or the name of the top-level public folder. In the latter case, it uses the getConnection function internally to retrieve a Connection to the store identified by the specified top-level public folder. The function is as follows:

[VBScript]

```
Const adModeReadWrite = 3

Function getConnection( relUrl )

  If not VarType(relUrl) = vbString Then
    Err.Raise &H80070057 ' E_INVALIDARG
  End If

  Dim Info
  Dim Domain
  Dim Url
  Set InfoNT = CreateObject("WinNTSystemInfo")
  Set Info   = CreateObject("ADSystemInfo")

  Dim Conn
  Set Conn = CreateObject("ADODB.Connection")

  Url = "http://" & lcase(InfoNT.ComputerName) & "." & _
  Info.DomainDNSName & relUrl
  wscript.echo Url
  Conn.Provider = "ExOLEDB.DataSource"
```

Using Relative URLs

```
 Conn.Open Url

 Set getConnection = Conn
End Function

' getRecord_ro
'
'   vSource is either the name of a top-level public folder or
'            an open ADO Connection object.
'   RelURI is the relative URI to an item within the store
'
Function getRecord_ro( relURL, Conn )

 If not VarType(relUrl) = vbString And ( (TypeName(Conn) =
"Connection") Or (TypeName(Conn) = "Nothing") ) Then
   Err.Raise &H80070057 ' E_INVALIDARG
 End If

 Dim Rec
 Set Rec = CreateObject("ADODB.Record")

 If Not TypeName(vSource) = "Connection" Then
   Set Conn = getConnection(relUrl)
 End If

 Rec.Open relURL, Conn

 Set getRecord_ro = Rec

End Function

' getRecord_rw
'   vSource is either the name of a top-level public folder or
'            an open ADO Connection object.
'   RelURI is the relative URI to an item within the store
'
Function getRecord_rw(relURL, Conn )

 If not VarType(relUrl) = vbString And ( (TypeName(Conn) =
"Connection") Or (TypeName(Conn) = "Nothing") ) Then
   Err.Raise &H80070057 ' E_INVALIDARG
 End If

 Dim Rec
 Set Rec = CreateObject("ADODB.Record")

 If Not TypeName(Conn) = "Connection" Then
   Set Conn = getConnection(relUrl)
```

Chapter 10 • Constructing Web Storage System URLs

```
End If

Rec.Open relURL, Conn, adModeReadWrite
Set getRecord_rw = Rec

End Function
```

Assume that you have a folder called "test1" below your Public Folders top-level folder in a public store and an item in "test1" called "item1.txt". To access the folder and the item, you could use these functions in the following way:

[VBScript]

```
Const adDefaultStream = -1

Dim Conn
Dim Rec
Dim Rec2

Set Conn = getConnection("/apps")
Set Rec  = getRecord_rw("/apps/test1/Schema",    Conn)
Set Rec2 = getRecord_ro("/apps/test1/item1.txt", Conn)

WScript.Echo Rec.Fields("DAV:href")
Wscript.Echo Rec.Fields("DAV:contentclass")

wscript.echo

WScript.Echo Rec2.Fields("DAV:href")
wscript.echo Rec2.fields("DAV:contentclass")
Set Stm = Rec2.Fields(adDefaultStream).Value
stm.charset = "us-ascii"
WScript.Echo Stm.readText
```

Note that the string "Public Folders" does not appear in the relative URLs. This name is used to connect to the appropriate public folder tree. After you have connected, you no longer need to specify this information in your relative URLs.

Getting the Host Domain Name

When you use the `file:` URL scheme to identify the location of items in the Web Storage System, you need the fully qualified domain name of the host. The programming task that follows demonstrates how to retrieve the domain name of the host on which the code is running.

To increase performance, you should retrieve this name once, store it, and then use the stored version when constructing URLs. For example, if you are writing an ASP application, retrieve the domain name and then place the information in the ASP Application collection for subsequent use by other scripts. The code is as follows:

[VBScript]

```
Function GetDomainName()

 Dim Info
 Set Info = CreateObject("AdSystemInfo")
 GetDomainName = Info.DomainDNSName

End Function

Function GetComputerName()

 Dim InfoNT
 Set InfoNT = CreateObject("WinNTSystemInfo")
 GetComputerName = lcase(InfoNT.ComputerName)

End Function

Function GetForestDNSName()

 Dim Info
 Set Info = CreateObject("AdSystemInfo")
 GetForestDNSName = Info.ForestDNSName

End Function
```

[Visual Basic]

```
Function GetDomainName()

 Dim Info As New ADSystemInfo
 GetDomainName = Info.DomainDNSName

End Function

Function GetComputerName()

 Dim InfoNT As New WinNTSystemInfo
 GetComputerName = LCase(InfoNT.ComputerName)

End Function

Function GetForestDNSName()
```

```
Dim Info As New ADSystemInfo
GetForestDNSName = Info.ForestDNSName

End Function
```

   [C++]

```cpp
#define _WIN32_WINNT 0x0500
#define _UNICODE
#define UNICODE

#include <windows.h>
#include <comdef.h>
#define BUF_SIZE 4096

bstr_t getHostDomainName() {

   HRESULT hr     = S_OK;
   BSTR    domainName;
   DWORD dwSize   = 0;
   wchar_t* pBuf = new wchar_t[BUF_SIZE];
   if(pBuf == NULL)
      _com_issue_error(E_OUTOFMEMORY);


if(!GetComputerNameEx((COMPUTER_NAME_FORMAT)ComputerNameDnsDomain,
                     pBuf,
                     &dwSize)) {
      if(GetLastError() == ERROR_MORE_DATA) {
         delete [] pBuf;
         pBuf = new wchar_t[dwSize+1];
         if(pBuf == NULL)
            _com_issue_error(E_OUTOFMEMORY);


if(!GetComputerNameEx((COMPUTER_NAME_FORMAT)ComputerNameDnsDomain, pBuf, &dwSize) ) {
            hr =   HRESULT_FROM_WIN32(GetLastError());
            delete [] pBuf;
            pBuf     = NULL;
            _com_issue_error(hr);
         }
      }
      else

_com_issue_error(HRESULT_FROM_WIN32(GetLastError()));
   }

   domainName = SysAllocString(pBuf);
```

```
    delete [] pBuf;

    return bstr_t(domainName, false);
}

#define _WIN32_WINNT 0x0500
#define _UNICODE
#define UNICODE

#include <windows.h>
#include <comdef.h>
#define BUF_SIZE 4096

bstr_t getHostName() {

    HRESULT hr        = S_OK;
    BSTR     hostName;
    DWORD    dwSize   = 0;
    wchar_t* pBuf = new wchar_t[BUF_SIZE];
    if(pBuf == NULL)
       _com_issue_error(E_OUTOFMEMORY);


if(!GetComputerNameEx((COMPUTER_NAME_FORMAT)ComputerNameDns
Hostname,
                    pBuf,
                    &dwSize)) {
      if(GetLastError() == ERROR_MORE_DATA) {
          delete [] pBuf;
          pBuf = new wchar_t[dwSize+1];
          if(pBuf == NULL)
             _com_issue_error(E_OUTOFMEMORY);


if(!GetComputerNameEx((COMPUTER_NAME_FORMAT)ComputerNameDns
Hostname, pBuf, &dwSize) ) {
             hr =   HRESULT_FROM_WIN32(GetLastError());
             delete [] pBuf;
             pBuf    = NULL;
             _com_issue_error(hr);
          }
      }
      else

_com_issue_error(HRESULT_FROM_WIN32(GetLastError()));
   }

   hostName = SysAllocString(pBuf);
   delete [] pBuf;
```

Chapter 10 • Constructing Web Storage System URLs

```cpp
    return bstr_t(hostName, false);
}

#define _WIN32_WINNT 0x0500
#define _UNICODE
#define UNICODE

#include <windows.h>
#include <comdef.h>
#define BUF_SIZE 4096

bstr_t getFQDName() {

    HRESULT hr         = S_OK;
    BSTR    fqdname;
    DWORD   dwSize     = 0;
    wchar_t* pBuf = new wchar_t[BUF_SIZE];
    if(pBuf == NULL)
        _com_issue_error(E_OUTOFMEMORY);


    if(!GetComputerNameEx((COMPUTER_NAME_FORMAT)ComputerNameDnsFullyQualified,
                    pBuf,
                    &dwSize)) {
        if(GetLastError() == ERROR_MORE_DATA) {
            delete [] pBuf;
            pBuf = new wchar_t[dwSize+1];
            if(pBuf == NULL)
                _com_issue_error(E_OUTOFMEMORY);


            if(!GetComputerNameEx((COMPUTER_NAME_FORMAT)ComputerNameDnsFullyQualified, pBuf, &dwSize) ) {
                hr =   HRESULT_FROM_WIN32(GetLastError());
                delete [] pBuf;
                pBuf   = NULL;
                _com_issue_error(hr);
            }
        }
        else

_com_issue_error(HRESULT_FROM_WIN32(GetLastError()));
    }

    fqdname = SysAllocString(pBuf);
    delete [] pBuf;

    return bstr_t(fqdname, false);
}
```

Getting Well-Known Mailbox Folder URLs

Each user's mailbox folder has a set of properties that you can use to retrieve URLs for well-known subfolders such as Inbox, Calendar, Drafts, and Tasks. Additionally, you can retrieve the Exchange mail submission URI that is used to send messages through HTTP/WebDAV or the ExOLEDB provider. The returned URLs are localized into the language that is used by the client.

Table 10–7 lists the properties that return these URLs and that are retrieved from a user's root mailbox folder.

TABLE 10–7 *Getting Well-Known Mailbox Folder URLs*

Property	Well-known folder (English)
urn:schemas:httpmail:calendar	Calendar
urn:schemas:httpmail:contacts	Contacts
urn:schemas:httpmail:deleteditems	Deleted Items
urn:schemas:httpmail:drafts	Drafts
urn:schemas:httpmail:inbox	Inbox
urn:schemas:httpmail:journal	Journal
urn:schemas:httpmail:notes	Notes
urn:schemas:httpmail:outbox	Outbox
urn:schemas:httpmail:sentitems	Sent Items
urn:schemas:httpmail:tasks	Tasks
urn:schemas:httpmail:sendmsg	Exchange Mail Submission URI
urn:schemas:httpmail:msgfolderroot	Mailbox Folder (root)

To access the properties listed in Table 10–7,

1. Bind to the user's root mailbox folder. You can either request the server and username from the client to construct this initial URL or search Active Directory for the user's homeMDB attribute. From the value of this attribute, you can get the server on which the user's private mailbox is stored.
2. Use the values of these properties to bind to these folders in a mailbox folder. The following code is illustrative:

   [VBScript]

```
<Job id="printMailboxURLs">

<reference object="ADODB.Record"/>
<reference object="CDO.Message"/>
```

```vbscript
<script language="VBScript">

userName   = WScript.Arguments.Item(0)

set info   = createobject("adsysteminfo")
set infoNT = CreateObject("WinNTSystemInfo")

urls = getStdWellKnownMailboxURLs("http://" &
lcase(infoNT.ComputerName) & "." & _
                                  Info.domaindnsname & "/
exchange/" & userName, _
                                  "ExOLEDB.DataSource")

wscript.echo "Well-known mailbox file: URLs for local
mailbox: " & userName
wscript.echo "======================================="

For i = LBound(urls) to UBound(urls) step 2
 wscript.stdout.write urls(i)
 if Len(urls(i)) > 7 then
  wscript.stdout.write vbTab
 else
  wscript.stdout.write vbTab & vbTab
 end if
 wscript.stdout.write urls(i+1) & vbCrLf
next

Function getStdWellKnownMailboxURLs( mailboxFolderURL,
provider )

 If Not TypeName(mailboxFolderURL) = "String" Then
  Err.Raise   &H80070057 ' E_INVALIDARG
 End If


 Dim Rec
 Set Rec = CreateObject("ADODB.Record")
 Dim Conn
 Set Conn = CreateObject("ADODB.Connection")
 Conn.Provider =  provider
 Conn.Open mailboxFolderURL

 Rec.Open mailboxFolderURL, Conn
 Set Flds = Rec.Fields

 ' The constants used here are defined in the CDOEx.dll
type library.
 ' They are imported using the <reference> element above.
```

```
            getStdWellKnownMailboxURLs = Array( _
                    "Calendar" , Flds(cdoCalendarFolderURL), _
                    "Contacts" , Flds(cdoContactFolderURL), _
                    "DeletedIt", Flds(cdoDeletedItems), _
                    "Inbox"    , Flds(cdoInbox), _
                    "Journal"  , Flds(cdoJournal), _
                    "MsgRoot"  , Flds(cdoMsgFolderRoot), _
                    "Notes"    , Flds(cdoNotes), _
                    "Outbox"   , Flds(cdoOutbox), _
                    "SendMsg"  , Flds(cdoSendMsg), _
                    "SendItems", Flds(cdoSentItems), _
                    "Tasks"    , Flds(cdoTasks) )

End Function

</script>

</Job>
```

[C++]

```cpp
#import <msado15.dll> no_namespace
#import <c:\program files\common files\microsoft shared\cdo\cdoex.dll> no_namespace
#include <iostream.h>

void printMailboxFolders(bstr_t mailtoUrl) {

    IMailboxPtr iMbx;
    try {
        iMbx = getIMailbox(mailtoUrl);
    }
    catch(_com_error e) {
        throw e;
    }

    cout << "BaseFolder: " << iMbx->BaseFolder << endl;
    cout << "Inbox: "      << iMbx->Inbox << endl;
    cout << "Calendar: "   << iMbx->Calendar << endl;
    cout << "Drafts: "     << iMbx->Drafts << endl;

    //...

    IDataSourcePtr iDsrc;
    iDsrc = iMbx;
    cout << iDsrc->SourceURL << endl;
    _RecordPtr Rec(__uuidof(Record));
    _ConnectionPtr Conn(__uuidof(Connection));
    Conn->Provider = "ExOLEDB.DataSource";
    bstr_t sSendMsgUrl;
```

```
    try {
        Conn->Open(iMbx->BaseFolder, bstr_t(),bstr_t(), -1);
        Rec->Open(iMbx->BaseFolder,
variant_t((IDispatch*)Conn, true), adModeRead,
adFailIfNotExists, adOpenRecordUnspecified, bstr_t(),
bstr_t());
        sSendMsgUrl = bstr_t(Rec->Fields-
>Item["urn:schemas:httpmail:sendmsg"]->Value);
    }
    catch(_com_error e) {
        cout << "Error binding to user's base mailbox folder.
" << endl;
        throw e;
    }
    cout << "Mail Submission URI: " << sSendMsgUrl << endl;

}

IMailboxPtr getIMailbox( bstr_t mailtoUrl) {

    IPersonPtr Per(__uuidof(Person));
    IDataSourcePtr Dsrc;
    Dsrc = Per;
    try {
        Dsrc->Open(mailtoUrl, NULL, adModeRead,
adFailIfNotExists, adOpenRecordUnspecified,
bstr_t(),bstr_t());
    }
    catch(_com_error e) {
        throw e;
    }

    return Per;
}
```

ELEVEN

Working with Folders and Items

The following sections describe how to work with items in the Web Storage System:

- Creating Folders
- Creating Items
- Getting Existing Items
- Accessing Item Streams
- Copying Items
- Deleting Items
- Moving Items
- Working with Item Properties
- Getting a List of Folders
- Using Transactions

Creating Folders

The examples that follow show how to create a folder in the Web Storage System. The function in each example performs the following steps:

1. The function attempts to create a folder at this URL. If an error occurs, the function fails.
2. If the function is successful, it sets the new folder's DAV:contentclass property to the value "urn:content-classes:folder".
3. The function returns a reference to the Record object that is bound to the new folder.

Chapter 11 • Working with Folders and Items

The code used to create folders is as follows:

[VBScript]

```
<job id="createfolder">
<reference object="adodb.record"/>
<script language="vbscript">

If WScript.Arguments.Count < 1 Then
 WScript.Echo "Usage: cscript createfolder.wsf URL [content class]"
 WScript.Quit
End If

Dim sUrl
Dim sContentClass
sUrl = WScript.Arguments(0)
sContentClass = WScript.Arguments(1)

Dim Rec
Wscript.Echo "Creating folder at URL: " & sUrl
Set Rec = CreateFolder(sUrl, sContentClass, Nothing)
Wscript.Echo "Succeeded."

Function CreateFolder( sUrl, sContentClass, Conn )

 Dim Rec
 Set Rec    = CreateObject("ADODB.Record")

 ' Did caller pass a Connection object reference?
 If Not ( VarType(Conn) = vbObject AND TypeName(Conn) = "Connection" ) Then
    Set Conn = CreateObject("ADODB.Connection")
    Conn.Provider = "ExOLEDB.DataSource"
    Conn.Open sUrl
 End If

 If sContentClass = "" Then
   sContentClass = "urn:content-classes:folder" ' The Default is urn:content-classes:folder.
 End If

 ' Try to create the folder

 Rec.Open sUrl, Conn, adModeReadWrite, adCreateCollection
 Rec.Fields("DAV:contentclass") = sContentClass
 Rec.Fields.Update

 Set CreateFolder = Rec
```

Creating Folders

```
End Function
</script>
</job>
```

[C++]

The following example creates a new folder by using the native OLE DB interfaces directly in C++.

```cpp
#include <oledb.h>
#include <msdasc.h>
#include <comdef.h>

#pragma comment(lib,"oledb.lib")
#pragma comment(lib,"msdasc.lib")

#define BUF_SIZE    4096

HRESULT CreateFolder( BSTR url, IRow** ppRow )
{

    if(url == NULL)
        return E_INVALIDARG;

    HRESULT           hr              = S_OK;
    DWORD             dwBindStatus    = 0;
    IBindResource*    pBRes           = NULL;
    ICreateRow*       pCrRow          = NULL;
    CLSID             clsid_ExOLEDBProviderBinder;

    if(FAILED(hr = CLSIDFromProgID(L"ExOLEDB.Binder",
&clsid_ExOLEDBProviderBinder)))
        return hr;

    hr = CoCreateInstance(
        clsid_ExOLEDBProviderBinder,
        NULL,
        CLSCTX_INPROC_SERVER,
        IID_IBindResource,
        (void**)&pBRes);

    if(FAILED(hr))
        return hr;

    hr = pBRes->Bind(
        NULL,
        url,
        DBBINDURLFLAG_READWRITE,
        DBGUID_SESSION,
        IID_ICreateRow,
        NULL,
```

```
        NULL,
        &dwBindStatus,
        (IUnknown**) &pCrRow);

    if(FAILED(hr)){
        pBRes->Release();
        return hr;
    }

    pBRes->Release();

    dwBindStatus      =    0;
    IRow*      pRow   =    NULL;
    wchar_t*   newUrl      =    NULL;
    hr = pCrRow->CreateRow(
        NULL,
        url,
        (DBBINDURLFLAG_READWRITE | DBBINDURLFLAG_COLLECTION
),
        DBGUID_ROW,
        IID_IRow,
        NULL,
        NULL,
        &dwBindStatus,
        &newUrl,
        (IUnknown**)&pRow
    );
    if(FAILED(hr)){
        pCrRow->Release();
        return hr;
    }

    *ppRow = pRow;
    pCrRow->Release();

    return hr;
}
```

Creating Items

The example that follows shows how to create a noncollection item in the Web Storage System. The example function performs the following steps:

1. It attempts to create the item at this URL. If an error occurs, the function fails.
2. If successful, it sets the new item's DAV:contentclass property to the value "urn:content-classes:item".
3. It returns a reference to the Record object bound to the new item.

Creating Items

The code for creating items is as follows:

[VBScript]

```
<job id="createitem">
<reference object="adodb.record"/>
<script language="vbscript">

If WScript.Arguments.Count < 1 Then
 WScript.Echo "Usage: cscript createitem.wsf URL [content class] [content type [, file contents name]]"
 Wscript.Echo "For example:"
 WScript.Echo " cscript createitem.wsf ""http://server/path/item.txt"" """" ""text/plain; charset=iso-8859-1"" <filename>"
 WScript.Quit
End If

Dim sUrl
Dim sContentClass
Dim sContentType
Dim sFileName

sUrl = WScript.Arguments(0)
sContentClass = WScript.Arguments(1)
sContentType  = WScript.Arguments(2)
sFileName = Wscript.Arguments(3)

Dim Rec
Wscript.Echo "Creating item at URL: " & sUrl
Set Rec = CreateItem(sUrl, sContentClass, sContentType, sFileName, Nothing)
Wscript.Echo "Succeeded."
Wscript.Echo Rec.Fields("DAV:href")
WScript.Echo Rec.Fields("DAV:contentclass")
Wscript.Echo Rec.Fields("urn:schemas:mailheader:content-type")

Function CreateItem( sUrl, sContentClass, sContentType, sFileName, Conn )

 Dim Rec
 Set Rec    = CreateObject("ADODB.Record")

 ' Did caller pass a Connection object reference?
 If Not ( VarType(Conn) = vbObject AND TypeName(Conn) = "Connection" ) Then
    Set Conn = CreateObject("ADODB.Connection")
    Conn.Provider = "ExOLEDB.DataSource"
    Conn.Open sUrl
```

Chapter 11 • Working with Folders and Items

```
  End If

  If sContentClass = "" Then
    sContentClass = "urn:content-classes:item" ' The default
content class is urn:content-classes:item.
  End If

  If sContentType = "" Then
    sContentClass = "application/octet-stream"
  End If

  ' Try to create the item

  Rec.Open sUrl, Conn, adModeReadWrite,
adCreateNonCollection
  Rec.Fields("DAV:contentclass") = sContentClass
  Rec.Fields("urn:schemas:mailheader:content-type") =
sContentType
  Rec.Fields.Update

  If Not sFileName = "" Then
    Set Stm = Rec.Fields(adDefaultStream).Value
    sContentType = LCase(sContentType)
    If InStr(sContentType, "text") > -1 Then
      Stm.Type = adTypeText
      pos = InStr(sContentType, "charset=") + 8
      wscript.echo pos
      If pos > 8 Then
        sCharset = Mid(sContentType, pos)
        wscript.echo "charset: " & sCharset
        Stm.Charset = sCharset
      Else
        Stm.Charset = "US-ASCII"
      End If
    Else
      Stm.Type = adTypeBinary
    End If

    Stm.LoadFromFile sFileName
    Stm.Flush
  End If

  Set CreateItem = Rec

End Function
</script>
</job>
```

Creating Items

[C++]

The following example illustrates how to create a new noncollection item and get an existing item by using the native OLE DB interfaces directly in C++:

```
#include <oledb.h>
#include <msdasc.h>
#include <comdef.h>

#pragma comment(lib,"oledb.lib")
#pragma comment(lib,"msdasc.lib")

HRESULT CreateItem( BSTR url, IRow** ppRow )
{
   HRESULT            hr             = S_OK;
   DWORD              dwBindStatus   = 0;
   IBindResource*     pBRes          = NULL;
   ICreateRow*        pCrRow         = NULL;
   ITransactionLocal* pTrans         = NULL;
   CLSID              clsid_ExOLEDBProviderBinder;

   if(FAILED(hr = CLSIDFromProgID(L"ExOLEDB.Binder",
&clsid_ExOLEDBProviderBinder)))
      return hr;

   hr = CoCreateInstance(
      clsid_ExOLEDBProviderBinder,
      NULL,
      CLSCTX_INPROC_SERVER,
      IID_IBindResource,
      (void**)&pBRes);

   if(FAILED(hr))
      return hr;

   hr = pBRes->Bind(
      NULL,
      url,
      DBBINDURLFLAG_READWRITE,
      DBGUID_SESSION,
      IID_ICreateRow,
      NULL,
      NULL,
      &dwBindStatus,
      (IUnknown**) &pCrRow);

   if(FAILED(hr)){
      pBRes->Release();
      return hr;
```

```
    }
    pBRes->Release();

    hr=pCrRow-
>QueryInterface(IID_ITransactionLocal,(void**)&pTrans);
    if(FAILED(hr))
        pTrans = NULL;
    else
    {
        DWORD dwLevel = 0;
        hr = pTrans-
>StartTransaction(ISOLATIONLEVEL_UNSPECIFIED,0,NULL,
&dwLevel);
    }

    IUnknown*  pUnk   = NULL;
    wchar_t* newUrl;
    hr = pCrRow->CreateRow(
        NULL,
        url,
        DBBINDURLFLAG_READWRITE,
        DBGUID_ROW,
        IID_IRow,
        NULL,
        NULL,
        &dwBindStatus,
        &newUrl,
        &pUnk
    );

    if(FAILED(hr)){
        if(pTrans != NULL) {
            pTrans->Abort(NULL,FALSE,FALSE);
            pTrans->Release();
        }
        pCrRow->Release();
        return hr;
    }

    hr = pUnk->QueryInterface(ppRow);

    hr = pTrans->Commit(FALSE, 0, 0 );
    pTrans->Release();
    pCrRow->Release();
    pUnk->Release();

    return hr;
}
```

Getting Existing Items

The example that follows shows how to get an existing item in the Web Storage System. The example function performs the following steps:

1. It attempts to bind to the item at this URL. If an error occurs, the function fails.
2. It returns a reference to the Record object bound to the new item.

The code used to get an existing item in the Web Storage System is as follows:

[VBScript]

```
<job id="getitem">
<reference object="adodb.record"/>
<script language="vbscript">

Dim Rec
Dim InfoNT
Dim sUrl
Dim sRelPath
Set InfoNT = CreateObject("WinNTSystemInfo")

sRelPath = "/public/test_folder/item1.txt"
sUrl = "http://" & InfoNT.Computername & sRelPath

Set Rec = getItem_rw(sUrl, Nothing)
WScript.echo "Opened " & Rec.Fields("DAV:displayname") & " 
at URL: " & Rec.Fields("DAV:href")
' ...

Dim Conn
Set Conn = CreateObject("ADODB.Connection")
Conn.Provider = "ExOLEDB.DataSource"
Conn.Open sUrl
Set Rec = getItem_ro(sUrl, Conn)
WScript.echo "Opened " & Rec.Fields("DAV:displayname") & " 
at URL: " & Rec.Fields("DAV:href")

'''''''''''''''''''''''''''''''''''''''''''''''''''''''
' getItem_rw
'    sUrl - The URL to the item (http).
'    Conn  - An open Connection object, or Nothing.
'
'''''''''''''''''''''''''''''''''''''''''''''''''''''''

Function getItem_rw( sUrl, Conn )
```

```
  Dim Rec
  Set Rec = CreateObject("ADODB.Record")

  ' Did caller pass a Connection object reference?
  If Not ( VarType(Conn) = vbObject AND TypeName(Conn) =
"Connection" ) Then
    Set Conn = CreateObject("ADODB.Connection")
    Conn.Provider = "ExOLEDB.DataSource"
    Conn.Open sUrl
  End If

  ' Try to bind to the item.
  Rec.Open sUrl, Conn, adModeReadWrite

  Set getItem_rw = Rec

End Function

'''''''''''''''''''''''''''''''''''''''''''''''''''
' getItem_ro
'    sUrl - The URL to the item (http).
'    Conn  - An open Connection object, or Nothing.
'
'''''''''''''''''''''''''''''''''''''''''''''''''''

Function getItem_ro( sUrl, Conn )

  Dim Rec
  Set Rec = CreateObject("ADODB.Record")

  ' Did caller pass a Connection object reference?
  If Not ( VarType(Conn) = vbObject AND TypeName(Conn) =
"Connection" ) Then
    Set Conn = CreateObject("ADODB.Connection")
    Conn.Provider = "ExOLEDB.DataSource"
    Conn.Open sUrl
  End If

  ' Try to bind to the item.
  Rec.Open sUrl, Conn

  Set getItem_ro = Rec

End Function
</script>
</job>
```

Getting Existing Items

[C++]

The example that follows demonstrates how to bind to an existing item using the native OLE DB interfaces directly when using C++. If the item is successfully bound, the OLE DB IRow interface address is returned.

```
#include <oledb.h>
#include <msdasc.h>
#pragma comment(lib,"oledb.lib")
#pragma comment(lib,"msdasc.lib")

#define BUF_SIZE    4096

HRESULT getItem(BSTR url, IRow** ppRow)
{
   if(url == NULL)
      return E_INVALIDARG;

   HRESULT           hr             = S_OK;
   IBindResource*    pBRes          = NULL;
   IUnknown*         pUnk           = NULL;
   DBBINDURLSTATUS   dwBindStatus   = 0;
   CLSID             clsid_ExOLEDBProviderBinder;

   if(FAILED(hr = CLSIDFromProgID(L"ExOLEDB.Binder",
&clsid_ExOLEDBProviderBinder)))
      return hr;

   hr = CoCreateInstance(
      clsid_ExOLEDBProviderBinder,
      NULL,
      CLSCTX_INPROC_SERVER,
      IID_IBindResource,
      (void**)&pBRes);

   if(FAILED(hr))
      return hr;

   hr = pBRes->Bind(
      NULL,
      url,
      DBBINDURLFLAG_READWRITE,
      DBGUID_ROW,
      IID_IRow,
      NULL,
      NULL,
      &dwBindStatus,
      (IUnknown**) &pUnk);

   if(FAILED(hr)){
```

```
        pBRes->Release();
        return hr;
    }

    hr = pUnk->QueryInterface(ppRow);
    pBRes->Release();
    return hr;

}
```

Accessing Item Streams

You can get an item's stream by using a Record or Recordset object's Fields collection. To request the stream, pass the index value of -1 adDefaultStream to the Fields.Item method.

When using CDO, you must use the CDO object's GetStream method. You cannot retrieve the stream using the Fields collection.

Items that are collections, such as folders, do not have streams. Requesting the stream for these types of items causes an exception to be raised.

In the following example, the function receives a URL to an inbox item, gets the item's stream, and saves it to a file on disk:

[VBScript]

```
<job id="getstream">
<reference object="adodb.record"/>
<script language="vbscript">

Dim Stm
Dim Conn
Dim InfoNT
Dim sUrl
Dim sRelPath
Set InfoNT = CreateObject("WinNTSystemInfo")

sRelPath = "/public/test_folder/item4.txt"
sUrl = "http://" & InfoNT.Computername & sRelPath
Set Conn = CreateObject("ADODB.Connection")
Conn.Provider = "ExOLEDB.DataSource"
Conn.Open sUrl

Set Stm = getStream(sUrl, Conn)

If Stm.Type = adTypeText Then
  Wscript.echo Stm.ReadText
End If
```

```
' ...

'\\\\\\\\\\\\\\\\\\\\\\\\\\\\\\\\\\\\\\\\\
' getStream
'    sUrl - URL to item
'    Conn - Active Connection or Nothing
'
'\\\\\\\\\\\\\\\\\\\\\\\\\\\\\\\\\\\\\\\\\
Function getStream( sUrl, Conn)

 Dim Rec
 Dim Flds
 Dim sContentType

 Set Rec    = CreateObject("ADODB.Record")

 ' Did caller pass a Connection object reference?
 If Not ( VarType(Conn) = vbObject AND TypeName(Conn) = "Connection" ) Then
    Set Conn = CreateObject("ADODB.Connection")
    Conn.Provider = "ExOLEDB.DataSource"
    Conn.Open sUrl
 End If

 ' Try to open the item

 Rec.Open sUrl, Conn, adModeReadWrite
 Set Flds = Rec.Fields
 If Flds("DAV:isfolder") = True Or Flds("DAV:iscollection") = True Then
    Err.Raise &H80070057, "GetStream", "Item at URL is a collection."    ' E_INVALIDARG
 End If

 sContentType = flds("urn:schemas:mailheader:content-type")
 set stm = Flds(adDefaultStream).Value
 If Not sContentType = "" And InStr(sContentType, "text") > -1 Then
    Stm.Type = adTypeText
    If InStr(sContentType,"charset=") > -1 Then
     Stm.Charset = Mid(sContentType, InStr(sContentType, "charset=") + 8)
    End If
 End If

 Set getStream = Stm

End Function
</script>
</job>
```

Chapter 11 • Working with Folders and Items

[C++]

The following example demonstrates how to use native OLE DB interfaces in C++ to write an item's stream and print an item's stream:

```cpp
#include <oledb.h>
#include <msdasc.h>
#include <comdef.h>

#pragma comment(lib,"oledb.lib")
#pragma comment(lib,"msdasc.lib")

HRESULT writeItemStream( IRow* pRow, BYTE* pBytes, DWORD dwSize, ITransactionLocal* pTrans )
{

    if(pRow == NULL || pBytes == NULL)
        return E_INVALIDARG;

    HRESULT         hr              =   S_OK;
    DWORD           dwBindStatus    =   0;
    DWORD           dwLevel         =   0;

    IStream*        pStm            =   NULL;
    ULONG           cColumns        =   1;
    DBCOLUMNACCESS  rgColumns[1];

    VARIANT         vStm;

    if(pTrans != NULL) {
        hr = pTrans->StartTransaction(ISOLATIONLEVEL_UNSPECIFIED,0,NULL,&dwLevel);
        if(FAILED(hr))
            return hr;
    }

    VariantInit(&vStm);
    rgColumns[0].pData      = &vStm;
    rgColumns[0].columnid   = DBROWCOL_DEFAULTSTREAM;
    rgColumns[0].wType      = DBTYPE_VARIANT;
    rgColumns[0].cbDataLen  = sizeof(VARIANT);
    hr = pRow->GetColumns(cColumns, rgColumns);
    if(FAILED(hr))
        return hr;

    hr = vStm.punkVal->QueryInterface(&pStm);
    if(FAILED(hr)) {
        VariantClear(&vStm);
        return hr;
    }
```

```c
    ULONG    cbWritten   =    0;
    if( FAILED( hr = pStm->Write((void*)pBytes, dwSize,
&cbWritten) ) ) {
        VariantClear(&vStm);
        return hr;
    }

    ULARGE_INTEGER uLargeInt;
    uLargeInt.LowPart = dwSize;
    uLargeInt.HighPart = 0;
    if( FAILED(hr = pStm->SetSize(uLargeInt) ) ) {
        VariantClear(&vStm);
        return hr;
    }

    if(FAILED(hr = pStm->Commit(1)) ) {
        VariantClear(&vStm);
        return hr;
    }

    if(pTrans != NULL)
        hr = pTrans->Commit(FALSE, 0 , 0);

    VariantClear(&vStm);

    return hr;
}

#include <oledb.h>
#include <msdasc.h>
#pragma comment(lib,"oledb.lib")
#pragma comment(lib,"msdasc.lib")

#include <stdio.h>

#define BUF_SIZE   4096

HRESULT printStream(BSTR itemURL) {


    HRESULT         hr              =   S_OK;
    DWORD           dwBindStatus    =   0;
    IBindResource*  pBRes           =   NULL;
    IStream*        pStrm           =   NULL;
    char*           buf             =   new char[BUF_SIZE];
    ULONG           cbToRead        =   BUF_SIZE;
    ULONG           cbRead          =   0;
    CLSID           clsid_ExOLEDBProviderBinder;
```

Chapter 11 • Working with Folders and Items

```
    if(FAILED(hr = CLSIDFromProgID(L"ExOLEDB.Binder",
&clsid_ExOLEDBProviderBinder)))
        return hr;

    if(itemURL == NULL)
        return E_INVALIDARG;

    hr = CoCreateInstance(
        clsid_ExOLEDBProviderBinder,
        NULL,
        CLSCTX_INPROC_SERVER,
        IID_IBindResource,
        (void**)&pBRes);

    if(FAILED(hr))
        goto Exit;

    hr = pBRes->Bind(
        NULL,
        itemURL,
        DBBINDURLFLAG_READ,
        DBGUID_STREAM,
        IID_IStream,
        NULL,
        NULL,
        &dwBindStatus,
        (IUnknown**) &pStrm);

    if(FAILED(hr))
        goto Exit;

    while(1) {
       hr=pStrm->Read((void*)buf,cbToRead,&cbRead);
       if(FAILED(hr)) {
          goto Exit;
       }

       if(hr==S_FALSE || cbRead == 0)
          break;

       for(unsigned int i = 0;i<cbRead;i++)
          printf("%c",buf[i]);
    }

Exit:

    delete [] buf;

    if(pBRes)
       pBRes->Release();
```

```
   if(pStrm)
      pStrm->Release();

   return hr;
}
```

Copying Items

To copy an item from one location to another within the same store, use the Record.CopyRecord method. If you copy a folder, all items and subfolders are also copied. You cannot use the Record.CopyRecord method to copy items from one public or mailbox store to another. The code example is as follows:

[VBScript]

```
<job id="copy_item">
<reference object="adodb.record"/>

<script language='vbscript'>

Dim Rec
Dim Info
Dim InfoNT
Dim sUrlRoot
Dim sUrl
Dim sUrlDest
Set Info   = CreateObject("ADSystemInfo")
Set InfoNT = CreateObject("WinNTSystemInfo")

SUrlRoot = "http://" & InfoNT.Computername & "." &
Info.DomainDNSName & "/public/"
sUrl     = sUrlRoot & "test_folder/test1.txt"
SurlDest = sUrlRoot & "test_folder2/test1.txt"

copyItem sUrl, sUrlDest, Nothing

Sub copyItem( sUrl, sUrlDest, Conn )

  Dim Rec

  ' Did caller pass a Connection object reference?
  If Not ( VarType(Conn) = vbObject AND TypeName(Conn) =
"Connection" ) Then
    Set Conn = CreateObject("ADODB.Connection")
    Conn.Provider = "ExOLEDB.DataSource"
    Conn.Open sUrl
  End If
```

```
    Set Rec = CreateObject("ADODB.Record")

    Rec.Open sURL, Conn, adModeReadWrite
    Rec.CopyRecord ,sUrlDest

    Rec.Close

End Sub
</script>
</job>
```

   [C++]

```cpp
#import <msado15.dll> no_namespace
#import <cdoex.dll> no_namespace

void copyitem(bstr_t urlfrom, bstr_t urlto) {

   _RecordPtr Rec(__uuidof(Record));
   _ConnectionPtr Conn(__uuidof(Connection));
   Conn->Provider = "ExOLEDB.DataSource";
   cout << urlfrom << endl;
   try {
      Conn->Open(urlfrom, bstr_t(""), bstr_t(""),-1);
   }
   catch(_com_error e) {
      // handle error or throw...
      throw e;
   }

   try {
      Rec->Open(
            variant_t(urlfrom),
            variant_t((IDispatch*)Conn, true),
            adModeReadWrite,
            adFailIfNotExists,
            adOpenSource,
            bstr_t(""),
            bstr_t(""));
   }
   catch(_com_error e) {
      // handle error or throw...
      throw e;
   }

   try {
      Rec->CopyRecord(
         bstr_t(),
         urlto,
```

```
            bstr_t(),
            bstr_t(),
            (CopyRecordOptionsEnum)adMoveOverWrite,
            VARIANT_FALSE);
   }
   catch(_com_error e) {
      // handle error or throw...
      throw e;
   }
}
```

Deleting Items

To delete an item from a folder, use the Record.DeleteRecord method. If you delete a folder item, all items within the folder are also deleted. The code is as follows:

[VBScript]

```
<job id="delete_record">
<reference object="adodb.record"/>

<script language='vbscript'>

Dim Rec
Dim Info
Dim InfoNT
Dim sUrl
Set Info   = CreateObject("ADSystemInfo")
Set InfoNT = CreateObject("WinNTSystemInfo")

sUrl = "http://" & InfoNT.Computername & "." & _
Info.DomainDNSName & "/public/test_folder2/test1.txt"

deleteItem sUrl, Nothing

Sub deleteItem( sUrl, Conn )

  Dim Rec

 ' Did caller pass a Connection object reference?
 If Not ( VarType(Conn) = vbObject AND TypeName(Conn) = "Connection" ) Then
    Set Conn = CreateObject("ADODB.Connection")
    Conn.Provider = "ExOLEDB.DataSource"
    Conn.Open sUrl
 End If
```

```
    Set Rec = CreateObject("ADODB.Record")

    Rec.Open sURL, Conn, adModeReadWrite
    Rec.DeleteRecord

    Rec.Close

End Sub
</script>
</job>
```

   [Visual Basic]

```
' Reference to Microsoft ActiveX Data Objects 2.5 Library
' Reference to Microsoft CDO for Exchange 2000 Library

Sub DeleteRecord( sUrl as String )

   Dim Rec As New ADODB.Record
   Dim Conn as New ADODB.Connection

   Conn.Provider = "ExOLEDB.DataSource"
   Conn.Open sURL

   Rec.Open sURL, Conn, adModeReadWrite
   Rec.DeleteRecord

End Sub
```

Deleting Items Using a Recordset

To delete all items in a folder, you can use a Recordset object's Delete method. The following example deletes all the items in a folder, except for subfolders that are stipulated by a WHERE clause:

   [VBScript]

```
<job id="delete_record">
<reference object="adodb.record"/>

<script language='vbscript'>

Dim Info
Dim InfoNT
Dim sFolderUrl
Dim sQuery
Set Info   = CreateObject("ADSystemInfo")
```

Deleting Items Using a Recordset

```
Set InfoNT = CreateObject("WinNTSystemInfo")

sFolderUrl = "http://" & InfoNT.Computername & "." &
Info.DomainDNSName & "/public/test_folder2/"

' Delete all non-folder items from folder.
sQuery = "SELECT * FROM scope('shallow traversal of " &
Chr(34) & sURL & Chr(34) & "')" & _
        " WHERE ""DAV:isfolder"" = FALSE"

Dim cItems
cItems = deleteItemsMatchSQL(sFolderUrl, sQuery, Nothing)
wscript.echo "Deleted " & cItems & " Items from " &
sFolderUrl

Function deleteItemsMatchSQL( sUrl, sQuery, Conn )

  Dim Rs
  Dim cItems

  ' Did caller pass a Connection object reference?
  If Not ( VarType(Conn) = vbObject AND TypeName(Conn) =
"Connection" ) Then
     Set Conn = CreateObject("ADODB.Connection")
     Conn.Provider = "ExOLEDB.DataSource"
     Conn.Open sUrl
  End If

  Set Rs = CreateObject("ADODB.Recordset")

  With Rs
     .Open sQuery, Conn
     .MoveFirst
     cItems = .RecordCount
     While Not Rs.EOF
     .Delete 1  ' Current record
     .MoveNext
     Wend
     .Close
  End With

  deleteItemsMatchSQL = cItems

End Function
</script>
</job>
```

    [C++]

```
#import <msado15.dll> no_namespace
#import <cdoex.dll> no_namespace
```

Chapter 11 • Working with Folders and Items

```cpp
void deleteitems(bstr_t url, bstr_t sqlCondition) {

   _RecordsetPtr Rs(__uuidof(Recordset));
   _ConnectionPtr Conn(__uuidof(Connection));
   Conn->Provider = "ExOLEDB.DataSource";

   bstr_t sqlStatement;
   sqlStatement = "select \"DAV:href\" from scope('shallow traversal of \"";
   sqlStatement += url;
   sqlStatement += "\"') ";
   sqlStatement += sqlCondition;

   try {
      Conn->Open(url, bstr_t(), bstr_t(),-1);
      Rs->Open(
            variant_t(sqlStatement),
            variant_t((IDispatch*)Conn, true),
            (CursorTypeEnum)-1,
            (LockTypeEnum) -1,
            -1
            );
   }
   catch(_com_error e) {
      // handle error or throw...
      throw e;
   }

   long numRec = Rs->RecordCount;
   cout << "Record count: " << numRec << endl;
   try {
      Rs->MoveFirst();
      for(long i = 1 ; i <= numRec;  i++ ) {
         Rs->Delete(adAffectCurrent);
         Rs->MoveNext() ;
      }
   }
   catch(_com_error e) {
       cerr << "Error deleting item using Recordset." << endl;
   }
}
```

Moving Items

To move items within a public store, use the Record.MoveRecord method. If you move a folder item, all items within the folder are also moved. You cannot use the Record.MoveRecord method to move items from one public or mailbox store to another. The code to use is as follows:

[VBScript]

```
<job id="moveitems">
<reference object="adodb.record"/>
<script language="vbscript">

Function MoveItem( UrlFrom, UrlTo )

 Dim Rec
 Dim Conn
 Dim NewURL

 Set Conn = CreateObject("ADODB.Connection")
 Conn.Provider = "ExOLEDB.DataSource"
 Conn.Open UrlFrom

 Set Rec = CreateObject("ADODB.Record")
 Rec.Open URLFrom, Conn, adModeReadWrite
 NewURL = Rec.MoveRecord( , URLTo, , , adMoveOverWrite)
 MoveItem = NewURL

End Function
</script>
</job>
```

[C++]

```
#import <msado15.dll> no_namespace
#import <cdoex.dll> no_namespace

void moveitem(bstr_t urlfrom, bstr_t urlto) {

   _RecordPtr Rec(__uuidof(Record));
   _ConnectionPtr Conn(__uuidof(Connection));
   Conn->Provider = "ExOLEDB.DataSource";
   cout << urlfrom << endl;
   try {
      Conn->Open(urlfrom, bstr_t(""), bstr_t(""),-1);
   }
   catch(_com_error e) {
      // handle error or throw...
      throw e;
```

```
    }

    try {
       Rec->Open(
               variant_t(urlfrom),
               variant_t((IDispatch*)Conn, true),
               adModeReadWrite,
               adFailIfNotExists,
               adOpenSource,
               bstr_t(""),
               bstr_t(""));
    }
    catch(_com_error e) {
       // handle error or throw...
       throw e;
    }

    try {
       Rec->MoveRecord(
             bstr_t(),
             urlto,
             bstr_t(),
             bstr_t(),
             (MoveRecordOptionsEnum)adMoveOverWrite,
             VARIANT_FALSE);
    }
    catch(_com_error e) {
       // handle error or throw...
       throw e;
    }
}
```

Working with Item Properties

The following sections outline how to go about working with item properties:

- Printing Item Property Names, Types, and Values
- Working with Multivalued Properties
- Setting and Retrieving Custom Properties

Printing Item Property Names, Types, and Values

The example that follows demonstrates how to print the name, type, and value for each of an item's properties. In this routine, a bound Microsoft ADO Record object is passed, the Fields collection for the Record is enumerated, and the type for each Field is echoed to the console. Where appropriate, the value for the property is also printed. Properties that are binary or arrays of bytes are not printed.

When binding to an item in this way, the list of properties present within the Fields collection is determined by using the following information:

- The value of the item's DAV:contentclass and the parent folder's schema scope. If the item's content class is not defined within the parent folder's schema scope, only the properties actually set for the item appear in the Fields collection. If the content class is defined within the parent folder's schema scope, all properties defined by this class appear within the Fields collection.
- The properties that are set on the item, but that are not defined by the item's content class. You can always get all properties set for an item, whether or not these properties are part of the item's content class definition.

Note All properties defined by the item's content class appear in the Fields collection, even if the properties have not been set (are empty).

The following is the code to use:

[VBScript]

```
Sub printPropsAndType( Rec )

 If Not (VarType(Rec) = vbObject And TypeName(Rec) = "Record") Then
    Err.Raise   &H80070057 ' E_INVALIDARG
 End If

 Dim Flds
 Set Flds = Rec.Fields

 Dim vt

 For Each Fld in Flds
  vt = VarType(Fld.Value)
  WScript.Echo Fld.Name
  If vt = 14 Then
    WScript.Echo "   (Unsupported VARIANT type for VBScript)"
  Else
    WScript.Echo "   " & TypeName(Fld.Value)
  End If

  If IsArray(Fld.Value) Then
   WScript.Echo VarType(Fld.Value)
```

```
            If VarType(Fld.Value) = 14 Then
               WScript.Echo "   " & "<array of unprintable>"
            ElseIf Not IsPrintable(TypeName(Fld.Value)) Then
               WScript.Echo "   " & "<array of unprintable>"
            Else
               temp = Fld.Value
               For i = LBound(temp) to UBound(temp)
                  WScript.Echo "   " & temp(i)
               Next
            End If
          Else
            If VarType(Fld.Value) = 14 Then
                Wscript.Echo "   " & "<value unprintable>"
             ElseIf Not IsPrintable(TypeName(Fld.Value)) Then
                Wscript.Echo "   " & "<value unprintable>"
             Else
                Wscript.Echo "   " & Fld.Value
             End If
          End If
          wscript.echo
       Next
    End Sub

    Function IsPrintable(sTypeName)

       dim result

       Select Case sTypeName
         Case "Object"
           result = False
         Case "Object()"
           result = False
         Case "Byte"
           result = False
         Case "Byte()"
           result = False
         Case "Null"
           result = False
         Case ""Error"
           result = False
         Case "Error()"
           result = False
         Case Else
           result = True
       End Select

       IsPrintable = result
    End Function
```

Working with Multivalued Properties

Properties for items in the Web Storage System can have multiple values. In this case, you set or retrieve the property using an Array (SAFEARRAY). Even if the multivalued property has only one value, you still use an Array.

Each value in the array must be of the same type. For example, a property can be a multivalued array of Strings (string or BSTR) or Longs (i4 or long), but not both strings and integers.

The following example demonstrates how to set and retrieve multivalued properties for items:

[VBScript]

```
' Assume URL is defined and points to a folder.

Const adModeReadWrite = 3

Dim Rec
Dim Conn
Set Conn = CreateObject("ADODB.Connection")
Set Rec  = CreateObject("ADODB.Record")
Conn.Provider = "ExOLEDB.DataSource"

Conn.Open URL
Rec.Open URL, Conn, adModeReadWrite

Dim Flds
Set Flds = Rec.Fields

Dim rgBaseSchema
rgBaseSchema = Flds("urn:schemas-microsoft-com:exch-data:baseschema").Value

' ...

Flds("urn:schemas-microsoft-com:exch-data:expected-content-class").Value = _
   Array("urn:content-classes:item", "urn:schemas-domain-tld:content-classes:special")

Flds.Update

[Visual Basic]
' Reference to ActiveDs Type Library
' Reference to ActiveX Data Objects 2.5 Library

Sub MultiValPropsExample()

    Dim sUrl As String
```

Chapter 11 • Working with Folders and Items

```
    Dim Info As New ADSystemInfo
    Dim InfoNT As New WinNTSystemInfo

    sUrl = "http://" & InfoNT.ComputerName & "." & _
Info.DomainDNSName & _
            "/public/test_folder3/"

    Dim Conn As New ADODB.Connection
    Dim Rec As New ADODB.Record
    Conn.Provider = "ExOLEDB.DataSource"
    Conn.Open sUrl
    Rec.Open sUrl, Conn, adModeReadWrite

    Dim Flds As ADODB.Fields
    Set Flds = Rec.Fields

    Dim rgExpectedContClass As Variant
    rgExpectedContClass = Flds("urn:schemas-microsoft-com:exch-data:expected-content-class").Value

    If IsArray(rgExpectedContClass) Then
        For I = LBound(rgExpectedContClass) To UBound(rgExpectedContClass)
            Debug.Print rgExpectedContClass(I)
        Next I
        ' ...
    Else
        Debug.Print "Error...VarType for returned VARIANT:"
        Debug.Print VarType(rgExpectedContClass)
    End If

    Dim rgCCs(2) As Variant
    rgCCs(0) = "urn:content-classes:item"
    rgCCs(1) = "urn:schemas-domain-tld:content-classes:special"
    Flds("urn:schemas-microsoft-com:exch-data:expected-content-class").Value = rgCCs
    Flds.Update

End Sub
```

   [C++]

```
#import <msado15.dll> no_namespace
#import "c:\program files\common files\microsoft shared\cdo\cdoex.dll" no_namespace
#include <iostream.h>

void setBaseSchema(bstr_t sFolderUrl) {
```

```cpp
    _RecordPtr Rec(__uuidof(Record));
    _ConnectionPtr Conn(__uuidof(Connection));

    Conn->Provider = "ExOLEDB.DataSource";
    try {
       Conn->Open(sFolderUrl, bstr_t(), bstr_t(), -1);
    }
    catch(_com_error e) {
       cout << "Error opening connection." << endl;
       //..
       throw e;
    }

    wchar_t* url1 =  L"http://server/public/test_folder2";
    wchar_t* url2 =  L"http://server/public/test_folder3";
    wchar_t* url3 =  L"http://server/public/
non_ipm_subtree/Schema";

    VARIANT     vVal;
    VariantInit(&vVal);
    vVal.vt = VT_ARRAY | VT_VARIANT;

    SAFEARRAY* psa  = NULL;
    psa = SafeArrayCreateVector(VT_VARIANT, 0, 3);
    if(psa == NULL) {
       // handle error here.
    }

    VARIANT* pVal;
    HRESULT hr = S_OK;
    hr = SafeArrayAccessData(psa, (void**)&pVal);
    if(FAILED(hr)) {
       // handle error
    }

    VariantInit(&(pVal[0]));
    pVal[0].vt = VT_BSTR;
    pVal[0].bstrVal = SysAllocString(url1);
    VariantInit(&(pVal[1]));
    pVal[1].vt = VT_BSTR;
    pVal[1].bstrVal = SysAllocString(url2);
    VariantInit(&(pVal[2]));
    pVal[2].vt = VT_BSTR;
    pVal[2].bstrVal = SysAllocString(url3);

    SafeArrayUnaccessData(psa);

    vVal.parray = psa;

    try {
```

Chapter 11 • Working with Folders and Items

```cpp
        Rec->Open(sFolderUrl,
            variant_t((IDispatch*)Conn,true),
            adModeReadWrite,
            adFailIfNotExists,
            adOpenSource,
            bstr_t(),
            bstr_t());
    }
    catch(_com_error e) {
        cout << "Error opening item" << endl;
        //..
    }

    FieldsPtr Flds;
    Flds = Rec->Fields;
    FieldPtr Fld;
    Fld = Flds->Item["urn:schemas-microsoft-com:exch-data:baseschema"];
    Fld->Value = vVal;

    SafeArrayDestroy(psa);
    VariantClear(&vVal);
    psa = NULL;

    try {
        Flds->Update();
    }
    catch(_com_error e) {
        cout << "update failed" << endl;
        cout << e.Description() << endl;
    }

    // Now, read the props back and print the values...
    variant_t vBaseSchema;
    vBaseSchema = Flds->Item["urn:schemas-microsoft-com:exch-data:baseschema"]->Value;
    if( ! (vBaseSchema.vt == (VT_ARRAY | VT_VARIANT))) {
        cout << "Unexpected..." << endl;
        // handle error
    }

    hr = SafeArrayAccessData(vBaseSchema.parray, (void**)&pVal);
    if(FAILED(hr)) {
        cout << "access data failed!!" << endl;
    }

    cout << "Set the baseschema property for the folder at \r\n   " << sFolderUrl;
    cout << " \r\nto the following URLS: " << endl;
```

```
    cout << bstr_t(pVal[0].bstrVal) << endl;
    cout << bstr_t(pVal[1].bstrVal) << endl;
    cout << bstr_t(pVal[2].bstrVal) << endl;

    SafeArrayUnaccessData(vBaseSchema.parray);

}
```

Setting and Retrieving Custom Properties

The following example demonstrates how to set properties on items in the Web Storage System:

[VBScript]

```
<job id="custom_props">
<reference object="adodb.record"/>

<script language='vbscript'>

Dim InfoNT
Set InfoNT = CreateObject("WinNTSystemInfo")

SetProps "http://" & InfoNT.ComputerName & "/public/
test_folder/test1.txt"
GetProps "http://" & InfoNT.ComputerName & "/public/
test_folder/test1.txt"

Sub SetProps(sUrl)

    Dim Rec
    Set Rec = CreateObject("ADODB.Record")
    Dim Conn
    Set Conn = CreateObject("ADODB.Connection")
    Conn.Provider = "ExOLEDB.DataSource"
    Conn.Open sUrl
    Rec.Open sUrl, Conn, adModeReadWrite

    Dim Flds
    Set Flds = Rec.Fields
    With Flds
       .Item("urn:schemas-domain-tld:modified") = Now
       .Item("urn:schemas-domain-tld:status") = "Behind
Schedule"
       .Item("urn:schemas-domain-tld:author") = "Paul West"
       .Item("urn:schemas-domain-tld:author-email") =
"""Paul west"" <pw@somewhere.microsoft.com>"
       .Item("urn:schemas-domain-tld:editor") = "Wendy
Wheeler"
       .Item("urn:schemas-domain-tld:editor-email") =
```

```
      """"Wendy Wheeler"" <ww@somewhere.microsoft.com>"
        .Update
      End With

End Sub

Sub GetProps(sUrl)

   ' This example shows how to retrieve custom property
values
   ' set in the previous snippet.

      Dim Rec
      Set Rec = CreateObject("ADODB.Record")
      Dim Conn
      Set Conn = CreateObject("ADODB.Connection")
      Conn.Provider = "ExOLEDB.DataSource"
      Conn.Open sUrl
      Rec.Open sUrl, Conn, adModeReadWrite

      Dim Flds
      Set Flds = Rec.Fields
      Dim Props(10)
      Props(1) = "urn:schemas-domain-tld:modified"
      Props(2) = "urn:schemas-domain-tld:status"
      Props(3) = "urn:schemas-domain-tld:author"
      Props(4) = "urn:schemas-domain-tld:author-email"
      Props(5) = "urn:schemas-domain-tld:editor"
      Props(6) = "urn:schemas-domain-tld:editor-email"
      For I = 1 To 6
        WScript.Echo Props(I) & vbCrLf
        WScript.Echo Flds(Props(I))
      Next

End Sub
</script>
</job>
```

[Visual Basic]

```
Sub SetProps(sUrl)

    Dim Rec As New Record
    Dim Conn As New Connection
    Conn.Provider = "ExOLEDB.DataSource"
    Conn.Open sUrl
    Rec.Open sUrl, Conn, adModeReadWrite

    Dim Flds As Fields
    Set Flds = Rec.Fields
```

Working with Item Properties

```
   With Flds
      .Item("urn:schemas-domain-tld:modified") = Now
      .Item("urn:schemas-domain-tld:status") = "Behind
Schedule"
      .Item("urn:schemas-domain-tld:author") = "Paul West"
      .Item("urn:schemas-domain-tld:author-email") = """Paul
west"" <pw@somewhere.microsoft.com>"
      .Item("urn:schemas-domain-tld:editor") = "Wendy
Wheeler"
      .Item("urn:schemas-domain-tld:editor-email") = """Wendy
Wheeler"" <ww@somewhere.microsoft.com>"
      .Update
   End With

End Sub

Sub GetProps(sUrl)

   ' This example shows how to retrieve custom property
values
   ' set in the previous snippet.

   Dim Rec As New Record
   Dim Conn As New Connection
   Conn.Provider = "ExOLEDB.DataSource"
   Conn.Open sUrl
   Rec.Open sUrl, Conn, adModeReadWrite

   Dim Flds As Fields
   Set Flds = Rec.Fields
   Dim Props(10) As Variant
   Props(1) = "urn:schemas-domain-tld:modified"
   Props(2) = "urn:schemas-domain-tld:status"
   Props(3) = "urn:schemas-domain-tld:author"
   Props(4) = "urn:schemas-domain-tld:author-email"
   Props(5) = "urn:schemas-domain-tld:editor"
   Props(6) = "urn:schemas-domain-tld:editor-email"
   For I = 1 To 6
      Debug.Print Props(I) & vbCrLf
      Debug.Print Flds(Props(I))
   Next I

End Sub
```

Getting a List of Folders

This example demonstrates how to get a list of folders within a folder. When constructing the SQL query, you must require that the DAV:isfolder property is TRUE and the DAV:ishidden property is FALSE in the WHERE clause—for example,

```
select "DAV:displayname", "DAV:contentclass", "DAV:href" from
scope('shallow traversal of "/myfolders/myfolder"')
where "DAV:ishidden" = False AND
      "DAV:isfolder" = True
```

    Note that a relative URL is used in the SCOPE portion of the SQL statement. Searches occur within the context of a connection to a particular public or private store. Therefore, you need not use the entire URL in the query. The path is relative to the root folder for a public store and "MBX" for a private store. The beginning forward slash is required. For example, the folder at the URL file://./backofficestorage/domain.tld/Public Folders/myfolders/myfolder can be referred to by using the relative URL /myfolders/myfolder; the path is anchored from the Public Folders root public store folder, as in the following code:

[VBScript]

```
Function getFolderList( sUrl, Conn )

  ' Did caller pass a Connection object reference?
  If Not ( (VarType(Conn) = vbObject Or VarType(Conn) = vbString) AND TypeName(Conn) = "Connection" ) Then
     Set Conn = CreateObject("ADODB.Connection")
     Conn.Provider = "ExOLEDB.DataSource"
     Conn.Open sUrl
  End If

  Dim Rs
  Set Rs = CreateObject("ADODB.Recordset")

  Dim sql
  sql = "select ""DAV:displayname"", ""DAV:contentclass"", ""DAV:href"" from"
  sql = sql & " scope('shallow traversal of """ & sUrl & """')"
  sql = sql & " where ""DAV:ishidden"" = False and ""DAV:isfolder"" = True"

  Rs.Open sql, Conn
  Set GetFolderList = Rs

End Function
```

Getting a List of Folders

[C++]

```cpp
#import <msado15.dll> no_namespace

_RecordsetPtr getFolderList(bstr_t sFolderUrl,
_ConnectionPtr Conn) {

   _RecordsetPtr Rs(__uuidof(Recordset));

   if(Conn == NULL) {
      Conn.CreateInstance(__uuidof(Connection));
      Conn->Provider = "ExOLEDB.DataSource";
      try {
         Conn->Open(sFolderUrl, bstr_t(), bstr_t(),-1);
      }
      catch(_com_error e) {
         // handle error or throw...
         throw e;
      }
   }

   bstr_t sQuery = "select \"DAV:displayname\",
\"DAV:contentclass\", \"DAV:href\" from \"";
      sQuery += sFolderUrl;
      sQuery += "\" where \"DAV:ishidden\" = False And
\"DAV:isfolder\" = True";

   try {
      Rs->Open(
            variant_t(sQuery),
            variant_t((IDispatch*)Conn, true),
            adOpenUnspecified,
            adLockUnspecified,
            -1);
   }
   catch(_com_error e) {
      // handle error or throw...
      throw e;
   }

    return Rs;

}
```

Using Transactions

When you use the server-side Microsoft Exchange 2000 Server OLE DB Provider, you can perform operations on items in a store as a single transaction. To do so, you first create an ADO Connection object and bind to a particular store. Next, you invoke the _Connection.BeginTrans method. All operations that you subsequently perform within the context of this connection are not committed to the store until the transaction has been committed. To commit the transaction, you invoke the _Connection.CommitTrans method. To cancel the transaction, you invoke the _Connection.RollbackTrans method.

You cannot perform transactions across multiple stores. For example, you cannot create items in two public stores as part of the same transaction.

The example demonstrates how to perform the following operations, all within the context of a transaction:

1. Create an application folder and set properties on the folder.
2. Create a schema subfolder to house schema information for the application.
3. Create three schema items — one content class definition and two property definitions.
4. Create a test item in the application folder.

If the transaction is successful, the example then tests the schema information by using the test item created in the application folder. Because none of the operations are actually committed to the store before the transaction has been committed, the schema test operations cannot be performed in the transaction. Here is the code that is used:

[VBScript]

```
<Job id="createFoldersAndSchemaFolders_Trans">

<reference object="adodb.record"/>

<script language="vbscript">
option explicit
Const s     = "urn:schemas-microsoft-com:exch-data:"
Const dt        = "urn:schemas-microsoft-com:datatypes#"
Const x     = "urn:schemas-microsoft-com:xml-data#"
Const cc        = "urn:content-classes:"
Const d     = "DAV:"
Const pcc       = "urn:schemas-myorg-tld:content-classes:"
Const p         = "urn:schemas-myorg-tld:"

Const vRoot     = "/apps"
Const appfldr   = "/apps/a2"
```

Using Transactions

```
Const pcc_1     = "class1"
Const pcc_1_fn  = "class1_pcc"
Const pp_1      = "prop1"
Const pp_1_fn   = "prop1_pp"
Const pp_2      = "prop2"
Const pp_2_fn   = "prop2_pp"

Const test_fn   = "item.txt"

createFoldersAndSchema_Trans vRoot, appfldr
createTestItem appfldr & "/" & test_fn
testSchema1 appfldr & "/" & test_fn
testSchema2 appfldr

' -- createFolderAndSchema_Trans --
'
' This routine creates the following within a local
transaction:
' - an application folder,
' - a schema folder "Schema" (child of app folder)
' - one custom content class definition
' - two custom property definitions (referenced by content
class)
' - one test item in app folder with the custom content
class
'
'
Sub createFoldersAndSchema_Trans( vRootURL, appfolderURL )

 WScript.Echo ""
 WScript.Echo "-- createFoldersAndSchema_Trans --"

 Dim Rec
 Dim Conn
 Dim info
 Dim infoNT
 Dim URL

  ' Get the fully qualified domain name from the
ADSystemInfo object.
  Set info = CreateObject("ADSystemInfo")
  Set InfoNT = CreateObject("WinNTSystemInfo")
  Set Conn = CreateObject("ADODB.Connection")

  URL = "http://" & lcase(infoNT.computername) & _
                  "." & info.domaindnsname & _
                  appfolderURL

  wscript.echo url
  Conn.Provider = "ExOLEDB.DataSource"
```

Chapter 11 ● Working with Folders and Items

```
Conn.Open URL

' We now have a connection to the appropriate store
' Begin transaction
Dim lvl
lvl = Conn.BeginTrans

Set Rec = CreateObject("ADODB.Record")

' Try to create the app folder. Use Connection with
transaction
With Rec
   .Open appfolderURL, Conn , adModeReadWrite,
adCreateCollection Or adCreateOverwrite
     With .Fields
       .Item(d & "contentclass")            = cc & "folder"
       .Item(s & "schema-collection-ref")   =
appfolderURL & "/Schema"
       .Item(s & "expected-content-class").Value   =
Array(pcc & pcc_1)         'urn:schemas-myorg-tld:content-
classes:class1
       .Update
     End With
   .Close


' Now create the folder for the schema items. By
convention, this is the "Schema" folder below the App
folder
   .Open appfolderURL & "/Schema", Conn, adModeReadWrite,
adCreateCollection Or adCreateOverwrite
     With .Fields
       .Item(d & "contentclass").Value      = cc &
"folder"
       .Item(s & "expected-content-class").Value  = _
         Array("urn:content-classes:propertydef",
"urn:content-classes:contentclassdef","urn:content-
classes:item")
       .Item(s & "baseschema").Value        = _
         Array(vRootURL & "/non_ipm_subtree/Schema")
       .Update
     End With
   .Close

   wscript.echo vRootURL & "/non_ipm_subtree/Schema"

' Create the first property definition. This property
definition has the name
'    urn:schemas-myorg-tld:prop1
   .Open appfolderURL & "/Schema/" & pp_1_fn, Conn,
```

```
adModeReadWrite, adCreateNonCollection Or adCreateOverwrite
   With .Fields
      .Item(x  & "name")                    = p & pp_1
      .Item(d  & "contentclass")            = cc &
"propertydef"
      .Item(dt & "type")                    = "date"
      .Item(s  & "isindexed")               = False
      .Item(s  & "ismultivalued")           = False
      .Item(s  & "isreadonly")              = False
      .Item(s  & "synchronize")             = False
      .Item(s  & "isrequired")              = False
      .Item(s  & "isvisible")               = True
      .Update
   End With
   .Close

   ' Create the second property definition. This property
definition has the name
   '   urn:schemas-myorg-tld:prop2
   .Open appfolderURL & "/Schema/" & pp_2_fn, Conn,
adModeReadWrite, adCreateNonCollection Or adCreateOverwrite
   With .Fields
      .Item(x  & "name")                    = p & pp_2
      .Item(d  & "contentclass")            = cc &
"propertydef"
      .Item(dt & "type")                    = "string"
      .Item(s  & "isindexed")               = False
      .Item(s  & "ismultivalued")           = False
      .Item(s  & "isreadonly")              = False
      .Item(s  & "synchronize")             = False
      .Item(s  & "isrequired")              = False
      .Item(s  & "isvisible")               = True
      .Update
   End With
   .Close

   ' Create the content class definition. This class has the
name
   '   urn:schemas-myorg-tld:content-classes:class1
   .Open appfolderURL & "/Schema/" & pcc_1_fn, Conn,
adModeReadWrite, adCreateNonCollection Or adCreateOverwrite
   With .Fields
      .Item(d & "contentclass")             = cc &
"contentclassdef"
      .Item(x & "name")                     = pcc &
pcc_1
      .Item(x & "extends").Value            = Array(cc
& "object")
      .Item(x & "element").Value            = Array(p &
pp_1, p & pp_2)
```

```
            .Item(s & "closedexpectedcontentclasses")   = False
            .Update
        End With
        .Close

    End with

    If Err.Number <> 0 Then
     wscript.echo "Error!"
     wscript.echo err.number
     wscript.echo err.description
     wscript.echo "Transaction Aborted"
     Conn.RollbackTrans
    Else
     Conn.CommitTrans
     wscript.echo "No Error. Transaction Completed"
    End if


    ' Create a test item. Set it's content class to our
    private class.
    ' When we open this item, the properties we defined for
    our content class
    ' should appear in Fields collection even though they
    have not been set.
       Rec.Open appfolderURL & "/" & test_fn, Conn,
    adModeReadWrite, adCreateNonCollection Or adCreateOverwrite
       With Rec.Fields
           .Item(d & "contentclass") = pcc & pcc_1
           .Item(adDefaultStream).Value.WriteText "Here is the
    text for the item."
           .Update
       End With
       Rec.Close

End Sub

Sub CreateTestItem( itemRelURL )
  Dim Rec
  Dim Conn
  Dim info
  Dim infoNT
  Dim URL

    ' Get the fully qualified domain name from the
    ADSystemInfo object.
    Set info    = CreateObject("ADSystemInfo")
    Set InfoNT  = CreateObject("WinNTSystemInfo")
    Set Conn    = CreateObject("ADODB.Connection")
    Set Rec     = CreateObject("ADODB.Record")
```

Using Transactions

```
    URL = "http://" & lcase(infoNT.computername) & _
                 "." & info.domaindnsname & _
                 itemRelURL

wscript.echo url
 Conn.Provider = "ExOLEDB.DataSource"
 Conn.Open URL

  ' Create a test item. Set it's content class to our
private class.
  ' When we open this item, the properties we defined for
our content class
  ' should appear in Fields collection even though they
have not been set.
    Rec.Open URL, Conn, adModeReadWrite,
adCreateNonCollection Or adCreateOverwrite
    With Rec.Fields
      .Item(d & "contentclass") = pcc & pcc_1
      .Item(adDefaultStream).Value.WriteText "Here is the
text for the item."
      .Update
    End With
    Rec.Close

End Sub


' -- testSchema1 --
' This routine checks the schema information set using the
above routine.
' If the schema scope has been set up properly, the
properties
' defined by our custom content class urn:schemas-myord-
tld:content-classes:class1
' should appear in the Fields collection for the item even
though values have not
' been set for these. If values have been set for these
properties, this test
' tells us nothing.
'

Sub testSchema1( Path )

  WScript.Echo ""
  WScript.Echo "-- testSchema1 --"

  Dim Rec
  Set Rec = CreateObject("ADODB.Record")
  Dim Conn
  Set Conn = CreateObject("ADODB.Connection")
```

Chapter 11 • Working with Folders and Items

```
     Dim Info
     Set Info = CreateObject("ADSystemInfo")
     Dim InfoNT
     Set InfoNT = CreateObject("WinNTSystemInfo")

     Dim URL
     URL = "http://" & _
        lcase(InfoNT.ComputerName) & "." & _
           Info.DomainDNSName & _
           Path

     Conn.Provider = "ExOLEDB.DataSource"
     Conn.Open URL
     WScript.Echo "Testing schema using item at URL: " & URL
     Rec.Open URL, Conn

     Dim Fld
     For Each Fld in Rec.Fields
        If Fld.Name = (p & pp_1) Then
           WScript.Echo p & pp_1 & " returned in schema!"
        ElseIf Fld.Name = (p & pp_2) Then
           WScript.Echo p & pp_2 & " returned in schema!"
        End If
     Next

     Rec.Close
  End Sub


' -- testSchema2 --
' This routine checks the schema information set using the
above routine.
' If the schema scope has been set up properly, the
properties
' defined by our custom content class urn:schemas-myord-
tld:content-classes:class1
' should appear in the results of a "select *" in the
appfolder.
'
Sub testSchema2( path )

     WScript.Echo ""
     WScript.Echo "-- testSchema2 --"

     Dim Conn
     Set Conn = CreateObject("ADODB.Connection")
     Dim Info
     Set Info = CreateObject("ADSystemInfo")
     Dim InfoNT
     Set InfoNT = CreateObject("WinNTSystemInfo")
```

```
    Dim URL
    URL = "http://" & _
      infont.computername & "." & _
          info.domaindnsname & "/" & _
          path

    Conn.Provider = "ExOLEDB.DataSource"
    Conn.Open URL

    Dim Rs
    Set Rs = CreateObject("ADODB.Recordset")
    Set Rs.ActiveConnection = Conn
    Rs.Open "select * from """ & path & """"

    Dim Fld
    For Each Fld In Rs.Fields
     If Fld.Name = (p & pp_1) Then
        WScript.Echo p & pp_1 & " returned in schema!"
     ElseIf Fld.Name = (p & pp_2) Then
        WScript.Echo p & pp_2 & " returned in schema!"
     End IF
    Next

End Sub

</script>
</job>
```

Using the HTTP/WebDAV Protocol

This section describes how to access Web Storage System content using the HTTP/WebDAV protocol. Many of the examples in this section use an instance of the Microsoft.XMLHTTP COM class to send and receive HTTP/WebDAV requests to the Web Storage System. In addition, many examples use an instance of the Microsoft.XMLDOM COM component to construct and manipulate the XML bodies that are used for HTTP/WebDAV protocol requests. The XMLHTTP COM object is part of the Microsoft MSXML 2.0 or later COM component and integrates directly with the other components. For example, you can retrieve the XML body of a successful PROPFIND command directly from the XMLHTTP object as a DOMDocument object.

Important Use the XMLHTTP COM class only on clients. If you are creating applications on the server where the Web Storage System is located, use the ExOLEDB provider.

Creating Items (HTTP/WebDAV)

To create nonfolder items using the HTTP/WebDAV protocol, perform the following steps:

1. Create a PUT or PROPPATCH HTTP/WebDAV request. The request URI for the command is the URI to the item that you are creating.
2. When using a PUT command, set the Translate: HTTP header to the value "f" (false).
3. When using a PUT command, send the stream for the item as the request body.

Chapter 12 • Using the HTTP/WebDAV Protocol

4. When using a PROPPATCH command, send the values of the properties in the request body.
5. Set the Content-Type: header to the appropriate value, for example "text/html; charset=\"iso-8859-1\"" or "text/xml".
6. Send the request.
7. If successful, the response status will be "201 Created."

The following code shows a typical PUT request:

```
PUT /pub2/folder1/folder2/item1.txt HTTP/1.1
Host: hostname
Translate: f
Content-Type: text/plain
Content-Length: 4

abcd
```

The following example uses an instance of the Microsoft.XMLHTTP COM class to send a PUT protocol command to a Web Storage System server:

[JScript]

```
function createItem( uri, vXML ) {

 var Req = new ActiveXObject("Microsoft.XMLHTTP");
 Req.open("PROPPATCH", uri, false);
 if(vXML != "") {
  Req.setRequestHeader("Content-Type","text/xml");
  Req.send(vXML);
 }
 else {
  Req.send();
 }
 return Req;

}

/*
** This example uses a PUT command to put the stream for an item.
** If the item does not exist, it is created.
*/
function putItemStream( uri, text ){
 var Req = new ActiveXObject("Microsoft.XMLHTTP");
 Req.open("PUT", uri, false);
 Req.setRequestHeader("Translate","f");
 if(text != "") {
  Req.setRequestHeader("Content-Type","text/plain");
  Req.send(text);
 }
```

```
    else {
     Req.send("");
    }
    return Req;

}
```

To create a folder item, use the MKCOL protocol command. See "Creating Folders" in Chapter 11, "Working with Folders and Items."

Creating Folders (HTTP/WebDAV)

To create nonfolder items using the HTTP/WebDAV protocol, perform the following steps:

1. Create a MKCOL HTTP/WebDAV request. The request URI for the command is the URI to the folder that you are creating.
2. Optionally, set properties for the new folder by sending an XML body in the request. You format the XML the same way as when sending a PROPPATCH command—for example,

```
<d:propertyupdate xmlns:d="DAV:">
 <d:set>
   <d:prop>
    <d:displayname>Folder 1</d:displayname>
   </d:prop>
 </d:set>
</d:propertyupdate>
```

When sending a request body with the MKCOL command, set the Content-Type header to "text/xml" and set the Content-Length header to the appropriate value.
3. Send the request.
4. If successful, the response status will be "201 Created."

The following example shows a typical MKCOL request:

```
MKCOL /pub2/folder1/folder2/ HTTP/1.1
Host: hostname
Content-Type: text/xml
Content-Length: XXX

<?xml version="1.0"?>
<g:propertyupdate xmlns:g="DAV:" >
    <g:set>
        <g:prop>
            <g:displayname>value</g:displayname>
```

```
        </g:prop>
        <g:prop>
            <f:myprop xmlns:f="urn:schemas-mydomain-tld:">Test</f:myprop>
        </g:prop>
    </g:set>
</g:propertyupdate>
```

The following example uses an instance of the Microsoft.XMLHTTP COM class to send a MKCOL protocol command to a Web Storage System server:

[JScript]

```
function createFolder( urisource, vXML ) {

 var Req = new ActiveXObject("Microsoft.XMLHTTP");
 Req.open("MKCOL", urisource, false);
 if(vXML != "") {
  Req.setRequestHeader("Content-Type","text/xml");
  Req.send(vXML);
 }
 else {
  Req.send();
 }
 return Req;

}
```

Getting an Item's Stream (HTTP/WebDAV)

To create nonfolder items using the HTTP/WebDAV protocol, perform the following steps:

1. Create a GET HTTP/WebDAV request. The request URI for the command is the URI to the item.
2. Set the Translate: HTTP header to the value "f" (false).
3. Send the request.
4. If successful, the response status will be "200 OK."

The following example shows a typical GET request:

```
GET /pub2/folder1/folder2/item1.txt HTTP/1.1
Host: hostname
Translate: f
```

The following example uses an instance of the Microsoft.XMLHTTP COM class to send a GET protocol command to a Web Storage System server:

[JScript]

```
/*
** The getStream function returns a reference to an
** XMLHTTP object that should contain the stream for the
** specified item.
*/
function getStream( uri ){
 var Req = new ActiveXObject("Microsoft.XMLHTTP");
 Req.open("GET", uri, false);
 Req.setRequestHeader("Translate","f");
 Req.send();
 return Req;
}
```

Deleting Items (HTTP/WebDAV)

To delete items using the HTTP/WebDAV protocol, perform the following steps:

1. Create a DELETE HTTP/WebDAV request. The request URI for the command is the URI to the item that you want to delete.
2. Send the request. The body of the request should be empty.
3. If successful, the response status will be "200 OK."

The following example shows a typical DELETE request:

```
DELETE /pub2/folder1/folder2 HTTP/1.1
Host: hostname
Content-Length: 0
```

The following example uses an instance of the Microsoft.XMLHTTP COM class to send a DELETE protocol command to a Web Storage System server:

[JScript]

```
function deleteItem( uri ) {

 var Req = new ActiveXObject("Microsoft.XMLHTTP");
 Req.open("DELETE", uri, false);
 Req.send();
 return Req;

}
```

Copying Items (HTTP/WebDAV)

To copy items using the HTTP/WebDAV protocol, perform the following steps:

1. Create a COPY HTTP/WebDAV request. The request URI for the command is the URI to the item that you want to copy.
2. Set the Destination: HTTP header to the URI for the copied item.
3. Send the request. The body of the request should be empty.
4. If successful, the response status will be "201 Created."

The following example shows a typical COPY request:

```
COPY /pub2/folder1/folder2 HTTP/1.1
Destination: /pub2/folder1/folder3
Host: hostname
```

The following example uses an instance of the Microsoft.XMLHTTP COM class to send a COPY protocol command to a Web Storage System server:

[JScript]
```
function copyItem( urisource, urito ) {

var Req = new ActiveXObject("Microsoft.XMLHTTP");
Req.open("COPY", urisource, false);
Req.setRequestHeader("Destination",urito);
Req.send();
return Req;

}
```

Moving Items (HTTP/WebDAV)

To move items using the HTTP/WebDAV protocol, perform the following steps:

1. Create a MOVE HTTP/WebDAV request. The request URI for the command is the URI to the item that you want to move.
2. Set the Destination: HTTP header to the URI for the moved item.
3. Send the request. The body of the request should be empty.
4. If successful, the response status will be "201 Created."

The following example shows a typical MOVE request:

```
MOVE /pub2/folder1/folder2 HTTP/1.1
Destination: /pub2/folder1/folder3
Host: hostname
```

The following example uses an instance of the Microsoft.XMLHTTP COM class to send a MOVE protocol command to a Web Storage System server:

[JScript]

```
function copyItem( urisource, urito ) {

  var Req = new ActiveXObject("Microsoft.XMLHTTP");
  Req.open("MOVE", urisource, false);
  Req.setRequestHeader("Destination",urito);
  Req.send();
  return Req;

}
```

Getting Item Property Values (HTTP/WebDAV)

This example shows how you can manually construct the XML body of a PROPFIND HTTP/WebDAV request. In the example, you are requesting the DAV:displayname for a folder. After the request has been constructed, the code passes the XML string to an XMLHTTP COM object and sends the PROPFIND request to the server.

The following example shows what the request might look like (the code has been formatted for clarity):

```
PROPFIND /public/docs/ HTTP/1.1
Content-Type: text/xml;   charset="UTF-8"
Content-Length: XXX
Depth: 1
...

<?xml version="1.0" encoding="UTF-8"?>
<d:propfind xmlns:d="DAV:">
 <d:prop><d:displayname/></d:prop>
</d:propfind>
```

The example that follows is provided mainly for illustration. It is easy to make errors when constructing XML streams manually, so you should use an XML DOM implementation to do so.

[VBScript]

```
<HTML>
<HEAD>
<META NAME="GENERATOR" Content="Microsoft Visual Studio 6.0">
<TITLE>Simple PROPFIND</TITLE>
</HEAD>
<BODY LANGUAGE="VBScript" onLoad="doXML">
<SCRIPT FOR=WINDOW LANGUAGE=VBSCRIPT>
<!--

Sub DoXML
Dim objX, strR, objXD, objDE
Set objX = CreateObject("Microsoft.XMLHTTP")
objX.Open "PROPFIND", "http://myServer/public/docs/", FALSE, "ADOMAIN\Administrator", ""
strR = "<?xml version='1.0'?>"
strR = strR & "<d:propfind xmlns:d='DAV:'>"
strR = strR & "<d:prop><d:displayname/></d:prop></d:propfind>"
objX.SetRequestHeader "Content-type:", "text/xml"
objX.SetRequestHeader "Depth", "1"
objX.send(strR)

set docback = objX.responseXML

Dim objNodeList
Set objNodeList = docback.getElementsByTagName("*")
For i = 0 TO (objNodeList.length -1)
  Set objNode = objNodeList.nextNode
  Document.Write("<b>" & objNode.NamespaceURI & " " & objNode.NodeName & "</b> - ")
  Document.Write(objNode.Text & "<hr>")
Next
End Sub

//-->
</SCRIPT>

<P> </P>

</BODY>
</HTML>
```

Constructing XML with XMLDOM

This topic shows how you can construct the body of a PROPFIND HTTP/WebDAV request by using the MSXML 2.0 COM component. In the XMLDOM object model, you use the AppendChild method to create nodes and add them to the XML document. After the request has been constructed as an XML DOM Document, you then pass a reference to an XMLHTTP COM object and send the PROPFIND request to the server. The following example illustrates the code used:

[VBScript]

```
<HTML>
<HEAD>
<META NAME="GENERATOR" Content="Microsoft Visual Studio 6.0">
<TITLE>PROPFIND</TITLE>
</HEAD>
<BODY>

<SCRIPT FOR=window EVENT=onload LANGUAGE=VBScript>
<!--

Set req = CreateObject("Microsoft.XMLHTTP")
Set domin = CreateObject("Microsoft.XMLDOM")
Set domback = CreateObject("Microsoft.XMLDOM")

req.Open "PROPFIND", "http://microsoft.com/public/docs/myFile.doc", False,
"TheDomain\Administrator", "thepassword"

req.setRequestHeader "Content-Type", "text/xml; charset=""UTF-8"""

Set oPi = domin.createProcessingInstruction("xml", "version='1.0'")
domin.appendChild(opi)

Set PFind = Domin.CreateNode(1, "d:propfind", "DAV:")
domin.AppendChild PFind

Set DProp = Domin.CreateNode(1, "d:prop", "DAV:")
PFind.AppendChild DProp

Set Author = Domin.CreateNode(1, "O:Author", "urn:schemas-microsoft-com:office:office")
DProp.AppendChild Author
MsgBox domin.XML, ,"IN: PROPFIND"
```

```
req.Send Domin

MsgBox req.StatusText, ,"PROPFIND"
Set domback = req.ResponseXML
MsgBox domback.XML, ,"OUT: PROPFIND"
MsgBox domback.Text, ,"OUT: PROPFIND (text)"

//-->
</SCRIPT>

</BODY>
</HTML>
```

Modifying Item Property Values (HTTP/WebDAV)

This topic shows how to construct the body of a Web Storage System PROPFIND HTTP/WebDAV request by using the MSXML 2.0 COM component. In the XMLDOM object model, you use the AppendChild method to create nodes and add them to the XML document. After the request body has been constructed as an XML DOM Document, you pass a reference to an XMLHTTP COM object and send the PROPFIND request to the server.

The following example illustrates the results of an HTTP request (the code has been formatted for clarity):

```
PROPPATCH /public/docs/myFile.doc HTTP/1.1
Content-Type: text/xml;    charset="UTF-8"
Content-Length: XXX
...

<?xml version="1.0" encoding="UTF-8"?>
<d:propertyupdate xmlns:d="DAV:">
  <d:set>
   <d:prop>
     <o:Author
        xmlns:o="urn:schemas-microsoft-com:office:office"
     >
        Ray Zambroski
     </o:Author>
   </d:prop>
  </d:set>
</d:propertyupdate>
```

If the request was successful, a message box displays the XMLHTTP.StatusText property, followed by the XML of the XMLDOM object that is returned from the XMLHTTP object:

[VBScript]

```
<HTML>
<HEAD>
<META NAME="GENERATOR" Content="Microsoft Visual Studio 6.0">
<TITLE>PROPPATCH</TITLE>
</HEAD>
<BODY>

<SCRIPT FOR=window EVENT=onload LANGUAGE=VBScript>
<!--

Set req = CreateObject("Microsoft.XMLHTTP")
Set domin = CreateObject("Microsoft.XMLDOM")
Set domback = CreateObject("Microsoft.XMLDOM")

req.Open "PROPPATCH", "http://myServer/public/docs/myfile.doc", False,
"TheDomain\Administrator", "thepassword"

req.SetRequestHeader "encoding", "utf-8"

req.setRequestHeader "Content-Type", "text/xml; charset=""UTF-8"""

Set oPi = domin.createProcessingInstruction("xml", "version='1.0'")
domin.appendChild(opi)

Set PUpdate = Domin.CreateNode(1, "d:propertyupdate", "DAV:")
domin.AppendChild PUpdate

Set DSet = Domin.CreateNode(1, "d:set", "DAV:")
PUpdate.AppendChild DSet

Set DProp = Domin.CreateNode(1, "d:prop", "DAV:")
DSet.AppendChild DProp

Set Author = Domin.CreateNode(1, "O:Author", "urn:schemas-microsoft-com:office:office")
DProp.AppendChild Author

Set AuthorName = Domin.CreateTextNode("Ray Zambroski")
Author.AppendChild AuthorName

MsgBox domin.XML, ,"IN: PROPPATCH"

req.Send Domin
```

```
MsgBox req.StatusText, ,"PROPPATCH"

Set domback = Req.ResponseXML
MsgBox domback.XML, ,"OUT: PROPPATCH"
//-->
</SCRIPT>

</BODY>
</HTML>
```

Searching Folders (HTTP/WebDAV)

This topic shows how to construct and send an HTTP/WebDAV SEARCH request. The SQL query is packaged as a value of an XML element that is sent to the server by using the XMLHTTP COM component.

The following example shows an HTTP search request:

```
SEARCH /public/folder1/ HTTP/1.1
Content-Type: text/xml
Content-Length: XXX
...

<?xml version="1.0"?>
<D:searchrequest xmlns:D = "DAV:" >
   <D:sql>
SELECT "dav:displayname",
"urn:schemas:mailheader:textdescription"   FROM
"http://myserver/vroot/folder1/"') where "DAV:ishidden" = false AND "DAV:isfolder" = false
   </D:sql>
</D:searchrequest>
```

See the Web Storage System SQL Reference for supported SQL grammar syntax, indexed properties, unsupported SQL, and other search reference topics.

You can get search result values by manipulating the returned DOMDocument object. Use its getItemsbyTagName method to create a collection of nodes containing values for one of the properties in your SQL SELECT statement. The method is demonstrated in the task.

The prefix for the property, such as "d" in <d:yourproperty>, is not entirely predictable. For more information, see "Property Names and HTTP/WebDAV" in the MS Exchange SDK. The code for getting search results is as follows:

Searching Folders (HTTP/WebDAV)

[VBScript]

```
Sub Search

   set doc = createobject("microsoft.xmldom")
   set docback = createobject("microsoft.xmldom")
   dim strURL
   strURL = "http://myServer1/public/folder1/"
   set pi =
doc.createProcessingInstruction("xml","version=""1.0""")
   doc.appendChild pi

   set node = doc.createNode(1,"searchrequest","DAV:")
   set doc.documentElement = node

   set node2 = doc.createNode(1,"sql","DAV:")
   node.appendChild node2
   set query = doc.createTextNode("select
""DAV:displayname"" from """ & strURL & """ WHERE
CONTAINS(*,'""1998 Tax Return""')")
   node2.appendChild query

   set req = createobject("microsoft.xmlhttp")
   req.open "SEARCH", strURL, false,
"NYCDomain\Administrator", "pw4me"
   req.setrequestheader "Translate", "f"
   req.setrequestheader "Content-Type", "text/xml"
   req.setrequestheader "Depth", "0"
   req.send doc

   set docback = req.responseXML

   'save the XML to disk to study
   docback.Save "d:\xml\docback.xml"

   Dim objNodeList

   'Typically the DAV namespace get the 'a' prefix.
   'If specifying multiple properties in a search
   'examine the returned XML beforehand to determine
prefixes for your code

   Set objNodeList =
docback.getElementsByTagName("a:displayname")
   For i = 0 To (objNodeList.length -1)
     Set objNode = objNodeList.nextNode
     Document.Write(objNode.Text & "<hr>")
   Next

   '******
```

```
'*   If you also selected urn:schemas:httpmail:sendername
in your SQL,
'*   the code to get the values might be like this:
'*
'*       Set objNodeList2 =
docback.getElementsByTagName("d:sendername")
'*       For i = 0 To (objNodeList2.length -1)
'*           Set objNode = objNodeList2.nextNode
'*           Document.Write(objNode.Text & "<hr>")
'*       Next
'*
'******

End Sub
```

Specifying Row Ranges in a Search

By including a range header in a WebDAV search request, you can obtain selected ranges in your search result using a variety of patterns—for example,

```
Range: rows=20-39
Range: rows=0-5, 10-15, 20-25, 30-35
```

For more examples, see "Range Header" in the Web Storage System SQL reference.

Rendering Search Results with XSL

You can use the XSL capabilities of the MSXML 2.0 COM component to render the results of a PROPFIND method.

The following example uses a simple XSL style sheet to transform the XML body returned by the PROPFIND command into HTML for display in a browser:

[JScript]

```
<html>

<head>
<meta http-equiv="Content-Type" content="text/html;
charset=windows-1252">
<meta name="GENERATOR" content="Microsoft FrontPage 4.0">
<meta name="ProgId" content="FrontPage.Editor.Document">
<title>Demo DAV Request</title>
```

Rendering Search Results with XSL

```
<meta name="Microsoft Theme" content="none, default">
</head>

<xml id=calxsl>
<xsl:template   xmlns:xsl="uri:xsl" xmlns:d="DAV:">
<table
     id="thetable"
     onclick="clickrow();"
     border="4"
     width="100%"
     style="border-style: groove"
     cellspacing="0" bordercolor="#808080"
bordercolorlight="#808080" bordercolordark="#000080">
  <tr>
    <td width="25%" onclick="resort(0, 'd:displayname');"
bgcolor="silver"><font face="Tahoma" size="1"><b>Name</b>
</font></td>
    <td width="25%" onclick="resort(1, 'd:propstat/d:prop/
d:creationdate');" bgcolor="silver"><font face="Tahoma"
size="1"><b>Creation Date</b></font></td>
    <td width="25%" onclick="resort(2, 'd:propstat/d:prop/
d:getlastmodified');" bgcolor="silver"><font face="Tahoma"
size="1"><b>Last Modified</b></font></td>
  </tr>
  <xsl:for-each select="d:multistatus/d:response" order-
by="d:href">
  <tr>
     <td><xsl:value-of select="d:href" /></td>
     <td><xsl:for-each select="d:propstat/d:prop/
d:creationdate">
<xsl:eval>this.nodeTypedValue</xsl:eval></xsl:for-each></td>
     <td><xsl:value-of select="d:propstat/d:prop/
d:getlastmodified" /></td>
  </tr>
  </xsl:for-each>

</table>
</xsl:template>
</xml>

<body>
<h1>Simple DAV request</h1>

<p>URL: <INPUT type="text" id=urlid name=urlid
value="http://myServer1/" size=128></p>
<p>Depth: <SELECT id=depthid name=depthid>
<OPTION value="0">0</OPTION>
<OPTION value="1" SELECTED>1</OPTION>
<OPTION value="1,noroot">1,noroot</OPTION>
<OPTION value="infinity">infinity</OPTION>
```

```
</SELECT><INPUT type="button" value="Go" id=button1
name=button1 onclick="update()"></p>

<div id=xsldest>
</div>

<script>

function clickrow()
{
   src = event.srcElement;
   while(src.tagName != "TR")
      src = src.parentElement;
   if(src == thetable.rows[0])
      return;
   for(i=0; i < thetable.rows.length; i++)
   {
      onerow = thetable.rows[i];
      for(j = 0; j < onerow.cells.length; j++)
      {
         onecell = onerow.cells[j];
         onecell.style.backgroundColor = "white";
         onecell.style.color = "black";
      }
   }
   for(j = 0; j < src.cells.length; j++)
   {
      onecell = src.cells[j];
      onecell.style.backgroundColor = "black";
      onecell.style.color = "white";
   }
}

function resort(col, sortby)
{
   thenode =
calxsl.selectSingleNode("xsl:template/table/xsl:for-each");
   thenode.setAttribute("order-by", sortby);
   xsldest.innerHTML =
thexml.transformNode(calxsl.documentElement);
   therow = thetable.rows[0];
   therow.cells[col].style.backgroundColor = "gray";
}

</script>

<script>

var request;
var thexml;
```

```
function dostatechange()
{
   if(request == null || request.readystate != 4)
      return;
   if(request.status != 207)
   {
      xsldest.innerText = "Error, status = " +
request.status + " " + request.statusText;
   }
   else
   {
      thexml = request.responseXML;
      xsldest.innerHTML =
thexml.transformNode(calxsl.documentElement);
   }
   request = null;
}

function update()
{
   request = new ActiveXObject("microsoft.xmlhttp");
   request.open("PROPFIND", urlid.value, true);
   request.setRequestHeader("depth", depthid.value   );
   request.onreadystatechange = dostatechange;
   xsldest.innerHTML = "<h4>loading...</h4>";
   request.send("");
}

update();

</script>

</body>

</html>
```

Creating Search Folders

To create a search folder using the HTTP/WebDAV protocol, perform the following steps:

1. Create an MKCOL HTTP/WebDAV request. The request URI should be the location of the new search folder—for example, *http://myserver/pub2/folders/search_folder*.

Chapter 12 ● Using the HTTP/WebDAV Protocol

2. In the body of the request, send a DAV:propertyupdate XML stream. Specify the SQL statement in the DAV:sql portion of the DAV:search-request property.
3. Send the request to the HTTP service on the machine that hosts the Web Storage System in which the new search folder is to be created.
4. If successful, the HTTP service will respond with the status "207 Multi-Status," the new folder creation will have the status "201 Created," and the property update will have the status "200 OK."

Note Search folders *cannot* be created in the one public folder tree (and associated public store) designated for MAPI clients. If you attempt to create a search folder in this public folder tree, the web server will return an error. This public folder tree is, by default, made available through the '/public' HTTP virtual root.

The following example shows what the request body might look like:

```
MKCOL /pub2/search_folder/ HTTP/1.1
Host: somedomain.microsoft.com
Content-Length: XXX
Content-type: text/xml

<?xml version="1.0"?>
<a:propertyupdate xmlns:a="DAV:" >
    <a:set>
        <a:prop>
            <a:searchrequest>
                <a:sql>
                    Select "DAV:displayname"
                    FROM Scope('shallow traversal of "/pub2/folder1 "')
                    WHERE ""DAV:ishidden"" = false AND
                          ""DAV:isfolder"" = false
                </a:sql>
            </a:searchrequest>
        </a:prop>
    </a:set>
</a:propertyupdate>
```

In addition, a successful response might be as follows:

```
HTTP/1.1 207 Multi-Status
Server: Microsoft-IIS/5.0
Date: Tue, 22 Feb 1999 12:54:46 GMT
WWW-Authenticate: Negotiate AADAB...
MS-Exchange-Permanent-URL: http://hostname/pub2/-
FlatUrlSpace-/ab7e2af09631
b745981c6d39445456f2-17/
```

Creating Search Folders 295

```
Location: http://hostname/pub2/search_folder/
Timeout: Infinity
Repl-UID:
<rid:ab7e2af09631b745981c6d39445456f2000000001371>
Content-Type: text/xml
Content-Length: XXX
ResourceTag:
<rt:ab7e2af09631b745981c6d39445456f2000000001371ab7e2af0963
1b745981
c6d39445456f2000000001573>

<?xml version="1.0"?>
<a:multistatus xmlns:a="DAV:">
  <a:response>
    <a:href>http://hostname/pub2/search_folder</a:href>
    <a:status>HTTP/1.1 201 Created</a:status>
    <a:propstat>
       <a:status>HTTP/1.1 200 OK</a:status>
       <a:prop><a:searchrequest/></a:prop>
    </a:propstat>
  </a:response>
</a:multistatus>
```

Note   To reiterate, you can create search folders in all mailbox stores and all public folder trees, except the public folder tree designated for MAPI clients. This public folder tree is the default made available through the '/public' virtual root.

The example that follows uses an instance of the Microsoft.XMLHTTP COM class to create and send the request to the server. It then returns a reference to the object. The XML stream for the request body is hard coded by using a string variable. You can also use an instance of the Microsoft.XML-DOM COM class to create the XML stream for the request body. Here's what the codes might look like:

[JScript]

```
function createSearchFolder( folderURL, SQL ) {
  var Req;
  Req = new ActiveXObject("Microsoft.XMLHTTP");

  Req.Open("MKCOL", folderURL, false);
  strR = "<?xml version='1.0'?>";
  strR += "<d:propertyupdate xmlns:d='DAV:'>";
  strR += "<d:set><d:prop><d:searchrequest><d:sql>" + SQL +
"</d:sql>";
  strR += "</d:searchrequest></d:prop></d:set>
</d:propertyupdate>";
```

```
Req.SetRequestHeader("Content-type:", "text/xml");

Req.send(strR);

if(! Req.Status == "207") { // Multi-Status response
   // handle error
}

return Req;
}z
```

THIRTEEN

Search Tasks

This section contains common search tasks used with the Web Storage System. The examples presented here use the Microsoft ADO 2.5 COM component running on the same computer as the Web Storage System.

The search condition scope for most of these tasks is a shallow traversal, which is the default scope if no scope is specified. The Simple Query programming task contains commented code to show how to explicitly specify a shallow traversal. You can also search subfolders using a deep traversal.

You can improve search performance by employing the following techniques:

- Take advantage of Web Storage System property and full-text indexing.
- Use relative URLs to improve performance and simplify coding.
- Pass one ADO Connection object to routines that open record sets and process search results.
- If you are searching on a property that you defined with a property definition, you should cast its data type to a known XML data type to prevent any properties from being unrecognized by the Web Storage System. Custom strings and Boolean properties, however, do not require casting.

See Web Storage System SQL Reference for supported SQL grammar syntax, indexed properties, unsupported SQL, and other search reference topics.

Simple Query

The following example shows how to construct and run a query on the Web Storage System, the results of which are passed to a function that enumerates the search results:

[VBScript]

```
'Finds items from a sender
'Passes search result recordset to DoResults (see
Enumerating Results)

'get computer and domain information
Set info   = CreateObject("ADSystemInfo")
Set infoNT = CreateObject("WinNTSystemInfo")
cName = infoNT.ComputerName
dName = info.DomainDNSName

'create connection object
Set Conn = CreateObject("ADODB.Connection")
Conn.Provider = "Exoledb.DataSource"

'URL for connection object
'is at the virtual directory root
cURL = "http://" & _
     cName & "." & _
     dName & "/" & _
     "public"

Conn.Open cURL

'relative URL is the folder to search
relURL = "Reports"

sender = "Jane Clayton"

FindMsgsFrom sender, relURL, Conn

Sub FindMsgsFrom(sender, relURL, Conn)

    Const adErrNoCurrentRecord = 3021

    Set rs = CreateObject("ADODB.Recordset")

    'construct the SQL query
    strQ = "SELECT ""urn:httpmail:subject"" "
    strQ = strQ & "FROM """ & relURL & """ "

    '* ------
```

```
    '* A shallow traversal is the default scope. To explicitly
    '* specify a shallow traversal, the code would be:
    '* 'strQ = strQ & "FROM scope('shallow traversal of """ & strURL & """ ')"
    '*-------

    strQ = strQ & "WHERE ""urn:schemas:httpmail:sendername""" = '" & sender & "'"

    Rs.Open strQ, Conn

    'If empty recordset, return error
    'If successful call DoResults routine passing the recorset
    If Rs.EOF = True Then
        On Error Resume Next
        Err.Raise adErrNoCurrentRecord
        Response.Write "No items found, run another query."
    Else
        Response.Write "Success! Found " & Rs.RecordCount
        DoResults Rs
    End If
    Rs.Close

End Sub
```

Schema Scope

Each folder in the Microsoft Web Storage System has a schema scope. The schema scope is a set of folders, traversed in a particular order, which can contain schema definition items. Each folder can have a different schema scope. The scope can be simple, consisting of only the global schema folder, or complex, containing a large list of folder URLs.

The following two properties from the urn:schemas-microsoft-com:exch-data: namespace are examined on folder items to define a schema scope:

- *schema-collection-ref.* This property is a URL for a folder in which you search for content class and property definitions. This is the first folder searched for schema definition items and is always the first folder in a folder's schema scope. If this property is not set, the default is that store's non_ipm_subtree/Schema folder, which contains the Web Storage System default schema definition items.

- *baseschema*. This property is a multivalue string containing URLs for one or more folders. You extend the schema scope for a folder by identifying other folders that contain schema definition items.

Applying these two properties to folders, you create a virtual tree of folders in a store that contains schema definition items, starting with the folder identified by schema-collection-ref. When a schema-aware application constructs the schema information for a particular folder, it traverses the entire scope, breadth first, collecting definition items as they are encountered. Figure 13–1 presents one possible schema scope for a folder.

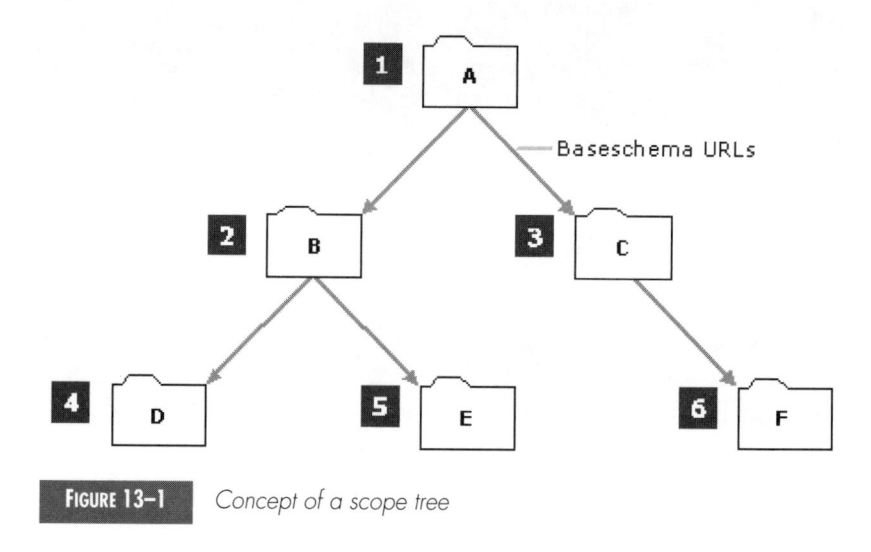

FIGURE 13–1 *Concept of a scope tree*

In Figure 13–1:

- An application folder (not shown in the diagram) identifies folder A as its schema collection folder in its schema-collection-ref property.
- Folder A is the first folder searched for schema definition items.
- Folder A has baseschema URLs pointing to folders B and C, which are subsequently searched (in that order) for schema definition items.
- Folder B has baseschema URLs pointing to folders D and E, which are subsequently searched (in that order) for schema definition items.
- Folder C has a baseschema URL pointing to folder F, which is the last folder in the scope and the last one searched. Typically, this folder is set to the non_ipm_subtree/Schema folder for that store.

Note The scope tree descends in breadth-first fashion. A breadth-first search works as follows: A is searched first, followed by B and C, and then D, E, and F. This algorithm is not of the recursive-descent type (that is, A, B, D, E, C, and F).

Also notice that the scope tree need not, and normally does not, correlate to the actual folder hierarchy in the Web Storage System. This scope tree is virtual in that sense.

In most cases, you should have one folder in your application folder's schema scope that has a baseschema property with one entry pointing to the non_ipm_subtree/Schema folder in that store. This folder contains the default global schema provided by the Web Storage System. If your scope does not contain the non_ipm_subtree/Schema folder, the global schema definition items are not included in your application folder's schema definition.

Specifying a Deep Traversal

A deep traversal is a scope that includes any and all subfolders. You cannot perform a deep traversal in the MAPI client public store installed by Microsoft Exchange 2000 Server, but you can perform deep traversals in private stores and in any new public folder tree.

[VBScript]

```
'Finds items from a sender, searching subfolders
'Passes search result recordset to DoResults (see
Enumerating Results)

'get computer and domain information
Set info   = CreateObject("ADSystemInfo")
Set infoNT = CreateObject("WinNTSystemInfo")
cName = infoNT.ComputerName
dName = info.DomainDNSName

'create connection object
Set Conn = CreateObject("ADODB.Connection")
Conn.Provider = "Exoledb.DataSource"

'URL for connection object
'is at the virtual directory root
cURL = "http://" & _
    cName & "." & _
    dName & "/" & _
    "public"

Conn.Open cURL

'relative URL is the folder to search
relURL = "Reports"
```

```
sender = "Jane Clayton"

FindMsgsFrom sender, relURL, Conn

Sub FindMsgsFrom(sender, relURL, Conn)

    Const adErrNoCurrentRecord = 3021

    Set rs = CreateObject("ADODB.Recordset")

    'construct the SQL query, note the scope for deep traversal
    strQ = "SELECT ""urn:httpmail:subject"" "
    strQ = strQ & "FROM scope('deep traversal of """ & strURL & """ ')"
    strQ = strQ & "WHERE ""urn:schemas:httpmail:sendername"" = '" & sender & "'"

    Rs.Open strQ, Conn

    'If empty recordset, return error
    'If successful call DoResults routine passing the recorset
    If Rs.EOF = True Then
        On Error Resume Next
        Err.Raise adErrNoCurrentRecord
        Response.Write "No items found, run another query."
    Else
        Response.Write "Success! Found " & Rs.RecordCount
        DoResults Rs
    End If
    Rs.Close

End Sub
```

Word and Character Matching

You can find items based on word and character matches of a specified search string. The example that follows shows how to construct an SQL query using the predicates in Table 13–1.

Table 13-1 Word and Character Matching

Predicate	Usage
CONTAINS	Finds words in the order specified, such as "Romeo and Juliet."
FREETEXT	Finds one or more words specified, such as "apples oranges pears."
FORMSOF	Finds word variations, such as "gardening" and "garden."
LIKE	Finds characters that match a specified string. The percent character (%) matches any or no characters adjacent to the specified string. For example, "%he ca%" matches "the cat."

The following is the code used to construct an SQL query:

[VBScript]

```
'Finds items based on CONTAINS, FREETEXT, FORMS, or LIKE
predicate
'This example uses FREETEXT to find reports with names of
cities
'Passes search result recordset to DoResults (see
Enumerating Results)

'get computer and domain information
Set info   = CreateObject("ADSystemInfo")
Set infoNT = CreateObject("WinNTSystemInfo")
cName = infoNT.ComputerName
dName = info.DomainDNSName

'create connection object
Set Conn = CreateObject("ADODB.Connection")
Conn.Provider = "Exoledb.DataSource"

'URL for connection object
'is at the virtual directory root
cURL = "http://" & _
      cName & "." & _
      dName & "/" & _
      "public"

Conn.Open cURL

'relative URL is the folder to search
relURL = "Reports/FieldOffices"

'search specification variable
searchspec = "Tokyo London Bogata Honolulu Cairo Sydney
Chicago"
```

Chapter 13 ● Search Tasks

```
'predicate to use in search
predicate = "FREETEXT"

FindSearchSpec searchspec, predicate, relURL, Conn

Sub FindSearchSpec(sender, relURL, Conn)

    Const adErrNoCurrentRecord = 3021

    Set rs = CreateObject("ADODB.Recordset")

    'construct the SQL query
    strQ = "SELECT ""urn:httpmail:subject"" "
    strQ = strQ & "FROM """ & relURL & """ "


    'Construct a query based on the search predicate.
    Select Case predicate
        Case "CONTAINS"
            strQ = strQ & "WHERE CONTAINS(*, '" & Chr(34) & searchspec & Chr(34) & "') "
        Case "FREETEXT"
            strQ = strQ & "WHERE FREETEXT(*, '" & Chr(34) & searchspec & Chr(34) & "') "
        Case "LIKE"
            strQ = strQ & "WHERE ""urn:schemas:httpmail:textdescription"" LIKE '" & searchspec & "'"
        Case "FORMSOF"
            strQ = strQ & "WHERE CONTAINS('FORMSOF(INFLECTIONAL," & Chr(34) & searchspec & Chr(34) & ")')"
        Case Else
            strQ = strQ & "WHERE CONTAINS(*, '" & Chr(34) & searchspec & Chr(34) & "') "
    End Select

    Rs.Open strQ, Conn

    'If empty recordset, return error
    'If successful call DoResults routine passing the recorset
    If Rs.EOF = True Then
        On Error Resume Next
        Err.Raise adErrNoCurrentRecord
        Response.Write "No items found, run another query."
    Else
        Response.Write "Success! Found " & Rs.RecordCount
```

```
        DoResults Rs
    End If
    Rs.Close

End Sub
```

Specifying a Date Range

This example filters for items based on a date range:

Note Because Web Storage date values use the DBTYPE_TIMESTAMP data type; you must include an exact time specification to match a particular date. For example, the following WHERE clause will not match items created on 2000-04-05:

```
WHERE "DAV:creationdate" = '2000-04-05'
```

To match, the clause must include the complete timestamp of an item:

```
WHERE "DAV:creationdate" = '2000-04-05 11:38:39.275'
```

A practical way to match a date is to define the range between the day before and the day after, as shown in this clause:

```
WHERE "DAV:creationdate" > '2000-04-04' AND
"DAV:creationdate" < '2000-04-06'
```

The following is the code to use to filter items based on date range:

[VBScript]

```
'Finds items matching a date range
'Passes search result recordset to DoResults (see
Enumerating Results)

'get computer and domain information
Set info   = CreateObject("ADSystemInfo")
Set infoNT = CreateObject("WinNTSystemInfo")
cName = infoNT.ComputerName
dName = info.DomainDNSName

'create connection object
Set Conn = CreateObject("ADODB.Connection")
Conn.Provider = "Exoledb.DataSource"

'URL for connection object
'is at the virtual directory root
cURL = "http://" & _
```

Chapter 13 ● Search Tasks

```
            cName & "." & _
            dName & "/" & _
            "public"

Conn.Open cURL

'relative URL is the folder to search
relURL = "Reports"

'date range variable:
DateRng = " > 2000-06-12"

FindMsgsByDate relURL, DateRng, Conn

Sub FindMsgsByDate(relURL, DateRng, Conn)

    Const adErrNoCurrentRecord = 3021

    Set rs = CreateObject("ADODB.Recordset")

    'construct the SQL query
    strQ = "SELECT ""urn:httpmail:subject"" "
    strQ = strQ & "FROM """ & relURL & """ "

    strQ = strQ & "WHERE
""urn:schemas:httpmail:datereceived"" " & DateRng

    Rs.Open strQ, Conn

    'If empty recordset, return error
    'If successful call DoResults routine passing the
recorset
    If Rs.EOF = True Then
        On Error Resume Next
        Err.Raise adErrNoCurrentRecord
        Response.Write "No items found, run another
query."
    Else
        Response.Write "Success! Found " & Rs.RecordCount
        DoResults Rs
    End If
    Rs.Close

End Sub
```

Getting Item Counts with GROUP BY

You can use the GROUP BY clause to get a tally of particular items, such as the number of messages with low, normal, or high importance. The DAV:visiblecount property contains the total for each group in the returned record set.

The example that follows could hypothetically return tallies of 3 low-importance, 207 normal-importance, and 27 high-importance messages. The property values are shown in Table 13–2.

TABLE 13–2 *Getting Item Counts with GROUP BY*

Property	Value
DAV:visiblecount	3
urn:schemas:httpmail:importance	0 (low importance)
DAV:visiblecount	207
urn:schemas:httpmail:importance	1 (normal importance)
DAV:visiblecount	27
urn:schemas:httpmail:importance	2 (high importance)

[VBScript]

```
'Tallies number of high, normal, and low importance msgs

'get computer and domain information
Set info   = CreateObject("ADSystemInfo")
Set infoNT = CreateObject("WinNTSystemInfo")
cName = infoNT.ComputerName
dName = info.DomainDNSName

'create connection object
Set Conn = CreateObject("ADODB.Connection")
Conn.Provider = "Exoledb.DataSource"

'URL for connection object
'is at the virtual directory root
cURL = "http://" & _
     cName & "." & _
     dName & "/" & _
     "exchange/userA"

Conn.Open cURL

'relative URL is the folder to search
relURL = "Inbox"
```

Chapter 13 • Search Tasks

```
TallyMsgsByImportance relURL, Conn

Sub TallyMsgsByImportance(relURL, Conn)

    Const adErrNoCurrentRecord = 3021

    Set rs = CreateObject("ADODB.Recordset")

    'construct the SQL query
    strQ = "SELECT ""DAV:visiblecount"", "
    strQ = strQ & " ""urn:schemas:httpmail:importance"" "
    strQ = strQ & "FROM """ & relURL & """ "
    strQ = strQ & "GROUP BY
""urn:schemas:httpmail:importance"" "

    Rs.Open strQ, Conn
    'If empty recordset, return error
    'If successful, display results
    If Rs.EOF = True Then
            On Error Resume Next
            Err.Raise adErrNoCurrentRecord
            WScript.Echo "No items found, run another
query."
        Else
            Rs.MoveFirst
            Do Until Rs.EOF
            Select Case
Rs("urn:schemas:httpmail:importance")
                Case 2
                    strI = "High"
                Case 1
                    strI = "Normal"
                Case 0
                    strI = "Low"
            End Select
            WScript.Echo Rs("DAV:visiblecount") & " " &
strI & " importance messages"
            Rs.MoveNext
        Loop
    End If
    Rs.Close

End Sub
```

Enumerating Search Results

This example shows how to process a returned record set, accommodating for multivalued and null properties, and how to render the results:

[VBScript]

```
'writes property values from a recordset (Rs)
'returned from a SQL query

'The DoResults function writes an HTML table
'for each record (item) in the recordset. In that table
'each property and value are written to a table cell,
'accommodating for null and multi-valued properties.

Function DoResults(Rs)
    'If empty recordset, return error
    If Rs.EOF = True Then
     On Error Resume Next
     Err.Raise adErrNoCurrentRecord
     Response.Write "<br><FONT FACE=Arial SIZE=2><B>No items found, run another query.</B><p>"
        Else
            Rs.MoveFirst
            Do Until Rs.EOF
            'Create a HTML table for each record, make table headings stand out
            Response.Write "<FONT FACE=Arial SIZE=2><TABLE BORDER=1 cellpadding=5 cellspacing=5>"
            Response.Write "<TR><TH bgcolor=#0000ff><FONT color=#ffffff><B>Property</B></TH>"
            Response.Write "<TH bgcolor=#0000ff><FONT color=#ffffff><B>Value</B></TH></TR>"

            For Each f In Rs.Fields
               'for every field in the record
               Response.Write "<TR><TD><FONT SIZE=1>"
               Response.Write f.Name
               Response.Write "</TD><TD><FONT SIZE=1>"

               'accommodate null and multi-valued properties
               If Not IsNull(f.Value) Then
                   If IsArray(f.Value) Then
                     'a multi-valued  property
                     Dim V
                     For Each V In f.Value
                        On Error Resume Next
                        Response.Write(V & "<br>")
                     Next
```

```
            Else
                On Error Resume Next
                Response.Write f.Value
            End If
        Else
           'Field is null
           Response.Write "Null"
        End If
        Response.Write "</TD></TR>"
        Next
        Response.Write "</TABLE><br><hr><br>"
        Rs.MoveNext
    Loop
  End If
End Function
```

FOURTEEN

Using Schema

Creating schemas for your application can be broken down into the following two steps:

1. Create schema definition items for your application.
   Schema definition items are items that define properties and content classes for your application. These items can be in any folder in the private or public store in which your application runs. Normally, you designate one or more folders to contain your application's schema definition items, and you add each folder to your application folder's schema scope.
2. Configure the schema scope of your application folders.
   After you have created your schema definition items and placed them in a folder in the public or private store where your application runs, you need to configure the scope of your application and schema folders. In doing so, you make your schema definition items visible to your application and to others that rely on a folder's schema scope, such as the Web Storage System SQL query processor for SELECT * requests.

The following sections describe how to perform those steps:
- Creating Property Definitions
- Creating Content Class Definitions
- Configuring a Folder's Schema Scope

The location of the folder(s) that contains your schema definition items is up to you.

Creating Property Definitions

To create a property definition, perform the following steps:

1. Create an item in one of your application's schema folders. You must place the item in a folder that is in your application folder's schema scope.
2. Set the item's DAV:contentclass to the value "urn:content-classes:propertydef". This identifies the item as a property definition.
3. Set the name of the property by using the urn:schemas-microsoft-com:xml-data#name property for the item. This name is used to refer to the property definition. Note that this name is not the URL for the item. For example, a property definition located at the URL *http://server/public/myapplication/schema/property1* may have the name "urn:schemas-myschema-tld:propA". This name is used to refer to the property in applicable item fields, such as the urn:schemas-microsoft-com:xml-data#element property for a content-class definition item.
4. Set the property's data type by using the urn:schemas-microsoft-com:datatypes#type field.
5. Define whether the property is multivalued by setting the urn:schemas-microsoft-com:exch-data:ismultivalued property for the item.

The following is an example of the codes used:

[VBScript]

```
<job id="createpropdefs">
<reference object="adodb.record"/>
<script language="vbscript">

Dim InfoNT
Set InfoNT = CreateObject("WinNTSystemInfo")
Dim sPath
sPath = "/public/test_folder/schema/"

CreatePropDefs "http://" & InfoNT.ComputerName & sPath

Sub CreatePropDefs( sSchemaFolderUrl )

'
' This example creates the following property definitions:
'    urn:schemas-domain-tld:submitdate
'    urn:schemas-domain-tld:cuisine
'    urn:schemas-domain-tld:title
'    urn:schemas-domain-tld:ingredients
'    urn:schemas-domain-tld:instructions
'    urn:schemas-domain-tld:rating
```

Creating Property Definitions

```
' These properties are used in the urn:schemas-domain-
tld:content-classes:recipe
' content class.
'
' A URN scheme is used for the namespace: "urn:schemas-
domain-tld:"
'  where "tld" refers to "top-level domain".

Dim Conn
set Conn = CreateObject("ADODB.Connection")
conn.Provider = "ExOLEDB.DataSource"
Conn.Open sSchemaFolderUrl

Dim Rec
Set Rec = CreateObject("ADODB.Record")

' Create the property definition in the schema folder for
submitdate
Rec.Open sSchemaFolderUrl & "submitdate", Conn,
adModeReadWrite, adCreateNonCollection
Set Flds = Rec.Fields
With Flds
   .Item("DAV:contentclass") = "urn:content-
classes:propertydef"
   .Item("urn:schemas-microsoft-com:xml-data#name") =
"urn:schemas-domain-tld:submitdate"
   .Item("urn:schemas-microsoft-com:datatypes#type") =
"dateTime"
   .Item("urn:schemas-microsoft-com:exch-
data:ismultivalued") = False
  .Item("urn:schemas-microsoft-com:exch-data:isindexed")
= True
  .Item("urn:schemas-microsoft-com:exch-data:isreadonly")
= False
   .Update
End With
Rec.Close

' Create the property definition in the schema folder for
cuisine
Rec.Open sSchemaFolderUrl & "cuisine", Conn,
adModeReadWrite, adCreateNonCollection
Set Flds = Rec.Fields
With Flds
   .Item("DAV:contentclass") = "urn:content-
classes:propertydef"
   .Item("urn:schemas-microsoft-com:xml-data#name") =
"urn:schemas-domain-tld:cuisine"
   .Item("urn:schemas-microsoft-com:datatypes#type") =
"string"
```

Chapter 14 • Using Schema

```
    .Item("urn:schemas-microsoft-com:exch-
data:ismultivalued") = False
    .Item("urn:schemas-microsoft-com:exch-data:isindexed")
= False
    .Item("urn:schemas-microsoft-com:exch-data:isreadonly")
= False
     .Update
 End With
 Rec.Close

 ' Create the property definition in the schema folder for
title
 Rec.Open sSchemaFolderUrl & "title", Conn,
adModeReadWrite, adCreateNonCollection
 Set Flds = Rec.Fields
 With Flds
    .Item("DAV:contentclass") = "urn:content-
classes:propertydef"
    .Item("urn:schemas-microsoft-com:xml-data#name")   =
"urn:schemas-domain-tld:title"
    .Item("urn:schemas-microsoft-com:datatypes#type") =
"string"
    .Item("urn:schemas-microsoft-com:exch-
data:ismultivalued") = False
    .Item("urn:schemas-microsoft-com:exch-data:isindexed")
= True
    .Item("urn:schemas-microsoft-com:exch-data:isreadonly")
= False
     .Update
 End With
 Rec.Close

 ' Create the property definition in the schema folder for
ingredients
 Rec.Open sSchemaFolderUrl & "ingredients",
Conn,adModeReadWrite, adCreateNonCollection
 Set Flds = Rec.Fields
 With Flds
    .Item("DAV:contentclass") = "urn:content-
classes:propertydef"
    .Item("urn:schemas-microsoft-com:xml-data#name")   =
"urn:schemas-domain-tld:ingredients"
    .Item("urn:schemas-microsoft-com:datatypes#type") =
"string"

    ' Note that ismultivalued is set to true for handling
multiple ingredients
    .Item("urn:schemas-microsoft-com:exch-
data:ismultivalued") = True
```

Creating Property Definitions 315

```
  .Item("urn:schemas-microsoft-com:exch-data:isindexed")
= True
  .Item("urn:schemas-microsoft-com:exch-data:isreadonly")
= False
    .Update
 End With
 Rec.Close

 ' Create the property definition in the schema folder for
 instructions
 Rec.Open sSchemaFolderUrl & "instructions",
 Conn,adModeReadWrite, adCreateNonCollection
 Set Flds = Rec.Fields
 With Flds
    .Item("DAV:contentclass") = "urn:content-
classes:propertydef"
    .Item("urn:schemas-microsoft-com:xml-data#name") =
"urn:schemas-domain-tld:instructions"
    .Item("urn:schemas-microsoft-com:datatypes#type") =
"string"

    ' Note that ismultivalued is set to true for handling
multiple instructions
    .Item("urn:schemas-microsoft-com:exch-
data:ismultivalued") = True
  .Item("urn:schemas-microsoft-com:exch-data:isindexed")
= False
  .Item("urn:schemas-microsoft-com:exch-data:isreadonly")
= False
    .Update
 End With
 Rec.Close

 ' Create the property definition in the schema folder for
 rating
 Rec.Open sSchemaFolderUrl & "rating", Conn,
 adModeReadWrite, adCreateNonCollection
 Set Flds = Rec.Fields
 With Flds
    .Item("DAV:contentclass") = "urn:content-
classes:propertydef"
    .Item("urn:schemas-microsoft-com:xml-data#name") =
"urn:schemas-domain-tld:rating"
    .Item("urn:schemas-microsoft-com:datatypes#type") =
"int"
    .Item("urn:schemas-microsoft-com:exch-
data:ismultivalued") = False
  .Item("urn:schemas-microsoft-com:exch-data:isindexed")
= True
```

```
        .Item("urn:schemas-microsoft-com:exch-data:isreadonly")
= False
         .Update
  End With
  Rec.Close

End Sub
</script>
</job>
```

Creating Content Class Definitions

To create a content-class definition item, follow these steps:

1. Create a nonfolder item to hold the content-class definition. You must place the item in a folder that is in your application folder's schema scope.
2. Set the item's DAV:contentclass field to the value urn:content-classes:content–classdef. This identifies the item as a content-class definition.
3. Set the content class's *name* using the urn:schemas-microsoft-com:xml-data#name property for the item. This name refers to the content-class definition. Note that this name is not the URL for the item. For example, a content-class definition located at the URL *http://server/public/myapplication/schema/contentclass1* could have the name "urn:schemas-myschema-tld:content-classes:class1". This name refers to the content class in applicable item fields—for example, a folder's *expected-content-class* or an item's DAV:contentclass property.
4. Optionally, you can extend other content classes by setting the urn:schemas-microsoft-com:xml-data#extends property for the item. This property is an array of strings, in which each string is the name of a content class as designated by the class's urn:schemas-microsoft-com:xml-data#name field. When you extend other content-class definition items, your class inherits the property definitions set for each of these classes.
5. You can also specify the names of property definitions to associate with the content class. If this class extends others, you do not need to specify property names for those classes; they are inherited. To specify the names of property definitions, you set the urn:schemas-microsoft-com:xml-data#element property for the item. This property is an array of strings, in which each string is the name of a property definition in the schema scope.

Creating Content Class Definitions

The following is an example of codes used:

[VBScript]

```vbscript
<Job id="CreateCCDef">
<reference object="adodb.record"/>
<script language="vbscript">

Dim Conn
Dim Info
Dim InfoNT
Dim sSchemaFolderURL

Set Info   = CreateObject("ADSystemInfo")
Set InfoNT = CreateObject("WinNTSystemInfo")

sVrootURL        = "http://" & InfoNT.ComputerName & "." & Info.DomainDNSName & "/public"
sSchemaFolderURL = sVrootURL & "/test_folder/schema"

Set Conn = CreateObject("ADODB.Connection")
Conn.Provider = "ExOLEDB.DataSource"
Conn.Open sVrootURL

CreateCCDef sSChemaFolderURL, Conn

Sub CreateCCDef( sSchemaFolderURL, Conn )

   Const adModeReadWrite       = 3
   Const adFailIfNotExists     = -1
   Const adCreateNonCollection = 0

   Dim Rec
   Set Rec = CreateObject("ADODB.Record")

   Rec.Open sSchemaFolderURL & "/ccdef-recipe", Conn, adModeReadWrite, adCreateNonCollection

   Dim Flds
   Set Flds = Rec.Fields

   With Flds

     ' Name the content class.
     .Item("urn:schemas-microsoft-com:xml-data#name").Value = _
        "urn:schemas-domain-tld:content-classes:recipe"

     ' The content class of the definition item.
     .Item("DAV:contentclass") = "urn:content-
```

```
classes:contentclassdef"

    ' The content classes it extends (inherits from).
    .Item("urn:schemas-microsoft-com:xml-
data#extends").Value = _
        Array("urn:content-classes:item", "urn:content-
classes:person")

    ' The properties to belong to this content class.
    .Item("urn:schemas-microsoft-com:xml-
data#element").Value = _
        Array("urn:schemas-domain-tld:submitdate",_
            "urn:schemas-domain-tld:cuisine", _
            "urn:schemas-domain-tld:title", _
            "urn:schemas-domain-tld:ingredients", _
            "urn:schemas-domain-tld:instructions", _
            "urn:schemas-domain-tld:rating")

    .Update
End With

Rec.Close

End Sub
</script>
</Job>
```

Specifying Expected Content Classes for Folders

Each folder item has a list of content-class names in its urn:schemas-microsoft-com:exch-data:expected-content-class property. These names refer to the names of content-class definition items that reside in the folder's schema scope. When you set this property for folders, you are indicating to schema-aware applications the list of content class names to expect items within the folder to be instances of. For example, the Web Storage System SQL query processor uses this list of names, along with definition items in the folder's schema scope, to determine which properties it should return when a client issues a SELECT * command. The list of content-class names identified in this property does not restrict the possible values that you can set for an item's DAV:contentclass property. It merely acts as an indicator to schema-aware applications what class of content to expect in the folder.

The following example demonstrates how to set the urn:schemas-microsoft-com:exch-data:expected-content-class property on a folder:

[VBScript]

```vbscript
' Update the application folder to specify the schema scope

Const adModeReadWrite   = 3
Const adFailIfNotExists = -1

Dim sURL
sURL =
"file://./backofficestorage/microsoft.com/pubtreeroot"

Dim Rec
Dim Conn
Dim Flds

Set Conn = CreateObject("ADODB.Connection")
Set Rec  = CreateObject("ADODB.Record")

Conn.Provider = "ExOLEDB.DataSource"
Conn.Open sURL
Rec.Open  sURL & "/myapp/myappfolder/", Conn, 
adModeReadWrite

Set Flds = Rec.Fields
With Flds

  ' Specify which content classes are expected for this
folder.
  ' Here, a custom content class is specified along with
the standard folder
  ' content class urn:content-classes:folder.

    .Item("urn:schemas-microsoft-com:exch-data:expected-
content-class").Value = _
        Array("urn:schemas-domain-tld:content-
classes:mycontentclass", "urn:content-classes:folder")
    .Update
End With

Rec.Close
```

Configuring a Folder's Schema Scope

A *schema scope* is defined as the set of folders, identified by URI, that are traversed when searching for schema definition items. You need to define your application folder's schema scope so that your schema definition items are in the schema scope. You configure a folder's schema scope by using two folder properties:

- *urn:schemas-microsoft-com:exch-data:schema-collection-ref.* This single-valued property, which can be set on any folder, specifies the URL that points to the first folder which contains applicable schema definition items. If this property is empty, the default location is the *non_ipm_subtree/Schema* folder of the public or private store. When you want to create your own schema definition items and apply them to items in your application folders, you set this property on each of your application folders.

    The schema scope for any folder always starts with a single folder in the store. You can further expand the scope by setting the urn:schemas-microsoft-com:exch-data:baseschema field on the first and subsequent schema folders. Normally, applications terminate the schema scope with the *non_ipm_subtree/Schema* folder, which contains the global Web Storage System schema definition items.

- *urn:schemas-microsoft-com:exch-data:baseschema.* This multivalued field, which can be set on any folder, specifies the URLs for folders that contain additional, or base, schema definition items. When an application constructs the list of folders that are in a particular folder's schema scope, each folder identified by this property is added to the list in the order in which it appears in this field. Note that, by convention, you set the field for designated application schema folders and *not* for the application folder itself.

Note: The order in which folders are searched is significant: If two or more definition items exist that have the same name set in the definition item's urn:schemas-microsoft-com:xml-data#name property, only the first definition is used. See "Schema Scope" in Chapter 13, "Search Tasks," for more information.

The following sections demonstrate how to set and examine these properties on folders in an application folder's schema scope:

- Setting the Schema Collection Reference for a Folder
- Setting the Base Schema Path for a Folder

Setting the Schema Collection Reference for a Folder

The example that follows demonstrates how to set the urn:schemas-microsoft-com:schema-collection-ref property for a folder. This property indicates the URI of the first folder in which to search for schema definition items. If the property is not set, the default location is the *non_ipm_subtree/Schema* folder

Configuring a Folder's Schema Scope

in the public or private store where the folder resides. The code to use is as follows:

[VBScript]

```
<Job id="SetupFolderschema">
<reference object="adodb.record"/>

<script language="vbscript">

 Option Explicit

 Dim Info
 Dim InfoNT
 Dim oRec
 Dim oRec2
 Dim Conn
 Dim sVrootURL
 Dim sFolderURL
 Dim sSchemaFolderURL

 Set Info   = CreateObject("ADSystemInfo")
 Set InfoNT = CreateObject("WinNTSystemInfo")
 Set Conn   = CreateObject("ADODB.Connection")

 sVrootURL = "http://" & InfoNT.ComputerName & "/public/"
 sFolderURL = "appfolder/"
 sSchemaFolderURL = "schema/"

 Conn.Provider = "ExOLEDb.DataSource"
 Conn.Open   sVrootURL

 Set oRec = CreateObject("ADODB.Record")
 oRec.Open sVrootURL & sFolderURL, Conn, adModeReadWrite,
adCreateCollection OR adCreateOverWrite

 oRec.Fields("DAV:contentclass") = "urn:content-classes:folder"

 '''''''''''''''''''''''''''''''''''''''''''
 ' Here the schema-collection-ref URL is set.'
 '                                          '
 '''''''''''''''''''''''''''''''''''''''''''
 oRec.Fields("urn:schemas-microsoft-com:exch-data:schema-collection-ref") = _
    sVrootURL & sFolderURL & sSchemaFolderURL

 oRec.Fields.Update

 Set oRec2 = CreateObject("ADODB.Record")
```

Chapter 14 • Using Schema

```
 oRec2.Open sVrootURL & sFolderURL & sSchemaFolderURL,
Conn, adModeReadWrite, adCreateCollection OR
adCreateOverWrite
 oRec2.Fields("DAV:contentclass") = "urn:content-
classes:folder"
 oRec2.Fields("urn:schemas-microsoft-com:exch-
data:baseschema").Value = Array( sVrootURL &
"non_ipm_subtree/Schema")
 oRec2.Fields.Update

 wscript.echo oRec.Fields("urn:schemas-microsoft-com:exch-
data:schema-collection-ref")

</script>
</Job>
```

[C++]

```cpp
#import <msado15.dll> no_namespace
#import "c:\program files\common files\microsoft
shared\cdo\cdoex.dll" no_namespace
#include <iostream.h>

void setSchemaColRef(bstr_t sFolderUrl) {

   _RecordPtr Rec(__uuidof(Record));
   _ConnectionPtr Conn(__uuidof(Connection));

   Conn->Provider = "ExOLEDB.DataSource";
   try {
      Conn->Open(sFolderUrl, bstr_t(), bstr_t(), -1);
   }
   catch(_com_error e) {
      cout << "Error opening connection." << endl;
      //..
      throw e;
   }

   try {
      Rec->Open(sFolderUrl,
            variant_t((IDispatch*)Conn,true),
            adModeReadWrite,
            adFailIfNotExists,
            adOpenSource,
            bstr_t(),
            bstr_t());
   }
   catch(_com_error e) {
      cout << "Error opening item" << endl;
      //..
```

```
   }

   FieldsPtr Flds;
   Flds = Rec->Fields;
   FieldPtr Fld;
   Fld = Flds->Item["urn:schemas-microsoft-com:exch-
data:schema-collection-ref"];
   Fld->Value = bstr_t("http://server.microsoft.com/vroot/
path/to/collection/");

   try {
      Flds->Update();
   }
   catch(_com_error e) {
      cout << "update failed" << endl;
      cout << e.Description() << endl;
   }

}
```

Setting the Base Schema Path for a Schema Folder

The example that follows demonstrates how to set the urn:schemas-microsoft-com:baseschema property for a folder. This property indicates the URIs of folders that contain additional schema definition items. The order in which these folder URIs appear in the property is the order in which these folders are searched.

If you define your own schema definition items and place them in your own set of schema folders, make sure that one of your schema folders has the base schema property set to the *non_ipm_subtree/Schema* folder for that store. If not, the global schema definitions will not be in the schema scope. Here is the code used:

[VBScript]

```
<Job id="SetupFolderschema">
<reference object="adodb.record"/>

<script language="vbscript">

 Option Explicit

 Dim Info
 Dim InfoNT
 Dim oRec
 Dim oRec2
 Dim Conn
 Dim sVrootURL
 Dim sFolderURL
```

Chapter 14 • Using Schema

```
Dim sSchemaFolderURL

Set Info   = CreateObject("ADSystemInfo")
Set InfoNT = CreateObject("WinNTSystemInfo")
Set Conn   = CreateObject("ADODB.Connection")

sVrootURL = "http://" & InfoNT.ComputerName & "/public/"
sFolderURL = "appfolder/"
sSchemaFolderURL = "schema/"

Conn.Provider = "ExOLEDb.DataSource"
Conn.Open   sVrootURL

Set oRec = CreateObject("ADODB.Record")
oRec.Open sVrootURL & sFolderURL, Conn, adModeReadWrite,
adCreateCollection OR adCreateOverWrite

oRec.Fields("DAV:contentclass") = "urn:content-
classes:folder"
oRec.Fields("urn:schemas-microsoft-com:exch-data:schema-
collection-ref") = _
   sVrootURL & sFolderURL & sSchemaFolderURL
oRec.Fields.Update

Set oRec2 = CreateObject("ADODB.Record")
oRec2.Open sVrootURL & sFolderURL & sSchemaFolderURL,
Conn, adModeReadWrite, adCreateCollection OR
adCreateOverWrite
oRec2.Fields("DAV:contentclass") = "urn:content-
classes:folder"

'''''''''''''''''''''''''''''''''''''''''''''''
' Here the baseschema array of URLs is set. '
'                                             '
'''''''''''''''''''''''''''''''''''''''''''''''
oRec2.Fields("urn:schemas-microsoft-com:exch-
data:baseschema").Value = Array( sVrootURL &
"non_ipm_subtree/Schema")

oRec2.Fields.Update

wscript.echo oRec.Fields("urn:schemas-microsoft-com:exch-
data:schema-collection-ref")

</script>
</Job>
```

   [C++]

```
#import <msado15.dll> no_namespace
#import "c:\program files\common files\microsoft
```

Configuring a Folder's Schema Scope

```cpp
shared\cdo\cdoex.dll" no_namespace
#include <iostream.h>

void setBaseSchemaForFolder(bstr_t sFolderUrl) {

   _RecordPtr Rec(__uuidof(Record));
   _ConnectionPtr Conn(__uuidof(Connection));

   Conn->Provider = "ExOLEDB.DataSource";
   try {
      Conn->Open(sFolderUrl, bstr_t(), bstr_t(), -1);
   }
   catch(_com_error e) {
      cout << "Error opening connection." << endl;
      //..
      throw e;
   }

   wchar_t* url1 =   L"http://server/public/test_folder2";
   wchar_t* url2 =   L"http://server/public/test_folder3";
   wchar_t* url3 =
   L"http://server/public/non_ipm_subtree/Schema";

   VARIANT      vVal;
   VariantInit(&vVal);
   vVal.vt = VT_ARRAY | VT_VARIANT;

   SAFEARRAY* psa  = NULL;
   psa = SafeArrayCreateVector(VT_VARIANT, 0, 3);
   if(psa == NULL) {
      // handle error here.
   }

   VARIANT* pVal;
   HRESULT hr = S_OK;
   hr = SafeArrayAccessData(psa, (void**)&pVal);
   if(FAILED(hr)) {
      // handle error
   }

   VariantInit(&(pVal[0]));
   pVal[0].vt = VT_BSTR;
   pVal[0].bstrVal = SysAllocString(url1);
   VariantInit(&(pVal[1]));
   pVal[1].vt = VT_BSTR;
   pVal[1].bstrVal = SysAllocString(url2);
   VariantInit(&(pVal[2]));
   pVal[2].vt = VT_BSTR;
   pVal[2].bstrVal = SysAllocString(url3);
```

```
        SafeArrayUnaccessData(psa);

        vVal.parray = psa;

        try {
           Rec->Open(sFolderUrl,
                   variant_t((IDispatch*)Conn,true),
                   adModeReadWrite,
                   adFailIfNotExists,
                   adOpenSource,
                   bstr_t(),
                   bstr_t());
        }
        catch(_com_error e) {
           cout << "Error opening item" << endl;
           //..
        }

        FieldsPtr Flds;
        Flds = Rec->Fields;
        FieldPtr Fld;
        Fld = Flds->Item["urn:schemas-microsoft-com:exch-
        data:baseschema"];
        Fld->Value = vVal;

        SafeArrayDestroy(psa);
        VariantClear(&vVal);
        psa = NULL;

        try {
           Flds->Update();
        }
        catch(_com_error e) {
           cout << "update failed" << endl;
           cout << e.Description() << endl;
        }

        // Now, read the props back and print the values...
        variant_t vBaseSchema;
        vBaseSchema = Flds->Item["urn:schemas-microsoft-
        com:exch-data:baseschema"]->Value;
        if( ! (vBaseSchema.vt == (VT_ARRAY | VT_VARIANT))) {
           cout << "Unexpected..." << endl;
           // handle error
        }

        hr = SafeArrayAccessData(vBaseSchema.parray,
        (void**)&pVal);
        if(FAILED(hr)) {
```

```
        cout << "access data failed!!" << endl;
    }

    cout << "Set the baseschema property for the folder at
\r\n  " << sFolderUrl;
    cout << " \r\nto the following URLS: " << endl;
    cout << bstr_t(pVal[0].bstrVal) << endl;
    cout << bstr_t(pVal[1].bstrVal) << endl;
    cout << bstr_t(pVal[2].bstrVal) << endl;

    SafeArrayUnaccessData(vBaseSchema.parray);

}
```

Testing Your Schema

The following is the code to test your schema:

[VBScript]

```
<job id="testschema">
<reference object="adodb.record"/>
<script language="vbscript">

Dim InfoNT
Dim Conn
Dim Rec
Dim Rs
Dim strQ
Dim strURL
Set Conn = CreateObject("ADODB.Connection")
Conn.Provider = "ExOLEDB.DataSource"

Set Rs = CreateObject("ADODB.Recordset")
Set Rec = CreateObject("ADODB.Record")
Set InfoNT = CreateObject("WinNTSystemInfo")

strURL = "http://" & InfoNT.ComputerName & "/public/
test_folder/"
Conn.Open strURL

Rec.Open strURL, Conn, adModeReadWrite
Rec.Fields("urn:schemas-microsoft-com:exch-data:schema-
collection-ref") = strUrl & "schema"
Rec.Fields("urn:schemas-microsoft-com:exch-data:expected-
content-class") = _
   Array("urn:schemas-domain-tld:content-classes:recipe")
```

Chapter 14 • Using Schema

```
Rec.Fields.Update
Rec.Close

Rec.Open strURL & "schema", Conn, adModeReadWrite
Rec.Fields("urn:schemas-microsoft-com:exch-
data:baseschema") = Array(CStr("/public/non_ipm_subtree/
Schema"))
Rec.Fields.Update
Rec.Close

Rec.Open strURL & "test1.txt", Conn, adModeReadWrite,
adCreateNonCollection Or adCreateOverWrite
Rec.Fields("urn:schemas-domain-tld:title").Value       =
"Title Here"
Rec.Fields("urn:schemas-domain-tld:submitdate").Value
= Now
Rec.Fields("urn:schemas-domain-tld:rating").Value
= CLng(4)
Rec.Fields("urn:schemas-domain-tld:cuisine").Value     =
CStr("Cuisine Here")
Rec.Fields("urn:schemas-domain-tld:ingredients").Value =
Array("this", "that", "something-else")
Rec.Fields("urn:schemas-domain-tld:instructions").Value =
CStr("The instructions here.")
Rec.Fields("DAV:contentclass") = "urn:schemas-domain-
tld:content-classes:recipe"
Rec.Fields.Update
Rec.Close

Rec.Open strURL & "test1.txt", Conn
For Each Fld in Rec.Fields
 wscript.echo Fld.Name
  if not isarray(fld.value) then
    wscript.echo fld.value
  end if
Next

wscript.quit

strQ = "SELECT * from scope('shallow traversal of "
strQ = strQ & Chr(34) & strURL & Chr(34) & "') WHERE
""DAV:isfolder"" = False AND ""DAV:ishidden"" = False"

Rs.Open strQ, Conn
Rs.MoveFirst
Do Until Rs.EOF
   For x = 0 To Rs.Fields.Count - 1
      Wscript.Echo "Name: " & Rs(x).Name
      If VarType(Rs(x).Value) = vbString _
            Or VarType(Rs(x).Value) = vbInteger _
```

```
                        Or VarType(Rs(x).Value) = vbLong _
                        Or VarType(Rs(x).Value) = vbDate Then
            Wscript.Echo "Value: " & Rs(x).Value
                    Else
                        wscript.echo vartype(Rs(x).Value)
                    End If
    Next
    Wscript.Echo "Next Record----------------------"
    Rs.MoveNext
Loop

Rs.Close
</script>
</job>
```

Displaying Icons Based on Item Content Class

All Web Storage System items have content classes that denote their intended purpose. Applications can use this value to determine how to process the data that an item contains. Each item's content class is identified by its DAV:contentclass property.

The following example demonstrates how to select appropriate icons for items in a folder using ADO:

[Visual Basic]

```
' Assume oRecSub is an ADO Record object of a selected item
in a folder;
' Use the content class to select a picture.

Select Case oRecSub.Fields("DAV:contentclass").Value

    'evaluate content-class value
    'and display appropriate icon

    Case "urn:content-classes:message"
        Image1.Picture = LoadPicture("mail01a.ico")
    Case "urn:content-classes:mailfolder"
        Image1.Picture = LoadPicture("mail01a.ico")
    Case "urn:content-classes:appointment "
        Image1.Picture = LoadPicture("clock01.ico")
    Case "urn:content-classes:contact"
        Image1.Picture = LoadPicture("crdfle10.ico")
    Case "urn:content-classes:mailfolder"
        Image1.Picture = LoadPicture("crdfle10.ico")
    Case "urn:content-classes:contactfolder"
        Image1.Picture = LoadPicture("crdfle10.ico")
```

```
        Case "urn:content-classes:calendarfolder"
            Image1.Picture = LoadPicture("crdfle10.ico")
        Case Else
            Image1.Picture = LoadPicture("unknown.ico")
End Select
```

Using Folder Content Class

All Web Storage System folders and items have content-class values that denote their intended purpose. A folder is an item that is a collection of other items. Web Storage System applications can use content-class values to determine how to process the data that an item contains.

You can check the content class using an ADO Record object before you create instances of any CDO objects. To do so, you can check the value of the DAV:contentclass property. Alternatively, if you know the item is a folder by checking its DAV:iscollection property values, you can create an instance of a CDO Folder object from a URL or from an ADO Record object and then check the IFolder.ContentClass property. The code to use is as follows:

[Visual Basic]

```
Dim CC as String
Dim Rec As New ADODB.Record
With Rec
  .Open strFolderURL
  CC = .Fields("DAV:contentclass")
  If CC = "urn:content-classes:contactfolder" Then
    '
  Else If CC = "urn:content-classes:mailfolder" Then
    '
  End If
  Rec.Close
End With

  'To check a folder Content-Class using a CDO Folder object
Dim iFldr As New CDO.Folder
Dim iDsrc as CDO.IDataSource
Set iDsrc = iFldr
iDsrc.Open strFolderURL
If iFldr.ContentClass = "urn:content-classes:mailfolder" Then
    '
End If
```

FIFTEEN

Security Tasks

The following sections describe how to manage security for items in the Web Storage System:

- Getting an Item's XML Security Descriptor
- Creating Web Storage System Descriptors in XML
- Updating an Item's Security Descriptor

Getting an Item's XML Security Descriptor

You can get an item's XML security descriptor by requesting the *http://schemas.microsoft.com/exchange/security/descriptor* property. The following example shows what the HTTP/WebDAV request might look like:

```
PROPFIND /path/to/item.txt HTTP/1.1
Content-Type: text/xml
Depth: 0
Translate: f
Content-Length: XXX

<?xml version="1.0"?>
<propfind xmlns="DAV:">
 <prop xmlns:S="http://schemas.microsoft.com/exchange/security/">
   <S:descriptor/>
 </prop>
</propfind>
```

Chapter 15 ● Security Tasks

The following example demonstrates how to send this request by using the XMLHTTP COM object:

[JScript]

```
function getSecurityDescForItem( url , username, password)
{

 var xmlDom = new ActiveXObject("Microsoft.XMLDOM");
 var pi     = xmlDom.createProcessingInstruction("xml","version=\"1.0\"");
 var e1     = xmlDom.createNode(1, "propfind", "DAV:");
 var e2     = xmlDom.createNode(1, "prop","DAV:");

 xmlDom.appendChild(pi);
 xmlDom.documentElement = e1;
 e1.setAttribute("xmlns:S","http://schemas.microsoft.com/exchange/security/");
 e1.appendChild(e2);
 e2.appendChild(xmlDom.createNode(1, "S:descriptor", "http://schemas.microsoft.com/exchange/security/"));

 var Req = new ActiveXObject("Microsoft.XMLHTTP");

 Req.open("PROPFIND",url, false, username, password);
 Req.setRequestHeader("Content-Type","text/xml");
 Req.setRequestHeader("Depth","0");
 Req.setRequestHeader("Translate","f");

 Req.send(xmlDom.xml);

 if(Req.status != "207") {
    var errstr = "ERR: HTTP server returned status=" + Req.status
    errstr    += "\r\nError: HTTP server returned status=" + Req.status;
    errstr    += "        Status text: " + Req.statusText;
    errstr    += "        Response Text: " + Req.responseText;
    throw errstr;
 }

 var resItem  = findDescriptorInDOM(Req.responseXML);
 if(resItem == null)
    throw "ERR: Could not locate prop in response!!";
 else
    return resItem;
}
```

Getting an Item's XML Security Descriptor

```
function findDescriptorInDOM( Doc ) {

 var item;
 var root = Doc.documentElement;
 if(root.namespaceURI != "DAV:")
   return null;

 var prefix = root.prefix;
 var propElem = root.selectSingleNode("//" + prefix + ":" +
"prop");
 if(propElem == null)
   return null;

 var descProp = propElem.childNodes.item(0);
 if(descProp.baseName != "descriptor" ||
descProp.namespaceURI != "http://schemas.microsoft.com/
exchange/security/")
   return null;

 var desc = descProp.childNodes.item(0);
 WScript.Echo(desc.nodeName);
 return desc;

}
```

The following example demonstrates how to get the item's security descriptor by using ADO and the Microsoft Exchange 2000 Server OLE DB provider:

[VBScript]

```
Function getSecDescForItem( vSource )

  Dim Rec
  Dim vtype
  dim typenam
  vtype = VarType(vSource)
  typenam = TypeName(vSource)

 ' Check arguments
  If Not ( _
    ( vtype = vbString) OR  _
    (  ( vtype = vbObject)  And  _
    (  ( typenam = "Record") ) ) _
    ) Then
    Err.Raise &H80070057 ' E_INVALIDARG
  End If

  if vtype = vbString Then
    Set Rec = CreateObject("ADODB.Record")
```

```
    Rec.Open vSource
elseif vtype = vbObject And typename = "Record" Then
    Set Rec = vSource
End If

Dim Flds
Set Flds = Rec.Fields
getSecDescForItem = Flds("http://schemas.microsoft.com/
exchange/security/descriptor").Value

End Sub
```

Creating Web Storage System Descriptors in XML

To construct Web Storage System item security descriptors in XML, you need only create the appropriate XML elements and XML document described in Web Storage System Security. The following sections show how to create various XML descriptor elements using the Microsoft MSXML DOM parser:

- Creating an ACE
- Modifying an Item's DACL

Creating an ACE in XML

There are two types of ACEs used in the XML security descriptor format. The access_allowed_ace element grants a trustee an access right, and the access_denied_ace element denies a trustee an access right.

The following example demonstrates how to create an ACE for a Web Storage System XML-formatted security descriptor:

[JScript]

```
function createXMLAce(  XMLDom, prefix, bAccessAllowed,
username, mask ) {

  var eAce;
  var eMask;
  var eId;

  if(XMLDom == null)
    throw "ERR: XMLDOMDocument passed was null";

  if(prefix != "")
    prefix += ":";

  if(bAccessAllowed)
```

```
    eAce = XMLDom.createNode(1,prefix +"access_allowed_ace",
"http://schemas.microsoft.com/security/");
 else
    eAce = XMLDom.createNode(1,prefix +"access_denied_ace",
"http://schemas.microsoft.com/security/");

 if(eAce == null)
    throw "ERR: created ACE was null!";

 eMask = getXMLMask(XMLDom, prefix, mask);
 eSid  = getXMLSID(XMLDom, prefix, username);
 eAce.appendChild(eMask);
 eAce.appendChild(eSid);
 return eAce;
}

function getXMLMask(XMLDom, prefix, mask) {

 var eMask = XMLDom.createNode(1, prefix + "access_mask",
"http://schemas.microsoft.com/security/");
 eMask.appendChild(XMLDom.createTextNode(mask));
 return eMask;
}

function getXMLSID(XMLDom, prefix, username) {

 var eSid = XMLDom.createNode(1,prefix + "sid",
"http://schemas.microsoft.com/security/");
 var eName;
 eName = XMLDom.createNode(1, prefix +
"nt4_compatible_name",
"http://schemas.microsoft.com/security/");
 eName.appendChild(XMLDom.createTextNode(username));
 eSid.appendChild(eName);

 return eSid;

}
```

Modifying an Item's DACL

To modify an item's DACL, you manage the access control entries in the effective_aces, subcontainer_inheritable_aces, and subitem_inheritable_aces sections of the DACL.

The following example demonstrates how to add access-allowed and access-denied ACEs to an item's DACL:

[JScript]

```
function addAccessAllowedAce( XMLDomDescriptor, sdACEElem )
{
 var p = XMLDomDescriptor.documentElement.prefix;
 WScript.Echo("descriptor prefix: " + prefix);
 if(p != "")
  p += ":";
 var daclElem = XMLDomDescriptor.selectSingleNode
("/"+p+"security_descriptor/"+p+"dacl");
 if(daclElem == null)
   throw "ERR: No discretionary access control list in
descriptor";

 var effAcesElem =
daclElem.selectSingleNode(p+"effective_aces");
 if(effAcesElem == null)
    throw "ERR: No effective aces!";

 effAcesElem.appendChild(sdACEElem);

 return;
}

function addAccessDeniedAce( XMLDomDescriptor, sdACEElem )
{
 var p = XMLDomDescriptor.documentElement.prefix;
 WScript.Echo("descriptor prefix: " + prefix);
 if(p != "")
  p += ":";
 var daclElem = XMLDomDescriptor.selectSingleNode
("/"+p+"security_descriptor/"+p+"dacl");
 if(daclElem == null)
   throw "ERR: No discretionary access control list in
descriptor";

 var effAcesElem =
daclElem.selectSingleNode(p+"effective_aces");
 if(effAcesElem == null)
    throw "ERR: No effective aces!";

 effAcesElem.insertBefore( sdACEElem ,
effAcesElem.firstChild);

 return;
}
```

Updating an Item's Security Descriptor

To update an item's security descriptor, you need only modify the XML representation of the descriptor and save the updated XML back to the item's *http://schemas.microsoft.com/exchange/security/descriptor* property. To update the respective parts of the item's descriptor, you must have the proper access rights (READ_CONTROL, WRITE_DAC, or WRITE_OWNER).

If you want to update only a portion of an item's security descriptor, you can leave out the other sections of the descriptor in the XML stream. For example, if you want to update only the DACL for an item, you can leave out the <S:owner>, <S:group>, and <S:sacl> portions in the XML stream. When an entire section is not present in the update XML, this portion of the item's descriptor does not change.

The following example demonstrates how to update an item's security descriptor:

[JScript]

```
/*
** putSecurityDescForItem

** This function uses the HTTP/WebDAV protocol to update
** an item's
http://schemas.microsoft.com/exchange/security/descriptor
** property.
**    url       - URL to the item.
**    vSource   - Either XML text or an XMLDOM object reference.
**    username  - Username used to authenticate with IIS.
**    password  - Password used to authenticate with IIS.
*/
function putSecurityDescForItem( url , vSource , username, password) {

  var sendXMLDOM;
  if(typeof(vSource) == "string") {
    sendXMLDOM = new ActiveXObject("Microsoft.XMLDOM");
    sendXMLDOM.loadXML(vSource);
  }
  else if(typeof(vSource) == "object") {
    sendXMLDOM = vSource;
  }
  else {
    throw "ERR-putSecurityDescForItem: Invalid Argument";
  }

  var xmlDom = new ActiveXObject("Microsoft.XMLDOM");
```

Chapter 15 ● Security Tasks

```
  var pi      = xmlDom.createProcessingInstruction("xml","version=\"1.0\"");
  var root    = xmlDom.createNode(1, "propertyupdate", "DAV:");
  var e1      = xmlDom.createNode(1, "set","DAV:");
  var e2      = xmlDom.createNode(1, "prop", "DAV:");
  var e3      = xmlDom.createNode(1, "a:descriptor", "http://schemas.microsoft.com/exchange/security/");

  root.appendChild(e1);
  e1.appendChild(e2);
  e2.appendChild(e3);
  e3.appendChild(sendXMLDOM.documentElement);

  xmlDom.appendChild(pi);
  xmlDom.documentElement = root;

  var Req = new ActiveXObject("Microsoft.XMLHTTP");
  Req.open("PROPPATCH", url, false, username, password);
  Req.setRequestHeader("Content-Type","text/xml");
  Req.setRequestHeader("Translate","f");
  Req.send(xmlDom.xml);

  if(Req.status != "207") {
     var errstr = "ERR: HTTP server returned status=" + Req.status
     errstr    += "\r\nError: HTTP server returned status=" + Req.status;
     errstr    += "      Status text: " + Req.statusText;
     errstr    += "      Response Text: " + Req.responseText;
     throw errstr;
  }

  return Req.responseXML;

}
```

SIXTEEN

Using Web Storage System Forms

Registering a Web Storage System Form

Custom Web Storage System Forms can be registered in the Web Storage System in the MS Exchange SDK. Once forms are properly registered, Microsoft Exchange 2000 Server displays the custom forms.

To manually register a Web Storage System Form,

1. Create the form in Microsoft FrontPage or the editor most appropriate to your needs.
2. Modify the form to add the functionality that you want. You can also choose to add the form itself to the store.
3. Log on to the Exchange server as a user with rights to write to the intended directory.
4. Register the Web form in the store.

Form Definition Properties

A form registration consists of a collection of form definition properties. The properties define other properties such as the browser version, information about data binding, and information about events performed on an object. The content class property is required and all other form definition properties are optional. The most basic form registration can consist of the following properties:

Chapter 16 • Using Web Storage System Forms

The content class of the form registration.
- The form's content class.
- The form's Uniform Resource Locator (URL).
- The executeURL.

Syntax

Property name = item
urn:schemas-microsoft-com:office:forms#browser = "Microsoft Internet Explorer"

TABLE 16–1 *Property List*

Property name	Description
urn:schemas-microsoft-com:office:forms#binding	Case-insensitive; indicates the binding type. Possible values are server, client, and Web-client.
urn:schemas-microsoft-com:office:forms#browser	Case-insensitive; indicates the type of browser. An asterisk (*) indicates a wildcard. Example: urn:schemas-microsoft-com:office:forms#browser = Internet Explorer.
urn:schemas-microsoft-com:office:forms#cmd	Case-insensitive; string denoting the action or behavior being performed on an object. This is the first parameter after the command (?cmd= of the URL returned from Microsoft Internet Information Services roughly corresponding to the Internet Server Application Programming Interface (ISAPI) QUERY_STRING.) The QUERY_STRING is delimited by ampersands (&) that represent modifiers of the action. Example: urn:schemas-microsoft-com:office:forms#cmd = NewArt.
urn:schemas-microsoft-com:office:forms#contentclass	Case-insensitive; associated with a set of schemas and a set of forms. The content class for which the form is registered. Example: urn:schemas-microsoft-com:office:forms#contentclass = urn:content-classes:message.
urn:schemas:microsoft-com:office:forms#contentstate	Case-insensitive. http://schemas.microsoft.com/exchange/contents. Example: urn:schemas:microsoft-com:office:forms#contentstate = "mySample".
urn:schemas-microsoft-com:office:forms#execute-parameters	Parameters that are passed to the rendering engine specified by the executeURL property. The parameters must be URL escaped. An ampersand (&) is used to separate multiple values. Examples: param1=mySample& m2=url%20escaped.

Form Definition Properties 341

TABLE 16-1 *Property List (continued)*

Property name	Description
urn:schemas-microsoft-com:office:forms#executeurl	The URL to execute to render a form. An ISAPI filter or Active Server Pages (ASP) page. Example: process.asp.
urn:schemas-microsoft-com:office:forms#formurl	The URL of the form or template being handled and rendered; the item that is denoted by the current URL. Example: ExpenseForm.htm.
urn:schemas-microsoft-com:office:forms#language	Automatically provided as part of the HTTP request headers, this is the language of the form. This attribute corresponds to a case-insensitive ISO language-country/region value in the Accept-Language HTTP header. Example: en.
urn:schemas-microsoft-com:office:forms#majorver	Indicates the major version of the browser. Example: <5.
urn:schemas-microsoft-com:office:forms#messagestate	Case-insensitive; values include normal, submitted, read, unread, and importance. Status of the item.
urn:schemas-microsoft-com:office:forms#minorver	The minor version of the browser. Example: =5.
urn:schemas-microsoft-com:office:forms#platform	Case-insensitive. The platform of the browser matched against forms registrations. The platform information is in the same format as it is in browscap.ini. Example: Microsoft® Windows NT® 4.0.
urn:schemas-microsoft-com:office:forms#request	Case-insensitive. Property used to specify whether the form uses GET or POST requests. There are two possible values: GET and POST. GET queries for information, POST writes information. Examples: GET, POST.
urn:schemas-microsoft-com:office:forms#version	Value includes relational operator. Example: >5.

Registering a Web Storage System Form Using PROPPATCH

This example assumes a Web page with a button that triggers the DoDocRegister function. Log on as a user authorized to write to the store before you run the code:

```
function DoDocRegister()
{
m_httpsaverequest = new ActiveXObject("microsoft.xmlhttp");
bstrRequestXML = "<?xml version='1.0'?><a:propertyupdate
xmlns:a='DAV:' xmlns:b='urn:schemas:mailheader:'>";
bstrRequestXML +="<a:set><a:prop>";
```

```
bstrRequestXML +="<a:contentclass>urn:schemas-microsoft-
com:office:forms#registration</a:contentclass>";
bstrRequestXML += "</a:prop></a:set></a:propertyupdate>";
m_httpsaverequest.open("PROPPATCH", docform.url, false);
m_httpsaverequest.setRequestHeader("Content-type",
"text/xml");
// send takes one parameter which is the requestBody to use
// if status property is in 200 range, then everything's OK
m_httpsaverequest.send(bstrRequestXML);
//Response is XML DOM object that can be inspected
bstrXML = m_httpsaverequest.responseXML;
// idMsgViewer2.update();   // do whatever updates are
necessary
m_httpsaverequest = null;
}
```

The XML example that follows illustrates useful fields in XML format that you need to register a form. For an explanation of each of the fields, see "Form Definition Properties" earlier in this chapter. The form uses a custom content class named myclass. Processing is handled by an ASP file named *Process.asp*:

```
<prop>
<b:contentclass>urn:schemas-microsoft-
com:office:forms#registration</b:contentclass>
<f:formurl>process.asp</f:formurl>
<f:cmd></f:cmd>
<f:contentclass>urn:contentclasses:myclass</f:contentclass>
<f:executeurl>process.asp</f:executeurl>
<f:browser>*</f:browser>
<f:contentstate>*</f:contentstate>
<f:language>*</f:language>
<f:majorver>=5</f:majorver>
<f:minorver>*</f:minorver>
<f:platform>*</f:platform>
<f:request>GET</f:request>
</prop>
```

Using ADO to Set the SCR and Default Document Properties

Web items can be registered in the store as the default page for a particular folder. You can do this by setting the DAV:defaultdocument to the name of the item.

When the user opens the folder, the default page appears instead of the usual list of files. (The default page is set with the default document properties.)

The next example uses an ASP Web page to create an ActiveX Data Objects database (ADODB) object. It updates the Schema-Collection-Ref (SCR) and the default document properties.

Before you run the code, make sure that you log on as a user authorized to write to the store:

> **Note**
> 1. To return to the original default folder, set the default document property to "".
> 2. Registering the form will override the default document setting.

```
<HTML>
<HEAD>
<%@ LANGUAGE = "VBScript" %>
<%
Const adModeReadWrite       = 3
Const adFailIfNotExists     = -1
Const adCreateNonCollection = 0

Dim strURL
strURL =
"file://./backofficestorage/ServerName.microsoft.com/public
folders/myappfolder3/"

Dim Rec
Set Rec = CreateObject("ADODB.Record")

response.write strURL

Rec.Open strURL,,adModeReadWrite, adFailIfNotExists
response.write "<P>"

Dim Flds
Set Flds = Rec.Fields

' Set the SCR and the default document
Flds("urn:schemas-microsoft-com:exch-data:schema-
collection-ref") = strURL & "schema5h/"
Flds("DAV:defaultdocument") = "default2.htm"
Flds.Update

Response.write(Err.number) & "<P>"
response.write"<H3>SUCCESS</H3>"

Rec.Close
%>

</HEAD>
<BODY>
</BODY>
</HTML>
```

Binding Messages to Custom Forms

Developers often want a user to view a custom form when the user opens a message.

The custom form example consists of two files, *InstallMessage.VBS* and *CustomMessage.ASP*. *InstallMessage.VBS* creates the necessary folders, sets the SCR, and performs the form registration. The ASP file is executed whenever the user opens a message in that particular folder.

To run the custom form example,

1. Copy *InstallMessage.VBS* and *CustomMessage.ASP* to your server.
2. Run the VBS file, typing in the desired URL when requested.
3. Copy the *CustomMessage.ASP* file into the resulting Bin directory.
4. Go to that folder inside Outlook Web Access and create a new message.
5. While still inside Outlook Web Access, click the icon to check for new messages and then double click on the message.
6. Now you see the custom form.

The form itself is intentionally very simple. It only shows some HTML-generated text and the subject of the opened message:

Note In Exchange System Manager: Turn on Script Execute Permissions for ASP pages and Scripts and Executables for ISAPI filters. Otherwise, you will get a "403 Permission Denied" error.

InstallMessage.VBS

```
Install
Sub Install
'Get the folder
sFolder = InputBox("Please enter the URL to the folder:
example http://serverName/public/foldername","Setup
Instructions")
If Trim(sFolder) = "" Then
    Exit Sub
End If

'Create the app folder, pointing its SCR to the BIN
subfolder
Set oDest = CreateObject("CDO.Folder")
oDest.Fields("urn:schemas-microsoft-com:exch-data:schema-
collection-ref") = sFolder + "\bin"
odest.Fields("DAV:contentclass") = "urn:content-
classes:folder"
oDest.Fields.Update
oDest.DataSource.SaveTo sFolder
```

Form Definition Properties

```
'Create the BIN folder and make it invisible
Set oDest = CreateObject("CDO.Folder")
oDest.Fields("DAV:ishidden") = True
oDest.Fields.Update
oDest.DataSource.SaveTo sFolder +  "/bin"

'Fill the BIN folder with form registrations

Set oCon = CreateObject("ADODB.Connection")
oCon.ConnectionString = sFolder + "/bin"
oCon.Provider = "ExOledb.Datasource"
oCon.Open


'-------------------------------------------------
'Register the default page for the folder
Set oRec = CreateObject("ADODB.Record")
oRec.Open "default.reg", oCon, 3, 0
oRec.Fields("DAV:contentclass") = "urn:schemas-microsoft-
com:office:forms#registration"
oRec.Fields("urn:schemas-microsoft-
com:office:forms#contentclass") = "urn:content-
classes:message"
oRec.Fields("urn:schemas-microsoft-com:office:forms#cmd") =
"open"
oRec.Fields("urn:schemas-microsoft-
com:office:forms#formurl") = "CustomMessage.asp"
oRec.Fields("urn:schemas-microsoft-
com:office:forms#executeurl") = "CustomMessage.asp"
oRec.Fields.Update
oRec.Close

'Further instructions
MsgBox "Copy CustomMessage.ASP into the BIN directory.
Enable script execution on the directory.", 64, "Further
Instructions"

End Sub
```

CustomMessage.ASP

```
<%@Language=VBScript%>
<html>
<body>

<%

dataurl = request.querystring("dataurl")
Set c = Server.CreateObject("ADODB.Connection")
c.ConnectionString = dataurl
c.Provider = "ExOledb.Datasource"
```

```
c.Open
Set r = Server.CreateObject("ADODB.Record")
r.Open dataurl, c, 3

%>

<form class="form" method="post"
action="<%=request.querystring("dataurl")%>?Cmd-save">

<h3> Message</h3>
Subject:<input type="text"
name="urn:schemas:mailheader:subject"
value="<%=r("urn:schemas:mailheader:subject")%>"

<input type="submit" value="Save">
</form>

<%
r.Close
c.Close
%>
</body>
</html>
```

Reusing Outlook Web Access Components in a Web Page

Microsoft Outlook Web Access views can be added to a Web page. They can be nested inside frames, iframes, and tables. Nesting allows the Web designer to control the appearance and the functionality of the page. Adjusting the URL parameters modifies the appearance of the view.

Loading an Outlook Web Access View in an IFrame

IFrames allow the Web page author to place a frame at a precise location on the Web page. IFrames also allow the author to control the height and width of the frame.

IFrames were introduced in Microsoft Internet Explorer 4. More information about IFrames is available on the "Microsoft MSDN Library."

The following example loads the user's Exchange inbox into a frame and provides links to the user's inbox and outbox:

Note This example requires Microsoft Internet Explorer 4 or later.

```
<HTML>
<HEAD>
</HEAD>
<BODY>
<HR>
Example of displaying Exchange Web form in an iFrame.<P>

<a href="http://ServerName1/exchange/user1/
inbox?Cmd=contents" target= "main" >Inbox</a>
<a href="http://ServerName1/exchange/user1/
outbox?Cmd=contents" target= "main" >Outbox</a>
<P>
<IFRAME name = "main", src="http://ServerName1/exchange/
user1/inbox?Cmd=contents",
width = 90%, height = 70%> </IFRAME>
</BODY>

</HTML>
```

Loading an Outlook Web Access View in a Frame

Frames are available in both Microsoft Internet Explorer and Netscape.

The next example creates a frameset and two frames. A table of contents is loaded in the left frame. The table of contents lets the user choose an inbox and outbox, which will appear in the frame on the right side.

Three files are used: *frame.htm*, *toc.htm*, and *main.htm*. *Frame.htm* creates the frameset, *toc.htm* is the table of contents, and *main.htm* holds the inbox and outbox views:

frame.htm

```
<HTML>
<FRAMESET FRAMEBORDER = 1 bordercolor= "000000" cols="80,
300">
  <FRAME FRAMEBORDER=1 src="toc.htm" name="toc">
  <FRAME FRAMEBORDER=1 src="frmain.htm" name="main">
</FRAMESET>
<NOFRAMES>Need a browser that supports Frames</NOFRAMES>
</HTML>
toc.htm
<HTML>
<BODY>
<H1>Logo</H1>
<HR>
Select One<P>
<a href="http://ServerName1/exchange/user1/
inbox?Cmd=contents" target= "main" >Inbox</a><p>
<a href="http://ServerName1/exchange/user1/
outbox?Cmd=contents" target= "main" >Outbox</a><p>
```

```
<a href="http://ServerName1/public/common/phonelist.htm"
target= "main" >Phone List</a><P>
</BODY>
</HTML>
main.htm
<HTML>
<BODY>
<BR>
<I><CENTER>Click on a menu choice to the left<I>
</CENTER><P>
</BODY>
</HTML>
```

SEVENTEEN

Using Store Events

You can include the EXOLEDB-type library (EXOLEDB.DLL) in any Microsoft Visual Basic project.

In implementing your Visual Basic event sinks in a COM class, you name event methods by prefixing the event names with the interface name. Use the following event-method names:

```
IExStoreSyncEvents_OnSyncSave
IExStoreSyncEvents_OnSyncDelete
IExStoreAsyncEvents_OnSave
IExStoreAsyncEvents_OnDelete
IExStoreSystemEvents_OnMDBStartUp
IExStoreSystemEvents_OnMDBShutDown
IExStoreSystemEvents_OnTimer
```

When implementing event methods as scripts, you prefix all event methods with "ExStoreEvents_". For example, the OnSyncSave event in a script would be ExStoreEvents_OnSyncSave.

For examples of how to implement event sink methods in a script or event sink interfaces in a COM class, see the following sections:

- Implementing Synchronous Event Sinks
- Implementing Asynchronous Event Sinks
- Implementing System Event Sinks

For examples of how to create and manage event registrations, see the following sections:

- Managing Event Registrations
- Managing Event Registrations with RegEvent.vbs

Implementing Synchronous Event Sinks

A synchronous event occurs before the specified event is committed to the store, thus giving you a chance to abort the event if necessary. The OnSyncSave event also gives you a chance to check or modify the data before you save it. For examples of implementing synchronous event sinks, see the following sections:

- Implementing an OnSyncSave Event Sink
- Implementing an OnSyncDelete Event Sink

Implementing an OnSyncSave Event Sink

A synchronous event is called once for the beginning phase of the specified event and then again to either commit or abort it. The EVT_NEW_ITEM flag is set for the first time this specific event is called for this event registration. The following example illustrates the basic structure of a synchronous event:

[Visual Basic]

```
Private Sub IExStoreSyncEvents_OnSyncSave(ByVal pEventInfo
As Exoledb.IExStoreEventInfo, ByVal bstrURLItem As String,
ByVal lFlags As Long)

    Dim FSO         As Object
    Dim EvtLog      As String
    Dim EvtFile
    Dim DispEvtInfo As IExStoreDispEventInfo
    Dim ADODBRec    As ADODB.Record

    Set DispEvtInfo = pEventInfo

'Log file
    EvtLog = Environ("SystemDrive") & "\OnSyncSave.log"

'Creates new log file %SystemDrive%\OnSyncSave.log or opens
it if exists
    Set FSO = CreateObject("Scripting.FileSystemObject")
    Set EvtFile = FSO.OpenTextFile(EvtLog, 8, True)

'Append incoming event info into log file
    EvtFile.WriteLine ("[VB Event Sink]
OnSyncSave()")
    EvtFile.WriteLine ("   URL Item:                " &
bstrURLItem)
    EvtFile.WriteLine ("   lFlags:                  " & "0x" &
Hex(lFlags))
```

Implementing Synchronous Event Sinks

```
'Small sample that shows how to use ADO Record Object and
Fields inside events
    Set ADODBRec = DispEvtInfo.EventRecord
    EvtFile.WriteLine ("  DAV:Displayname Value: " &
ADODBRec.Fields("DAV:displayname").Value)

'To determine type of incoming OnSyncSave notifications:

    'Case 1: EVT_SYNC_BEGIN
    If lFlags And EVT_SYNC_BEGIN Then
        'Perform your tasks
        'Begin phase of OnSyncSave for a resource
        EvtFile.WriteLine ("  Flag contains EVT_SYNC_BEGIN
bit set")

    'Case 2: EVT_SYNC_COMMITTED
    ElseIf lFlags And EVT_SYNC_COMMITTED Then
        'Perform your tasks
        'Commit phase of OnSyncSave for a resource
        EvtFile.WriteLine ("  Flag contains
EVT_SYNC_COMMITTED bit set")

    'Case 3: EVT_SYNC_ABORTED
    ElseIf lFlags And EVT_SYNC_ABORTED Then
        'Perform your tasks
        'Abort phase of OnSyncSave for item that is getting
aborted
        EvtFile.WriteLine ("  Flag contains
EVT_SYNC_ABORTED bit set")

    End If


'To determine cause of OnSyncSave

    'Case 1: EVT_IS_DELIVERED
    If lFlags And EVT_IS_DELIVERED Then
        'Perform your tasks
        'OnSyncSave for delivered mail item
        EvtFile.WriteLine ("  Flag contains
EVT_IS_DELIVERED bit set")

    'Case 2: EVT_MOVE
    ElseIf lFlags And EVT_MOVE Then
        'Perform your tasks
        'OnSyncSave for moved item
        EvtFile.WriteLine ("  Flag contains EVT_MOVE bit
set")

    'Case 3: EVT_COPY
```

352 Chapter 17 • Using Store Events

```
    ElseIf lFlags And EVT_COPY Then
        'Perform your tasks
        'OnSyncSave for copied item
        EvtFile.WriteLine ("  Flag contains EVT_COPY bit
set")

    End If


    'Check if it is folder notification
    If lFlags And &H2 Then
        'Perform your tasks
        'OnSyncSave for a folder
        EvtFile.WriteLine ("  Flag contains
EVT_IS_COLLECTION bit set")
    End If

    EvtFile.WriteBlankLines (1)

'Before Quit
    EvtFile.Close
    Set FSO = Nothing
    Set DispEvtInfo = Nothing

End Sub
```

Implementing an OnSyncDelete Event Sink

The following example handles the OnSyncDelete event:

[Visual Basic]

```
Private Sub IExStoreSyncEvents_OnSyncDelete(ByVal
pEventInfo As Exoledb.IExStoreEventInfo, ByVal bstrURLItem
As String, ByVal lFlags As Long)

    Dim FSO         As Object
    Dim EvtLog      As String
    Dim EvtFile

'Log file
    EvtLog = Environ("SystemDrive") & "\OnSyncDelete.log"

'Creates new log file %SystemDrive%\OnSyncDelete.log or
opens it if exists
    Set FSO = CreateObject("Scripting.FileSystemObject")
    Set EvtFile = FSO.OpenTextFile(EvtLog, 8, True)

'Append incoming event info into log file
    EvtFile.WriteLine ("[VB Event Sink]
```

```
OnSyncDelete()")
    EvtFile.WriteLine ("  URL Item:              " &
bstrURLItem)
    EvtFile.WriteLine ("  lFlags:                " & "0x" &
Hex(lFlags))

'To determine type of incoming OnSyncDelete notifications:

    'Case 1: EVT_SYNC_BEGIN
    If lFlags And EVT_SYNC_BEGIN Then
        'Perform your tasks
        'Begin phase of OnSyncDelete
        EvtFile.WriteLine ("  Flag contains EVT_SYNC_BEGIN
bit set")

    'Case 2: EVT_SYNC_COMMITTED
    ElseIf lFlags And EVT_SYNC_COMMITTED Then
        'Perform your tasks
        'Commit phase of OnSyncDelete
        EvtFile.WriteLine ("  Flag contains
EVT_SYNC_COMMITTED bit set")

    'Case 3: EVT_SYNC_ABORTED
    ElseIf lFlags And EVT_SYNC_ABORTED Then
        'Perform your tasks
        'Abort phase of OnSyncDelete
        EvtFile.WriteLine ("  Flag contains
EVT_SYNC_ABORTED bit set")

    End If

'To determine type of OnSyncDelete

    'EVT_SOFTDELETE
    If lFlags And EVT_SOFTDELETE Then
        'Perform your tasks
        EvtFile.WriteLine ("  Flag contains EVT_SOFTDELETE
bit set")
    End If

    'EVT_HARDDELETE
    If lFlags And EVT_HARDDELETE Then
        'Perform your tasks
        EvtFile.WriteLine ("  Flag contains EVT_HARDDELETE
bit set")
    End If

    'Check if it is a folder notification
    If lFlags And EVT_IS_COLLECTION Then
        'Perform your tasks
```

```
            'OnSyncDelete for a folder
            EvtFile.WriteLine ("  Flag contains
EVT_IS_COLLECTION bit set")
        End If

        EvtFile.WriteBlankLines (1)

    'Before Quit
        EvtFile.Close
        Set FSO = Nothing

End Sub
```

Implementing Asynchronous Event Sinks

An asynchronous event occurs after the specified event is committed to the store. For examples of implementing asynchronous event sinks, see the following sections:

- Implementing an OnSave Event Sink
- Implementing an OnDelete Event Sink

Note The naming convention for event methods is always Interfacename_Eventname.

Implementing an OnSave Event Sink

The following code receives the OnSave event and returns information about it:

[Visual Basic]

```
Private Sub IExStoreAsyncEvents_OnSave(ByVal pEventInfo As
Exoledb.IExStoreEventInfo, ByVal bstrURLItem As String,
ByVal lFlags As Long)

    Dim FSO         As Object
    Dim EvtLog      As String
    Dim EvtFile
    Dim DispEvtInfo As IExStoreDispEventInfo
    Dim ADODBRec    As ADODB.Record

    Set DispEvtInfo = pEventInfo

'log file
    EvtLog = Environ("SystemDrive") & "\OnSave.log"
```

Implementing Asynchronous Event Sinks 355

```
'Creates new log file %SystemDrive%\OnSave.log or opens it
if exists
    Set FSO = CreateObject("Scripting.FileSystemObject")
    Set EvtFile = FSO.OpenTextFile(EvtLog, 8, True)

'Append incoming event info into log file
    EvtFile.WriteLine ("[VB Event Sink]        OnSave()")
    EvtFile.WriteLine ("  URL Item:            " &
bstrURLItem)
    EvtFile.WriteLine ("  lFlags:              " & "0x" &
Hex(lFlags))

'Small sample that shows how to use ADO Record Object and
Fields inside events
    Set ADODBRec = DispEvtInfo.EventRecord
    EvtFile.WriteLine ("  DAV:Displayname Value: " &
ADODBRec.Fields("DAV:displayname").Value)

'To determine cause of OnSyncSave

    'Case 1: EVT_IS_DELIVERED
    If lFlags And EVT_IS_DELIVERED Then
        'Perform your tasks
        'OnSave for delivered mail item
        EvtFile.WriteLine ("  Flag contains
EVT_IS_DELIVERED bit set")

    'Case 2: EVT_MOVE
    ElseIf lFlags And EVT_MOVE Then
        'Perform your tasks
        'OnSave for moved item
        EvtFile.WriteLine ("  Flag contains EVT_MOVE bit
set")

    'Case 3: EVT_COPY
    ElseIf lFlags And EVT_COPY Then
        'Perform your tasks
        'OnSave for copied item
        EvtFile.WriteLine ("  Flag contains EVT_COPY bit
set")

    End If

    'Check if it is a folder notification
    If lFlags And &H2 Then
        'Perform your tasks
        'OnSave for a folder
        EvtFile.WriteLine ("  Flag contains
EVT_IS_COLLECTION bit set")
```

```
    End If

    EvtFile.WriteBlankLines (1)

    'Use the sink context (custom contextual info saved in
the registration item)
    Dim case_switch As Integer
    Dim notify_group As String

    Const customnamespace = "mycustomnamespace:eventsinks/
notifyingevents/"
    Dim propname As String

    propname = customnamespace + "caseswitch"
    case_switch = ADODBRec.Fields(propname)

    propname = customnamespace + "notifygroup"
    notify_group = ADODBRec.Fields(propname)

    'Call some program here to use the custom data to
notify people of an event
    'Something like: handle_notifyevent(case_switch,
notify_group)

'Before Quit
    EvtFile.Close
    Set FSO = Nothing
    Set DispEvtInfo = Nothing

End Sub
```

Implementing an OnDelete Event Sink

The following code receives the OnDelete event and returns information about it:

[Visual Basic]

```
Private Sub IExStoreAsyncEvents_OnDelete(ByVal pEventInfo
As Exoledb.IExStoreEventInfo, ByVal bstrURLItem As String,
ByVal lFlags As Long)

    Dim FSO        As Object
    Dim EvtLog     As String
    Dim EvtFile

'log file
    EvtLog = Environ("SystemDrive") & "\OnDelete.log"
```

```
'Creates new log file %SystemDrive%\OnDelete.log or opens
it if exists
    Set FSO = CreateObject("Scripting.FileSystemObject")
    Set EvtFile = FSO.OpenTextFile(EvtLog, 8, True)

'Append incoming event info into log file
    EvtFile.WriteLine ("[VB Event Sink]      OnDelete()")
    EvtFile.WriteLine ("  URL Item:              " &
bstrURLItem)
    EvtFile.WriteLine ("  lFlags:                " & "0x" &
Hex(lFlags))

'To determine type of OnDelete

    'Case 1: EVT_SOFTDELETE
    If lFlags And EVT_SOFTDELETE Then
        'Perform your tasks
        EvtFile.WriteLine ("  Flag contains EVT_SOFTDELETE
bit set")
    End If

    'Case 2: EVT_HARDDELETE
    If lFlags And EVT_HARDDELETE Then
        'Perform your tasks
        EvtFile.WriteLine ("  Flag contains EVT_HARDDELETE
bit set")
    End If

    'Check if it is a folder notification
    If lFlags And EVT_IS_COLLECTION Then
        'Perform your tasks
        'OnDelete for a folder
        EvtFile.WriteLine ("  Flag contains
EVT_IS_COLLECTION bit set")
    End If

    EvtFile.WriteBlankLines (1)

'Before Quit
    EvtFile.Close
    Set FSO = Nothing

End Sub
```

Implementing System Event Sinks

For examples of how to handle and log system events, see the following sections:

- Implementing an OnMdbStartup Event Sink
- Implementing an OnMdbShutdown Event Sink
- Implementing an OnTimer Event Sink

Implementing an OnMdbStartup Event Sink

The following code handles and logs the OnMdbStartup system event:

[Visual Basic]

```
Private Sub IExStoreSystemEvents_OnMDBStartUp(ByVal
bstrMDBGuid As String, ByVal bstrMDBName As String, ByVal
lFlags As Long)

    Dim FSO         As Object
    Dim EvtLog      As String
    Dim EvtFile

'Log file
    EvtLog = Environ("SystemDrive") & "\OnMDBStartUp.log"

'Creates new log file %SystemDrive%\OnMDBStartUp.log or
opens it if exists
    Set FSO = CreateObject("Scripting.FileSystemObject")
    Set EvtFile = FSO.OpenTextFile(EvtLog, 8, True)

'Append incoming event info into log file
    EvtFile.WriteLine ("[VB Event Sink]
OnMDBStartUp()")
    EvtFile.WriteLine ("    MDB Guid              " &
bstrMDBGuid)
    EvtFile.WriteLine ("    MDB Name              " &
bstrMDBName)
    EvtFile.WriteLine ("    lFlags:               " & "0x" &
Hex(lFlags))

    EvtFile.WriteBlankLines (1)

'Before Quit
    EvtFile.Close
    Set FSO = Nothing

End Sub
```

Implementing an OnMdbShutdown Event Sink

The following code handles and logs the OnMdbShutdown system event:

[Visual Basic]

```
Private Sub IExStoreSystemEvents_OnMDBShutDown(ByVal
bstrMDBGuid As String, ByVal lFlags As Long)

    Dim FSO         As Object
    Dim EvtLog      As String
    Dim EvtFile

'log file
    EvtLog = Environ("SystemDrive") & "\OnMDBShutDown.log"

'Creates new log file %SystemDrive%\OnMDBShutDown.log or
opens it if exists
    Set FSO = CreateObject("Scripting.FileSystemObject")
    Set EvtFile = FSO.OpenTextFile(EvtLog, 8, True)

'Append incoming event info into log file
    EvtFile.WriteLine ("[VB Event Sink]
OnMDBShutDown()")
    EvtFile.WriteLine ("   MDB Guid              " &
bstrMDBGuid)
    EvtFile.WriteLine ("   lFlags:               " & "0x" &
Hex(lFlags))

    EvtFile.WriteBlankLines (1)

'Before Quit
    EvtFile.Close
    Set FSO = Nothing

End Sub
```

Implementing an OnTimer Event Sink

The following code handles and logs the OnTimer system event:

[Visual Basic]

```
Private Sub IExStoreSystemEvents_OnTimer(ByVal bstrURLItem
As String, ByVal lFlags As Long)

    Dim FSO         As Object
    Dim EvtLog      As String
    Dim EvtFile
```

```
'Log file
    EvtLog = Environ("SystemDrive") & "\OnTimer.log"

'Creates new log file %SystemDrive%\OnTimer.log or opens it
if exists
    Set FSO = CreateObject("Scripting.FileSystemObject")
    Set EvtFile = FSO.OpenTextFile(EvtLog, 8, True)

'Append incoming event info into log file
    EvtFile.WriteLine ("[VB Event Sink] OnTimer()")
    EvtFile.WriteLine ("   lFlags:                  " & "0x" & Hex(lFlags))

    EvtFile.WriteBlankLines (1)

'Before Quit
    EvtFile.Close
    Set FSO = Nothing

End Sub
```

Managing Event Registrations

For examples of how to add, enumerate, and delete event sink registrations, see the following sections in the MS Exchange SDK:

- Adding an Event Registration for a Folder
- Removing an Event Registration for a Folder
- Enumerating Event Registrations for a Folder

Adding an Event Registration for a Folder

The code that follows creates a store item, sets its content class and schema, and saves it to the store. The store then processes the event registration. For more information, see "Event Registration" in the MS Exchange SDK. Here is the code:

[Visual Basic]

```
'==========================================================
====================='
' This subroutine creates the event binding in the meta-
database
' by setting properties in an event registration item and
```

```
committing it to the
' store.  The event of saving the item triggers the event registration
' event sink, which processes the event registration and sets the registration
' to hidden so that it does not appear in the store folder.
'===========================================================================
Sub AddNewStoreEvent(Server As String)
    On Error Resume Next

    'heres a list of the properties you can set for the registration event item
    'not all of these are used in this example
    Const propcontentclass = "DAV: contentclass"

    Const propCriteria = "http://schemas.microsoft.com/exchange/events/Criteria"
    Const propEnabled = "http://schemas.microsoft.com/exchange/events/Enabled"
    Const propEventMethod = "http://schemas.microsoft.com/exchange/events/EventMethod"
    Const propMatchScope = "http://schemas.microsoft.com/exchange/events/MatchScope"
    Const propPriority = "http://schemas.microsoft.com/exchange/events/Priority"
    Const propScriptURL = "http://schemas.microsoft.com/exchange/events/ScriptUrl"
    Const propSinkClass = "http://schemas.microsoft.com/exchange/events/SinkClass"
    Const propTimerExpiryTime = "http://schemas.microsoft.com/exchange/events/TimerExpiryTime"
    Const propTimerInterval = "http://schemas.microsoft.com/exchange/events/TimerInterval"
    Const propTimerStartTime = "http://schemas.microsoft.com/exchange/events/TimerStartTime"


    Dim cn As New ADODB.Connection
    Dim rEvent As New ADODB.Record
    Dim strGuid
    Dim strBaseUrl
    Dim strEvent


    'This will serve as the scope as well
    '(Where you save it is where the event fires)
    strBaseUrl = "file://./backofficestorage/" + _
                 Server + _
                 "/public folders/internet newsgroups"
```

Chapter 17 • Using Store Events

```
    strEvent = strBaseUrl + "/evtreg1" 'evtreg1 is the item name

    ' Create the connection
    cn.Provider = "exoledb.datasource"
    cn.ConnectionString = strBaseUrl
    cn.Open
    If Err.Number <> 0 Then
      MsgBox "Error Opening Connection : " & Err.Number & " " & Err.Description & vbCrLf
       Exit Sub
    End If

    cn.BeginTrans
    rEvent.Open strEvent, cn, 3, 0      ' adModeReadWrite, adCreateNonCollection
    If Err.Number <> 0 Then
      MsgBox "Error Opening Record : " & Err.Number & " " & Err.Description & vbCrLf
       Exit Sub
    End If

    'set the properties in the item
    With rEvent.Fields
      .Item(propcontentclass) = "urn:content-class:storeeventreg"
      .Item(propEventMethod) = "onsave;ondelete" 'register for both save and delete events
      .Item(propSinkClass) = "VB_OutProc.sink"  'your registered event handler sink class ProgID


      'match scope
      .Item(propMatchScope) = "deep"
      .Item(propCriteria) = "WHERE $DAV:ishidden$ = FALSE"

      'Add custom properties which the event sink can use to
      'determine the context of this event registration

      Const customnamespace = "mycustomnamespace:eventsinks/notifyingevents/"
      Dim propname As String
      propname = customnamespace + "caseswitch"
      .Append propname, adInteger, , , 2         'for a case switch in the event sink
      propname = customnamespace + "notifygroup"
      .Append propname, adChar, , , "Marketing"  'a group you've created in exchange
```

```
    MsgBox "New Event Binding with custom properties
created."

      .Update   'get the ADO object current
      If Err.Number <> 0 Then
        MsgBox "Error Updating Props : " & Err.Number & " "
& Err.Description & vbCrLf
        Exit Sub
      End If

   End With
   cn.CommitTrans   'commit transaction to the store

   If Err.Number <> 0 Then
     MsgBox "Error Commiting Transaction : " & Err.Number
& " " & Err.Description & vbCrLf
     Exit Sub
   End If

End Sub
```

During the process of adding an event registration for a folder, contextual information about this specific registration is also added. You can access this information from within the event sink. For more information, see "Contextual Information in an Event Registration" in the MS Exchange SDK.

Removing an Event Registration for a Folder

To remove an event sink, you delete the item, using code similar to the following sample:

[Visual Basic]

```
  'All you have to do is delete the registration item

Private Sub DeleteEvent(Server As String)
    On Error Resume Next

    'heres a handy list of the properties you can set for
the registration event item
    'not all of these are used in this example

    Dim cn    As New ADODB.Connection
    Dim rEvent As New ADODB.Record
    Dim strGuid
    Dim strBaseUrl
    Dim strEvent
```

```
    'this will serve as the scope as well
    strBaseUrl = "file://./backofficestorage/" + _
                Server + _
                "/public folders/internet newsgroups"

    strEvent = strBaseUrl + "/evtreg1"  'evtreg1 is the item
name

    ' Create the connection
    cn.Provider = "exoledb.datasource"
    cn.ConnectionString = strBaseUrl
    cn.Open
    If Err.Number <> 0 Then
      MsgBox "Error Opening Connection : " & Err.Number & "
" & Err.Description & vbCrLf
       Exit Sub
    End If

    cn.BeginTrans

    rEvent.Open strEvent, cn, 3, 0     ' adModeReadWrite,
adCreateNonCollection
    If Err.Number <> 0 Then
      MsgBox "Error Opening Record : " & Err.Number & " " &
Err.Description & vbCrLf
       Exit Sub
    End If

    rEvent.DeleteRecord

    cn.CommitTrans   'commit transaction to the store

    If Err.Number <> 0 Then
      MsgBox "Error Committing Transaction : " & Err.Number
& " " & Err.Description & vbCrLf
       Exit Sub
    End If

End Sub
```

Enumerating Event Registrations for a Folder

The following code opens an event registration item and lists the events it is registering:

Managing Event Registrations

[Visual Basic]

```vb
Public Sub Enum_Event(Server As String)
  On Error Resume Next
  Dim Query
  Dim fld

  Dim rs As New ADODB.Recordset
  Dim strParentFolder
  Dim strEventRegistrationName
  Dim aPropNames

  aPropNames = Array( _
    "DAV:contentclass", _
    "http://schemas.microsoft.com/exchange/events/Criteria", _
    "http://schemas.microsoft.com/exchange/events/Enabled", _
    "http://schemas.microsoft.com/exchange/events/EventMethod", _
    "http://schemas.microsoft.com/exchange/events/MatchScope", _
    "http://schemas.microsoft.com/exchange/events/Priority", _
    "http://schemas.microsoft.com/exchange/events/ScriptUrl", _
    "http://schemas.microsoft.com/exchange/events/SinkClass", _
    "http://schemas.microsoft.com/exchange/events/TimerExpiryTime", _
    "http://schemas.microsoft.com/exchange/events/TimerInterval", _
    "http://schemas.microsoft.com/exchange/events/TimerStartTime")

  ' Specify the event folder and the event registration name
  strParentFolder = "file://./backofficestorage/" + _
                    Server + "/mbx/user1/inbox"

  strEventRegistrationName = "evtreg1"  'If you want to enum all the events, then leave this blank

  'Build the sql query to get the events
  'This section gets all event types so that you don't have to change this per event type
  'To limit the event types, remove the unwanted event types from aPropNames
  Dim i
```

```
  Query = "SELECT "
  For i = LBound(aPropNames) To UBound(aPropNames)
     Query = Query + Chr(34) + aPropNames(i) + Chr(34)
     If i <> UBound(aPropNames) Then
        Query = Query + ", "
     End If
  Next
  Query = Query + " FROM SCOPE('shallow traversal of " +
Chr(34) + strParentFolder + Chr(34) + "')"
  Query = Query + " WHERE " + Chr(34) + "DAV:contentclass"
+ Chr(34) + " = 'urn:content-class:storeeventreg'"
  If strEventRegistrationName <> "" Then
     'event folder name specified
     Query = Query + " AND " + Chr(34) + "DAV:displayname" +
Chr(34) + " = '" + strEventRegistrationName + "'"
  End If


  Dim rec As New ADODB.Record
  rec.Open strParentFolder   'root binder will select the
correct provider
  If Err.Number <> 0 Then
     Debug.Print "Error Executing Query : " & Err.Number & "
" & Err.Description & vbCrLf
     Exit Sub
  End If

  rs.Open Query, rec.ActiveConnection
  If Err.Number <> 0 Then
     Debug.Print "Error Executing Query : " & Err.Number & "
" & Err.Description & vbCrLf
     Exit Sub
  End If

  ' Go thru each entry in the recordset
  Do While (rs.BOF <> True And rs.EOF <> True)
     For Each fld In rs.Fields
        If fld.Value <> vbNull Then
           Debug.Print fld.Name & ", " & fld.Value & vbCrLf
        End If
     Next
     Debug.Print
"*************************************************" & vbCrLf
     rs.MoveNext
     If Err.Number <> 0 Then
        Debug.Print "Error Moving To Next Record : " &
Err.Number & " " & Err.Description & vbCrLf
        Exit Sub
     End If
  Loop
```

```
    Set rs = Nothing

End Sub
```

Managing Event Registrations with RegEvent.vbs

This topic covers the following information:
- Registering for an Asynchronous Event
- Registering for an OnSyncSave Event
- Registering for a System Event
- Registering for an OnTimer Event
- Deleting Event Registrations
- Enumerating Event Registrations

You can manage event sinks by using the Visual Basic script RegEvent.vbs. For more information, see "The RegEvent Script" in the VBScript file in the MS Exchange SDK.

Registering for an Asynchronous Event

The following example uses the RegEvent script to register for an OnSave event and an OnDelete event:

Example

```
cscript RegEvent.vbs add "onsave;ondelete"
Exoledb.ScriptEventSink.1
    file://./backofficestorage/exchange.microsoft.com/user1/
    inbox/EventRegItem1
    -m deep -file d:\test.vbs
```

Registering for an OnSyncSave Event

The following example uses the RegEvent script to register for an OnSyncSave event:

Example

```
cscript RegEvent.vbs Add OnSyncSave ExOleDB.ScriptEventSink.1
    file://./backofficestorage/mydomain.com/user1/inbox/
    EventRegItem5
    -file c:\script3.vbs
```

Registering for a System Event

The example that follows uses the RegEvent script to register for an OnMdb-Startup system event. The command specifies the script host sink class (ExOleDB.ScriptEventSink.1), which then runs the script specified with the -url option:

Example

```
cscript RegEvent.vbs add onmdbstartup
ExOleDB.ScriptEventSink.1
http://mystore/public/myfolder/startupevent
-url http://mystore/myeventscripts/script.vbs
```

Registering for an OnTimer Event

The example that follows uses the RegEvent script to register for an OnTimer event.

Timers have scope, in the same way as other events. With timers, however, no event occurs in that location to cause the specified event to occur (such as a save event or a delete event). Note that scope does define a specific location for the registration event item, which can affect the security context of the event sink, and guarantees that the event will be deleted if the folder containing the timer event registration is deleted.

For more information about registering and managing event registrations, see "Event Registration" in the MS Exchange SDK. Here is the code:

Examples

Add an OnTimer event to occur every minute for one hour:

```
cscript RegEvent.vbs add ontimer sink1.sink1.1
    file://./backofficestorage/mydomain/public%20folders/
    events/EventRegTimerItem1
    "8/4/98 01:50:00 AM" 1 -e "8/4/98 02:50:00 AM"
```

Register for an event handled by a script:

```
cscript RegEvent.vbs add ontimer ExOleDB.ScriptEventSink.1
    file://./backofficestorage/mydomain/mbx/user1/inbox/
    TimerEventReg2
    "09/15/98 02:35:00 PM" 1  -e "09/15/98 03:35:00 PM"
    -url http://public.microsoft.com/my_script_location/
    script2.vbs
```

Deleting Event Registrations

You can use the RegEvent script to delete event registrations.

Remarks

RegEvent does not recursively delete events in child folders.

Examples

```
'delete an item via its URL
cscript RegEvent.vbs delete
  file://./backofficestorage/exchange.microsoft.com/mbx/
user1/inbox/evtreg1

'delete all items in a folder via the folder's URL
cscript RegEvent.vbs delete
  file://./backofficestorage/exchange.microsoft.com/mbx/
user1/inbox all
```

Enumerating Event Registrations

You can use the RegEvent script to enumerate event registrations. The enumeration includes a list of properties for each registration item.

Remarks

RegEvent does not recursively enumerate events in child folders.

Examples

'Enum an event by specifying an item URL

```
cscript RegEvent.vbs enum
  file://./backofficestorage/exchange.microsoft.com/mbx/
  user1/inbox/evtreg1

'Enumerate events in a folder by specifying a folder URL
cscript Regevent.vbs enum
  file://./backofficestorage/exchange.microsoft.com/mbx/
  user1/inbox all
```

EIGHTEEN

Messaging

Creating a Message

To build a new message, you must first create an instance of the Message COM class, as shown in the following example:

[Visual Basic]

```
' Reference to Microsoft ActiveX Data Objects 2.5 Library
' Reference to Microsoft CDO for Exchange 2000 Server
Library
Dim iMsg as new CDO.Message
```

[C++,IDL]

```
#import "c:\program files\common
files\system\ado\msado15.dll" no_namespace
#import "c:\program files\common files\microsoft
shared\cdo\cdoex.dll" no_namespace
// ...
MessagePtr iMsg(__uuidof(Message));
```

[VBScript]

```
Dim iMsg
Set iMsg = CreateObject("CDO.Message")
```

You can create and send or post a simple message by using only the IMessage interface:

- To send an SMTP message, you must at least set the To and From properties on the IMessage interface.

- To post an NNTP message, you must at least set the IMessage.Newsgroups and IMessage.Subject properties.
- To send or post multiple messages efficiently, create a single Message object and reuse it for each message.
- To send individual messages with the same content to several recipients, change the address and call the IMessage.Send or IMessage.Post method for each message.
- To send different content in each message, use the IBodyParts.DeleteAll method to clear all of the body parts associated with a Message object.

Configuring the Message Object

To configure a Message object,

1. Create an instance of the Configuration COM class.
2. Populate the configuration settings in the IConfiguration.Fields collection.
3. Set the IMessage.Configuration property to the IConfiguration object reference on the Configuration object.

The following example demonstrates how to configure a message object:

[Visual Basic]

```
' Reference to Microsoft ActiveX Data Objects 2.5 Library
' Reference to Microsoft CDO for Exchange 2000 Server
Library
' ..
Dim iConf As New CDO.Configuration
Dim Flds  As ADODB.Fields
Set Flds = iConf.Fields

' Set the configuration
Flds(cdoSendUsingMethod) = cdoSendUsingPort
Flds(cdoSMTPServer) = "mail.microsoft.com"
' ... other settings
Flds.Update

Dim iMsg As New CDO.Message
Set iMsg.Configuration = iConf

' go on to use Message instance
```

Setting Language and Time-Zone Information

Language code and time-zone information is stored in the Message object's associated Configuration object. These values are stored in the *http://schemas.microsoft.com/cdo/configuration/languagecode* and urn:schemas:calendar:timezoneid fields.

The language code is used when constructing the response text for reply and forwarded messages. The time-zone identifier is used when converting date and time values to local times.

To configure the language code and time zone that are used for messaging, set the *http://schemas.microsoft.com/cdo/configuration/languagecode* and urn:schemas:calendar:timezoneid fields to appropriate values in the associated Configuration object:

[Visual Basic]

```
' Reference to Microsoft ActiveX Data Objects 2.5 Library
' Reference to Microsoft CDO for Exchange 2000 Server
Library
' ..
Dim iConf As New CDO.Configuration
Dim Flds  As ADODB.Fields
Set Flds = iConf.Fields

' Set the configuration for Network Send
Flds(cdoLanguageCode) = "en-us"
Flds(cdoTimezoneId) = cdoMountain
' .. set additional fields
Flds.Update

Dim iMsg As New CDO.Message
Set iMsg.Configuration = iConf
```

Both of these fields have default values that depend on the current computer locale and system settings. In many cases, you will not need to set these values explicitly.

Setting the Send and Post Methods

With the Message object, you have the option of choosing how messages are sent or posted for delivery. These options are determined by the software installed on the computer running your CDO application. Table 18–1 lists these methods and describes when the method is available.

TABLE 18-1 *Send and Post Methods*

Method	Description
Pickup Directory	If the application is running on a computer that has SMTP or NNTP services, you can use the pickup directory for those services.
Network via SMTP or NNTP protocol	You can connect directly to an SMTP or NNTP service and use the SMTP or NNTP protocol to send or post a message.
Microsoft Exchange	You can send and post messages using Microsoft Exchange 2000 Server. In this case, the item is submitted by using the ExOLEDB provider mail transmission URI when the sender's mailbox is on a local machine, or through the HTTP/WebDAV mail transmission URI if the user's mailbox is on a remote Exchange service.

To set the send or post method for messaging objects,

1. Set the *http://schemas.microsoft.com/cdo/configuration/sendusing* and *http://schemas.microsoft.com/cdo/configuration/postusing* fields to the desired method in the associated Configuration object. The methods listed in the previous table are identified with CdoSendUsing and CdoPostUsing enumerations.
2. Set any required or optional configuration fields that correspond to the send or post method.

The required and optional fields depend upon the send or post mechanism. The following example illustrates the code used:

[Visual Basic]

```
' Reference to Microsoft ActiveX Data Objects 2.5 Library
' Reference to Microsoft CDO for Exchange 2000 Server
Library
' ..
Dim iConf As New CDO.Configuration
Dim Flds  As ADODB.Fields
Set Flds = iConf.Fields

' Set the configuration for Network Send
Flds(cdoSendUsingMethod) = cdoSendUsingPort
Flds(cdoSMTPServer) = "server.domain.tld"
' .. set additional fields
Flds.Update

Dim iMsg As New CDO.Message
Set iMsg.Configuration = iConf
```

Sending or Posting Using the Network

To send messages over the network,

1. Set the *http://schemas.microsoft.com/cdo/configuration/sendusing* or *http://schemas.microsoft.com/cdo/configuration/postusing* field to cdoSendUsingPort or CdoPostUsingPort in the Configuration object.
2. Set the *http://schemas.microsoft.com/cdo/configuration/smtpserver* or *http://schemas.microsoft.com/cdo/configuration/nntpserver* field to a resolvable name (DNS or NetBIOS) for an SMTP or NNTP service on the network.
3. Set the following additional fields used with network configurations:

TABLE 18-2 *SMTP and NNTP Services*

Name	Description
smtpserverport nntpserverport	The port to use when connecting the service. Defaults are 25 and 119.
smtpconnectiontimeout nntpconnectiontimeout	The timeout in seconds for attempted connections to the service. Default is 30 seconds.
smtpaccountname nntpaccountname	The account name.
smtpauthenticate nntpauthenticate	The mechanism (if any) used to authenticate the service.
smtpusessl nntpusessl	Indicates whether or not to use Secure Sockets Layer (SSL) for the connection.
sendusername senduserpassword postusername postpassord	The username and password that are needed to authenticate the Basic Authentication mechanism. These fields are also used when sending mail by using Exchange 2000 Server to look up the user's mailbox URI.

The following example demonstrates explicitly setting various fields that are used when sending messages over the network:

[Visual Basic]

```
' Reference to Microsoft ActiveX Data Objects 2.5 Library
' Reference to Microsoft CDO for Exchange 2000 Server
Library
' ..
Dim iConf As New CDO.Configuration
Dim Flds  As ADODB.Fields
Set Flds = iConf.Fields

' Set the configuration for Network Send
Flds(cdoSendUsingMethod) = cdoSendUsingPort
```

```
Flds(cdoSMTPServer) = "server.microsoft.com"
Flds(cdoSMTPServerPort) = 25           'standard port for
SMTP (default)
Flds(cdoSMTPConnectionTimeout) = 30
Flds(cdoSMTPAccountName) = "My Name"
Flds(cdoSendUserReplyEmailAddress) = """User""
<user@microsoft.com>"
Flds(cdoSendEmailAddress) = """User"" <user@microsoft.com>"
' ... other settings
Flds.Update

Dim iMsg As New CDO.Message
Set iMsg.Configuration = iConf

' go on to use Message instance
```

Many of these settings can be loaded if Microsoft Outlook Express is installed on the local computer. Only the settings for the default account, default identity can be used. See "Using Default Configuration Settings" in the MS Exchange SDK for more information.

Sending or Posting Using the Pickup Directory

To send messages using a local SMTP pickup directory,

1. Set the *http://schemas.microsoft.com/cdo/configuration/sendusing* or *http://schemas.microsoft.com/cdo/configuration/postusing* field to cdoSendUsingPickup and CdoPostUsingPickup in the Configuration object, respectively.
2. Set the following fields that are used with pickup directories:

TABLE 18-3 *SMTP and NNTP Pickup Directory Services*

Name	Description
Smtppickupdirectory nntppickupdirectory	The full paths to the pickup directories for the SMTP and NNTP services. These values are normally automatically loaded when the Configuration object is created, if local services are installed.
Flushbuffersonwrite	Indicates whether to override file system buffering when writing the messages to the pickup directory. If set to True, the messages are committed directly to disk when written. Setting this field to True can cause performance degradation.

The following example demonstrates explicitly setting various fields that are used when sending messages using the SMTP pickup directory on the local computer:

[Visual Basic]

```
' Reference to Microsoft ActiveX Data Objects 2.5 Library
' Reference to Microsoft CDO for Exchange 2000 Server
Library
' ..
Dim iConf As New CDO.Configuration
Dim Flds  As ADODB.Fields
Set Flds = iConf.Fields

' Set the configuration for Network Send
Flds(cdoSendUsingMethod) = cdoSendUsingPickup
Flds(cdoSendUserReplyEmailAddress) = """User""
<user@microsoft.com>"
Flds(cdoSendEmailAddress) = """User"" <user@microsoft.com>"
' ... other settings
Flds.Update

Dim iMsg As New CDO.Message
Set iMsg.Configuration = iConf

' go on to use the Message object.
```

Many of these settings can be loaded if an SMTP service is installed on the local machine. See "Using Default Configuration Settings" for more information.

Sending or Posting Using Exchange

To send messages using Exchange 2000 Server,

1. Set the *http://schemas.microsoft.com/cdo/configuration/sendusing* or *http://schemas.microsoft.com/cdo/configuration/postusing* field to cdoSendUsingExchange and CdoPostUsingExchange in the Configuration object.
2. Set the *http://schemas.microsoft.com/cdo/configuration/sendusername* and *http://schemas.microsoft.com/cdo/configuration/postusername* fields to the e-mail address of the sender. These values are used to look up the Exchange service on which the sender's mailbox resides. Mail can only be submitted to the Exchange service containing the sender's mailbox.
3. If desired, set the *http://schemas.microsoft.com/cdo/configuration/activeconnection property* to an open ADO Connection object. The object must be bound to the user's mailbox.
4. If desired, set the *http://schemas.microsoft.com/cdo/configuration/mailboxurl* to the user's mailbox URL. If set, this value is used to bind to the user's mailbox and send the message. If it is not set, the user's Exchange server is found in Active Directory and the URL to the mailbox is constructed.

Note that the "mailbox" in this context is the user's root private store mailbox folder, not their inbox. For example—*"file://./backofficestorage/domain.tld/mbx/user1"*.

5. Set the following additional fields used when posting with Exchange:

Name   *http://schemas.microsoft.com/exchange/hardlinklist*
Description   A multi-valued string containing the URLs to folders into which the item should be posted. Currently, only one URL can be specified.

The following example demonstrates explicitly setting various fields that are used when sending messages using Exchange 2000 Server:

[Visual Basic]

```
' Reference to Microsoft ActiveX Data Objects 2.5 Library
' Reference to Microsoft CDO for Exchange 2000 Server
Library
' ..
Dim iConf As New CDO.Configuration
Dim Flds  As ADODB.Fields
Set Flds = iConf.Fields

Dim Conn As New ADODB.Connection
Conn.Provider = "ExOLEDB.DataSource"
' Note here: showing an HTTP URL but the
' location must be local to use the
' Exchange OLE DB Provider
Conn.Open "http://server/exchange/user1"

' Set the configuration for Network Send
Flds(cdoSendUsingMethod) = cdoSendUsingExchange
Flds(cdoSendUserReplyEmailAddress) = """User""
<user1@microsoft.com>"
Flds(cdoSendEmailAddress) = """User""
<user1@microsoft.com>"
Flds(cdoSendUserName) = "mailto:user1@microsoft.com"
Flds(cdoActiveConnection) = Conn
Flds(cdoMailboxURL) = "http://server/exchange/user1"
' ... other settings
Flds.Update

Dim iMsg As New CDO.Message
Set iMsg.Configuration = iConf

' go on to use the Message object

iMsg.Send ' Message is sent using the sender's local
Exchange mailbox.
```

Configuring Network Authentication Information

When sending or posting messages over the network, many SMTP and NNTP services require clients to authenticate themselves.

To configure a messaging object for authentication,

1. Set the *http://schemas.microsoft.com/cdo/configuration/smtpauthenticate* or *http://schemas.microsoft.com/cdo/configuration/nntpauthenticate* fields in the Configuration object's IConfiguration.Fields collection. The possible values are defined by the CdoProtocolsAuthentication enumeration.
2. If the mechanism is set to cdoBasic, set the username and password. For SMTP, set the *http://schemas.microsoft.com/cdo/configuration/sendusername* and *http://schemas.microsoft.com/cdo/configuration/sendpassword* configuration fields. For NNTP, set the *http://schemas.microsoft.com/cdo/configuration/postusername* and *http://schemas.microsoft.com/cdo/configuration/postpassword fields.*

For the NTLM setting, the current process/thread security context is used to authenticate. The following example illustrates the code used:

[Visual Basic]

```
' Reference to Microsoft ActiveX Data Objects 2.5 Library
' Reference to Microsoft CDO for Exchange 2000 Server
Library
' ..
Dim iConf As New CDO.Configuration
Dim Flds  As ADODB.Fields
Set Flds = iConf.Fields

' Set the configuration
' Use string constants provided in the type library
' for field names (they are long)
Flds(cdoSendUsingMethod) = cdoSendUsingPort
Flds(cdoSMTPServer) = "mail.microsoft.com"
Flds(cdoSMTPServerPort) = 26
Flds(cdoSMTPConnectionTimeout) = 30
Flds(cdoSMTPAccountName) = "My Name"
Flds(cdoSendUserReplyEmailAddress) = """User""
<user@microsoft.com>"
Flds(cdoSendEmailAddress) = """User"" <user@microsoft.com>"
Flds(cdoSMTPAuthenticate) = cdoBasic
Flds(cdoSendUserName) = "name"
Flds(cdoSendPassword) = "password"
Flds.Update

Dim iMsg As New CDO.Message
Set iMsg.Configuration = iConf

' go on to use Message instance
```

Setting Network Proxy Information

When using methods such as IMessage.AddAttachment and IMessage.CreateMHTMLBody, you may need to access network resources through a proxy server.

To set up the proxy configuration for a Message object,

1. Set the *http://schemas.microsoft.com/cdo/configuration/urlproxyserver* field in the Configuration object's IConfiguration.Fields collection.
2. Set the *http://schemas.microsoft.com/cdo/configuration/urlproxybypass* field to the value "<local>". With this setting, the proxy service will be bypassed for local addresses. (This is an optional setting.)
3. Set the *http://schemas.microsoft.com/cdo/configuration/urngetlatestversion* field to force direct retrieval of resources and bypass the cache. (This is an optional setting.)

The following example illustrates the codes used:

[Visual Basic]

```
' Reference to Microsoft ActiveX Data Objects 2.5 Library
' Reference to Microsoft CDO for Exchange 2000 Server Library
' ..
Dim iConf As New CDO.Configuration
Dim Flds  As ADODB.Fields
Set Flds = iConf.Fields

' Set the configuration
Flds(cdoSendUsingMethod) = cdoSendUsingPort
Flds(cdoSMTPServer) = "mail.microsoft.com"
Flds(cdoSMTPServerPort) = 26
Flds(cdoSMTPConnectionTimeout) = 30
Flds(cdoSMTPAccountName) = "My Name"
Flds(cdoSendUserReplyEmailAddress) = """User"" <user@microsoft.com>"
Flds(cdoSendEmailAddress) = """User"" <user@microsoft.com>"
Flds(cdoURLProxyServer) = "proxyserver:80"
Flds(cdoURLProxyBypass) = "<local>"
Flds(cdoURLGetLatestVersion) = True
Flds(cdoHTTPCookies) = "cookies here"
' ... other settings
Flds.Update

Dim iMsg As New CDO.Message
Set iMsg.Configuration = iConf

' go on to use Message instance
```

Using Default Configuration Settings

Default values are loaded when a Configuration object is created. The following sections discuss these default configuration values.

Local SMTP/NNTP Service

If the SMTP or NNTP Service is installed on the local computer, CDO sets the SMTP pickup directory to the directory defined in the service properties, and sets the delivery method to use the pickup directory.

Outlook Express

If Outlook Express is installed on the local computer, CDO gets default configuration settings from the Outlook Express properties that are defined for the default identity of the default account.

Because CDO automatically collects configuration information from the computer, you may not need to set these values manually. For example, if either the SMTP service or Outlook Express is installed, your application can send messages without having to explicitly configure the Message object. To change these settings, you can start with the default values and modify the fields you desire. Use the IConfiguration.Load method to load particular default settings on demand.

Note For performance reasons, it is recommended that you set up a single Configuration object and associate it with all messages rather than having CDO load the defaults for each sent message. For example, if using CDO in an ASP application, you can store the Configuration class instance in the Session object, and then reuse it for each message sent during that session. If you use global settings, you could also place the object in the Application object.

Addressing the Message

To send a message, you must specify at least one recipient address by using the IMessage.To, IMessage.CC, or IMessage.BCC property. To post an NNTP message, you must specify at least one newsgroup address by using the IMessage.Newsgroups property.

Address Formats

The address formats are defined by various Internet standards:

SMTP Addresses

```
recipient@microsoft.com
<recipient@microsoft.com>
"Display Name" <recipient@microsoft.com>
```

NNTP Newsgroup Names
```
comp.os.windows
comp.microsoft.newsgroup1
```

> **Note** Multiple addressees for a message are separated with *commas* only. The semicolons used with MAPI clients such as Microsoft Outlook are not used.

```
"Mr. A" <a@microsoft.com>, "Mr. B" <b@microsoft.com>
A@microsoft.com, <B@microsoft.com>, "Mr. C"
<c@microsoft.com>
comp.microsoft.newsgroup1, comp.microsoft.newsgroups2
```

All addresses must be complete addresses or newsgroup names. The following examples show how to address a message by using the IMessage.To or IMessage.Newsgroup property:

[**Visual Basic**]

```
' Reference to Microsoft ActiveX Data Objects 2.5 Library
' Reference to Microsoft CDO for Exchange 2000 Server
Library
' ..
Dim iMsg as New CDO.Message

iMsg.To         = "someone@microsoft.com"
iMsg.Newsgroups = "comp.microsoft.newsgroup"
```

[**C++,IDL**]
```
#import "c:\program files\common
files\system\ado\msado15.dll" no_namespace
#import "c:\program files\common files\microsoft
shared\cdo\cdoex.dll" no_namespace
// ...
IMessagePtr iMsg(__uuidof(Message));

iMsg->To         = "someone@microsoft.com";
iMsg->Newsgroups = "comp.microsoft.newsgroup";
```

[**VBScript**]

```
Dim iMsg
Set iMsg = CreateObject("CDO.Message")

iMsg.To         = "someone@microsoft.com"
iMsg.Newsgroups = "comp.microsoft.newsgroup"
```

Note Trailing commas are removed from address strings by the address field parser each time you set an address property. To concatenate address fields, place the comma at the beginning of the string being added. You can also concatenate the addresses prior to setting the value of the address field. This note applies to the To, CC, BCC, FollowUpTo, and Newsgroup properties.

```
iMsg.To = "someone@microsoft.com"
iMsg.To = iMsg.To & ",another@microsoft.com"
```

The IMessage interface exposes properties that relate to the most common mail header fields, such as To, From, CC, BCC, Newsgroups, and FollowUpTo. However, the complete list of headers for the message is contained in the IMessage.Fields collection. Fields that are used with a Message object reside in the urn:schemas:mailheader: and urn:schemas:httpmail: namespaces. Consequently, you can use the Fields collection to set mail header fields used to address the message:

[Visual Basic]

```
' Reference to Microsoft ActiveX Data Objects 2.5 Library
' Reference to Microsoft CDO for Exchange 2000 Server
Library
' ..
Dim iMsg As New CDO.Message

Dim Flds As ADODB.Fields
Set Flds = iMsg.Fields
With Flds
  .Item("urn:schemas:mailheader:to") = "someone@microsoft.com"
  .Item("urn:schemas:mailheader:from") = "<another@microsoft.com>"
  .Item("urn:schemas:mailheader:cc") = "<thirdperson@microsoft.com>"
  .Update
End With
' ..
```

[C++,IDL]

```
#import "c:\program files\common files\system\ado\msado15.dll" no_namespace
#import "c:\program files\common files\microsoft shared\cdo\cdoex.dll" no_namespace
// ...
IMessagePtr iMsg(__uuidof(Message));

FieldsPtr Flds;
Flds = iMsg->Fields;
```

```cpp
Flds->Item["urn:schemas:mailheader:to"]->Value =
_variant_t("someone@microsoft.com");
Flds->Item["urn:schemas:mailheader:from"]->Value =
_variant_t("<another@microsoft.com>");
Flds->Item["urn:schemas:mailheader:cc"]->Value =
_variant_t("<thirdperson@microsoft.com>");
Flds->Update();
```

[VBScript]

```
Dim iMsg
Set iMsg = CreateObject("CDO.Message")

Dim Flds
Set Flds = iMsg.Fields
With Flds
   .Item("urn:schemas:mailheader:to")   =
"someone@microsoft.com"
   .Item("urn:schemas:mailheader:from") =
"<another@microsoft.com>"
   .Item("urn:schemas:mailheader:cc")   =
"<thirdperson@microsoft.com>"
   .Update
End With
```

Setting Subject and TextBody Fields

When sending a message, setting the subject field is optional, but usually specified. For posting a message to a newsgroup, setting the subject field is required. For both message types, setting the text body field is optional, but also typically provided. You can set the subject and text body fields using the IMessage.Subject and IMessage.TextBody properties. The following example illustrates the codes used:

[Visual Basic]

```
' Reference to Microsoft ActiveX Data Objects 2.5 Library
' Reference to Microsoft CDO for Exchange 2000 Server
Library
' ..
Dim iMsg As New CDO.Message

With iMsg
   .To = "someone@microsoft.com"
   .Newsgroups = "comp.microsoft.newsgroup1"
   .Subject = "Agenda for staff meeting"
```

Setting Subject and TextBody Fields

```
    .TextBody = "Please plan to present your status for the
following projects..."
End With
```

[C++,IDL]

```
#import "c:\program files\common
files\system\ado\msado15.dll" no_namespace
#import "c:\program files\common files\microsoft
shared\cdo\cdoex.dll" no_namespace
// ...
IMessagePtr iMsg(__uuidof(Message));

iMsg->To         = "someone@microsoft.com";
iMsg->Newsgroups = "comp.microsoft.newsgroup1";
iMsg->Subject    = "Agenda for staff meeting";
iMsg->TextBody   = "Please plan to present your status for
the following projects...";
```

[VBScript]

```
Dim iMsg
Set iMsg = CreateObject("CDO.Message")

With iMsg
  .To         = "someone@microsoft.com"
  .Newsgroups = "comp.microsoft.newsgroup1"
  .Subject    = "Agenda for staff meeting"
  .TextBody   = "Please plan to present your status for
the following projects..."
End With
```

You can use the IMessage.Fields collection to set the subject and text body fields of the message. The field names are urn:schemas:mailheader:subject, urn:schemas:httpmail:subject, and urn:schemas:httpmail:textdescription, respectively. The subject field within the urn:schemas:mailheader: returns the subject with any non-US-ASCII characters encoded according to RFC 1522. The subject field within the urn:schemas:httpmail: namespace contains the subject in unicode characters. This example illustrates the codes used:

[Visual Basic]

```
' Reference to Microsoft ActiveX Data Objects 2.5 Library
' Reference to Microsoft CDO for Exchange 2000 Server
Library
' ..
Dim iMsg As New CDO.Message

Dim Flds As ADODB.Fields
```

```
Set Flds = iMsg.Fields
With Flds
  .Item("urn:schemas:httpmail:to") =
"someone@microsoft.com"
  .Item("urn:schemas:httpmail:from") =
"<another@microsoft.com>"
  .Item("urn:schemas:httpmail:cc") =
"<thirdperson@microsoft.com>"

  .Item("urn:schemas:httpmail:subject") = "Agenda for the
staff"
meeting ""
  .Item("urn:schemas:httpmail:textdescription") = "Please
plan to present your status for the following projects..."
  .Update
End With
```

[C++,IDL]

```
#import "c:\program files\common
files\system\ado\msado15.dll" no_namespace
#import "c:\program files\common files\microsoft
shared\cdo\cdoex.dll" no_namespace
// ...
IMessagePtr iMsg(__uuidof(Message));

FieldsPtr Flds;
Flds = iMsg->Fields;
Flds->Item["urn:schemas:mailheader:to"] =
_variant_t("someone@microsoft.com");
Flds->Item["urn:schemas:mailheader:from"] =
_variant_t("<another@microsoft.com>");
Flds->Item["urn:schemas:mailheader:cc"] =
_variant_t("<thirdperson@microsoft.com>");
Flds->Item["urn:schemas:mailheader:subject"]->Value
    = _variant_t("Agenda for the staff meeting");
Flds->Item["urn:schemas:mailheader:textdescription"]->Value
    = _variant_t("Please plan to present your status for
the following
projects...");
Flds->Update();
```

[VBScript]

```
Dim iMsg
Set iMsg = CreateObject("CDO.Message")

Dim Flds
Set Flds = iMsg.Fields
With Flds
```

```
  .Item("urn:schemas:httpmail:to")    =
"someone@microsoft.com"
  .Item("urn:schemas:httpmail:from") =
"<another@microsoft.com>"
  .Item("urn:schemas:httpmail:cc")    =
"<thirdperson@microsoft.com>"

  .Item("urn:schemas:httpmail:subject")         = "Agenda
for the staff
meeting"
  .Item("urn:schemas:httpmail:textdescription") = "Please
plan to present
your status for the following projects..."
  .Update
End With
```

In addition to a plain text body, you can use HTML-formatted text using the IMessage.HTMLBody property. By default, the IMessage.AutoGenerateTextBody property in the object is set to True (VARIANT_TRUE), and therefore a plain text body is automatically generated from the HTML body text to support recipients whose clients cannot display HTML-formatted messages. For more information on creating attachments, see "Creating MIME-Formatted Messages" in the MS Exchange SDK.

Setting Message Header Fields

The most common message header fields are exposed as properties on the IMessage interface. However, all header fields are accessible in the IMessage.Fields collection. The header fields you can set by using this collection reside in the urn:schemas:mailheader: and urn:schemas:httpmail: namespaces. Additionally, the *http://schemas.microsoft.com/exchange/sensitivity* field is available.

You can add other headers not present in the provided default schema by adding the header to the collection within the urn:schemas:mailheader: field namespace.

Note Make sure to encode non-US-ASCII characters when using the urn:schemas:mailheader: namespace by using the mechanism defined in RFC 1522.

The following illustrates the codes used:

[Visual Basic]

```
' Reference to Microsoft ActiveX Data Objects 2.5 Library
' Reference to Microsoft CDO for Exchange 2000 Server
Library
```

```vb
' ..
Dim iMsg As New CDO.Message

Dim Flds As ADODB.Fields
Set Flds = iMsg.Fields

With Flds
  .Item("urn:schemas:httpmail:to") = "someone@microsoft.com"
  .Item("urn:schemas:httpmail:from") = "another@microsoft.com"
  .Item("urn:schemas:httpmail:cc") = "thirdperson@microsoft.com"
  .Item("urn:schemas:httpmail:sender") = "myaddress@microsoft.com"

  .Item("urn:schemas:mailheader:myhdr") = "some value"
  .Item("urn:schemas:mailheader:X-Hdr") = "less value"

  .Update
End With
```

[C++,IDL]

```cpp
#import "c:\program files\common files\system\ado\msado15.dll" no_namespace
#import "c:\program files\common files\microsoft shared\cdo\cdoex.dll" no_namespace
// ...
IMessagePtr iMsg(__uuidof(Message));

FieldsPtr Flds;
Flds = iMsg->Fields;

Flds->Item["urn:schemas:httpmail:to"]->Value
    = _variant_t("someone@microsoft.com");
Flds->Item["urn:schemas:httpmail:from"]->Value
    = _variant_t("another@microsoft.com");
Flds->Item["urn:schemas:httpmail:cc"]->Value
    = _variant_t("thirdperson@microsoft.com");
Flds->Item["urn:schemas:httpmail:sender"]->Value
    = _variant_t("myaddress@microsoft.com");

Flds->Item["urn:schemas:mailheader:myhdr"]->Value
    = _variant_t("some value");
Flds->Item["urn:schemas:mailheader:X-Header"]->Value
    = _variant_t("another value");
Flds->Update();
```

[VBScript]

```
Dim iMsg
Set iMsg = CreateObject("CDO.Message")

Dim Flds
Set Flds = iMsg.Fields

With Flds
  .Item("urn:schemas:httpmail:to")      = "someone@microsoft.com"
  .Item("urn:schemas:httpmail:from")    = "another@microsoft.com"
  .Item("urn:schemas:httpmail:cc")      = "thirdperson@microsoft.com"
  .Item("urn:schemas:httpmail:sender")  = "myaddress@microsoft.com"
  .Item("urn:schemas:mailheader:myhdr") = "some value"
  .Item("urn:schemas:mailheader:X-Hdr") = "less value"
  .Update
End With
```

Tip — When using the Fields collection, remember to invoke the Update method to commit any changes, deletions, or additions. If the CDO object is currently bound, invoke IDataSource.Save to commit the changes to the data source.

Note that in the preceding example, the Field.Item method was used to retrieve the Field object from the collection. You can also use the Fields.Append method. For CDO applications, the Item method will return the appropriate Field object regardless of whether it currently exists in the collection.

Adding Attachments

The IMessage.AddAttachment method adds an attachment to a message. The AddAttachment method accepts a file, ftp, http, or https URL parameter that identifies the location of the attachment. The method returns a reference to the newly added BodyPart object that houses the attachment so that it can be further manipulated, if necessary.

Chapter 18 • Messaging

The following example shows how to add a GIF graphic and a Microsoft Word file as attachments to a message:

[Visual Basic]

```
' Reference to Microsoft ActiveX Data Objects 2.5 Library
' Reference to Microsoft CDO for Exchange 2000 Server
Library
' ..
Dim iMsg As New CDO.Message
' configure message here if necessary
With iMsg
    .To = "someone@microsoft.com"
    .From = "another@microsoft.com"
    .Newsgroups = "comp.microsoft.newsgroup1"
    .Subject = "Agenda for staff meeting"
    .TextBody = "See attached docs for more info."
    .AddAttachment "http://example.microsoft.com/picture.gif"
    .AddAttachment "file://d:/temp/test.doc"
    .AddAttachment "C:\files\another.doc"
    ' finish and send
End With
```

[C++,IDL]

```
#import "c:\program files\common files\system\ado\msado15.dll" no_namespace
#import "c:\program files\common files\microsoft shared\cdo\cdoex.dll" no_namespace
// ...
IMessagePtr iMsg(__uuidof(Message));

/*
** configure message here if necessary
*/

iMsg->To         = "someone@microsoft.com";
iMsg->From       = "another@microsoft.com";
iMsg->Newsgroups = "comp.microsoft.newsgroup1";
iMsg->Subject    = "Agenda for staff meeting";
iMsg->TextBody   = "See attached docs for more info.";

try {
  iMsg->AddAttachment("http://example.microsoft.com/picture.gif","","");
  iMsg->AddAttachment("file://d:/temp/test.doc","","");
  iMsg->AddAttachment("C:\files\another.doc","","");
}
catch(_com_error err) {
```

```
  // handle exception
}
// finish and send
```

[VBScript]

```
Dim iMsg
Set iMsg = CreateObject("CDO.Message")
' configure message here if necessary
With iMsg
   .To   = "someone@microsoft.com"
   .From = "another@microsoft.com"
   .Newsgroups = "comp.microsoft.newsgroup1"
   .Subject  = "Agenda for staff meeting"
   .TextBody = "See attached docs for more info."
   .AddAttachment "http://example.microsoft.com/
picture.gif"
   .AddAttachment "file://d:/temp/test.doc"
   .AddAttachment "C:\files\another.doc"
   ' ..
End With
```

Note — If you attach a Web page using the AddAttachment method, you attach only the file specified in the URL. If the page contains image links or other content, they are not included. To attach a full Web page with embedded graphics, use the IMessage.CreateMHTMLBody method. For more information on attaching Web pages, see "Creating MHTML Messages" in the MS Exchange SDK.

Manually Adding Attachments

You can manually add attachments directly to the IMessage.Attachments or IBodyPart.BodyParts collection that is exposed by the Message object. This approach is useful if you have content that is not on the file system or URL addressable. When manually adding an attachment, use the IMessage.Attachments collection as described in the following procedure:

1. Create a new BodyPart object in the Attachments collection using IBodyParts.Add. (The Attachments property on the object returns a BodyParts collection object reference.)
2. Set appropriate MIME header fields for the body part.
3. Obtain the content stream for the attachment using IBodyPart.GetDecodedContentStream and write the content to it
4. Call _Stream.Flush to commit written data to the body part.

Chapter 18 • Messaging

The following example shows how to manually add attachments:

[Visual Basic]

```
Dim iMsg As New CDO.Message

Dim iBp As CDO.IBodyPart
Dim Stm As ADODB.Stream
Dim Flds As ADODB.Fields

With iMsg
   .To = "someone@microsoft.com"
   .From = "another@microsoft.com"
   .Newsgroups = "comp.microsoft.newsgroup1"
   .Subject = "Agenda for staff meeting"
   .TextBody = "Please plan to present your status for the following projects..."
   Set iBp = .Attachments.Add
   Set Flds = iBp.Fields

   With Flds
       .Item("urn:schemas:mailheader:content-type") = "text/plain; name=test.txt"
       .Item("urn:schemas:mailheader:content-transfer-encoding") = "quoted printable """
       .Update
   End With            ' Flds
   Set Flds = Nothing
   Set Stm = iBp.GetDecodedContentStream
   ' Because body part content-type is "text", the returned Stream
   '    is of type adTypeText.  Use WriteText to fill the stream
   Stm.WriteText "Here is the text in the ""attachment"" called text.txt"
   ' commit the changes into the BodyPart object
   Stm.Flush
   Set Stm = Nothing
End With             ' iMsg
```

[C++,IDL]

```
#import "c:\program files\common files\system\ado\msado15.dll" no_namespace
#import "c:\program files\common files\microsoft shared\cdo\cdoex.dll" no_namespace
// ...
IMessagePtr iMsg(__uuidof(Message));
IBodyPartPtr iBp;
_StreamPtr Stm;
```

Manually Adding Attachments

```cpp
FieldsPtr Flds;

iMsg->To         = "someone@microsoft.com";
iMsg->From       = "another@microsoft.com";
iMsg->Subject    = "Agenda for staff meeting";
iMsg->TextBody   = "Please plan to present your status for
the following
projects...";

iBp = iMsg->Attachments->Add(-1);
Flds = iBp->Fields;
Flds->Item["urn:schemas:mailheader:content-type"]->Value
    = _variant_t("text/plain; name=\"test.txt\"");
Flds->Update();

Stm = iBp.GetDecodedContentStream();
  /*
  **  Because body part content-type is "text", the
returned Stream
  **  is of type adTypeText.  Use WriteText to fill the
stream
  */
Stm->WriteText("Here is the text in the ""attachment""
called
text.txt",adWriteChar);
    ' commit the changes into the BodyPart object
Stm->Flush();

// ...
if(g_Debug)
    cout << iMsg->GetStream()->ReadText(-1);
```

[VBScript]

```vbscript
Dim iMsg
Set iMsg = CreateObject("CDO.Message")
Dim iBp
Dim Stm
Dim Flds

With iMsg
    .To        = "someone@microsoft.com"
    .From      = "another@microsoft.com"
    .Subject   = "Agenda for staff meeting"
    .TextBody  = "Please plan to present your status for
the following
projects..."
    Set iBp = .Attachments.Add
    Set Flds = iBp.Fields
```

```
    With Flds
      .Item("urn:schemas:mailheader:content-type") = _
"text/plain; name=test.txt"
      .Item("urn:schemas:mailheader:content-transfer-
encoding") = "quoted
printable"
      .Update
    End With             ' Flds
    Set Flds = Nothing
    Set Stm = iBp.GetDecodedContentStream
    ' Because body part content-type is "text", the returned Stream
    '    is of type adTypeText.  Use WriteText to fill the stream
    Stm.WriteText "Here is the text in the ""attachment""
called text.txt"
    ' commit the changes into the BodyPart object
    Stm.Flush
    Set Stm = Nothing
End With              ' iMsg
```

You can add any type of attachment to a message. For MIME-formatted messages, attachments are added as MIME body parts. CDOs automatically sets the MIME Content-Type and Content-Transfer-Encoding values for some attachments. Depending on the attachment type, you may need to set these values explicitly.

If you want to have the message sent with attachments formatted and encoded with UUENCODE, set the IMessage.MIMEFormatted property to false before sending the message.

In many cases, you may need to specify credentials to access a resource on the network. In these cases, you will need to add this information to the Message object's associated Configuration object. See "Configuring the Message Object" in the MS Exchange SDK for more information.

Creating MIME-Formatted Messages

By default, the CDO components construct message body content using MIME encoding format. This process is controlled by using the IMessage.MIMEFormatted property, which defaults to True. There are many ways to create the MIME-content hierarchy in a message. In most cases, when adding an attachment or creating an MHTML message, the IMessage interface exposes methods that automatically structure the MIME content and manage the underlying details. These methods include IMessage.AddAttachment and IMessage.CreateMHTMLBody. To add attachments to a message in UUEncoded format, you set

IMessage.MIMEFormatted to False. In many cases, you may need to manually construct the entire body part hierarchy, or portions of it.

Objects that participate in the body part hierarchy for a message expose implementations of the IBodyPart interface. For example, each instance of the BodyPart and Message COM classes represents one body part in the hierarchy of a MIME-encoded message. Both BodyPart and Message instances expose the IBodyPart interface to facilitate manipulation of the body part's content and properties. The IBodyPart.BodyParts collection contains the child BodyPart objects for the object and is therefore used to navigate down the hierarchy of objects. To navigate up the hierarchy from an object, you use the IBodyPart.Parent property.

The Message object acts as the root of the MIME hierarchy. In standard object-oriented fashion, the hierarchies extend in patterns of BodyPart -> BodyParts -> BodyPart until a terminating (leaf) node in the hierarchy is reached.

When using methods such as IMessage.CreateMHTMLBody or IMessage.AddAttachment, or the HTMLBody property on the message, the MIME hierarchy is constructed automatically. You do not need to manually add the BodyPart objects that contain the various content parts.

In many cases, you may want to manually create the BodyPart hierarchy. To do so, you can use the IBodyPart.AddBodyPart method to add child body parts to the object. Alternately, you can access the IBodyPart.BodyParts collection explicitly and use the IBodyParts.Add method to add the new body part. Both methods create a new BodyPart instance and return an object reference on the newly added object. Using this returned interface, you can then set any fields for the object using the IBodyPart.Fields collection. For body parts that contain content, you use the appropriate Stream object to populate the content. You access the BodyPart Stream object by using either IBodyPart.GetEncodedContentStream or IBodyPart.GetDecodedContentStream.

Adding BodyPart Objects to the MIME Hierarchy

The following example demonstrates creating a common MIME hierarchy for a message that contains two alternate representations of the message text: text/plain and text/html. The steps are as follows:

1. Create the Message object, and retrieve its IBodyPart interface.
2. Use the IBodyPart.AddBodyPart method to create and add a child BodyPart object.
3. Use the returned IBodyPart object reference to set fields for the object by using its IBodyPart.Fields collection.
4. If this body part is to directly contain content, you can add this content by retrieving a Stream object by using the IBodyPart.GetDecodedContentStream method. Write the data to the Stream object, and call _Stream.Flush to commit the stream to the BodyPart object.

Chapter 18 • **Messaging**

The following example illustrates the codes used to add Body Part Objects to the MIME hierarchy:

[Visual Basic]

```
' Reference to Microsoft ActiveX Data Objects 2.5 Library
' Reference to Microsoft CDO for Exchange 2000 Server
Library
' ..
Dim iMsg As New CDO.Message
Dim iBp  As CDO.IBodyPart
Dim iBp1 As CDO.IBodyPart
Dim Flds As ADODB.Fields
Dim Stm  As ADODB.Stream

' Get IBodyPart on the Message object
Set iBp = iMsg

' TEXT BODYPART
' Add the body part for the text/plain part of message
Set iBp1 = iBp.AddBodyPart

' set the fields here
Set Flds = iBp1.Fields
Flds("urn:schemas:mailheader:content-type") = "text/plain; charset=""iso-8859-1"""
Flds.Update

' get the stream and add the message
Set Stm = iBp1.GetDecodedContentStream
Stm.WriteText "this is the message in text format"
Stm.Flush

' HTML BODYPART
' Do the HTML part here
Set iBp1 = iBp.AddBodyPart

' set the content-type field here
Set Flds = iBp1.Fields
Flds("urn:schemas:mailheader:content-type") = "text/html"
Flds.Update

' get the stream and add message HTML text to it
Set Stm = iBp1.GetDecodedContentStream
Stm.WriteText "<HTML><H1>this is some content for the body part object</H1></HTML>"
Stm.Flush

' Now set the Message object's Content-Type header
' to multipart/alternative
```

Creating MIME-Formatted Messages

```
Set Flds = iBp.Fields
Flds("urn:schemas:mailheader:conent-type") = "multipart/
alternative"
Flds.Update
```

[C++,IDL]

```
#import "c:\program files\common
files\system\ado\msado15.dll" no_namespace
#import "c:\program files\common files\microsoft
shared\cdo\cdoex.dll" no_namespace
// ...
IMessagePtr iMsg(__uuidof(Message));
IBodyPartPtr iBp;
IBodyPartPtr iBp1;
FieldsPtr Flds;
_StreamPtr Stm;

// Get IBodyPart on the Message object
iBp = iMsg;

// TEXT BODYPART
// Add the body part for the text/plain part of message
iBp1 = iBp->AddBodyPart(-1);

' set the fields here
Flds = iBp1->Fields();
Flds->Item["urn:schemas:mailheader:content-type"]->Value
   = _variant_t("text/plain; charset=""iso-8859-1""");
Flds->Update();

// get the stream and add the message
Stm = iBp1->GetDecodedContentStream();
Stm->WriteText("this is the message in text format",
adWriteLine);
Stm->Flush();

// HTML BODYPART
// Do the HTML part here
iBp1 = iBp->AddBodyPart(-1);

// set the content-type field here
Flds = iBp1->Fields;
Flds->Item["urn:schemas:mailheader:content-type"]->Value
   = _variant_t("text/html");
Flds->Update();

// get the stream and add message HTML text to it
Stm = iBp1->GetDecodedContentStream();
Stm->WriteText("<HTML><H1>this is some content for the body
```

```
part
object</H1></HTML>",adWriteLine);
Stm->Flush();

// Now set the Message object's Content-Type header
// to multipart/alternative
Flds = iBp->Fields;
Flds->Item["urn:schemas:mailheader:conent-type"]->Value
    = _variant_t("multipart/alternative");
Flds->Update();
```

[VBScript]

```
Dim iMsg
Dim iBp
Dim iBp1
Dim Flds
Dim Stm

Set iMsg = CreateObject("CDO.Message")
' Get IBodyPart on the Message object
Set iBp = iMsg.BodyPart

' TEXT BODYPART
' Add the body part for the text/plain part of message
Set iBp1 = iBp.AddBodyPart

' set the fields here
Set Flds = iBp1.Fields
Flds("urn:schemas:mailheader:content-type") = "text/plain;
charset=""iso
8859-1"""
Flds.Update

' get the stream and add the message
Set Stm = iBp1.GetDecodedContentStream
Stm.WriteText "this is the message in text format"
Stm.Flush

' HTML BODYPART
' Do the HTML part here
Set iBp1 = iBp.AddBodyPart

' set the content-type field here
Set Flds = iBp1.Fields
Flds("urn:schemas:mailheader:content-type") = "text/html"
Flds.Update

' get the stream and add message HTML text to it
Set Stm = iBp1.GetDecodedContentStream
```

```
Stm.WriteText "<HTML><H1>this is some content for the body
part
object</H1></HTML>"
Stm.Flush

' Now set the Message object's Content-Type header
' to multipart/alternative
Set Flds = iBp.Fields
Flds("urn:schemas:mailheader:conent-type") = "multipart/
alternative"
Flds.Update
```

Setting Header Fields on Body Parts

CDO automatically sets the fields needed for typical MIME messages. For example, when you create IMessage.HTMLBody with the IMessage.AutoGenerateTextBody property set to True, IMessage.TextBody is automatically generated along with the appropriate MIME structure. The IBodyPart.ContentMediaType for the root part is automatically set to multipart/alternative, with the two subparts being set to text/plain and text/html.

For more complex MIME-formatted messages, you may need to set the header fields directly. All fields are stored in an ADO Fields collection as name/value pairs. The mail header fields used with body parts reside in the urn:schemas:mailheader: namespace. Common fields such as urn:schemas:mailheader:content-type are also exposed as properties of the IBodyPart interface.

The following example shows how to set the ADO field urn:schemas:mailheader:content-language of the root body part of a simple message to German ("de"):

[Visual Basic]

```
' Reference to Microsoft ActiveX Data Objects 2.5 Library
' Reference to Microsoft CDO for Exchange 2000 Server
Library
' ..
Dim iMsg As New CDO.Message
Dim iBp  As CDO.IBodyPart
Set iBp = iMsg

Dim Flds As ADODB.Fields
Set Flds = iBp.Fields
Flds("urn:schemas:mailheader:content-language") = "de"
Flds.Update
```

[C++,IDL]

```
#import "c:\program files\common
files\system\ado\msado15.dll" no_namespace
```

```
#import "c:\program files\common files\microsoft
shared\cdo\cdoex.dll" no_namespace
// ...
IMessagePtr iMsg(__uuidof(Message));
IBodyPartPtr iBp;
FieldsPtr Flds;

iBp = iMsg;
Flds = iBp->Fields;
Flds->Item["urn:schemas:mailheader:content-language"] =
_variant_t("de");
Flds->Update();
```

[VBScript]

```
Dim iMsg
Dim iBp
Set iBp = iMsg.BodyPart

Dim Flds
Set Flds = iBp.Fields
Flds("urn:schemas:mailheader:content-language") = "de"
Flds.Update
```

Creating MHTML-Formatted Messages

MIME Encapsulation of Aggregate HTML Documents (MHTML) formatting provides a simple way to send an entire Web page, or portions of one, as a message. The message includes all of the HTML formatting, graphics, and other elements that are contained in the original page. You can also choose to exclude one or more types of elements from the message.

The IMessage.CreateMHTMLBody method accepts a URL parameter and a flags parameter. The URL specifies the Web page being sent, and the optional flags specify the types of elements to exclude from the message. CDO makes the file specified by the URL the IMessage.HTMLBody of the message, and each graphic or other element referenced in that file becomes a MIME body part. By default, CDO automatically generates the text body that contains a plain text version of the HTMLBody content.

CDO must be able to access the specified source URL to create the message. If CDO needs to use a proxy server to reach a URL outside a firewall, set this location for the *http://schemas.microsoft.com/cdo/configuration/urlproxyserver* field in the Message object's associated Configuration object.

The following example shows how to create a message from a Web page:

Creating MIME-Formatted Messages

[Visual Basic]

```vb
' Reference to Microsoft ActiveX Data Objects 2.5 Library
' Reference to Microsoft CDO for Exchange 2000 Server
Library
' ..
Dim iMsg   As New CDO.Message
Dim iConf  As New CDO.Configuration
Dim Flds   As ADODB.Fields

Set Flds = iConf.Fields
Flds("http://schemas.microsoft.com/cdo/configuration/urlproxyserver") = "proxyname:80"
Flds("http://schemas.microsoft.com/cdo/configuration/urlproxybypass") = "<local>"
Flds("http://schemas.microsoft.com/cdo/configuration/urlgetlatestversion") = True
Flds.Update

Set iMsg.Configuration = iConf

iMsg.CreateMHTMLBody "http://example.microsoft.com", _
                    cdoSuppressAll, _
                    "domain\username", _
                    "password"

' ...
```

[C++, IDL]

```cpp
#import "c:\program files\common files\system\ado\msado15.dll" no_namespace
#import "c:\program files\common files\microsoft shared\cdo\cdoex.dll" no_namespace
// ...
IMessagePtr        iMsg(__uuidof(Message));
IConfigurationPtr  iConf(__uuidof(Configuration));
FieldsPtr          Flds;

Flds = iConf->Fields;
Flds
>Item["http://schemas.microsoft.com/cdo/configuration/urlproxyserver"]
>Value
   = _variant_t("myproxyserver:80");
Flds
>Item["http://schemas.microsoft.com/cdo/configuration/urlproxybypass"]
>Value
   = _variant_t("<local>");
```

```cpp
Flds
>Item["http://schemas.microsoft.com/cdo/configuration/
urlgetlatestversion
]->Value
  = _variant_t(VARIANT_TRUE);
Flds->Update();
iMsg->Configuration = iConf;
try
{
  iMsg->CreateMHTMLBody(
          "http://example.microsoft.com",
          cdoSuppressAll,
          "domain\\username",
          "password");
}
catch(_com_error err)
{
  // handle exception
}
```

[VBScript]

```
Dim iMsg
Dim iConf
Dim Flds

Set iMsg = CreateObject("CDO.Message")
Set iConf = CreateObject("CDO.Configuration")

Set Flds = iConf.Fields
Flds("http://schemas.microsoft.com/cdo/configuration/
urlproxyserver") =
"proxyname:80"
Flds("http://schemas.microsoft.com/cdo/configuration/
urlproxybypass") =
"<local>"
Flds("http://schemas.microsoft.com/cdo/configuration/
urlgetlatestversion")
= True
Flds.Update

Set iMsg.Configuration = iConf

iMsg.CreateMHTMLBody "http://example.microsoft.com", _
                    cdoSuppressAll, _
                    "domain\username", _
                    "password"
```

Note To suppress multiple elements, add the values of the flag constants. For example, to suppress images and style sheets, specify the flags parameter as (cdoSuppressImages + cdoSuppressStyleSheets).

Specifying the Header Fields Character Set

A MIME-formatted message can use one character set for the text or HTML body parts and another character set for the message header fields. In this case, the character set for the header fields must be explicitly set so that the fields are properly encoded using the mechanism defined by RFC 1522.

The following example demonstrates how to explicitly set the character set for the message header fields to iso-2022-jp, whereas the explicit character set for an included html body part is iso-8859-9:

[Visual Basic]

```
' Reference to Microsoft ActiveX Data Objects 2.5 Library
' Reference to Microsoft CDO for Exchange 2000 Server
Library
' ..
Dim iMsg As New CDO.Message
With iMsg
  .From = """[Japanese Unicode characters]""
<sender@microsoft.com>"
  .To = """[Japanese Unicode characters]""
<recipient@microsoft.com>"
  .Subject = "[Japanese Unicode characters]"

  ' The character set is iso-8859-1 for the HTML in
included Web page
  ' and for the text/plain alternative message text
  .CreateMHTMLBody "http://www.microsoft.com"

  ' The next line sets the character set for the message
header fields
  ' to iso-2022-jp.
  .BodyPart.Charset = "iso-2022-jp"
  .Send
End With
```

[C++,IDL]

```
#import "c:\program files\common
files\system\ado\msado15.dll" no_namespace
#import "c:\program files\common files\microsoft
shared\cdo\cdoex.dll" no_namespace
// ...
IMessagePtr iMsg(__uuidof(Message));
```

```cpp
iMsg->To   = """[Japanese Unicode characters]""
<sender@microsoft.com>";
iMsg->From = """[Japanese Unicode characters]""
<recipient@microsoft.com>";
iMsg->Subject = "[Japanese Unicode characters]";
   /*
   ** The character set is iso-8859-1 for the HTML in the
   ** included Web page and for the text/plain alternative
message text
   */
iMsg->CreateMHTMLBody("http://
www.microsoft.com",cdoSuppressNone,"","");

   /*
   ** Now, set the character set for the message header
fields
   ** so that they are encoded properly (RFC 1522).
   */
IBodyPartPtr iBp;
iBp = iMsg;
iBp->Charset = "iso-2022-jp";

iMsg->Send();
```

[VBScript]

```vbscript
Dim iMsg
Set iMsg = CreateObject("CDO.Message")
With iMsg
   .From    = """[Japanese Unicode characters]""
<sender@microsoft.com>"
   .To      = """[Japanese Unicode characters]""
<recipient@microsoft.com>"
   .Subject = "[Japanese Unicode characters]"

   ' The character set is iso-8859-1 for the HTML in
included Web page
   ' and for the text/plain alternative message text
   .CreateMHTMLBody "http://www.microsoft.com"

   ' This next line sets the character set for the message
header fields
   ' to iso-2022-jp.
   .BodyPart.Charset = "iso-2022-jp"
   .Send
End With
```

Sending and Posting Messages

To send a message, use the IMessage.Send method. Before you can send a message, you must set at least one recipient address and one sender address. You can use the To and From properties for the Message object to do so.

To post a message, use the IMessage.Post method. Before you can post a message, you must set at least the From, Subject, and Newsgroups message header fields for the object. You can use either the IMessage.From, IMessage.Subject, and IMessage.Newsgroups properties for the Message object.

The following example demonstrates these steps using IMessage interface properties and fields in the IMessage.Fields collection:

[Visual Basic]

```
' Reference to Microsoft ActiveX Data Objects 2.5 Library
' Reference to Microsoft CDO for Exchange 2000 Server
Library
' ..
Dim iMsg As New CDO.Message
' configure object here if necessary
With iMsg
   .From = "Someone@Somewhere.microsoft.com"
   .CC = "Another@microsoft.com"
   .Subject = "Your lights are on, but no one is home"
   .TextBody = "You left your lights on this morning."
   .Newsgroups = "somewhere.general"
   .Post
   .Newsgroups = ""
   .To = "SomeoneElse@Somewhere.microsoft.com"
   .Fields(cdoDispositionNotificationTo) =
"Someone@somewhere.microsoft.com"
   .Fields.Update
   .Send
End With

Set iMsg = Nothing
```

[C++,IDL]

```
#import "c:\program files\common
files\system\ado\msado15.dll" no_namespace
#import "c:\program files\common files\microsoft
shared\cdo\cdoex.dll" no_namespace
// ...
IMessagePtr iMsg(__uuidof(Message));
iMsg->From    = "Someone@Somewhere.microsoft.com";
iMsg->CC      = "Another@microsoft.com";
iMsg->Subject = "Your lights are on, but no one is home";
```

```cpp
iMsg->TextBody = "You left your lights on this morning.";
iMsg->Newsgroups = "somewhere.general";
iMsg->Post();
iMsg->Newsgroups = "";
iMsg->To         = "SomeoneElse@Somewhere.microsoft.com";
iMsg->Fields->Item[cdoDispositionNotificationTo]->Value =
_variant_t("someone@somewhere.microsoft.com");
iMsg->Fields->Update();
iMsg->Send();
iMsg = NULL;
```

[VBScript]

```
Dim iMsg
Set iMsg = CreateObject("CDO.Message")
' configure object here if necessary
With iMsg
    .From     = "Someone@Somewhere.microsoft.com"
    .CC       = "another@microsoft.com"
    .Subject  = "Your lights are on, but no one is home"
    .TextBody = "You left your lights on this morning."
    .Newsgroups = "somewhere.general"
    .Post

    .Newsgroups = ""
    .To       = "SomeoneElse@Somewhere.microsoft.com"
    .Fields(cdoDispositionNotificationTo) =
"someone@somewhere.microsoft.com"
    .Fields.Update
    .Send
End With

Set iMsg = Nothing
```

The mechanism for sending or posting messages is controlled through configuration settings associated with the object. For more information, see Configuring the Message Object.

Sending Using Exchange

When sending mail by using Microsoft Exchange 2000 Server, CDO uses the Exchange Mail Submission URI for the user to transmit the message. This URI is available from the urn:schemas:httpmail:sendmsg property for the user's root private mailbox folder. When sending a message using Exchange, an OLE DB provider is used.

A special set of configuration properties can be set when sending messages using Exchange. Each property in the following table is within the *http://schemas.microsoft.com/cdo/configuration/ namespace,* unless denoted otherwise.

TABLE 18-4 *Special Configuration Properties for Sending Messages Using Exchange*

Property Name	Description
mailboxurl	The URL to the user's Exchange mailbox. This URL can be in either file: or http: URL scheme format. If the property is not set, CDO looks up the user's mailbox URL using Active Directory and the user principle name (UPN) in the sendusername property.
activeconnection	An open ADO Connection object to the user's mailbox. If this property is set, the connection is used to look up the user's mail submission URI, to bind to the user's mail submission URI, and transmit the message. Set this property if you do not want a currently bound Message object to rebind to the user's mailbox when sending a message using Exchange. When messages are sent using Exchange, CDO normally binds to the user's mailbox, and the current DataSource binding is changed.
urlsource	What source the URL in the mailboxurl property is set to. Currently, the only supported value is cdoExchangeMailboxURL, which is the default.
sendusername	The user's user principle name. For example, mailto:user1@domain.tld or user1@domain.tld.
sendpassword	The user's password.

The following examples demonstrate sending messages using Exchange:

[VBScript]

```
' Assume constants have been imported into scripting host.
' For example,
' <reference object="adodb.record"/>
' <reference object="cdo.message"/>
' when using Windows Scripting Host

Sub SendMailUsingExchange(sMailboxURL, sTo, sFrom, sSubject, sText)

  ' Assume type information has been imported into the scripting host.
  ' e.g. <reference object="CDO.Message"/> in .wsf script file.
  Set Msg = CreateObject("CDO.Message")
```

```
   Set Conf = Msg.Configuration

   Conf("http://schemas.microsoft.com/cdo/configuration/
sendusing")  = cdoSendUsingExchange
   Conf("http://schemas.microsoft.com/cdo/configuration/
mailboxurl") = sMailboxURL
   Conf.Fields.Update

   Msg.To       = sTo
   Msg.From     = sFrom
   Msg.Subject  = sSubject
   Msg.TextBody = sText

   Msg.Send

End Sub

Sub SendMailWithConnectionTrans( sMailboxURL, Conn, sTo,
sFrom, sSubject, sText)

   ' Assume type information has been imported into the
scripting host.
   ' e.g. <reference object="CDO.Message"/> in .wsf script
file.

   Set Msg  = CreateObject("CDO.Message")
   Set Conf = CreateObject("CDO.Configuration")
   Set Msg.Configuration = Conf

   Conf("http://schemas.microsoft.com/cdo/configuration/
sendusing")  = cdoSendUsingExchange
   Conf("http://schemas.microsoft.com/cdo/configuration/
mailboxurl") = sMailboxURL
   Conf("http://schemas.microsoft.com/cdo/configuration/
activeconnection") = Conn
   Conf.Fields.Update

   Msg.To       = sTo
   Msg.From     = sFrom
   Msg.Subject  = sSubject
   Msg.TextBody = sText

   Conn.BeginTrans
   Msg.Send
   Conn.CommitTrans

End Sub
```

```
Sub SendMailWithConnection( sMailboxURL, Conn, sTo, sFrom,
sSubject, sText)

  ' Assume type information has been imported into the
scripting host.
  ' e.g. <reference object="CDO.Message"/> in .wsf script
file.

  Set Msg  = CreateObject("CDO.Message")
  Set Conf = CreateObject("CDO.Configuration")
  Set Msg.Configuration = Conf

  Conf("http://schemas.microsoft.com/cdo/configuration/
sendusing")          = cdoSendUsingExchange
  Conf("http://schemas.microsoft.com/cdo/configuration/
mailboxurl")         = sMailboxURL
  Conf("http://schemas.microsoft.com/cdo/configuration/
activeconnection") = Conn
  Conf.Fields.Update

  Msg.To       = sTo
  Msg.From     = sFrom
  Msg.Subject  = sSubject
  Msg.TextBody = sText

  Msg.Send

End Sub
```

Posting Using Exchange

When posting using Microsoft Exchange 2000 Server, CDO uses either the NNTP protocol or posts the message directly to a folder specified in the hardlinklist configuration property.

A special set of configuration properties can be set when posting messages using Exchange. Each property in the following table is within the *http://schemas.microsoft.com/cdo/configuration/namespace*, unless denoted otherwise.

Chapter 18 • Messaging

TABLE 18–5 Special Configuration Properties for Posting Messages Using Exchange

Property Name	Description
http://schemas.microsoft.com/exchange/hardlinklist	An array of URLs that identify public folders in which to post the message. Currently, only one URL can be set in the array. If set, the Newsgroups property is ignored, and an OLE DB provider is used to post the message directly to the public folder. To avoid rebinding the object's data source, specify an open Connection object to use when posting in the activeconnection property.
activeconnection	An open ADO Connection object to the public store in which the folder specified in the hardlinklist property resided. If this property is set, the connection is used to post the message to the public folder. You set this property if you do not want a currently bound Message object to rebind to the folder when posting. Normally, when messages are posted using Exchange to the folders in the hardlinklist property, CDO binds to the folder x, and the current DataSource binding for the object is therefore changed.
postusername	The user's UPN—for example, mailto:user1@domain.tld or user1@domain.tld. This username is used along with the password to post messages directly to folders on remote Exchange servers.
postpassword	The user's password.

The following examples demonstrate posting messages using Exchange directly to a particular folder:

[VBScript]

```
Sub PostToFolderUsingExchange(sURL, sMailboxURL, sFrom, sSubject, sText)

  ' Assume type information has been imported into the scripting host.
  ' e.g. <reference object="CDO.Message"/> in .wsf script file.
  Set Msg = CreateObject("CDO.Message")
  Set conf = CreateObject("CDO.Configuration")
  Set Msg.Configuration = Conf

  With Conf.Fields
    .Item("http://schemas.microsoft.com/cdo/configuration/postusing")   = cdoPostUsingExchange
    .Item("http://schemas.microsoft.com/cdo/configuration/mailboxurl") = sMailboxURL
```

```
        .Item("http://schemas.microsoft.com/exchange/hardlinklist")
             = Array(sURL)
        .Update
    End With
    With Msg
        .From     = sFrom
        .Subject  = sSubject
        .TextBody = sText
        .Post
    End With

End Sub
```

Replying to Messages

You can easily reply to a message using the IMessage.Reply or IMessage.ReplyAll methods. These methods mimic the behavior of email programs such as Microsoft Outlook.

Both methods return a new Message object reference. The difference in the two methods is that the ReplyAll method retains the original message's CC line in the new message. You must set the From property in the new message before you send the message.

If the *http://schemas.microsoft.com/cdo/configuration/usemessageresponsetext* field is set to True (VARIANT_TRUE), the TextBody of the reply method contains standard reply formatting—for example,

```
----Original Message----
From: "A Person" <person@microsoft.com>
Sent:  Sat, 23 Jan 1998 12:34:34 -0800
To:   "Another" <another@microsoft.com>
Subject: See this attached message

(body of the message here)
```

This message response text is localized into the language specified by using the *http://schemas.microsoft.com/cdo/configuration/languagecode* field in the Configuration object.

The Reply method puts the sender of the original message in the To property of the new message, but removes all other recipients and any attachments. If the message contains a ReplyTo field, the Reply method sets the IMessage.To property to this ReplyTo field; otherwise, it sets the To property to the From field.

The ReplyAll method fills in the To line and removes any attachments as does the Reply method, but retains any recipients in the appropriate To or CC properties.

Chapter 18 • Messaging

The following example illustrates the code used:

[Visual Basic]

```
' Reference to Microsoft ActiveX Data Objects 2.5 Library
' Reference to Microsoft CDO for Exchange 2000 Server
Library
' ..
Sub ReplyToMessage(iMsg As CDO.Message)

    ' Assume we want to reply to all recipients.
    Dim iMsg2 As CDO.Message
    Set iMsg2 = iMsg.ReplyAll
    '   or Set iMsg2 = iMsg.Reply
    '       Set iMsg2 = iMsg.PostReply
    ' ..configure message object.
    '    Add any other recipients.
    iMsg2.TextBody = "I agree...please proceed." & vbCrLf &
iMsg2.TextBody
    iMsg2.Send

End Sub
```

[C++,IDL]

```
#import "c:\program files\common
files\system\ado\msado15.dll" no_namespace
#import "c:\program files\common files\microsoft
shared\cdo\cdoex.dll" no_namespace

void replyToMessage( IMessagePtr& iMsg ) {

    // want to reply all

    IMessagePtr iMsg2;
    iMsg2 = iMsg->ReplyAll();
    // iMsg2 = iMsg->Reply();
    // iMsg2 = iMsg->PostReply();
    //     add any other recipients
    iMsg2->TextBody = "I agree...please proceed." + "\r\n" +
iMsg2->TextBody;

    try {
        iMsg2->Send();
    }
    catch(_com_error e) {
        throw e;
    }
}
```

[VBScript]

```
Dim iDropDir
Dim iMsgs
Dim iMsg

Set iDropDir = CreateObject("CDO.DropDirectory")
Set iMsgs =
iDropDir.GetMessages("c:\Inetpub\mailroot\Drop")
Set iMsg = iMsgs(1)

' want to reply all

Dim iMsg2
Set iMsg2 = iMsg.ReplyAll
' or Set iMsg2 = iMsg.Reply
'     Set iMsg2 = iMsg.PostReply
' ... configure message object
'     add any other recipients
iMsg2.TextBody = "I agree...please proceed." & vbCrLf &
iMsg2.TextBody
iMsg2.Send
```

Forwarding Messages

You can forward an existing message by using the IMessage.Forward method. The Forward method retains all the attachments from the original message, but does not set any recipients on the new message. You must set the To property in the new message before you send the message. The codes used are as follows:

[Visual Basic]

```
' Reference to Microsoft ActiveX Data Objects 2.5 Library
' Reference to Microsoft CDO for Exchange 2000 Server
Library
' ..
Sub ForwardMessage(iMsg As CDO.Message)

    Dim iMsg2 As CDO.Message
    Set iMsg2 = iMsg.Forward
    ' ..configure message object
    '    Add any other recipients
    iMsg2.TextBody = "You missed this:  " & vbCrLf &
iMsg2.TextBody
    iMsg2.Send

End Sub
```

[C++,IDL]

```cpp
#import "c:\program files\common files\system\ado\msado15.dll" no_namespace
#import "c:\program files\common files\microsoft shared\cdo\cdoex.dll" no_namespace

void forwardMessage( IMessagePtr& iMsg ) {

    // want to reply all

    IMessagePtr iMsg2;
    iMsg2 = iMsg->Forward();
    // iMsg2 = iMsg->Reply();
    // iMsg2 = iMsg->PostReply();
    //     add any other recipients
    iMsg2->TextBody = "I agree...please proceed." + "\r\n" + iMsg2->TextBody;

    try {
        iMsg2->Send();
    }
    catch(_com_error e) {
        throw e;
    }
}
```

[VBScript]

```vbscript
Dim iDropDir
Dim iMsgs
Dim iMsg

Set iDropDir = CreateObject("CDO.DropDirectory")
Set iMsgs = iDropDir.GetMessages("c:\\Inetpub\\mailroot\\Drop")
Set iMsg = iMsgs(1)

' want to reply all

Dim iMsg2
Set iMsg2 = iMsg.Forward
' ... configure message object
'     add any other recipients
iMsg2.TextBody = "You missed this: " & vbCrLf & iMsg2.TextBody
iMsg2.Send
```

Extracting Embedded Messages

Use the IDataSource.OpenObject method to extract messages that are contained within other objects, such as Message or BodyPart objects, and move them into another Message object. This method is most useful when you want to extract an embedded message from another Message object's BodyPart hierarchy. The process is analogous to opening files in Microsoft Word: the content in the opened file is copied from the disk into the open application. Embedded messages are contained in body parts with Content-Media-Type set to "message." When you encounter such a message in a body part, you can open it in the following way:

1. Find the BodyPart (IBodyPart interface) object that contains the embedded message. Call the Message object with the embedded message "message A." The urn:schemas:mailheader:content-type (Content-Type) for the body part should contain the "message" media type. The full content-type is normally "message/rfc822" for a fully embedded message (as opposed to partial or external-body subtypes).
2. Create a new instance or use an existing instance of the Message COM class. Use this object to extract and hold the embedded message. Call this object Message B.
3. Using the IDataSource interface on Message B, invoke its IDataSource.OpenObject method, passing the IBodyPart interface retrieved in step 1 as the first argument and the string "IBodyPart" as the second argument. The string "IBodyPart" notifies the implementation that the passed interface reference is of type IBodyPart and therefore to expect a body part content stream to exist in the object.
4. If the call is successful, the entire contents of the embedded message (including all attachments) in Message A are now present in Message B. In effect, Message B is a duplicate of that message.
5. If you want to alter the contents of the embedded message with changes you make in Message B, you simply call the IDataSource.Save method and the changes are copied back to source object from which you opened the message.

The following example illustrates how to extract embedded messages:

[Visual Basic]

```
' Reference to Microsoft ActiveX Data Objects 2.5 Library
' Reference to Microsoft CDO for Exchange 2000 Server
Library
' ..
Function ExtractMessage(iBp As IBodyPart) As Message
    Dim iMsg As New CDO.Message
    Dim iDsrc As IDataSource
```

```
        Set iDsrc = iMsg
        iDsrc.OpenObject iBp, "IBodyPart"
        Set ExtractMessage = iMsg
End Function
```

[C++,IDL]

```
#import "c:\program files\common
files\system\ado\msado15.dll" no_namespace
#import "c:\program files\common files\microsoft
shared\cdo\cdoex.dll" no_namespace
// ...
IMessagePtr ExtractMessage(IBodyPartPtr iBp)
{
      IMessagePtr iMsg(__uuidof(Message));
      IDataSourcePtr iDsrc;
      iDsrc = iMsg;

      try
      {
            iDsrc->OpenObject(iBp,_bstr_t("IBodyPart"));
      }
      catch(_com_error error)
      {
            throw error;
      }
      return iMsg;
}
```

[VBScript]

```
Function ExtractMessage(iBp As IBodyPart) As Message
    Dim iMsg
    Set iMsg = CreateObject("CDO.Message")
    Dim iDsrc
    Set iDsrc = iMsg.DataSource
    iDsrc.OpenObject iBp, "IBodyPart"
    Set ExtractMessage = iMsg
End Function
```

Embedding a Message

You can use the IDataSource.SaveToObject method to "copy" an entire Message object into another Message object. This is most useful when you want to embed the message into another as a body part. If you embed Message A into Message B, Message B would then contain message A in its entirety in its MIME hierarchy as a body part with Content-Type "message/rfc822."

To embed one message in another, perform the following steps:

1. Obtain an IMessage object reference on the Message object containing the message you want to embed.
2. Obtain the IDataSource interface on that object.
3. Obtain the IBodyPart object reference on the BodyPart object within the body part hierarchy of the Message object in which you want to embed the message.
4. Call IDataSource.SaveToObject on the first Message object, passing the IBodyPart object reference as the first parameter and the string "IBodyPart" as the second. This step embeds the message and creates a binding between the Message and BodyPart objects.
5. If you make changes to the message, you can save them by reembedding the message. Because the Message and BodyPart objects are currently bound, you need only call IDataSource.Save.

The following is the code used to embed one message into another:

[Visual Basic]

```
' Reference to Microsoft ActiveX Data Objects 2.5 Library
' Reference to Microsoft CDO for Exchange 2000 Server
Library
' ..
Sub EmbedMessage(iMsg As CDO.Message, iBp As IBodyPart)
    Dim iDsrc As IDataSource
    Set iDsrc = iMsg
    iDsrc.SaveToObject iBp, "IBodyPart"
End Sub
```

[C++,IDL]

```
#import "c:\program files\common files\system\ado\msado15.dll" no_namespace
#import "c:\program files\common files\microsoft shared\cdo\cdoex.dll" no_namespace
// ...
void EmbedMessage( IMessagePtr& iMsg, IBodyPartPtr& iBp)
{
    IDataSourcePtr iDsrc;
    iDsrc = iMsg;

    try
    {
        iDsrc->SaveToObject(iBp,_bstr_t("IBodyPart"));
    }
    catch(_com_error error)
```

```
        {
            throw error;
        }
}
```

[VBScript]

```
Sub EmbedMessage(iMsg As CDO.Message, iBp As IBodyPart)
    Dim iDsrc
    Set iDsrc = iMsg.DataSource
    iDsrc.SaveToObject iBp, "IBodyPart"
End Sub
```

Loading Messages from within ADO Stream Objects

To load a serialized message into a CDO Message object from an ADO Stream object, perform the following steps:

1. Retrieve the IDataSource interface on the Message object.
2. Create or otherwise obtain a _Stream object reference on an ADO Stream object.
3. Using the IDataSource interface on the Message object, call OpenObject, passing the _Stream object reference as the first argument and the string "_Stream" as the second.

This example illustrates how to load serialized messages into CDO message objects from an ADO Stream object:

[Visual Basic]

```
' Reference to Microsoft ActiveX Data Objects 2.5 Library
' Reference to Microsoft CDO for Exchange 2000 Server
Library
' ..
Function LoadMessageFromFile(Path As String) As Message
    Dim Stm As New Stream
    Stm.Open
    Stm.LoadFromFile Path
    Dim iMsg As New CDO.Message
    Dim iDsrc As IDataSource
    Set iDsrc = iMsg
    iDsrc.OpenObject Stm, "_Stream"
    Set LoadMessageFromFile = iMsg
End Function
```

[C++,IDL]

```cpp
#import "c:\program files\common files\system\ado\msado15.dll" no_namespace
#import "c:\program files\common files\microsoft shared\cdo\cdoex.dll" no_namespace
// ...
IMessagePtr Load_Message_from_File(_bstr_t path)
{
      /*
      ** This example shows a common use of the ADO Stream
      ** object with CDO, namely, opening a serialized
      ** message from a file on disk and loading it into
      ** a CDO Message object.
      **/

      _StreamPtr  pStm(__uuidof(Stream));
      _variant_t varOptional(DISP_E_PARAMNOTFOUND,VT_ERROR);
      try {
            pStm->raw_Open(varOptional, adModeUnknown, adOpenStreamUnspecified,NULL,NULL);
            pStm->LoadFromFile(path);
      }
      catch(_com_error e)
      {
            throw e;
      }

      IMessagePtr iMsg(__uuidof(Message));
      IDataSourcePtr iDsrc;
      iDsrc = iMsg;

      try {
            iDsrc->OpenObject(pStm,_bstr_t("_Stream"));
      }
      catch(_com_error e)
      {
            throw e;
      }

      // ....

      return iMsg;
}
```

[VBScript]

```vbscript
Function LoadMessageFromFile(Path) As Message
    Dim Stm
    Set Stm = CreateObject("ADODB.Stream")
```

```
        Stm.Open
        Stm.LoadFromFile Path
        Dim iMsg
        Set iMsg = CreateObject("CDO.Message")
        Dim iDsrc
        Set iDsrc = iMsg
        iDsrc.OpenObject Stm, "_Stream"
        Set LoadMessageFromFile = iMsg
End Function
```

Saving Messages into ADO Stream Objects

To save a serialized message from a CDO Message object to an ADO Stream object, perform the following steps:

1. Retrieve the IDataSource interface on the Message object.
2. Create or otherwise obtain a _Stream object reference on an ADO Stream object.
3. Using the IDataSource interface on the Message object, call OpenObject, passing the _Stream object reference as the first argument and the string "_Stream" as the second.

The following example illustrates how to save a serialized message from a CDO Message object to an ADO Stream object:

[**Visual Basic**]

```
' Reference to Microsoft ActiveX Data Objects 2.5 Library
' Reference to Microsoft CDO for Exchange 2000 Server
Library
' ..
Sub SaveMessageToFile(iMsg As CDO.Message, Filepath As
String)
    Dim Stm As New Stream
    Stm.Open
    Stm.Type = adTypeText
    Stm.Charset = "US-ASCII"

    Dim iDsrc As IDataSource
    Set iDsrc = iMsg
    iDsrc.SaveToObject Stm, "_Stream"

    Stm.SaveToFile Filepath, adSaveCreateOverWrite

End Sub
```

[C++,IDL]

```
#import "c:\program files\common files\system\ado\msado15.dll" no_namespace
#import "c:\program files\common files\microsoft shared\cdo\cdoex.dll" no_namespace
// ...
void Save_Message_to_File(IMessagePtr iMsg, bstr_t filename)
{
    /*
    ** This example shows a common use of the ADO Stream
    ** object with CDO, namely, saving a serialized
    ** message to disk using an ADO Stream object.
    **/
    _StreamPtr  pStm(__uuidof(Stream));
    IDataSourcePtr iDsrc;
    iDsrc = iMsg;

    _variant_t varOptional(DISP_E_PARAMNOTFOUND,VT_ERROR);
    pStm->raw_Open(varOptional, adModeUnknown, adOpenStreamUnspecified,NULL,NULL);
    pStm->Type = adTypeText;
    pStm->Charset = "US-ASCII"; // apparently, we need this!
    try
    {
        iDsrc->SaveToObject(pStm,_bstr_t("_Stream"));
    }
    catch(_com_error error)
    {
        throw error;
    }

    try {
        pStm->SaveToFile(filename,adSaveCreateOverWrite);
    }
    catch(_com_error e)
    {
        throw e;
    }
}
```

[VBScript]

```
Sub SaveMessageToFile(iMsg, Filepath)
    Dim Stm
    Set Stm = CreateObject("ADODB.Stream")
```

Chapter 18 • Messaging

```
        Stm.Open
        Stm.Type = adTypeText  ' 2
        Stm.Charset = "US-ASCII"

        Dim iDsrc
        Set iDsrc = iMsg.DataSource
        iDsrc.SaveToObject Stm, "_Stream"

        Stm.SaveToFile Filepath, adSaveCreateOverWrite

End Sub
```

Listing Inbox Contents Using ADO

The example that follows demonstrates how to create a common item listing of a user's inbox. This list, or "view," is normally presented when a user selects a folder in their mailbox that contains messages:

[Visual Basic]

```
' Reference to Microsoft ActiveX Data Objects 2.5 Library
' Reference to Microsoft CDO for Exchange 2000 Server
Library
' ..
Dim Rec    As New ADODB.Record
Dim Rs     As New ADODB.Recordset
Dim strURLInbox As String

strURLMailbox =
"file://.//backofficestorage/microsoft.com/MBX/user1/"
Rec.Open strURLMailbox
sURLInbox = Rec.Fields("urn:schemas:httpmail:inbox")
Rec.Open sURLInbox, Rec.ActiveConnection

Dim strView As String
strView = "select " _
& "  ""DAV:href""" _
& ", ""DAV:content-class""" _
& ", ""urn:schemas:httpmail:datereceived""" _
& ", ""DAV:isfolder""" _
& ", ""DAV:getcontentlength""" _
& ", ""urn:schemas:httpmail:from""" _
& ", ""urn:schemas:httpmail:subject""" _
& ", ""urn:schemas:mailheader:importance""" _
& ", ""urn:schemas:httpmail:hasattachment""" _
& ", ""urn:schemas:httpmail:read""" _
& " from scope ('shallow traversal of """ _
```

Listing Inbox Contents Using ADO

```
    & strURLInbox & """') " _
    & " WHERE ""DAV:isfolder"" = false AND ""DAV:ishidden"" = false" _
    & " ORDER BY ""urn:schemas:httpmail:datereceived"" DESC"

Rs.Open strView, Rec.ActiveConnection

If Rs.RecordCount = 0 Then
  ' no items in inbox
Else
  Rs.MoveFirst
  While Not Rs.EOF
    ' render view data here
      Rs.MoveNext
  Wend
End If
```

NINETEEN

Calendaring and Contacts

Creating Appointments and Meeting Requests

You can add an appointment to your calendar and request that others join you by sending them meeting requests. You add an appointment by creating a CDO Appointment object, setting information about the appointment by using the object, and then saving the item to a folder. You create a meeting request from the Appointment object by using the IAppointment.CreateRequest method. CDO creates a special message within a CalendarMessage object that you then send to attendees to invite them to the appointment.

Adding an Appointment to the Calendar

You can add appointments to a user's personal calendar folder and to a public folder.

To add an appointment to a folder,

1. Create an Appointment object.
2. Set the properties of the appointment. A StartTime is required.
3. Save the appointment to the designated folder by using the Appointment object's IDataSource interface.

The following example shows how to create an appointment and then save it to a specified folder:

[Visual Basic]

```
' Reference to Microsoft ActiveX Data Objects 2.5 Library
' Reference to Microsoft CDO for Exchange 2000 Library
Function CreateAppointment(StartTime As Date, _
```

Chapter 19 • Calendaring and Contacts

```
                            EndTime As Date, _
                            Subject As String, _
                            Location As String, _
                            TextBody As String, _
                            iMbx As IMailbox) As
Appointment

    Dim iAppt      As New Appointment
    Dim Conn       As New ADODB.Connection
    Conn.Provider = "ExOLEDB.DataSource"

    'Set the appointment properties
    With iAppt
        .StartTime = StartTime
        .EndTime = EndTime
        .Subject = Subject
        .Location = Location
        .TextBody = TextBody
        'Save the appointment
        Conn.Open iMbx.BaseFolder
        .DataSource.SaveToContainer iMbx.Calendar, Conn
    End With

    Set CreateAppointment = iAppt
End Function
```

[C++]

```
/*

Assume that the following paths are in your
INCLUDE path.
%CommonProgramFiles%\system\ado
%CommonProgramFiles%\microsoft shared\cdo
*/

#import <msado15.dll> no_namespace
#import <cdoex.dll> no_namespace
#include <iostream.h>

IAppointmentPtr CreateAppointment(DATE startTime, DATE
endTime, bstr_t subject, bstr_t location, bstr_t textbody,
const IMailboxPtr& iMbx) {

    IAppointmentPtr   iAppt(__uuidof(Appointment));
    _ConnectionPtr    Conn(__uuidof(Connection));
    IDataSourcePtr    iDsrc;

    Conn->Provider = "ExOLEDB.DataSource";

    try {
```

```
    //Set the appointment properties
    iAppt->StartTime = startTime;
    iAppt->EndTime   = endTime;
    iAppt->Subject   = subject;
    iAppt->Location  = location;
    iAppt->TextBody  = textbody;
    //Save the appointment
    iDsrc = iAppt;

    Conn->Open(iMbx->BaseFolder, bstr_t() , bstr_t(), -
1);
    cout << "save to container here" << endl;
    iDsrc->SaveToContainer(iMbx->Calendar, Conn,
adModeReadWrite, adCreateNonCollection, adOpenSource,
bstr_t(), bstr_t() );

    }
    catch(_com_error e) {
        cout << "Error setting props on appointment??" <<
endl;
        throw e;
    }
    return iAppt;
}
```

Sending a Meeting Request

A meeting request is a message sent by the meeting organizer to invite other users to a meeting. A meeting request contains a description of the meeting, including the start time, end time, and location. CDO creates a meeting request from an Appointment object by using the IAppointment.CreateRequest method.

To send a meeting request,

1. Create or open an Appointment object.
2. Add attendees to the meeting by adding Attendee objects to the Appointment's Attendees collection.
3. Save the Appointment to the organizer's calendar (optional).
4. Create a CalendarMessage object using the IAppointment.CreateRequest method.
5. Send the message requesting that the users attend the meeting.

The following example shows how to add attendees to an appointment and send a meeting request to the specified users:

   [Visual Basic]

```
' Reference to Microsoft ActiveX Data Objects 2.5 Library
' Reference to Microsoft CDO for Exchange 2000 Library
```

Chapter 19 • **Calendaring and Contacts**

```
Sub SendMeetingRequest(iAppt As CDO.Appointment, _
                      iMbx As IMailbox, _
                      strAttnMandatory() As String, _
                      strAttnOptional() As String)

    Dim iCalMsg     As CalendarMessage
    Dim Config      As New Configuration
    Dim iAttendee   As New Attendee
    Dim iPers       As CDO.Person

    'Set the configuration fields
    Set iPers = iMbx
    Config(cdoSendEmailAddress) = iPers.Email
    Config(cdoMailboxURL) = iMbx.BaseFolder
    Config.Fields.Update

    With iAppt
        .Configuration = Config

        'Add attendees
        Dim I As Long
        For I = LBound(strAttnMandatory) To UBound(strAttnMandatory)
            Debug.Print "Mandatory Attendee Email:" & strAttnMandatory(I)
            Set iAttendee = .Attendees.Add
            iAttendee.Address = CStr(strAttnMandatory(I))
            iAttendee.Role = cdoRequiredParticipant
        Next I

        For I = LBound(strAttnOptional) To UBound(strAttnOptional)
            Debug.Print "Optional Attendee Email:" & strAttnOptional(I)
            Set iAttendee = .Attendees.Add
            iAttendee.Address = CStr(strAttnOptional(I))
            iAttendee.Role = cdoOptionalParticipant
        Next I


        'Create the calendar message and send it
        Set iCalMsg = .CreateRequest

        'Save these changes to the appointment
        .DataSource.Save

        iCalMsg.Message.Send
    End With

End Sub
```

Creating Appointments and Meeting Requests

[C++]

```cpp
/*
 Assume that the following paths are in your
 INCLUDE path.
 %CommonProgramFiles%\system\ado
 %CommonProgramFiles%\microsoft shared\cdo
*/

#import <msado15.dll> no_namespace
#import <cdoex.dll> no_namespace
#include <iostream.h>
#include <vector>
using namespace std;

void sendMeetingRequest(
                IAppointmentPtr& iAppt,
                IMailboxPtr& iMbx,
                vector<bstr_t>& AttnMand,
                vector<bstr_t>& AttnOpt
                ) {

    ICalendarMessagePtr iCalMsg(__uuidof(CalendarMessage));
    IConfigurationPtr   iConf(__uuidof(Configuration));
    IAttendeePtr        iAttn;
    IPersonPtr          iPer;

    try {
        iPer = iMbx;
    }
    catch(_com_error e ) {
        cerr << "Invalid or unbound Person object reference passed. " << endl;
        _com_issue_error(E_INVALIDARG);
    }

    iConf->Fields->Item[cdoSendEmailAddress]->Value = variant_t(iPer->Email);
    iConf->Fields->Item[cdoMailboxURL]->Value = variant_t(iMbx->BaseFolder);
    iConf->Fields->Update();

    iAppt->Configuration = iConf;

    typedef vector<bstr_t>::const_iterator CI;
    for(CI p = AttnMand.begin(); p != AttnMand.end(); p++) {
        iAttn = iAppt->Attendees->Add(bstr_t());
        iAttn->Address = _bstr_t(*p);
        iAttn->Role = cdoRequiredParticipant;
        cout << "Added " << bstr_t(*p) << " as required
```

```
        attendee to meeting" << endl;
      }

      for(p = AttnOpt.begin(); p != AttnOpt.end(); p++) {
         iAttn = iAppt->Attendees->Add(bstr_t());
         iAttn->Address = _bstr_t(*p);
         iAttn->Role = cdoOptionalParticipant;
         cout << "Added " << bstr_t(*p) << " as optional
      attendee to meeting" << endl;
      }

      try {
         iCalMsg = iAppt->CreateRequest();
         iCalMsg->Message->Send();
      }
      catch(_com_error e) {
         cerr << "Error creating and sending request" << endl;
         throw e;
      }

      try {
         iAppt->DataSource->Save();
      }
      catch(_com_error e) {
         cerr <<  "Error saving appointment!" << endl;
         throw e;
      }

   }
```

Note By default, calendar messages are sent by using the SMTP pick-up directory.

ADDRESSING A CALENDAR MESSAGE

You can add attendees to a meeting by using the Attendees collection of the Appointment object. The Attendees collection can contain one or more attendees. You can use the same Attendee object to add each attendee.

When you create a CalendarMessage object requesting a meeting, the message is automatically addressed to each attendee in the Attendees collection:

To add attendees to an appointment,

1. Create an Attendee object.
2. Set the properties of the Attendee object.
3. Add each attendee by using the same Attendee object.

The following example shows how to add attendees to an appointment and then generate a meeting request:

[Visual Basic]

```
Dim iAppt       As New Appointment
Dim iAttendee   As Attendee

'Add a required attendee
Set iAttendee = iAppt.Attendees.Add
iAttendee.Address = "someone@microsoft.com"
iAttendee.Role = cdoRequiredParticipant

'Add an optional attendee
Set iAttendee = iAppt.Attendees.Add
iAttendee.Address = "another@microsoft.com"
iAttendee.Role = cdoOptionalParticipant
' ...
```

[C++]

```
IAppointmentPtr iAppt(__uuidof(Appointment));
IAttendeePtr iAttn;

//Add a required attendee
// Set email address during addition step.
iAttn = iAppt->Attendees->Add(bstr_t(strEmailAddr));
iAttn->Role = cdoRequiredParticipant;
cout << "Attendee email address (MAILTO:): " << iAttn->Address << endl;

//Add an optional attendee
iAttn = iAppt->Attendees->Add(bstr_t());
iAttn->Address = "another@microsoft.com";
iAttn->Role = cdoOptionalParticipant;
// ...
```

CHECKING FREE/BUSY STATUS

Before you send a meeting request, you can check an attendee's calendar to see when the attendee is available. The IAddressee.GetFreeBusy method returns a string of numbers that indicate the attendee's availability for a requested period of time.

Each number in the free/busy string represents an interval of time (every 1/2 hour in this example). Free time returns 0, Tentative returns 1, Busy returns 2, and Out of Office (OOF) returns 3. If appointments overlap, the highest number is returned. If no free/busy data is available for the interval, the value 4 is returned.

Figure 19–1 shows part of an attendee's calendar and the corresponding free/busy string.

To get an attendee's free/busy status for a specific time, you can create an Addressee object and execute the IAddressee.GetFreeBusy method. You

Chapter 19 • Calendaring and Contacts

Monday, July 12

```
8:00  9:00  10:00 11:00 12:00  1:00   2:00   3:00   4:00   5:00   6:00
 |-----|-----|-----|-----|-----|-----|-----|-----|-----|-----|
                   | Tentative |
                         |   Busy   |
```

Tuesday, July 13

```
8:00  9:00  10:00 11:00 12:00  1:00   2:00   3:00   4:00   5:00   6:00
 |-----|-----|-----|-----|-----|-----|-----|-----|-----|-----|
             | Busy |  Tentative  |           |  OOF  |
```

Attendee's calendar

GetFreeBusy (#7/12/1999 8:00:00 AM#, #7/13/1999 6:00:00 PM#, 3C
000000111222200000000000000000000000
000000000002220011000033333

FIGURE 19–1 *Checking free/busy status*

can also get the free/busy status for longer intervals and parse the string to find times the attendee is free.

Note You must first call the IAddressee.CheckName method and resolve the addressee before you can use the IAddressee.GetFreeBusy method.

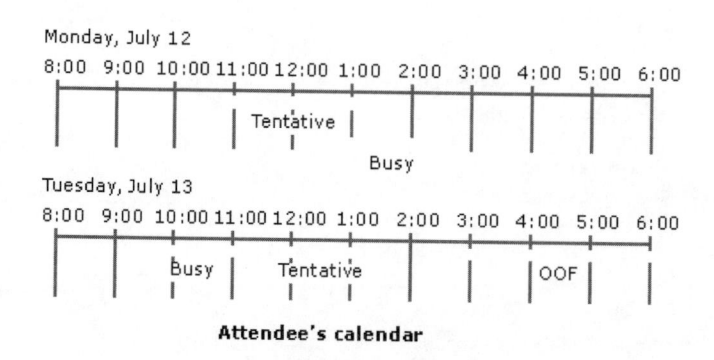

The following example returns the free/busy status of the specified user:

[Visual Basic]

```
' Reference to Microsoft ActiveX Data Objects 2.5 Library
' Reference to Microsoft CDO for Exchange 2000 Library

Function GetFreeBusyString(strUserUPN As String,
dtStartDate As Date, dtEndDate As Date, Interval As
Integer) As String

    Dim iAddr     As New CDO.Addressee
    Dim freebusy  As String
    Dim Info      As New ADSystemInfo

    iAddr.EmailAddress = strUserUPN
    If Not iAddr.CheckName("LDAP://" & Info.DomainDNSName)
Then
        ' handle error
    End If
```

Creating Appointments and Meeting Requests

```
    'Get the free/busy status in Interval minute intervals
from dtStartDate to dtEndDate
    freebusy = iAddr.GetFreeBusy(dtStartDate, dtEndDate,
Interval)
    GetFreeBusyString = freebusy

End Function
```

[C++]

```cpp
/*
Assume that the following paths are in your
INCLUDE path.
%CommonProgramFiles%\system\ado
%CommonProgramFiles%\microsoft shared\cdo
*/

#import <msado15.dll> no_namespace
#import <cdoex.dll> no_namespace
#include <iostream.h>

bstr_t getFreeBusyString( const bstr_t& userUPN, const
bstr_t& domainDNSName, DATE startDate, DATE endDate, long
Interval) {

    IAddresseePtr iAddr(__uuidof(Addressee));

    iAddr->EmailAddress = userUPN;
    if(iAddr->CheckName(bstr_t("LDAP://") + domainDNSName,
bstr_t(), bstr_t()) == VARIANT_FALSE) {
        cerr << "Error looking up name!" << endl;
        _com_issue_error(E_FAIL);
    }

    //Get the free/busy status in Interval minute intervals
from startDate to endDate
    return iAddr->GetFreeBusy(startDate, endDate, Interval,
bstr_t(), bstr_t(), bstr_t(), bstr_t());

}
```

Note An automated process in Microsoft Exchange 2000 Server periodically updates the free/busy status of users. Microsoft Outlook updates the free/busy status of Outlook users. CDO synchronizes the Outlook free/busy cache with free/busy information from CDO clients. The free/busy status is not updated immediately when a meeting is added to a user's calendar. By default, three months' worth of free/busy status is maintained in a system folder in the Web Storage System.

PUBLISHING AN APPOINTMENT

When you publish an appointment, the appointment is available to others without requiring a response from them. For example, you can publish your company's holidays, charity drives, and upcoming conferences.

You can save a published appointment to a public folder or a file, or you can send a published appointment by email. Published appointments have no attendees. To publish an appointment, perform the following steps:

1. Create an Appointment object.
2. Set the properties of the appointment.
3. Create a CalendarMessage object derived from the Appointment object by using the IAppointment.Publish method.
4. Send the CalendarMessage by using the IMessage methods and save the Appointment object by using the IDataSource.SaveToContainer method.

In the following example, an organizer publishes an appointment to the "team" alias and saves it to the TeamCalendar public folder:

[Visual Basic]

```
' Reference to Microsoft ActiveX Data Objects 2.5 Library
' Reference to Microsoft CDO for Exchange 2000 Library

Sub PublishMeetingToFolder(iAppt As CDO.Appointment, _
                           iMbx As IMailbox, _
                           strTeamCalendarFolderURL As String, _
                           strTeamEmail As String)

    Dim iCalMsg      As CalendarMessage
    Dim Config       As New Configuration
    Dim iPer         As CDO.Person
    Dim Conn         As New ADODB.Connection
    Conn.Provider = "ExOLEDB.DataSource"

    'Set the configuration fields
    Set iPer = iMbx
    Config.Fields(cdoSendEmailAddress) = iPer.Email
    Config.Fields(cdoMailboxURL) = iMbx.BaseFolder
    Config.Fields.Update

    With iAppt
        Set .Configuration = Config
        'Publish the appointment

        ' Get CalendarMessage and send to the team.
        Set iCalMsg = .Publish
        iCalMsg.Message.To = strTeamEmail
        iCalMsg.Message.Send
```

Creating Appointments and Meeting Requests

```
        'Save the appointment to a public folder
        Conn.Open strTeamCalendarFolderURL
        .DataSource.SaveToContainer
strTeamCalendarFolderURL, Conn

    End With

End Sub
```

   [C++]

```cpp
/*
 Assume that the following paths are in your
 INCLUDE path.
 %CommonProgramFiles%\system\ado
 %CommonProgramFiles%\microsoft shared\cdo
*/

#import <msado15.dll> no_namespace
#import <cdoex.dll> no_namespace
#include <iostream.h>

void publishAppointmentToFolder(
                    const IAppointmentPtr& iAppt,
                    const IMailboxPtr& iMbx,
                    const bstr_t&
strTeamCalendarFolderURL,
                    const bstr_t& strTeamEmail)
{

    ICalendarMessagePtr iCalMsg;
    IConfigurationPtr   iConf(__uuidof(Configuration));
    IPersonPtr          iPer;
    _ConnectionPtr      Conn(__uuidof(Connection));

    Conn->Provider = "ExOLEDB.DataSource";

    try {
        iPer = iMbx;
    }
    catch(_com_error e ) {
        cerr << "Invalid or unbound Person object reference
passed. " << endl;
        _com_issue_error(E_INVALIDARG);
    }

    iConf->Fields->Item[cdoSendEmailAddress]->Value =
variant_t(iPer->Email);
    iConf->Fields->Item[cdoMailboxURL]->Value =
```

```
   variant_t(iMbx->BaseFolder);
iConf->Fields->Update();

iAppt->Configuration = iConf;

try {
   iCalMsg = iAppt->Publish();
   iCalMsg->Message->To = strTeamEmail;
   iCalMsg->Message->Send();

   // Save the appointment to a public folder
}
catch(_com_error e) {
   cerr << "Failed to send email to " << strTeamEmail << endl;
   throw e;
}

try {
    Conn->Open(strTeamCalendarFolderURL, bstr_t(), bstr_t(), -1);
    iAppt->DataSource->SaveToContainer(strTeamCalendarFolderURL,
                              Conn,
                              adModeReadWrite,
                              adCreateNonCollection,
                              adOpenSource,
                              bstr_t(),
                              bstr_t());
}
catch(_com_error e) {
   cerr << "Failed to save appointment to folder at URL: " << strTeamCalendarFolderURL << endl;
   throw e;
}

}
```

Creating Recurring Appointments and Meetings

Recurring appointments and meetings occur more than once and follow a pattern in time. For example, a department meeting on the first Tuesday of each month can be defined as a recurring meeting.

In CDO, a single Appointment object and one or more Recurrence-Pattern objects represent a recurring appointment or meeting. The Appointment object defines the first appointment or meeting, and the Recurrence-Pattern objects define the pattern for additional appointments

Creating Appointments and Meeting Requests 437

or meetings. You can also specify modifications to the recurring meeting pattern by using one or more Exception objects:

1. Create an Appointment object.
2. Set the properties of the first appointment or meeting.
3. Create a RecurrencePattern object and add it to the Appointment's RecurrencePatterns collection. You do this by using the IRecurrence Patterns.Add method.
4. Set the properties of the RecurrencePattern object to create the desired recurrence pattern.
5. For meetings, create one or more Attendee objects and specify the attendees.
6. For meetings, create a CalendarMessage object by using the IAppointment.CreateRequest method and send the message.
7. Save the appointment to the organizer's calendar (optional).

The following example creates a recurring meeting and then invites the specified attendees to the meeting:

[Visual Basic]

```
' Reference to Microsoft ActiveX Data Objects 2.5 Library
' Reference to Microsoft CDO for Exchange 2000 Library

Sub CreateRecurringMeeting(iAppt As CDO.Appointment, _
                           Frequency As CDO.CdoFrequency, _
                           Interval As Long, _
                           dtEndDate As Date, _
                           iMbx As IMailbox, _
                           strAttnMandatory() As String, _
                           strAttnOptional() As String)

    Dim Config      As New Configuration
    Dim RRULE       As IRecurrencePattern
    Dim iCalMsg     As CalendarMessage
    Dim iAttendee   As New Attendee
    Dim CalendarURL As String
    Dim iPer        As CDO.Person
    Dim Conn        As New ADODB.Connection

    Conn.Provider = "ExOLEDB.DataSource"


    'Set the configuration fields
    Set iPer = iMbx
    Config.Fields(cdoSendEmailAddress) = iPer.Email
    Config.Fields(CDO.cdoMailboxURL) = iMbx.BaseFolder
    Config.Fields.Update
```

```
    With iAppt
        .Configuration = Config

        'Create the RecurrencePattern object
        Set RRULE = .RecurrencePatterns.Add("Add")

        'Define the recurrence pattern
        ' Frequency, such as cdoWeekly or cdoDaily
        RRULE.Frequency = Frequency
        ' Interval, for example "2"
        RRULE.Interval = Interval
        ' The pattern end date.
        RRULE.PatternEndDate = dtEndDate

        ' Add attendees
        Dim I As Long
        For I = LBound(strAttnMandatory) To UBound(strAttnMandatory)
            Set iAttendee = .Attendees.Add
            iAttendee.Address = CStr(strAttnMandatory(I))
            iAttendee.Role = cdoRequiredParticipant
        Next I

        For I = LBound(strAttnOptional) To UBound(strAttnOptional)
            Set iAttendee = .Attendees.Add
            iAttendee.Address = CStr(strAttnOptional(I))
            iAttendee.Role = cdoOptionalParticipant
        Next I


        ' Create Meeting Request Message and Send (to attendees).
        Set iCalMsg = .CreateRequest

        'Save the appointment to the organizer's calendar
        Conn.Open iMbx.BaseFolder
        .DataSource.SaveToContainer iMbx.Calendar, Conn

        iCalMsg.Message.Send
    End With
End Sub
```

   [C++]

```
/*
Assume that the following paths are in your
INCLUDE or Directories path:
%CommonProgramFiles%\system\ado
%CommonProgramFiles%\microsoft shared\cdo
```

```cpp
*/

#import <msado15.dll> no_namespace
#import <cdoex.dll> no_namespace
#include <iostream.h>
#include <vector>
using namespace std;

void createRecurringMeeting(
                    IAppointmentPtr& iAppt,
                    IMailboxPtr& iMbx,
                    CdoFrequency Frequency,
                    long Interval,
                    DATE endDate,
                    vector<bstr_t>& AttnMand,
                    vector<bstr_t>& AttnOpt
                    )
{

    if(iAppt == NULL || iMbx == NULL)
        _com_issue_error(E_INVALIDARG);

    IConfigurationPtr iConf(__uuidof(Configuration));
    _ConnectionPtr Conn(__uuidof(Connection));
    IRecurrencePatternPtr RRULE;
    ICalendarMessagePtr iCalMsg;
    IAttendeePtr iAttn;
    IPersonPtr   iPer;

     Conn->Provider = "ExOLEDB.DataSource";

    try {
        iPer = iMbx;
    }
    catch(_com_error e ) {
        cerr << "Invalid or unbound Person object reference passed." << endl;
        _com_issue_error(E_INVALIDARG);
    }

    iConf->Fields->Item[cdoSendEmailAddress]->Value = variant_t(iPer->Email);
    iConf->Fields->Item[cdoMailboxURL]->Value = variant_t(iMbx->BaseFolder);
    iConf->Fields->Update();

    iAppt->Configuration = iConf;

     //Create the RecurrencePattern object
     RRULE = iAppt->RecurrencePatterns->Add("Add");
```

Chapter 19 • Calendaring and Contacts

```cpp
   /*
    Define the recurrence pattern
      Frequency, such as cdoWeekly or cdoDaily
    */
   RRULE->Frequency = Frequency;

   // Interval, for example "2"
   RRULE->Interval = Interval;

   // The pattern end date.
   RRULE->PatternEndDate = endDate;

   typedef vector<bstr_t>::const_iterator CI;
   for(CI p = AttnMand.begin(); p != AttnMand.end(); p++) {
      iAttn = iAppt->Attendees->Add(bstr_t());
      iAttn->Address = _bstr_t(*p);
      iAttn->Role = cdoRequiredParticipant;
      cout << "Added " << bstr_t(*p) << " as required
attendee to meeting." << endl;
   }

   for(p = AttnOpt.begin(); p != AttnOpt.end(); p++) {
      iAttn = iAppt->Attendees->Add(bstr_t());
      iAttn->Address = _bstr_t(*p);
      iAttn->Role = cdoOptionalParticipant;
      cout << "Added " << bstr_t(*p) << " as optional
attendee to meeting." << endl;
   }

   try {
      iCalMsg = iAppt->CreateRequest();
   }
   catch(_com_error e) {
      cerr << "Error creating the request" << endl;
      throw e;
   }

   //Save the appointment to the organizer's calendar
   try {
      Conn->Open(iMbx->BaseFolder, bstr_t(), bstr_t(), -1);
      iAppt->DataSource->SaveToContainer(
                     iMbx->Calendar,
                     Conn,
                     adModeReadWrite,
                     adCreateNonCollection,
                     adOpenSource,
                     bstr_t(),
                     bstr_t());
   }
```

```
   catch(_com_error e) {
      cerr << "Error saving recurring appointment to user's
calendar folder." << endl;
      throw e;
   }

   try {
      iCalMsg->Message->Send();
   }
   catch(_com_error e) {
      cerr << "Error sending calendar message." << endl;
      throw e;
   }

}
```

SPECIFYING EXCEPTIONS TO RECURRING APPOINTMENTS AND MEETINGS

Exceptions are specific appointments that are added, modified, or deleted from the pattern of a recurring appointment or meeting. For example, if a recurring pattern generates a meeting that falls on a holiday, you can define an exception to that one instance of the recurring pattern.

CDO uses IRecurrencePattern objects and IException objects to define exceptions to recurring appointments and meetings. The following table shows how each object can be used:

TABLE 19-1 *Objects to Define Exceptions to Recurring Appointments and Meetings*

Object	Type	Action
IRecurrencePattern	Add	Adds a set of instances.
IRecurrencePattern	Delete	Deletes a set of instances.
IException	Add	Adds a single instance.
IException	Delete	Deletes a single instance.
IException	Modify	Changes the properties of one or more instances (equivalent to an Outlook exception).

To define an exception to the recurring pattern,

1. Create the recurring appointment or meeting.
2. Create an Exception object by using the Add method on the Exceptions collection of the Appointment object, or create a RecurrencePattern object by using the Add method on the RecurrencePatterns collection.
3. Set the properties of the Exception or RecurrencePattern object to specify appointment instances that are being added, deleted, or modified.

Chapter 19 • Calendaring and Contacts

The following example creates a recurring meeting, deletes the meeting instance on November 26, 2000, and adds a meeting instance on November 29, 2000.

[Visual Basic]

```vb
' Reference to Microsoft ActiveX Data Objects 2.5 Library
' Reference to Microsoft CDO for Exchange 2000 Library

Function CreateApptWithException(iMbx As IMailbox) As CDO.Appointment

    Dim iAppt       As New Appointment
    Dim Config      As New Configuration
    Dim RRULE       As IRecurrencePattern
    Dim iCalMsg     As CalendarMessage
    Dim EXDATE      As IException
    Dim RDATE       As IException
    Dim Conn        As New ADODB.Connection
    Conn.Provider = "ExOLEDB.DataSource"

    With iAppt
        'Set the first appointment properties
        .StartTime = Now
        .EndTime = DateAdd("n", 60, Now)   ' 60 minute appointment starting now
        .Subject = "Read the MS Exchange SDK Docs."
        .Location = "My Office"

        'Create the RecurrencePattern object
        Set RRULE = .RecurrencePatterns.Add("Add")

        'Define the recurrence pattern
        RRULE.Frequency = cdoDaily   'use a daily pattern
        RRULE.Interval = 1   'every day
        RRULE.PatternEndDate = DateAdd("d", 7, Now) 'the last appointment, 7 days from now at this time.

        'Delete an appointment instance
        Set EXDATE = .Exceptions.Add("Delete")
        'The ID is the start time of the instance being deleted
        EXDATE.RecurrenceID = DateAdd("d", 7, Now) ' Except the 7th day...reschedule.

        'Add an appointment instance
        Set RDATE = .Exceptions.Add("Add")
        ' Start 2 hours later on the seventh day
        RDATE.StartTime = DateAdd("n", -60, DateAdd("d", 7, Now))
```

```
        RDATE.EndTime = DateAdd("d", 7, Now)

        'Save the appointment to the organizer's calendar
        Conn.Open iMbx.BaseFolder
        .DataSource.SaveToContainer iMbx.Calendar, Conn
    End With
    Set CreateApptWithException = iAppt

End Function
```

USING CALENDAR FOLDER QUERY

The Web Storage System expands recurring appointments and meetings when the calendar folder is queried through an SQL statement. The instances are expanded within the range specified by the query. For example, if you query a calendar folder for all entries in the month of November, the Web Storage System creates the November instances of all recurring appointments and meetings. Although appointments and meetings can be stored in any folder, the Web Storage System expands only recurring appointments and meetings that are stored in calendar folders.

To expand recurring appointments, query the calendar folder by using a SELECT statement. Use the WHERE clause of the SELECT statement to specify the range of dates that are expanded with each recurring appointment. The dates must be adjusted from local time to UTC (because dates are stored in UTC), and then converted to International Standards Organization (ISO) format, and finally cast to the DateTime data type, as shown in the following query:

```
SELECT "DAV:href",
"urn:schemas:calendar:dtend","urn:schemas:calendar:dtstart"
FROM scope('shallow traversal of """ & CalendarURL & """')
WHERE ("urn:schemas:calendar:dtstart" >= CAST("1999-10-
25T16:00:00Z" as 'dateTime'))
AND ("urn:schemas:calendar:dtend" <= CAST("1999-10-
30T01:00:00Z" as 'dateTime'))
```

The example that follows shows how to query a calendar for a specific user. It prints the subject, start time, and end time of each appointment and meeting found. The example also includes functions to convert time zones and ISO format; you must change the time-zone constants to the appropriate values for your clients. The codes used are as follows:

[Visual Basic]

```
' Reference to Microsoft ActiveX Data Objects 2.5 Library
' Reference to Microsoft CDO for Exchange 2000 Library

Function QueryCalendarFolder(dtStartDate As Date, dtEndDate
As Date, iMbx As IMailbox) As ADODB.Recordset
```

Chapter 19 • Calendaring and Contacts

```
    Dim Rs          As New ADODB.Recordset
    Dim Rec         As New ADODB.Record
    Dim Conn        As New ADODB.Connection

    'Open the record set for the items in the calendar
folder
    Conn.Provider = "ExOLEDB.DataSource"
    Conn.Open iMbx.Calendar
    Rec.Open iMbx.Calendar, Conn
    Set Rs.ActiveConnection = Rec.ActiveConnection

    Rs.Source = "SELECT """DAV:href""", " & _
                    " ""urn:schemas:calendar:dtstart""," & _
                    " ""urn:schemas:calendar:dtend""," & _
                    " ""urn:schemas:calendar:duration""," & _
                    " ""urn:schemas:httpmail:subject""", " & _
                    "
""urn:schemas:calendar:instancetype""," & _
                    " ""urn:schemas:calendar:busystatus""
" & _
                " FROM scope('shallow traversal of """ & iMbx.Calendar & """')" & _
                " WHERE (""urn:schemas:calendar:dtstart"" >= CAST(""" & GetISODate(ConvertDate(dtStartDate)) & """ as 'dateTime')) AND " & _
                    "(""urn:schemas:calendar:dtend"" <= CAST(""" & GetISODate(ConvertDate(dtEndDate)) & """ as 'dateTime'))"

    Rs.Open

    Set QueryCalendarFolder = Rs
End Function

Function GetISODate(dtDate As Date)
    GetISODate = Format(CStr(dtDate), "yyyy-mm-ddThh:mm:ssZ")
End Function

Function ConvertDate(dtSrc As Date, _
                                Optional dstTzId As CdoTimeZoneId = cdoPacific, _
                                Optional srcTzId As CdoTimeZoneId = cdoPacific, _
                                Optional srcTz As String
```

```
                                    Optional dstTz As String
= "") As Date

    Dim obAppt      As New CDO.Appointment
    Dim obConfig    As New CDO.Configuration
    Dim bTz         As Boolean

    obAppt.Configuration = obConfig

    bTz = ((srcTz <> "") Or (dstTz <> ""))

    If (Not bTz) Then
        obConfig.Fields(cdoTimeZoneIDURN) = srcTzId
    Else
        obConfig.Fields(cdoTimeZoneURN) = srcTz
    End If
    obConfig.Fields.Update

    obAppt.StartTime = dtSrc

    If (Not bTz) Then
        obConfig.Fields(cdoTimeZoneIDURN) = dstTzId
    Else
        obConfig.Fields(cdoTimeZoneURN) = dstTz
    End If
    obConfig.Fields.Update

    ConvertDate = obAppt.StartTime

End Function
```

Adding Attachments to Appointments and Meetings

You can add attachments to appointments and meetings. For example, you could attach an image of a map to a meeting to show where the meeting is located. Attachments are added by using the Attachments collection of the Appointment object. Attachments are saved with the Appointment object in the Web Storage System.

To add attachments to appointments and meetings,

1. Create the Appointment object and set its properties.
2. Create the attachment body part by calling the Add method on the attachments collection.
3. Set the content-type and content-transfer encoding fields of the body part.
4. Get the default stream from the attachment body part.

5. Load the file being attached into the default stream, and save it back to the attachment body part.
6. For meetings, create a calendar message, add attendees, and send the meeting request.
7. Save the appointment or meeting to the organizer's calendar folder (optional).

The following example shows how to add the attachment d:\maps\directions.gif to a meeting:

[Visual Basic]

```
' Reference to Microsoft ActiveX Data Objects 2.5 Library
' Reference to Microsoft CDO for Exchange 2000 Library

Sub AddAttachmentToAppt(iAppt As CDO.Appointment,
strFilePath As String, strContentType As String,
strEncoding As String)

    Dim iBp As CDO.IBodyPart
    Set iBp = iAppt.Attachments.Add
    'Set the fields for the attachment
    Set Flds = iBp.Fields
    Flds.Item("urn:schemas:mailheader:content-type") =
strContentType
    Flds.Item("urn:schemas:mailheader:content-transfer-
encoding") = strEncoding
    Flds.Update

    'Get the stream interface on the body part
    Set Stm = iBp.GetDecodedContentStream

    'Load the attachment file into the stream and flush
    '  the stream to save it back to the body part
    Stm.LoadFromFile strFilePath
    Stm.Flush

End Sub
```

Processing a Calendar Message

When a meeting organizer sends a meeting request, Microsoft Exchange 2000 Server stores the calendar message in the recipient's inbox. Responses to meeting requests, meeting updates, and cancellations are all received as calendar messages in the inbox. You can use ADO and CDO to retrieve calendar messages from the inbox and process them.

Processing a Calendar Message

You can identify an item in an Exchange 2000 folder by the item's content class. The content class is a property of items in the Web Storage System. The content class of calendar messages is contained in the DAV:contentclass field of the message. All calendar messages have the content class urn:content-classes:calendarmessage.

You typically open calendar messages by using the ICalendarPart.GetUpdatedItem method. This method checks the Web Storage System to verify if the meeting in the calendar message already exists. If the meeting already exists, the calendar message is probably an update to that meeting. The GetUpdatedItem method returns an Appointment object in memory that contains the most current meeting information, either from the Web Storage System or the calendar message. When you save the meeting, it overwrites the existing meeting in the Web Storage System.

Note If the calendar part contains an exception to an existing recurring meeting, the GetUpdatedItem method returns the exception in memory. If you accept or decline the exception, the meeting response is based on the exception. However, when you call the IDataSource.Save method on the exception, it merges the exception into the master recurring meeting and saves the updated master to the Web Storage System.

This topic explains how to identify and open calendar messages. Other topics in this section explain how to process the calendar message after it has been opened.

To open calendar messages in the inbox,

1. Open the inbox folder by using an ADODB record.
2. Open an ADO Recordset containing the items in the inbox. Use a SELECT statement to include the item URL and content class in the record set. Specify a WHERE clause to select only calendar messages.
3. Get the URL of the message from the record set and then open the URL by using a CDO CalendarMessage object.
4. Open each calendar part in the calendar parts collection by using a CDO Appointment object and process the Appointment object as needed.
5. Delete the calendar message from the inbox (optional).

The following example gets all calendar messages from the inbox of a specific user. It prints the subject of each calendar part and deletes the message. The examples under other topics in this section explain how to process the calendar parts:

[Visual Basic]

```
' Reference to Microsoft ActiveX Data Objects 2.5 Library
' Reference to Microsoft CDO for Exchange 2000 Library
```

Chapter 19 • Calendaring and Contacts

```
Sub ProcessCalMsgs(iMbx As IMailbox)

    Dim Rs As ADODB.Recordset
    Set Rs = QueryInboxFolderForCalMsgs(iMbx)
    Debug.Print Rs.RecordCount
    While Not Rs.EOF
        Debug.Print Rs(0)
        Debug.Print Rs(1)
        ProcessCalMsg Rs(0), Conn, iMbx, False
        Rs.MoveNext
    Wend

End Sub

Function QueryInboxFolderForCalMsgs(iMbx As IMailbox) As ADODB.Recordset

    Dim Rs          As New ADODB.Recordset
    Dim Rec         As New ADODB.Record
    Dim Conn        As New ADODB.Connection

    'Open the record set for the items in the calendar folder
    Conn.Provider = "ExOLEDB.DataSource"
    Conn.Open iMbx.BaseFolder
    Rec.Open iMbx.Inbox, Conn
    Set Rs.ActiveConnection = Rec.ActiveConnection


    Rs.Source = "SELECT ""DAV:href"", " & _
                " ""DAV:contentclass"", " & _
                " ""urn:schemas:httpmail:subject"" " & _
                " FROM scope('shallow traversal of """ & iMbx.Inbox & """')" & _
                " WHERE ""DAV:ishidden"" = False AND ""DAV:isfolder"" = False AND ""DAV:contentclass"" = 'urn:content-classes:calendarmessage'"
    Rs.Open

    Set QueryInboxFolderForCalMsgs = Rs
End Function

Sub ProcessCalMsg(itemURL As String, Conn As ADODB.Connection, iMbx As CDO.IMailbox, fDelete As Boolean)

    Dim iCalMsg     As New CalendarMessage
    Dim iAddre      As New Addressee
    Dim iCalPart    As ICalendarPart
    Dim iAppt       As Appointment
    Dim iDsrc       As CDO.IDataSource
```

```
    Dim Index        As Integer
    Dim Rec As New ADODB.Record


    Dim Config As New CDO.Configuration
    Config("CalendarLocation") = iMbx.Calendar
    Config.Fields.Update

    Set iCalMsg.Configuration = Config
    iCalMsg.DataSource.Open itemURL, Conn, adModeReadWrite

    'Get each calendar part
    For Each iCalPart In iCalMsg.CalendarParts
      Set iAppt = iCalPart.GetUpdatedItem
      Debug.Print "Subject: " & iAppt.Subject

      'Process the appointment as necessary
      Select Case iCalPart.CalendarMethod
        Case "REQUEST"
          ' Handle a meeting request
        Case "REPLY"
          ' Handle meeting request reply
        Case "CANCEL"
          ' Handle cancelled meeting.
      End Select
    Next iCalPart

    'If flagged, delete the calendar message from the inbox
    If fDelete Then
        Rec.Open itemURL, Conn, adModeReadWrite
        Debug.Print iMbx.DeletedItems
        Rec.DeleteRecord
        ' Or move the Record:
        ' Rec.MoveRecord , iMbx.DeletedItems, , ,
adMoveOverWrite
    End If
End Sub
```

Responding to a Meeting Request

When you receive a meeting request in your inbox, you can accept it, accept it tentatively, reject it, or delete it. You typically save the meeting to your calendar folder after accepting the response.

Meeting requests are calendar messages that are identified by the ICalendarPart.CalendarMethod value REQUEST.

The CDO Appointment object provides three methods for responding to meeting requests: Accept, AcceptTentative, and Decline. Each method returns a CalendarMessage object that is addressed to the meeting requestor. Each method also updates the status of the meeting in memory so that if you save the meeting to your calendar, the status corresponds to the response you sent. You can also modify the message before sending it.

> **Note** None of the response methods changes the meeting request message in the inbox. Typically, the program deletes the meeting request message after a response is sent.

To respond to a meeting request,

1. Open each meeting in the calendar message as shown in Processing a Calendar Message.
2. Based on the programming logic or user input, call the appropriate response method: Accept, AcceptTentative, or Decline.
3. Make any desired changes to the response message (optional).
4. Call the ICalendarMessage.Message.Send method to send the response.
5. Save the meeting to the calendar folder.
6. When you have finished processing all meetings in a calendar message, delete the message from the inbox.

The example that follows checks the inbox of a specific user. It accepts any meeting request with the word "lunch" in the subject line and declines all other meetings. Then it deletes the calendar message from the inbox:

[Visual Basic]

```
' Reference to Microsoft ActiveX Data Objects 2.5 Library
' Reference to Microsoft CDO for Exchange 2000 Library

Dim InboxURL       As String
Dim CalendarURL    As String
Dim itemURL        As String
Dim Rs             As New ADODB.Recordset
Dim Rec            As New ADODB.Record
Dim iCalMsg        As New CalendarMessage
Dim iCalMsg2       As CalendarMessage
Dim iCalPart       As ICalendarPart
Dim iAppt          As Appointment
Dim Index          As Integer
Dim ContentClass   As String
Dim Config         As New Configuration

InboxURL = "file://./backofficestorage/" & DomainName & _
"/MBX/" & Username & "/inbox/"
CalendarURL = "file://./backofficestorage/" & DomainName & _
"/MBX/" & Username & "/calendar/"

'Set the configuration fields for the appointment objects
```

Processing a Calendar Message

```
Config.Fields(cdoSendEmailAddress) = Username & "@" &
DomainName
Config.Fields.Update

'Open the record set for the calendar messages in the inbox
folder
Rec.Open InboxURL
Set Rs.ActiveConnection = Rec.ActiveConnection
Rs.Source = "SELECT ""DAV:href"",""DAV:contentclass"" " & _
  "FROM scope('shallow traversal of """ & InboxURL & """')" & _
  "WHERE (""DAV:contentclass"" = 'urn:content-classes:calendarmessage')"
Rs.Open

'Enumerate the record set and process each calendar message
Rs.MoveFirst
Do Until Rs.EOF
  'Open the calendar message
  itemURL = Rs.Fields(CdoDAV.cdoHref).Value
  iCalMsg.DataSource.Open itemURL, , adModeReadWrite
  iCalMsg.Configuration = Config
  'Get each calendar part
  For Index = 1 To iCalMsg.CalendarParts.Count
    Set iCalPart = iCalMsg.CalendarParts(Index)
    Set iAppt = iCalPart.GetUpdatedItem(CalendarURL)
    Select Case iCalPart.CalendarMethod
      Case "REQUEST"
        'Accept any meeting with "lunch" in the subject text
        If InStr(1, iAppt.Subject, "lunch", 1) Then
          Set iCalMsg2 = iAppt.Accept
        Else
          Set iCalMsg2 = iAppt.Decline
        End If
        'Save the meeting
        iAppt.DataSource.SaveToContainer CalendarURL
        'Send the response
        iCalMsg2.Message.Send
      Case Else
        'See the other examples in this section
    End Select

  Next Index
  'Delete the calendar message
  Rs.Delete

Rs.MoveNext
Loop
```

Processing Meeting Responses

The organizer of a meeting receives the responses to meeting requests from attendees. The organizer then needs to process all the responses to update their status. Because attendees can invite other attendees, a meeting organizer should be able to process responses from attendees the organizer did not invite.

When you call the ICalendarPart.GetUpdatedItem method, CDO searches your calendar folder for an existing meeting that matches a meeting in the calendar part. CDO builds an appointment object in memory that contains the latest information from the saved meeting and the new meeting. The response to your meeting request (accepted, declined, or tentative) is merged into the existing meeting. When you save the appointment object in memory using the Datasource.Save method, the meeting in your calendar folder contains the updated attendee status.

Meeting responses are calendar messages identified by the ICalendarPart.CalendarMethod value "REPLY."

To process meeting responses,

1. Open each meeting in the calendar message as shown in Processing a Calendar Message.
2. Save the meeting returned by GetUpdatedItem.
3. Delete the calendar message after processing all calendar parts.

The code in the example that follows checks the inbox of a specific user. It then opens all meeting responses and saves the updated attendee status. Finally, it deletes the calendar message from the inbox:

[Visual Basic]

```
' Reference to Microsoft ActiveX Data Objects 2.5 Library
' Reference to Microsoft CDO for Exchange 2000 Library

Sub ProcessResponse(iCalMsg As CDO.CalendarMessage, iMbx As IMailbox)

    Dim Rec         As New ADODB.Record
    Dim Conn        As New ADODB.Connection
    Dim iCalMsg     As New CalendarMessage
    Dim iCalPart    As ICalendarPart
    Dim iAppt       As CDO.Appointment

    Conn.Provider = "ExOLEDB.DataSource"
    Conn.Open iMbx.BaseFolder

    For Each iCalPart In iCalMsg.CalendarParts
        Set iAppt = iCalPart.GetUpdatedItem(iMbx.Calendar)
        Select Case iCalPart.CalendarMethod
```

```
            Case "REPLY" ' Make sure this is a reply
                iAppt.DataSource.Save
        End Select
    Next

End Sub
```

Processing Meeting Cancellations

As the organizer of a meeting, you can send a calendar message to cancel a meeting. Cancellation messages are calendar messages identified by the ICalendarPart.CalendarMethod value "CANCEL."

Instead of deleting the meeting from their calendars, attendees save the updated appointment object that has a MeetingStatus property set to Cancelled. Calendar client programs typically do not display canceled meetings. For example, Microsoft Outlook ignores canceled meetings when building calendar views. CDO does not automatically delete canceled meetings from the Web Storage System.

To process meeting cancellations,

1. Open each meeting in the calendar message as shown in Processing a Calendar Message.
2. Save the meeting returned by the GetUpdatedItem method.
3. Delete the calendar message after processing all calendar parts.

The code in the example that follows checks the inbox of user12 on a Microsoft Exchange 2000 Server named exsvr3, in the exchange.microsoft.com domain. It opens all meeting cancellations and saves the updated meeting. Then it deletes the calendar message from the inbox:

[Visual Basic]

```
Dim InboxURL      As String
Dim CalendarURL   As String
Dim ItemURL       As String
Dim Rs            As New ADODB.Recordset
Dim Rec           As New ADODB.Record
Dim iCalMsg       As New CalendarMessage
Dim iCalPart      As    ICalendarPart
Dim iAppt         As    Appointment
Dim Index         As    Integer
Dim ContentClass  As    String
Dim Config        As New Configuration

InboxURL = "file://./backofficestorage/exchange.microsoft.com/MBX/user12/inbox/"
CalendarURL = "file://./backofficestorage/exchange.microsoft.com/MBX/user12/calendar/"
```

Chapter 19 — Calendaring and Contacts

```
'Set the configuration fields for the appointment objects
Config.Fields(cdoSendEmailAddress) =
"user12@exchange.microsoft.com"
Config.Fields("CalendarLocation") = CalendarURL
Config.Fields.Update

'Open a recordset for the items in the inbox folder
Rec.Open InboxURL
Set Rs.ActiveConnection = Rec.ActiveConnection
Rs.Source = "select ""DAV:href"",""DAV:contentclass"" from
scope('shallow traversal of """ & InboxURL & """')"
Rs.Open

'Enumerate the recordset, checking each item's content
class
Rs.MoveFirst
Do Until Rs.EOF
  'get the content class of each item
  ContentClass = Rs.Fields("DAV:contentclass").Value
  'test content class for calendar message
  If ContentClass = "urn:content-classes:calendarmessage"
Then
    'open calendar message
    ItemURL = Rs.Fields(CdoDAV.cdoHref).Value
    iCalMsg.DataSource.Open ItemURL
    iCalMsg.Configuration = Config
    Debug.Print "Message subject: " &
iCalMsg.Message.Subject
    'get each calendar part
    For Index = 1 To iCalMsg.CalendarParts.Count
      Set iCalPart = iCalMsg.CalendarParts(Index)
      Set iAppt = iCalPart.GetUpdatedItem
      Select Case iCalPart.CalendarMethod
        Case "CANCEL"
          'Save the appointment
          iAppt.DataSource.Save
        Case Else
          'see other examples in this section
      End Select

    Next Index

    'Delete the calendar message
    Rs.Delete
  End If

Rs.MoveNext
Loop
```

Processing Recurring Meeting Exceptions

There are two ways to process exceptions in recurring meetings. If the meeting does not contain exceptions with a RecurrenceIDRange property value of ThisAndFuture or ThisAndPrior, you can process each exception exactly once. This is an efficient way to process exceptions.

If the meeting contains ThisAndFuture or ThisAndPrior exceptions, you must loop through the exceptions multiple times. This is less efficient.

The code in the following example works for exceptions that do not contain ThisAndFuture or ThisAndPrior values:

[Visual Basic]

```
Dim recurid As Date
Dim obExAppt As CDO.Appointment
Dim obReq As CDO.CalendarMessage
Dim obEx As CDO.IException

For Each obEx In obAppt.Exceptions
   'To make sure we process next exception if we can't process this one
   On Error GoTo NextException
   If obEx.Type = "Modify" Then
     recurid = obEx.RecurrenceID
     'Found an exception: process it
     Set obExAppt = obAppt.GetFirstInstance(recurid, recurid)
     Set obReq = obExAppt.CreateRequest ' OR Invite OR Cancel, etc.
     obReq.Message.Send
   End If
NextException:
   End
```

The code in the following example works for exceptions that contain ThisAndFuture or ThisAndPrior values:

[Visual Basic]

```
While (1)
  On Error GoTo NextInstance
  obExAppt = obAppt.GetNextInstance
  If obExAppt.Fields("urn:schemas:calendar:instancetype") = cdoException Then
    Found an exception: process it
    Set obExAppt = obAppt.GetFirstInstance(recurid, recurid)
    Set obReq = obExAppt.CreateRequest ' OR Invite OR Cancel, etc.
```

```
         obReq.Message.Send
      End If
NextInstance:
   'Check for err.Number = DISP_E_BADINDEX: 0x8002000b
(winerror.h)
   If Err.Number = 2147614731# Then GoTo Quit
   End
Quit:
```

Updating Appointments and Meetings

You can update the properties and fields of an appointment or meeting that is saved in your calendar folder. For appointments, you overwrite the original appointment in the Microsoft Web Storage System with the updated appointment. For meetings, in addition to saving the changes to the Web Storage System, you must send the updates to attendees. If you are not the meeting organizer and you update a meeting in your calendar folder, any updates you accept from the meeting organizer overwrite your updates.

To update appointments or meetings,

1. Open an appointment or meeting in the Calendar folder as shown in Getting Appointments and Meetings from Folders in Exchange. Be sure to open the appointment in read or write mode by using adModeReadWrite.
2. Change the properties and fields of the appointment or meeting.
3. Save the appointment or meeting to the calendar folder using the IAppointment.Datasource.Save method.

The code in the example that follows checks all of the appointments and meetings in the calendar of user12 on the Microsoft Exchange 2000 Server named exsvr3 in the exchange.microsoft.com domain. It changes any appointment or meeting scheduled in the "Flamingo Room" to the "Mount Rainier Room" and saves the appointment:

[Visual Basic]

```
Dim CalendarURL  As       String
Dim ItemURL      As       String
Dim Rs           As New   ADODB.Recordset
Dim Rec          As New   ADODB.Record
Dim Conn         As New   ADODB.Connection
Dim iAppt        As New   Appointment
Dim Target       As       String
Dim NewValue     As       String
Dim Location     As       String
```

```
Target = "Flamingo Room"
NewValue = "Mount Rainier Room"

  'Using the Exchange OLE DB provider
  CalendarURL = "file://./backofficestorage/
gberg2.extest.microsoft.com/MBX/user12/calendar/"

'Open a record set for the items in the calendar folder
Rec.Open CalendarURL
Set Rs.ActiveConnection = Rec.ActiveConnection
Rs.Source = "SELECT ""DAV:href"",
""urn:schemas:calendar:location"" from scope('shallow
traversal of """ & CalendarURL & """')"
Rs.Open

'Enumerate the record set, checking each item's location
Rs.MoveFirst
Do Until Rs.EOF
  'get the location of each item
  Location = Rs.Fields(CdoCalendar.cdoLocation).Value
  'test for desired location
  If (Location = Target) Then
    'open appointment in read/write mode and update the
location property
    ItemURL = Rs.Fields(CdoDAV.cdoHref).Value
    iAppt.DataSource.Open ItemURL, , adModeReadWrite
    iAppt.Location = NewValue
    iAppt.DataSource.Save
  End If
  Rs.MoveNext
Loop
```

Getting Appointments and Meetings from Folders in Exchange

Microsoft Exchange 2000 Server stores appointments and meetings in a user's calendar folder or in a public folder. By using a CDO Appointment object, you can open, view, and modify appointments and meetings in the Web Storage System. Individual appointments and meetings are stored as single items in the Web Storage System.

Recurring appointments are expanded into individual instances when the calendar folder is queried in the Web Storage System. If you want to modify one or more instances of a recurring appointment, you can modify the master appointment. You can also modify the individual instances directly. The urn:schemas:calendar:instancetype field identifies master recurring appointments, recurring instances, single appointments, or exceptions to recurring appointments.

Chapter 19 • Calendaring and Contacts

Although appointments and meetings can be stored in any Exchange folder, the Web Storage System expands only recurring appointments and meetings that are stored in calendar folders.

To get appointments from a calendar folder,

1. Open the calendar folder using an ADODB record.
2. Open an ADODB record set containing the items in the calendar folder. Use a SELECT statement to include the item URL and the appointment date or other desired fields in the record set. To expand recurring meetings, include a WHERE clause in the SELECT statement that specifies the range of dates where recurring instances are expanded.
3. Enumerate the record set, and then test each item's fields, as appropriate.
4. For appointments that match your selection criteria, get the URL from the record set, and then open the URL using a CDO Appointment object.
5. Process the Appointment objects as needed.

The code in the example that follows lists appointments in the calendar folder of user12, on the Exchange 2000 Server named exsvr3 in the exchange.microsoft.com domain. The code example selects appointments within a specific date range that have the subject "Department Meeting." It also prints the start and end times of the appointment, the subject, and the instance type:

[Visual Basic]

```
Dim CalendarURL     As      String
Dim ItemURL         As      String
Dim Rs              As New  ADODB.Recordset
Dim Rec             As New  ADODB.Record
Dim Conn            As New  ADODB.Connection
Dim iAppt           As New  Appointment
Dim dateStartDate   As      Date
Dim Subject         As      String

CalendarURL = "file://./backofficestorage/
exchange.microsoft.com/MBX/user12/calendar/"

'Open a record set for the items in the calendar folder
Rec.Open CalendarURL
Set Rs.ActiveConnection = Rec.ActiveConnection
Rs.Source = "SELECT ""DAV:href"", " & _
            " ""urn:schemas:httpmail:subject"", " & _
            " ""urn:schemas:calendar:dtstart"", " & _
            " ""urn:schemas:calendar:dtend"" " & _
            "FROM scope('shallow traversal of """ & _
CalendarURL & """') " & _
            "WHERE (""urn:schemas:calendar:dtstart"" >= CAST(""1999-08-01T08:00:00Z"" as 'dateTime')) " & _
            "AND (""urn:schemas:calendar:dtend"" <=
```

```
CAST(""1999-09-01T08:00:00Z"" as 'dateTime'))"
Rs.Open

'Enumerate the record set, checking each item's subject
Rs.MoveFirst
Do Until Rs.EOF
    'get the subject of each item
    Subject = Rs.Fields(CdoHTTPMail.cdoSubject).Value
    If Subject = "Department Meeting" Then
        'open appointment
        ItemURL = Rs.Fields(CdoDAV.cdoHref).Value
        iAppt.DataSource.Open ItemURL
        Debug.Print iAppt.StartTime & " - " & iAppt.EndTime
        Debug.Print "Subject: " & iAppt.Subject
        'print the type of appointment
        Select Case
iAppt.Fields(CdoCalendar.cdoInstanceType).Value
            Case cdoSingle
                Debug.Print "Single appointment"
            Case cdoMaster
                Debug.Print "Master recurring appointment"
            Case cdoInstance
                Debug.Print "Instance of recurring
appointment"
            Case cdoException
                Debug.Print "Exception to recurring
appointment"
            Case Else
                Debug.Print "Unknown"
        End Select
    End If

    Rs.MoveNext

Loop
```

Sending Meeting Updates

If you are the organizer of a meeting, you can send updates to the attendees of the meeting using a calendar message. CDO returns an error if you call the IAppointment.CreateRequest method for a meeting of which you are not the organizer.

Attendees process the update messages the same way they process any other calendar message. The ICalendarMessage.CalendarParts.GetUpdatedItem method compares the new calendar message with the existing meeting. It returns an Appointment object that can be saved to the calendar folder. The updated meeting overwrites the existing meeting. For more information on processing meeting updates, see "Responding to a Meeting Request," in the MS Exchange SDK.

To send meeting updates,

1. Open the meeting and then update the desired properties and fields as shown in Updating Appointments and Meetings. Verify that you are the organizer of the meeting.
2. Set the meeting configuration and then create a Calendar Message object using the IAppointment.CreateRequest method. For a published appointment, use the Publish method instead of the CreateRequest method.
3. Add any text you want to the Calendar Message object.
4. Send the Calendar Message using the IMessage.Send method.
5. Save the meeting update to the calendar folder.

The code in the example that follows checks all of the meetings in the calendar of user12, located on server exsvr3 in the exchange.microsoft.com domain. For meetings originated by user12, this code changes any meeting in the "Flamingo Room" to the "Mount Rainier Room" and sends an update to all attendees:

[Visual Basic]

```
Dim CalendarURL As         String
Dim ItemURL     As         String
Dim Rec         As New ADODB.Record
Dim Rs          As New ADODB.Recordset
Dim iDsrc       As         CDO.IDataSource
Dim iAtnds      As         CDO.IAttendees
Dim Config      As New CDO.Configuration
Dim iAppt       As New CDO.Appointment
Dim iCalMsg     As         CDO.CalendarMessage
Dim iMsg        As         CDO.Message
Dim Target      As         String
Dim NewValue    As         String
Dim Location    As         String
Dim Address     As         String
Dim Index       As         Integer

Target = "Flamingo Room"
NewValue = "Mount Rainier Room"

  'Using the Exchange OLE DB provider
  CalendarURL = "file://./backofficestorage/
exchange.microsoft.com/MBX/user12/calendar/"

'Set the configuration for the message
Config.Fields(cdoSendEmailAddress) =
"user12@exchange.microsoft.com"
Config.Fields("CalendarLocation") = CalendarURL
```

```
Config.Fields.Update

'set address of user for comparing with attendee value
Address = "MAILTO:" & Config.Fields(cdoSendEmailAddress)

'Open a record set for the items in the calendar folder
Rec.Open CalendarURL
Set Rs.ActiveConnection = Rec.ActiveConnection
Rs.Source = "SELECT ""DAV:href"",
""urn:schemas:calendar:location"" from scope('shallow
traversal of """ & CalendarURL & """')"
Rs.Open

'Enumerate the record set, checking each item's location
Rs.MoveFirst
Do Until Rs.EOF
  'get the location of each item
  Location = Rs.Fields(CdoCalendar.cdoLocation).Value
  'test for organizer and desired location
  If (Location = Target) Then
    'open appointment in read/write mode
    ItemURL = Rs.Fields(CdoDAV.cdoHref).Value
    Set iDsrc = iAppt
    iDsrc.Open ItemURL, , adModeReadWrite
    'verify this user is organizer by checking attendee
property
    Set iAtnds = iAppt.Attendees
    'If appointment has attendess and this user is
organizer send an update
    'otherwise just save update to calendar
    If iAtnds.Count > 1 Then
      For Index = 1 To iAtnds.Count
        If iAtnds.Item(Index).IsOrganizer And
iAtnds.Item(Index).Address = Address Then
          'update the appointment location
          iAppt.Location = NewValue
          'save the appointment
          iDsrc.Save
          'set the configuration
          iAppt.Configuration = Config
          'create a calendar message
          Set iCalMsg = iAppt.CreateRequest
          'send the update to the attendees
          Set iMsg = iCalMsg.Message
          iMsg.TextBody = "Automated update - please note
new location"
          iMsg.Send
        End If 'user is organizer
      Next Index
    Else 'appointment has only one attendee
```

```
            iAppt.Location = NewValue
            iDsrc.Save
        End If 'appointment has attendees
    End If 'location = target
    Rs.MoveNext
Loop
```

Canceling Appointments and Meetings

There are four possible scenarios for canceling appointments and meetings:
- The organizer cancels an appointment.
- The organizer cancels a meeting or removes some attendees from a meeting.
- The organizer cancels a single instance or all instances of a recurring appointment or meeting.
- The attendee declines a previously accepted meeting.

Only the organizer of a meeting can cancel that meeting. However, attendees can remove themselves from a meeting by sending a decline response (even if they previously accepted it). The following sections describe each of these scenarios in detail.

CANCELING AN APPOINTMENT

To cancel an appointment, you delete the appointment from the calendar folder. It is a good idea to verify that you are deleting an appointment and not a meeting. Unlike Microsoft Outlook, CDO does not warn you to notify attendees when the item you are deleting has attendees. If the object being deleted has attendees, it is a meeting; see "Canceling a Meeting" in the MS Exchange SDK.

To cancel an appointment,

1. Open the calendar folder by using an ADODB record set.
2. Locate the appointment that you want to delete. Open the appointment, and then check the attendee count to verify that there are no other attendees.
3. Delete the appointment using the Recordset.Delete method.

The code in the following example gets all of the appointments with the subject "Documentation Review Meeting" in the calendar of a specific user. It then verifies that each appointment has no other attendees and deletes it:

[Visual Basic]

```
' Reference to Microsoft ActiveX Data Objects 2.5 Library
' Reference to Microsoft CDO for Exchange 2000 Library

Sub CancelAppt(iAppt As CDO.Appointment, iMbx As IMailbox)
```

```
    Dim Conn        As New ADODB.Connection
    Dim iPer        As New CDO.Person
    Dim Rec         As New ADODB.Record

    Conn.Provider = "ExOLEDB.DataSource"
    Conn.Open iMbx.BaseFolder
    Rec.Open iAppt.DataSource.SourceURL, Conn,
adModeReadWrite
    Rec.DeleteRecord
    Rec.Close

End Sub
```

CANCELING A MEETING

The organizer of a meeting can cancel a meeting and notify all of the attendees. To do so, the organizer changes the meeting status to Canceled and then sends an updated Calendar Message to the attendees.

The organizer can also remove some of the attendees from the meeting without canceling the entire meeting. To remove only some of the attendees, the organizer specifies the attendees' email addresses in the string passed to the IAppointment.Cancel method. To cancel the entire meeting, the organizer calls the Cancel method without any parameters.

To cancel a meeting,

1. Open the calendar folder by using an ADODB record set.
2. Locate the meeting that you want to delete and then open it using an Appointment object. Verify that you are the organizer. Be sure to open the appointment in read/write mode by using adModeReadWrite.
3. Create a Calendar Message object using the IAppointment.Cancel method. Pass a list of attendees to be removed, or, to cancel the entire meeting, do not pass any parameters.
4. Add text to the Calendar Message object, if necessary.
5. Send the Calendar Message object using the IMessage.Send method.
6. Delete the canceled meeting from the calendar folder (optional).

The code in the example that follows gets all the meetings with the subject "Documentation Review Meeting" in the calendar of a specific user. It verifies that the user is the organizer, sends the cancellation message to the attendees, and then deletes the meeting from the calendar folder:

[Visual Basic]

```
' Reference to Microsoft ActiveX Data Objects 2.5 Library
' Reference to Microsoft CDO for Exchange 2000 Library

Sub CancelMeeting(iAppt As CDO.Appointment, iMbx As
IMailbox)
```

```
    Dim Conn        As New ADODB.Connection
    Dim iPer        As New CDO.Person
    Dim iCalMsg     As CDO.CalendarMessage
    Dim Config      As CDO.Configuration

    Conn.Provider = "ExOLEDB.DataSource"
    Conn.Open iMbx.BaseFolder

    Set iCalMsg = iAppt.Cancel
    With iCalMsg
        Set Config = .Configuration
        Config(cdoSendUsingMethod) = cdoSendUsingExchange
        Config(cdoMailboxURL) = iMbx.BaseFolder
        Config(cdoActiveConnection) = Conn
        Config.Fields.Update
        .Message.TextBody = "Sorry, the meeting has been cancelled"
        .Message.Send
    End With
    'Delete the appointment from the calendar folder (optional)
End Sub
```

CANCELING RECURRING APPOINTMENTS AND MEETINGS

Recurring appointments and meetings have one master and one or more recurring instances. To cancel an entire series of a recurring appointment or meeting, you need to cancel the master appointment or meeting. Each recurring instance has a GetRecurringMaster method that returns its master appointment or meeting.

To cancel a single instance of a recurring appointment or meeting, open the instance and cancel it. You cancel single instances the same way you cancel a single appointment or meeting; see "Canceling an Appointment or Canceling a Meeting" in the MS Exchange SDK.

To cancel a recurring appointment or meeting,

1. Open the calendar folder by using an ADODB record set. Specify start and end times in the query so that instances are expanded in the calendar folder; see "Calendar Folder Query" in the MS Exchange SDK.
2. Locate any instance of the recurring appointment or meeting that you want to cancel and then open it using an Appointment object.
3. Open the master appointment using the IAppointment.GetRecurringMaster method. Verify that you are the organizer. Be sure to open the appointment or meeting in read/write mode by using adModeReadWrite.
4. Set the configuration, and then create a Calendar Message object using the IAppointment.Cancel method.

Updating Appointments and Meetings

5. Add text to the Calendar Message object, if you want.
6. Send the Calendar Message object by using the IMessage.Send method.
7. Delete the master appointment or meeting from the calendar folder (optional).

Note After you delete the master appointment or meeting for an instance, do not try to delete the master again for another instance of the same master.

The code in the example that follows gets meetings in the specified date range with the subject "Documentation Review Meeting" from the calendar of a specific user. Then it gets the master meeting, verifies that the user is the organizer, and finally cancels all instances of the recurring meeting:

[Visual Basic]

```
' Reference to Microsoft ActiveX Data Objects 2.5 Library
' Reference to Microsoft CDO for Exchange 2000 Library

Sub CancelRecurringAppointment(iAppt As CDO.Appointment, iMbx As IMailbox)
    Dim Rec         As New ADODB.Record
    Dim Rec2        As New ADODB.Record
    Dim iAppt       As New CDO.Appointment
    Dim iAppt2      As CDO.Appointment
    Dim iAtnds      As CDO.IAttendees
    Dim Config      As New CDO.Configuration
    Dim iCalMsg     As CDO.CalendarMessage
    Dim Address     As String
    Dim Index       As Integer
    Dim iPer        As CDO.Person

    Set iPer = iMbx

    'Set the configuration fields
    Config.Fields(cdoSendEmailAddress) = Username & "@" & DomainName
    Config.Fields.Update
    Set iAppt.Configuration = Config

    'Set the address of the user for comparing with the attendee value
    Address = "MAILTO:" & Username & "@" & DomainName

    'Open the record set for the items in the calendar folder
    Rec.Open CalendarURL
```

Chapter 19 • Calendaring and Contacts

```
    Set Rs.ActiveConnection = Rec.ActiveConnection
    Rs.Source = "SELECT ""DAV:href""," & _
                    " ""urn:schemas:httpmail:subject""," & _
                    " ""urn:schemas:calendar:dtstart""," & _
                    " ""urn:schemas:calendar:dtend"" " & _
                "FROM scope('shallow traversal of """ & CalendarURL & """') " & _
                "WHERE (""urn:schemas:calendar:dtstart"" >= CAST(""1999-10-01T08:00:00Z"" as 'dateTime')) " & _
                    "AND (""urn:schemas:calendar:dtend"" <= CAST(""1999-11-01T08:00:00Z"" as 'dateTime'))" & _
                    "AND (""urn:schemas:httpmail:subject"" = 'Documentation Review Meeting')"
    Rs.Open

    'Enumerate the record set
    Rs.MoveFirst
    Do Until Rs.EOF
      itemURL = Rs.Fields(CdoDAV.cdoHref).Value
      iAppt.DataSource.Open itemURL, , adModeReadWrite
      Set iAtnds = iAppt.Attendees
      For Index = 1 To iAtnds.Count
      'Check if this user is the organizer
      If iAtnds.Item(Index).IsOrganizer And iAtnds.Item(Index).Address = Address Then
        'This user is the organizer
        Set iAppt2 = iAppt.GetRecurringMaster(CalendarURL) 'Get the master
                                                            'If already master, returns itself
        'Create a cancelation message
        iAppt2.Configuration = Config
        Set iCalMsg = iAppt2.Cancel
        iCalMsg.Message.TextBody = "This meeting is canceled."
        iCalMsg.Message.Send

        'Delete the master from the calendar folder (optional)
        itemURL = iAppt2.Fields(CdoDAV.cdoHref)
        Rec2.Open itemURL, , adModeReadWrite
        Rec2.DeleteRecord

        Exit Do 'Stop processing meeting instances
      End If
    Next Index
```

```
            Rs.MoveNext
            Loop

End Sub
```

DECLINING A PREVIOUSLY ACCEPTED MEETING

Attendees who want to remove themselves from a meeting can open the meeting in their calendar folder and send a decline response message to the organizer. The meeting remains in the attendees' calendar with a status of Declined, unless the attendees delete the meeting from their calendar folders.

If you want to remove the meeting from your calendar without notifying the organizer, delete the meeting as shown in Canceling an Appointment.

> **Note** It is a good idea to verify that you are not the organizer of a meeting before trying to decline that meeting.

The basic procedure for declining a previously accepted meeting is as follows:

1. Open the calendar folder by using an ADODB record set.
2. Locate the meeting that you want to decline, and then open it using an Appointment object. Verify that you are not the organizer. Be sure to open the meeting in read/write mode by using adModeReadWrite.
3. Create a Calendar Message object by using the IAppointment.Decline method.
4. Add text to the Calendar Message object, if you want.
5. Send the Calendar Message object by using the IMessage.Send method.
6. Delete the declined meeting from the calendar folder (optional).

The code in the example that follows gets all of the meetings in the calendar of a specific user with the subject "Documentation Review Meeting." It verifies that the user is not the organizer, sends the Decline message, and then deletes the meeting from the calendar folder.

[Visual Basic]

```
' Reference to Microsoft ActiveX Data Objects 2.5 Library
' Reference to Microsoft CDO for Exchange 2000 Library

Sub DeclineAcceptedMeeting(iAppt As CDO.Appointment, iMbx _
As IMailbox)

      Dim Conn         As New Connection
      Dim Config       As New Configuration
      Dim iCalMsg      As CDO.CalendarMessage
```

```
    Dim iPer        As CDO.Person
    Dim Rec         As New ADODB.Record

    Set iPer = iMbx
    Conn.Provider = "ExOLEDB.DataSource"
    Conn.Open iMbx.BaseFolder
    Config.Fields(cdoSendEmailAddress) = iPer.Email
    Config.Fields(CDO.cdoActiveConnection) = Conn
    Config.Fields.Update


    With iAppt
        .Configuration = Config
        Set iCalMsg = .Decline
    End With

    iCalMsg.Message.TextBody = "Sorry, I cannot attend this
meeting."
    iCalMsg.Message.Send

    iAppt.DataSource.Save

    Rec.Open iAppt.DataSource.SourceURL, Conn,
adModeReadWrite
    Set iAppt = Nothing
    Rec.DeleteRecord

End Sub
```

Inviting Additional Attendees

Both organizers and attendees can invite additional attendees to a meeting. You can invite attendees to a meeting in your calendar folder, and you can also forward meeting requests from your inbox.

If an attendee invites another attendee, the organizer's attendee list is not automatically updated. Therefore, when the new attendee responds to the meeting request, the organizer can choose to add the new attendee by processing the response message and saving the updated meeting. A meeting organizer should be able to process responses from attendees the organizer did not invite.

Inviting Attendees to a Meeting in the Calendar Folder

You can invite additional attendees to a meeting that already exists in your calendar folder. The IAppointment.Invite method returns a Calendar Message object that you send to the attendees being added.

For information on how to forward a meeting request from your inbox, see "Forwarding a Meeting Request" in the MS Exchange SDK.

If the organizer of the meeting invites additional attendees, the meeting in the organizer's calendar folder is updated with the new attendees' names. If an attendee invites additional attendees, the attendee list is not updated in the attendees' or organizer's calendars. When the new attendees respond to the meeting request, the organizer can choose whether or not to add them to the attendee list.

Because a new meeting request is not automatically sent to existing attendees, their calendars are not updated with the new attendee names.

The basic procedure for inviting attendees to a meeting in the calendar folder is as follows:

1. Open a meeting in the Calendar folder as shown in Getting Appointments and Meetings from Folders in Exchange. Be sure to open the appointment in read/write mode by using adModeReadWrite.
2. Create a Calendar Message object.
3. Call the IAppointment.Invite method, and then pass the list of attendees to invite by using the Calendar Message object.
4. Call the ICalendarMessage.Message.Send method to send the message.
5. Save the updated meeting.

The code in the example that follows opens a meeting in the calendar folder of a specific user, forwards the meeting to two new attendees, and then saves the updated meeting. In this example, the meeting is selected based on subject:

[Visual Basic]

```
' Reference to Microsoft ActiveX Data Objects 2.5 Library
' Reference to Microsoft CDO for Exchange 2000 Library

Sub InviteOthers(iAppt As CDO.Appointment, iMbx As IMailbox, NewList As String)

    Dim Conn As New ADODB.Connection
    Conn.Provider = "ExOLEDB.DataSource"
    Conn.Open iMbx.BaseFolder

    Dim Config As New CDO.Configuration
    'Set the configuration fields
    Config.Fields(cdoActiveConnection) = Conn
```

Chapter 19 • Calendaring and Contacts

```
Config(cdoMailboxURL) = iMbx.BaseFolder
Config.Fields.Update

iAppt.Configuration = Config
Set iCalMsg = iAppt.Invite(NewList)

iCalMsg.Message.Send

'Save the meeting
iAppt.DataSource.Save

End Sub
```

Forwarding a Meeting Request

Forwarding a meeting request is similar to forwarding any message. If an attendee forwards a meeting request to someone else and that person responds to the meeting request, the response is sent to the meeting organizer.

For information on how to invite new attendees to a meeting that is already saved to your calendar, see "Inviting Attendees to a Meeting in the Calendar Folder" in the MS Exchange SDK.

The basic procedure for forwarding a meeting request is as follows:

1. Open the meeting request in your inbox by using a Calendar Message object, as shown in Processing a Calendar Message.
2. Create a new Message object from the Calendar Message object by using the IMessage.Forward method.
3. Address the new message, and then add any text you want.
4. Call the IMessage.Send method to send the new message.

The code in the example that follows gets calendar messages with the subject "Documentation Review Meeting" from the inbox of a specific user. If the calendar message is a meeting request, it is automatically forwarded to the other users:

[Visual Basic]

```
' Reference to Microsoft ActiveX Data Objects 2.5 Library
' Reference to Microsoft CDO for Exchange 2000 Library

Sub ForwardRequest(iCalMsg As CDO.CalendarMessage, iMbx As
IMailbox, EmailAddrs As String, strComment As String)

    Dim iCalPart As CDO.ICalendarPart
    Dim iMsg As CDO.Message
    Dim Conn As New ADODB.Connection
    Conn.Provider = "ExOLEDB.DataSource"
```

```
    Conn.Open iMbx.BaseFolder

    Dim Config As New CDO.Configuration
    Config(cdoActiveConnection).Value = Conn
    Config(cdoMailboxURL) = iMbx.BaseFolder
    Config.Fields.Update

    ' Make sure the message is a request.
    For Each iCalPart In iCalMsg.CalendarParts
        If iCalPart.CalendarMethod = "REQUEST" Then
            Set iMsg = iCalMsg.Message.Forward
            Set iMsg.Configuration = Config
            iMsg.To = EmailAddrs
            iMsg.TextBody = strComment
            iMsg.Send
            Exit For
        End If
    Next

End Sub
```

Configuring the Appointment Object

The CDO Configuration object contains the configuration information needed by other CDO objects and methods. The *http://schemas.microsoft.com/cdo/configuration* namespace lists the fields defined for the Configuration object.

The sendemailaddress field is required for sending meeting requests and responses. This field should be set to the email address of the user.

You can set other configuration fields, such as the sendusing field, if you need to. If your program creates multiple appointments or messages, you should create a single configuration object and reuse it for each appointment or message. This reduces the overhead involved in creating a new configuration object each time you create a new Appointment or Message object.

The example that follows uses the default private store name "MBX." The code demonstrates how to set the configuration object for user12 in the exchange.microsoft.com domain:

[Visual Basic]

```
Dim Config As New CDO.Configuration
CalendarURL = "file://./backofficestorage/
exchange.microsoft.com/MBX/user12/calendar/"

'Set the configuration for calendar messages
Config.Fields(cdoSendEmailAddress) =
"user12@exchange.microsoft.com"
```

```
Config.Fields("CalendarLocation") = CalendarURL
Config.Fields.Update
```

CDO automatically gets some configuration information from the computer on which it is running. The information from the computer includes how messages are sent. To control how meeting requests and responses are sent, set the *http://schemas.microsoft.com/cdo/configuration/sendusing* field.

Using Contacts

The following topics explain how to program contacts:
- Creating Contacts
- Searching for Contacts
- Getting a Contact's VCard Stream

Creating Contacts

Creating a contact using the CDO Person object involves setting informational properties and saving the contact to either the Microsoft Web Storage System or Microsoft Active Directory.

The following sections describe how to create contacts:
- Creating a Contact in the Web Storage System
- Creating a Contact in Active Directory

Creating a Contact in the Web Storage System

Creating a contact involves setting informational properties and saving the contact to the Web Storage System.

The example that follows uses an Exchange OLE DB Provider URL to save the contact.

This example creates a contact using the CDO Person object and saves it to the Web Storage System:

[Visual Basic]

```
Sub CreateContactWebStore()

Dim oPerson As New CDO.Person
Dim strURL As String
```

```
oPerson.FirstName = "John"
oPerson.LastName = "Smith"
oPerson.HomeCity = "Redmond"
oPerson.HomeState = "Washington"
oPerson.Email = "jsmith@somewhere.microsoft.com"
oPerson.Fields("objectClass").Value = "contact"
oPerson.Fields.Update

'URL to save the contact using Exchange OLE DB Provider
strURL = "file://./backofficestorage/
fullyqualifieddomain.Microsoft.Com/MBX/User1/Contacts/
JohnSmith"

'Save the contact to Web Store
oPerson.DataSource.SaveTo strURL

End Sub
```

By default the CDO person object creates a user. In the preceding code, the oPerson.Fields("objectClass").Value is set to type "contact" in order to create a contact.

The objectClass value is an array of variants. However, the property can accept a single value. The value might be one of the following:

```
oPerson.Fields("objectClass").Value = "contact"
oPerson.Fields("objectClass").Value = Array("top",
"person", _ "organizationalPerson", "contact")
```

Creating a Contact in Active Directory

Creating a contact involves setting informational properties and saving the contact to Active Directory.

The LDAP URL consists of prefixes and distinguishing names for the contact that address its placement in Active Directory's hierarchy. Use the prefix CN for common names, DC for domains, and O or OU for organizations to refer to the object.

CN is used to uniquely identify the object's common name, as well as to indicate its classification, such as users.

Use as many DCs as necessary for each qualification in the domain name, including a DC for subdomains.

Example LDAP URL for a Person Object

If James Smith is a person with an Exchange mailbox in the domain named somewhere.microsoft.com and the name of the Microsoft Exchange 2000 Server is the server, then the LDAP URL would be

```
LDAP://theserver/
cn=jamessmith,cn=users,dc=somewhere,dc=microsoft,dc=com
```

The following example creates a contact using the CDO Person object and saves it to Active Directory:

[Visual Basic]

```
Dim oPerson As New CDO.Person
Dim strURL As String

oPerson.FirstName = "John"
oPerson.LastName = "Smith"
oPerson.HomeCity = "Redmond"
oPerson.HomeState = "Washington"
oPerson.Email = "jsmith@somewhere.microsoft.com"
oPerson.Fields("objectClass").Value = "contact"
oPerson.Fields.Update

strURL = "LDAP://theserver/
cn=johnsmith,cn=users,dc=somwhere,dc=microsoft,dc=com"

'Save the contact
oPerson.DataSource.SaveTo strURL
```

By default the CDO person creates a user. In the preceding code the oPerson.Fields("objectClass").Value is set to type "contact" in order to create a contact.

The objectClass value is an array of variants. However, the property can accept a single value. Thus, the value might be one of the following:

```
  oPerson.Fields("objectClass").Value = "contact"
  oPerson.Fields("objectClass").Value = Array("top",
"person", "organizationalPerson", "contact")
```

Searching for Contacts

When using the CDO Person object, you can search contacts for specific properties and fields. For example, a recruiter may want to search a contact list for candidates who live in California.

The following example uses the CDO Person object to search for candidates who live in California:

[Visual Basic]

```
Function SearchContacts( strWhereClause as String, iMbx as
CDO.IMailbox, Conn as ADODB.Connection )

  Dim Rs as New ADODB.Recordset
  Set Rs.ActiveConnection = Conn
```

```
  strSQL = "select ""DAV:href"", " & _
              """urn:schemas:contacts:fileas"", " & _
              """urn:schemas:contacts:email1""" & _
              "from "

  strSQL = strSQL & """" & iMbx.Contacts & """ "
  strSQL = strSQL & strWhereClause

  Rs.Open strSQL, Conn

End Function
```

Getting a Contact's VCard Stream

Exchange 2000 supports the Internet-industry VCard standard for obtaining contact information through the CDO Person object. You can import contact information from any VCard-compliant contact application.

The GetVCardStream method on the IPerson interface returns contact information by returning an ADO stream object.

The following example uses the CDO Person object to obtain a contact's VCard information:

[Visual Basic]

```
Dim oPerson As New CDO.Person
Dim strm As New ADODB.Stream

'Assume strURL is a valid URL to a person contact item
oPerson.DataSource.Open strURL

'you can set the ADO Stream object to the returned VCard
stream
Set strm = oPerson.GetVcardStream

'Save the stream to a file
strm.SaveToFile "d:\vcard.txt", adSaveCreateOverwrite

'You don't have to set a Stream object,
'just use the Stream methods off GetVCardStrem directly
oPerson.GetVcardStream.SaveToFile "d:\vcard.txt", _
adSaveCreateOverwrite
```

TWENTY

Managing Workflow

Using the WorkflowSession Object

The typical workflow application developer implements business logic by using the WorkflowSession object. This object provides access to the workflow item and messaging without requiring that the developer have object creation privileges. The developer does not need to create this object, because the workflow engine passes the WorkflowSession object to the script host. Scripts can immediately call WorkflowSession methods and properties by using the object name. There is only one WorkflowSession object per transition, and that is the one the engine passes to the script host. For restricted workflow authors, this is the only object they need to work with. Privileged workflow authors can create other objects in the script.

The typical workflow developer also uses the Microsoft Exchange 2000 Server Workflow Designer. The Exchange Workflow Designer enables the developer to create a graphic representation of the workflow. The developer adds script conditions and actions to the graphic representation to create the rules for the workflow. See the "Exchange Workflow Designer" in the MS Exchange SDK documentation for information on how to use this tool.

The following topics explain some of the things you can do with the WorkflowSession object:

- Managing Run-Time Errors
- Caching Custom Properties
- Accessing Active Directory Properties
- Using WorkflowSession Item Security
- Using Audit Trail
- Deleting Workflow Items
- Working with ReceivedMessage
- Accessing and Modifying a ProcessInstance

Managing Run-Time Errors

To log a run-time error, set the IWorkflowSession ErrorNumber property to a negative value in your script. You can use decimal or hexadecimal notation, such as −2147467259 or &H80004005. When the workflow engine sees a negative value in the ErrorNumber property, it writes an error message to the audit trail. The engine gets the message from the ErrorDescription property. The ErrorDescription property should contain the string that you want written to the audit trail for the associated error number.

For example, if the call to CreateObject fails in the code that follows, the workflow state transition ends; this happens because you set the WorkflowSession ErrorNumber to a negative value. The workflow engine generates an entry in the application log of the event viewer with the error message that reads in part: *State transition error: Error in action: I'm testing this*. Note that the rest of the code in the procedure is executed, and any other procedure calls in the current action field are completed:

[VBScript]

```
on error resume next
Dim fso
Set fso = CreateObject("Scripting.FileSystemObject")
if err.number <> 0 then
   with WorkflowSession
      .ErrorNumber = &H80004005   ' (-2147467259)
      .ErrorDescription = "I'm testing this..."
   end with
end if

'Message generated in Application log of Event Viewer:
' "State transition error: Error in action: I'm testing
this..."
```

Caching Custom Properties

You can make custom properties available from one script function to the next by caching your custom properties. There are two main scenarios where this feature is useful:

- During any OnChange transition, the workflow engine looks for matching OnExit and OnEnter rules in the ActionTable. The engine evaluates the conditions and actions for each rule in a predetermined evaluation order. You can cache custom properties during the entire OnChange transition, so that they can be used by any condition or action scripts.

- An OnChange transition from a given state, for example state A, can have many possible outcomes. The outcomes in this example are state B, state C, state D, and so on. Each path from A to the respective outcome states—B, C, D, and so on—has condition scripts that must be tested. These conditions can contain functions that impair server performance if they are repeated too many times. After running the function one time, you can cache the result, so that subsequent condition scripts can use it without having to call the function.

You can cache your own properties for the duration of one transition. Use the IWorkflowSession Properties property to cache your custom properties. In the example that follows, the OnExit action caches a custom property. The custom property is used in the OnChange action, the OnEnter condition, and the OnEnter action. The OnEnter action completes the transition and is the last place the custom property can be used. The following is the code used:

[VBScript]

```
''''''''
'EventType: OnExit
'Condition Expression:
True
'Action Script Procedure:
Dim oItem
Set oItem = CreateObject("CDO.Item")
'do something with oItem
WorkflowSession.Properties.Put "CustomPropertyName", oItem
''''''''
'EventType: OnChange
'Condition Expression:
   True
'Action Script Procedure
   dim MyCustomProperty
   Set MyCustomProperty = CreateObject("CDO.Item")
   Set MyCustomProperty =
WorkflowSession.Properties.Get("CustomPropertyName")
   ProcedureThatUses MyCustomProperty
''''''''
'EventType: OnEnter
'Condition Expression:
   UseCustomProperty(WorkflowSession.Properties.Get
("CustomPropertyName"))
'Action Script Procedure
   Dim MyCustomProperty
   Set MyCustomProperty = CreateObject("CDO.Item")
   Set MyCustomProperty =
WorkflowSession.Properties.Get("CustomPropertyName")
   ProcedureThatUses MyCustomProperty
```

```
'''''''
'Shared Script:
Function UseCustomProperty(CustomPropertyValue)
    'do something with CustomPropertyValue
    UseCustomProperty = True
End Function

Sub ProcedureThatUses(varProp)
    'do something with varProp
end sub
```

A transition may include a compensating action. Compensating actions are called if your transition is aborted for any reason. However, you cannot use custom properties in a compensating action, because the Properties property is not available to compensating actions.

Accessing Active Directory Properties

The Active Directory directory service in Microsoft Windows 2000 contains information about users, groups, organizations, and services in your enterprise. You can locate Active Directory information by querying for properties of an Active Directory object. You can access Active Directory properties with the IWorkflowSession GetUserProperty method. For example, a user may submit a form to a workflow-enabled folder. You may want the workflow to notify the user's manager when a new form is submitted. One way to obtain the manager's email address is to look it up in the Active Directory by using the manager property of the user object. The code used in the example that follows gets the email address for the manager of the user who submitted the form. The code first gets the distinguished name of the manager from Active Directory, and then it uses the manager's distinguished name to get the manager's email address:

[VBScript]

```
'Action Script Procedure:
mgr = GetUserMgr(WorkflowSession.Sender)

'Shared Script:
Function GetUserMgr(UserAddress)
    with WorkflowSession
        mgrDN = .GetUserProperty(UserAddress, "manager", 0)
'0 = cdowfUserEmailAddress
        GetUserMgr = .GetUserProperty(mgrDN, "mail", 1) '1 = cdowfDistinguishedName
    end with
End Function
```

Using WorkflowSession Item Security

You can control access to individual workflow items using IWorkflowSession ItemAuthors and ItemReaders collections. You populate these collections with either email addresses or folder roles.

ITEMAUTHORS

You can allow individual users, groups, or roles to modify and delete specific workflow items by using the ItemAuthors collection. Adding a user, group, or role to the collection gives exclusive Author access to the item. To add a user to the ItemAuthors collection, use the following code:

[VBScript]

```
'In Action field:
AddAuthor "someone@microsoft.com", 0
'MemberType=cdowfEmailAddress

'In Shared Script
Sub AddAuthor(MbrName,MbrType)
   WorkflowSession.ItemAuthors.Add MbrName, MbrType
End Sub
```
To delete this user from the ItemAuthors collection, use the following code:
```
[VBScript]
'In Action field:
DeleteAuthor "someone@microsoft.com"

'In Shared Script
Sub DeleteAuthor(MbrName)
   WorkflowSession.ItemAuthors.Delete mbrname
End Sub
```

To clear the ItemAuthors collection, use the following code:

[VBScript]

```
WorkflowSession.ItemAuthors.Clear
```

The following code writes the list of ItemAuthors to the audit trail and enumerates the members of the ItemAuthors collection:

[VBScript]

```
'In the Action field:
WriteAuthorsToAudit

'In the Shared Script:
Sub WriteAuthorsToAudit()
   Dim str
   Dim mbr
```

```
    str = vbcrlf
    with WorkflowSession
       for each mbr in .ItemAuthors
          str = str & .ItemAuthors(mbr) & vbcrlf
       next
       .AddAuditEntry str
    end with
End Sub
```

ITEMREADERS

You can give a collection of users or roles exclusive read access to specific workflow items by using the ItemReaders property. If you are not a member of ItemReaders,

- The item will not appear in any of your views, folders, or queries.
- You cannot open the item even if you know the URL.

To add a user to the ItemReaders collection, use the following code:

[VBScript]

```
'In Action field:
AddReader "someone@microsoft.com", 0
'MemberType=cdowfEmailAddress

'In Shared Script
Sub AddReader(MbrName,MbrType)
   WorkflowSession.ItemReaders.Add MbrName, MbrType
End Sub
```

To delete this user from the ItemReaders collection, use the following code:

[VBScript]

```
'In Action field:
DeleteReader "someone@microsoft.com"

'In Shared Script
Sub DeleteReader(MbrName)
   WorkflowSession.ItemReaders.Delete mbrname
End Sub
```

To clear the ItemReaders collection, use the following code:

[VBScript]

```
WorkflowSession.ItemReaders.Clear
```

The following code writes the list of ItemReaders to the audit trail and enumerates the members of the ItemReaders collection:

[VBScript]

```
'In the Action field:
WriteReadersToAudit

'In the Shared Script:
Sub WriteReadersToAudit()
   Dim str
   Dim mbr
   str = vbcrlf
   with WorkflowSession
      for each mbr in .ItemReaders
         str = str & .ItemReaders(mbr) & vbcrlf
      next
      .AddAuditEntry str
   end with
End Sub
```

In the next example, you want to give a user's manager exclusive read privileges on an item. The following code demonstrates how to give the user's manager author and read permission:

```
'Action Script Procedure:
ManagerLockOut

'Shared Script:
Sub ManagerLockOut()
   Dim str
   with WorkflowSession
      str = GetUserMgr(.Sender)
      .ItemAuthors.Add str,0 'cdowfEmailAddress
      .ItemReaders.Clear
      .ItemReaders.Add str,0 'cdowfEmailAddress
   end with
End Sub

Function GetUserMgr(UserAddress)
   with WorkflowSession
      mgrDN = .GetUserProperty(UserAddress, "manager", 0)
'0 = cdowfUserEmailAddress
      GetUserMgr = .GetUserProperty(mgrDN, "mail", 1) '1 = cdowfDistinguishedName
   end with
End Function
```

Notice that the ManagerLockOut procedure clears the ItemReaders collection before adding the manager to the ItemReaders collection. This makes the manager the only member of the collection, thus giving the manager exclusive read access to the item.

Using Audit Trail

You can use the audit trail for logging custom messages during script execution. This might be useful as a debugging tool. The IWorkflowSession AddAuditEntry method provides the ability to log messages to the current audit trail provider.

The following code builds a debug string that is entered in the log when the script runs:

[VBScript]

```
Sub SendAuditedMail (MySubject)
   Dim strDebug
   strDebug = vbCrLf
   set WFMsg = WorkflowSession.GetNewWorkflowMessage()
   with WFMsg
      .From = WorkflowSession.Sender
      .To = "someone@microsoft.com"
      .Subject = MySubject
      .TextBody = WorkflowSession.StateFrom & " -> " & WorkflowSession.StateTo
      .SendWorkflowMessage 0 'cdowfNoTracking
      strDebug = strDebug & _
                 "From: " & .from & "; " & _
                 "To: " & .to & "; " & _
                 "Subject: " & .subject & "; " & _
                 "TextBody: " & .textbody & "."
   end with
   WorkflowSession.AddAuditEntry strDebug
End Sub
```

Deleting Workflow Items

You can delete a workflow item during any transition, except during OnReceive events, by using the IWorkflowSession DeleteWorkflowItem method. Deleting a workflow item during a transition will not raise an OnDelete event. If you want to take special delete action, do it in the same script in which you use the DeleteWorkflowItem method.

You can use the following code in an action or condition script:

[VBScript]

```
WorkflowSession.DeleteWorkflowItem
```

Working with ReceivedMessage

In workflow, a ReceivedMessage is a reply posted to a folder as part of an existing workflow process. You receive the reply in response to an email initiated by the workflow process. The reply contains information necessary to advance the workflow. The ReceivedMessage property of the IWorkflow-Session interface returns the IWorkflowMessage interface of a reply to an email sent by using the SendWorkflowMessage method. The ReceivedMessage property is available only in an OnReceive event. This is known as email workflow and is used in a situation where users do not have a direct connection to the corporate database.

In email workflow, you use the IWorkflowMessage interface with the SendWorkflowMessage method to send email whose reply can be matched with an existing workflow process. Use GetNewWorkflowMessage method to get an IWorkflowMessage interface. SendWorkflowMessage adds two fields to the message that are used to match a reply with an existing workflow process. The following two fields are added by SendWorkflowMessage:

- *http://schemas.microsoft.com/cdo/workflow/workflowmessageid*
- *http://schemas.microsoft.com/cdo/workflow/parentprocinstance*

These two fields and values must be properties of the reply form; they are required in the reply form so that the workflow engine can correlate the reply to the original workflow process. When the workflow engine matches a reply, the ReceivedMessage property contains the IWorkflowMessage interface in the reply. You can access and modify the Fields collection of the reply to advance the workflow.

In the code that follows, SendWorkflowMessage creates and populates the workflowmessageid and parentprocinstance fields on the message that it sends. When the client, such as Microsoft Outlook, receives the message, a macro embedded in MyForm copies the values from the fields on the message to fields of the same name on the reply. When the workflow engine handles the reply from the client form, it correlates the reply to the original item based on workflowmessageid and parentprocinstance fields. An OnReceive event triggers the UpdateWorkflowItem procedure, which consolidates the message body into a TrackingTable field.

If you want to track responses—for example, voting—do the following:

- Make sure your form contains the field *http://schemas.microsoft.com/cdo/workflow/response*.
- Make sure you bind the form control containing the response data to the *http://schemas.microsoft.com/cdo/workflow/response* field on the form.

If your form contains the field *http://schemas.microsoft.com/cdo/workflow/response*, the workflow engine writes the value of this field to the response field of the TrackingTable. Response tracking is automatic and requires no coding on your part.

The code in the following example assumes that you have created and published a form in Outlook called MyForm with the workflowmessageid and parentprocinstance properties:

[VBScript]

```
'In Form script for MyForm:
Sub Item_Reply(ByVal Response)
   set CurrentProp = Response.UserProperties.Add(
"http://schemas.microsoft.com/cdo/workflow/
parentprocinstance", 1)
   CurrentProp.Value =
Item.UserProperties("http://schemas.microsoft.com/cdo/
workflow/parentprocinstance").Value
   set CurrentProp = Response.UserProperties.Add
("http://schemas.microsoft.com/cdo/workflow/
workflowmessageid", 1)
   CurrentProp.Value =
Item.UserProperties("http://schemas.microsoft.com/cdo/
workflow/workflowmessageid").Value
End Sub

'EventType: OnChange (original workflow item)
'Action Script Procedure::
SendWorkflowItem 2 '"cdowfStrict"

'EventType: OnReceive (reply to sendworkflowitem)
'Action Script Procedure:
UpdateWorkflowItem

'In Shared Script:
Sub SendWorkflowItem(cdowfMethod)
     Set WFMsg = WorkflowSession.GetNewWorkflowMessage
     with WFMsg
        .To = WorkflowSession.Sender
        .Subject = "Workflow Item"
        .TextBody = "Workflow Item body"

        .Fields("http://schemas.microsoft.com/mapi/proptag/
0x001A001E").Value = "IPM.Note.MyForm"
        .Fields.Update
        .SendWorkflowMessage cdowfMethod
     end with
End Sub

Sub UpdateWorkflowItem()
   with WorkflowSession
      .TrackingTable.Fields("custom0") =
.TrackingTable.Fields("custom0") & vbCrLf & _

.ReceivedMessage.TextBody
      .TrackingTable.Fields.Update
   end with
End Sub
```

Accessing and Modifying a ProcessInstance

A ProcessInstance is an individual workflow item in a Microsoft Web Storage System folder. You can access and modify properties of a ProcessInstance with the Fields collection of the IWorkflowSession interface. The workflow engine provides the WorkflowSession object to the script host without you having to do anything. The following code illustrates how to access a field by using the field name as an index to the Fields collection on the IWorkflowSession interface.

[VBScript]

```
Function GetFieldValue(Name)
   GetFieldValue = WorkflowSession.Fields(CStr(Name)).Value
End Function
```

The Fields collection also enables you to append new fields to a ProcessInstance. Use the Append method of the Fields collection, as shown in the following example:

[VBScript]

```
Sub AddFieldToItem (Name, Value)
   Dim FieldType
   FieldType = 8 ' BSTR
   with WorkflowSession
      .Fields.Append CStr(Name), FieldType, , , CStr(Value)
      .Fields.Update
   end with
End Sub
```

You may decide to send notification with a different subject depending on the importance flag of a ProcessInstance. You can use the Fields collection of the IWorkflowSession interface to obtain the value for the urn:schemas:httpmail:importance property on the item. The following code shows the action script that calls shared scripts in Exchange Workflow Designer.

[VBScript]

```
'This goes in the action pane of Workflow Designer
dim x
x = GetImportance()
if x=2 then 'High Importance
   SendMail "Alert!"
else 'Normal or Low Importance
   SendMail "At ease."
end if

'These go on the Shared Script tab
Function GetImportance()
```

```
      GetImportance = WorkflowSession.Fields
("urn:schemas:httpmail:importance").Value
End Function

Sub SendMail(MySubject)
   Set WFMsg = WorkflowSession.GetNewWorkflowMessage()
   With WFMsg
      .From = WorkflowSession.Sender
      .To = GetUserMgr(WorkflowSession.Sender)
      .Subject = MySubject
      .TextBody = WorkflowSession.StateFrom & " -> " &
WorkflowSession.StateTo
      .SendWorkflowMessage 0 'cdowfNoTracking
   End With
End Sub

Function GetUserMgr(UserAddress)
   with WorkflowSession
      mgrDN = .GetUserProperty(UserAddress, "manager", 0)
'0 = cdowfUserEmailAddress
      GetUserMgr = .GetUserProperty(mgrDN, "mail", 1) '1 =
cdowfDistinguishedName
   end with
End Function
```

Advanced Developer Tasks

Advanced developers may want to write their own event sink or design tool. This section contains examples of the fundamental tasks involved in writing an event sink or design tool. These tasks include the following:

- Creating Action Table Columns
- Adding Action Table Rows
- Specifying the CommonScript File
- Creating the ProcessDefinition
- Registering a Workflow Event Sink in a Folder

Creating Action Table Columns

Creating action table columns is the first step in creating an action table for a workflow.

In workflow terms, an action table is a set of rules that define how workflow items can change state. Each row in the table represents a possible state transition in the workflow. In an expense report example, one row in the table defines how an item gets from submitted state to pending state. Another row defines how an item gets from pending state to approved state.

The columns in an action table define the properties that the workflow engine uses to advance a workflow.

In programming terms, an action table is a record set. To create an action table, you create an ADODB record set. You begin by appending Fields to the Fields collection of a new Recordset object. You append Fields before opening the Recordset object or a Connection object. The workflow engine requires and recognizes 14 fields exclusively. In the Append method, you provide the field name and type as arguments. The following example shows how to append the action table fields to a Recordset object:

[Visual Basic]

```
Dim Rs As ADODB.Recordset
Set Rs = New ADODB.Recordset

With Rs.Fields
 .Append "ID", adBSTR
 .Append "Caption", adBSTR
 .Append "State", adBSTR
 .Append "NewState", adBSTR
 .Append "EventType", adBSTR
 .Append "Condition", adBSTR
 .Append "EvaluationOrder", adBSTR
 .Append "Action", adBSTR
 .Append "ExpiryInterval", adBSTR
 .Append "RowACL", adBSTR
 .Append "TransitionACL", adBSTR
 .Append "DesignToolFields", adBSTR
 .Append "CompensatingAction", adBSTR
 .Append "Flags", adBSTR
End With

Dim varColumnNames As Variant

varColumnNames = Array(Rs.Fields.Item(0).Name, _
                       Rs.Fields.Item(1).Name, _
                       Rs.Fields.Item(2).Name, _
                       Rs.Fields.Item(3).Name, _
                       Rs.Fields.Item(4).Name, _
                       Rs.Fields.Item(5).Name, _
                       Rs.Fields.Item(6).Name, _
                       Rs.Fields.Item(7).Name, _
                       Rs.Fields.Item(8).Name, _
                       Rs.Fields.Item(9).Name, _
                       Rs.Fields.Item(10).Name, _
                       Rs.Fields.Item(11).Name, _
                       Rs.Fields.Item(12).Name, _
                       Rs.Fields.Item(13).Name)
```

Adding Action Table Rows

After you have a record set with the columns required by the workflow engine, you can begin adding records. To do this, you first open the record set with the fields previously appended, then use the AddNew method to add records. After you have added your records to the record set, you can assign the Recordset object to the ActionTable property of the ProcessDefinition. The code used is as follows:

[Visual Basic]

```
Rs.Open
If Err.Number <> 0 Then
    Debug.Print "Failed to open ActionTable Recordset" & Err.Description
End If

With Rs
    .AddNew varColumnNames, Array("1", "OnCreate", "", "Submitted", "OnCreate", "true", "", "sendmail(""new ProcessInstance"")", "", "", "", "", "", "0")
    .AddNew varColumnNames, Array("2", "OnEnter", "", "Submitted", "OnEnter", "true", "", "sendmail(""entered submitted state"")", "", "", "", "", "", "0")
    .AddNew varColumnNames, Array("3", "OnExpiry", "Submitted", "Submitted", "OnExpiry", "true", "", "sendmail(""submitted state expired"")", "", "", "", "", "", "0")
    .AddNew varColumnNames, Array("4", "OnDelete", "Submitted", "", "OnDelete", "true", "", "sendmail(""deleted ProcessInstance"")", "", "", "", "", "", "0")
End With
```

Specifying the Common Script File

The common script file is a text document containing script functions that you can share among many workflow applications. To specify the common script file, you can

- Use the CommonScriptURL property of the IProcessDefinition interface.
- Load the common script text as the default Stream property of the ProcessDefinition item.

Note You must set the Charset property of the Stream to Unicode.

The following code shows how to load the common script as the default Stream property of the ProcessDefinition item:

[Visual Basic]

```
Dim fso As New Scripting.FileSystemObject
Dim file1 As TextStream

Set file1 = fso.OpenTextFile(cstPath)

Dim commonscripttext As String
commonscripttext = file1.ReadAll

Dim Rec As New ADODB.Record
Dim Conn As New ADODB.Connection
Dim Stm As New ADODB.Stream

With Conn
   .Provider = "Exoledb.datasource"
   .ConnectionString = wfFolder
   .Open
End With

Rec.Open pdURL, Conn, adModeReadWrite, adCreateOverwrite

With Stm
   .Open Rec, adModeReadWrite, adOpenStreamFromRecord
   .Charset = "unicode"
   .Type = adTypeText
   .Position = 0
   .SetEOS
   .WriteText commonscripttext
   .Position = 0
   .Flush
   .Close
End With
```

Creating the ProcessDefinition

The ProcessDefinition object encapsulates your business logic and defines how the engine will advance a workflow item. The ProcessDefinition object also determines the privileges that your scripts have and the audit trail that the engine uses.

The example that follows shows how to create a new ProcessDefinition object and an ADO Connection. It binds to the target folder with a Connection object. With the open connection, it sets the desired properties on the ProcessDefinition object. Then, it uses the Recordset object that was built at runtime and sets the ActionTable property on the ProcessDefinition object. See "Creating ActionTable Columns and Adding ActionTable Rows" in the MS

Exchange SDK for examples of how to create the action table record set. Finally, it saves the ProcessDefinition properties to the URL and commits the transaction. The code used to create the ProcessDefinition is as follows:

[Visual Basic]
```
Dim iPD As New CDOWF.ProcessDefinition
Dim conn As New ADODB.Connection

sDomainURL = "file://./backofficestorage/" _
             & Environ("USERDNSDOMAIN") & _
             "/Public Folders/"
sFolderURL = sDomainURL & sFolderName
sProcDefURL = sFolderURL & "/" & sProcDef

conn.Provider = "ExOleDb.DataSource"
conn.Open sFolderURL
conn.BeginTrans

With iPD
  .ActionTable = Rs
'Rs is an open ADODB.Recordset built at runtime

  .AuditTrailProvider = "CdoWf.AuditTrailEventLog"
  .CommonScriptURL = sCommonScriptURL
  .Mode = cdowfPrivilegedMode
  .Fields("DAV:ishidden") = True
End With

iPD.DataSource.SaveTo sProcDefURL, _
                      conn, _
                      adModeReadWrite, _
                      adCreateOverwrite Or
adCreateNonCollection

conn.CommitTrans
```

Registering a Workflow Event Sink in a Folder

The workflow event sink handles OnSyncSave, OnSyncDelete, and OnTimer events in any Microsoft Web Storage System folder where it is registered. When a user saves or deletes an item in a folder, an event occurs. When the event occurs in a folder, the Web Storage System process looks for an event registration item in the folder. The registration item tells the Web Storage System which process handles the event. You need to tell the Web Storage System that you want the workflow event sink process to handle OnSyncSave, OnSyncDelete, and OnTimer events in your folder. This is called registering the workflow event sink in a folder.

The following rules govern the registration of an event sink:

- The event type must be one of the three supported types: OnSyncSave, OnSyncDelete, or OnTimer.
- The user who registers the workflow must be a member of the Can Register Workflow role. The Deployment topic explains how to do this.
- You cannot set the MatchScope of the registration to ANY.
- You cannot register the event sink for a synchronous event with DEEP MatchScope if it is already registered in a subfolder of the same folder.
- You cannot register the event sink in a folder where it is already registered by a DEEP MatchScope registration in a parent folder.
- When you set the OnTimer interval, it should not be smaller than necessary, because the OnTimer event occurs for every workflow folder on your server.
- OnTimer events can have DEEP MatchScope only on a public folder tree that you create. DEEP MatchScope for OnTimer events is not supported in the default public folder tree.

Note — The store event registrations set the criteria field with an SQL WHERE clause to prevent other registrations, ProcessDefinitions, and CommonScripts from raising events in the folder.

The following code registers your workflow application folder for the OnTimer system event, the OnSyncSave store event, and the OnSyncDelete store event. In this example, the OnTimer event causes the workflow event sink to run every 15 minutes:

[Visual Basic]

```
Dim EventRuleItem As String
Dim sEvtRegURL As String
Dim ProcessDefinitionURL As String

'''''''''''''''''''Register OnTimer Event

EventRuleItem = "OnTimerRule"

sEvtRegURL = sFolderURL & EventRuleItem

'The event registration item (sEvtRegURL) must be saved
'in the folder for which you want to register
'the workflow sink.

Dim Rec As ADODB.Record
Set Rec = New ADODB.Record
```

Chapter 20 • Managing Workflow

```
   Rec.Open sEvtRegURL, , adModeReadWrite, _
                adCreateNonCollection Or adCreateOverwrite, _
                adDelayFetchFields
   If Err.Number <> 0 Then
      Debug.Print "Failed to open event registration record." & Err.Description
   End If

   Dim Flds As ADODB.Fields
   With Rec
     Set Flds = .Fields
Flds("DAV:contentclass") = "urn:content-class:storeeventreg"
Flds("http://schemas.microsoft.com/exchange/events/EventMethod") = "OnTimer"

Flds("http://schemas.microsoft.com/exchange/events/SinkClass") = "CdoWfEvt.EventSink.1"

Flds("http://schemas.microsoft.com/exchange/events/TimerStartTime") = #5/1/1999#

Flds("http://schemas.microsoft.com/exchange/events/TimerInterval") = 720

Flds("http://schemas.microsoft.com/exchange/events/TimerExpiryTime") = #8/4/2000#
      Flds.Update
      .Close
   End With

'''''''''''''''''''''Register OnSyncSave and OnSyncDelete Events

   EventRuleItem = "OnSyncSave_OnSyncDelete_Rule"

   sEvtRegURL = sFolderURL & EventRuleItem

   ProcessDefinitionURL = sProcDefURL

   Rec.Open sEvtRegURL, , adModeReadWrite, _
                adCreateNonCollection Or adCreateOverwrite, _
                adDelayFetchFields
   If Err.Number <> 0 Then
      Debug.Print "Failed to open event registration record." & Err.Description
   End If
```

Advanced Developer Tasks

```
  With Rec
    Set Flds = .Fields
    Flds("DAV:contentclass") = "urn:content-
class:storeeventreg"

Flds("http://schemas.microsoft.com/exchange/events/
EventMethod") = "OnSyncSave;OnSyncDelete"

Flds("http://schemas.microsoft.com/exchange/events/
SinkClass") = "CdoWfEvt.EventSink.1"

Flds("http://schemas.microsoft.com/exchange/events/
Criteria") = "WHERE $DAV:ishidden$ AND $DAV:iscollection$ =
FALSE"

Flds("http://schemas.microsoft.com/cdo/workflow/
defaultprocdefinition") = ProcessDefinitionURL

Flds("http://schemas.microsoft.com/cdo/workflow/
adhocflows") = 0

Flds("http://schemas.microsoft.com/cdo/workflow/
enabledebug") = True

Flds("http://schemas.microsoft.com/cdo/workflow/
disablesuccessentries") = False
      Flds.Update
      .Close
  End With
```

TWENTY ONE

Server and Recipient Management

The following programming tasks demonstrate the use of CDOEXM objects and CDOEXM interfaces that are aggregated into other CDO and ADSI objects. For conceptual discussions of CDOEXM objects and interfaces, see "Server and Recipient Management" in the MS Exchange SDK.

Server Management Tasks

The following tasks use the CDOEXM objects to configure Microsoft Exchange 2000 Server:

- Enumerating Storage Groups and Stores
- Retrieving Folder Tree URLs
- Creating a Folder Tree
- Deleting a Folder Tree
- Creating a Storage Group
- Deleting a Storage Group
- Creating a Public Store
- Deleting a Public Store
- Creating a Mailbox Store
- Deleting a Mailbox Store
- Checking for CDOEXM Errors

Enumerating Storage Groups and Stores

The example that follows shows how you can use each CDOEXM object to enumerate storage groups, public and private stores in the storage groups, and the folder trees in which the stores appear. Various parts of this sample can be useful for locating such objects in the Exchange 2000 server:

[Visual Basic]

```
Private Sub EnumerateStore()

  Dim iExs As New CDOEXM.ExchangeServer
  Dim isg As New CDOEXM.StorageGroup
  Dim ipsDB As New CDOEXM.PublicStoreDB
  Dim imbxDB As New CDOEXM.MailboxStoreDB
  Dim ift As New CDOEXM.FolderTree

  Dim ds2 As IDataSource2
  Set ds2 = iExs

  Debug.Print Chr(13) + Chr(13) + Chr(13) +
"================================="

  Dim server_nm As String
  server_nm = Environ("COMPUTERNAME") 'The computer name is the servername.

  ds2.Open server_nm
  Debug.Print "ExchangeVersion = " + iExs.ExchangeVersion

  Debug.Print "DirectoryServer = " + iExs.DirectoryServer

  Dim storegroup As Variant
  Dim pubstore As Variant
  Dim mbx As Variant


  For Each storegroup In iExs.StorageGroups
    Debug.Print "StorageGroup   = " + storegroup + Chr(13)
    isg.DataSource.Open storegroup

    For Each pubstore In isg.PublicStoreDBs

      Debug.Print "Public Store   = " + pubstore
      ipsDB.DataSource.Open pubstore
      Debug.Print "             Name    = " + ipsDB.Name + Chr(13)

      Debug.Print "FolderTree    = " + ipsDB.FolderTree
      ift.DataSource.Open ipsDB.FolderTree
      Debug.Print " RootFolderURL = " + ift.RootFolderURL
      Debug.Print "             Name    = " + ift.Name + Chr(13)

    Next 'public store
```

```
   For Each mbx In isg.MailboxStoreDBs

      Debug.Print "Mailbox         = " + mbx
      imbxDB.DataSource.Open mbx
      Debug.Print "            Name = " + imbxDB.Name +
Chr(13)

   Next 'mailbox
  Next 'storage group


  Set iExs = Nothing
  Set isg = Nothing
  Set ipsDB = Nothing
  Set imbxDB = Nothing
  Set ift = Nothing

End Sub
```

Retrieving Folder Tree URLs

Folder tree URLs are required for various store management operations. The following code, which will locate a folder tree by name on a given server, will return the full URL, which you can use when creating a store:

[Visual Basic]

```
'////////////////////////////////////////////////////////
////////////////////////
'// Function:   GetFolderTreeURL
'// Purpose:    To get the Folder Tree Hierarchies URL
'// Input:      strComputerName = contains the name of the
Exchange 2000 Server
'//             strFHName = contains the name of the Folder
Tree Hierarchy to be found
'// Output:     True = the Folder Tree Hierarchy was found
'//             False = there were errors and Folder Tree
Hierarchy wasn't found
'//
'// Notes:     The function is useful for checking to see
if this folder tree url
'//            is already in use.  Also it is useful when
creating a new
'//            public or mailbox store (since they require
a folder tree URL).
'//
'////////////////////////////////////////////////////////
////////////////////////
```

Chapter 21 • Server and Recipient Management

```
Public Function GetFolderTreeURL(ByVal strComputerName As String, _
                                 ByRef strFHName As String) As Boolean
    On Error Resume Next
    Dim Result     As Boolean
    Dim RootDSE    As IADs
    Dim conf       As IADs

    Dim conn       As New ADODB.Connection
    Dim comm       As New ADODB.Command
    Dim rs         As ADODB.Recordset

    'Get the default IExchangeServer interface
    Dim iServer         As New CDOEXM.ExchangeServer

    Dim strPath            As String
    Dim strDSAdminName     As String
    Dim strDSAdminPass     As String
    Dim strDNFolder        As String

    Result = True

    strFHName = ""

    ' Bind to the Exchange Server
    iServer.DataSource.Open strComputerName
    Result = Result And CheckError("Open Server in function GetFolderTreeURL")

    Set RootDSE = GetObject("LDAP://" + iServer.DirectoryServer + "/RootDSE")
    strPath = "LDAP://" & iServer.DirectoryServer & "/" & RootDSE.Get("configurationNamingContext")

    ' Set the Provider for the connection object
    conn.Provider = "ADsDSOObject"

    'You will need to provide login credentials if you are not logged in
    'with an administrator security context.
'    conn.Properties("user id") = "Administrator"
'    conn.Properties("Password") = ""
'    conn.Properties("Bind Flags") = 1

    ' Open connection
    conn.Open
    Result = Result And CheckError("Open Connection in function GetFolderTreeURL")
```

```
    ' Set command to connection object
    Set comm.ActiveConnection = conn
    Result = Result And CheckError("Set Active Connection
in function GetFolderTreeURL")


    comm.CommandText = "<" & strPath & ">" &
";(objectClass=msExchPFTree);ADsPath,distinguishedName,Name
;subtree"

    ' Execute command
    Set rs = comm.Execute
    Result = Result And CheckError("Execute Command in
function GetFolderTreeURL")

    ' Get the Default FolderTreeHierarcy
    Do While Not (rs.EOF)
        'You can print access folder tree information here
        'Debug.Print rs.Fields("ADsPath").Value
        'Debug.Print rs.Fields("distinguishedName")
        'Debug.Print rs.Fields("Name")
        strDNFolder = rs.Fields("distinguishedName")
        'cut the folder name to get the Folder Hierarchies
        strFHName = Mid(strDNFolder, InStr(2, strDNFolder,
"CN="))
        If strFHName <> "" Then
            Exit Do
        Else
            rs.MoveNext
        End If
    Loop
    ' test if the URL to the FolderTreeHierarcy is empty
    If strFHName = "" Then
        Debug.Print "No Folder Hierarchy Name Found."
        Result = False
    End If

    'Cleanup
    Set RootDSE = Nothing
    Set conf = Nothing

    Set conn = Nothing
    Set comm = Nothing
    Set rs = Nothing
    Set iServer = Nothing

    GetFolderTreeURL = Result
End Function
```

Creating a Folder Tree

The following example creates a folder tree in the Microsoft Web Storage System. (See "Web Storage System Configuration" in the MS Exchange SDK for an explanation of the folder tree).

[Visual Basic]

```
'////////////////////////////////////////////////////////////////////////////////////////
'// Function:    CreatePublicFolderTree
'// Purpose:     To create a new PublicFolderTree with a given name
'// Input:       strFolderName = contains name of the New Folder to be created
'//              strComputerName = contains the name of the Exchange 2000 server
'//              strFolderUrl (Optional ByRef) = contains the URL to the New Folder created;
'// Output:      True = the Folder Tree was created
'//              False = there were errors and Folder Tree wasn't created
'//
'////////////////////////////////////////////////////////////////////////////////////////

Public Function CreatePublicFolderTree(ByVal strFolderName As String, _
                                       ByVal strComputerName As String, _
                                       Optional ByRef strFolderURL As String) As Boolean
    On Error Resume Next
    Dim iServer         As New CDOEXM.ExchangeServer
    Dim iPFTree         As New CDOEXM.FolderTree
    Dim strFHName       As String

    Dim Result      As Boolean

    Result = True
    ' Get the URL to the FolderTreeHierarchy
    Result = Result And GetFolderTreeURL(strComputerName, strFHName)

    ' Bind to the Exchange Server
    iServer.DataSource.Open strComputerName
    Result = Result And CheckError("Open Server in function CreatePublicFolderTree")

    ' Build the URL to the PublicFolderTree
```

```
    strFolderURL = "LDAP://" & iServer.DirectoryServer &
"/CN=" & strFolderName & "," & strFHName

    ' Set the name of the PublicFolderTree
    iPFTree.Name = strFolderName

    ' Save the PublicFolderTree
    iPFTree.DataSource.SaveTo strFolderURL
    Result = Result And CheckError("SaveTo " &
strFolderName & " in function CreatePublicFolderTree")

    ' Cleanup
    Set iServer = Nothing
    Set iPFTree = Nothing

    CreatePublicFolderTree = Result
End Function
```

The preceding function calls GetFolderTreeURL to build a proper URL for creating a folder tree. See "Retrieving Folder Tree URLs" in the MS Exchange SDK for a description of the function call GetFolderTreeURL().

See "Checking for CDOEXM Errors," also in the MS Exchange SDK, to see the function CheckError().

Deleting a Folder Tree

The following example deletes a folder tree from the Microsoft Web Storage System. See "Web Storage System Configuration" in the MS Exchange SDK for an explanation of the folder tree.

[Visual Basic]

```
'///////////////////////////////////////////////////////////
//////////////////////
'// Function:    DeletePublicFolderTree
'// Purpose:     To delete a Public Folder Tree
'// Input:       strFolderName = contains the name of the
Folder Tree to be deleted
'//              strComputerName = contains the name of the
Exchange 2000 server
'// Output:      True = the Folder Tree was deleted
'//              False = there were errors and Folder Tree
wasn't deleted
'//
'///////////////////////////////////////////////////////////
//////////////////////
```

```
Public Function DeletePublicFolderTree(ByVal strFolderName
As String, _
                                       ByVal
strComputerName As String) As Boolean
    On Error Resume Next
    Dim iServer        As New CDOEXM.ExchangeServer
    Dim iPFTree        As New CDOEXM.FolderTree
    Dim strFolderURL   As String
    Dim strFHName      As String
    Dim Result         As Boolean

    Result = True
    ' get the URL to the FolderTreeHierarchy
    Result = Result And GetFolderTreeURL(strComputerName,
strFHName)

    ' Bind to Exchange Server
    iServer.DataSource.Open strComputerName
    Result = Result And CheckError("Open Server in function
DeletePublicFolderTree")

    ' Build the URL to the PublicFolderTree
    strFolderURL = "LDAP://" & iServer.DirectoryServer &
"/CN=" & strFolderName & "," & strFHName

    ' Bind to the Public Folder Tree
    iPFTree.DataSource.Open strFolderURL
    Result = Result And CheckError("Open PublicFolderTree "
& strFolderName & " in function DeletePublicFolderTree")

    ' Delete the Public Folder Tree
    iPFTree.DataSource.Delete
    Result = Result And CheckError("Delete PublicFolderTree
" & strFolderName)

    ' Cleanup
    Set iServer = Nothing
    Set iPFTree = Nothing

    DeletePublicFolderTree = Result
End Function
```

The preceding function calls GetFolderTreeURL to build a proper URL for creating a folder tree. See "Retrieving Folder Tree URLs" in the MS Exchange SDK for a description of the function call GetFolderTreeURL().

See "Checking for CDOEXM Errors" in the MS Exchange SDK, to see the function CheckError().

Creating a Storage Group

The following example creates a storage group. See "Server and Recipient Management" in the MS Exchange SDK for further information.

[Visual Basic]

```
'///////////////////////////////////////////////////////////////////////////////
'// Function:    CreateNewStorageGroup
'// Purpose:     To create a new Storage Group with a given name
'// Input:       strSGName = contains name of the New Storage Group to be created
'//              strComputerName = contains the name of the Exchange 2000 server
'//              strSGUrl (Optional ByRef) = contains the URL to the New Storage Group created;
'// Output:      True = the Storage Group was created
'//              False = there were errors and Storage Group wasn't created
'//
'///////////////////////////////////////////////////////////////////////////////

Public Function CreateNewStorageGroup(ByVal strSGName As String, _
                        ByVal strComputerName As String, _
                        Optional ByRef strSGUrl As String) As Boolean
    On Error Resume Next
    Dim iServer         As New CDOEXM.ExchangeServer
    Dim iStGroup        As New CDOEXM.StorageGroup
    Dim Result          As Boolean
    Dim strTemp         As String

    Result = True

    ' Set the name of the StorageGroup
    iStGroup.Name = strSGName
    Result = Result And CheckError("Set StorageGroup.Name to " & strSGName & " in function CreateNewStorageGroup")

    ' Bind to the Exchange Server
    iServer.DataSource.Open strComputerName
    Result = Result And CheckError("Open Server in function CreateNewStorageGroup")
```

```
    'cut out the Storage Group name from URL
    strTemp = iServer.StorageGroups(0)
    strTemp = Mid(strTemp, InStr(2, strTemp, "cn"))
    ' Build the URL to the StorageGroup
    strSGUrl = "LDAP://" & iServer.DirectoryServer & "/CN="
& strSGName & "," & strTemp

    ' Save the StorageGroup
    iStGroup.DataSource.SaveTo strSGUrl
    Result = Result And CheckError("SaveTo " & strSGName &
" in function CreateNewStorageGroup")

    ' Cleanup
    Set iServer = Nothing
    Set iStGroup = Nothing

    CreateNewStorageGroup = Result
End Function
```

See "Checking for CDOEXM Errors" in the MS Exchange SDK to see the function CheckError().

Deleting a Storage Group

The following example deletes a storage group. See "Server and Recipient Management" in the MS Exchange SDK for further information.

[Visual Basic]

```
'//////////////////////////////////////////////////////
////////////////////////
'// Function:    DeleteStorageGroup
'// Purpose:     To delete a Storage Group
'// Input:       strSGName = contains the name of the
Storage Group to be deleted
'//              strComputerName = contains the name of the
Exchange 2000 server
'// Output:      True = the Storage Group was deleted
'//              False = there were errors and Storage Group
wasn't deleted
'//
'// Notes:       Dismount is performed automatically when
deleted.
'//
'//////////////////////////////////////////////////////
////////////////////////

Public Function DeleteStorageGroup(ByVal strSGName As
String, _
```

```
                                ByVal strComputerName As
String) As Boolean
    On Error Resume Next
    Dim iServer         As New CDOEXM.ExchangeServer
    Dim iStGroup        As New CDOEXM.StorageGroup
    Dim arrStGroup()    As Variant
    Dim Result          As Boolean
    Dim strSGUrl        As String
    Dim i               As Integer

    Result = True
    strSGUrl = ""

    ' Bind to the Exchange Server
    iServer.DataSource.Open strComputerName
    Result = Result And CheckError("Open Server in
DeleteStorageGroup function")

    ' Set variant array to the ExchangeServer.StorageGroups
    arrStGroup = iServer.StorageGroups

    ' Look for a Storage Group with strSGName name in the
StorageGroups array
    For i = 0 To UBound(arrStGroup)
        If InStr(1, UCase(arrStGroup(i)), UCase(strSGName))
<> 0 Then
            strSGUrl = arrStGroup(i)
        End If
    Next
    ' Verify if StorageGroup was found
    If strSGUrl = "" Then
        LogComment "The Storage Group >" & strSGName & "<
is not being found."
        Result = False
    Else
        ' Bind to the StorageGroup
        iStGroup.DataSource.Open "LDAP://" &
iServer.DirectoryServer & "/" & strSGUrl
        Result = Result And CheckError("Open Storage Group
" & strSGName & " in function DeleteStorageGroup")

        ' Delete the StorageGroup
        iStGroup.DataSource.Delete
        Result = Result And CheckError("Delete Storage
Group " & strSGName)
    End If

    ' Cleanup
    Set iServer = Nothing
    Set iStGroup = Nothing
```

```
        DeleteStorageGroup = Result
End Function
```

See "Checking for CDOEXM Errors" in the MS Exchange SDK to see the function CheckError().

Creating a Public Store

The code in the example that follows creates a public store in a storage group. Note that when creating a public store, you must specify a folder tree. The folder tree specifies where the data in the store is to appear in the Web Storage System. See "Web Storage System Configuration" in the MS Exchange SDK for more information. The code is as follows:

[Visual Basic]

```
'//////////////////////////////////////////////////////////
//////////////////////////
'// Function:    CreateNewPublicStore
'// Purpose:     To create a new PublicStoreDB with a given name
'// Input:       strPSName = contains name of the New PublicStoreDB to be created
'//              strFolderName = contains the name of the related Public Folder
'//              strComputerName = contains the name of the Exchange 2000 server
'//              blnMount (Optional) = True if New PublicStoreDB will be Mounted after creation
'//                                  = False if New PublicStoreDB will not be Mounted
'//              strSGName (Optional) = contains the name of the Storage Group to create New PublicStoreDB in;
'//                                   if it's empty then the new PublicStoreDB will be created in the default Storage Group
'//              strMDBUrl (Optional ByRef) = contains the URL to the New PublicStoreDB created;
'// Output:      True = the PublicStoreDB was created
'//              False = there were errors and PublicStoreDB wasn't created
'//
'//////////////////////////////////////////////////////////
//////////////////////////

Function CreateNewPublicStore(ByVal strPSName As String, _
                              ByVal strFolderName As String, _
```

```
                                ByVal strComputerName As
String, _
                                Optional ByVal blnMount As
Boolean, _
                                Optional ByVal strSGName As
String, _
                                Optional ByRef strPSUrl As
String) As Boolean
    On Error Resume Next
    Dim iServer         As New CDOEXM.ExchangeServer
    Dim iPbStoreDB      As New CDOEXM.PublicStoreDB
    Dim Result          As Boolean
    Dim arrStGroup()    As Variant
    Dim i               As Integer
    Dim strTemp         As String
    Dim strFolderURL    As String
    Dim strFHName       As String
    Result = True

    ' Bind to the Exchange Server
    iServer.DataSource.Open strComputerName
    Result = Result And CheckError("Open Server in function
CreateNewPublicStore")

    ' Get the FolderTreeHierarcy to build the URL to the
Public Folder
    Result = Result And GetFolderTreeURL(strComputerName,
strFHName)

    ' Build the URL to the PublicFolderTree
    strFolderURL = "LDAP://" & iServer.DirectoryServer &
"/CN=" & strFolderName & "," & strFHName

    ' Set the variant array to the array of StorageGroups
from Server object
    arrStGroup = iServer.StorageGroups
    ' Start to build the URL to the PublicStore - first
part
    strTemp = "LDAP://" & iServer.DirectoryServer & "/CN="
& strPSName & ","

    ' Set the name of the PublicStoreDB
    iPbStoreDB.Name = strPSName
    Result = Result And CheckError("Set PublicStoreDB.Name
for " & strPSName & " in function CreateNewPublicStore")
    ' Set the name of the PublicFolderTree
    iPbStoreDB.FolderTree = strFolderURL
    Result = Result And CheckError("Set
PublicStoreDB.FolderTree for " & strFolderName & " in
function CreateNewPublicStore")
```

```
    ' Verify if the StorageGroup strSGName exist in the
StorageGroups array
    If strSGName = "" Then
        ' Finish to build the URL to the PublicStoreDB -
add last part
        strPSUrl = strTemp & iServer.StorageGroups(0)
    Else
        For i = 0 To UBound(arrStGroup)
            If InStr(1, arrStGroup(i), strSGName) <> 0 Then
                ' Finish to build the URL to the
PublicStoreDB -  add last part
                strPSUrl = strTemp & arrStGroup(i)
            End If
        Next
        If strPSUrl = "" Then
            LogComment "The Storage Group >" & strSGName &
"< was not found."
            Result = False
            Exit Function
        End If
    End If

    ' Save the PublicStoreDB
    iPbStoreDB.DataSource.SaveTo strPSUrl
    Result = Result And CheckError("SaveTo PublicStoreDB "
& strPSName & "in function CreateNewPublicStore")

    ' Mount the PublicStoreDB if thr blnMount is True
    If blnMount = True Then
        iPbStoreDB.Mount
        Result = Result And CheckError("Mount PublicStoreDB
" & strPSName & " in function CreateNewPublicStore")
    End If

    ' Cleanup
    Set iServer = Nothing
    Set iPbStoreDB = Nothing

    CreateNewPublicStore = Result
End Function
```

The preceding sample calls GetFolderTreeURL(). This retrieves the folder tree full URL that is used to specify the location of the store data in the Web Storage System. See "Retrieving Folder Tree URLs" in the MS Exchange SDK for an explanation of GetFolderTreeURL.

See "Checking for CDOEXM Errors," also in the MS Exchange SDK, to see the function CheckError().

Deleting a Public Store

The code in the example that follows deletes a public store in a storage group. The function searches the server for the specified storage group from which to delete the public store.

[Visual Basic]

```
'//////////////////////////////////////////////////////////////////////////////
'// Function:   DeletePublicStore
'// Purpose:    To delete a PublicStoreDB with a given name
'// Input:      strPSName = contains name of the PublicStoreDB to be deleted
'//             strComputerName = contains the name of the Exchange 2000  server
'//             strSGName (Optional) = contains the name of the Storage Group where PublicStoreDB is in;
'//                                  if it's empty then Storage Group will be considered the first one in the list
'// Output:     True = the PublicStoreDB was deleted
'//             False = there were errors and PublicStoreDB wasn't deleted
'//
'// Notes:      It is not necessary to dismount the store. The store will be
'//             automatically dismounted before deletion.
'//
'//////////////////////////////////////////////////////////////////////////////

Function DeletePublicStore(ByVal strPSName As String, _
                      ByVal strComputerName As String, _
                      Optional ByVal strSGName As String) As Boolean
    On Error Resume Next
    Dim iServer         As New CDOEXM.ExchangeServer
    Dim iPbStoreDB      As New CDOEXM.PublicStoreDB
    Dim Result          As Boolean
    Dim arrStGroup()
    Dim i               As Integer
    Dim strTemp         As String
    Dim strFolderURL    As String
    Dim strFHName       As String
    Dim strPSUrl        As String

    Result = True
```

```
    ' Bind to the Exchange Server
    iServer.DataSource.Open strComputerName
    Result = Result And CheckError("Open Server in function
DeletePublicStore")

    ' Set the variant array to the array of StorageGroups
from Server object
    arrStGroup = iServer.StorageGroups

    ' Start to build the URL to the PublicStore - first
part
    strTemp = "LDAP://" & iServer.DirectoryServer & "/CN="
& strPSName & ","

    ' Verify if the StorageGroup strSGName exist in the
StorageGroups array
    If strSGName = "" Then
        ' Finish to build the URL to the PublicStoreDB -
add last part
        strPSUrl = strTemp & iServer.StorageGroups(0)
    Else
        For i = 0 To UBound(arrStGroup)
            If InStr(1, arrStGroup(i), strSGName) <> 0 Then
                ' Finish to build the URL to the
PublicStoreDB -  add last part
                strPSUrl = strTemp & arrStGroup(i)
            End If
        Next
        If strPSUrl = "" Then
            LogComment "The Storage Group >" & strSGName &
"< was not found."
            Result = False
            Exit Function
        End If
    End If

    ' Bind to the PublicStoreDB
    iPbStoreDB.DataSource.Open strPSUrl
    Result = Result And CheckError("Open PublicStoreDB " &
strPSName & " in function DeletePublicStore")

    ' Delete the PublicStoreDB
    iPbStoreDB.DataSource.Delete
    Result = Result And CheckError("Delete PublicStoreDB "
& strPSName)

    ' Cleanup
    Set iServer = Nothing
    Set iPbStoreDB = Nothing
```

```
        DeletePublicStore = Result
End Function
```

See Checking for CDOEXM Errors to see the function CheckError().

Creating a Mailbox Store

The example that follows creates a mailbox store in a storage group. Note that when creating a mailbox store, you must specify a folder tree. The folder tree specifies where the mailboxes appear in the Web Storage System. See "Web Storage System Configuration" in the MS Exchange SDK for more information. The code is as follows:

[Visual Basic]

```
'///////////////////////////////////////////////////////
///////////////////////
'// Function:    CreateNewMailboxStoreDB
'// Purpose:     To create a new Mailbox Store (MDB) with a given name
'// Input:       strMDBName = contains name of the New MDB to be created
'//              blnMount = True if New MDB will be Mounted after creation or False if New MDB will not be Mounted
'//              strComputerName = contains the name of the Exchange 2000  server
'//              strSGName (Optional) = contains the name of the Storage Group to create New MDB in; if it's empty then the new MDB will be created in the default Storage Group
'//              strMDBUrl (Optional ByRef) = contains the URL to the New MDB created;
'// Output:      True = the MDB was created
'//              False = there were errors and MDB wasn't created
'//
'///////////////////////////////////////////////////////
///////////////////////

Public Function CreateNewMailboxStoreDB(ByVal strMDBName As String, _
                                        ByVal strComputerName As String, _
                                        Optional ByVal blnMount As Boolean, _
                                        Optional ByVal strSGName As String, _
                                        Optional ByRef strMDBUrl As String) As Boolean
    On Error Resume Next
```

Chapter 21 • Server and Recipient Management

```
    Dim iServer         As New CDOEXM.ExchangeServer
    Dim iMDB            As New CDOEXM.MailboxStoreDB
    Dim arrStGroup()    As Variant
    Dim Result          As Boolean
    Dim i               As Integer
    Dim strTemp         As String

    Result = True

    ' Set the name of the MailboxStoreDB
    iMDB.Name = strMDBName
    Result = Result And CheckError("Set MailboxStoreDB.Name
to " & strMDBName & " in function CreateNewMailboxStoreDB")

    ' Bind to the Exchange Server
    iServer.DataSource.Open strComputerName
    Result = Result And CheckError("Open Server in function
CreateNewMailboxStoreDB")

    ' Start to build the URL to the MailboxStoreDB - first part
    strTemp = "LDAP://" & iServer.DirectoryServer & "/" &
"cn=" & strMDBName & ","

    ' Set variant array to the ExchangeServer.StorageGroups
    arrStGroup = iServer.StorageGroups

    ' Look in the StorageGroups array if the StorageGroup
with strSGName exists
    If strSGName = "" Then
        ' Finish to build the URL to the MailboxStoreDB -
add last part
        strMDBUrl = strTemp & iServer.StorageGroups(0)
    Else
        For i = 0 To UBound(arrStGroup)
            If InStr(1, UCase(arrStGroup(i)),
UCase(strSGName)) <> 0 Then
                strMDBUrl = arrStGroup(i)
            End If
        Next
        If strMDBUrl = "" Then
            LogComment "The Storage Group >" & strSGName &
"< was not found."
            Result = False
            Exit Function
        Else
            ' Finish to build the URL to the MailboxStoreDB
- add last part
            strMDBUrl = strTemp & strMDBUrl
        End If
    End If
```

```
    ' Save the New MailboxStoreDB
    iMDB.DataSource.SaveTo strMDBUrl
    Result = Result And CheckError("SaveTo for" &
strMDBName)

    ' Mount the MailboxStoreDB if blnMount is True
    If blnMount = True Then
        iMDB.Mount
        Result = Result And CheckError("Mount " &
strMDBName)
    End If

    ' Cleanup
    Set iServer = Nothing
    Set iMDB = Nothing

    ' Return the boolean value
    CreateNewMailboxStoreDB = Result
End Function
```

The preceding code calls GetFolderTreeURL(). This retrieves the folder tree full URL that is used to specify the location of the store data in the Web Storage System. See "Retrieving Folder Tree URLs" in the MS Exchange SDK for an explanation of GetFolderTreeURL.

See "Checking for CDOEXM Errors," also in the MS Exchange SDK, to see the function CheckError().

Deleting a Mailbox Store

The code in the example that follows deletes a mailbox store in a storage group. The function searches the server for the specified storage group from which to delete the mailbox store:

[Visual Basic]

```
'////////////////////////////////////////////////////////
////////////////////////
'// Function:    DeleteMailboxStoreDB
'// Purpose:     To delete a Mailbox Store (MDB)
'// Input:       strMDBName = contains the name of the MDB
to be deleted
'//              strSGName = contains the name of the
Storage Group which contains the MDB
'//              strComputerName = contains the name of the
Exchange 2000  server
'// Output:      True = the MDB was deleted
'//              False = there were errors and MDB wasn't
deleted
```

Chapter 21 ● Server and Recipient Management

```
'//
'// Notes:     Dismount is performed automatically when
deleted.
'//
'///////////////////////////////////////////////////////
////////////////////////

Public Function DeleteMailboxStoreDB(ByVal strMDBName As
String, _
                                    ByVal strSGName As
String, _
                                    ByVal strComputerName
As String) As Boolean

    On Error Resume Next
    Dim iServer        As New CDOEXM.ExchangeServer
    Dim iMDB           As New CDOEXM.MailboxStoreDB
    Dim arrStGroup()
    Dim Result         As Boolean
    Dim i              As Integer
    Dim strTemp        As String
    Dim strMDBUrl      As String


    Result = True

    ' Bind to the Exchange Server
    iServer.DataSource.Open strComputerName
    Result = Result And CheckError("Open Server in function
DeleteMailboxStoreDB")

    ' Build the first part of the URL to the MailboxStoreDB
    strTemp = "LDAP://" & iServer.DirectoryServer & "/" &
"cn=" & strMDBName & ","

    ' Set variant array to the ExchangeServer.StorageGroups
    arrStGroup = iServer.StorageGroups

    ' Look in the StorageGroups array if the StorageGroup
with strSGName exists
    If strSGName = "" Then
        ' Add last part to the URL to the MailboxStoreDB
        strMDBUrl = strTemp & iServer.StorageGroups(0)
    Else
        For i = 0 To UBound(arrStGroup)
            If InStr(1, UCase(arrStGroup(i)),
UCase(strSGName)) <> 0 Then
                strMDBUrl = arrStGroup(i)
            End If
```

Server Management Tasks

```
        Next
        If strMDBUrl = "" Then
            LogComment "The Storage Group >" & strSGName &
"< was not found."
            Result = False
            Exit Function
        Else
            ' Add last part to the URL to the
MailboxStoreDB
            strMDBUrl = strTemp & strMDBUrl
        End If
    End If

    ' Bind to the MailboxStoreB
    iMDB.DataSource.Open strMDBUrl   ', , ,
adCreateOverwrite
    Result = Result And CheckError("Open " & strMDBName & "
in function DeleteMailboxStoreDB")

    ' Delete the MailboxStoreDB
    iMDB.DataSource.Delete
    Result = Result And CheckError("Delete MailboxStoreDB "
& strMDBName)

    ' Cleanup
    Set iServer = Nothing
    Set iMDB = Nothing

    DeleteMailboxStoreDB = Result
End Function
```

See Checking for CDOEXM Errors to see the function CheckError( ).

Checking for CDOEXM Errors

CDOEXM objects support the Microsoft Visual Basic IsupportErrorInfo, which logs errors into the global VBA.ErrorObject. The following function accesses this object, reports any errors, and clears the errors from the object.

[Visual Basic]

```
'///////////////////////////////////////////////////////
///////////////////////
'// Function:   CheckError
'// Purpose:    Checks last error and prints a comment if
one is given
'// Input:      Action = Whatever you want to print if an
error occurred.
'// Output:     True = Pass
```

```
'//                False = Fail
'//
'///////////////////////////////////////////////////////
////////////////////////

Public Function CheckError(Action As String) As Boolean
    Dim strLineNum          As String
    Dim iErrLine            As Long
    Dim strErrorNum         As String
    Dim ErrDescription      As String

    ErrDescription = Err.Description

    On Error Resume Next

    If Err.Number < 0 And Err.Number > -2147483648# Then
        strErrorNum = "0x" + Hex(Err.Number)
    Else
        strErrorNum = Err.Number & ""
    End If

    CheckError = True

    'Print line num if it's available
    iErrLine = Erl()
    If iErrLine <> 0 Then
        strLineNum = " (line " & iErrLine & ")"
    Else
        strLineNum = ""
    End If

    If Err.Number <> 0 Then
        CheckError = False
        LogComment "Error" & strLineNum & ": Error #" &
strErrorNum & " (" & Replace(ErrDescription, vbCrLf, " ") &
"): " & Action
    End If
    Err.Clear
End Function
```

The function CheckError() is used in the examples in this section to check whether errors have occurred.

Recipient Management Tasks

The tasks in this section demonstrate the use of the CDOEXM aggregated interfaces to create and manage recipients in Exchange 2000 Server.

Creating a Mail-Enabled Recipient

To create a mail-enabled recipient, you must first create an object that supports the IMailRecipient interface:

- Person
- Folder
- ADSI Contact (IADS)
- ADSI Group (IADSGroup)
- ADSI User (IADSUser)

In most cases, you create an instance of a Person object. Note that if the user does not have an Exchange mailbox, you must set his or her address by using the IMailRecipient.MailEnable method.

Example (CDOEXM)

The next example creates a mail recipient who can access mail through HTTP. The recipient is limited to sending and receiving messages no larger than 50 KB. The code used is as follows:

[Visual Basic]

```
Function MailEnableCDOPerson(strFirstName As String, _
                            strLastName As String, _
                            strTargetMailAddress As String) As Boolean

    Dim oPerson            As New CDO.Person
    Dim oRecipient         As CDOEXM.IMailRecipient
    Dim strUserName        As String
    Dim strURL             As String
    Dim strContainerName   As String
    Dim Result             As Boolean
    Dim forward_email      As String


    Result = True
    'Target address should look like this
    'strTargetMailAddress = strLastName & "@somewhere.com"

    strUserName = strFirstName & strLastName
    strContainerName = "Users"
    ' Create URL for the user
    Result = Result And CreateUserURL(strURL, strContainerName, False, strUserName)

    oPerson.FirstName = strFirstName
    oPerson.LastName = strLastName

    oPerson.DataSource.SaveTo strURL
```

```
        Result = Result And CheckError("SaveTo " & strURL)

        Set oPerson = New CDO.Person

        ' Bind
        oPerson.DataSource.Open strURL
        Result = Result And CheckError("Bind to CDO User " &
strUserName)

        ' MailEnable
        Set oRecipient = oPerson
        oRecipient.MailEnable strTargetMailAddress
        Result = Result And CheckError("Mail Enable CDO User "
& strUserName)

        If oRecipient.TargetAddress = "" And
oRecipient.X400Email = "" Then
            forward_email = "smtp:" + recipname + "@" +
forward_domain
            oRecipient.MailEnable forward_email  'where to
forward the mail to
            oRecipient.IncomingLimit = 50
            oRecipient.OutgoingLimit = 50
            ' Save
            oPerson.DataSource.Save
            Result = Result And CheckError("Save CDO User " &
strUserName)

            MsgBox recipname + " mail enabled successfully"
        Else
            MsgBox recipname + " is already mail enabled"
        End If

        'CleanUp
        Set oPerson = Nothing
        Set oRecipient = Nothing

        MailEnableCDOPerson = Result
End Function
```

Creating a Mailbox-Enabled Recipient

The example that follows creates a new recipient and an accompanying mailbox. The IMailboxStore interface is aggregated onto the Person object. This allows the person information to be used when creating the mailbox. The code is as follows:

Example (CDOEXM)

Create a mailbox for a mail recipient.

Recipient Management Tasks

[Visual Basic]

```vb
Function CreateMailboxCDOPerson(strFirstName As String, _
                                strLastName As String, _
                                strHomeMDBUrl As String) As Boolean
'strHomeMDBUrl should look like this
'strHomeMDBUrl = "CN=Mailbox Store (MYSTORE),CN=First Storage Group,
'
CN=InformationStore,CN=MYSTORE,CN=Servers,
'                CN=First Administrative Group,CN=Administrative Groups,
'                CN=IASI,CN=Microsoft Exchange,CN=Services,CN=Configuration,
'
DC=mydomain,DC=extest,DC=microsoft,DC=com"

    Dim oPerson          As New CDO.Person
    Dim oMailbox         As CDOEXM.IMailboxStore
    Dim strUserName      As String
    Dim strURL           As String
    Dim strContainerName As String
    Dim Result           As Boolean

    Result = True

    strUserName = strFirstName & strLastName

    strContainerName = "Users"
    ' Create URL for the user
    Result = Result And CreateUserURL(strURL, strContainerName, False, strUserName)

    oPerson.FirstName = strFirstName
    oPerson.LastName = strLastName

    oPerson.DataSource.SaveTo strURL
    Result = Result And CheckError("SaveTo " & strURL)

    Set oPerson = New CDO.Person
    ' Bind
    oPerson.DataSource.Open strURL
    Result = Result And CheckError("Bind to CDO User " & strUserName)

    ' Create Mailbox
    Set oMailbox = oPerson
    oMailbox.CreateMailbox strHomeMDBUrl
    Result = Result And CheckError("Create Mailbox for CDO
```

```
                       User " & strUserName)

                           ' Save
                           oPerson.DataSource.Save
                           Result = Result And CheckError("Save CDO User " &
                       strUserName)

                           'CleanUp
                           Set oPerson = Nothing
                           Set oMailbox = Nothing

                           CreateMailboxCDOPerson = Result
                       End Function
```

[VBScript]

```
Sub CDOCreateMailBoxRecipient(serverName, _
                              domainName, _
                   exchangeOrg, _
                       adminGroup, _
                   storageGroup, _
                       storeName, _
                                   emailname, _
                                   firstName, _
                                   lastName)

' serverName    - the server name, for example "MyServer6"
' domainName    - the server's domain, for example
"MYDOMAIN3.microsoft.com"
' exchangeOrg   - the Exchange organization housing the
mailbox store. For example "First Organization"
' adminGroup    - the Exchange administrative group name,
for example "First Administrative Group"
' storageGroup  - the storage group for the mailbox store,
for example "First Storage Group"
' storeName     - the mailbox store name, for example
"Mailbox Store (SERVERNAME)"
' emailname     - the user's email name, for example
"jamessmith"
' firstName     - the user's first name, for example "James"
' lastName      - the user's last name, for example "Smith"

Dim objPerson
Set objPerson = CreateObject("CDO.Person")
Dim objMailbox

Dim domTokens
domTokens    = split(domainName,".",-1,1)
domainDN     = join(domTokens,",dc=")
domainDN     = "dc=" & domainDN
```

```
' First, create the user in Active Directory
objPerson.FirstName = FirstName
objPerson.LastName  = LastName
objPerson.Fields("userPrincipalName") = LastName
objPerson.Fields("userAccountControl") = 512
objPerson.Fields("userPassword") = "password"
objPerson.Fields.Update
objPerson.DataSource.SaveTo "LDAP://" + ServerName + _
                            "/CN=" + emailname + _
                            ",CN=users," + domainDN

' Now, create mailbox in specified location.

Set objMailbox = objPerson.GetInterface("IMailboxStore")
objMailbox.CreateMailbox "LDAP://" + _
                         ServerName + _
                         "/CN=" + _
                         StoreName + _
                         ",CN=" + _
                         StorageGroup + 
",CN=InformationStore,CN=" + _
                         ServerName + _
                         ",CN=Servers,CN=" + _
                         AdminGroup + "," + _
                         "CN=Administrative Groups,CN=" + _
                         ExchangeOrg + "," + _
                         "CN=Microsoft
Exchange,CN=Services," + _
                         "CN=Configuration," + domainDN

 objPerson.DataSource.Save

End Sub
```

Creating a Recipient Using ADSI

The ADSI example that follows creates a new mail recipient. The accompanying mailbox is created using an CDOEXM interface aggregated onto the ASDI.user object. The code is as follows:

Example
 Create a mailbox for a mail recipient.

[Visual Basic]

```
Function ADSICreateMailBoxRecipient(ServerName As String, _
                                    DomainName As String, _
                                    emailname As String, _
                                    FirstName As String, _
                                    LastName As String) As
Integer
```

Chapter 21 • Server and Recipient Management

```
'ServerName is something like "MyServer6"
'DomainName is something like
"DC=MYDOMAIN3,DC=microsoft,DC=com"
'emailname is something like "jamessmith"

'this assumes the MDB to be "Private MDB"

Dim objUser As IADsUser
Dim objContainer As IADsContainer
Dim objMailbox As CDOEXM.IMailboxStore
Dim recipname As String, recip As String

recip = "CN=" & emailname

' get the container
Set objContainer = GetObject("LDAP://" + ServerName + "/" + _
                             "CN=users," + DomainName)

' create a recipient
Set objUser = objContainer.Create("User", recip)
objUser.Put "samAccountName", emailname
objUser.Put "sn", LastName
objUser.Put "givenName", FirstName
objUser.Put "userPrincipalName", emailname

objUser.SetInfo
objUser.SetPassword "password"   'let user change it later
objUser.AccountDisabled = False

Set objMailbox = objUser

'Create a mailbox for the recipient
'You cannot create a mailbox using ADSI, so use CDOEXM
objMailbox.CreateMailbox "LDAP://" + ServerName + _
                        "/CN=Private MDB" + _
                        ",CN=First Storage Group,CN=InformationStore,CN=" + _
                        ServerName + _
                        ",CN=Servers,CN=First Administrative Group," + _
                        "CN=Administrative Groups,CN=First Organization," + _
                        "CN=Microsoft Exchange,CN=Services," + _
                        "CN=Configuration," + DomainName
objUser.SetInfo

End Function
```

Disabling a Mail Recipient

Call the IMailRecipient.MailDisable method to disable a mail recipient. The IMailRecipient interface is aggregated onto the Person object. The following is the code used:

Example

[Visual Basic]

```
Function MailDisableCDOPerson(strFirstName As String, _
                              strLastName As String) As Boolean

    Dim oPerson          As New CDO.Person
    Dim oRecipient       As CDOEXM.IMailRecipient
    Dim strUserName      As String
    Dim strConatinerName As String
    Dim strURL           As String
    Dim Result           As Boolean

    Result = True

    strUserName = strFirstName & strLastName

    strContainerName = "Users"
    ' Create URL for the user
    Result = Result And CreateUserURL(strURL, strContainerName, False, strUserName)

    Set oPerson = New CDO.Person
    ' Bind
    oPerson.DataSource.Open strURL
    Result = Result And CheckError("Bind to CDO User " & strUserName)

    ' MailDisable
    Set oRecipient = oPerson
    oRecipient.MailDisable
    Result = Result And CheckError("Mail Disablee CDO User " & strUserName)

    ' Save
    oPerson.DataSource.Save
    Result = Result And CheckError("Save CDO User " & strUserName)

    'CleanUp
    Set oPerson = Nothing
```

```
        Set oRecipient = Nothing

        MailDisableCDOPerson = Result
End Function
```

Creating a Contact

The examples that follow create a mail-enabled contact. The respective CDO and ADSI objects expose the IMailRecipient interface. Note that these examples use the LDAP protocol to access the Microsoft Active Directory directory service in Microsoft Windows 2000. Any information that needs to be updated in Exchange 2000 Server is updated behind the scenes as part of CDOEXM management. The code is as follows:

Example (CDO)

[Visual Basic]

```
'///////////////////////////////////////////////////////////////////////////////
'// Function:   CreateNewCDOUserOrContact
'// Purpose:    To create a user in a given Container in the DS via CDO.
'// Input/Output:
'//     strUserName  = contains name of user to be created;
'//                    If not provided CreateUserURL() will create a name such as DSIPerson_12345600
'//     strUserOrContact = contains the type: "User" or "Contact"
'//     strContainerName [Optional] = contains name of container to create user in.
'//                          If nothing passed in then user created at domain level.
'// Notes:
'//  Caller needs to verify user is unique before calling this function
'//
'///////////////////////////////////////////////////////////////////////////////


Public Function CreateNewCDOUserOrContact(ByVal strUserName As String, _
                                          ByVal strUserOrContact As String, _
                                          Optional ByVal strContainerName As String) As Boolean
```

Recipient Management Tasks

```
    On Error Resume Next

    Dim oPerson     As New CDO.Person

    Dim strURL      As String

    Dim Result      As Boolean


    Result = True


    Result = Result And CreateUserURL(strURL,
strContainerName, False, strUserName)


    oPerson.FirstName = strUserName

    Result = Result And CheckError("Set FirstName prop of
Person to " & strUserName)

    If StrComp(LCase(strUserOrContact), "contact",
vbTextCompare) = 0 Then

        oPerson.Fields("objectClass") = "contact"

        oPerson.Fields.Update
        oPerson.Fields.Resync
    End If

    oPerson.DataSource.SaveTo strURL
    Result = Result And CheckError("SaveTo " & strURL)

    'CleanUp
    Set oPerson = Nothing
    CreateNewCDOUserOrContact = Result
End Function
```

[VBScript]

```
Function CreateContact_CDO( _
                            serverName, _
                            domainName, _
                            emailAddr, _
                            firstName, _
                            lastName )
```

Chapter 21 • Server and Recipient Management

```
    ' serverName   - Server used to create contact. Example: "MyServer6"
    ' domainName   - Domain for contact.          Example: "mydomain3.microsoft.com"
    ' emailAddr    - Contact's SMTP email address. Example: "jsmith@mydomain4.microsoft.com"
    ' firstName    - Contact's first name,        Example: "James"
    ' lastName     - Contact's last name.         Example: "Smith"

    Dim iPerson     ' IPerson Interface
    Dim iRecip      ' IMailRecipient Interface
    Dim domainDN    ' Distinguished name for Domain
    Dim recipN      ' Recipient email name. Used to construct DN for contact.

    ' Construct the DN for the domain
    Dim domTokens
    domTokens   = split(domainName,".",-1,1)
    domainDN    = join(domTokens,",dc=")
    domainDN    = "dc=" & domainDN

    'Get recipient name to construct DN for contact
    recipN = Mid(emailAddr,1,InStr(1,emailAddr,"@",1) - 1)

    Set iPerson = CreateObject("CDO.Person")

    ' Now create the object in Active Directory
    With iPerson
      .FirstName = firstName
      .LastName  = lastName
      .Fields("objectClass") = "contact"
      .Fields.Update
      .DataSource.SaveTo "LDAP://" + serverName + "/CN=" + recipN + _
                        ",CN=Users," + domainDN

      Set iRecip = .GetInterface("IMailRecipient")
      iRecip.MailEnable "smtp:" & emailAddr
      .DataSource.Save
    End With

    Set CreateContact_CDO = iPerson

End Function
```

Example (ADSI)

[Visual Basic]

```
Sub CreateADSI_Contact(ServerName As String, _
                      DomainName As String, _
                      recipname As String, _
                      ForwardingDomain As String, _
                      FirstName As String, _
                      LastName As String)


'ServerName is something like "MyServer6"
'DomainName is something like
"DC=MYDOMAIN3,DC=microsoft,DC=com"
'recipname is is the email alias eg. "jamessmith"
'ForwardingDomain is a domain like
"somewhere.microsoft.com"

Dim objContact As IADs
Dim objContainer As IADsContainer
Dim objRecip As CDOEXM.MailRecipient
Dim recip As String

'recipname is contact name (eg. jamessmith)
'ForwardingAddress is full forwarding address,
'such as jamessmith@somewhere_else.microsoft.com
recip = "CN=" & recipname

' get the container
Set objContainer = GetObject("LDAP://" + ServerName + "/" + _
                             "CN=users," + DomainName)

' create a Contact
Set objContact = objContainer.Create("contact", recip)
objContact.Put "sn", recipname
objContact.Put "givenName", recipname
objContact.SetInfo

Set objRecip = objContact
Dim FwdAddress As String
FwdAddress = "smtp:" + recipname + "@" + ForwardingDomain
objRecip.MailEnable FwdAddress
objContact.SetInfo

End Sub
```

Moving a Mailbox

The examples that follow move a mailbox. Note that the second private mailbox store has already been created. LDAP protocol is used to access Active Directory. Modifications in Exchange 2000 Server are handled behind the scenes as part of CDOEXM management. The code is as follows:

Example (CDO)

[Visual Basic]

```
Sub CDOMove_Mailbox(ServerName As String, _
                   DomainName As String, _
                   recipname As String, _
                   Moveto_MDB As String)

'ServerName is something like "MyServer6"
'DomainName is something like
"DC=MYDOMAIN3,DC=microsoft,DC=com"
'recipname is is the email alias (eg. "jamessmith")."
'This assumes you have created the MDB Moveto_MDB (with a
name like "PrivateMDB2")

Dim objPerson As New CDO.Person
Dim objMailbox As CDOEXM.IMailboxStore

On Error GoTo Error

objPerson.DataSource.Open "LDAP://" + ServerName + _
                         "/CN=" + recipname + _
                         ",CN=users," + DomainName

Set objMailbox = objPerson
If objMailbox.HomeMDB = "" Then
    Debug.Print "No mailbox to move."
Else
   Debug.Print "Current MDB: " + objMailbox.HomeMDB
    'Moveto_MDB is the MDB name to move the mailbox to (eg.
PrivateMDB2)

   objMailbox.MoveMailbox "LDAP://" + ServerName + "/CN=" + Moveto_MDB + _
                         ",CN=First Storage Group,CN=InformationStore,CN=" + _
                         ServerName + _
                         ",CN=Servers,CN=First Administrative Group," + _
                         "CN=Administrative Groups,CN=First Organization," + _
                         "CN=Microsoft
```

Recipient Management Tasks

```
Exchange,CN=Services,CN=Configuration," + _
                    DomainName
  objPerson.DataSource.Save
  Debug.Print "Mailbox has been moved to " + Moveto_MDB + "
successfully."
End If
GoTo Ending

Error:
If Err.number = -2147016656 Then
   Debug.Print "Recipient " + recipname + " does not exist
in the default container."
   MsgBox "Recipient " + recipname + " is not found."
   Err.Clear
Else
   MsgBox "Run time error: " + Str(Err.number) + " " +
Err.Description
   Err.Clear
End If

Ending:
End Sub
```

Example (ADSI)

[Visual Basic]

```
Sub ADSIMove_Mailbox(ServerName As String, _
                    DomainName As String, _
                    recipname As String, _
                    Moveto_MDB As String)

'ServerName is something like "MyServer6"
'DomainName is something like
"DC=MYDOMAIN3,DC=microsoft,DC=com"
'recipname is is the email alias (eg. "jamessmith")."
'This assumes you have created the MDB Moveto_MDB (with a
name like "PrivateMDB2")

Dim objUser As IADsUser
Dim objMailbox As CDOEXM.IMailboxStore

On Error GoTo Error

Set objUser = GetObject("LDAP://" + ServerName + _
                    "/CN=" + recipname + _
                    ",CN=users," + DomainName)

Set objMailbox = objUser
If objMailbox.HomeMDB = "" Then
```

```
      Debug.Print "No mailbox to move."
   Else
      Debug.Print "Current MDB: " + objMailbox.HomeMDB

      'Moveto_MDB is the MDB name to move the mailbox to (eg.
PrivateMDB2)

      objMailbox.MoveMailbox "LDAP://" + ServerName + "/CN=" +
Moveto_MDB + _
                            ",CN=First Storage
Group,CN=InformationStore,CN=" + _
                            ServerName + _
                            ",CN=Servers,CN=First
Administrative Group," + _
                            "CN=Administrative Groups,CN=First
Organization," + _
                            "CN=Microsoft
Exchange,CN=Services,CN=Configuration," + _
                            DomainName

     objUser.SetInfo
     Debug.Print "Mailbox has been moved to " + Moveto_MDB + "
successfully."
End If
GoTo Ending

Error:
If Err.number = -2147016656 Then
    Debug.Print "Recipient " + recipname + " does not exist
in the default container."
    MsgBox "Recipient " + recipname + " is not found."
    Err.Clear
Else
    MsgBox "Run time error: " + Str(Err.number) + " " +
Err.Description
    Err.Clear
End If

Ending:

End Sub
```

Deleting a Mailbox

The following code deletes a user's mailbox and account:

Example (CDO)

[Visual Basic]

```
Function DeleteMailboxCDOPerson(strFirstName As String, _
                                strLastName As String) As Boolean

    Dim oPerson            As New CDO.Person
    Dim oMailbox           As CDOEXM.IMailboxStore
    Dim strUserName        As String
    Dim strURL             As String
    Dim strContainerName   As String
    Dim Result             As Boolean

    Result = True

    strUserName = strFirstName & strLastName
    strContainerName = "Users"
    ' Create URL for the user
    Result = Result And CreateUserURL(strURL, strContainerName, False, strUserName)

    Set oPerson = New CDO.Person
    ' Bind
    oPerson.DataSource.Open strURL
    Result = Result And CheckError("Bind to CDO User " & strUserName)

    ' Delete Mailbox
    Set oMailbox = oPerson
    oMailbox.DeleteMailbox
    Result = Result And CheckError("Delete Mailbox for CDO User " & strUserName)

    ' Save
    oPerson.DataSource.Save
    Result = Result And CheckError("Save CDO User " & strUserName)

    'CleanUp
    Set oPerson = Nothing
    Set oMailbox = Nothing

    DeleteMailboxCDOPerson = Result
End Function
```

Chapter 21 — Server and Recipient Management

Example (ADSI)

[Visual Basic]

```
Sub Delete_MailBoxADSI(ServerName As String, _
                      DomainName As String, _
                      recipname As String)

'ServerName is something like "MyServer6"
'DomainName is something like
"DC=MYDOMAIN3,DC=microsoft,DC=com"
'recipname is something like "jamessmith"

Dim objUser As IADsUser
Dim objMailbox As CDOEXM.IMailboxStore

Set objUser = GetObject("LDAP://" + ServerName + _
                       "/CN=" + recipname + _
                       ",CN=users," + DomainName)

Set objMailbox = objUser
If objMailbox.HomeMDB = "" Then
   MsgBox "No mailbox found."
Else
   objMailbox.DeleteMailbox
   objUser.SetInfo
   MsgBox "Mailbox for " + recipname + " deleted
successfully"
End If

End Sub
```

Setting Mailbox Storage Limits

A common store policy is to limit the amount of disk space allocated for each mailbox. The IMailboxStore::StoreQuota property specifies the maximum size of the mailbox, in kilobytes. Once the user reaches this limit, a warning message appears every time he or she sends a message. If the amount of disk space that the user consumes is not important, retain this property's default value of –1.

If you do set StoreQuota, you might also set the IMailboxStore::OverQuotaLimit property. This property specifies the number of kilobytes over the StoreQuota limit that the user can go before he or she is restricted from sending mail. This is a "gentle reminder" to the user to clear some space in his or her mailbox.

Finally, set the IMailboxStore::HardLimit property to the number of kilobytes over the StoreQuota limit that the user can go before he or she is restricted from sending or receiving mail. This is a "final notice" to the user to clear some space in his or her mailbox.

Example

This example limits jamessmith to 10 MB, with a 2-MB soft limit and an additional 1-MB hard limit. He gets 13 MB before losing mail privileges. The code is as follows:

[Visual Basic]

```
Sub Set_Limits(ServerName As String, _
               DomainName As String, _
               recipname As String)

    'ServerName is something like "MyServer6"
    'DomainName is something like
"DC=MYDOMAIN3,DC=microsoft,DC=com"
    'recipname is something like "jamessmith"

    Dim objPerson As New CDO.Person
    Dim objMailbox As CDOEXM.IMailboxStore

    objPerson.DataSource.Open "LDAP://" + ServerName + _
                              "/CN=" + recipname + _
                              ",CN=users," + DomainName

    Set objMailbox = objPerson
    If objMailbox.HomeMDB = "" Then
       MsgBox "No Mailbox found."
    Else
       objMailbox.StoreQuota = 10
       objMailbox.OverQuotaLimit = 2
       objMailbox.HardLimit = 1
       objPerson.DataSource.Save
       MsgBox "Mailbox limits for " + recipname + " set successfully"
    End If

End Sub
```

Controlling Mailbox Cleanup

You can automatically clean up deleted messages from mailboxes by setting the garbage collection properties on the mailbox. To limit how long the store keeps deleted mail, set the IMailboxStore::DaysBeforeGarbageCollection property to the number of days to keep the deleted mail. The default is to keep the deleted mail indefinitely.

To require that the store is backed up before it removes deleted mail, set the IMailboxStore::GarbageCollectOnlyAfterBackup property to True.

Finally, to prevent the store from removing deleted mail, set the IMailboxStore::OverrideStoreGarbageCollection property to True.

See also the "DaysBeforeDeletedMailboxCleanup" property in the MS Exchange SDK on the IMailboxStoreDB interface.

Example

This example cleans up files seven days after a backup.

[Visual Basic]

```
Sub Set_Cleanup(ServerName As String, _
                DomainName As String, _
                recipname As String)

'ServerName is something like "MyServer6"
'DomainName is something like
"DC=MYDOMAIN3,DC=microsoft,DC=com"
'recipname is something like "jamessmith"

Dim objUser As IADsUser
Dim objMailbox As CDOEXM.IMailboxStore

Set objUser = GetObject("LDAP://" + ServerName + _
                        "/CN=" + recipname + _
                        ",CN=users," + DomainName)

Set objMailbox = objUser
If objMailbox.HomeMDB = "" Then
   MsgBox "No mailbox found."
Else
   objMailbox.GarbageCollectOnlyAfterBackup = True
   objMailbox.DaysBeforeGarbageCollection = 7
   'commit the changes
   objUser.SetInfo
End If

End Sub
```

Enumerating Recipients

The next example lists the recipients in an Exchange 2000 mailbox store. It opens the user information in Active Directory by using ADSI. It then uses the IMailboxStore interface aggregated onto the ADSI user object to access information in the Web Storage System. The following is the code used:

Example

[Visual Basic]

```
Sub List_Users(ServerName As String, DomainName As String)

'ServerName is something like "MyServer6"
'DomainName is something like
"DC=MYDOMAIN3,DC=microsoft,DC=com"

Dim objUser As IADsUser
Dim objContainer As IADsContainer
Dim objMailbox As CDOEXM.IMailboxStore
Dim i As Long
Dim name As String

On Error GoTo Error
' get the container
Set objContainer = GetObject("LDAP://" + ServerName + "/" + _
                             "CN=users," + DomainName)

objContainer.Filter = Array("User")
i = 0

Debug.Print

For Each objUser In objContainer
   name = objUser.name
   name = Right(name, Len(name) - 3)
   Set objMailbox = objUser
   If objMailbox.HomeMDB = "" Then
      Debug.Print name + "   (no mailbox)"
   Else
      Debug.Print name + "   (has mailbox)"
      Debug.Print objMailbox.HomeMDB
   End If
   i = i + 1
Next
Debug.Print "Number of users found in the DS (in the
default container): " + Str(i)
GoTo Ending

Error:
   Debug.Print "Failed while displaying the users in the
default container."
   MsgBox "Run time error: " + Str(Err.number) + " " +
Err.Description
```

```
    Err.Clear
Ending:

End Sub
```

Enumerating Groups

The next example lists the groups in an Exchange 2000 store. It opens group information in Active Directory by using ADSI. It then uses the IMailRecipient interface aggregated onto the ADSI group object to access information in the Web Storage System. The following is the code used:

Example

[Visual Basic]

```
Sub List_Groups(ServerName As String, DomainName As String)

'ServerName is something like "MyServer6"
'DomainName is something like
"DC=MYDOMAIN3,DC=microsoft,DC=com"

Dim objGroup As IADsGroup
Dim objContainer As IADsContainer
Dim objRecip As CDOEXM.MailRecipient
Dim i As Long
Dim name As String

On Error GoTo Error
' get the container
Set objContainer = GetObject("LDAP://" + ServerName + "/" + _
                             "CN=users," + DomainName)

objContainer.Filter = Array("Group")
i = 0

Debug.Print

For Each objGroup In objContainer
    name = objGroup.name
    name = Right(name, Len(name) - 3)
    Set objRecip = objGroup
    If objRecip.TargetAddress = "" And objRecip.X400Email = "" Then
        Debug.Print name + "    (mail disabled)"
    Else
        Debug.Print name + "    (mail enabled)"
    End If
    i = i + 1
```

Recipient Management Tasks

```
Next
Debug.Print "Number of groups found in the DS (in the
default container): " + Str(i)
GoTo Ending

Error:
   Debug.Print "Failed while displaying the groups in the
default container."
   MsgBox "Run time error: " + Str(Err.number) + " " +
Err.Description
   Err.Clear
Ending:

End Sub
```

Enumerating Contacts

The next example lists the contacts in an Exchange 2000 store. It opens contact information in Active Directory by using ADSI. It then uses the IMailRecipient interface aggregated onto the ADSI contacts object to access information in the Web Storage System. The code is as follows:

Example

[Visual Basic]

```
Sub List_Contacts(ServerName As String, DomainName As
String)

'ServerName is something like "MyServer6"
'DomainName is something like
"DC=MYDOMAIN3,DC=microsoft,DC=com"

Dim objContact As IADs
Dim objContainer As IADsContainer
Dim objRecip As CDOEXM.MailRecipient
Dim i As Long
Dim name As String

On Error GoTo Error
' get the container
Set objContainer = GetObject("LDAP://" + ServerName + "/" +
                              "CN=users," + DomainName)
objContainer.Filter = Array("Contact")
i = 0
Debug.Print
For Each objContact In objContainer
   name = objContact.name
   name = Right(name, Len(name) - 3)
```

```
    Set objRecip = objContact
    If objRecip.TargetAddress = "" And objRecip.X400Email =
"" Then
        Debug.Print name + "    (mail disabled)"
    Else
        Debug.Print name + "    (mail enabled)"
    End If
    i = i + 1
Next
Debug.Print "Number of contacts found in the DS (in the
default container): " + Str(i)
GoTo Ending

Error:
    Debug.Print "Failed while displaying the contacts in the
default container."
    MsgBox "Run time error: " + Str(Err.number) + " " +
Err.Description
    Err.Clear

Ending:

End Sub
```

Setting Proxy Addresses

The next example sets the proxy addresses for a mailbox-enabled user. The code used for the example is as follows:

Example

[Visual Basic]

```
Sub SetProxyAddress(ServerName As String, _
                    DomainName As String, _
                    recipname As String)

    'ServerName is something like "MyServer6"
    'DomainName is something like
"DC=MYDOMAIN3,DC=microsoft,DC=com"
    'recipname is something like "jamessmith"

    Dim objPerson As New CDO.Person
    Dim objMailRecip As CDOEXM.IMailRecipient
    Dim i

    objPerson.DataSource.Open "LDAP://" + ServerName + _
                              "/CN=" + recipname + _
                              ",CN=users," + DomainName
```

```
    'Capitalized proxy type for proxies(1) makes it the
primary (reply) address.
    'the others are receive only.
    Dim proxies(3) As Variant
    proxies(0) = "smtp:user@somewhere.microsoft.com"
    proxies(1) = "SMTP:user@somewhere.microsoft.com"
    proxies(2) = "x400:c=us;a= ;p=Domain;o=First
Organization;s=user;"

    Set objMailRecip = objPerson
    objMailRecip.ProxyAddresses = proxies

    'look at the results
    Debug.Print Chr(13) + Chr(13) + Chr(13) + Chr(13) +
Chr(13) 'add some space
    For i = LBound(objMailRecip.ProxyAddresses) To
UBound(objMailRecip.ProxyAddresses)
        Debug.Print objMailRecip.ProxyAddresses(i)
    Next

    objPerson.DataSource.Save
    MsgBox "Proxy addresses for " + recipname + " set
successfully"

End Sub
```

Building a Restricted Address List

The example that follows adds to the restricted address list for a recipient. It involves setting the IMailRecipient.RestrictedAddresses property to either cdoReject or cdoAccept and adding to the IMailRecipient.RestrictedAddressList list. The code used is as follows:

Example

[Visual Basic]

```
Sub RestrictAddresses(DomainName As String, _
                     FolderName As String)

    'DomainName is something like "MyDomain.wherever.com"
    'FolderName is something like "Public Folders/Folder3"

    Dim objFolder As New CDO.Folder
    Dim objMailRecip As CDOEXM.IMailRecipient
    Dim fullurl As String
    Dim i

    'fullurl might look like:
```

Chapter 21 • Server and Recipient Management

```
    ' "file://./backofficestorage/MyDomain.wherever.com/
Public Folders/Folder3"
    fullurl = "file://./backofficestorage/" + _
              DomainName + "/" + FolderName

    objFolder.DataSource.Open fullurl, , adModeReadWrite,
adFailIfNotExists

    Set objMailRecip = objFolder

    ' can build an accept or reject list
    objMailRecip.restrictedAddresses = cdoReject 'reject
these emails

    Dim list(3) As Variant

    list(0) = "user@" + DomainName
    list(1) = "user1@" + DomainName
    list(2) = "user2@" + DomainName

    objMailRecip.RestrictedAddressList = list
    objFolder.DataSource.Save

    'look at the results
    Debug.Print Chr(13) + Chr(13) + "View list"
    For i = LBound(objMailRecip.RestrictedAddressList) To
UBound(objMailRecip.RestrictedAddressList)
        Debug.Print objMailRecip.RestrictedAddressList(i)
    Next

    MsgBox "Mailbox restrictions for " + FolderName + " set
successfully"

End Sub
```

Enabling a Folder for Mail

The example that follows enables a folder for receiving mail. It uses the following codes:

Example

[Visual Basic]

```
Sub EnableFolder(DomainName As String, _
                 FolderName As String)

    'DomainName is something like "MyDomain.wherever.com"
    'FolderName is something like "Public Folders/Folder3"
```

```
    Dim objFolder As New CDO.Folder
    Dim objRecip As CDOEXM.IMailRecipient
    Dim fullurl As String

    'fullurl might look like:
' "file://./backofficestorage/MyDomain.wherever.com/
Public Folders/Folder3"
    fullurl = "file://./backofficestorage/" + _
            DomainName + "/" + FolderName

    objFolder.DataSource.Open fullurl, , adModeReadWrite,
adFailIfNotExists
    Set objRecip = objFolder
    objRecip.MailEnable
    objFolder.DataSource.Save

End Sub
```

APPENDIX

MIME, SMTP, and RFCs

MIME Encapsulation of Aggregate HTML Documents (MHTML)

MIME Encapsulation of Aggregate HTML Documents (MHTML) is an Internet standard that defines the MIME structure used to send HTML content in message bodies along with those resources referenced from within the HTML. The HyperText Markup Language (HTML) is a markup language used to create documents that are portable between various platforms. One of its key features is the ability to render a document composed of separate resources such as images, sound files, cascading style sheets, and Microsoft ActiveX objects, in-lined with the marked up text. Many email clients, such as Microsoft Outlook Express, are capable of displaying HTML pages just as they would appear in a Web browser. As email content, such HTML documents usually include links to other resources that are available on the network. These resources are identified by the HTML author for inclusion in the page using relative or absolute uniform resource locators (URLs) as attributes within HTML markup elements.

In many cases, it is desirable to include external resources referenced by the HTML document in the message body itself. The MHTML specification provides the architecture used to encapsulate referenced resources within the message body, and thereby allows the email client to construct and render the page without retrieving these resources directly over the network.

Key Concepts of MHTML

While HTML as a document format for MIME email has been available for years in the form of the text/HTML content type, the richness of HTML as an interoperable email format can be achieved only through the use of the MIME multipart/related content type. This content type allows the message to contain an HTML page and other resources such as pictures and sound included directly in the MIME hierarchy of the message. The data can be referenced through links from the HTML content and used to complete the rendering of the document. The usage lets the recipient resolve all the links "locally"—that is, without having to use the network.

MHTML defines the naming of objects that are normally referred to by URLs and the means of aggregating resources that go together. Two MIME headers, Content-Location and Content-Base, are defined in order to resolve references to other content stored locally in related body parts. Content-Base gives an absolute URL base, or "starting point," for relative URLs that appear in other MIME headers and in HTML documents that do not contain any BASE HTML elements. Content-Location specifies the URL that corresponds to the content of the body part that contains this header.

The following example shows an MHTML message with a relative reference to an embedded GIF:

```
From: user1@microsoft.com
To: user2@microsoft.com
Subject: An example
Mime-Version: 1.0
Content-Base: http://www.microsoft.com
Content-Type: Multipart/related; boundary="boundary-
example-1";type=Text/HTML

--boundary-example-1
Content-Type: Text/HTML; charset=ISO-8859-1
Content-Transfer-Encoding: QUOTED-PRINTABLE

... text of the HTML document, which might contain a
hyperlink
to the other body part, for example through a statement
such as:
<IMG SRC="/images/ie5.gif" ALT="Internet Explorer logo">
Example of a copyright sign encoded with Quoted-Printable:
=A9
Example of a copyright sign mapped onto HTML markup: &#168;

--boundary-example-1
Content-Location: /images/ie5.gif
Content-Type: IMAGE/GIF
Content-Transfer-Encoding: BASE64
```

```
AAAFFDDlhGAGgAPEAAP/////
ZRaCgoAAAACH+PUNvcHlyaWdodCAoQykgMTk5
NSBJRVRGLiBVbmF1dGhvcml6ZWQgZHVwbGljYXRpb24gcHJvaGliaXRlZC4A
etc...

--boundary-example-1 -
```

CDO Support for MHTML

The CDO COM components provide native support for MIME formatted content. As MHTML is based upon MIME, the CDO object model can be used to create MTHML formatted messages. To facilitate the easy construction of MHTML formatted messages, the IMessage interface defines two useful methods, IMessage.CreateMHTMLBody and IMessage.AddRelatedBodyPart. The CreateMHTMLBody method can construct the entire multipart/related MIME structure for you and you need only specify the URL to the page you want to add to the message. The appropriate multipart/related body part hierarchy is automatically created, complete with the necessary body part headers for each related part. If you want more control over constructing the MIME hierarchy itself, you can use the AddRelatedBodyPart method in conjunction with the IMessage.HTMLBody property. AddRelatedBodyPart automatically correlates the resource added as a body part to the message with the HTML that references it. This method will create the multipart/related hierarchy if required and, depending upon your preference, associate the referenced resource in the HTML with the related body part using Content-Location or Content-ID headers.

If you want to perform all of the steps manually, you can go about creating the multipart/related MIME hierarchy using the only the IBodyPart.Fields, IBodyPart.GetDecodedContentStream and IBodyPart.AddBodyPart methods. This approach provides the highest flexibility, but also requires the most code and understanding of the MHTML specification, as each body part must have its content stream populated with the appropriate resource, and all header fields manually set.

MIME Extensions to Internet Mail

MIME grew out of a need to encapsulate messages within messages. It now includes multipart messages that can consist of a variety of file types such as images, audio, and video.

MIME is consistent with Internet mail protocols using headers and bodies. It allows for transmission of 7-bit printable US-ASCII characters and maximum 1000-character lines in message bodies over all Internet mail transports.

It has become the most widely used extension to the simple email standard. (See "About Simple Internet (RFC 822) Messages" in the MS Exchange SDK.) It is also used as a transport mechanism in Web pages.

MIME Capabilities

MIME defines a message format that allows for:

- Textual message bodies in character sets other than US-ASCII
- Nontextual message bodies
- Multipart message bodies
- Textual header information in character sets other than US-ASCII.

MIME provides a mechanism for sending a variety of file types as a part of or along with regular mail messages. It uses the headers defined by RFC 822 and extensions to those header definitions. MIME does all this while following all the standard SMTP and RFC 822 mail rules. MIME messages can be constructed to transport mail over any mail transport system that is compliant with SMTP. MIME is able to transmit objects with varying ranges of complexity in a way that allows any MIME-compliant user agent (UA) to faithfully process them and hand them off to an appropriate application.

MIME accomplishes this simplifying and rebuilding of complex files by encoding a file (see "Content-Transfer-Encoding" in the MS Exchange SDK) and transporting it as a message body, or a series of messages with component parts of the file. A MIME-compliant UA on the receiving end can decode the message, presenting it to the reader, or providing it to another application as a file. A UA that is not MIME-compliant will be able to process a MIME-encoded mail message, but may not be able to decode the message.

MIME allows for multipart mail messages, ensuring that the mail reader (UA) with even the most limited capabilities can still process the message. The multiple parts are arranged so that the parts requiring the least sophisticated UA are at the beginning of the message. In fact, most MIME UAs include courtesy text when constructing messages to give users of non-MIME UAs an indication of the message content. This courtesy text is inserted ahead of any MIME parts.

Sample MIME Message

MIME works by using headers and separators that tell a UA what processing is required to recreate the message. An example with no encoded body parts is as follows:

```
From: Some One <someone@microsoft.com>
MIME-Version: 1.0
Content-Type: multipart/mixed;
        boundary="XXXXboundary text"
```

```
This is a multipart message in MIME format.

--XXXXboundary text
Content-Type: text/plain

this is the body text

--XXXXboundary text
Content-Type: text/plain;
Content-Disposition: attachment;
        filename="test.txt"

this is the attachment text

--XXXXboundary text--
```

The example shows the use of a MIME message to send a text message and an attached text file. Both are body parts of this message.

The `"MIME-Version:"` header tells the receiving UA to treat this as a MIME message.

The `"Content-Type:"` header specifies "multipart/mixed." It tells the receiving UA that the message has parts separated by the string argument defined in `"boundary="`. A MIME-compliant UA will only display or otherwise process content following the specified `"boundary="` text strings. The actual boundaries are constructed using the `"boundary="` string, prepended by `"--"`. The final body part is followed by the `"boundary="` string with the `"--"` both prepended and appended.

In the preceding example, the courtesy message `"This is a multipart message in MIME format."` will not be displayed or otherwise processed by the MIME UA since it does not follow a `"boundary="` string. A UA that does not support MIME will display it, and at least this part of the message will be readable no matter what features the reader supports. If our example had encoded parts, they would make no sense to the human reader using a non-MIME-compliant UA, but at least the courtesy message would give the user a hint as to why.

There are two message body parts in our example. Each body part has headers of its own, in addition to the overall message headers. Each body part begins with the boundary string. If there were no headers in the body parts, then the blank line that must follow headers in RFC 822 messages would follow the boundary string. The first body part is a plain text message. It is the message the sender might have typed into a UA. Its single "Content-Type:" header identifies it as "text/plain", meaning US-ASCII characters are used exclusively and any UA should be able to display this body part. Text/plain is the default content type.

The second body part in the example contains the file attachment. Since the file attachment is an ASCII text file, it is sent with no encoding and its content type is given as text/plain. The "Content-Disposition: attachment" header has a parameter, "filename=", which specifies a suggested name for the file. This header specifies that this body part is to be treated as a file rather than being displayed to the user and is to be saved on local storage under the suggested file name.

MIME Headers

MIME headers appear at the beginning of a MIME message as well as within the separate body parts. Some MIME headers can be used both as message headers and in MIME body parts. Some additional headers are defined for use only in body parts.

The following headers are defined in MIME:

- MIME-Version
- Content-Type
- Content-Transfer-Encoding
- Content-ID
- Content-Description
- Content-Disposition

There are additional headers that are applied in specialized situations, such as Content-Base and Content-Location. All of the "Content-xxx" headers have defined subheaders, fields, and/or parameters. Headers that begin with "Content-" are the only headers that have defined meaning in body parts. All other body part headers can be ignored and might actually be removed by message transfer agents (MTAs).

MIME-Version is a required header indicating that this message is to use the rules of MIME. "MIME-Version: 1.0" is the only currently defined MIME-Version header allowed. The MIME-Version header is a top-level header only and does not appear in body parts unless the body part is an encapsulated, fully formed message of content-type message/RFC 822, which might have its own MIME-Version header.

Content-Type headers are used to specify the media type and subtype of data in the body of a message and to fully specify the native representation of such data. The header embodies much of the power of MIME. The IETF can add new official content types. Additionally, private content-type values can be defined by anyone. Such private content types have values of "x-something" or "X-something", where "something" can take on any value.

Content-Transfer-Encoding headers can have two different meanings. If the value is "base64" or "quoted-printable", then the header indicates the encoding used for this body part. If the value is "7bit", "8bit", or "binary", then the header indicates that there is no encoding and that the value indicates only the type of content the body part contains. The default is "7bit". It should be noted that "8bit" and "binary" cannot be assured of being handled by all Internet (SMTP) MTAs, and are not actually valid in Internet mail. Provision is made for private Content-Transfer-Encoding headers. They have values that begin with "x-" or "X-". These are for specialized cases where the users have the tools to decode or otherwise process a specific "x-" encoding.

Content-ID headers are world-unique values that identify body parts, individually or as groups. They are necessary at times to distinguish body parts and allow cross-referencing between body parts.

Content-Description headers are optional and are often used to add descriptive text to nontextual body parts.

Content-Disposition headers provide information about how to present a message or a body part. When a body part is to be treated as an attached file, the Content-Disposition header will include a file name parameter.

CONTENT-TYPE

The example in Sample MIME Message shows how MIME uses headers and multiple body parts. But the real power of MIME is in its ability to handle a wide variety of content types. Some encoding schemes are defined by MIME. An even broader range of possibilities is anticipated, and organizational elements are provided to handle the rich set of possibilities inherent in MIME. The "Content-Type:" header field is specified to organize media types. This allows the UA to present the body part to the user in its appropriate form, to engage the services of a tool that can process the body part, or to save the body part as a file for offline processing. The content type can be either "composite" or "discrete."

The two composite top-level media types are:

- Multipart
- Message

The five discrete top-level media types are:

- Text
- Image
- Audio
- Video
- Application

CONTENT-TYPE: APPLICATION

The application content type allows for the transmission of application data or binary data, effectively allowing for specific handling of application data. The following application subtypes might be encountered:

- application/cals-1840 [RFC1895]
- application/marc [RFC2220]

- application/news-message-id [RFC1036]
- application/news-transmission [RFC1036]
- application/octet-stream [RFC1521]
- application/oda [RFC1521]
- application/pgp-encrypted [RFC2015]
- application/pgp-keys [RFC2015]
- application/pgp-signature [RFC2015]
- application/pkcs7-MIME [RFC2311]
- application/pkcs7-signature [RFC2311]
- application/pkcs10 [RFC2311]
- application/postscript [RFC1521]
- application/remote-printing [RFC1486]
- application/sgml [RFC1874]
- application/x400-bp [RFC1494]

CONTENT-TYPE: AUDIO

The audio content type allows standardized audio files to be included in messages. They are as follows:

- audio/32kadpcm [RFC1911]
- audio/basic [RFC1521]

CONTENT-TYPE: IMAGE

The image content type allows standardized image files to be included in messages. They are as follows:

- image/g3fax [RFC1494]
- image/gif [RFC1521]
- image/ief (Image Exchange Format) [RFC1314]
- image/jpeg [RFC1521]
- image/tiff (Tag Image File Format) [RFC2301]

CONTENT-TYPE: MESSAGE

The message content type allows messages to contain other messages or pointers to other messages. The following are a few examples:

- message/delivery-status [RFC1894]
  The message/delivery-status content type is defined for use in message delivery status notification, allowing automated information transmission.

- message/disposition-notification-to [RFC2298]
  The message/disposition-notification-to content type adds enhanced functionality to messaging. This works within the framework of the multipart/report content type.

- message/external-body [RFC1521]
  The message/external-body content type allows the contents of a message to be external to the message and only referenced in the message. The only required parameter of this content type is access-type, which can have values such as "FTP" and "LOCAL-ACCESS." If values are used that have not been registered with IANA, then they begin with "x-".

  Message/external-body parts must include a Content-ID header field with a unique identifier to reference the external data.

- message/http [RFC2068]
  The message/http content type is not strictly a MIME content type. Provisions are made in the definition of HTTP to allow it to be used over MIME transport mechanisms, but there must be a conversion between HTTP and MIME for strict MIME adherence.

- message/partial [RFC1521]
  The message/partial content type allows for large messages to be broken up into smaller messages. The full message can then be put back together by the UA. Only 7bit content-transfer-encoding is allowed for this content type. Three parameters are required:
  - *id*: a unique identifier used to match up the pieces.
  - *number*: an integer identifying which piece of the message this is.
  - *total*: an integer indicating the total number of parts the message has. This parameter is required only on the final fragment of the message, but should be used on all parts.

- message/rfc822 [RFC1521]
  The message/RFC 822 content type is used to enclose a complete message within a message. It is different from other MIME body parts in that it must be a fully formed RFC 822 message, complete with headers.

CONTENT-TYPE: MULTIPART

Multipart Content-Type headers identify multipart messages. They require that a subtype and other elements be included in the header. The following are examples of multipart content types:

- multipart/alternative [RFC1521]
  The multipart/alternative content type is used when the same information is presented in different body parts in different forms. The body parts are ordered by increasing complexity. For example, a message that consists of a heavily formatted Microsoft Word 97 document might also be presented in Microsoft Word 6.0 format, rich text format, and a plain text format. In this case, the plain text would be presented as the first alternative body part. The rich text version

would follow, then the Microsoft Word 6.0, then the most complex, Microsoft Word 97. Placing the plain text version first is the friendliest scheme for users with non-MIME-compliant UAs, because they will see the recognizable version first. The MIME-compliant UAs should present the most complex version that they can recognize or give the user a choice of which version to view.

Content-ID values should be different for each part where there are different levels of complexity between parts. The content-ID of each part should be different from the content-ID of the overall multipart/alternative. That is, one content-ID value will refer to the multipart/alternative entity, while one or more other content-ID values will refer to the parts inside it.

- multipart/byteranges [RFC2068]

  The multipart/byteranges content type is defined as a part of the HTTP message protocol. It includes two or more parts, each with its own Content-Type and Content-Range fields. The parts are separated using a MIME boundary parameter. It allows for binary as well as 7-bit and 8-bit files to be sent as multiple parts with the lengths of the parts being specified in the header of each part. Note that while HTTP makes provisions for using MIME for HTTP documents, HTTP is not strictly MIME-compliant.

- multipart/digest [RFC1521]

  The multipart/digest content type is used to send collections of plain-text messages. It is accomplished in the same way as the multipart/mixed content-type, but each body part is expected to be of content-type: message/RFC 822.

- multipart/form-data [RFC1867]

  The multipart/form-data content type is intended to allow information providers to express file upload requests uniformly, and to provide a MIME-compatible representation for file upload responses.

- multipart/mixed [RFC1521]

  The multipart/mixed content type is used when the body parts are independent and need to be bundled in a particular order. When a UA does not recognize a multipart subtype, it will treat the message as multipart/mixed.

- multipart/parallel [RFC1521]

  The purpose of the multipart/parallel content type is to display all of the parts simultaneously on hardware and software that can do so. For instance, an image file can be displayed while a sound file is playing.

- multipart/related [RFC2112]

The multipart/related content type is used for compound documents, those messages in which the separate body parts are intended to work together to provide the full meaning of the message. Additionally, multipart/related can be used to provide links to content not contained within the message.

Multipart/related can be used for compound documents where the object is built progressively from pieces, starting with the "root" body part as specified in the start parameter. If the start parameter is not specified, then the first body part is considered the starting point or "root" body part.

Multipart/related requires a type parameter. The type parameter specifies the content type of the first or "root" part.

Multipart/related processing takes precedence over content disposition. Many MIME user agents do not recognize multipart/related and treat these messages as multipart/mixed. To allow for this, some UAs will include the technically unnecessary Content-Disposition header in multipart/related body parts.

Content-Location and Content-Base headers are defined to resolve URL references to other body parts. Both headers are valid in any message or body part. They are valid for the content heading or message heading where they occur and for its content.

The Content-Location and Content-Base headers apply to headers and body parts where they occur and do not have meaning in multipart headings.

The Content-Base header gives a base for relative URIs occurring in other heading fields and in HTML documents that do not have any BASE element in its HTML code. Its value must be an absolute URI.

The Content-Location header contains a URL that specifies the body of that body part. The URL may be relative to a URL specified in a Content-Base header.

The following example shows how these headers are used:

```
Content-Type: Multipart/related; boundary="boundary-content_example";
type=Text/HTML; start=example@someplace.com
;Content-Base header not allowed here
;since this is a multipart MIME object
--boundary-content_example
Part 1:
Content-Type: Text/HTML; charset=US-ASCII
Content-ID: <example@someplace.com>
```

```
Content-Location: http://www.webpage/images/the.one
; This Content-Location must contain an absolute URL,
; since no base; is valid here.
--boundary-content_example
Part 2:
Content-Type: Text/HTML; charset=US-ASCII
Content-ID: <example2@someplace.com>
Content-Location: the.one ; The Content-Base below applies to
; this relative URL
Content-Base: http://www.webpage/images/
--boundary-content_example--
```

- multipart/report [RFC1892]

  The multipart/report content type was defined for returning delivery status reports, with optional included messages. It is finding wider use in machine-to-machine communication. The multipart/report is used for Message Disposition Notification.

- multipart/signed, multipart/encrypted [RFC1847]

  The multipart/signed and multipart/encrypted content types provide a security framework for MIME parts. These headers do not define security protocols, but exist to carry the protected documents. Each multipart/signed or multipart/encrypted body part is carried as two related parts, one with the control information describing the protocol and one with the protected document.

  The multipart/signed content type specifies how to support authentication and integrity services using digital signature. The control information is carried in the second of the two required body parts.

  The multipart/encrypted content type specifies how to support confidentiality using encryption. The control information is carried in the first of the two required body parts.

CONTENT-TYPE: TEXT

The text content type is used for message content that is primarily in human-readable text character format. The more complex text content types are defined and identified so that an appropriate tool can be used to display that body part.

- text/enriched [RFC1896]

  The text/enriched content type is intended to be simple enough to make multifont, formatted email widely readable. It uses a very limited set of formatting commands that all begin with <commandname> and end with </commandname>, affecting the formatting of the text between those two tokens.

- text/html [RFC1866]

    The text/html content type is an Internet Media Type as well as a MIME content type. Using HTML in MIME messages allows the full richness of Web pages to be available in email.

- text/plain [RFC1521]

    The text/plain content type is the generic subtype for plain text. It is the default specified by RFC 822.

- text/rfc822-headers [RFC1892]

    The text/RFC 822-headers content type provides a mechanism for an MTA to label and return only the RFC 822 headers of a failed message. Only the headers are returned, not the complete message. The returned headers are useful for identifying the failed message and for diagnosing delivery problems. All headers are to be returned, up to the blank line following the headers.

- text/richtext [RFC1521]

    The text/richtext content type has been made obsolete by text/enriched.

- text/sgml [RFC1874]

    The text/SGML content type is meant to be used when the contents of the SGML entity is meant to be read by a human and is in a readily comprehensible form—that is, the content can be easily discerned by someone without SGML display software. Each record in the SGML entity, delimited by record start (RS) and record end (RE) codes, must correspond to a line in the text/SGML body part.

CONTENT-TYPE: VIDEO

The video content type allows standardized video files to be included in messages:

- video/mpeg [RFC1521]

CONTENT-TRANSFER-ENCODING

Many message transfer agents properly handle only short lines of US-ASCII characters. This is referred to as "7bit" or sometimes as "7bit encoded" text. SMTP imposes this limit. In order to send a richer set of file types across the Internet so that all MTAs can properly process them, some sort of encoding must be used. The purpose of the encoding is to use only 7-bit characters and limited line lengths to represent the content of the file. The file can be an image file, an executable file, or any general binary file.

While there are five content-transfer-encoding values defined, along with the extensible X-token, the base64 and quoted-printable are the only actual encoding schemes defined by MIME. These two schemes offer the extremes in the tradeoff between the need for a compact and efficient scheme and the desire for a generally human-readable scheme. The base64 is a totally mapped and fairly efficient encoding scheme for binary files. The quoted-printable scheme is used for mostly 7-bit data and is readable by humans.

There are three values of content-transfer-encoding that can be used in Internet SMTP messages. The 7bit is the definitive SMTP mechanism. The base64 and quoted-printable are encoding schemes that ensure that the content will properly pass through all MTAs. The 8bit and binary content-transfer-encoding values are defined to explicitly identify content that may require processing or encoding before being packaged for Internet transfer.

CONTENT-TRANSFER-ENCODING: 7BIT

The 7bit is the most fundamental message encoding. Actually, 7bit is not encoded; 7bit encoded files are files that use only 7-bit characters and have lines no longer than 1000 characters. CR (carriage return) and LF (line feed) characters can only occur as pairs to limit the line length to 1000 characters, including the CRLF pair. NULL characters are not allowed. 7bit encoded files need no encoding or decoding. This is the default.

CONTENT-TRANSFER-ENCODING: 8BIT

8bit encoding has the same line-length limitations as the 7bit encoding. It allows 8bit characters. No encoding or decoding is required for 8bit files. Since not all MTAs can handle 8bit data, the 8bit encoding is not a valid encoding mechanism for Internet mail.

CONTENT-TRANSFER-ENCODING: BASE64

Base64 encoding is the scheme used to transmit binary data. Base64 processes data as 24-bit groups, mapping this data to four encoded characters. It is sometimes referred to as 3-to-4 encoding. Each 6 bits of the 24-bit group is used as an index into a mapping table (the base64 alphabet) to obtain a character for the encoded data. The encoded data has line lengths limited to 76 characters. The characters used in base64 encoding, the base64 alphabet, include none of the special characters of importance to SMTP or the hyphen used with MIME boundary strings.

CONTENT-TRANSFER-ENCODING: BINARY

Binary encoding is simply unencoded binary data. It has no line-length limitations. Binary encoded messages are not valid Internet messages.

CONTENT-TRANSFER-ENCODING: QUOTED-PRINTABLE

Quoted-printable encoding is used where data is mostly US-ASCII text. It allows for 8-bit characters to be represented as their hexadecimal values. For instance, a new line can be forced by using the following string: "=0D=0A".

Line lengths are limited to 76 characters. Using an equal sign as the last character on the line as a "soft" line break accommodates longer lines. The 76-character limit does not include the CRLF sequence or the equal sign.

Any character, except the CRLF sequence, can be represented by an equal sign followed by a two-digit hexadecimal representation. This is especially useful in getting mostly text messages to pass reliably through gateways such as EBCDIC where such characters as "{" and "}" have special meaning.

CONTENT-TRANSFER-ENCODING: X-TOKEN

Private or proprietary encoding schemes can be included in messages by having specialized UAs or applications available to both the sender and the receiver, each recognizing an agreed-upon x-token and providing their own encoding mechanism. The x-token can be any character string preceded by "x-" or "X-".

CONTENT-DISPOSITION

Content-Disposition headers are included to allow a message to be tagged to indicate its presentation mechanism or its archival disposition, a file name.

Some UAs may ignore Content-Disposition headers when they appear within multipart/related body parts.

Content-Disposition headers cannot contain comments.

CONTENT-DISPOSITION: ATTACHMENT

Body parts designated as containing attachments require user action to be displayed and are normally split out of the message. They are typically stored as files for subsequent access. The optional parameters for this header are file name, creation-date, modification-date, read-date, and size.

CONTENT-DISPOSITION: INLINE

Inline content is displayed to the user when the message is opened. The inline body parts are to be displayed in the order they appear in the message, subject to applicable rules for multipart content type. If a multipart body part has an inline header, the inline designation applies to the multipart as a whole, not to its subparts.

Internet Mail RFCs

The following RFCs address MIME: 822, 934, 1000, 1036, 1039, 1049, 1314, 1341, 1486, 1494, 1495, 1521, 1522, 1601, 1602, 1652, 1730, 1738, 1847, 1866, 1867, 1892, 1894, 1896, 1911, 2000, 2015, 2017, 2026, 2045, 2046, 2047, 2048, 2049, 2068, 2076, 2077, 2110, 2111, 2112, 2122, 2183, 2184, 2220, 2231, 2234, 2298, 2301, 2311, 2318.

Internet Messages and SMTP

Standard for the Format of ARPA Internet Text Messages is the title of RFC 822, the document that has defined the format of Internet mail messages since its publication in August of 1982. This straightforward format has been very successful. In fact, it has been adopted, wholly or partially, well beyond the confines of the Internet and the Internet SMTP transport, which is defined in RFC 821.

A basic understanding of RFC 822 messages and MIME extensions is useful for people who use CDO to create MIME formatted messages. Many properties and methods, for example, IBodyPart.ContentMediaType, require that you have some understanding of RFC 822 and MIME.

As the RFC 822 message format has seen wider use, a number of its limitations have proven increasingly restrictive. These limitations and the ways they were circumvented are described more fully in MIME Extensions to Internet Mail.

About Simple Internet (RFC 822) Messages

This section briefly describes the format of the simple Internet message. For the original in-depth description, see RFC 822 itself, *http://ds.internic.net/rfc/rfc822.txt*.

RFC 822 messages have two major parts:

- **Message envelope**. The message envelope contains all the information needed to accomplish transmission and delivery of the message. This information includes the email address of the message's creator—also known as the originator. This string matches the information in the *Sender:* header, if this header is present. The envelope is created by a user agent—such as Microsoft Outlook—and is meaningful only to the message transfer agents that move the message on the path to its destination.

- **Message contents**. The contents make up the object to be delivered to the recipient. Message contents consist of lines of ASCII text. This text is arranged in the classic "memo" format, in which the message contains one or more introductory headers and a body. Persons and/or applications that want to assemble or read email messages using CDO use the headers and the body.

This structure can be seen in Figure A–1.

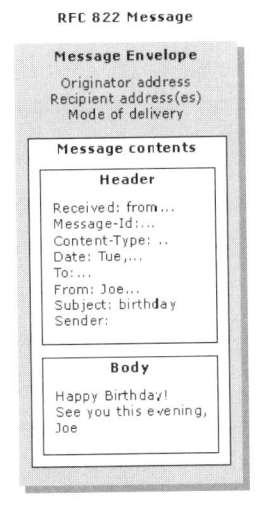

RFC 822 Message

Message Envelope
Originator address
Recipient address(es)
Mode of delivery

Message contents

Header
Received: from...
Message-Id:...
Content-Type: ..
Date: Tue,...
To:...
From: Joe...
Subject: birthday
Sender:

Body
Happy Birthday!
See you this evening,
Joe

FIGURE A-1 *Simple internet (RFC 822) messages*

You can identify the headers and body within the contents of the sample Internet mail message in the following topic.

Simple Internet Mail Message: An Example

As you can see in the sample that follows of a message's contents, the format described in RFC 822 produces messages readable with little difficulty by humans.

The first few lines, from the first instance of "Received" to "Precedence", are headers. These lines define the recipients, the sender, the date, and other information involved with message transmission.

Following the headers is a blank line. This is marked by the consecutive occurrence of the four characters CR, LF, CR, and LF. After this blank line starts the body of the message. In the following example, only the final few lines make up the message body:

```
Received: from someone@microsoft.com
Message-Id: <v0214040cad6a13935723@>
Mime-Version: 1.0
Content-Type: text/plain; charset="us-ascii"
Date: Thursday, 4 Jun 1998 09:43:14 -0800
To: project-discussion@microsoft.com
From: Nina Marton <nina@microsoft.com>
Subject: Happy Birthday
Precedence: bulk

Happy Birthday!
See you this evening,
Nina
```

About SMTP

As important as the format of electronic messages is the transfer protocol for which that format was created. This is SMTP, the Internet protocol for electronic mail. It is defined in RFC 821, the companion document to RFC 822.

SMTP is just one part of the TCP/IP protocol suite. SMTP standardizes communication between MTAs by defining how messages move from one computer's MTA to another computer's MTA, though it does not specify the message's path to the destination computer. This path can be direct or it can lead through intermediate computers, in a process known as store and forward. The SMTP protocol is concerned only with moving messages and with this as a goal, it limits the formatting attributes of messages. SMTP transfers only ASCII text—no fonts, colors, graphics, or attachments—though as mentioned earlier, MIME extensions provide workarounds for these limitations.

In the early days of the Internet, SMTP gained widespread use through its close connection to UNIX-based systems. At first it was used only with UNIX tools, such as the email program *sendmail*. Today SMTP is the still the standard email protocol for the Internet, but Internet hosts use a wide variety of operating systems, and people can read and send their mail with any user agent that can communicate with an MTA.

Summary of RFC 822

RFC 822 was revised by David H. Crocker, of the Department of Electrical Engineering at the University of Delaware, and published on August 13, 1982. It made RFC 733 (NIC #41952) obsolete.

The following topics summarize the major sections of RFC 822:

- RFC 822: Introduction
- RFC 822: Notational Conventions
- RFC 822: Lexical Analysis of Messages
- RFC 822: Message Specification
- RFC 822: Date and Time Specification
- RFC 822: Address Specification
- RFC 822: Appendixes

Note A few parts of the following summary are taken verbatim from RFC 822, while most parts are shortened and paraphrased. For complete details, see the original document.

RFC 822: INTRODUCTION

The purpose of RFC 822 is to revise the standards that had previously been codified, culminating in RFC 733. The document's scope is the syntax of email text messages. Messages contain two major parts, envelope and contents (see

"About Simple Internet [RFC 822] Messages"), though the envelope is specifically not described in the document.

In a forward-looking way, RFC 822 states that, although its specifications are intended for use on the ARPA Internet, "an attempt has been made to free it of any dependence on that environment, so that it can be applied to other network text message systems."

Also, RFC 822 defines only what information is passed between Internet hosts, not how messaging systems are used to store, create, or read messages or the information they contain.

About Message Contents and Framework

Messages consist of "lines of text," with no special provisions made for encoding drawings, facsimile, speech, or structured text. Little consideration is given to questions of data compression or to transmission and storage efficiency.

The RFC 822 message will use a general "memo" framework in which initial information is presented in a rigid, defined format (the headers section) followed by the main part of the message whose format is unspecified.

The described framework has limitations, specifically that its constraints on document tone and appearance make messages of this format "primarily useful for most intra-organization communications and well-structured, inter-organization communication, as well as for some types of interprocess communication, such as simple file transfer and remote job entry."

It is speculated that "a more robust framework might allow for multifont, multicolor, multidimensional encoding of information," whereas "a less robust one, as is present in most single-machine message systems, would more severely constrain the ability to add fields and the decision to include specific fields."

RFC 822: NOTATIONAL CONVENTIONS

The notation used in RFC 822 is based on the Backus-Naur Form (BNF) convention, but was recoded by Ken L. Harrenstien into an "augmented BNF that makes the representation smaller and easier to understand."

This section primarily describes how rules (which describe the syntax of the message format) are used in the rest of the document. It includes the following notes:

- Quotation marks enclose literal text, which may be upper- and/or lowercase.
- Certain basic rules are in uppercase, such as SPACE, TAB, CRLF, DIGIT, ALPHA, and so on.
- Elements separated by a forward slash (/) are alternatives.
- Elements enclosed in parentheses are treated as a single element.
- Square brackets enclose optional elements.
- The asterisk character (*) preceding an element indicates repetition of that element an unspecified number of times.

- Repetition a specified number of times is indicated by use of a digit: <n>(element) is equivalent to <n>*<n>(element)—that is, exactly <n> occurrences of (element). Thus, 2DIGIT is a 2-digit number, and 3ALPHA is a string of three alphabetic characters.
- Lists are made using the # character. The construct # is defined, similar to *, as follows: <l>#<m>element.
- A semicolon, set off some distance to the right of rule text, starts a comment that continues to the end of line.

RFC 822: LEXICAL ANALYSIS OF MESSAGES

A message consists of header fields and, optionally, a body. The body is simply a sequence of lines containing ASCII characters. It is separated from the headers by a null line, that is, a line with nothing preceding the carriage return/line feed (CR/LF).

About Header Fields

Each header field is a single line of ASCII characters, and it contains a field name and a field body. A header field can be viewed as being composed of a field name, followed by a colon (:), followed by a field body, and terminated by a CR/LF.

Wrapping Field Bodies

The field-body portion of a header can be wrapped into a multiple-line representation. The general rule is that wherever there is linear-white-space (not simply LWSP-characters), a CR/LF immediately followed by at least one LWSP-character can instead be inserted.

This word-wrap capability is referred to in RFC 822 as "folding," and the process of moving from the multiple-line representation of a header field to its single-line representation is called "unfolding." Unfolding is accomplished by regarding a CR/LF immediately followed by an LWSP-character as equivalent to the LWSP-character alone.

Structure of Header Fields

The name of a header field must be composed of printable ASCII characters (characters with ASCII values between decimal 33 and 126, except colons). The header field body can be composed of any ASCII characters except CR or LF. (While CR and/or LF can be present in the actual text, they are removed when the field is unfolded.)

Certain header field bodies such as those for dates and addresses have internal structure. Others, such as "Subject" and "Comments", are regarded simply as strings of text, and are defined as <text>.

The Structure of Header Field Bodies

In RFC 822, this section describes the structure of fields used for headers. It is assumed that "lexical analyzer" code exists to interpret the bodies of header fields and that those header fields consist of the following lexical symbols:

- Individual special characters
- Quoted-strings
- Domain-literals
- Comments
- Atoms

The usage rules for the elements and structure of header fields are supported in this section by an example.

Header Field Definitions

This section lists the syntax rules for header field names and header field bodies, for the purpose of detecting fields within messages.

Lexical Tokens

The rules in this section define a "lexical analyzer," which feeds tokens to higher level parsers. For example:

```
CHAR = <any ASCII character>
DIGIT       =  <any ASCII decimal digit>
LWSP-char   =  SPACE / HTAB
linear-white-space =  1*([CRLF] LWSP-char)
atom = 1*<any CHAR except specials, SPACE and CTLs>
comment = "(" *(ctext / quoted-pair / comment) ")"
word = atom / quoted-string
```

This section is followed by a Clarifications section, which gives more details about issues such as quoting, white space, comments, and case-sensitivity.

RFC 822: MESSAGE SPECIFICATION

This section explains the broader requirements of (and recommendations for) constructing a message. For example:

- Header fields are *not* required to occur in any particular order, except that the message body must occur *after* the headers.
- It is recommended that, if present, headers be sent in the order "Return- Path", "Received", "Date", "From", "Subject", "Sender", "To", "cc", and so on.
- message = fields *(CRLF *text)
- fields = dates

    source
    1*destination
    *optional-field

The section also describes the use of fields for forwarding messages, providing an audit trail to facilitate message handling (and to identify a route to the message's sender), and identifying the various hosts that sent and received the message en route. Header fields can also be used to provide information about the message's origination, in particular:

- **From**—The identity of the person(s) who initiated sending the message.
- **Sender**—The authenticated identity of the Agent (person, system or process) that sends the message.
- **Reply-to**—Mailboxes to which responses are to be sent.

Receiver fields are also described. These include the following:

- **To**—The identity of the primary recipients of the message.
- **Cc**—The identity of the secondary (informational) recipients of the message.
- **Bcc**—The identity of additional recipients of the message. The contents of this field are not included in copies of the message sent to the primary and secondary recipients.

Reference Fields

This section describes the fields Message-ID, In-Reply-To, References, and Keywords.

Other Fields

The Subject and Comments fields are briefly described, as are the fields used for encryption, extensions to standard fields, and user-defined fields.

RFC 822: DATE AND TIME SPECIFICATION

The syntax and semantics for the dates and times used in RFC 822 messages are defined in this section. For example, the days of the week and months of the year are enumerated, and the time is defined as:

```
time = hour zone ; ANSI and Military

hour = 2DIGIT ":" 2DIGIT [":" 2DIGIT] ; 00:00:00 - 23:59:59
Time zones are also specified, for example:
zone = "UT" / "GMT"
       / "EST" / "EDT"
```

RFC 822: ADDRESS SPECIFICATION

The syntax for addresses is given as follows:

```
address = mailbox ; one addressee / group ; named list
group = phrase ":" [#mailbox] ";"
mailbox = addr-spec ; simple address / phrase route-addr ;
name & addr-spec
route-addr = "<" [route] addr-spec ">"
route = 1#("@" domain) ":" ; path-relative
```

```
addr-spec = local-part "@" domain ; global address
local-part = word *("." word) ; uninterpreted ;
case-preserved
domain = sub-domain *("." sub-domain)
sub-domain = domain-ref / domain-literal
domain-ref = atom ; symbolic reference
```

For an example of addresses used in an RFC 822 message, see Simple Internet Mail Message: An Example.

Address Semantics

A mailbox is defined as a conceptual entity that receives mail and does not necessarily store files; a mailbox could, for example, pass mail directly on to a printer rather than storing it on disk.

A mailbox specification is defined as consisting of a person, system or process name reference, a domain-dependent string, and a name-domain reference, where the name reference is optional.

RFC 822: APPENDIXES

This section of RFC 822 provides a number of examples of addresses, written to illustrate both typical and borderline cases. Examples of message headers are given that show the use of both mandatory and optional headers.

An appendix is provided that describes the differences between the specifications of RFC 733 and those of RFC 822.

Finally, the syntax rules for the basic Internet message are listed alphabetically in a table.

SMTP/NNTP Transport Event Sinks with CDO

Implementing and managing SMTP/NNTP service transport event sinks using CDO is covered in the CDO for Microsoft Windows 2000 documentation.

Transport event sinks implemented with CDO for Windows 2000 will continue to function without alteration after the installation of Microsoft Exchange 2000 Server. No recompilation or reimplementation of the sink is required. The CDO for Exchange 2000 COM component has been designed to install cleanly over the CDO for Windows 2000 COM component, and all applications, including transport event sinks, will continue to function after the installation.

If you need to update or revise the code for applications written using CDO for Windows 2000, it is recommended that you update any references to the CDOSYS component and replace them with references to the CDOEX component.

INDEX

A

ActionTable, 5
    actions, 185
    columns, creating, 488-89
    conditions, 185-86
    defining, 169, 182-86
    event types, 184
    row evaluation order, 183-84
    rows, adding, 490
    using CdoWfEventTypes in calls to advance, 184
    using event types with, 184-85
Activeconnection property, 407, 410
Active Directory:
    creating contacts in, 473-74
    paths:
        building, 200-201
        email addresses stored as, 212-13
    properties, accessing, 480
Active Directory Services Interfaces (ADSI), 115
    and CDO, 122
    mail recipients using, creation of, 523-25
ActiveX controls, 5
AddRelatedBodyPart method, 547
Addressing calendar messages, 430-31
Ad hoc process definitions, 181
ADO (ActiveX Data Objects), 2, 34, 96
    and CDO, 119-20
        binding to items in the Web Storage System, 121
        differences between, 120-22
        synchronized streams and properties, 120-21
        updating items in the Web Storage System, 122
    messaging, when to use, 150
    using to set SCR and default document properties, 342-43
ADSI, *See* Active Directory Services Interfaces (ADSI)
Advanced developer tasks, 488-95
    action table columns, creating, 488-89
    action table rows, adding, 490
    common script file, specifying, 490-91
    ProcessDefinition object, creating, 491-92
Advanced workflow applications, developing, 168-72
Application architecture, 173-74
    business logic layer, 173-74
    presentation layer, 173
Application content type, 551-52
Application folders, 33-34

Appointment object, configuring, 471-72
Appointments, 151
    adding attachments to, 445-46
    attachments, 152, 445-46
    canceling, 462-63
    creating, 425-27
        in C++, 426-27
        in Visual Basic, 425-26
    exceptions, defined, 441
    getting from folders in Exchange, 457-59
    publishing, 434-36
        using C++, 435-36
        using Visual Basic, 434-35
    recurring, 436-45
    updating, 456-68
Asynchronous events, 96, 100
    details, 100
Asynchronous event sinks:
    implementing, 354-57
    OnDelete event sink, 356-57
    OnSave event sink, 354-56
Attachments, 389-91
    adding to appointments, 152, 445-46
    adding to meetings, 445-46
    manually adding, 391-94
Attendees:
    additional, inviting to meetings, 468-71
    inviting to a meeting in calendar folder, 469-70
Audio content type, 552
Audit trail:
    testing/debugging workflow applications using, 193
    using, 484
AuditTrailEventLog object, 167-68
AuditTrail provider, setting, 186
Automatic categorization, 93
Automatic message property promotion, 133-34

B

base64 encoding, 558
baseschema, 299
Base schema path, setting for schema folder, 323-27
Binary encoding, 558
Binding, 123-24
Binding messages to custom forms, 344-46
Body part fields and streams, and CDO messaging, 140-43
Body part object hierarchies, and CDO messaging, 137-40
Body parts, MIME message format, 128-29

Building paths, 200-201
Built-in workflow functionality, 165-68
Business critical applications, and CDOEXM, 196
Business logic layer, 173-74
Business processes, modeling, 166

C

Calendar folder query, 443-45
Calendaring, 151-60, 425-76
    Appointment object, configuring, 471-72
    appointments, 151
        attachments, 152, 445-46
        canceling, 462-63
        creating, 425-27
        getting from folders in Exchange, 457-59
        publishing, 152, 434-36
        recurring, 436-45
        updating, 456-68
    attendees:
        additional, inviting to meetings, 468-71
        inviting to a meeting in calendar folder, 469-70
    calendar messages:
        addressing, 430-31
        opening in inbox, 447
        processing, 446-56
    defined, 151
    free/busy status, checking, 431-33
    meeting cancellations, processing, 453-54
    meeting requests, 151
        attachments, 152
        forwarding, 470-72
        responding to, 449-51
        sending, 427-36
    meeting responses, processing, 452-53
    meetings, 151
        adding attachments to, 445-46
        canceling, 463-64
        getting from folders in Exchange, 457-59
        previously accepted, 467-68
        recurring, 436-45, 455-56
        updating, 456-68
    meeting updates, sending, 459-62
    previously accepted meeting, declining, 467-68
    recurring appointments, 436-45
        canceling, 464-67
    recurring meetings, 436-45
        canceling, 464-67
        processing exceptions, 455-56
    using with Exchange 2000 Server, 151
CalendarMessage object, 437
Calendar messages:
    addressing, 430-31
        in C++, 431
        in Visual Basic, 431
    opening in inbox, 447
    processing, 446-56
Calendars:
    Calendar object model, 154-55
    coordinated universal time (UTC), 155-56
    in Exchange 2000 Server, 152

    on the Internet, 152-54
    Time Zone to CdoTimeZoneId map, 158-60
    time zones, 155 56
        making work, with Outlook, 157
        recurring appointments and, 158
        specifying, 156-57
Canceling appointments, 462-63
Canceling meetings, 463-64
CDO, *See* Collaboration Data Objects (CDO)
CDOEX, 115
CDOEXM, 116, 118-19
    Active Directory paths:
        building, 200-201
        email addresses stored as, 212-13
    and ADSI, 200
    automated services, 196
    and business critical applications, 196
    CDOEXM objects, error checking, 213
    defined, 195
    DLLs, 196-97
    errors, checking, 517-18
    Exchange management security, 205
    Exchange Server, managing, 205-6
    folders, accessing, 211-12
    FolderTree COM class, 206
    folder trees, 198
        creating, 207
        replication, 199
        rules about, 198-99
    folder tree URLs, retrieving, 202-4
    installation, 197
    mailboxes, accessing, 211-12
    MailboxStoreDB COM class, 206
    mail recipients, managing, 208
    MDBs, 198
        rules about, 198-99
    and MMC snap-ins, 196
    public and mailbox stores, creating, 207
    PublicStoreDB COM class, 206
    recipient management interfaces, 208-9
        CDOEXM IDistributionList interface, 208
        CDOEXM IMailboxStore interface, 208-9
        CDOEXM IMailRecipient interface, 208-9
        using in context, 209-10
    recipients/folders/groups, 211
    and remote management, 196
    Server COM class, 205-6
    setting up a store, 206-8
    storage group, creating, 207
    StorageGroup COM class, 206
    and system administration, 196
    uses of, 196
    Web-based management, 204-5
    Web Storage System configuration, 197-98
CDOEXM IDistributionList interface, 208
CDOEXM IMailboxStore interface, 208-9
CDOEXM IMailRecipient interface, 208-9
CDOEXM objects, error checking, 213
CDOEX Server, 4, 115, 116-18
    COM classes/interfaces, 117
    uses of, 117-18

Index 571

CDO messaging, 136-50
    and ADO, 149-50
    body part fields and streams, 140-43
        BodyPart content streams, 141-42
        BodyPart streams, 142-43
    body part object hierarchies, 137-40
        examples, 138-40
    COM classes, 137
    COM interfaces, 136-37
    configuration, 146-48
        configuration fields, 147-48
CDO Person object, working with, 161
CdoWfEventTypes, using in calls to advance, 184
CDO Workflow Event Sink, 164
CDO Workflow Objects for Microsoft Exchange, 116, 164
Client-specified process definition, 180
Collaboration Data Objects (CDO), 3-4, 115-24
    and ADO, 119-20
        binding to items in the Web Storage System, 121
        differences between, 120-22
        synchronized streams and properties, 120-21
        updating items in the Web Storage System, 122
    and ADSI, 122
    CDOEXM, 116, 118-19
    CDOEX Server, 4, 115, 116-18
    CDOW, 118
    CDO Workflow Objects for Exchange (CDOWF), 116
    components, 116
    Configuration object, 124
    data sources and binding, 123-24
    IDataSource interface, 123
    messaging with, for Exchange 2000 Server, 136
Columns, creating, 488-89
COM classes, top-level, 124
Common script file, specifying, 490-91
Conditions, ActionTable, 185-86
Configuration object, 124
Contacts, 161, 472-76
    creating, 472-74
        in Active Directory, 473-74
        in the Web Storage System, 472-73
    searching for, 474-75
    using, 472
    VCard Stream, getting, 475
CONTAINS predicate, 303
Content-Base header, 546
Content class definitions, 29-30
    creating, 316-18
Content classes, 25-28
    compared to a content type, 25
    defined, 25
    example of, 25-26
    folder expected content class, 32-33
    inheritance, 27-28
        benefits of, 28
        multiple inheritance, 28
        single inheritance, 27
    messaging, 132-34
    uses of, 26
Content classes for folders, expected, specifying, 318-19
Content-Description headers, 551
Content-Disposition headers, 551, 559
    attachment header, 559
    inline header, 559
Content-ID headers, 551
Content-Location header, 546
Content-Transfer-Encoding headers, 550-51, 557-59
    base64 encoding, 558
    binary encoding, 558
    8bit encoding, 558
    quoted-printable encoding, 558-59
    7bit encoding, 558
    x-token encoding, 559
Content-Type headers, 550-57
    application content type, 551-52
    audio content type, 552
    message content type, 552-53
    multipart content type, 553-56
    text content type, 556-57
    video content type, 557
Coordinated universal time (UTC), 155-56
COPY command, HTTP/WebDAV, 6
Copying items, 249-50
Custom forms, binding messages to, 344-46
Custom item properties, 263-65
    setting:
        using VBScript, 263-64
        using Visual Basic, 264-65
CustomMessage.VBS, 345-46
Custom properties, 15-16
    caching, 478-88

▼ D

Data sources, 123-24
Data type mappings, 20-21
Date range, specifying, 305-6
Deep traversal:
    defined, 301
    specifying, 301-2
Default namespaces, 13
Default process definition, 180
Default stream, 21-22
Definition items, 29-30
    content class definitions, 29-30
    property definition items, 29, 30
Definition properties:
    forms, 339-41
        property list, 340-41
DELETE command, HTTP/WebDAV, 6
Deleting:
    folder trees, 503-4
    items, 251-52
    storage groups, 506-8
Deployment, managing, 189-92
.doc, 23
DSN content class, 133

E

8bit encoding, 558
Email Workflow, 179-80
    Web-based workflow compared to, 178-80
Embedded messages, extracting, 415-16
.eml, 23
Enumerating:
    contacts, 539-40
    event registrations, for a folder, 364-67
    groups, 538-39
    mail-enabled contacts, 539-40
    mail recipients, 536-38
    search results, 309-10
    storage groups, 497-501
    stores, 497-501
Event logs, 113
Event naming, 112-13
Event notification priority, 105-6
Event registration, 103-9
    guidelines, 108
    modification, 109
    security, 108
Event registrations:
    adding for a folder, 360-63
    enumerating for a folder, 364-67
    managing, 360-67
    and RegEvent.vbs, 367-68
        deleting event registrations, 369
        enumerating event registrations, 369
        registering for an asynchronous event, 367
        registering for an OnSyncSave event, 367-68
        registering for an OnTimer event, 368
        registering for a system event, 368
    removing for a folder, 363-64
Event reliability, 109
Event sink interfaces, 96-102
Event types, ActionTable, 184
Exceptions, defined, 441
Exchange 5.5, access rights, and the Web Storage System, 57-79
Exchange 2000 Server, calendars in, 152
Exchange 2000 Server Web storage system, 6
Exchange calls event methods, 93-94
Exchange Installable File System (ExIFS), 10
Exchange mail submission URI, 135
Exchange OLE DB provider (ExOLEDB), 2, 6-7, 11, 96
    and property names, 16-17
Exchange Web Storage System, and messaging, 132
Exchange Workflow Designer, 165-66, 477
Existing items, getting, 241-44
    using C++, 243-44
    using VBScript, 241-42
Expected content classes for folders, specifying, 318-19

F

Fields, 12
file: URL scheme, 216-17
File system, 2
Folder expected content class, 32-33
Folder item access rights, 46-47

Folders, 40-44
    accessing, 211-12
    configuring schema scope, 319-27
    content class, 330
    creating, using HTTP/WebDAV protocol, 279-80
    enabling for mail, 542-43
    getting a list of, 266
        using C++, 267
        using VBScript, 266
    searching, using HTTP/WebDAV protocol, 288-90
    setting base schema path for schema folder, 323-27
        using C++, 324-27
        using VBScript, 323-24
    setting schema collection reference for, 320-23
        using C++, 322-32
        using VBScript, 321-22
Folders, creating, 233-36
    with C++, 235-36
    with VBScript, 234-35
FolderTree COM class, 206
Folder trees, 198
    creating, 207, 502-3
    deleting, 503-4
    replication, 199
    rules about, 198-99
Folder tree URLs, retrieving, 202-4
Form definition properties, 84-85
Form registration, 81-89, 339
    content class of, 340
    default, 88-89
    examples of, 86-88
        HTTP/WebDAV example, 86-87
        Testapp example, 87-88
    form definition properties, 84-85
    forms registry, 82-83
    how forms work, 81-82
    namespaces, 86
    order of precedence, 88
    registering using PROPPATCH, 341-42
    registration security, 86
    schema collection ref (SCR), 83-84
    syntax, 340
Forms:
    ADO, using to set SCR and default document properties, 342-43
    custom forms, binding messages to, 344-46
    definition properties, 339-41
        property list, 340-41
    form registration, 339
        content class of, 340
        registering using PROPPATCH, 341-42
        syntax, 340
    Microsoft Outlook Web Access views:
        loading in an IFrame, 346-47
        loading in a frame, 347-48
        reusing in a Web page, 346-48
    using, 339-48
FORMSOF predicate, 303
Forms registry, 82-83
Forwarding meeting requests, 470-72

Index   573

Free/busy status:
    checking, 431-33
        C++ code, 433
        Visual Basic code, 432-33
FREETEXT predicate, 303
Full-text indexing, 38-40
    customizing, 39-40
        adding properties, 39-40
        editing noise words, 40

▼ G

GetNewWorkflowMessage method, 168
GetUpdatedItem method, 447
Globally unique identifier (GUID), 16
GROUP BY clause, 307-8
Groups, enumerating, 538-39
Guidelines:
    event registration, 108
    namespaces, 15-16

▼ H

Header fields, messages, 387-89
Headers:
    MIME, 550-59
        Content-Description headers, 551
        Content-Disposition headers, 551, 559
        Content-ID headers, 551
        Content-Transfer-Encoding headers, 550-51, 557-59
        Content-Type headers, 550-57
        MIME-Version header, 550
http: URL scheme, 218-20
HTTP/WebDAV protocol, 1-2, 3, 6, 11, 15, 17, 40, 277-96
    folders:
        creating, 279-80
        searching, 288-90
    items:
        copying, 282
        creating, 277-79
        deleting, 281
        getting an item's stream, 280-81
        getting property values, 283-84
        modifying property values, 286-88
        moving, 282-83
    MKCOL command, 42-44
    and property names, 17-18
    row ranges, specifying in a search, 290
    search folders, creating, 293-96
    search results, rendering with XSL, 290-93
    XMLDOM, constructing XML with, 285-86
HyperText Markup Language (HTML), defined, 545

▼ I

IAppointment.Cancel method, 463-64
IAppointment.CreateRequest method, 425, 427, 437, 459-60
IAppointment.Decline method, 467-68
IAppointment.Invite method, 469

IAuditTrail interface, 193
IBodyPart.BodyParts collection, 391, 395
IBodyPart.ContentMediaType, 399
IBodyPart.Fields collection, 395
ICalendarMessage.CalendarParts.GetUpdatedItem method, 459
ICalendarMessage.Send method, 469
ICalendarPat.GetUpdatedItem method, 452
ICreateRegistration interface method, 101-2
IDataSource interface, 123
IException objects, 441
IExStoreAsyncEvents, 96, 100
IExStoreSyncEvents, 96
IExStoreSystemEvents, 97
IMessage.AddAttachment method, 389-91, 395
IMessage.AddRelatedBodyPart, 547
IMessage.Attachments collection, 391
IMessage.AutoGenerateTextBody property, 387
IMessage.CreateMHTMLBody method, 395, 547
IMessage.Fields collection, 383, 405
IMessage.Forward method, 470
IMessage.From property, 405
IMessage.HTMLBody property, 387, 395, 399
IMessage.Newsgroups property, 405
IMessage.Send method, 465, 470
IMessage.Subject property, 384, 405
IMessage.TextBody property, 384, 399
Inheritance, content classes, 27-28
    benefits of, 28
    multiple inheritance, 28
    single inheritance, 27
InstallMessage.VBS, 344-45
Internet, calendars and, 152-55
Internet mail RFCs, 559
Internet Message Access Protocol version 4 (IMAP4), 11
Internet messages, 560-67
    simple (RFC 822), 560-61
        example, 561
Internet standard message formats, 126
IProcessDefinition interface, 186
IProcessInstance, 172-73
IRecurrencePattern objects, 441
Item access rights, 46-48
    folders, 46-47
    non-folders, 47-48
    standard, 48
ItemAuthors collection, 481-82
Item counts, getting with GROUP BY clause, 307-8
Item default stream property, 21-22
Item properties, 12-23, 256-65
    automatic property promotion from the stream, 22-23
    custom properties, 15-16, 263-65
    custom properties and MAPI, 16
    default namespaces, 13
    item default stream property, 21-22
    multivalued properties, 259-63
    namespace guidelines, 15-16
    namespace URLs/URNs, 13
    namespaces, 12-13, 14
    printing property names/types/values, 256-58
        using VBScript, 257-58

Item properties *(continued)*
    property data types, 19-21
    property names, 12-13
        and Exchange OLE DB provider, 16-17
        and HTTP/WebDAV, 17-18
        and XML, 18-19
    property names/types/values, 256-58
ItemReaders collection, 482-83
Items:
    copying, 249-50
        using C++, 250-51
        using HTTP/WebDAV protocol, 282
        using VBScript, 249-50
    creating, 236-40
        with C++, 239-40
        using HTTP/WebDAV protocol, 277-79
        with VBScript, 237-38
    deleting, 251-52
        using HTTP/WebDAV protocol, 281
        using VBScript, 251-52
        using Visual Basic, 252
    deleting using a recordset, 252-54
        using C++, 253-54
        using VBScript, 252-53
    existing items, getting, 241-44
    getting property values, using HTTP/WebDAV
        protocol, 283-84
    modifying property values, using HTTP/WebDAV
        protocol, 286-88
    moving, 255-56
        using C++, 255-56
        using HTTP/WebDAV protocol, 282-83
        using VBScript, 255
Item streams, accessing, 244-49
    using C++, 246-49
    using VBScript, 244-46
Item validation, 93
IWorkflowMessage interface, 168
IWorkflowSession GetUserProperty method, 480

▼ J

JScript, getting XML security descriptor using, 332-33

▼ K

Knowledge management, 2

▼ L

Lexical analysis of messages, RFC 822, 564-65
LIKE predicate, 303
Loop recursion, 110

▼ M

Mailbox:
    deleting, 533-34
    moving, 530-32
Mailbox cleanup, controlling, 535-36
Mailbox-enabled recipients, creating, 520-23

Mailboxes, accessing, 211-12
Mailbox storage limits, setting, 534-35
Mailbox store:
    creating, 513-15
    deleting, 515-17
MailboxStoreDB COM class, 206
Mailboxurl property, 407
Mail-enabled contacts:
    creating, 526-29
    enumerating, 539-40
Mail recipients:
    creating, 519-20
    disabling, 525-26
    enumerating, 536-38
    managing, 208
Manually adding attachments, 391-94
MAPI, 2, 6, 11, 19
    and custom properties, 16
MDBs, 198
    rules about, 198-99
MDB-wide events, registering, 104-5
MDN content class, 133
Meeting cancellations, processing, 453-54
Meeting requests, 151
    forwarding, 470-72
    responding to, 449-51
    sending, 427-36
        calendar message, addressing, 430-31
        free/busy status, checking, 431-33
        using C++, 429-30
        using Visual Basic, 427-28
Meeting responses, processing, 452-53
Meetings:
    adding attachments to, 445-46
    canceling, 463-64
    getting from folders in Exchange, 457-59
    previously accepted, declining, 467-68
    recurring, 436-45
    updating, 456-68
Meeting updates, sending, 459-62
Message content type, 552-53
Message fields, CDO, 143-44
Message object:
    configuring, 372-81
        default configuration settings, 381
        network authentication information, 379
        network proxy information, 380
        sending/posting using Exchange, 377-78
        sending/posting using the network, 375-76
        sending/posting using the pickup directory, 376-77
        setting language and time-zone information, 373
        setting send and post methods, 373-74
        using Visual Basic, 372
Messages:
    creating, 371-72
    posting, 405-6
        using Exchange, 409-11
    replying to, 411-14
    sending, 405-6
        using Exchange, 406-9
message streams, CDO, 143, 144-45

Index 575

Messaging, 125-50, 371-423
    attachments, 389-91
        manually adding, 391-94
    automatic message property promotion, 133-34
    with CDO for Exchange 2000 Server, 136
    CDO messaging:
        and ADO, 149-50
        body part fields and streams, 140-43
        body part object hierarchies, 137-40
        COM classes, 137
        COM interfaces, 136-37
        configuration, 146-48
        message fields, 143, 144
        message stream and property synchronization, 146
        message streams, 143, 144-45
        when to use, 150
    content classes, 132-34
    defined, 125
    embedded messages, extracting, 415-16
    Exchange mail submission URI, 135
    and Exchange Web Storage System, 132
    inbox contents, listing using ADO, 422-23
    Internet standard message formats, 126
    loading from within ADO Stream objects, 418-20
    Message object, configuring, 372-81
    messages:
        address formats, 381
        addressing, 381-84
        creating, 371-72
        embedding, 416-18
        header fields, 387-89
        NNTP newsgroup names, 382
        replying to, 411-14
        sending/posting, 405-11
        SMTP addresses, 381
        Subject field, 384-87
        TextBody field, 384-87
    MIME-formatted messages, creating, 394-404
    MIME message format, 127-32
        body parts, 128-29
        content body parts, 129-30
        hierarchies of body parts, 131
        multipart body parts, 130
        RFC 822 message format, 126
    saving into ADO Stream objects, 420-22
    UUENCODE attachment format, 127
MHTML, 545-47
    CDO support for, 547
    key concepts of, 546-47
Microsoft:
    Active Directory Services Interfaces (ADSI), 115
    ADO 2.5, 115
    CDOEXM and, 200
Microsoft Exchange 2000 Server Workflow Designer, 477
Microsoft MSXML DOM parser, 334
Microsoft Outlook Express, 545
Microsoft Outlook Web Access views:
    loading in an IFrame, 346-47
    loading in a frame, 347-48
    reusing in a Web page, 346-48

Microsoft's Software Development Kit (SDK), 16
Microsoft Web Storage System, *See* Web Storage System
Microsoft Workflow Designer for Exchange 2000 Server, 166-167
Microsoft XML (MSXML) COM components, 9
MIME:
    capabilities, 548
    extensions to Internet mail, 547-67
    headers, 550-59
        Content-Description headers, 551
        Content-Disposition headers, 551, 559
        Content-ID headers, 551
        Content-Transfer-Encoding headers, 550-51, 557-59
        Content-Type headers, 550, 551-57
        MIME-Version header, 550
    message format, 548
    sample MIME message, 548-50
MIME Encapsulation of Aggregate HTML Documents (MHTML), 400, 545-47
    CDO support for, 547
    key concepts of, 546-47
MIME-formatted messages:
    BodyPart Objects, adding to MIME hierarchy, 395-99
    creating, 394-404
    header fields, setting on body parts, 399-400
    header fields character set, specifying, 403-4
    MHTML-formatted messages, creating, 400-403
MIME message format, 127-32
    body parts, 128-29
    content body parts, 129-30
    hierarchies of body parts, 131
    multipart body parts, 130
MIME-Version header, 550
MKCOL command, HTTP/WebDAV, 6, 42-44
Modeling business processes, 166
Modeling tools, 164
MOVE command, HTTP/WebDAV, 6
Moving items, 255-56
Multipart content type, 553-56
Multiple events, 94-95
Multiple inheritance, content classes, 28
Multiple sinks, 95
Multivalued item properties, 259-63
    setting/retrieving:
        using C++, 260-63
        using VBScript, 259-60
MyForm, 485

▼ **N**

Namespace guidelines, 15-16
Namespaces, 12-13, 14, 15-16, 86
Namespace URLs/URNs, 13
Network authentication information, 379
Network proxy information, 380
Non-folder item access rights, 47-48
Notifications, 93, 100

O

OLE DB URLs, constructing, 215
OnDelete event sink, 356-57
OnMdbShutdown event sink, 359
OnMdbStartup event sink, 358
OnSave event sink, 354-56
OnSyncDelete, 170
OnSyncDelete event, 5
OnSyncDelete event sink, 352-54
OnSyncSave, 170
OnSyncSave event, 5
OnSyncSave event sink, 350-52
OnTimer, 170
OnTimer event sink, 359-60
Outlook, making time zones work with, 157
Outlook Web Access:
    default views, working with, 89
    Navigation Bar, controlling, 90
    reusing elements of, 89-91
    URL parameters, 90-91
        CMD examples, 91

P

performance monitor counters, 114
Post Office Protocol version 3.0 (POP3), 11
Postpassword property, 410
Postusername property, 410
.ppt, 23
Presentation layer, 173
Previously accepted meeting, declining, 467-68
Privilege Checking, 187, 188
Privileged mode, 189
Privileged workflow authors, 189, 192
PrivilegedWorkflowAuthors, 186-87, 192
ProcessDefinition, creating, 169-70
ProcessDefinition object:
    AuditTrailProvider property, 193
    creating, 491-92
Processing calendar messages, 446-56
Processing meeting responses, 452-53
ProcessInstance, 487
    accessing/modifying, 487-88
PROPPATCH, registering forms using, 341-42
Property data types, 19-21
Property definition items, 29, 30
Property definitions, creating, 312-16
Property indexing, 38
Property names, 12-13
    and Exchange OLE DB provider, 16-17
PROPFIND command, HTTP/WebDAV, 3, 6, 15, 17, 36
PROPPATCH command, HTTP/WebDAV, 6
Proxy addresses, setting, 540-41
Public folders and mailboxes, creating, 2
Public and mailbox stores, creating, 207
Public store:
    creating, 508-10
    deleting, 511-13
PublicStoreDB COM class, 206
Publishing appointments, 434-36

Q

Quoted-printable encoding, 558-59

R

recallmessage content class, 133
recallreport content class, 133
ReceivedMessage, working with, 484-86
Recipient management interfaces, 208-9
    CDOEXM IDistributionList interface, 208
    CDOEXM IMailboxStore interface, 208-9
    CDOEXM IMailRecipient interface, 208-9
    using in context, 209-10
Recipient management tasks, 518-43
    contacts:
        creating, 526-29
        enumerating, 539-40
    enabling a folder for mail, 542-43
    groups, enumerating, 538-39
    mailbox:
        deleting, 533-34
        moving, 530-32
    mailbox cleanup, controlling, 535-36
    mailbox-enabled recipients, creating, 520-23
    mailbox storage limits, setting, 534-35
    mail-enabled recipients, creating, 519-20
    mail recipients:
        disabling, 525-26
        enumerating, 536-38
        using ADSI, creating, 523-25
    proxy addresses, setting, 540-41
    restricted address list, building, 541-42
Recordset.Delete method, 462
Recurrence-Pattern objects, 436-47
Recurring appointments, 436-45
    calendar folder query, 443-45
    canceling, 464-67
    creating:
        using C++, 438-41
        using Visual Basic, 437-38
    specifying exceptions to, 441-43
Recurring meetings, 436-45
    canceling, 464-67
    processing exceptions, 455-56
Recursive events, 104-5
    scope, 104
Recursive sink firing order, 106
RegEvent script, 106-8
RegEvent.vbs, 367-68
Registering forms, 339
Registration security, and form registration, 86
Relative URLs, 221-24
Remote management, and CDOEXM, 196
Replication, folder trees, 199
reportmessage content class, 133
Responding to meeting requests, 449-51
Restricted address list, building, 541-42
Restricted mode, 188

Index 577

RFC 822, 560-67
  address specification, 566-67
  appendixes, 567
  date and time specification, 566
  introduction, 562-63
  lexical analysis of messages, 564-65
  message format, 126
  message specification, 565-66
  notational conventions, 563-64
  summary of, 562-67
RFC 822-formatted stream, 22
RFC 1522, 403
Row evaluation order, 183-84
  ActionTable, 183-84
Row ranges, specifying in a search, 290
Rows, adding, 490
Run-time errors, managing, 478

S

Schema:
  content class definitions, creating, 316-18
  creation steps, 311
  expected content classes for folders,
    specifying, 318-19
  folder content class, 330
  folders:
    configuring schema scope, 319-27
      setting base schema path for schema folder,
        323-27
      setting schema collection reference for, 320-27
  property definitions, creating, 312-16
  testing, 327-29
  using, 311-30
Schema collection ref (SCR), 83-84, 299
Schema folders, 33-34
Schema scope, 299-301
  configuring for folders, 319-27
  defined, 319
Scope tree, concept of, 300-301
Script debugger, testing/debugging workflow
  applications using, 193-94
Script functions, developing, 169
Script Host Sink, 112
SEARCH command, HTTP/WebDAV, 6
Search folders, creating, 293-96
Searching for contacts, 474-75
Search results:
  enumerating, 309-10
  rendering with XSL, 290-93
Search tasks, 297-310
  date range, specifying, 305-6
  deep traversal, specifying, 301-2
  GROUP BY clause, 307-8
  item counts, getting with GROUP BY clause, 307-8
  schema scope, 299-301
  search results, enumerating, 309-10
  simple query, 298-99
  word and character matching, 302-5
Security modes, workflow, 186-89

Security tasks, 331-38
  XML security descriptor, 331-34
    creating, 334-36
    creating an ACE in XML, 334-35
    modifying an item's DACL, 335-36
    updating, 337-38
SELECT* statement, 36
SELECT statement, 35-36
Sending meeting requests, 427-36
Sendpassword property, 407
Sendusername property, 407
SendWorkflowMessage method, 168, 485
Server COM class, 205-6
Server management tasks, 497-501
  CDOEXM errors, checking, 517-18
  folder tree:
    creating, 502-3
    deleting, 503-4
  mailbox store:
    creating, 513-15
    deleting, 515-17
  public store:
    creating, 508-10
    deleting, 511-13
  storage groups:
    creating, 505-6
    deleting, 506-8
    enumerating, 497-501
  stores, enumerating, 497-501
Server and recipient management, 195-223
7bit encoding, 558
Simple Internet (RFC 822) messages, 560-61
  example, 561
Single inheritance, a content classes, 27
Sink monitoring, 113-14
  event logs, 113
SMTP, defined, 562
SMTP/NNTP transport event sinks with CDO, 567
Standard access rights, 48
Storage group, creating, 207
StorageGroup COM class, 206
Storage groups:
  creating, 505-6
  deleting, 506-8
  enumerating, 497-501
Store events, 349-69
  asynchronous event sinks, implementing, 354-57
  event registrations, managing, 360-67
  synchronous event sinks, implementing, 350-54
  system event sinks, implementing, 358-59
Store maintenance, 93
Stores, enumerating, 497-501
Subject field, messages, 384-87
Support interfaces, 102
Synchronous events, 96, 97-99
  details, 97-98
  event sinks sequence for a Web Storage System
    item, 99
Synchronous event sinks:
  implementing, 350-54
  OnSyncDelete event sink, 352-54
  OnSyncSave event sink, 350-52

Index

Syntax, form registration, 340
System events, 97, 100-101
System event sinks:
    implementing, 358-59
    OnMdbShutdown event sink, 359
    OnMdbStartup event sink, 358
    OnTimer event sink, 359-60

▼ T

TextBody field, messages, 384-87
Text content type, 556-57
Timers, 93
Time zones, 155-56
    making work, with Outlook, 157
    recurring appointments and, 158
    specifying, 156-57
    Time Zone to CdoTimeZoneId map, 158-60
Top-level COM classes, 124
Transactions, 268-75

▼ U

Updating appointments, 456-68
URL, defined, 13
URLs:
    constructing, 215-32
    file: URL scheme, 216-17
    host domain name, getting, 224-28
    http: URL scheme, 218-20
    OLE DB URLs, 215
    relative URLs, 221-24
    well-known mailbox folder URLs, getting, 229-32
Urlsource property, 407
URN, defined, 13
UUENCODE attachment format, 127

▼ V

VCard Stream, of contact, getting, 475
Video content type, 557

▼ W

Web-based workflow, email Workflow compared to, 178-80
Web Distributed Authoring and Versioning (WebDAV), 34
Web Storage System, 1-23
    access APIs and protocols, 6-11
        file system access, 10-11
        HTTP/WebDAV access, 9-10
        Internet Message Access Protocol version 4 (IMAP4), 11
        MAPI access, 11
        OLE DB and ADO access, 7-9
        Post Office Protocol version 3.0 (POP3), 11
    Application Programming Interfaces (APIs) used by, 1

automatic message property promotion, 133-34
binding items to, with ADO Record object, 121
Collaboration Data Objects (CDO), 3-4
    CDOEX, 4
creating contacts in, 472-73
events, 4-5
Exchange 2000 Server Web storage system, 6
Exchange OLE DB provider (ExOLEDB), 2
existing items, getting, 241-44
file name extensions used in, 23
file system, 2
folders:
    creating, 233-36
    getting a list of, 266
form registration, 81-89
    default, 88-89
    examples of, 86-88
    form definition properties, 84-85
    forms registry, 82-83
    how forms work, 81-82
    HTTP/WebDAV example, 86-87
    namespaces, 86
    order of precedence, 88
    registration security, 86
    schema collection ref (SCR), 83-84
    Testapp example, 87-88
forms, 3
    using, 339-48
HTTP/WebDAV, 1-2
item properties, 12-23, 256-65
    automatic property promotion from the stream, 22-23
    custom properties, 15-16, 263-65
    custom properties and MAPI, 16
    default namespaces, 13
    item default stream property, 21-22
    multivalued properties, 259-63
    namespace guidelines, 15-16
    namespaces, 12-13, 14
    namespace URLs/URNs, 13
    property data types, 19-21
    property names, 12-13
    property names and Exchange OLE DB provider, 16-17
    property names and HTTP/WebDAV, 17-18
    property names/types/values, 256-58
    property names and XML, 18-19
items:
    copying, 249-50
    creating, 236-40
    deleting, 251-52
    deleting using a recordset, 252-54
    moving, 255-56
item streams, accessing, 244-49
knowledge management, 2
and messaging, 132
organization of, 1
protocols used by, 1
schema, 2-3
transactions, 268-75
updating items in, using ADO, 122

Index 579

URLs:
    accessing items using, 1-2
    constructing, 215-32
Web application development, 5
workflow support, 5
XML security descriptor format, 48-79
    accessing item descriptors, 56
    Discretionary Access Control Lists
        (DACLs) XML elements, 51-53
    example descriptor in XML, 55-56
    Exchange 5.5 access rights and the Web Storage System, 57-79
    new item descriptor inheritance, 57
    security identifiers in XML, 49-50
    system Audit Control Lists (system ACLs) XML elements, 53-54
    XML security descriptor XML elements, 50-51
Web Storage System events, 91-94
    asynchronous events, 96, 100
        details, 100
    automatic categorization, 93
    event naming, 112-13
    event notification priority, 105-6
    event registration, 103-9
        guidelines, 108
        item, 103
        modification, 109
        recursive events, 104-5
        registration steps, 104
        security, 108
    event reliability, 109
    event sink interfaces, 96-102
    events sinks, 110-12
        contextual information in an event registration, 110-11
        information passed to an event methods, 110
        loop recursion, 110
        security in an event sink, 111-12
    Exchange calls event methods, 93-94
    ICreateRegistration interface method, 101-2
    item validation, 93
    MDB-wide events, registering, 104-5
    multiple events, 94-95
    multiple sinks, 95
    notifications, 93
    OLE DB and ADO, 96
    overview, 92-93
    recursive events, 104-5
        scope, 104
    recursive sink firing order, 106
    RegEvent script, 106-8
    Script Host Sink, 112
    sink monitoring, 113-14
        event logs, 113
    store maintenance, 93
    support interfaces, 102
    synchronous events, 96, 97-99
        details, 97-98
        event sinks sequence for a Web Storage System item, 99
    system events, 97, 100-101
    timers, 93
    URL parameters, terms, 92
    workflow applications, 93
Web Storage System schema, 2-3, 25-34
    application and schema folders, 33-34
    content classes, 25-28
        compared to a content type, 25
        defined, 25
        example of, 25-26
        folder expected content class, 32-33
        inheritance, 27-28
        uses of, 26
    definition items, 29-30
        content class definitions, 29-30
        property definition items, 29, 30
    scope, 31-32
Web Storage System search, 34-44
    folders, 40-44
        client request, 43
        example search folder HTTP request and response, 43-44
        HTTP/WebDAV MKCOL command, 42-44
        items, 41-42
        properties, 41
        server response, 44
    full-text indexing, 38-40
        customizing, 39-40
    property indexing, 38
    search scope, 36-37
    SELECT* statement, 36
    SELECT statement, 35-36
Web Storage System security, 45-79
    item access rights, 46-48
        folders, 46-47
        non-folders, 47-48
        standard, 48
    Web Storage System XML security descriptor format, 48-79
        accessing item descriptors, 56
        Discretionary Access Control Lists
            (DACLs) XML elements, 51-53
        example descriptor in XML, 55-56
        Exchange 5.5 access rights and the Web Storage System, 57-79
        new item descriptor inheritance, 57
        security identifiers in XML, 49-50
        system Audit Control Lists (system ACLs) XML elements, 53-54
        XML security descriptor XML elements, 50-51
word and character matching, 302-5
Workflow, 163-94
    ad hoc process definitions, 181
    advanced workflow applications, 168-72
        calling IProcessInstance advance, 172-73
        creating a ProcessDefinition, 169-70
        defining an ActionTable, 169
        developing script functions, 169
        registering the Workflow Event Sink, 170-72
    application architecture, 173-74
        business logic layer, 173-74
        presentation layer, 173
    AuditTrail provider, setting, 186
    AuditTrailEventLog object, 167-68

Index

Workflow *(continued)*
　built-in workflow functionality, 165-68
　client-specified process definition, 180
　default process definition, 180
　deployment, managing, 189-92
　Exchange Workflow Designer, 165-66
　GetNewWorkflowMessage method, 168
　IWorkflowMessage interface, 168
　modeling business processes, 166
　modeling tools, 164
　overview, 163-65
　security modes, 186-89
　　Privilege Checking, 187, 188
　　privileged mode, 189
　　restricted mode, 188
　security properties, setting, 186
　SendWorkflowMessage, 168
　testing/debugging workflow applications, 193-94
　　using an audit trail, 193
　　using script debugger, 193-94
　variations, 178-81
　Web-based workflow, email Workflow compared to, 178-80
　workflow applications, developing, 167-68
　workflow components, 174-77
　　workflow engine, 175-76
　　workflow event sink, 176-77
　workflow event sinks:
　　creating, 168-86
　　registering, 190-92
　WorkflowMessage object, 168
　workflow process definition, 182-86
　　defining the ActionTable, 182-86
　WorkflowSession object, 167
　Workflow System Account, adding, 189-90
Workflow applications, 93
Workflow components, 174-77
Workflow engine, 175-76
Workflow event sinks, 176-77
　advanced workflow applications, 168-72
　　calling IProcessInstance advance, 172-73
　　creating a ProcessDefinition, 169-70
　　defining an ActionTable, 169
　　developing script functions, 169
　　registering the Workflow Event Sink, 170-72
　creating, 168-86
　registering, 170-72, 190-92
　registering in a folder, 492-95
Workflow items, deleting, 484
Workflow management, 477-95
　Active Directory properties, accessing, 480
　advanced developer tasks, 488-95
　　adding action table rows, 490
　　creating action table columns, 488-89
　　ProcessDefintion object, 491-92
　　registering a workflow event sink in a folder, 492-95
　　specifying the common script file, 490-91
　audit trail, using, 484
　custom properties, caching, 478-88
　ProcessInstance, accessing/modifying, 487-88
　ReceivedMessage, working with, 484-86
　run-time errors, managing, 478
　workflow items, deleting, 484
　WorkflowSession item security, 481-86
　　ItemAuthors collection, 481-82
　　ItemReaders collection, 482-83
WorkflowMessage object, 168
Workflow process definition, 182-86
　defining the ActionTable, 182-86
WorkflowSession item security, 481-86
WorkflowSession object, 167, 477
Workflow System Account, adding, 189-90

▼ X

.xls, 23
XML, 86
XMLDOM, constructing XML with, 285-86
XML (Extensible Markup Language), 6, 9, 34
　and property names, 18-19
XMLHTTP COM object, 332
XMLHTTPRequest COM class, 10
XML security descriptor, 331-34
　getting using JScript, 332-33
　getting using VBScript, 333-34
　HTTP/WebDAV request, 331
XML security descriptor format, 48-79
　accessing item descriptors, 56
　Discretionary Access Control Lists (DACLs) XML elements, 51-53
　example descriptor in XML, 55-56
　Exchange 5.5 access rights and the Web Storage System, 57-79
　new item descriptor inheritance, 57
　security identifiers in XML, 49-50
　system Audit Control Lists (system ACLs) XML elements, 53-54
　XML security descriptor XML elements, 50-51
XSL (Extensible Style Language) templates, 5
x-token encoding, 559

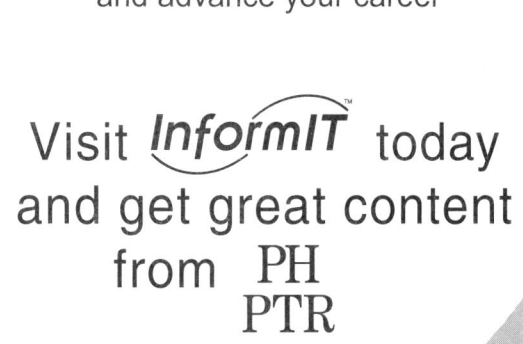

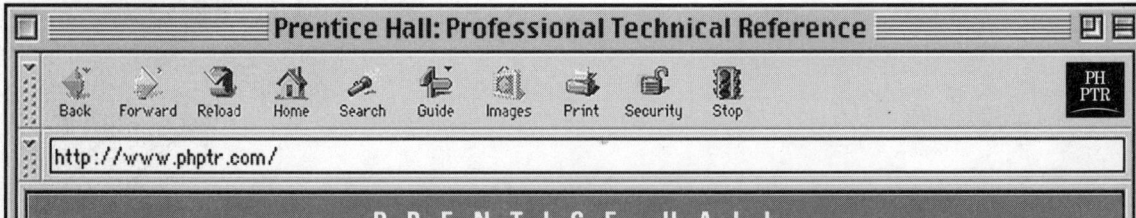

PRENTICE HALL
Professional Technical Reference
Tomorrow's Solutions for Today's Professionals.

Keep Up-to-Date with
PH PTR Online!

We strive to stay on the cutting edge of what's happening in professional computer science and engineering. Here's a bit of what you'll find when you stop by **www.phptr.com**:

@ Special interest areas offering our latest books, book series, software, features of the month, related links and other useful information to help you get the job done.

☞ Deals, deals, deals! Come to our promotions section for the latest bargains offered to you exclusively from our retailers.

$ Need to find a bookstore? Chances are, there's a bookseller near you that carries a broad selection of PTR titles. Locate a Magnet bookstore near you at www.phptr.com.

! What's new at PH PTR? We don't just publish books for the professional community, we're a part of it. Check out our convention schedule, join an author chat, get the latest reviews and press releases on topics of interest to you.

✉ Subscribe today! Join PH PTR's monthly email newsletter!

Want to be kept up-to-date on your area of interest? Choose a targeted category on our website, and we'll keep you informed of the latest PH PTR products, author events, reviews and conferences in your interest area.

Visit our mailroom to subscribe today! **http://www.phptr.com/mail_lists**